ENCRYPTED

UNLOCKING THE TIMELINE
REVELATION IN THE PSALMS

N. KARL LAWLEY

authorHOUSE®

AuthorHouse™
1663 Liberty Drive
Bloomington, IN 47403
www.authorhouse.com
Phone: 833-262-8899

Published by AuthorHouse   12/04/2023

ISBN: 979-8-8230-1748-0 (sc)
ISBN: 979-8-8230-1747-3 (e)

Library of Congress Control Number: 2023921538

Print information available on the last page.

Any people depicted in stock imagery provided by Getty Images are models, and such images are being used for illustrative purposes only. Certain stock imagery © Getty Images.

This book is printed on acid-free paper.

All scripture references are from the New King James Version unless otherwise stated.

CONTENTS

PREFACE

If it were discovered that God, the Creator of heaven and earth, encrypted a prophetic timeline in His word that revealed the final sequence of events of the "end of days," including the starting and ending years, and then hid it in plain sight in the middle of the Bible, it would be the discovery of the ages. Such a discovery should be made known to the world so that everyone who has eyes to see and ears to hear can have an opportunity to know about it and make a decision for, or against Christ before it's too late. The Psalms are at the literal center of the Bible, and many notable theologians and Church Fathers through the centuries, such as Saint Augustine himself, have recognized that there is an intentional, and yet concealed prophetic sequence and pattern to the organization of the Psalms. However, God, in His wisdom and sovereignty, has never allowed this encrypted sequence to be understood. That is until now...

Through a series of seemingly small but divine revelations, coupled with intense Bible study, our Heavenly Father has allowed me of all people to decode this mysterious and heretofore concealed timeline sequence in the Psalms. This sequence reveals that as of the infamous year of 2020, the world has, in fact, already been living in the final years of this present age. Beginning with that same year, there has been a definite convergence of prophetic signs that God encoded in the Psalms to be found and known, which match and connect to all of the end-time prophetic scriptures in both the Old and the New Testaments. According to these Psalms, we are witnessing a global chain of events that has begun and will continue until the year 2034 after the return of Jesus, the King of Kings and Lord of Lords.

So far, since 2020, the encrypted timeline revelation in the Psalms has proven itself to be exceptionally accurate and trustworthy. According to the timeline, this chain of events encoded in the Psalms will continue to and through the 7-year tribulation period, which will begin sometime around 2025. If this timeline continues to be correct, it goes without saying that time is very short. I believe that God has revealed this timeline now in our day to prove to the world that He is God and there is no other. It is also a last-minute wake-up call to Israel and to the Church. It is through prophecy that God reveals Himself and His power according to Isaiah 46, where He declares that, *"I am God, and there is no other; I am God, and there is none like me. I make known the end from the beginning, from ancient times, what is still to come."* Has God done just that? Has He made known from ancient times what is still to come in our day? I believe that He has. If God encrypted this timeline in His word and finally allowed it to be discovered and decoded at this time, then He obviously has a reason for it and a mission for everyone who will hear it. I believe that God is speaking personally to our generation through His ancient texts, revealing that we are truly living in Bible times. That should light a fire under each and every one of us who are eagerly awaiting the return of our Lord. That fire should ignite our resolve to be rebels for Jesus, rebel against the rising evil, and boldly spread the gospel around the world at any cost while we still have time because our time is running out. The final ignition of this gospel fire is the point and purpose of this book because at the end, nothing else will matter.

Why did God choose me? I ask myself that question every day. I am certainly no Saint Augustine, but I understand that God has a long track record of choosing the unexpected underdog to prove His power and glory. Other than that, all I can say is that I have been studying eschatology for over 20 years and love to research and teach Bible prophecy. It's not my profession, but my passion.

As I will expand on in the coming chapters, God set me on a new and amazing journey of discovery through the prophetic scriptures when He gave me an unexpected numerical two-number key that helped unlock the encrypted timeline in the Psalms. After that, He proved Himself to me over and over all the way through the researching and writing phase of the book by revealing connections throughout His word in many miraculous ways. I often told Him, "If He wasn't leading this, I wanted nothing to do with it." I document throughout the book the many miraculous and inspirational ways that God used to guide me to the knowledge that He wanted to reveal to me, and ultimately to everyone who is willing to listen in these final days.

Many have tried for centuries through calculations to figure out the "day and hour" when the Lord will return, and all have failed. The encrypted timeline in the Psalms does not set the specific "day or hour" for the Lord's return or any other prophetic event, but it does give a year range. It is also not based on calculations, although numbers are very important to God, as witnessed throughout the Bible. This timeline has always been in the Psalms since they were originally compiled in the second temple period before Jesus' first advent. Simply knowing to look in the Psalms, the starting point, and the overall prophetic context was what was required to unlock the Psalm's long-held secrets.

According to God's word, He demands at least two witnesses to settle a matter. As proof that the encrypted timeline is true, God placed two encrypted last days' timelines in the Psalms that complement each other and follow the same sequence. One of the witnesses is based on the Gregorian calendar, and the other is based on the prophetic re-birth of the nation of Israel, which happened in 1948.

If these two combined witnesses had been revealed prior to 2020, we would have known to expect lies and deception that year, along with a plague that caused us to wash our hands in affliction all day long, which continued into 2022. According to the timeline, the current year of 2023 foretells the coming judgment, distress, earthquakes, natural disasters, the bringing down of one, and the promotion of another. A major earthquake already happened in Turkey and Syria just north of Israel in February, and Benjamin Netanyahu regained power from Iyar Lapid in Israel at the beginning of this year. All of the related Psalms are Israel-centric. Even though both of these prophecies have been fulfilled this year, I do not believe they are fully complete. I believe that more fulfillments are still to come as the setup for the tribulation period continues this year.

According to my interpretation of the timeline that God encrypted in the Psalms, next year, in 2024, Israel will be invaded, fulfilling the Ezekiel 38 and 39 prophecies, and the "Rapture Season," as I call it, which we are currently in, will end. The tribulation will begin with the rise of the Antichrist in 2025, and the children of Israel will be regathered back to their land from all over the world in 2026. The long-awaited third temple will be built and completed in 2027, and the Antichrist will declare himself to be "god" in the temple in 2028, fulfilling Daniel 9:27 and Matthew 24:15. The remnant of Israel will then flee to a place prepared for them according to Revelation 12:14-16 and Matthew 24:16-21. At that time begins what Jesus called the "Great Tribulation," which will last for three and a half years, ending with the second coming of our Lord at Armageddon in late 2031. All of this is revealed in sequence in both witnesses in the Psalms!

Even though the timeline has already proven itself, and I firmly believe that we are living in it right now, I believe that after reviewing the evidence, you will be able to make up your own mind if it is real, or if it is simply a coincidence. The point of this book is not to set a date for the Lord's return for His Church or His second coming at the end of the tribulation because Jesus Himself said that, "No man knows the day or the hour." The point is that regardless of the exact day, time is extremely short, and God wants an abundant harvest when His Son returns. He doesn't want anyone to perish. We are the workers in His field, and unfortunately, most of us still have empty baskets because we are too busy with other priorities in our lives. So this book might just be the final wake-up call to a sleeping Church that God wants to rise and realize the late hour that we are living in. It is clear throughout His word that in these final days, our Lord desires that we fearlessly spread the Gospel around the world and shine His light in the darkness like never before.

Matthew 9:37-38

[37] Then He said to His disciples, "The harvest truly is plentiful, but the laborers are few. [38] Therefore pray the Lord of the harvest to send out laborers into His harvest."

CHAPTER 1

Introduction

It is a well-known fact that something unexpected, unprecedented, and quite cataclysmic happened in 2020. It seems that there was some sort of paradigm shift as the year got underway, and all of a sudden, the world that we knew ceased to exist. For a short time, we all thought it would come back if we could just "flatten the curve" and "follow the science." We all did what we could to get back to normal, but a few years later, I think we can all see that what we called normal isn't ever coming back. It's gone for good. Since then, the news has been the same all around the world, apostasy, wars and rumors of wars, civil unrest, wickedness intensifying, pestilence, drought, flooding, famine, fuel shortages, supply chain problems, high inflation, economic collapse, and the list goes on and on rolling in like the birth pains of an expectant mother. It seems that we have entered into a new era, a prophesied era that the Bible revealed would one day come, and it has arrived. Now what?

Believers in Jesus have been wondering about the signs and the timing of the prophesied end-time events for almost two thousand years. Just a few days before Jesus' crucifixion, several of His disciples asked Him privately, *"When will this happen, and what will be the sign of your coming and of the end of the age?"* What if I told you that our Heavenly Father left His children a last day's timeline revelation encrypted in the Psalms that answers these questions and more? It foretells major prophetic events by year and even in sequential order as a final wake-up call, not only to the Church but also to the nation of

Israel. This timeline may be the key to a better understanding of the prophetic timing of the end of the age, as well as a useful tool to navigate through the days ahead. In fact, He left us at least two timelines hidden in the Psalms that overlap and give a possible starting season for the end times, and a chronological sequence shedding more light on the timing and events of the final years. I will present the proof for the timeline revelation in the Psalms, along with other supporting scriptures and evidence, and then allow you to be the judge. However, I am confident that when you see these Psalms in context, and in their pattern, you will know and understand how great our God really is, that He is fully in control, and how much He wants us to know the time we are living in, and what that means for our lives and those around us.

As you probably know, according to both the Old and the New Testaments, it takes at least two witnesses to confirm a matter. So, of course, God left at least 2 timelines in the Psalms as confirmation of the truth and validity of His revelation. I'm not going to search out any more than those two for now since I believe time is short and this information is critical, but I do believe that there are more yet to be discovered.

This timeline revelation gives a yearly account of the seven-year tribulation period as well as the years leading up to it, the "Rapture Season," and even afterward into the Millennial Kingdom. In case you are new to biblical prophecy, the rapture is the promised escape of the Church, the Bride of Christ, prior to the outpouring of God's wrath on the unrepentant world. I promise to cover the rapture in much more detail in the coming chapters. The tribulation period is the 7-year period, also known as "Daniel's 70th week" from Daniel chapter 9 and the "Time of Jacobs Trouble" from Jeremiah chapter 30. It's the time of the outpouring of God's wrath in the judgment of the world, as well as the time of what will arguably be the greatest revival in world history. The tribulation period begins with the confirming of a covenant, possibly a peace covenant between Israel and many other nations, by the one we call the Antichrist. This 7-year period is made up of two 3 1/2-year periods, of which the second half is known as the "Great Tribulation." The Millennial Kingdom is the 1000-year reign of Christ following the current age.

Daniel 9:27 tells us, *"He (the Antichrist) will confirm a covenant with many for one seven. In the middle of the seven he will put an end to sacrifice and offering (speaking of the Jewish temple that will need to be rebuilt in Jerusalem). And at the temple, he will set up an abomination that causes desolation, until the end that is decreed is poured out on him."*

Jesus said in **Matthew 24:21** *"For then there will be great tribulation, such as has not been since the beginning of the world until this time, no, nor ever shall be. ²² And unless those days were shortened, no flesh would be saved; but for the elect's sake, those days will be shortened."*

According to Jesus' own words, the tribulation period will be the worst time in history, and that's saying something! Trust me, you do not want to be here for it. As you may remember from history, after the great fire of Rome in 64 AD, Emperor Nero had to find someone to pin the blame on, so he conveniently blamed the Christians and had them arrested and then executed by crucifixion, being thrown to the beasts, and by being burned alive as human torches to light his garden at dinner parties. As bad as that sounds, the final tribulation period is going to be even worse for those who are left after the rapture. In fact, not only did Jesus point out that it would be the worst time in all of history, but the prophet Daniel did as well.

Daniel 12:1
"At that time, Michael, the great prince who protects your people (Israel), will arise. There will be a time of distress such as has not happened from the beginning of nations until then..."

Historically, there have been some terrible times, and Christians have been persecuted and martyred for their faith for going on for two thousand years now. Remember how Saul, later known as Paul, was rounding up the early Christians and had them arrested and even put to death, as detailed in the book of Acts? Historical accounts show that all of the remaining 11 disciples were martyred except for John, who we know was exiled to the island of Patmos, where he wrote the book of Revelation, known as Apocalypse in Greek. According to prophecy, those days will return, and worse.

Christians are persecuted, oppressed, imprisoned, and killed for their faith even today in countries such as China, Afghanistan, North Korea, Somalia, Libya, Yemen, India, Mozambique, and many other countries. As horrible as all of that is, it's going to pale in comparison to what is coming soon on the whole earth. That is one of the reasons for writing this book. Many do not know what is coming, or how to escape it, but they have a sense that something is clearly wrong in the world today. Much of the Church is asleep and unaware of what is coming because churches are no longer teaching Bible prophecy out of the fear that it is too controversial. Yes, it is controversial, but I would say that leaving your flock unaware of what day they are living in, and what God expects from His own during this time is far more controversial.

To Reveal or Not to Reveal

This book will certainly be seen as very controversial. Some people think that I shouldn't reveal this timeline, and that we shouldn't know these mysteries. People may say that if the exact timing of the encrypted timeline isn't correct, especially as it relates to the possible "Rapture Season," it would be responsible for building up a false hope only to let people down. Some could even use that as an excuse to fall away from the faith. Many could misunderstand the sovereignty of God and forget that only He has the last word regarding His timing. I understand all of that very well, but Isn't it true, though, that I would be remiss if I didn't share what God allowed me to uncover? Daniel 2:28 says, *"There is a God in heaven who reveals mysteries,"* and Deuteronomy 29:29 says, *"The secret things belong to the LORD our God, but those things which are revealed belong to us and to our children forever, that we may do all the words of this law."* Even though God promises that He will reveal mysteries, and when He does reveal them they belong to us, it is still with some hesitancy that I share this revelation. However, I know that if God didn't want it revealed, He wouldn't have encrypted it within the Psalms and wouldn't have allowed it to be decoded.

Luke 8:17
For nothing is secret that will not be revealed, nor anything hidden that will not be known and come to light.

Didn't Jesus say that the last days would be "as the days of Noah?" Didn't God give Noah, the preacher of righteousness, a 120-year warning? So, according to scripture, even Noah and anyone who listened to him should have at least known the year of their impending destruction. They wouldn't have known the exact "day or hour," but they should have been able to know and understand what year destruction was coming upon their world. Through the encrypted and prophetic arrangement of the Psalms, God has also revealed to our generation the year destruction will begin in our world. And prophetically, through the Psalms, He has also revealed, once again, that it is on another 120-year warning. The question we have to ask ourselves is, would God give the ancient world such a warning, allowing them time to repent, but not us? They didn't heed the warning in Noah's time, will we?

Matthew 24:36-37
[36] *"But of that day and hour no one knows, not even the angels of heaven, but My Father only.* [37] *But as the days of Noah were, so also will the coming of the Son of Man be.*

Again, they certainly didn't know the day or the hour, but they should have been aware of the year unless they simply didn't take God, or His preacher, seriously to their demise. Like Noah and then later like the Sons of Issachar (1 Chronicles 12:32), I believe God wants us, in this final generation, to at least know and understand the times we are living in. It is only through understanding the times that we can help and warn others of the nearness of the coming of our Lord and the time of trouble that is close at hand.

Almost Out of Time

I am certain that many people, even some Christians, will scoff at the information that I am going to share. Some will say that it's all merely coincidence, or may even be offended because they think I'm setting dates. Some will certainly not want to accept it since it won't match their own eschatological timeline, and that's ok. You don't have to believe any of the sequences of events decoded from the Psalms as long as you realize that we are indeed running out of time to fulfill the Great Commission and that so many of our unsaved friends and loved ones around the world are at risk of perishing without the salvation that has been freely offered by our Lord Jesus, the one true Messiah.

Even in the face of ridicule and persecution, I know that I must present the timeline revelation that God allowed me to find in the Psalms. I have to sound the alarm because time is very short, even shorter than you can imagine. By allowing me to uncover this encrypted timeline, God has made me a "watchman on the wall," and therefore, I am fully aware that I am responsible for sharing this information regardless of the consequences. The prophet Ezekiel spoke of this responsibility in two different chapters of his book, both in chapter 3 and again in chapter 33. God made it clear through Ezekiel that if I do not warn the people of what is coming that their blood will be on my head. So, I'm sounding the trumpet as loud as possible to warn anyone who will listen. Time is short, the harvest is about to end, and the sword is coming. And now you are also a watchman responsible for spreading the word.

Ezekiel 33:1-6
¹Again the word of the LORD came to me, saying, ² "Son of man, speak to the children of your people, and say to them: 'When I bring the sword upon a land, and the people of the land take a man from their territory and make him their watchman, ³ when he sees the sword coming upon the land, if he blows the trumpet and warns the people, ⁴ then whoever hears the sound of the trumpet and does not

take warning, if the sword comes and takes him away, his blood shall be on his own head. ⁵ He heard the sound of the trumpet, but did not take warning; his blood shall be upon himself. But he who takes warning will save his life. ⁶ But if the watchman sees the sword coming and does not blow the trumpet, and the people are not warned, and the sword comes and takes any person from among them, he is taken away in his iniquity; but his blood I will require at the watchman's hand.'

Why Me?

Who am I to make such claims? You may have never heard of me. In fact, I would be surprised if you had. I have never written a book before. I do not have a prophecy channel on YouTube or social media with thousands of fans and followers, and I do not do large prophecy speaking engagements. However, I study God's prophetic word, write notebooks full of notes, and share my findings and ideas in classes that I teach about the end times with my brothers and sisters in Christ at a small but fantastic church in the Central Valley of California. Since the 90's, I've had a passion for God's prophetic word. It was really on 9/11/2001 when that passion exploded, and the researcher gene that God gave me really came alive. I knew in my spirit that there was more to it than met the eye. I needed to figure out why anyone would do such a thing, and what the prophetic significance was.

For years, my studying was simply for my own edification, and I found that most people didn't really want to talk about the end times. I believe, in America anyway, most people were so focused on the "American Dream" and where they were going in the "world" that they didn't want to hear about anything that would bring an end to their plans. A better career, a better car, a better house, or starting a family was the driving force for most. There's nothing wrong with those things as long as you are putting God first in your life. He deserves to be first! However, over the last few years, especially since the Covid lockdowns, a lot more people are asking, "What's going on in this world?" And I hear a lot of people saying that most churches are still silent on matters of end-time prophecy, which I know to be true firsthand.

My family and I were attending a church when we first moved from Florida to California (I know, moving to California sounded like a good idea at the time). One week, the pastor explained that he was going to start a new series of teaching on the book of Daniel. I was super excited! Finally, some prophetic teaching, I thought. Well, we spent the next few weeks going through the book of Daniel and never once discussed anything prophetic! That actually takes a lot of talent!

Over time, I knew in my spirit that if nobody else was going to teach it, then I had to. But I'm not a pastor, a professor, or a polished speaker. I'm not perfect or righteous, or any of the things that I would think would be prerequisites for such a mission from our Heavenly Father. I'm just an Air Force veteran with a business degree who now restores classic Porsches for a living! Additionally, I had an accident at work a few years ago, resulting in head trauma that has caused me to have some annoying memory recall problems. I have a chronic case of "it's on the tip of my tongue," so I write everything down, or I won't remember it. Considering all of that, I can't figure out why God chose me for this mission, but I know He did.

The process of studying these prophetic Psalms has been much like decoding encrypted military communications. The funny thing is that when I entered the Air Force, I was assigned to a specialty training course as a Cryptologic Language Analyst. That's a top-secret code breaker responsible for analyzing and decoding encrypted messages. Well, someone messed up and assigned that specialty career to me, but they forgot to give me the test required to enter the training. So, one day, when I was still in basic training/boot camp, my TI (training instructor) told me that I had to go to a certain office across the base to take a test. When I signed up for the Air Force, and even when I left for basic training, I had no idea what career they would place me in, so I had no idea what this test was all about.

So, I marched across the base to the office as instructed, and was told to take a cryptology test. I didn't even know what cryptology was!

Needless to say, I completely bombed that test. It was mostly difficult math, and I hadn't had a math class in three years by that time. After the test, I was told to wait in a room, and eventually, someone came in and told me the frightening news that I had failed the test for one of the best-enlisted careers in the Air Force, and would now probably get one of the worst. He pulled out a binder with reams of dot matrix paper in it and started flipping from page to page with a perplexed look on his face. He said that I could choose from any of these leftover career fields. Basically, these were the leftover jobs that nobody wanted, so they had plenty of openings. I thought, "Oh great, I'm going to be a garbage man in the Air Force!" As he flipped the pages he read the names of these careers out to me. None of them sounded very good; in fact, they sounded pretty terrible until he called out what was known then as a 906, which was a hospital administration specialist. I said, "I'll take it!" Considering the other options, it was really the only choice. So, I worked at a hospital at Eglin Air Force Base for 4 years and loved it! Needless to say, I never had to break any codes during my enlistment, though. I was, however, one of the only 906s with a top-secret clearance since the Air Force had already completed an entire background check on me before I took the test. After seeing my test score, I'm surprised they didn't take it away, too!

In my self-doubt, I think that surely God would have entrusted this encrypted timeline revelation in the Psalms to a real "code breaker," and not to a failure who couldn't pass the test. Why in the world would He use me? With my embarrassing and pathetic back story of not being good enough to be a real code breaker, it seems that I would have been His last choice for the job. That is unless we serve a God who "chooses the foolish things to confound the wise" (1 Corinthians 1:27). Well, He does have a long track record of doing just that.

I'm praying and believing that He will make a way for this information to get out and serve His intended purpose. Since I know that God doesn't make mistakes, I am confident that His plan will prevail regardless of my shortcomings. Perhaps If I had been a real military code breaker, or even maybe a theology professor like many other Christian authors, I would be tempted to use elaborate terms that only highly educated people would understand. The good news is that I don't know any! So, this book should be easy to read and easy to understand for the rest of us.

I've told you a lot about what I'm not. What I am is a digger! I love to dig into God's word and search out biblical wisdom in a matter, especially as it relates to prophecy. It's just what I do and who I am. Any time there is a biblical question that arises that I don't have an answer to, like a bloodhound hot on a scent; I love to search and search, and make sure that I find some answers to put my spirit at ease. That's just how God made me.

The Fig Tree Generation Revelation

One day, not unlike many others, I was studying and really seeking a greater understanding of the timing of the last day's events. Suppose you have studied Bible prophecy for a long time. In that case, you will have certainly realized that it's not exactly black and white, and there are many different interpretations of any given prophetic verse out there. However, I think it's safe to say that most students of biblical prophecy realize that we're in the end times, but how far in is the question?

The season of the rapture of the Church is a matter that I have been researching for a long time. It was 2022, and I had fully thought that the rapture would have already happened by now based on the signs of the times that we're living in, and on my previous understanding of "the fig tree generation," which comes from Jesus' teaching in Matthew 24 as well as from Psalm 90:10, where Moses states that *"The days of our lives are seventy years; and if by reason of strength they are eighty years, yet their boast is only labor and sorrow; for it is soon cut off, and we fly away.* In Matthew 24:32-34 Jesus says, *[32] "Now learn this parable from the fig tree: when its branch has already become tender and puts forth leaves, you know that summer is near. [33] So you also, when you see all these things (signs), know that it (He) is near—at the doors! [34] Assuredly, I say to you, **this generation** will by no means pass away till all these things take place."*

Many believe, myself included, that the fig tree in Matthew 24:32 represents Israel being reborn, which happened on May 14, 1948. How do we know that the fig tree represents Israel? I recently heard a very prominent prophecy teacher declare that everyone has misunderstood Matthew 24:32 and that Israel is not represented in the Bible by figs or by the fig tree. Needless to say, I was very surprised by this news since several Old Testament prophets, such as Jeremiah and Hosea, specifically related Israel to good and bad figs in baskets and to the first fruits on a fig tree in its first season. Also, remember that Jesus Himself cursed the fig tree in front of His disciples for not having any fruit on it just days before His crucifixion, as told in Matthew 21, and paralleled in Mark 11. It's not that Jesus was just angry with the fig tree that didn't have any fruit on it; He was connecting the prophetic scriptures with the time of His visitation and the generation that rejected Him as Messiah.

Since they didn't accept Jesus as their Messiah, that generation of Jews, and all generations since then, have been barren of any fruit. That's why, a few days later, Jesus said, "Now learn this parable from **the** fig tree" to His disciples. They would have certainly known what fig tree Jesus was referring to since it was only a few days earlier when they witnessed Jesus curse and wither **the** fruitless fig tree on their way into Jerusalem. However, now in Matthew 24:32, Jesus explains that the fruitless fig tree will be revived one day as a sign of His soon return. Did Israel wither just as the fig tree withered after the Jews rejected Jesus as their Messiah? Yes, the Jewish Temple was destroyed in 70 AD, and the Jews were driven from their land in 135 AD. Has Israel come back to life and started to bud and re-grow as a nation? Yes, as stated before, Israel became a nation again in 1948 and has continued to blossom as a powerful and prosperous nation ever since. Is reborn Israel the figurative "fig tree" that was prophesied by Jesus that would "become tender" and "put forth leaves" as a sign of His return? Absolutely! Also, I would like to point out one more important detail about how Jesus describes the last day's fig tree. Jesus said that it will become tender and put forth leaves, but notice that He doesn't mention any fruit! Yes. The fig tree is once again alive, but without Jesus the Messiah, it still cannot bear any fruit.

There is a day prophesied when the fruitlessness of Israel will be over. That wonderful day was spoken of by Jesus in Luke 13 and is the day of His glorious return.

Luke 13:35
35 See! Your house is left to you desolate; and assuredly, I say to you, you shall not see Me until the time comes when you say, 'Blessed is He who comes in the name of the LORD!'"

In Matthew 24:34, Jesus said, "This generation," I believe referring to the generation alive at the time of Israel's rebirth, will not pass away until all of the signs and end-time events happen and are completed. If you know from Psalm 90 that our lives are 70 to 80, years you can conclude that a generation is no more than 80 years. With that understanding, you can do some simple math and surmise that everything will have to be finished, including the rapture/resurrection of the church and the 7-year tribulation period, before Israel turns 81 years old in 2029. I realize that this is a little confusing, so I'll put it another way. On May 14, 2022, Israel celebrated their 74th birthday, which blew the "fig tree generation" theory since they couldn't reach 74 years old under this theory without the rapture/resurrection happening first, as well as the start of the tribulation period. As of May 2022, the theory no longer worked mathematically. If you add a 7-year tribulation period to 2022, you will land at 2029, which means that Israel will be 81 years old. Under this theory, Israel has to still be in their 80th year when all things are completed according to Jesus in Matthew 24, and my understanding of how long a generation is according to Psalm 90:10, which is no more than 80 years. In addition, it makes no sense that the rapture and the beginning of the tribulation period would happen simultaneously. There has to be some time in between for the Antichrist to rise to power. So, all the way through 2021, I kept thinking that Jesus was cutting it really close, but then, in 2022, I began to realize that there was definitely a flaw in the theory.

After this theory was no longer a possible solution to the rapture timing or the start of the tribulation period, I continued digging into my studies, trying to figure out what I had missed. I wasn't going to give up that easily! After all, I knew that the rapture had to be near because the signs were all around indicating that we were already in the final setup for the tribulation. I wasn't looking for a "day or an hour" for the rapture, or even for the start of the tribulation period, but a general timeframe, especially in the wake of the events of 2020, as well as the daily discussion of the war in Ukraine, which started to look like it was shaping up to be the precursor to World War 3. I knew that there had to be an answer encrypted in God's word somewhere because God told us through the prophets that He has hidden mysteries in His word.

The Key

I went to bed one night after studying and couldn't stop thinking about it. I was wrestling with God a bit and continued to pray fervently that God would give me a revelation, and the wisdom to figure it out. "Please Lord, help me to understand!" I had dots that I just couldn't connect. I then heard in my spirit, "5 and 10." However, I thought, "No, Lord, it should be 7 or 2 X 3.5!" But no, I understood, quite unexpectedly, I might add, that I was given "5 and 10." I didn't really want to believe it because it made no sense to me, but because it made no sense to me, I knew it wasn't from my own thoughts. It had to be God! OK, God gave me a couple of specific numbers, so I thought "Well, that's something I guess?" It didn't really seem like an answer or a key to unlocking anything, but it was a clue that caused me to dig even deeper, and I at least had a new direction. It looked like I was going to be a code breaker after all!

I'll be honest with you, I was really confused by the "5 and 10." I asked myself over and over, did I think that? Were those my thoughts, or was that a divine revelation? Those two numbers weren't even on my radar at all, so I can't see how they could have been my thoughts. I had already figured out that God uses numbers and patterns to communicate with us in His word, but when I was asking for a revelation and wisdom, I was thinking more along the lines of Him filling me with knowledge, and me thinking, "Oh wow, I all of a sudden understand everything!" That didn't happen at all, but looking back, I can see how perfectly He has managed my path toward understanding so many things. Instead of one moment of "oh wow," I've had many moments of "oh wow" along the way. So, to circle back to the question of "were those my thoughts, or was that a divine revelation," my conclusion is 100% that it was divine, and absolutely God gave me a little push in the right direction.

Since that first revelation, God has used many miraculous and inspirational ways to guide me to the knowledge that He wanted to reveal to me, and ultimately to the world in these final days. One evening on a day when I was seriously questioning all of what I was learning, and even my own sanity for that matter, God spoke to me in my spirit. Not with anything big, but as I was walking to the dinner table, I was prompted to say, seemingly out of nowhere, "Hey, let's read the devotional tonight before we eat." I was even surprised at the words that were coming out of my mouth! You see, I'm ashamed to say that I had never asked to read it before. I usually spend so much time in the word studying prophecy and writing in the mornings, then work all day that I just don't think about the family devotional that we're supposed to be reading together every night. I know I'm a terrible role model, but thankfully, my wife Tammy usually picks up my slack and reminds me. This devotional is sort of like a little flip chart, and each day has a Bible verse and a few discussion questions related to it. On that particular day when I was seriously doubting and crying out to the Lord saying, "Lord, if you are not in this, then I don't want anything to do with it," He divinely snuck in the most perfect scripture verse that really helped me to understand that He was truly the One leading me down this path. Not that I'm anyone worthy at all, but He was leading me nonetheless. Out of over 30,000 verses in the Bible, the verse that God put on the dinner table that evening was Jeremiah 33:3. It was exactly what I needed! There simply couldn't have been a more perfect word from the Lord that day. It was a miracle, and it gave me overwhelming peace and assurance that I had to keep going. Now I knew for certain that God was in this!

Jeremiah 33:3
*³ 'Call to Me, and I will answer you, and show you great
and mighty things, which you do not know.'*

I can testify that I called on Him and that He has been showing me
great and mighty things in amazing ways ever since!

Hidden Prophecies in the Psalms

Some time ago, I heard of a book written in the 80s by J. R. Church
titled *Hidden Prophecies in the Psalms* and that he had discovered a
prophetic correlation between the order of the Psalms and the Gregorian
calendar years starting with the year 1901, matching Psalm 1. I can't
remember when or where, but I had heard that his first example, which
he used to establish his concept in the opening of his book, was from
Psalm 48. He believed that Psalm 48 matched the historical events
surrounding the prophetic rebirth of the nation of Israel in 1948. I
figured this was just a coincidence and that he was reading too much
into it. Maybe he was seeing something that really wasn't there. Maybe
he wanted it to be there bad enough that he stretched the words to fit
his preconceived notions. I also really didn't want to believe any of it
because of my own biases and opposing preconceived notions.

After all, God has His own calendar, which He gave Moses to
follow, and He certainly wouldn't hide prophetic codes in a sequence
that matches the pagan Gregorian calendar, I thought. I discounted
this concept wholeheartedly for some time, but then I began to wrestle
with the thought that maybe God is bigger than I gave Him credit for,
and that maybe there is something to it after all. Maybe I didn't know
as much as I thought I did. I finally gave up my pride and arrogance
and purchased a used copy of J. R. Church's book and began to read
it and study the Psalms for myself for prophetic patterns. Since his
revised edition was published back in 1990, I knew I was a latecomer
to this concept, but God had placed a hunger for end-time prophetic

knowledge in my spirit that had been lacking some new nourishment for some time, so I dug into it.

My wrestling with the concept that God would encode a prophetic sequence of events into the Psalms, and match them to the Gregorian calendar was mainly due to a realization that I had as I was studying and writing for my prophetic teaching classes at church. Through my own studies and research, I realized that there are no coincidences in God's word or God's plan. In fact, the word "coincidence" never appears in the Bible. God has set everything in perfect order, even when it may appear to us that it's all messed up. I even did a teaching on the lack of the word "coincidence" in the Bible to illustrate how God is in complete control of everything. So, if He is really in complete control, then obviously, He was in control of the creation of the Gregorian calendar, as well as the corruption of God's calendar by the Jews. I'm not saying that He wanted it that way, but He certainly wasn't surprised, and ultimately it will serve His purposes.

The Bible Code Debate

One day, I was listening to a debate between two scholarly theologians; both were doctors of this, that, and the other from highly prestigious schools. They were debating the merits of the Bible Codes discovered in the Hebrew Masoretic texts of the Old Testament. The Masoretic text is what most of our current Bibles are based on, including the King James Bible. These codes use equal letter spacing (ELS) to find names, and other hidden codes in the Bible. By counting between an equal number of letters, you look for a pattern that spells a name, event, etc. As an example, let's say that in the book of Genesis, starting with the first letter of chapter 1, which is the Hebrew letter Bet, or our letter "B," we then count 10 letters to find the next letter in the pattern, then 10 more to find the next letter in the pattern. Then we put all of those letters together that appeared every 10 spaces to find that it spells "believe" in Hebrew. I totally made that example up, so don't go telling anyone that God encoded "believe" in the opening of Genesis.

Anyway, one of the doctors claimed that the codes were real, but the other claimed that they couldn't be real regardless of the overwhelming evidence for them. His claim that they can't be real, or inspired by God was based on his reasoning that the Masoretic text came after the Dead Sea Scroll text, so any ELSs found in the Masoretic text were invalid based on different spellings of words between the two, etc. These doctors would have chewed me up and spit me out in a debate because after my accident a few years ago, I cannot retain and recall information as I once could. But I think the hit that I took to my head may have actually knocked a little more common sense into me. For instance, I no longer climb 3 legged ladders, and I now know that I'm not invincible. What the big brains couldn't understand was that God would simply place the codes inside of the text used by those whom He wished to find it regardless of which was written first. So I think it's simple, just as with the Gregorian calendar used by current-day Gentiles, God knows all things, and is in control of all things, and will certainly use the text or calendar that we are using when He wants to convey a message to us. Why would He put it somewhere where we can't find it? That wouldn't make any sense at all. If current-day Jewish Rabbis are using the Masoretic text, then that's where God will meet them. If we Gentiles are using the Gregorian calendar, then that's where God will meet us. Maybe we need to stop putting God in a box of our own making!

The other realization that I had regarding God's calendar, is that no one is following it today. Even if they think they are, they probably aren't. Might I add that this is possibly one of the reasons why Jesus Himself said that *"no one knows the day or the hour"* of His return. How can you know if you don't have God's correct calendar? If you search online you will find that several versions of calendars claim to be God's calendar. Still, they all seem to follow the current Jewish calendar which was corrupted by the influence of the ancient pagan Babylonian calendar during the exile and also during the Hellenistic Period. The current Jewish calendar, which is used in Israel today was constructed by the Jewish Patriarch Hillel II around 360 AD and finalized by the Jewish scholar and Rabbi Maimonides in the Middle Ages around 1200 AD. So, at best, it's a man-made calendar and not God's calendar. The

Jews today even use the Babylonian names for their months and not the original Hebrew names, which should also be a clue that it isn't God's calendar.

The Israelites did follow God's calendar during their exodus from Egypt and afterward, but historically, we know that it was eventually corrupted. The only Israelites that we know of that were still keeping God's calendar during the time of Jesus were the Essenes. The Essenes were the ones who hid their scrolls in the caves of Qumran near the Dead Sea and then more or less disappeared from history.

Now that we know that basically no one and no nation is using God's calendar, the question then becomes this, if no one is following God's calendar any longer, and God wants to convey calendar-specific, prophetic end-time warnings and events to mankind, both Jews and Gentiles, how would He do it? After all, God revealed through the Prophet Amos, *"Surely the Lord God does nothing, unless He reveals His secret to His servants the prophets"* (Amos 3:7). So according to God's word, He has to reveal it in some way. There are really only two options: He would either reveal his true calendar by allowing mankind to unearth His hidden truth before the times in which the prophecies applied, or He would have to do it through the calendars that we use and understand today. Well, I believe He did both.

God's prophetic time clock really started ticking louder and louder starting in 1948 when the Nation of Israel was miraculously reborn just as prophesied, thereby officially starting the last minutes of the last days. Is it a coincidence that a Bedouin shepherd boy stumbled across the scrolls, which were hidden for nearly 2000 years in the caves of Qumran, only a year earlier in 1947? Is it a coincidence that he was specifically 15 years old when he discovered the scrolls (we'll come back to that question later)? This discovery revealed so many things regarding God's word. First, God's word can be trusted to still be accurate. After reviewing the scrolls and fragments and matching them up with the current-day Hebrew Bible, or Old Testament as we call it, scholars have found that great care was taken to preserve the accuracy of the Bible that we have today. God definitely wanted us to be able to prove His word to be unchanged in these last days, so He allowed the scrolls to be hidden and then discovered again in our time, just in time for the end of days.

The Dead Sea Scrolls also revealed how God's true calendar works and that it is a solar calendar and not a lunar calendar, as the Jews are now keeping and have been for several thousand years. This corruption of God's calendar was actually prophesied in the Book of Jubilees, which was also found among the Dead Sea Scrolls. In Exodus 12, God declared to Moses and Aaron, *"...This month shall be your beginning of months; it shall be the first month of the year to you."* But we never knew exactly when that was, and we also didn't know what year from creation we were in. Now we do.

Interestingly, neither the Jews nor the world have found God's calendar to be that important. No country has changed its calendars to match the calendar given to Moses personally by the Almighty. Most of the world doesn't even know that such a calendar exists. The discovery of God's ancient calendar wasn't important enough to make international news headlines or cause nations even to consider making a change. So, God, in His infinite grace and mercy, is communicating with a world that is in rebellion and ignorance through their own devised calendars.

Because of the world's apathy toward the Dead Sea Scrolls and all that they reveal, which I believe to be the most important discovery in all of history, I cannot help but be saddened as I am reminded of the first chapter of the Gospel of John. Jesus came into the world which He had created, but the world didn't even recognize Him, or care that the God of all creation was revealing Himself and literally walking among them.

John 1:10-11
He was in the world, and the world was made through Him, and the world did not know Him. He came to His own, and His own did not receive Him.

Knowing that man wasn't going to follow God's calendar, He perfectly arranged the Psalms and encrypted prophetic treasures in them, matching the years of the Gregorian calendar.

Literal or Allegorical?

The answer to a longstanding question of mine, and I believe of most prophecy students throughout history, has become much clearer in the course of my studies into the timeline revelation in the Psalms. Most wonder if Bible prophecy should be taken literally as the early Church fathers understood it, or if it should be treated as allegorical as the Augustinian view interprets it. I now believe the answer is Yes! Both sides can make a strong case for their view because they are both correct. The truth is somewhere in between these two polar opposites.

Prophetic visions, whether through dreams or in person, weren't meant to be literal, and they weren't meant as allegories to simply teach a spiritual lesson. I have finally realized that the prophets who had prophetic dreams, visions, and who were even transported into heaven itself to witness events unfold in front of them all saw real views of future people, places, and things; however, what they witnessed was an "encrypted" view of future reality. Just as the military encrypts messages so that their enemies cannot understand them and thereby be able to thwart their plans, God has also used a perfect balance of encrypted prophecy in His word for the same reason. Remember, we are at war!

No One Knows the Day or Hour

J. R. Church completed his prophetic study of the Psalms in 1990 by looking back at the history of the previous 90 years and matching them to the first 90 Psalms. Even though he had firmly established the concept that there was indeed a correlation between the numbering of the Psalms and the years in sequence, he was reluctant to use the same pattern and look ahead into the future to discover the future prophetic treasures found therein. He stated in his opening chapter that "it is with some degree of reluctance that I even approach the subject for fear of being labeled as a date setter. I do not wish to be classified in such a manner. On the other hand, if I were to shelve this entire study on the uncanny twentieth-century chronology apparent in the Psalms, would I not then be remiss in my calling?" I feel his pain! Even though this book does not attempt to set the "day or hour" of the rapture or the "day or hour" of any other specific eschatological event, but rather a timeline of years to and through the tribulation, as I have stated before, I am certain that many Christians will still be offended by this. Many Christians believe that no one can know anything about the timing of when the Lord is coming back to take His bride, the Church. I know, because I used to be one of them. When I would hear of anyone speaking of a possible year, season, or day of the Lord's return, I would say, "Well, I'm sure that it won't be then!" That's because the Lord Himself told us in Matthew 24:36, *"But of that day and hour no one knows, not even the angels of heaven, but My Father only."* So, if no one can know, then it stands to reason that if someone thinks they know, they're surely wrong! But wouldn't that way of thinking diminish all of the other scriptures that insist we should be watching and know when to expect our Lord?

I have not set out on this journey of writing and sharing these revelations that I have been allowed to uncover to convince anyone here and now of their validity. You will have to weigh the evidence and decide for yourself if they are just coincidences, or are indeed what I call "encrypted prophetic treasures" that have been hidden in the Psalms, which I believe reveal a lot more than what you see on the surface. If these revelations that I am going to share with you in this book are true and accurate, this could be one of the most important books you'll ever read, not including the Bible, of course! Regardless, I believe that this information will be very important soon during the tribulation period, which, as I mentioned before, is also known by many other names, including the "Time of Jacob's Trouble," "the 70th week of Daniel," and also the "Day of the Lord." From now on, I'm going to refer to this 7-year period simply as the "tribulation period." I would also like to point out that the tribulation period is global and will affect every nation on earth, but God's focus is on Israel. It's not the "time of the Church's Trouble," but specifically "Jacob's Trouble," according to Jeremiah 30.

Even if the starting year or season is off because God sovereignly allows the world more time, as He did with King Hezekiah when He granted him 15 more years of life, the sequence of events leading to and then through the tribulation is still confirmed by two sets of Psalms, which settles the matter in God's eyes according to scripture. I believe that this book could become a handbook for the remnant of Israel, and the Gentile "Tribulation Saints" who will be trapped here during the tribulation period. That is why I have given as many supporting scriptures and background information as possible. It is my view that not only do the correlating Psalms give the remnant, and the tribulation saints a prophetic word of what to expect, but also how to pray, and how to worship and praise our Holy Father during that time. They also reveal the general timeline of His Son's second coming and Millennial Kingdom reign, which can give many the strength to persevere through what will be the most difficult time known to man.

Before beginning, I would like to share two very important verses that I believe are foundational to the study of end-time prophecy. These are in addition to Amos 3:7, which I have already mentioned. As I am digging in God's word, I like to keep these scriptures in mind because they prove that the answers that I am looking for are there; I just have to be willing to put in the hard work of digging

them out.

Proverbs 25:2
It is the glory of God to conceal a matter, but the glory of kings is to search out a matter.

Isaiah 46:9-10
Remember the former things of old, For I am God, and there is no other; I am God, and there is none like Me, declaring the end from the beginning, and from ancient times things that are not yet done, saying, 'My counsel shall stand, and I will do all My pleasure,'

CHAPTER 2

Prophetic Patterns in Numbers

The discoveries in this book will simply not make any sense without having an understanding of how important numbers are in the Bible. When you are studying the Bible, it's a good idea to take note when you see a strange detail that seems like more information than necessary to tell the story. For instance, Exodus 7:7 says, *"and Moses was eighty years old and Aaron eighty-three years old when they spoke to Pharaoh."* Have you ever stopped to wonder why God decided to point their ages out to us? Later in Exodus 33 and 34 we're told that they lived to be 120 and 123 respectively. That means that they both lived exactly 40 more years after they left Egypt. Doesn't that make you curious? Is there a pattern hidden in there?

It's also a good idea to note any repeated numbers that you come across. Nothing is there by coincidence, and the repetition of certain numbers in the Bible is certainly not coincidental.

Coincidence in the Bible

I think that it's important as you read this book to understand that "coincidence" is not a biblical concept. Here are a few definitions of coincidence; a situation in which events happen at the same time in a way that is not planned or expected, the act or condition of coinciding, and also the occurrence of two or more things at the same time by accident but seem to have some connection.

The simple definition is that coincidence is something that happens by chance or without any planning. As I mentioned before, the word coincidence does not appear in the Bible. I do not think that it's a "coincidence" that coincidence isn't in the Bible. God is a God of order and precision, and not of chaos. The closest we get to coincidence in the Bible is the phrase "by chance" found in Luke 10, which is the story of the Good Samaritan. In verse 31, Luke states:

Luke 10:31
Now "by chance" a certain priest came down that road. And when he saw him, he passed by on the other side.

That is certainly not the best translation. The original Greek word for "by chance" was "synkyrian," which is actually two Greek words put together. The first part of the word is "Syn," which means together with, and the second part of the word is from the Greek word "Kurios," meaning supreme in authority. Together, the word Synkyrian actually means "providential guidance." That's the short version. According to Strong's Concordance, the long version is: what occurs together by God's providential arrangement of circumstances – all achieving His eternal purpose in each scene of life.

The point is that in God's arrangement of the Psalms, as well as His use of certain numbers in His word, God is telling a broader story as well as giving us more historical and prophetic insight. Nothing is by chance, and every number and placement is important. We just have to understand this and look for it.

I cannot overstate how important numbers are to God and how significant they are in His prophetic revelations. God consistently uses numbers throughout His scriptures to give greater meaning, context, and understanding to biblical accounts. He reveals patterns in prophecy by connecting past, present, and future events through the use of common numbers. Numbers usually reveal an encoded connection or an extra detail that you just might miss if you don't pay attention to them. We just have to be wise and look for these numbers and understand how they interconnect with other scriptures, and even with other characters in the Bible.

Have you ever noticed how many times certain numbers show up in the Bible? Take the number 7, for instance. The number 7 is used in the Bible over 700 times from Genesis to Revelation. Do you think that there is something significant about the number 7? If so, then how about other repeated numbers? Also, remember that the Old Testament was written in Hebrew, and the New Testament was written in Greek. Both of these languages are alphanumeric. Every letter in Hebrew and in Greek has a numerical value associated with it. As you will see, letters and their numerical values also have specific meanings and symbolism. Understanding this symbolism can be really helpful in deciphering the deeper meanings of scripture. I don't think it's a coincidence that God chose two alphanumeric languages for His word to be written in. We will be dealing with many such letters, numbers, and their symbolic meanings throughout this book.

Remember that God gave me two numbers in my time of distress over the timing of the "Rapture Season" and the tribulation. He gave me a 5 and a 10. Let's look at what God's word reveals about the number 5 and the number 10.

What is the Biblical significance of the number 5?

The number 5 is very significant in the Hebrew language and in the Bible. It is associated with God's grace. The 5th Hebrew letter is Hey and it also has the numerical value of 5. As a pictograph it represents breath, air, the "Rauch Ha Kodesh" or Holy Spirit in English, and once again, God's grace. It also represents the power that we are gifted to go out and complete the mission YHWH has given us individually and as the Church. Doesn't that sound like the Holy Spirit? The letter Hey is the only letter that appears in God's name twice: Yod, Hey, Vav, Hey, or YHWH in our English rendering.

There are 5 books of the Torah. The Psalms are divided into 5 sections matching the 5 books of the Torah. There are 5 other nations mentioned in Ezekiel 38 who will invade Israel along with the Gog of Magog. Jesus fed 5,000 with only 5 loaves of bread. There were 5 wise and 5 foolish virgins referenced in Jesus' parable in Matthew 25. Jesus pointed out that 5 of them had enough oil, and the other 5 did not. As you may know, oil typically represents the Holy Spirit in the Bible. The number 5 also relates to the anointing since there are specifically 5 ingredients in the anointing oil. You can see the connection between the Holy Spirit and anointing. The 5 ingredients are Myrrh, cinnamon, calamus, cassia, and olive oil.

Prophetically, I believe that the number 5 also represents the rapture of the Church. Since 5 represents the Holy Spirit that was poured out at Pentecost, 5 also represents the Holy Spirit, and our departure at the rapture. The 5th feast on God's calendar is the Feast of Trumpets, which is, of course, symbolic of the rapture and resurrection, and is the next feast day that will be fulfilled by Jesus. The 5th of 7 Churches in The Book of Revelation is Sardis, which has a few meanings such as "prince of joy," but also means "escaping" or "comes out."

The Church of Sardis in the Book of Revelation is known as the "dead" church even though they had a reputation of being alive. Jesus warned them that if they did not wake up and repent, He would come like a thief, and they would not know at what time He would come. That is definitely prophetic rapture language and ties together with 1 Thessalonians 5:2 and many other scriptures that indicate that Jesus will come like a thief in the night to those who are not watching and are not ready. That also means that He won't come like a thief and surprise those who are watching and are ready. What does a thief take? A thief takes treasures and valuables. We, the believing, repentant, and watching Church filled with the Holy Spirit, are the treasure that Jesus will come as a thief and take from this earth at the rapture. So, to those left behind, Jesus will be like a thief who came suddenly and took what was most valuable, even if they didn't realize its value.

Here's another interesting historical and prophetic sign relating to the number 5 that is playing out right now in our day. David picked up 5 smooth stones, but only needed 1 to slay the Nephilim giant Goliath. Recently, 5 perfect red heifers were shipped to Israel for the purification sacrifice according to Numbers 19, but they only needed 1. What are the odds of that? Do you think we are living in prophetic Bible times?

Mahalalel was the 5th in the Messianic line of Adam. Mahalalel means to shine or praise God. El, which we see in many Hebrew names, is the short form for Elohim, which is the plural title of God because God is 3 in 1, Father, Son, and Holy Spirit. El always represents God's strength and might. In Hebrew, Genesis 1:1 says that, "In the beginning, Elohim created the heavens and the earth." The use of Elohim lets us know that all three were at work, which ties to John 1:1-3 where Jesus is called the "Word," and we can clearly see that nothing was made without Him.

I don't believe that any of these facts related to the number 5 are by chance. I believe they are all pieces of a puzzle that our Heavenly Father wants us to study and piece together. Don't worry; we will dig out more as we progress through the prophetic Psalms.

What is the Biblical significance of the number 10?

You may have noticed in your Bible study time that there are lots of 10s in the Bible. The number 10 is a tricky one because it can be associated with both good and bad. For instance, God gave Israel the 10 Commandments as part of a covenant relationship between them and Himself, which is good. However, if they failed, and they certainly did repeatedly, there were dire consequences. So, there is typically a free-will choice involved with the number 10.

You may have also noticed that many times in the Bible, the number 10 has two 5s associated with it. For instance, God gave 10 Commandments to Israel, 5 written on one tablet, and 5 written on another. Jesus spoke of 10 virgins, 5 that were wise and ready, and 5 that were foolish and unprepared. There were 10 camels taken by Eleazar to find a bride for Isaac; he placed 2 bracelets on Rebekah's wrists weighing a total of 10 shekels of gold, or 5 shekels of gold each. Rebekah's brother and mother wanted Her to stay for another 10 days, but she agreed to go with Eleazar the next morning. The Philistines returned the Ark of the Covenant back to Israel with a guilt offering of 10 gold models of 5 tumors and 5 rats according to the number of the Philistine rulers who represented the whole of the Philistine people. Based on these stories and others, we know to be looking for 10s and 5s and to figure out what their importance is. Is there a repeating pattern that may help us unlock deeper meanings of prophetic events? We shall see...

Here are a few more important 10s from the Bible. Daniel and his friends were tested for 10 days to see if they withered from only eating vegetables and drinking water compared to the royal food. Job, who is a symbol of testing and tribulation, had 7 sons and 3 daughters, which, of course, equals 10. Noah was the 10th from Adam, and Jesus said the end times would be like the days of Noah. In Revelation 2:10, Jesus told the Church of Smyrna that they would be tested and suffer tribulation for 10 days. There are 10 Days of Awe (repentance) between the Feast of Trumpets (symbolic of the rapture) and the Day of Atonement (symbolic of Judgment Day), which happens to fall on the 10th day of Tishrei. Jesus ascended to the Father 10 days before the Jewish holiday that we call Pentecost, or Shavuot in Hebrew. There were 10 plagues poured out on Egypt, and evil Haman had 10 sons in the Book of Esther. The Passover lambs were selected on the 10th day of the month of Abib, or Nisan as it's now called in Hebrew. Jesus rode into Jerusalem on the colt of a donkey on the 10th of Abib fulfilling the prophecy of Zechariah 9:9 and showing himself as the Messiah, but was rejected by the majority of the Jews. There are a total of 10 enemies of Israel who will come against them, as indicated in Psalm 83. All of these are associated in some way with testing and choices, and that's just the shortlist! Do you think the Lord wants us to notice the number 10?

Here's one more. This is from Jewish history and the Jewish sage Rabbi Moshe ben Maimon (Maimonides, aka Rambam). There have only been a total of 9 red heifers sacrificed for the purification rituals required in Numbers 19 throughout history. The 10th will be the final red heifer, and according to Maimonides, it will be brought by the Messiah, which we know is the false messiah or Antichrist.

Here's an excerpt from Maimonides' writing called **Parah Adumah - Chapter 3:4:**

"...Nine red heifers were offered from the time that they were commanded to fulfill this mitzvah until the time when the Temple was destroyed a second time. The first was brought by Moses our teacher. The second was brought by Ezra. Seven others were offered until the destruction of the Second Temple. **And the tenth will be brought by the king *Mashiach*; may he speedily be revealed. *Amen*, so may it be G-d's will.**"

The 10th Hebrew letter is Yod and it also has the numerical value of 10. Yod is the first letter in the name of God. It has a pictographic symbol of a hand, representing a deed or action that can be good or bad. It can signify a snatching action, AKA harpazo in Greek or rapture in Latin, of the Church, and the trap for those remaining here during the tribulation. The rapture will be both a blessing and a curse: a blessing for those who are chosen to escape, according to Luke 21:36, and a curse for those who are left behind, according to Luke 21:35.

Another important attribute of the Biblical number 10 is that it is a symbol of the whole of something. For instance, a 10th of your earnings called a tithe, represents the whole of your earnings. So, as a biblical pattern, we have seen that 10 can represent a complete amount of something; it can be both good and bad, and typically involves a choice.

What are they together? 5 + 10 = 15 and 5 X 10 = 50

Let's start with the number 15. The first day of Passover, as well as the first day of Tabernacles, both start on the 15th of their respective months. It was at Passover that Jesus died for our sins, associating the number 15 with salvation and redemption. The Feast of Tabernacles is also associated with the future establishment of Jesus' Millennial Kingdom here on earth, which associates the number 15 with "ascending" from this age to the fullness of the next age.

Righteous King Hezekiah was granted another 15 years to live by God in 2 Kings 20. He was healed on the "3rd" day. King Hezekiah wrote 10 Psalms and added them to 4 Psalms written by King David, and 1 Psalm written by David's son, King Solomon, for a total of 15 Psalms called the 15 Songs of Ascent, one for each year that God added to his life. These 15 Psalms match the 15 steps up to the temple. They were sung by pilgrims and priests alike who came to worship at the temple each year at the Feast of Tabernacles. Can you see how intricately God has connected the number 15, and even the 15 Psalms of Ascent to represent ascension from the physical to the spiritual, salvation, healing, and redemption? Additionally, the prophet Hosea bought back, or "redeemed," his harlot wife, who represented Israel, for 15 silver shekels. Can all of that just be by coincidence?

The 15th letter in the Hebrew alphabet is Samech, which has the numeric value of 60. The number 15, however, is made up of both letters Yod and Hey, which is the short version of the name of God. Jews refer to God as HaShem (The Name) because His name is too holy to pronounce. Therefore, they also will not say the short version, or write the number 15 as 10 + 5 because that would also be Yod Hey. Instead, they write 15 as 9 + 6 so that they do not accidentally take God's name in vain. Remember that it was specifically a 15-year-old Bedouin boy who discovered the Dead Sea Scrolls in a cave in Qumran in 1947 as Israel was becoming a reborn nation. He wasn't 14 or 16, but he was specifically 15. Is that just a coincidence, or is that one way that God put his signature on possibly one of the most important discoveries in history? As you can see, it is already pretty clear that the number 15 is very important in the Bible and to God, and there's still more to discover.

Now let's look at the number 50 (5 X 10)

The number 50 is very important to us Christians. Pentecost, or Shavuot as it is known in Hebrew, is 50 days after the Feast of First Fruits (Leviticus 23:15-16). The First Fruits was the day that Jesus was resurrected from the grave, making Him the First Fruits of the resurrection harvest. Shavuot was the day when the Holy Spirit was poured out on 120 believers in the upper room beginning the Church

Age, as we see in Acts chapter 2. So, we can see that the number 50 is directly associated with the Holy Spirit.

The number 50 is also associated with paying a price or a ransom. As already stated, Jesus paid the price on the cross and then rose again; then, 50 days later, He sent the Holy Spirit to live inside of us. According to Deuteronomy 22:29, it takes 50 shekels of silver to make restitution and to pay the bride price to the father. Also, David purchased the threshing floor from Araunah the Jebusite to build an altar to the Lord for 50 shekels of silver (2 Samuel 24:24). You see, there's a reason why God's word gives us these numbers. It's so that we can connect them to other passages with like numbers to see a bigger picture. He could have just said that David purchased the threshing floor for a bag of silver, but He specifically told us that it was with 50 shekels of silver. He wants us to notice these numbers and put it all together!

Similar to paying a price, the number 50 also represents the release and the freedom granted from the price being paid. For example, the year of Jubilee is every 50 years. There are 7 Shmita cycles (7 X 7 = 49 years) followed by a Jubilee year. If the cycle was followed, which meant allowing the land to rest every 7 years and trusting in God to provide for the Israelites during the Sabbath year, then the 50th year, the Jubilee year, was to be a year of release. Prisoners and slaves were to be set free, debts were to be forgiven, and property was to be returned to its original owner. Similar to the Shmita years, there was to be no sowing or reaping of the land, which meant that the land rested as well as those who worked the land.

The number 50 is also associated with the Tabernacle. Not only was the number 50 prevalent in the items such as curtains in the construction of the tabernacle, but due to the labor involved in the erecting, dismantling, and transportation of the tabernacle from camp to camp, the Levite priests were to be no older than 50 years old (Numbers 4:23) at the completion of their service. So, through the Jubilee year, you can see that 50 relates to completion, a new beginning, the end of one cycle, and the beginning of another. Likewise, 50 is also related to the end of one age in a priest's life, and the beginning of another. His hard labor was over, and he was able to enter into a more restful time in his life.

There are only 22 letters in the Hebrew alphabet so there is no 50th letter. However, the 14th letter has the value of 50. That letter is Nun. As a pictograph, Nun is a seed or fish that symbolizes faithfulness, fruitfulness, and fullness. In Exodus 33, we are told that Joshua, Moses' protégé, was the "son of Nun." Joshua is Yeshua in Hebrew, which means God's Savior. That is Jesus' Hebrew name as well. Joshua was a "type" of messiah to Israel and was associated with the number 50, which also means a servant and a leader.

The number 50, and its relationship with other numbers is going to be very important in the coming chapters, but we're not quite there yet. What I've laid out so far about the biblical number 50 has been to give you a basic overview, and to whet your appetite to want to dig in a little deeper.

Other very important end-time numbers to understand:

I'm going to keep the remainder of the outlines of these important numbers shorter, and only give the general biblical idea of each of them, along with a few references, to keep this section as brief as possible. I will be adding to them as we progress through the pages of the timeline revelation.

The Biblical Symbolism of 3

Where to start? The number three is written hundreds of times throughout the Bible, and is also encoded throughout the Bible in less obvious ways, symbolized by 3 people such as Abraham, Isaac, and Jacob; 3 angels of Revelation 14; 3 categories of judgments - seals, trumpets, and bowls in Revelation; 3 pilgrimage festivals in Israel - Passover, Pentecost, and Tabernacles. Jesus was in the grave 3 days and 3 nights and was resurrected on the third of the annual festivals which is called the Feast of First Fruits, to be the first fruits of the resurrection, etc. The number 3 is one of the biblical numbers that represents divine completion and perfection, similar to the number 7. One example is the 3 in 1 Godhead - Father, Son, and Holy Spirit.

The Biblical Symbolism of 7

The biblical number 7 represents both physical and spiritual perfection and completion. It is by far the number found most often throughout the Old and the New Testaments. For the purpose of the timeline revelation, it is important to understand that God created the world around us over the course of 6 days, and then He rested from His work of creation on the 7th day, which He called the Sabbath day. This 7-day cycle established more than just a 7-day weekly pattern for the sake of marking days of the week on a calendar. More importantly, it also established a millennial pattern of 7 days (1 day = 1000 years) until the completion of prophecy (Psalm 90, 2 Peter 3). The beginning of the Bible, Genesis chapter 1, establishes the pattern, and the end of the Bible, Revelation chapters 20 and 21, tells of its completion. That means that mankind has 6 days, or 6000 years, until the beginning of the Millennial Sabbath, which is symbolized in Israel's 7th annual festival, known as the Feast of Tabernacles (Leviticus 23). A tabernacle is a booth or a tent, and it represents the Lord dwelling with us here on earth over the 1000-year Sabbath.

This was understood and taught by the ancient Hebrews as well as our Church Fathers in the early centuries of the Church Age; however, it isn't commonly taught any longer in churches, which lends to the confusion about what day we're actually living in. I find it ironic that at the very end of the 6th day, which is where we are now in the cycle, the very time that this information is most important, it is no longer taught or understood.

The Biblical Symbolism of 12

The number 12 commonly represents a perfect order and completeness both in time and organization. For example, there are 12 months in a year and 12 main constellations in the heavens, which God placed there for "signs and seasons" (Genesis 1:14). Jacob "Israel" had 12 sons, who were the patriarchs, or the "foundation" of the 12 tribes of Israel. Jesus specifically chose 12 disciples to teach and to become the "foundation" of His Church.

There was one of the 12 tribes who became apostates, the tribe of Dan. There was one disciple who became apostate, Judas Iscariot, who was probably from the tribe of Dan. There are 12 Psalms of Asaph, with 11 of the Psalms grouped together, but there is one "apostate," which isn't grouped with the other 11. The number 11 symbolizes judgment, rebellion, disorder, and chaos. The beast, aka Antichrist, is the 11th horn (Daniel 7).

The Biblical Symbolism of 30

The number 30, especially as it relates to age, is extremely important in Biblical history, as well as in prophecy. Numbers chapter 4 reveals that a Levite may not enter into priestly service until he is 30 years old. Jesus was 30 years old when He began His ministry. The number 30 is connected with both priests and kings, which I will greatly expand upon in the coming chapters.

The Biblical Symbolism of 40

The number 40 represents a period of testing, trial, and probation. For instance, Israel was tested in the desert for 40 years (Numbers 13, Joshua 1-4). It rained for 40 days and 40 nights during the flood (Genesis 7). Noah waited for 40 days after the water had receded below the tops of the mountains before he sent out a raven and a dove to see if the water had receded from the face of the ground (Genesis 8). Moses sent out 12 spies, including Caleb and Joshua, for 40 days to spy on the land that God had promised the Israelites (Numbers 13). Moses was on Mount Sinai for 40 days and nights, each of 3 times meeting with Yahweh (Deuteronomy 9 & 10). Moses led Israel for 40 years. He was 80 at the Exodus and died when he was 120 years old. King Saul ruled for 40 years (Acts 13). King David ruled for 40 years (2 Samuel 5). King Solomon ruled for 40 years (1 Kings 11). Goliath challenged the Israelite army for 40 days when David answered his challenge and defeated him (1 Samuel 17). The Ninevites were given a warning that their city would be destroyed in 40 days. They repented and were not destroyed (Jonah 3). Jesus fasted for 40 days and nights in the wilderness before being tempted by the Devil (Matthew 4, Mark 1, Luke 4). Jesus ascended to the Father 40 days after His resurrection (Acts 1).

Here's one more. Remember that God instructed Israel to have a weekly Sabbath, Moedim Sabbaths, Shmita Sabbaths every 7th year, and also a Jubilee Sabbath year every 50th year after 7 Shmita cycles. If Jesus' death, burial, and resurrection happened in 32 AD as prophesied by the Essenes in the Dead Sea Scrolls, then as of 2032, there will have been exactly 40 Jubilee cycles since then. Not only have the children of Israel been tested for the past 40 Jubilees, but we, the Church, have also been tested now for a 40 Jubilee probation period. Also, according to the Essenes, the end of the age will be in 2075. The end of their age was prophesied to be in 75 AD. They knew that the Messiah would come in 32 AD, which would have been at the end of the first Shmita cycle in the final Jubilee period of their age. If this was correct, and the Essenes were known to have been 100% correct in all of their prophesies, this means that in 2025, we will be entering into the final Jubilee period. That means that 2024 is the actual final Shmita year in the current Jubilee cycle. In the Jewish Rabbinical writings, they point out that war usually comes in the 7th year, and according to what you will see in the timeline revelation, this holds true.

The interesting thing is that the Pharisees of Jesus' time, and therefore today's Rabbis, are following a corrupted calendar, which was also prophesied in the Dead Sea Scrolls, so they do not know when the actual Shmita year or Jubilee year is. They think that the Shmita year was from September 2021 until September 2022. That means, according to their calculations, we are now at the beginning of a new Shmita cycle as of 2022/2023. They begin their Shmita calculations 1 year after the destruction of the temple, which they say was either in 68 AD, 69 AD, or 70 AD. You see how this gets really confusing! To keep it simple, if the temple was destroyed in 70 AD, that would mean that 71 AD was their first year in the cycle, and 77 AD was then the first Shmita year in the age since the destruction of the temple. Since all of this is debated by Rabbis and Jewish scholars, I can see how it will be open for the coming Antichrist to explain it to them, which will, of course, fit within his agenda. Remember that Daniel prophesies that the Antichrist will change times.

Daniel 7:25
*He shall speak pompous words against the Most High, shall persecute the saints of the Most High, and shall intend to change **times** and law. Then the saints shall be given into his hand for a time and times and half a time.*

According to Essene calculations, the Shmita year would have been in 74 AD, and the Jubilee year would have been in 75 AD. Personally, I believe that the Essene calendar and dates are correct.

The problem with the current Jewish count of Shmita cycles is compounded since they are also not counting Jubilee years. This is for a host of reasons, but mainly it's because they believe that all of the 12 Tribes of Israel have to be back in their land before they can observe the Jubilee years. That doesn't mean that God isn't counting them. God counts time by 7s and 50s. There are seven sevens in 50 years (7 X 7 = 49), with the 50th year being the Jubilee year all by itself. That means that the start of the next Shmita cycle wouldn't begin until the Jubilee year ended. If they aren't counting a Jubilee year every 50 years that will certainly throw off their count. For example, in a 2000-year period, there should be 40 Jubilee cycles of 50 years each. However, if you are counting by 49 and not 50, you end up with 40.82 in the same 2000-year period. There isn't anything prophetic about 40.82.

The Biblical Symbolism of 80

The number 80 represents a distinct period of time-related to Israel such as a lifespan, generation, or period of rulership. More importantly, 80 years specifically marks the end of those periods.

As I already mentioned, Moses was 80 years old when God poured out 10 plagues on Egypt, allowing Israel to set out on their journey to the promised land (Exodus 7:7). At that time, the nation of Israel was set free from captivity, and set out on a new course. So, through Moses, the number 80 is associated with the end of one period of time, and the beginning of another. Prior to that time, Joseph ruled over Egypt for 80 years. Exodus 41:46 says that Joseph was 30 years old when he entered the service of Pharaoh. Genesis 50:22 & 26 tell us that Joseph was 110 years old when he died. 110 - 30 = 80 years. Later, King David and then his son Solomon ruled for a total of 80 years, exactly 40 years each. According to ancient Jewish writings, Boaz, the Kinsman Redeemer, who was a messiah figure in the Bible, was 80 years old when he married Ruth, the Gentile bride. As patterned by Boaz and Ruth, Jesus came at the completion of 4,000 years of human history to take a Gentile bride, the Church. That was at the completion of 80 Jubilees. It has almost been another 40 Jubilees since Jesus' ascension. In simple math, 80 Jubilees + 40 Jubilees = 120 Jubilees. Does this connect back to Genesis 6:3, which says, *"My Spirit shall not strive with man forever, for he is indeed flesh; yet his days shall be one hundred and twenty years?"* Keep in mind that God interchanges days for years, etc. It's also interesting to note that according to Deuteronomy 34, Moses died when he was 120 years old, not 119, or 121, but specifically 120 years. That's God telling us something, it's significant!

So Moses was 80 at the Exodus when Israel was set free, but because of Israel's rebellion, they had to wander in the desert for 40 years of trials, testing, and probation until Moses was 120, then they were finally able to enter into the promised land. Jesus came at 80 Jubilees but was rejected by Israel, who rebelled against Him; they've endured trials, testing, and probation for almost 40 Jubilees, which will be complete in 2032 (2000 years/50 years = 40 Jubilees). Can you see the pattern? We're almost at the end of the 40 Jubilees since Jesus' ascension, which will equal a total of 120 Jubilees of human history, just as patterned by Moses' life.

Considering this strong pattern, will Israel enter into the promised land, meaning the Millennial Kingdom, where Jesus, Israel's true

Messiah, will reign from Jerusalem for 1000 years at the end of this current 2000-year period (40 Jubilees), which began in 32 AD? If the Millennial Kingdom begins after exactly 2000 years, or 40 Jubilees in 2032, then the 7-year tribulation period cannot start any later than 2025!

It's also very important to know that as a pattern, Israel has never in their history made it past 80 years as a unified, sovereign nation. The reborn nation of Israel will be 80 years old in 2028. If that pattern continues, 2028 marks the end of the nation of Israel as we know it today. All of these times and numbers, as well as signs of the times, are converging right now in our current world. Can all of this simply be a coincidence?

OK, let's put some numbers to good use. After studying the biblical texts and historical proofs, I'm still amazed by this one. The book of Daniel is a treasure trove of prophecy and is really an amazing book to study. For now, I want to focus on Daniel chapter 9, which ties a lot of the prophetic timing together. Understanding the portions of Daniel 9 that have already been fulfilled, and their timing, can give us reassurance that we can not only trust Bible prophecy but also the timing of it. If it was accurate in the past, it stands to reason that it will be accurate in the future. God doesn't make mistakes, and He's not a God of chaos or disorder. In fact, Bible prophecy has a perfect track record of fulfilled prophesies that foretold the future from the ancient past, and many of the yet-to-be-fulfilled prophesies are coming true right now in our generation.

The Daniel 9 prophecy is all about numbers, and I'm sorry to say that there is some math involved in this one, so as my 1st-grade teacher used to say, "Put on your thinking cap," and let's get started...

At the end of the Babylonian captivity of the Israelites, we find Daniel praying over the nation of Israel and the city of Jerusalem for the forgiveness of their sins. While Daniel is still praying, he is visited by the Angel Gabriel. Gabriel explains to Daniel that there will be a total of seventy weeks of sevens until the end, which will be broken into 3 periods. The first period was made up of seven sevens, or 49 years, which was the time it would take to rebuild

Jerusalem. Now, this is really important... A distinct time is given by Gabriel to pinpoint a specific date for the prophecy to begin. Gabriel explains that the prophecy begins when the decree goes forth to restore Jerusalem. That decree was detailed in Nehemiah 2:1-8, and we know the date of that decree, which was given by King Artaxerxes. That date was in the Jewish month of Nisan 1, 445 BC, or March 14 on our Gregorian calendar. Sorry, I'm getting ahead of myself. We'll move on with the other 2 periods of sevens, but we'll come back to this very important date.

The second period of sevens (weeks) was explained by Gabriel to be 62 sevens, which is a total of 434 years. The two periods combined, 49 + 434 = 483 years. In verse 26 Daniel states that after the 483 years from the time that the decree goes forth to rebuild Jerusalem, the Messiah would be "cut off," meaning killed, or executed, not for Himself, nor for His own sins, but for others. So, at the completion of 69 weeks, which equals 483, the Messiah was to come and be killed for others. But it's the 70 weeks prophecy, and not the 69 weeks prophecy, so what happened to the last week? It is still to come. It is the week of years known as the tribulation period. The two periods of time have been separated by 2000 years, or 40 Jubilee periods, to allow for Israel's rebellion during their time of testing, trial, and probation. That time is rapidly coming to a close.

There's more to Daniel's prophecy. In between the 483 years and the final 7 years of Daniel's 70 weeks, it was prophesied that the temple and Jerusalem would be destroyed again, this time by the "people of the prince that shall come." This prophecy was fulfilled in 70 AD by the Romans. The tragic yet amazing thing is that at the time that Daniel wrote this prophecy, the 2nd Temple hadn't been built yet, but it was already prophesied to be destroyed. Also, wars and desolations for Israel would be between the 69th and 70th week. That has certainly been true as the children of Israel were scattered all over the world and hated by many resulting in the Nazi holocaust, where over 6 million Jews were murdered.

As I mentioned, as of today, the final prophetic week of 7 years has yet to be fulfilled. We are currently still living in the mysterious age between week 69 and 70 of Daniel's 70 weeks prophecy given to him by the Angel Gabriel. The age we are living in is known as the Church Age.

So, was Daniel's messianic prophecy fulfilled by Jesus? This prophecy said that the Messiah would arrive at the end of 483 years, starting with the decree of Artaxerxes to rebuild Jerusalem. If it hadn't happened at that exact time, that failure of his prophecy would prove Daniel to be a false prophet and cast doubt on biblical prophecy as a whole.

Let's evaluate the biblical and historical records to determine the answer. The decree was given and is known historically to have occurred on Nisan 1, 445 BC, which is the 14th of March on the Gregorian calendar. These dates have been confirmed by historical records, as well as by the British Royal Observatory and astronomical calculations.

Now for some math... 69 weeks of years x 7-days per week x 360 days per year = 173,880 days. The prophetic calendar is based on a 360-day year. Starting with March 14th, 445 BC, which again was the day that the decree went forth, and adding the prophesied 173,880 days brings us to April 6th, 32 AD. That day lands on the Sunday before the Passover celebration in Jerusalem that year, which was Nisan 14 on the Hebrew calendar. That's the day we call Palm Sunday, when Jesus rode into Jerusalem on the colt of a donkey to proclaim that He is the Messiah as was prophesied in Zechariah 9:9! Daniel's 69 weeks prophecy, written in Daniel chapter 9 over 500 years before its fulfillment pinpoints the exact day that Jesus Christ, Yeshua HaMashiach, would arrive in Jerusalem as the Messiah, and thereby also pinpoint the time of His crucifixion as the Passover Lamb to atone for our sins. How could all of this be a coincidence?

I realize that Jesus' crucifixion date is debatable, but according to fulfilled Bible prophecy and these calculations, I think that we can be assured that Jesus was crucified in 32 AD. The year 32 AD becomes even more probable when you consider also that the Essenes, who left us the Dead Sea Scrolls, had also calculated, and prophesied that the Messiah would arrive in 32 AD. Once again, if we add 2000 years, which is 40 Jubilee periods, to that date, we land in 2032 for the end of the age. Also, when you consider it within the symbolism of human history as a one- week period of 7-days, Jesus came at the completion of the 4th day, meaning that the 6th day will also be completed in 2032 if 1 day is as 1000 years (Psalm 90, 2 Peter 3). The number 4, and the fact that Jesus came at the completion of the 4th day, is also very prophetically significant, as we shall discover in the coming chapters. For now, hang on to the thought that by many different metrics, it is clear that we are at the end of the current age known as the Church Age, and we are getting ready to enter into the 7th day, which is the Millennial Kingdom reign of Christ. But first, there has to be a 7-year tribulation period (the final week) to turn Israel back to God, and for them to accept His Son, the Lamb who was slain (Revelation 5).

CHAPTER 3

The Rapture and the Fig Tree Generation

Many throughout the past 2000 years have tried to figure out when the rapture of the Church will occur. I realize that there are some teachers out there who say that the rapture is a relatively new doctrine thought up by John Darby in the 1800s, but history tells a different story. In fact, early church fathers from the 2nd and 3rd centuries, such as Irenaeus, and Victorinus of Poetovio, plus other writings, including the Didache and the Shepherd of Hermas, all spoke of the church escaping the tribulation period. Many nonbelievers in the pre-tribulation rapture say that those who believe in a pre-tribulation rapture just want to escape the death and destruction of the apocalypse. Well, duh! Let's see, would I rather be with my Lord and Savior, or here facing the worst time in human history? Easy choice...

Many also teach that there is no such thing as a rapture and that the word "rapture" isn't even in the Bible. Yes, it is true that the term rapture doesn't appear in your English translation of the Bible. However, the original Greek writing of the New Testament includes the word Harpazo. The Greek word Harpazo means to seize, carry off by force, claim for one's self eagerly, and snatch out, or away. The Latin translation of the word Harpazo is Rapturo, which means to snatch or carry off. When you're reading your English Bible, and you see the phrase "caught up," that's Harpazo or Rapture.

In 2 Corinthians 12:2 and 12:4 Paul explained that he knew a man (probably himself) who was "caught up" (Harpazo) to the third heaven either in the body or out of the body.

Once again, Paul tells the believers in Thessalonica in 1 Thessalonians 4:17 that they/we would be "caught up" together in the clouds to meet the Lord in the air.

John the apostle reveals in one of the parenthetical chapters of Revelation, Revelation 12:5, that the man child (Jesus) was "caught up" unto God. For the sake of clarity, when I use the word "rapture," I'm talking about the day when the Lord returns for His bride, the true believing Church, and will snatch us away in the twinkling of an eye according to 1 Corinthians 15 prior to the tribulation period.

Worthy to Escape

In the conclusion of His "end of the age" teaching that we call the Olivet Discourse, after describing many of the signs and the horrific events of the tribulation period, Jesus gave us a very important commandment, which is found in Luke 21.

Luke 21:36
*36 Watch therefore, and pray always that you may be counted **worthy** to escape all these things that will come to pass, and to stand before the Son of Man.*

I hardly need to add any commentary to this scripture, as it pretty much says it all! According to Jesus Himself, we should be watching and praying always to be counted worthy to "escape" the terrible things that are coming on this earth. The word that really stands out to me in this text isn't actually "escape," but it's the word "worthy." Knowing the timeline, and at least having a rough idea of when the final events will happen should cause everyone who reads this book to refocus their lives on what really matters, which is our salvation, repentance, our relationship with the Lord, and the salvation of all of those whom God has brought into our lives. After all, in the end, there is only saved or unsaved, Heaven or Hell. Nothing else will even matter.

Remember the parable that Jesus taught in Matthew 25, and ask yourself, "Why am I here?"

Matthew 25:14-30

[14] *"For the kingdom of heaven is like a man traveling to a far country, who called his own servants and delivered his goods to them.* [15] *And to one he gave five talents, to another two, and to another one, to each according to his own ability; and immediately he went on a journey.* [16] *Then he who had received the five talents went and traded with them, and made another five talents.* [17] *And likewise he who had received two gained two more also.* [18] *But he who had received one went and dug in the ground, and hid his lord's money.* [19] *After a long time the lord of those servants came and settled accounts with them.*

[20] *"So he who had received five talents came and brought five other talents, saying, 'Lord, you delivered to me five talents; look, I have gained five more talents besides them.'* [21] *His lord said to him, 'Well done, good and faithful servant; you were faithful over a few things, I will make you ruler over many things. Enter into the joy of your lord.'* [22] *He also who had received two talents came and said, 'Lord, you delivered to me two talents; look, I have gained two more talents besides them.'* [23] *His lord said to him, 'Well done, good and faithful servant; you have been faithful over a few things, I will make you ruler over many things. Enter into the joy of your lord.'*

[24] *"Then he who had received the one talent came and said, 'Lord, I knew you to be a hard man, reaping where you have not sown, and gathering where you have not scattered seed.* [25] *And I was afraid, and went and hid your talent in the ground. Look, there you have what is yours.'*

²⁶ "But his lord answered and said to him, 'You wicked and lazy servant, you knew that I reap where I have not sown, and gather where I have not scattered seed. ²⁷ So you ought to have deposited my money with the bankers, and at my coming I would have received back my own with interest. ²⁸ So take the talent from him, and give it to him who has ten talents.

²⁹ 'For to everyone who has, more will be given, and he will have abundance; but from him who does not have, even what he has will be taken away.³⁰ And cast the unprofitable servant into the outer darkness. There will be weeping and gnashing of teeth.'

We are servants and are here to multiply! Not just physically, but spiritually. We are here to multiply the Kingdom of God. That's how we serve Him. He has given us each unique abilities and placed us among certain people in a certain place and time. He has given each of us a mission to complete. Are we living to complete that mission for the Kingdom, or are we keeping the treasure that He has given us to ourselves, perhaps not wanting to offend anyone with our Jesus?

I'm not saying that you won't be found worthy to escape the coming tribulation if you don't complete your mission, but are you even working on it? That is the question. The wicked servant in the parable wasn't even working on it. I believe that time is very short, and it's time to take our mission seriously.

To sum up many of Jesus' parables and teachings, we need to be watching, praying, and preparing ourselves, as well as those around us, so that we can be found worthy by our Lord no matter when He comes for us. You may think that we are saved by grace and not by our works, and you would be correct. However, I believe there is a difference between saying a prayer, as if speaking some magic words, versus truly believing in the finished work of Jesus on the cross and allowing the Holy Spirit to work in you and through you. As a born-again believer, shouldn't there be some evidence in your life as a witness to your belief?

Do you desire a relationship with your Savior, or are you still wanting a relationship with the world (Romans 8:7-9, James 4:4)?

What if being found *"worthy to escape"* the tribulation isn't the same as being saved? After all, death is final, being left behind isn't. Remember the 10 virgins of Jesus' parable in Matthew 25? Of the 10, 5 were taken to the wedding, and 5 were left behind. They all had some oil in their lamps, but some didn't have enough. Remember what Jesus said about the Laodicean Church in Revelation 3? They were neither hot nor cold, so Jesus spit them out. I can give other examples, especially from Matthew chapters 13 and 25 and Revelation chapters 2 and 3; however, the point is that I believe Jesus is returning to carry away His spotless bride and not for a lazy prostitute. I realize this seems a little harsh, but I have had to wrestle with these scriptures and their meaning in my own life, and then ask myself some hard questions. Have I made Jesus the real Lord of my life? Have I turned away from my sinful nature? Am I keeping His commandments, or am I lukewarm and living with one foot in the world and one foot in the Church? Am I using what God has given me to multiply the Kingdom of God? Am I giving God my best every day, or am I more concerned with the things of the world, such as work, entertainment, politics, etc...

We are absolutely saved by grace through faith as stated by the Apostle Paul in Ephesians 2.

Ephesians 2:8-9
[8] For by grace you have been saved through faith, and that not of yourselves; it is the gift of God, [9] not of works, lest anyone should boast.

However, most people leave off the following verse, verse 10, when quoting this scripture.

Ephesians 2:10
*[10] For we are His workmanship, created in Christ Jesus for **good works**, which God prepared beforehand that we should walk in them.*

So, we have been saved by grace to do good works that God had prepared for each of us. I don't want anyone to think I'm suggesting it's our works that get us to heaven. That's not what I'm saying at all. What I'm saying is this: when we were saved and were born-again, our hearts and our deeds should reflect the transformation that has taken place within each of us. It should be our heart's desire to do the good works that God prepared for us. He simply wants us to bear good fruit. If not, perhaps you will be given a chance to bear good fruit while being tested through the fire of the tribulation period. Only God can judge each of our hearts to determine who will be found worthy to escape as Jesus described in Luke 21. As for me, I don't want to be found wanting. I want to live with purpose and do the work that He has called me to do, not out of religious obligation, but to make my Savior happy. I want to put a smile on His face and then one day hear Him say "Well done."

The Month of Elul

In the Jewish custom, the month of Elul, which would be the 6th month on God's calendar, is a month of turning back to God in spiritual preparation for the coming High Holy Days of the Feast of Trumpets, Day of Atonement, and the Feast of Tabernacles, all of which represent the coming end of the age. As we know, in God's timing, "a day is as a thousand years," the 6th month represents the 6th day or final 1 thousand years before the 7th day, which is the Sabbath, also known as the Millennial Kingdom. We're at the tail end of the 6th day! From the beginning of Elul until the Day of Atonement there are 40 days known as Yemei Ratzon, which is Hebrew for Days of Favor, but they are also known as a time of Teshuvah, which means repent and return. During the month of Elul, religious Jews spend time in the study of the Torah, spend time in personal reflection, seek forgiveness from God and from others whom they have wronged, say special prayers, sing Psalm 27 daily, blow the shofar to awaken their souls, and get their lives and their houses in order before the coming of the Yamim Nora'im, which, as I have already mentioned, are the 10 days of Awe between the Feast of Trumpets until the Day of Atonement.

I had planned to expand on the prophetic importance of the Feast Days at the end of this book, but that added almost another 200 pages. So, for now, it is important to know that there are 7 Feast Days that were given to Israel to observe. They are listed in Leviticus 23 and combined they are all prophetic of God's redemption plan. The first 4 were fulfilled by Jesus through His death, burial, and resurrection at His first coming, as well as the outpouring of the Holy Spirit 10 days after His ascension. That leaves the final 3 to be fulfilled at His second coming. It is also important to understand that the 5th Feast/Festival is the Feast of Trumpets, which is symbolic of the Rapture, and the 6th Feast/Festival is the Day of Atonement, which is symbolic of the Day of Judgment following the return of the King. Following those two special days is the 7th Feast/Festival, which is the Feast of Tabernacles, which is symbolic of the Millennial Kingdom when we "tabernacle" with Christ. There are 10 days total from the Feast of Trumpets until the Day of Atonement, and then 5 more days until the Feast of Tabernacles. Just as God showed me, here we have both a 10 and a 5 for a total of 15!

It seems that the Israelites are aware that prior to the final feast days of God's calendar, they should be prepared spiritually through repentance and a time of fervently seeking the Lord. Is this just a coincidence, or is it symbolic of what we should be doing at the end of the age? God has given us every chance to wake up. As I mentioned, we are at the end of the symbolic month of Elul, and it's time for each of us to get our house in order. God has given us his prophetic word and so many signs and seasons so that we can know that we're in the final moments of the final "Elul" before the return of His son Jesus at the sound of the trumpet. Unfortunately, much of the church is still asleep. They forgot that we should be "watching" and "praying" to be found "worthy" to escape what is coming. At the most critical time, many churches will not teach about Bible prophecy to warn their congregations of what is ahead and to prepare them on how to be found worthy. Many have spent their time worried about worldly things and have forgotten about the Great Commission. They have spent the time that God gave them, and the gift they were freely given on themselves instead of sharing it with others as Jesus instructed us to do. I was once such a person, but after realizing just how short time really is, and what is truly important in this life, I am trying my best to serve the Lord now every day until He comes for me. Maybe He will come for me at the rapture, but maybe I don't even have that long. None of us are promised tomorrow. Regardless, I so desperately want to hear, "Well done, good and faithful servant." My heart is crushed over the thought of anyone hearing, "You wicked and lazy servant..." "Cast the unprofitable servant into outer darkness."

The Rebirth of Israel (Isaiah 66, Ezekiel 37)

How do we know that time is short and that we are in the final month of Elul? After all, haven't many Christians before us thought that they were living in the last days? For example, many Christians in the 1800s thought that the Lord would come back in their time, but that couldn't have happened because they were missing the fact that there was one main prophecy that had to be fulfilled prior to the Lord's return. Remember earlier that I said God had given us His prophetic word, which reveals signs and seasons. Well, the number one super sign that we are in the end times has to be the unprecedented rebirth of the nation of Israel in 1948. After all, Israel is the focal point of the Bible and the end times, so the end of the world cannot start without her!

Before I proceed, I would like to go over some basics for studying and understanding God's prophetic word without straying too far off course. The first thing to understand is that the Bible is a book of prophecy, with over 25 percent of the verses in the Bible being prophetic. Secondly, you have to study and know biblical and world history, and lastly, you have probably noticed that God never speaks to us in plain black-and-white English, so you have to really study, dig, and let scripture interpret scripture. It's sort of like peeling an onion. Every time you peel a layer away, a new layer appears, and it seems endless, layer after layer. Wouldn't we love to have everything laid out in simple bullet statements right on the top layer? There are reasons that future events aren't spoken of in that way. Bible prophecy is written in patterns, parables, rich metaphors, symbolism, types, shadows, and numbers. From Genesis chapter 1 through the last chapter of Revelation, God has given us just enough information and clues to form a basic understanding and to be able to anticipate things to come if we only have ears to hear and eyes to see. However, He doesn't give it so clearly that the enemy has enough detail to be able to change God's appointed times and events. In a nutshell, Proverbs 25:2 tells us that *it is the glory of God to conceal a thing, but the honor of kings is to search out a matter."* So, our heavenly Father wants us to search out His truth. He also uses prophecy to declare and reveal His authority over human history past, present and future for His glory.

Here's a perfect example from Isaiah's foretelling of the re-establishment or "re-birth" of the nation of Israel, but encrypted metaphorically in the imagery of childbirth. Remember, as I said earlier, Israel becoming a nation again is the number 1 super sign of the end times!

Isaiah 66:8
8 Who has heard such a thing? Who has seen such things? Shall the earth be made to give birth in one day? Or shall a nation be born at once? For as soon as Zion was in labor, she gave birth to her children.

Just as prophesied, Israel became a nation again in one day on May 14, 1948, which was unprecedented in world history. After the Jewish holocaust of World War II by the Nazis, Israel was once again a nation. On that day in May, David Ben-Gurion, the head of the Jewish Agency, proclaimed the establishment of the State of Israel. To make it official, U.S. President Harry S. Truman recognized Israel as a new nation on that very same day fulfilling the prophecy of Isaiah 66 and the dry bones prophecy of Ezekiel 37.

Ezekiel 37:11-14

Then He said to me, "Son of man, these bones are the whole house of Israel. They indeed say, 'Our bones are dry, our hope is lost, and we ourselves are cut off!' Therefore prophesy and say to them, 'Thus says the Lord GOD: "Behold, O My people, I will open your graves and cause you to come up from your graves, and bring you into the land of Israel. Then you shall know that I am the LORD, when I have opened your graves, O My people, and brought you up from your graves. I will put My Spirit in you, and you shall live, and I will place you in your own land. Then you shall know that I, the LORD, have spoken it and performed it," says the LORD.'"

You can see the horror of the holocaust pictured in the symbolism of the dry bones. It's out of the ashes of WWII that Israel was re-born.

Fig Tree Generation (Luke 21:29-32, Matthew 24:32-35, Mark 13:28-31)

The next sign goes hand in hand with the re-birth of Israel...

Matthew 24:32-35

"Now learn this parable from the fig tree: When its branch has already become tender and puts forth leaves, you know that summer is near. So you also, when you see all these things, know that it is near—at the doors! Assuredly, I say to you, this generation will by no means pass away till all these things take place."

The nations around Israel were known symbolically by their native trees. For instance, you will find that Lebanon was always biblically associated with the cedar tree. Even today, the cedar tree is proudly displayed on their national flag. As I have mentioned before, the nation of Israel is the prophetic and symbolic fig tree. The fig tree has been "putting forth leaves" or blossoming and re-gathering against all odds since the re-birth of Israel in 1948. Even though they are surrounded by enemy Arab nations that all want their destruction, they have thrived and continue to thrive.

In 1948 the surrounding Arab nations of Jordan (Transjordan), Egypt, Lebanon, Syria, Iraq, Saudi Arabia, and Yemen all attacked Israel one day after Israel's rebirth on May 15th with firepower and manpower far greater than what the newly founded nation of Israel had. Israel miraculously fought off all of the attackers and managed to hold their fledgling nation together. Since then, Israel has been in 8 recognized wars and countless armed conflicts with their Arab neighbors. Every time, they are like David fighting against Goliath, and every time, God miraculously makes a way for Israel to prevail.

Remember that Jesus said that the generation that sees the fig tree blossom (Israel's rebirth) would not pass away before all of the before-mentioned signs and prophesies were fulfilled. Also, remember that Israel is already 74 years old at the time of writing this. So, how long is a biblical generation? Well, here's the kicker: Psalm 90:10 says, *"The days of our lives are seventy years; and if by reason of strength they are eighty years,"* So, if you take it literally that all will be fulfilled within an 80-year generation which started at the re-birth of Israel, and you know that the clock started 74 years ago and there's still a 7-year tribulation period that has to fit in before all is fulfilled, that means that the tribulation period should have started already. Does that get your attention? Especially with the crazy state of the world right now...

Israel was reborn in one day in 1948+80 years = 2028 - 7-year tribulation period = 2021! But it didn't happen, now what?

The Bible gives us many genealogical accounts that help us to know how long it's been since Adam and Eve and the times in which many other Bible characters lived, which also helps us to date many of the major biblical events. It's a bit of a puzzle and we don't always have all the pieces, so it's impossible to be exact. However, I am confident that our Heavenly Father is exact, and has established everything with great detail and precision. Terms like "fullness of time" and "Moedim", which is Hebrew for "appointed times," help us to understand that God has a time for everything, as we also discover in Ecclesiastes 3.

Ecclesiastes 3:1

¹To everything there is a season, a time for every purpose under heaven.

As I have already pointed out, according to the Dead Sea Scrolls as well as our early Church Fathers, our human history is broken down into a 7-day week, with the first day of the week being Sunday, and then the Sabbath is on the 7th day, or our Saturday. Remember, Peter stated in 2 Peter 3: *"But do not forget this one thing, dear friends: with the Lord a day is like a thousand years, and a thousand years are like a day."* Psalm 90:4, yes, the same Psalm 90 that we have been talking about, also tells us that *"for a thousand years in Your sight are like yesterday when it is past, and like a watch in the night."* The concept of a day for a thousand years is a very important key to understanding Bible history and prophecy, and that concept, along with the 70 or 80 year life span/generation, are both found in Psalm 90. Coincidence?

Timeline of our biblical human history

It was believed by early Christian theologians such as Bishop Irenaeus of the 2nd century AD, who had been taught by Polycarp, who in turn had been taught by the apostle John, who wrote the book of Revelation, that Jesus came and died for man's sins at the fulfillment of 4000 years from Adam. In the 7-day week of 1000 years for a day, it's been almost 2000 years since then.

Even Jesus taught this timeline in His parable of the barren fig tree (there's that fig tree that represents Israel again!) in Luke 12. However, in this parable, Jesus represented 1 year to equate to 1000 years instead of 1 day for 1000 years. I had missed this scripture in my studies by simply reading over it and never really stopping long enough to ask what this parable even means. Early one morning, while I had the Bible playing on the tablet by my bed, I was awakened with my ear super tuned to the Word being spoken about 1 second before this parable:

Luke 12:39

*[6] He also spoke this parable: "A certain man had a **fig tree** planted in his vineyard, and he came seeking fruit on it and found none. [7] Then he said to the keeper of his vineyard, 'Look, for **three years** I have come seeking fruit on this fig tree and find none. Cut it down; why does it use up the ground?' [8] But he answered and said to him, 'Sir, let it alone **this year** also, until I dig around it and fertilize it. [9] And if it bears fruit, well. But if not, after that you can cut it down.'"*

There may be other interpretations of this parable, but I couldn't help but notice the timeline that Jesus encoded into this parable, which matches the timeline of human history up until the time when He spoke it. There had been "3 years" with no fruit for Him in this world. Then, the fig tree (Israel) was fertilized with the Law and the Covenant for "1 year." According to the parable, Israel was given "1 year" (1000 years) to bear fruit in this world. If the fig tree had borne fruit over that period of time, then it would not have been cut down. However, we know that it didn't bear fruit, which is why Israel was "cut down" after that fourth year. Hang on to this understanding of the fig tree, as it will continue to be important throughout the timeline.

So once again, we can see that God has human history laid out symbolically on a 7-day, 7-year, or 7000-year timeline. Doing some simple math, where does that place us in that timeline? As we have already seen, we're in the evening of the 6th day, and the Jewish Sabbath starts at sundown of the 6th day as we know it. So, according to this, time is very short. Once again, the Sabbath period, or the 7th day, is the Millennial Kingdom and the reign of Jesus Christ, the Messiah.

Here's a little more detail now that we know that in God's timeline, it might just be that the end of this age, and the beginning of the Millennial Kingdom is 2000 years or two days (Thursday and Friday) after His death and resurrection. So, when was that?

We have already established that the Essenes were expecting the Messiah to arrive in 32 AD based on their writings found in the Dead Sea Scrolls. We've also seen how that year is also a likely candidate for the Messiah's triumphal entry into Jerusalem, even based on the Book of Daniel and astronomical calculations. But can we arrive at the year 32 AD based purely on the Biblical account? Well, sort of. We also have to use some historically known dates to put it all together.

From known historical dates and the gospel accounts, we know that King Herod died sometime between 4 BC and 1 BC. Herod was alive when Jesus was born, and it was Herod who ordered that all boys 2 years old and under be put to death. So, for the sake of argument, let's say that Jesus was born around 1 year prior to Herod's death. Remember that Joseph was shown in a dream that Herod was dead and that they could return to Israel from Egypt. So, that would put Jesus' birth between 5 BC and 2 BC. We believe that Jesus was 33.5 years old when He was crucified because Luke told us that Jesus was around 30 years old when He started His 3-year ministry. You can also arrive at these time frames by using the known dates of the reign of Tiberius Caesar and John the Baptist based on Luke's account. So, what does all of that mean? Based on these possible dates, Jesus would have been crucified sometime between 28 AD and 32 AD. If you add 2000 years to that date you arrive at a timeframe between 2028 and 2032.

Suppose you take away the 7-year tribulation period yet to come before the 7th day Sabbath, aka Millennial Kingdom. In that case, you arrive at a possible pre-tribulation rapture time frame between the year 2021 and 2025. So, for the sake of argument, the most probable rapture "season" appears to be between the year 2021 and no later than 2025 based on all of these calculations and patterns.

Israel's rebirth in 1948 plus 80 years brings us to 2028 for the start of the 7th day, also known as the 1000-year Millennial Kingdom. And Jesus' possible resurrection date of 28 AD plus 2 days or 2000 years also brings us to 2028 for the start of the Millennial Kingdom. If we then subtract 7 years from 2028 for the 7-year tribulation period prophesied in Daniel and Revelation, both calculations bring us to a possible pre-tribulation rapture year of 2021, but as I said before, it didn't happen!

Based on Psalm 90:10, we know that the average lifespan, and therefore a generation, is 70 to 80 years, and then *"we fly away."* We know from history that Israel has never survived as a sovereign undivided nation past 80 years, so as a prophetic pattern, I do not believe that the re-born Israel will survive past 80 years. We know that the number 80 appears prophetically throughout the Bible, and there is no prophetic 81 or 82, so 80 years prophetically is the answer to how many years past Israel's rebirth that Israel will survive. Again, this equates to 2028!

Here's where it gets tricky! For the end of the tribulation period to occur in Israel's 80th year (2028), as you can see, the rapture should have already happened in 2021 to leave at least a few months of setup time for the Antichrist to come to power. Keep the year 2021 in mind as an important rapture-related year as we progress through the pages of this book. So, for 2028 to be the end of the tribulation and the year of the second coming of Christ, we only had until Israel's birthday on May 14th, 2022, for the rapture to happen, but it didn't, so it makes no prophetic sense... or does it?

So how does all of this workout?

Since it is now mathematically impossible to have a 7-year tribulation period before 2028, it is only logical that 2028, no matter what the prophetic evidence suggests, cannot be the end of the tribulation. I believe that the nation of Israel doesn't end at the end of the 7-year Tribulation Period, as many of us have previously concluded. Israel's 80-year curse for unbelief will strike again, however, not at the end, but at the middle, or 3.5-year mark, aka 42 months, or 1260 days from the confirming of the covalent by the Antichrist. This also matches Daniel 7:25.

Daniel 7:25
He shall speak pompous words against the Most High, shall persecute the saints of the Most High, and shall intend to

change times and law. Then the saints shall be given into
his hand for a time and times and half a time.

A "time, times and half a time" is 3.5 years. When the Antichrist takes control in the middle of the tribulation and sets himself up as God in the Temple, Israel will again cease to exist as a sovereign, undivided nation. It will be under the control of the Antichrist at the midpoint of the tribulation, and no longer under Israel's control. We know this because God tells us that the nation will be "desolate" at that time. Millions of Jews will be killed, and the remaining will have to flee as prophesied in Matthew 24:15, Mark 13:14-19, 2 Thessalonians 2:3-4, Revelation 12:14-15, Daniel 9:27, 11:31, and 12:11, etc...

This understanding shifts the 7-year tribulation period forward in time by 3.5 years, which means that the end of the Tribulation Period would be sometime in late 2031 or maybe 2032 and not 2028, as previously speculated. That still fits within the timeframe of Jesus' crucifixion plus 2000 years.

Based on this understanding, there will be 3.5 years of tribulation before 2028/2029, and 3.5 years of tribulation after 2028/2029. It's beginning to look like Israel's 80th anniversary year will be the year that the Antichrist sets himself up in the Temple and declares that he is God for the entire world to see.

The only problem with this new calculation is our traditional understanding of Jesus' Fig Tree Generation prophecy from Matthew 24.

Matthew 24:34

"Assuredly, I say to you, this generation will by no means
pass away till all these things take place."

According to what Jesus told us, all of the end-time prophecies had to be fulfilled by the end of the Generation that saw Israel reborn, which, of course, was in 1948. Our understanding of the length of a generation comes from Psalm 90:10, which again tells us: *"The days of our lives are seventy years; and if by reason of strength, they are eighty years, yet their boast is only labor and sorrow; for it is soon cut off, and we fly away."*

Maybe those of us watching and anxious for the rapture read something that wasn't there in Jesus' Fig Tree Prophecy. What Jesus really said was that there would still be people alive, when everything is complete, who had been born prior to Israel's rebirth in 1948. He specifically said that the generation "would not pass away" before everything is complete. His prophecy doesn't actually limit the time frame to 80 years, and there are certainly many people still alive in Israel who were born prior to May 14, 1948, and there will be many still alive after 2028.

CHAPTER 4

Decoding the Prophetic Songs
of Ascent - Psalm 120 - 134

As I mentioned in the introduction, J. R. Church chronicled the historical connections and patterns that he found between the first 90 Psalms and the first 90 years of the twentieth century. He was definitely on to something. He had certainly uncovered one of God's "concealed matters" by diligently searching it out. He did a masterful job of connecting all of the prophetic and historical dots and explaining them in an easy-to-follow and understandable way. As he mentioned, he was, however, reluctant to continue to follow the same chronological pattern that the first 90 Psalms matching 90 years established into future prophecy for fear of being labeled a "date setter." However, I believe he knew if the first 90 years were accurately depicted in Psalms 1 - 90, then it stood to reason that the following Psalms would also continue in the same pattern.

J. R. Church was also wise to point out that Jesus Himself stated that there were prophecies in the Psalms that He came to fulfill.

Luke 24
*⁴⁴ Then He said to them, "These are the words which I spoke to you while I was still with you, that all things must be fulfilled which were written in the Law of Moses and the Prophets and the **Psalms** concerning Me."*

He's not finished fulfilling His prophesies. Based on this verse alone, we should know to look to the Psalms to find prophetic insight into these last days in which we are now living. In fact, it has long been recognized that there is a pattern within the Psalms. They are not just a random grouping of 150 songs or poems, but they seem to have a distinct and purposeful arrangement to them. The problem is that no one has ever been able to decipher the encrypted arrangement beyond breaking them down into sections to match the 5 books of the Torah, that is until J. R. Church took a crack at it. His research and writing made it clear that the Psalms were the key to understanding the timeline of the last days, which was hiding in plain sight all this time, waiting to be decoded.

Scholars have figured out that the middle chapter, and the middle verse of the Christian Bible are in the Psalms, as well as the longest chapter of the Bible, which follows directly behind the shortest chapter in the Bible. I wish I could say that those are keys to unlocking greater hidden prophetic wisdom, but they aren't. They do, however, at least draw our attention to the Psalms as a prophetic resource, just as Jesus indicated, and even to the general area where things start to get interesting in the timeline revelation.

I am not going to go through Psalms 91 through 116 for the sake of brevity and because I believe that the validity of the pattern has already been established by J. R. Church. However, I would like to take a closer look at the three Psalms at the center point of the Bible, which are just prior to the first of the 15 Psalms of Ascension. These are Psalms 117, 118, and 119.

According to J. R. Church, Psalm 117 would match the year 2017. Interestingly, Psalm 117 is the shortest Psalm and is also the shortest chapter in the Bible. It only has 2 verses.

Psalm 117
¹ Praise the LORD, all you Gentiles! Laud Him, all you peoples! ² For His merciful kindness is great toward us, and the truth of the LORD endures forever. Praise the LORD!

As I said before, it's not exactly the key to unlocking the deeper mysteries of prophecy. However, I do think God wants us to notice it, and perhaps the year that it corresponds to, and that's why it's different. I also find it interesting and different since it specifically says, "Praise the Lord, **all you Gentiles**!" Of course, we know that the Psalms are centered around the Children of Israel, but in this short Psalm, we Gentiles are at center stage. According to this Psalm, as well as the Apostle Paul's quoting of it in Romans 15:11, the Lord's merciful kindness is great toward us Gentiles. That makes me wonder why specifically. Was there something that happened in 2017 pertaining to Israel that we Gentiles took part in? The answer is absolutely yes!

The year 2017 was the 50th anniversary of the Six-Day War when Israel once again gained control over the city of Jerusalem and even the Temple Mount. However, they then gave control over the Temple Mount to Jordan, but that's another story. In 2017, President Trump officially recognized Jerusalem as Israel's rightful capital and vowed to move the US Embassy from Tel Aviv to Jerusalem. Of course, this has great prophetic implications. As we know, Israel was reborn in 1948, but without Jerusalem as its capital city because the United Nations declared that Jerusalem would be under international control and not Israeli control. Remember that King David took Jerusalem as Israel's capital city, and that according to Bible prophecy, the city of Jerusalem is a central focus in the end times. Finally, after almost 70 years, Jerusalem would once again be recognized as the rightful capital of Israel.

The year 2017 was also the year that many of us remember as the year of the Revelation 12 sign. On September 23, right after the Feast of Trumpets, the Revelation 12 sign appeared in the sky as a sign of things soon to come.

Remember that Genesis 1 tells us that the lights in the sky are not only to divide the day from night, and for days and years, but also for "signs" and seasons. As the Three Wise Men were looking for signs in the sky, we too, should be looking for signs such as the one that happened in 2017. Will there be more prophetic signs in the heavens before the rapture of the Church and the start of the tribulation period?

I'm not an astronomer, but based on God's word, I'm certain there will be.

Genesis 1:14

*14 Then God said, "Let there be lights in the firmament of the heavens to divide the day from the night; and let them be for **signs** (Moedim) and seasons, and for days and years;*

Revelation 12:1-2

1 Now a great sign appeared in heaven: a woman clothed with the sun, with the moon under her feet, and on her head a garland of twelve stars. 2 Then being with child, she cried out in labor and in pain to give birth.

This sign appeared above Israel exactly as stated in Revelation 12. On September 23rd, 2017, the sun was in the constellation of Virgo, appearing to clothe her in sunlight. The moon was at her feet, and she had 12 stars, made-up-of 3 planets and the 9 brightest stars of the constellation Leo, at her head. The planet Jupiter had been in her center, or abdomen area, by that time for 9 months when it appeared to be birthed out of the womb of the virgin. Could it be this was a 7-year warning until the fulfillment of the next "Moedim" on God's prophetic calendar? If we add 7 years to 2017, we land in 2024. Hang on to that thought. It will be important later. I'm not going to give all of the extra astrological details of the Revelation 12 sign as it appeared in 2017, but if you are not familiar with it, please search to see how this prophetic sign was fulfilled in September of 2017 above Israel.

Revelation 12, verse 3 speaks of another sign that appeared in heaven, along with the woman giving birth. This was the sign of the fiery red dragon.

Revelation 12:3-4

3 And another sign appeared in heaven: behold, a great, fiery red dragon having seven heads and ten horns, and seven diadems on his heads. ⁴ His tail drew a third of the stars of heaven and threw them to the earth. And the dragon stood before the woman who was ready to give birth, to devour her Child as soon as it was born.

So, was there also a fiery red dragon in the sky in 2017, along with the woman who was to give birth? Yes, however, for some strange reason, this image was literally blacked out by GoogleSky. It makes me wonder why they would black out a section of the sky. What are they trying to hide? Apparently, it could, however, be seen by viewing NASA's SkyView virtual online telescope set to infrared mode, and there are plenty of pictures of it available online.

Many have debated whether the Revelation 12 sign is about Israel, or is it about the Church. I believe that the answer to that debate is yes! It's about both. Based on its connection to Psalm 117 through the timeline revelation in the Psalms, it has become clear to me that it is indeed a pattern for both Israel and the Church. Psalm 117 references both Gentiles as well as "us" being Israel. After all, it was certainly written by a Jew and not a Gentile;, therefore, "us" could only refer to the Jews or possibly "all people," which is also stated. So, I believe that it is a warning and that it foretells the escape of the remnant of Israel at the "abomination of desolation," as well as the escape of the Church in the rapture. And the timeline revelation in the Psalms gives us the year range of both events, and once again, numbers and patterns are important as you will see in the coming chapters.

Psalm 118

There is a lot to talk about in Psalm 118; however, most of it is outside of the purview of this book. However, I have to point out that Psalm 118 is the center of our Christian Bible. It has 594 chapters before it, and 594 chapters after it. That means that there are a total of 1188 chapters combined before and after Psalm 118. Isn't that interesting?

The numbers 118 and 1188 are certainly very coincidental, or are they? Let's see what verse 118:8 has to say, and if it might be important.

Psalm 118:8
⁸ It is better to take refuge in the LORD than to trust in man.

As general godly wisdom and guidance, this verse can certainly stand alone. However, I believe that it is also prophetic and that we will see its ultimate wisdom and guidance fulfilled in 10 years from 2018 in the timeline revelation. Regardless, it is clear that God wants us to pay attention to these Psalms here in the middle of His word.

For brevity's sake, I want to focus on only one more, but very important prophetic Messianic element of Psalm 118, and its relationship to the time in which we are living.

Verses 22-23
²² The stone which the builders rejected has become the chief cornerstone. ²³ This was the LORD's doing; it is marvelous in our eyes.

Obviously, these verses were prophetic of Jesus and His first coming, as He was the stone which the builders rejected. In Matthew 21, Jesus quoted specifically from this verse in Psalm 118, thereby connecting it to His Parable of the Wicked Vinedressers.

Matthew 21:33-45
³³ "Hear another parable: There was a certain landowner who planted a vineyard and set a hedge around it, dug a winepress in it and built a tower. And he leased it to vinedressers and went into a far country. ³⁴ Now when vintage-time drew near, he sent his servants to the vinedressers, that they might receive its fruit. ³⁵ And the vinedressers took his servants, beat one, killed one, and stoned another. ³⁶ Again he sent other servants, more than the first, and they did likewise to them. ³⁷ Then last of all

he sent his son to them, saying, 'They will respect my son.'
38 But when the vinedressers saw the son, they said among themselves, 'This is the heir. Come, let us kill him and seize his inheritance.' 39 So they took him and cast him out of the vineyard and killed him.

40 "Therefore, when the owner of the vineyard comes, what will he do to those vinedressers?"

41 They said to Him, "He will destroy those wicked men miserably, and lease his vineyard to other vinedressers who will render to him the fruits in their seasons."

42 Jesus said to them, "Have you never read in the Scriptures:

'The stone which the builders rejected has become the chief cornerstone. This was the LORD's doing, and it is marvelous in our eyes'?

43 "Therefore I say to you, the kingdom of God will be taken from you and given to a nation bearing the fruits of it. 44 And whoever falls on this stone will be broken; but on whomever it falls, it will grind him to powder."

45 Now when the chief priests and Pharisees heard His parables, they perceived that He was speaking of them.

In this parable, the Landowner is symbolic of God the Father. The vineyard is Jerusalem. The hedge and tower represent God's protection and the walls around the city of Jerusalem. The winepress that the Landowner dug represents God's provision as, He gives us everything we need to succeed. The evil vinedressers refer to the unrighteous kings, religious rulers of Israel, and the unbelieving children of Israel who took the vineyard as their own possession. The servants who are sent to collect the fruit are the Old Testament prophets ending with John the Baptist. The son of the Landowner is the Son of God. Notice that the evil vinedressers cast the son outside of the vineyard and killed him, prophetically symbolic of Jesus' death on the cross, which we know from all 4 gospels happened outside of the city walls of Jerusalem. Now that we know the symbols and characters, let's look at the prophetic word that Jesus gave us in verse 43.

Matthew 21:43

"Therefore I say to you, the kingdom of God will be taken from you and given to a nation bearing the fruits of it."

So what "nation" do you think Jesus was referring to whom the Kingdom of God will be given to that would bear the fruit of it? The key to this parable is "the bearing of fruit. But first let's look at the original Greek word for "nation." When our Western ears hear the word "Nation," we think of nations such as the US, Mexico, England, Germany, Spain, and so on. However, the Greek word that our English Bible translated into "nation" is the word Ethnei and in Hebrew, it's Goyim. The root of Ethnei is Ethnos. You may recognize that it's the word that we get "ethnic" from. Here's the definition of the Greek word ethnos:

Éthnos– people joined by practicing similar customs or common culture; *nation(s)*, usually referring to non-Jew *Gentiles.*

This word shows up again in Matthew 24 when Jesus predicts some of the signs before the "end" when He says, "nation will rise against nation, and kingdom against kingdom." Again, He is speaking of non-Jewish, Gentile ethnic groups and cultures in addition to "kingdoms," or as we would say today, "countries."

Keep in mind that Jesus was a Jew, the Lion of the Tribe of Judah, and He was telling His parable to a Jewish audience. In fact, at the time that Jesus was speaking this parable, it would have been very insulting and offensive to the Jewish ears hearing it since the Jews boasted the fact that they were God's chosen people. Keep in mind also that their idea of the Messianic Kingdom didn't necessarily include Gentiles as part of God's "in-crowd," or at best, the Israelites would be ruling over all of the Gentile nations. So, the thought of having to even share in the things of God with the "unclean" Gentiles was pretty repulsive to the religious Jews of Jesus' time. The reason that I say "unclean" is because of Israel's purity laws. Under the Old Covenant Law given to the Children of Israel, Jews were not allowed to mingle with Gentiles, enter the homes of Gentiles, eat with Gentiles, etc...

We can now see that the nation, or "ethnos," that Jesus was speaking of, that the kingdom of God would be given to after being taken from

Israel (but only for a time) due to unbelief, was the "Gentile nation." We can now also understand that it isn't really a nation with borders and such as we normally think of it, but it's the body of believers from all nations, tribes, and tongues, and yes, that also includes a small but growing population of believing Messianic Jews.

So according to Jesus' parable, we, the church, have been given a great gift. We have been chosen and adopted into God's family. We have also been given a great mission and responsibility as the new vinedressers for this Church Age season.

Matthew 28:19-20

"Therefore go and make disciples of all nations (Ethnos), baptizing them in the name of the Father and of the Son and of the Holy Spirit, and teaching them to obey everything I have commanded you. And surely I am with you always, to the very end of the age."

So, according to the parable and the Great Commission, our mission as Christians, and as part of His Church, is to bear fruit and make disciples of all nations.

Jesus said that He would be with us always "To the very end of the age." I believe from all of the prophetic signs all around us today that the age that we know as the "Church Age" is coming to a close right now in our generation. Then, after the Church Age and the 7-year tribulation period, Jesus taught from Psalm 118:26 that the Remnant of Israel would cry out: *"Blessed is he who comes in the name of the LORD!"* at His return (Matthew 23:39, Luke 13:35).

Psalm 119

Year 2019 - Jesus is the Word

This Psalm is not only the longest Psalm in the Bible, but it is also the longest chapter in the Bible, with 176 verses. As such, I'm not even going to attempt to cover them all. In fact, I'm barely going to touch on it because it deserves more attention than what I can give to it right now, especially since I personally haven't had any great revelations about it. I have a feeling that there is much encrypted in its acrostic pattern of 22 sections, matching the 22 letters of the Hebrew alphabet, each of which has exactly 8 verses. That's truly fertile ground for deeper hidden meaning, but I am aware that much has already been discussed and written about this Psalm, and I honestly do not see how I can add any further value to the discussion other than to say that it may be so different from other Psalms for a reason. Unlike the Psalms previous to it, Psalm 119 doesn't seem to have any relation to the year 2019, as far as I can tell. That means to me that it may be a marker like a road sign to signify that what has been before it will be very different from what will come after it.

I would also like to point out, in view of the timeline revelation, that this Psalm is primarily about loving God and loving His word. We know who His word is; He's Jesus (John 1). However, many do not know Him, and many do not want to know Him. Love Him or hate Him, according to the timeline revelation, everyone will be meeting Him very soon. That means that we who know the truth have only a little time left to share it with others.

To me, it seems that God really wanted us to notice these three Psalms right before the 15 Songs of Ascent. They are right in the middle of the Bible, and they certainly stand out due to their unusual characteristics. Psalm 117 is the shortest Psalm and chapter in the Bible, then Psalm 118, which is the center of the Bible, followed by Psalm 119, which is the longest Psalm, and chapter in the Bible. Personally, I don't think any of this is a coincidence.

4 Important Understandings

Now, we are ready to move on to Psalm 120, which should match the Gregorian calendar year of 2020 according to the timeline revelation. Needless to say, that was the year that our entire world was turned upside down by a virus. First, however, there are four very important details that I need to cover before proceeding.

1.—The first is that I believe we should always take God at His word. Some scripture verses are clearly metaphorical, some are poetic, and some are straight-forward; however, they are all truthful. Most of the time, it's easy enough to distinguish between them if we let the Bible interpret the Bible. I believe that we make mistakes when we use too much of our imagination and perhaps expand too much on what is being said, and even sometimes put words in our Lord's mouth that He didn't say. For example, Israel ceased to exist in 135 AD when the Romans expelled the Israelites from their country after the Jewish Bar Kokhba Revolt. There are many prophecies declaring that Israel would come back into their land, and once again be a nation. Of course, we know that Israel was re-born in 1948. However, prior to 1948 many Christians mistakenly attributed the blessings, and even end-time prophesies, to the Church instead of Israel since they couldn't imagine that Israel would ever exist again. They were mistaken because they thought that Israel had become a symbol for the Church. They should have taken God at His word!

So, if Jesus says, for example, that we can't know the day or the hour, I believe that. However, that doesn't mean we can't know the week, month, or year. He only specifically said that we wouldn't know the day or the hour, so maybe we shouldn't make that mean that we cannot know anything about it, or that we can't have a rough estimate based on scripture. In fact, Jesus stated many times that we should be "watching" so that "that day" will not overtake us like a thief in the night. Obviously, this means that we should be conducting ourselves according to His purposes, and carrying out the Great Commission, or "occupying" until He returns so that we are not caught off guard. However, how can you be "watching" if you don't know what you are watching for? I believe that our Lord wants us to not only know the signs of the times that we're living in, but we should also know the times as well.

I believe that knowing makes true Christians more excited and more ambitious to carry out the Great Commission because we know that time is short. Knowing that there may be very little time left to procrastinate and put off talking to your friends, neighbors, and loved ones about the free gift of salvation should light a fire in all of us to finally be the witness that God has called us to be in word and in deed.

2.—The second detail that is very important to understand before we proceed is that not all of the verses in any given Psalm are prophetic of the times in which we are living. The 150 Psalms contain verses of praise, thanksgiving, adoration, devotion, petition, deliverance, laments, historical details, and eschatological foresight. Many Psalms may contain several of these elements within one Psalm. Have you ever noticed how some of the Psalms seem to go in different directions? They may start out as praise and worship, and then all of a sudden, in the next stanza, it shifts, and the author relays some past historical event, usually related to Israel, seemingly out of nowhere, or he drops in a little prophetic treasure when you least expect it. You didn't see it coming, and it may seem out of place because there was no natural progression to it. Maybe it's because at least a verse, or even a few verses, were designed to align with a greater prophetic truth than what's on the surface, sort of like a code. My point is this: don't expect the entire Psalm to be prophetic, or to even be about one subject. They weren't intended to be that simplistic. You have to use some spiritual discernment and biblical literacy as your tools to pull out the encrypted prophetic treasures.

3.—The third important detail that must be understood before biblical prophecy can make any sense at all is that prophecy is usually found in patterns. Many view prophecy as having a 1 to 1 relationship, meaning 1 prophecy will equal 1 fulfillment. However, God is not that simple. He gave us repeated patterns throughout Biblical history to show us the interconnections between different times, people, and events in biblical history, and thus give us greater clarity of times, people, and events still to come.

Here's an example of a messianic pattern that has already played out in biblical history. I also believe that this established pattern will in part, play out again in the future to some degree, but this time it will be with the false messiah.

It is well established that Jacob's son Joseph was a type and shadow of the Messiah, but have you ever really looked at all of the similarities to see how God interwove Joseph's story with Jesus' story to not only establish a messianic pattern but to also prove that Jesus was the true Messiah.

Here's a short list of similarities between Joseph and Jesus:

1. Joseph was the "first fruit" born of Rachel, who was a symbol of the nation of Israel through the power and intervention of God. Jesus was the "first fruit" of Mary through the power and intervention of God, as well as the "first fruit" of the resurrection through the power and intervention of God.
2. Joseph was beloved by his father - Genesis 37. Jesus was beloved by His Father - Matthew 3:17.
3. Joseph was a shepherd. Jesus was the Good Shepherd.
4. Joseph's brothers hated and betrayed him. Jesus' brothers (Israelites) hated and betrayed Him.
5. Joseph was sent by his father to his brothers when they betrayed him. Jesus was sent by His Father to His brothers when they betrayed Him.
6. Joseph was stripped of his robe. Jesus was stripped of His robe.
7. Joseph was sold for 20 shekels of silver. Jesus was sold for 30 shekels of silver. Together, they equal 50 shekels, representing the bride price and the price for the threshing floor where the Holy Temple was built.
8. Joseph was taken to Egypt, sparing his life. Jesus was taken to Egypt, sparing His life.
9. Joseph was tempted but didn't sin. Jesus was tempted but didn't sin.

10. Joseph was betrayed by someone who was close to him. Jesus was betrayed by someone who was close to him.

11. Joseph was falsely accused. Jesus was falsely accused.

12. Joseph was in prison with two others, of which one was sentenced to death, and one was given life. Jesus was on the cross with two others, of which one was sentenced to eternal death because he rejected the Messiah, and one was given eternal life because he accepted the Messiah.

13. Joseph was given a Gentile bride. Jesus was given a Gentile bride, the Church.

14. Joseph was 30 years old when he became ruler. Jesus was 30 years old when He started His ministry.

15. Joseph was the savior of the world - Genesis 45:7. Jesus is the savior of the world - John 4:42.

16. Joseph revealed himself to his brothers after testing them. Jesus will reveal Himself to His brothers (Israel) after testing them.

17. Every knee had to bow before Joseph. Every knee will bow before Jesus.

There are more similarities to list, but I'm sure that you can already see that there was a specific messianic pattern revealed through the life of Joseph, which was a shadow that pointed specifically to Jesus. Since this is an established messianic pattern, as I mentioned before, I would expect much of this pattern to be mimicked by the coming false messiah soon to be revealed.

4.—The fourth very important detail to understand and remember when digging deeper into Bible prophecy is that God speaks through numbers, as previously discussed. Is it just a coincidence that both of the languages that God chose to have His word written in are alphanumeric? Meaning that they have numerical values associated with every letter. Therefore, keep in mind that unlike English, and most of the world's languages, both Hebrew and Greek letters also have a numerical meaning which can be very important when doing a prophetic deep scriptural dig.

We have already covered some of the meanings of prophetic numbers in the Bible, such as 3, 5, 7, 10, 12, 30, 40, 50, and so on. We have also already established through J. R. Church's research that God has used the numbering sequence of the Psalms in correlation to the years of the 20th and 21st centuries as we know them on the Gregorian calendar. However, I don't believe that it ends there... I also believe that God has used number sequences, and sometimes the numbered verses encoded in the Psalms to tie pieces of the prophetic puzzle together.

You might be tempted to say, "Wait a minute, the original manuscripts didn't have chapters and verses in them?" "I thought the numbering system was added to the Old Testament and the New Testament between 1200 - 1500 AD, so how could God speak to us through those numbering patterns?" Well, is our Lord and Savior in control of all things, or is He not? I know that His word tells us that He is, and I believe that the sequences found in the Psalms prove it.

Psalm 120 - 134 Songs of Ascent

Psalm 120 is the first of 15 special Songs of Ascent. Remember that God revealed a 5 and a 10 to me? I believe that this is certainly a big part of that revelation. The 15 Songs of Ascent align with the years 2020 through 2034 in the encrypted timeline revelation. I know that sounds like a total of 14, but we're counting the "0" (the year 2020), so it adds up to 15. It so happens that the numerical value of the short form of God's name, Yah, equals 15 and is specifically made up of 5 and 10. Considering that, coupled with the fact that there are these special 15 Psalms, specifically called "Songs of Ascent," should have been enough to cause us prophecy students to take notice. These 15 special songs were sung by pilgrims and priests alike while "ascending" up to the Temple during the third annual pilgrimage festival in Jerusalem. The three pilgrimage festivals in Hebrew are Pesach (Passover or Feast of Unleavened Bread), Shavuot (Pentecost or Feast of Weeks), and the third is Sukkot (Feast of Tabernacles or Booths). By the current corrupted Jewish calendar, Sukkot would be the first of the pilgrimage festivals because the Rabbis moved the new year (Rosh Hashanah) to the seventh month of God's calendar. However, according to God's word in Leviticus 23, Passover should be the first of the three pilgrimage festivals.

This would be a good time to briefly explain the fulfillment of God's feast days given to Israel as described in Leviticus 23, Exodus 12, 23, 34, and Deuteronomy 16, among others. God encoded His plan for salvation in the feast days that He called "Moedim," which means "appointed times." As I have previously mentioned, out of the 7 feast days, Jesus has fulfilled the first 4 exactly to the day, leaving a final 3 yet to be fulfilled. Those represent the future rapture, the second coming, judgment, and His Millennial Kingdom reign.

Our focus is on the final feast known as Sukkot, or the Feast of Tabernacles, which starts on the 15th day of the month following the Feast of Trumpets and the Day of Atonement. Historically, it is known that the Jewish pilgrims would sing the 15 Songs of Ascent on their journey up to the Temple at Sukkot and possibly during their pilgrimages to Jerusalem for Passover as well as Pentecost.

According to the Jewish Talmud, the 15 Songs of Ascent were also sung on the 15th day of the month by Priests as they descended and then presumably ascended the 15 steps from the lower courtyard up to the upper courtyard of the Temple. It seems that God really wants us to notice the number 15, and these 15 Psalms or Songs of Ascent!

As I previously mentioned, the short form of God's name is Yod Hey in Hebrew, which we would pronounce as Yah. The short form of God's name has a numerical value of 15. Jews will not say God's name, even the short form, because it is too holy, and they don't want to accidentally take His name in vain. They say "HaShem" instead, which simply means "The Name." The 15 is made up of a 10 and a 5 since Yod's numerical value is 10 and Hey's numerical value is 5. It is indicated in the Jewish Talmud that historically, the priests would stop on the 10th step on their journey down to the Shiloach Springs to draw water for their ceremony, beginning the feast of Tabernacles. They paused and blew trumpets on the 10th step in honor of "The Name," which, as I've stated, is divided into two parts, 10 and 5, corresponding to Yod and

Hey. Their journey to the Shiloach Springs from the temple would place them on the 5th step from the bottom when they would stop and blow their trumpets. In the timeline revelation, that step would correspond to the year 2024 because we are counting 2020 as the first step. Is this significant? Could there be a trumpet-blowing event in 2024?

King Hezekiah

Remember that God showed me a 5 and a 10 when I was desperately seeking wisdom from Him regarding the last days? At that time, I didn't understand that the short form of His name in Hebrew is numerically a 5 and a 10. I also didn't understand the significance of the sum of His name as 15. Why didn't He just say 15? Could it be that the end times are divided in this exact same way? What about the product of 5 and 10, which is 50? Is there any prophetic significance to 50? Before we search out these mysteries, we will need to understand the origin and historical relevance of the 15 Songs of Ascent. To do that, we will have to do a little study into the time of King Hezekiah in 2 Kings 20.

King Hezekiah, who was one of the few righteous kings over Judah, was sick and about to die, but he turned his face to the wall, and wept bitterly and prayed to the Lord. He reminded the Lord that he had been a good and righteous king over Judah. Here's God's reply to the prophet Isaiah for King Hezekiah:

> **2 Kings 20:4-6**
> *"And it happened, before Isaiah had gone out into the middle court, that the word of the LORD came to him, saying, ⁵ "Return and tell Hezekiah the leader of My people, 'Thus says the LORD, the God of David your father: "I have heard your prayer, I have seen your tears; surely I will heal you.* **On the third day you shall go up to the house of the LORD.** *⁶ And I will add to your days* **fifteen years.** *I will deliver you and this city from the hand of the king of*

Assyria; and I will defend this city for My own sake, and
for the sake of My servant David."

Then King Hezekiah asked the prophet Isaiah *"What is the sign that the*
LORD will heal me, and that I shall go up to the house of the LORD the third day?"

2 Kings 20:9-11
⁹ Then Isaiah said, "This is the sign to you from the LORD,
that the LORD will do the thing which He has spoken: shall
the shadow go forward ten degrees or go backward ten
degrees?" ¹⁰ And Hezekiah answered, "It is an easy thing for
the shadow to go down ten degrees; no, but let the shadow go
backward ten degrees." ¹¹ So Isaiah the prophet cried out to
the LORD, and He brought the shadow ten degrees backward,
by which it had gone down on the sundial of Ahaz.

There are so many prophetic patterns in these few verses from 2
Kings 20! We see a 3ʳᵈ day, a 10, and a 15 all together. Notice that King
Hezekiah was granted another 15 years to live. Not 14 or 16, but 15.
Obviously, God has a plan, and there's a lot more to the story.

You may have noticed that God instructed Hezekiah to go "up" to the
house of the Lord on the 3ʳᵈ day. There are many scriptures related to the
number 3 as we know, but there are also numerous prophetic scriptures
relating specifically to the "3ʳᵈ day." Let's compare Hezekiah's 3ʳᵈ day to
some other 3ʳᵈ days, and see how God is tying events and prophecy together.

Hosea 6:2
*² After two days He will revive us; on the **third day** He*
will raise us up, that we may live in His sight.

Exodus 19:11
*¹¹ And let them be ready for the **third day**. For on the*
***third day** the LORD will come down upon Mount Sinai*
in the sight of all the people.

Exodus 19:16-17
*¹⁶Then it came to pass on the **third day**, in the morning, that there were thunderings and lightnings, and a thick cloud on the mountain; and the sound of the trumpet was very loud, so that all the people who were in the camp trembled. ¹⁷And Moses brought the people out of the camp to meet with God, and they stood at the foot of the mountain.*

John 2:1-2
*¹ On the **third day** there was a wedding in Cana of Galilee, and the mother of Jesus was there. ² Now both Jesus and His disciples were invited to the wedding.*

As you can see, the 3rd day is about going up to the house of the Lord, healing, marriage, and living in the sight of the Lord. All of those connect to the Millennial Kingdom, which I will expand on in the coming chapters.

Labor Pains

In addition to the two groupings (5 and 10) of the 15 Psalms of Ascent that we discussed when the priests would stop and blow the trumpet on the steps of the temple, it has long been recognized that they also seem to be assembled in another specific grouping as well. They appear to be divided into 3 groups of 5. Each of the 3 groups of 5 follows a similar pattern. The first pattern, starting with Psalm 120, is that of distress. The distress pattern includes Psalms 120, 123, 126, 129, and 132.

The second pattern shows God's deliverance, which can be seen in Psalms 121, 124, 127, 130, and 133. The third pattern of 5 Psalms represents God's peace and blessing. This third and final pattern includes Psalms 122, 125, 128, 131, and 134.

I believe that these patterns are reminiscent of the labor process of child-birth. Remember that Jesus associated His second coming, and the establishment of His Kingdom with the same 3 patterns. The first is "distress" in labor pains, the second is "deliverance," or the birth of a child, and the third is the "peace and blessing" after the child has been born. Jesus lays this template out for us in John 15.

John 16:21-22
[21] A woman, when she is in labor, has sorrow because her hour has come; but as soon as she has given birth to the child, she no longer remembers the anguish, for joy that a human being has been born into the world. [22] Therefore you now have sorrow; but I will see you again and your heart will rejoice, and your joy no one will take from you.

Can it be just a coincidence that Jesus likened the last days to "birth pains," that there are medically 3 distinct stages of childbirth labor, and that there is a unique repeating pattern of these 3 with 5 Psalms each within the 15 Songs of Ascent similar to the 3 stages of childbirth?

CHAPTER 5

Psalm 120 A Song of Ascents

The Year 2020 - The Year of Deception

For clarification, I am not typically going to list all of the verses of each of the Psalms because not all of them are prophetic of this time. However, the majority of them are, so I will pull those out and list the ones that pertain to the days in which we are now living. Then, I will connect them to other related prophetic scriptures based on their context as well as keywords, phrases, numbers, patterns, and interconnected imagery. As you will see, this will help to establish and also to fill in the timeline for a better view of the last days.

Distress of the World

It is presumed that King Hezekiah wrote this first Song of Ascent, but there's no way to be certain. Regardless of who the author was, I believe that Psalm 120, which, according to J. R. Church's established pattern, would align with the year that saw so many changes on our planet, is the infamous year of 2020. During 2020, we all felt the distress of the "birth pains" intensify worldwide, and the pains of looming economic destruction, wars, and rumors of wars, and global famine have been intensifying ever since. I also believe that 2020 was the official start of what I call "the last minutes of the last days," and it won't be long before 2020 will seem like the "good ole days" for those who will be caught off guard.

Of course, we have already established that prophecy is a pattern, so even though this Psalm was probably written based on historical events, it was also partly prophetic of future events that align with the year 2020. In addition, I believe that this first Song of Ascents not only hits the highlights of 2020, but also gives a foreshadowing of things yet to come.

Lying Lips and Deceitful Tongues

If you think that our governments and our media were all telling us the truth about world events, the virus, lockdowns, vaccines, elections, etc..., you should take a look at what God has to say about the widespread deception in 2020 through this Psalm.

Verse 1
*¹ In my **distress** I cried to the LORD, and He heard me. Deliver my soul, O LORD, from **lying lips** and from a **deceitful tongue**.*

Did we have *"distress"* in 2020? Yes! Did we have *"deception"* in 2020? Yes! It's no coincidence that this Psalm speaks about deliverance from these *"lying lips"* and a *"deceitful tongue."* Jesus and the Apostle Paul both spoke of deception in the last days in Matthew 24 and in 2 Thessalonians 2, respectively, just to name a few places.

Of course, as we know Matthew 24 is about the last days. At the beginning of Matthew 24 several of Jesus' disciples came to Him and asked what would be the signs of His coming, and the end of the age. In response Jesus first warned of deception; in fact, He bookended His prophetic description about the final period of time just before His return with several warnings about deception.

Matthew 24:4

*⁴ And Jesus answered and said to them: "Take heed that no one **deceives** you.*

Then toward the end of His prophetic teaching to the disciples, Jesus again warns them of deception.

Matthew 24:24

*²⁴ For false christs and false prophets will rise and show great signs and wonders to **deceive**, if possible, even the elect.*

Paul also gave us many warnings of end-time deception. In 2 Thessalonians chapter 2 Paul connects the deceptions of the last days with the Antichrist and with Satan himself. He also explains that some of these deceptions will be in the form of power, signs, and lying wonders. I believe that in our present time, especially as of 2020, we can clearly see that the deceiving spirit of the Antichrist is alive and well, and growing exponentially even from week to week.

2 Thessalonians 2:9-10

*⁹ The coming of the lawless one is according to the working of Satan, with all power, signs, and lying wonders, ¹⁰ and with all unrighteous **deception** among those who perish, because they did not receive the love of the truth, that they might be saved.*

Here are a few more key verses in the New Testament, where Paul warns of deception from deceiving spirits, and from demons taught by hypocritical liars, causing even some Christians to fall away from their faith.

1 Timothy 4:1-2

*¹ The Spirit clearly says that in later times some will abandon the faith and follow **deceiving spirits** and things taught by demons. ² Such teachings come through*

*hypocritical liars, whose consciences have been seared as
with a hot iron.*

When I read these scriptures I cannot help but think about the
multiple globalist agendas that are being taught, or should I say pushed,
all over the world by the World Economic Forum, as well as the Vatican,
the United Nations, and most governments of the world. I believe
that it is clear that we are witnessing the prophesied rise of the global
"Babylon" system all around us today.

Paul points out that these teachings are really from deceiving
demonic spirits, but then he goes on to say that they are brought into
our world through "hypocritical liars." Paul's description has come to
life in our time as we watch on the news, and through social media
as the global elites fly on their private jets to far-off places to gather
together, make plans, and preach to the masses about how we, the
common people, are responsible for the demise of their "mother earth."

The reality is that they, through their wars, industries, mining,
ridiculous laws, and social policies, contribute more to what they deem
as evil than any of us combined. That fact is certainly never discussed,
because it's all about control, and they have given themselves the power
to pick the winners and the losers of the world, and they don't plan on
being the losers.

In their hypocrisy they insist that the sea levels are rising and that
the coastal lands will be flooded soon, all while they purchase expensive
ocean front property for themselves. They have the audacity to declare
that they are the appointed saviors of the planet while leaving their
hypocrisy out in the open for the entire world to see. Unfortunately,
too few have the discernment to see it.

These elites are mostly unelected leaders of industry, media,
technology, banking, pharmaceuticals, as well as religion and
government. They have appointed themselves to control, and monitor,
the world's temperature, population, health, finances, religions,
governments, and the global narrative, all of which are pushing for a
one-world system of control over governance, society, economics, and
religion, just to name a few.

A Prayer of Distress

Of the three patterns of the 15 Songs of Ascent, Psalm 120 is a prayer of distress. The writer is crying out for the Lord to deliver him from the lying lips and from the deceitful tongue of an unknown adversary. That fact that the identity of the enemy isn't delineated in the Psalm, or known historically through the scriptures, gives me some extra assurance that this Psalm is speaking of a future prophetic adversary. Knowing that God is just, the writer ponders what the fate of the deceiver will be once he is judged.

Judgment of the False Tongue

Verses 3-4
³What shall be given to you, or what shall be done to you, you false tongue? ⁴Sharp arrows of the warrior, with coals of the broom tree!

The answer to his fate along with all of those who were part of the deception, is written clearly in the book of Revelation. I believe that "Babylon" in the book of Revelation is symbolic of not only a location, but also of a system of global tyranny and control. There are many books and teachings that speculate the location of the end-time Babylon as well as those people, governments, and secret societies who are part of the Babylonian system, so I won't add my two cents to the debate since it isn't specified in the Psalms or through the biblical prophets. What we do know is that it's called "Mystery Babylon" for a reason. There are good reasons to believe that it could be Rome, London, maybe New York, or even Washington DC, but it will not be known until the time of the tribulation when the mystery will be revealed. Certainly, God will reveal the mystery in His time, but we are definitely witnessing this global control system of Babylon being established all over the world right now in our day.

We naturally associate Babylon with the world's mystery religions, which are alive and well even today through many different names, but they all have their foundations in Babylon, and they are all designed by the enemy as decoys to lead the masses away from the one true Savior. When I think about ancient Babylon, I also think about the ruler known as Nimrod, who we read about in Genesis 10, and the tower of Babel, which we read about in Genesis 11. Babylon was man's first attempt at unifying mankind in opposition to God. God instructed Noah and his sons to "Be fruitful and multiply, and fill the earth." However, it wasn't long until man decided to defy God in their pride and arrogance. They did not want to spread out and fill the earth as God had intended, so they built a type of global city and a tower in an act of rebellion against God and as a show of their own power and accomplishments without God. Of course, we know that God then confused their languages and scattered them all over the world, according to Genesis 11. However, the Bible does not say that God destroyed Babylon at that time.

Many of the Old Testament books, including Jeremiah and Daniel, tell of Babylon later around 600 BC. During this time a powerful King ruled over the Babylonian empire by the name of King Nebuchadnezzar. This is the king who attacked both Israel and Judea, took the children of Israel into captivity, looted, and then destroyed the temple of Solomon.

God used the Babylonians, also known as the Chaldeans, a people even more wicked than Israel, to punish and correct the children of Israel by allowing His children to be taken captive by the Babylonian Empire. However, once Israel's captivity was over after 70 years in Babylon to repay for their rebellion and disobedience, God also had a plan for Babylon. Jeremiah 51 and Isaiah 13 both give us a very vivid account of the destruction of Babylon in recompense for her sins against God's people. Just as prophesied, Babylon fell to the Persians around 540 BC. Though Babylon was once the most majestic and modern city in all of the world, through the course of time, looting, and conflicts, the great city of Babylon was left in ruins, and is only inhabited by jackals and other wild beasts even today.

Jeremiah 51:36-37

Therefore thus says the LORD: "Behold, I will plead your case and take vengeance for you. I will dry up her sea and make her springs dry. ³⁷Babylon shall become a heap, a dwelling place for jackals, an astonishment and a hissing, without an inhabitant.

Isaiah 13:19-22

¹⁹And Babylon, the glory of kingdoms, the beauty of the Chaldeans' pride, will be as when God overthrew Sodom and Gomorrah. ²⁰It will never be inhabited, Nor will it be settled from generation to generation; nor will the Arabian pitch tents there, nor will the shepherds make their sheepfolds there. ²¹But wild beasts of the desert will lie there, and their houses will be full of owls; ostriches will dwell there, and wild goats will caper there.²²The hyenas will howl in their citadels, and jackals in their pleasant palaces. Her time is near to come, and her days will not be prolonged."

Because of Babylon's history of opposing God and His people, many other sins, including their worship of demon gods such as Marduk, Enlil, Enki, Inanna, and Utu, the name Babylon is even today synonymous with a rebellious world government, idolatry, wickedness, blasphemy, and the persecution of Israel. History is repeating itself, and it is clear that Babylon is rising again as the world power. However, at this time, it isn't a place on a map, but a hidden world super power of deception and control that is infecting every part of our world today. Governments, societies, leaders, industries, religions, and individuals are all bowing down to this unseen force, which takes on many shapes. But just as ancient Babylon's days were numbered by God, it has been prophesied for ages that this resurrected Babylon shall also fall.

Revelation 18:1-2

¹After these things I saw another angel coming down from heaven, having great authority, and the earth was illuminated with his glory. ²And he cried mightily with a loud voice, saying, "Babylon the great is fallen, is fallen, and has become a dwelling place of demons, a prison for every foul spirit, and a cage for every unclean and hated bird!

Many Bible Prophecy teachers say that the actual City of Babylon will eventually rise again in the desert sands of Iraq in the end times since Babylon is mentioned in Revelation. I am usually one to take things literally in the prophetic scriptures with the understanding that they are also encrypted; however, in this case, God's judgment on the location of Babylon is already fully complete. Just as God prophesied through the Prophets Isaiah and Jeremiah, Babylon is no longer inhabited by humans, but is a literal habitation of only wild beasts of the desert. Isaiah 13:20 makes it clear that Babylon will never be inhabited again. Saddam Hussein started the building of a palace in what was the location of the ancient City of Babylon; however, it was never completed due to the Iraq War. Can you see the hand of God at work in all of this?

We are not waiting for the city of Babylon to be rebuilt for the end times to begin, as many would declare. That view point never made any sense to me anyway since the remains of what was the Great City of Babylon is now in a desert of Iraq and not on many waters as described in the prophetic scriptures. How could the captains of ships and sailors watch as the city burns if it's in a desert with no water, as described in Revelation 18? Obviously, God could move that mountain, but not against His own completed prophetic word.

The Fate of Mystery Babylon

Even if we don't know the exact location of this "Mystery Babylon," we do know her ultimate fate, as well as that of the false messiah and the false prophet. The fall of Mystery Babylon is detailed in Revelation 17 and 18. Based on current technology, it appears to me that the description of what destroys Mystery Babylon closely resembles that of a nuclear attack. In Revelation 18:21, we are given a glimpse into the violent, destructive ending that awaits this Babylon. The description is of a large boulder thrown into the sea by a mighty angel. As I have mentioned before, I believe that it is always best to take the prophetic events, people, places, and things in the scriptures literally, along with the understanding that they are encrypted. For instance, many times, you will see the word "like" used to describe something that isn't being specifically named. Let's look at Revelation 8:8 as an example.

Revelation 8:8

*[8] The second angel sounded his trumpet, and something **like** a huge mountain, all ablaze, was thrown into the sea. A third of the sea turned into blood, [9] a third of the living creatures in the sea died, and a third of the ships were destroyed.*

Because of the word "like" we know that it isn't necessarily a huge mountain that will be thrown into the sea, but it could be something "like" it, such as an asteroid or even perhaps a missile. The point is that it will have the same destructive power as a huge mountain being thrown into the sea, and any generation could understand that power.

The ultimate demise of Babylon is described in a similar way, but not with the use of the word "like." Here, we are told that John was shown an angel casting a large boulder down to symbolize the violence of the end that awaits Babylon, but not necessarily the exact means by which it will be destroyed.

Revelation 18:21

[21] Then a mighty angel picked up a boulder the size of a large millstone and threw it into the sea, and said:"With such violence the great city of Babylon will be thrown down, never to be found again..."

My hunch is that Revelation 18 is describing a nuclear strike. How else could John have described nuclear destruction almost 2,000 years ago? In addition, there are a few other very interesting aspects to the description that no other generation before ours could understand. After Babylon's destruction, Revelation 18:9-10 as well as Revelation 18:17, indicates that mourners will stand far away and mourn over the destruction of this great city. Could it be that they cannot approach due to radioactive fallout? Notice that no one goes to even sift through the rubble to find survivors or any remaining riches.

Revelation 18:9-10

*9 "When the kings of the earth who committed adultery with her and shared her luxury see the smoke of her burning, they will weep and mourn over her.10 Terrified at her torment, **they will stand far off** and cry:" 'Woe! Woe to you, great city, you mighty city of Babylon! In one hour your doom has come!'*

Revelation 18:17

*17 In one hour such great wealth has been brought to ruin!' "Every sea captain, and all who travel by ship, the sailors, and all who earn their living from the sea, **will stand far off**.*

When we add the description of Babylon's destruction from John's Revelation to Psalm 120:3-4, which reveals the answer to the question of how God will soon judge the unnamed lying and deceiving adversary, I am once again left with the belief that it will be with nuclear annihilation. Verse 4 says that the judgment will be with "sharp arrows of the warrior" and then also says, "with coals of the broom tree!"

Verses 3-4

3 What shall be given to you, or what shall be done to you, you false tongue? 4Sharp arrows of the warrior, with coals of the broom tree!

"Sharp arrows of the warrior" is certainly a fitting description of missiles made for war. In fact, I can't think of a more fitting description of a missile attack, considering that the Psalms were written around 3000 years ago. Then add to that the description of "coals of the broom tree." The broom tree, also known as the white broom, is a desert shrub that was used to make long-lasting charcoal because it burns exceptionally hot compared to other trees and shrubs found in the Judean wilderness.

Revelation 18:8
*Therefore in one day her plagues will overtake her: death, mourning and famine. She will be **consumed by fire**, for mighty is the Lord God who judges her.*

The charcoal of the broom tree is exceptionally hot and long-lasting. A fire that can consume a large city or land mass would also need to be exceptionally hot, as represented by the broom tree coals. In addition, the fire that one day will consume the future Babylon will have to be long-lasting as well so that the kings of the earth, the merchants, and the sea captains and sailors all stand far off and see her burning and mourn. Revelation 19:3 tells us that *"the smoke from her goes up forever and ever."* Through these scriptures in Revelation, you can see how the imagery from Psalm 120 comes to life foretelling of a future event still to come after the year 2020. How do we know it will be after 2020? Because in Psalm 120:1, the writer calls out to the Lord, pleading, *"Deliver my soul, O LORD, from lying lips and from a deceitful tongue."* His request is in the present tense. However, in Psalm 120:3, we can see that the writer is pondering what will be the still future judgment of the owner of those lying lips.

Verse 3
³What shall be given to you, or what shall be done to you, you false tongue?

Not just the mystery land known as Babylon will be destroyed by fire, but there is also a judgment of fire reserved for the false messiah, as well as the false prophet, who will certainly have lying lips and deceitful tongues. At the second coming of our Lord and Savior, they will both be thrown into the fiery lake of burning sulfur as described in Revelation 19:19-20.

Revelation 19:19-20

[19] Then I saw the beast and the kings of the earth and their armies gathered together to wage war against the rider on the horse and his army. [20] But the beast was captured, and with it the false prophet who had performed the signs on its behalf. With these signs he had deluded those who had received the mark of the beast and worshiped its image. ***The two of them were thrown alive into the fiery lake of burning sulfur.***

Meshech and Kedar

Verses 5-7

[5]Woe is me, that I dwell in Meshech, that I dwell among the tents of Kedar![6] My soul has dwelt too long with one who hates peace. [7] I am for peace; but when I speak, they are for war.

Keep in mind that the Psalms as well as all biblical scriptures, are best understood first from a Jewish perspective. This Psalm was probably written by King Hezekiah, who was a righteous king over Judea around 700 BC. Historically I cannot find any account of King Hezekiah or his fellow Judeans living among the nomadic, wild tribes of Kedar, who were descendants of Abraham's son Ishmael according to Genesis 16:12. They also didn't dwell in Meshech who were descendants of Japheth according to Genesis 10:2. However, this is a perfect prophetic description of Israel's current neighbors, as well as those who live among them who hate them, and want to see their destruction today.

Israel is surrounded by hostile Muslim countries, and has hostile Palestinians living among them in Gaza, the West Bank, and other settlements within Israel. Most, if not all, of these countries and individuals would rejoice if Israel no longer existed, just as the descendants of Esau, who were the Edomites, rejoiced when the descendants of Jacob were taken into captivity.

Obadiah 1:12

"But you [Edom] should not have gloated on the day of your brother [Jacob or Israel] in the day of his captivity; nor should you have rejoiced over the children of Judah in the day of their destruction; nor should you have spoken proudly in the day of distress.

There are other references to the coming judgment of the Edomites. Not only did they not act like a brother and help Israel, but they literally rejoiced over the captivity and destruction of their brothers - the children of Israel. Even worse, they actually helped the enemies of Israel who took them into captivity. More scripture concerning the coming judgment of the Edomites can be found in Obadiah, Lamentations 4, and Jeremiah 49.

Israel's 12th Prime Minister, Benjamin Netanyahu, is quoted as saying, "If the Arabs put down their weapons today, there would be no more violence. If the Jews put down their weapons today, there would be no more Israel."

Perhaps a more true statement has never been spoken by a politician! This struggle between Israel and the Arabs is nothing new. There has been an ongoing conflict for thousands of years between the descendants of Ishmael and Esau against their brothers Isaac and Jacob. This conflict still carries on today.

To sum up and simplify a lengthy genealogy, Ishmael and Esau are the fathers of today's Arab Muslims. Of course, we know that Isaac and Jacob are the fathers of the nation of Israel. Both groups are fathered by Abraham, so in a biblical sense, both are brothers.

Verse 6 says, *"My soul has dwelt too long with one who hates peace,"* indicating that as of 2020, Israel has already dwelt too long with their enemy. Israel has a promise that they will never again be destroyed;

however, unfortunately for the descendants of Esau, they do not have such a promise. In fact, they have a harsh judgment coming for their sins against their brother, and I believe that their day of reckoning is fast approaching.

Lamentations 4:21-22
21Rejoice and be glad, O daughter of Edom, you who dwell in the land of Uz! The cup shall also pass over to you and you shall become drunk and make yourself naked. 22 The punishment of your iniquity is accomplished, O daughter of Zion; He will no longer send you into captivity. He will punish your iniquity, O daughter of Edom; He will uncover your sins!

Obadiah 1:10-11
"For violence against your brother Jacob, shame shall cover you, and you shall be cut off forever. 11 In the day that you stood on the other side—In the day that strangers carried captive his forces, when foreigners entered his gates and cast lots for Jerusalem— even you were as one of them.

Obadiah 1:18
The house of Jacob shall be a fire, and the house of Joseph a flame; but the house of Esau shall be stubble; they shall kindle them and devour them, and no survivor shall remain of the house of Esau," for the LORD has spoken.

Psalm 120, which matches the year 2020 in the timeline revelation, indicates that it would be a year of distress, lies, and deception. It speaks of a future judgment, which is still to come for the deceivers. It also points out that Israel has lived too long with nations and people who hate them, and who prefer war over peace. Not only does this align with what we lived through in 2020, but it also fits perfectly into the encrypted timeline of prophetic events still to come, as you will see in the coming chapters.

CHAPTER 6

Psalm 121 A Song of Ascents

The Year 2021 - The Rapture Season Begins

Of the three patterns of "birth pains found in the 15 Psalms of Ascent, Psalm 121 is the second type in the theme of proclaiming God's help and deliverance.

After the deception and lies of 2020, it makes sense that God's help and deliverance is proclaimed in Psalm 121, corresponding to the year 2021. Along with the discussion of the prophetic implications of Psalm 121, as it relates to the year 2021, I'm going to also try to connect a lot of "dots" between Bible prophecy and world events, especially as they relate to Israel. Fortunately, 2021 is now in the past, which makes it even easier to see the larger prophetic picture that has been revealed in this Psalm.

I'm going to start by making a bold statement! This was the year that the "Rapture Season," as I call it, was opened. As of 2021, I believe that the Messiah, Jesus is standing at the door, and is ready to return just as the Jewish Rabbis prophesied that He would in the wake of the political turmoil in Israel, which culminated in 2021, leading to Benjamin Netanyahu being re-elected for a 3rd term at the end of 2022. Hang on as I explain what I'm talking about...

A prophecy was spoken over Netanyahu back in 2008 that he would serve as the Prime Minister of Israel for 3 terms: "And then the time of the end." As of the end of 2022, Benjamin Netanyahu will begin his unprecedented 3rd term in office. His first term was from 1996 to 1999, his second term was from 2009 to 2021, and as prophesied, his new term will be from late 2022 until the end! We are witnessing the convergence of so many end-times prophesies in our day, but much of the world doesn't see it, and unfortunately, much of the church doesn't know it.

You may be wondering why I am talking about prophesies that are not in the Bible. Well, let me answer that question with some truth directly from the Bible. First, remember what the Prophet Amos says:

Amos 3:7
*"Surely the Lord G*OD *does nothing, unless He reveals His secret to His servants the prophets."*

Is God still revealing His plans and secrets in our day? Personally, I don't think there has ever been a time when a prophetic word has been more important. Daniel 12 also reveals that there will be an increase of knowledge in the end times, and he was told not to reveal what he had written until the time of the end. That tells me that we should certainly be expecting new prophetic revelations during our generation. I think you will find this book as a good example of that. It seems to me that we are witnessing the puzzle pieces, which were very difficult to place even a few years ago, now finally starting to fall into place - glory to God!

Daniel 12:4
[4] *"But you, Daniel, shut up the words, and seal the book **until the time of the end**; many shall run to and fro, and **knowledge shall increase**."*

So, we should be expecting new revelation in our day, but how do we know if we can trust a prophecy not written in God's word? Remember that in Acts chapter 2, Peter made it clear from the prophet Joel that in the last days, or as Joel put it "those days," we should expect an outpouring of the Holy Spirit and to expect to hear prophesies and visions. Again, according to Peter, "those days" started almost 2000 years ago and have not ended.

The acid test for a true or false prophecy, and therefore a true or false prophet, is found in Deuteronomy 18:21. Moses revealed that we aren't the only ones to ever question what, or who to trust.

Deuteronomy 18:21

"But you may wonder, 'How will we know whether or not a prophecy is from the LORD?' If the prophet speaks in the LORD's name but his prediction does not happen or come true, you will know that the LORD did not give that message. That prophet has spoken without my authority and need not be feared (listened to or obeyed in the future).

Now that we have that cleared up, let's look at a few more recent prophecies from several Jewish Rabbis that have come true in amazing detail.

Israel's most prominent modern era Rabbi Yitzhak Kaduri, prophesied in 1979 the following: "On the eve of the year 5780 (primarily 2020 by the Jewish calendar), the year of correction, there will not be a government in Israel for an extended period, and the various camps will be quarrelling much without a decision on either side, and then, on Rosh Hashana itself, they will fight in heaven, the holy side against the side of evil, and God and His entourage will decide between them. And this is all I can say, and from here, I swore not to reveal more secrets and hidden things."

This prophecy wasn't understood at the time, because it didn't make sense that there wouldn't be a government in Israel, but it became clear after an unheard-of 4 election cycles between 2019 and 2021 when no government was able to be formed.

Here's an interesting side note. Rabbi Kaduri, who didn't speak very often, but rather spent most of his time studying the Torah, and other Jewish religious texts, stated late in his life that He had met the Messiah, and that he wrote the name of the Messiah down on a small note and sealed it to be opened 1 year after his death. One year later, the note was anxiously opened to reveal the encoded name of the Messiah. Much to the dismay of the anxious Jewish Rabbis, it revealed that the

Messiah's name is Yeshua, which is Jesus in Hebrew. That's the name that they have rejected for almost 2000 years now!

Another Jewish Rabbi, Sasson Hai Shoshani, prophesied decades ago: "There will come on the day that two ministers win the government in the land of Israel. Both their names will be Benjamin, and neither of them will succeed in establishing their government or kingship. On that day, know and understand that the King Messiah already stands "at the doorway," and on the Sabbath afterwards, he will come and be revealed. Understand this and remember it."

As with the previous prophecy from Rabbi Kaduri, it refers to the critical years in Israeli politics from around 2019 until 2022 and lets us know what time we're living in. Simply put, neither PM Benjamin Netanyahu, nor Benjamin Gantz could form a government on their own since neither could get the needed 61 Knesset votes. The Knesset is Israel's legislature, sort of like our Congress, and it is required that they reach a majority of 61 votes to form a new government. The two Benjamins' tried to form a shared prime-ministership; however, it was dissolved on June 13, 2021.

This prophesy from Rabbi Shoshani stating that there would be two Benjamins who wouldn't be able to form a government was extremely specific and couldn't have made any sense to anyone over the decades until it actually came to pass.

The first part of the prophecy came true in amazing detail. The second part of the prophecy reveals that at this time, the Messiah is already "standing at the door" and on the Sabbath afterwards, will be revealed. This part of the prophecy is less detailed because it just states, "on the Sabbath afterwards." God gave Israel many different Sabbaths detailed in the Torah, which is the first 5 books of the Old Testament. Sabbath in Hebrew simply means to rest. There are weekly Sabbaths, 7 yearly festival Sabbaths, also known as High Holy Days, Shmita Sabbaths every 7th year, and Jubilee Sabbaths every 50th year after 7 Shmita Sabbath cycles. So, it's hard to know which type of Sabbath the prophecy is referring to.

Being a student of these things, I was glued to the Israeli news on the weekly Sabbath after the new Prime Minister, Naphtali Bennett, was sworn in on June 13, 2021. That weekly Sabbath fell on Saturday, June 19, 2021. Unfortunately, nothing much happened that day, and no Messiah figure was revealed. I wasn't necessarily expecting the real Messiah, Jesus to us English speakers, or Yeshua in Hebrew, to come and rapture us that day, but I was hoping! However, with all of the signs and end-time prophesies that were already coming into focus during 2021, I was thinking that perhaps the Antichrist would be revealed to the watching and discerning few in some small way as the "little horn" of Daniel 7:8. However, on the following weekly Sabbath after the swearing in of the new Prime Minister, Naphtali Bennett, no messiah figure was revealed.

According to 2 Thessalonians chapter 2, I do not believe that the Antichrist can be fully revealed until after the rapture of the Church. However, that doesn't mean that he isn't out there already, and that we won't be able to get a glance at him as he is rising to prominence in these final days of the Church Age.

After the weekly Sabbath, the next type of Sabbath was the High Holy Day Sabbath of the Feast of Trumpets. The Feast of Trumpets is better known now in Israel as Rosh Hashanah (Jewish New Year) on the corrupted Jewish calendar. It typically falls in September or October on our Gregorian calendar. As I mentioned previously, God's calendar given to Moses and Aaron begins in the spring-time and not in the fall. On God's original calendar, the Feast of Trumpets falls on the first of the 7th month, but again, on that Sabbath, the Feast of Trumpets in 2021, no messiah figure was revealed in any discernible way in the media.

The next type of Sabbath that the Rabbi's prophecy could have been related to would have been the Shmita Sabbath. Ironically, the Shmita Sabbath was also calculated to start on Rosh Hashanah at the start of the Jewish new year of 5782. The start of the year was on September 7th, 2021, according to the corrupted Jewish calendar. If a messiah figure was going to be revealed on a Shmita Sabbath, that would mean that he could be revealed anytime during the Sabbath year. That, however, also did not happen.

The Shmita year is a Sabbatical year and is known in Hebrew as the year of release. You can read about God's Shmita year Sabbaths in

Exodus 23:10-11, Leviticus 25: 1-7 and 20-22, Deuteronomy 15:1-6 and 31:10-13. It is the final year in a seven-year cycle while the children of Israel inhabit their land. The Jews are to give the land a 1 year rest from planting and harvesting every seventh year to let the land recover from agriculture, and to show their faith in the provision of God. They are, however, to allow the poor, and even animals, to eat freely from the naturally growing crops in the fields, groves, orchards, and vineyards during the Shmita year.

I have a couple of final notes on the Shmita year and God's commandments regarding the 7-year cycle. Rabbis have tried to calculate the Shmita cycle going back to the 2nd Temple period in the first century AD and using the Torah to figure out the true Shmita year. There are different historical opinions from Rabbis and scholars regarding how to calculate it, and when to start calculating it. As we know, Israel became a nation again in 1948. So, should they start calculating from that year based on Leviticus 25, which ties the keeping of this commandment to Israel being in the land, as God said to keep the Shmita: "When you come to the land that I am giving you?" Or should the cycle have continued from the time of Joshua when the children of Israel first entered the land of Israel?

The Essenes, who I have mentioned before, who were descendants of the Zadok Priesthood, and were responsible for hiding the Dead Sea Scrolls in the caves of Qumran, continued to keep God's calendar. They also had records of all of the ages and of the Jubilees. If you know when the Jubilee years have occurred and will occur, then it's easy to figure out when the Shmita years will be. Modern-day Jewish Rabbis believe 2021/2022 (Jewish year 5782) is a Shmita year and 2022/2023 (Jewish year 5783) will be a Jubilee year. However, according to the Essenes, the year starting in the spring of 2024 until the spring of 2025 (Essene year 5949) will be a Shmita year, and the year beginning in the spring of 2025 until the spring of 2026 (Essene year 5950) will be a Jubilee year. Hang on to that information, as it is very important to our timeline revelation.

So, needless to say, there was no messiah figure revealed in 2021, which makes sense because it wasn't actually a biblical Shmita year, just a Rabbinical Shmita year. That means that according to the decades-old prophecy from Rabbi Shoshani, which has already partially come true, it could happen in the year 2024, the year of the true Shmita, which will then be followed by the Year of Jubilee in 2025. Also, according to the Essenes, 25 AD was a Jubilee year and the Messiah was expected to come and be revealed in the first Shmita of that new Jubilee, which was in 32 AD. That would correlate to the fulfillment of Zechariah 9:9 when Jesus rode into Jerusalem on the colt of a donkey, thereby proclaiming Himself as Messiah.

Could it be that the 7-year tribulation period is on a 7-year Shmita cycle? Could it be that the tribulation period will end 2000 years, or 40 Jubilees after Jesus' death and resurrection, which would be 2032? Could it be that the rapture of the Church, which has to happen prior to the start of the tribulation, will happen during a Shmita year prior to the Jubilee year? That would be the year 2024. Could it be even sooner? The signs are all around us.

Verses 1-2
¹I will lift up my eyes to the hills—from whence comes my help? ²My help comes from the LORD, Who made heaven and earth.

These two verses connect with what John wrote in Revelation chapter 4. John described that he "looked" and saw "a door standing open in heaven." Lifting up your eyes or lifting up your head is a more descriptive and poetic way of saying look, but the meaning is ultimately the same.

Revelation 4:1
*After these things **I looked**, and behold, **a door standing open in heaven**. And the first voice which I heard was like a trumpet speaking with me, saying, "Come up here, and I will show you things which must take place after this."*

Again, we see the "door" as a recurring theme, just as in Rabbi Shoshani's prophecy. Remember that it was Jesus who also connected the "door," and specifically being "at the door" even with the Fig Tree Generation.

> **Matthew 24:32-34**
> [32] *"Now learn this parable from the fig tree: when its branch has already become tender and puts forth leaves, you know that summer is near. [33] So you also, when you see all these things, know that it ("He" in other translations) is near—**at the doors!** [34] Assuredly, I say to you, this generation will by no means pass away till all these things take place.*

Can you see how all of these prophetic details are interconnected? What is truly exciting about this, as we are connecting some of the prophetic scriptures, is that Jesus is not only standing at the door; Jesus is the door according to His own words.

> **John 10:7-10**
> *Then Jesus said to them again, "Most assuredly, I say to you, **I am the door** of the sheep. All who ever came before Me are thieves and robbers, but the sheep did not hear them. **I am the door**. If anyone enters by Me, he will be saved, and will go in and out and find pasture. The thief does not come except to steal, and to kill, and to destroy. I have come that they may have life, and that they may have it more abundantly.*

In the Hebrew alphabet, the 4th letter is the "dalet," which has a numerical value of 4. In the ancient Hebrew, the dalet as a pictogram is a door, and it is known as the portal to heaven. Providentially, we know of Jesus, who is our doorway, or portal to heaven, through the "4" Gospels of Jesus Christ. Coincidence?

How else does Jesus relate to the number 4 other than being the "door?" Here are just 4 of the many ways that Jesus is connected to the Hebrew number 4.

- Jesus is from the tribe of Judah, who was the 4th son born to Jacob and Leah.
- Jesus came to save the world at the completion of 4 thousand years, also known as the 4th day.
- On the 4th day of creation He created the sun, moon and stars in heaven for signs, seasons (Moedim), and to light the world (Genesis 1:14-19). Jesus is the light of the world (John 8:12).
- The 4th commandment says to rest on the Sabbath Day (Exodus 20:8-11). Jesus declared that He is the Lord of the Sabbath (Matthew 12:8), and Jesus also declared that He is the one who would give us rest (Matthew 11:28).

There are many more, but that could be a chapter all by itself. The point is that Jesus declares to us that He is the only "door" by which we can be saved. I believe that in this time, He is also anxiously standing at the door and is ready to come for His Bride, the Church.

I have to add one more! Remember that Jesus said that the end times would be like the days of Noah in Matthew 24? That interconnects with Genesis 6:1-4 and the Nephilim, but that's a different story also. What I want to point out is found in Genesis 6:16 and Genesis 7:16:

Genesis 6:16

*16 You shall make a window for the ark, and you shall finish it to a cubit from above; and set **the door** of the ark in its side.*

Genesis 7:16

*16 So those that entered, male and female of all flesh, went in as God had commanded him; **and the LORD shut him in.***

Notice that God only allowed for one door in the side of the ark, and that He Himself shut the door, thereby saving all those inside, but also preventing anyone else from outside from being able to enter in. Is it just a coincidence that there was only one way into the wooden ark that saved those who obeyed God, and had faith in God? Is it a coincidence that once the door was shut by the hand of God that no one else was able to enter in? Can you see the pattern of Christ in Genesis 6 and 7?

Compare that to Jesus, who says He is the door (John 10:7) and is the only way (John 14:6) to be saved. He accomplished this through a wooden cross for all who are obedient and have faith in Him (James 2:14-26). You can see the parallels, but there's even more to it. So far, we've only looked at the prophetic patterns that have already been fulfilled. There is another pattern that has yet to be fulfilled.

God Himself closed the door of the ark with the obedient faithful on the inside and the disobedient unfaithful on the outside. This sets a pattern of a future event that Jesus describes in Matthew 25 in His parable of the 10 wise and foolish virgins. Remember that 5 had enough oil in their lamps, and the other 5 didn't. The 5 foolish virgins went to buy more oil after they heard the shout that the bridegroom was coming, but they were too late.

Matthew 25:10-11

*[10] And while they went to buy, the bridegroom came, and those who were ready went in with him to the wedding; **and the door was shut**.[11] "Afterward the other virgins came also, saying, 'Lord, Lord, open to us!'[12] But he answered and said, 'Assuredly, I say to you, I do not know you.'*

Once the door was shut, it wasn't opened for them for one very specific reason. Jesus says, "I do not know you," meaning they had no relationship with Him. Maybe they had some religion, but no relationship. We must have a relationship with our Savior. Religion is not the doorway into the wedding; it's only though a relationship with Jesus!

The coming world religious system will tell you that all roads lead to God, but that is a lie. We can already see the setup of this system that praises all of the many religions and ways to God except the "only way" that God actually designed and accepts, which is through His Son, the Messiah. Remember, in the Exodus story, it specifically took a lamb, some blood, and a "door" for the firstborn of the Israelites to be saved. Without it, they would have never passed from the world that they knew into the land promised to them by God. That pattern still exists for us today. There's only one "Lamb," and only His "blood" can save us (John 1:29). There's only one "Door" that we can go through (John 10:7) to enter into the Kingdom promised to us so that we can abide with the Father (John 14:6) and that's through Jesus.

After These Things

Backing up for a moment, there is one more thing that I would like to point out in Revelation 4 as it relates to the timeline revelation. Notice John's choice of words when he said, "after these things." It makes you wonder, "after what things?" Well, the previous 2 chapters were devoted to the Church Age, represented by 7 specific churches as models of the 7 types of churches now, and throughout the Church Age.

John used the Greek words Meta Tauta, which literally means "after these things." It implies a chronological order. So, after the Church Age John saw the door "standing" open, and he heard a voice that sounded like a trumpet (1 Corinthians 15:52, 1 Thessalonians 4:16), which told him to "come up here!" If that's not a symbol of the rapture based on other prophetic scriptures and patterns, I don't know what is!

The Last Trumpet

Remember that these 15 Psalms were sung as the pilgrims ascended Mount Zion to worship at the temple on the third main Jewish Festival, which we call the Feast of Tabernacles. It's also probable that they sang these 15 Songs of Ascent on the other two High Holy Days, when God also required all able-bodied men to travel to Jerusalem to worship and bring offerings. Of course, we know that the priests also sang these 15 songs on the 15 steps at the Holy Temple in Jerusalem and blew trumpets on the 10th step on their way down to draw water, according to Jewish history.

In 1 Corinthians 15 Paul calls the trumpet the "Last Trumpet." Many Christians have confused this trumpet with the last trumpet of the 7 trumpets of Revelation. However, when you study this from a Jewish perspective, you realize that the "Last Trumpet" is specifically the long and sustained last trumpet blast in a series of 100 blasts of the Shofar on Yom Teruah or Feast of Trumpets as we call it. It's specifically called the "Last Trumpet." As I have mentioned previously, the Feast of Trumpets is the next Feast Day to be fulfilled on the prophetic calendar, and it is symbolic of the rapture in many ways.

Of course, we already know that Jesus fulfilled all of the 4 spring feasts at His first coming. The feast days are known as "appointed times" and as "dress rehearsals" for future events. Jesus perfectly fulfilled the spring feasts in every way, exactly to the day, and even the hour. The spring feasts told of God's perfect plan for our redemption through the sacrificial death, burial, and resurrection of His spotless Lamb, as well as the outpouring of the Holy Spirit at Pentecost, which was a gift to the Bride of Christ, the Church. But that's only half of the redemption plan. There is still more to come. The Church Age has not yet come to a close at the blast of the "last trumpet" (1 Corinthians 15:52). All of Israel has not yet been saved (Romans 11:26), every knee has not yet bowed, and every tongue has not yet confessed He is Lord (Romans 14:11), the Messiah has not yet fought against the nations, or stood on the Mount of Olives, and split the mountain in two from east to west (Zechariah 14:3-4), and Jesus is not yet dwelling with us or ruling from the throne of David (2 Samuel 7:16-17, Zechariah 14:9, Isaiah 9:7).

As you can see, we're still waiting on the fulfillment of the final Messianic prophecies, which are patterned in the final 3 feast days to be completed at Jesus' second coming. According to scripture, His second coming will usher in the Millennial Kingdom of God with Jesus on the throne over all of the earth.

All together, the 7 feasts are God's encrypted redemption plan for all of mankind, both Jews and Gentiles, through His one and only Son, our Messiah, Jesus, Yeshua HaMashiach. Paul sums all of this up nicely in his letter to the Colossians:

Colossians 2:16-17
So let no one judge you in food or in drink, or regarding a festival or a new moon or Sabbaths, **which are a shadow of things to come, but the substance is of Christ.**

They were a foreshadowing of the soon to be completed work of the Messiah. Let's remember that God is the one who declares the end from the beginning, which proves Him to be the one true God.

Isaiah 46:9-10
Remember the former things of old, For I am God, and there is no other; I am God, and there is none like Me, ***declaring the end from the beginning****, and from ancient times things that are not yet done, saying, 'My counsel shall stand, and I will do all My pleasure,'*

As we know, the 7 Feasts are God's Feasts. He gave them to the Children of Israel to observe. All of them are Sabbaths. They also all have some connection to agricultural harvest seasons in Israel. Three of them are specific harvest festivals when it is required that all able-bodied men in Israel travel to Jerusalem to bring offerings and partake in the festival. Most of them have a connection to past events when God moved on Israel's behalf. In Leviticus chapter 23, all of the feast days have a specific stated meaning, whether it's theological, agricultural, or memorial. However, there's one exception: The Feast of Trumpets!

The fall feasts begin with the Feast of Trumpets, known as Yom Teruah in Hebrew. Yom Teruah means Day of Shouting, or making a loud noise, which could be either by a congregation or by trumpet blasts. Yom Teruah is a Sabbath and is also a Miqra, or dress rehearsal for a future event.

This feast day is a bit of a mystery in the Torah since there isn't much meaning assigned to it in Exodus, Leviticus, Numbers, or Deuteronomy. Even though Leviticus 23 calls it a memorial, there isn't any specific historical significance assigned to it. When you compare the Feast of Trumpets to another Feast, such as the Passover, you can see a stark contrast. Passover is, of course, in memory of when Israel escaped Egyptian slavery, as well as the sacrifice of our Lord and Savior. In comparison, the Feast of Trumpets is about making a loud noise and blowing a trumpet!

In addition, there isn't any stated harvest significance associated with it as there is with other feast days, even though it does land in the fall harvest season. So, based on all of this evidence, and the lack of any historical meaning, I think it's pretty clear that as one of God's 7 appointed feast days, it must be about a mysterious future event still on the horizon. So, it's truly a dress rehearsal for a day soon to come, and I believe that it will only be a true "memorial" when we look back on it in the Millennial Kingdom.

Rosh Hashanah

Before I go any further, let me add that many in Israel call the Feast of Trumpets, Rosh Hashanah. However, Rosh Hashanah means "Head of the Year" in Hebrew. That means that the Jews celebrate the day that God called Yom Teruah as New Year's Day now instead. This all comes from their Babylonian captivity and the mixing of pagan influences into their rabbinical version of Judaism. This is very confusing since God clearly proclaimed to Moses that the beginning of the year was in the month of Abib, which is in the spring and is now known more commonly in Israel by its pagan Babylonian name, Nisan.

God never said that the year should start in the fall at the beginning of the 7th month, which is called Tishrei. Remember that the Book of Jubilees prophesied the corruption of the calendar by the Jews, and the Old Testament Prophets Ezekiel, Isaiah, and Zephaniah all prophesied that when the Children of Israel return to their land, they will return in unbelief. Not only is Israel today a very secular society, but the majority of the religious Jews have rejected Jesus as their Messiah. So, even counting all of the religious Jews in Israel, we still have to conclude that they are living in unbelief. Their redemption through the acceptance of Jesus as their true Messiah is the primary goal of the coming 7-year tribulation period.

Here's what God instructed Moses regarding the Feast of Trumpets:

Leviticus 23:24-25
*Then the LORD spoke to Moses, saying, "Speak to the children of Israel, saying: 'In the **seventh month**, **on the first day** of the month, you shall have a sabbath-rest, a **memorial of blowing of trumpets**, a holy convocation. You shall do no customary work on it; and you shall offer an offering made by fire to the LORD.'"*

So, the Feast of Trumpets is on the 1st day of the 7th month and is a day of blowing trumpets. Could it be a coincidence that it falls on the 1st day of the 7th month? After all, the number 7, as it relates to time, and represents the coming Millennial Kingdom Sabbath. It makes me wonder if God considers the Feast of Trumpets to be the first prophetic feast day, out of the remaining three yet to be fulfilled, that will bring a close to the 6th millennium and start the 7th millennium.

Does the number 7 relate to the 7 Churches of Revelation and the Church in general, which doesn't appear to be present on earth during the tribulation period in the book of Revelation? You see, the Church is mentioned in the book of Revelation 19 times prior to Chapter 4, but not again by name until the final chapter, which is chapter 22. So, during all of the catastrophic events happening during the 7-year tribulation period, we, the Church, are never mentioned as being here on Earth. We are, however, seen in Revelation 19 coming out of Heaven, following Jesus back to Earth dressed in fine linen, white and clean.

Note: Revelation 19 also tells us that fine linen stands for the righteous acts of God's holy people, so we know that it's the Church that is being shown and not an army of angels.

What about the Trumpets?

At Mount Sinai, a long and very loud trumpet blast was heard signaling Moses to bring the Children of Israel to meet God, who had descended to the top of Mount Sinai.

Exodus 19:16-17
On the morning of the third day (wedding day) there was thunder and lightning, with a thick cloud over the mountain, and a very loud trumpet blast. Everyone in the camp trembled. Then Moses led the people out of the camp to meet with God,

Doesn't that sound like a typology of the rapture?

1 Thessalonians 4:16
[16]For the Lord Himself will descend from heaven with a shout, with the voice of an archangel, and with the trumpet of God. And the dead in Christ will rise first.

1 Corinthians 15:52
[52]In a moment, in the twinkling of an eye, at the last trumpet. For the trumpet will sound, and the dead will be raised incorruptible, and we shall be changed.

As we can see, the trumpet is a symbol of the resurrection, and the rapture of the Church. Trumpets were also used by Israel to call assemblies, for breaking camp during the exodus, military signals on the battle-field, and they used trumpets at the destruction of Jericho as well. Trumpets were also signs of judgment and warnings to God's people, as well as the signaling of the coronation of a new king.

There were two types of horns described in the Old Testament and used by Israel. There was the Ram's horn, and the 2 silver trumpets that God instructed Moses to have made. We're not going to have time to cover the differences, so we'll keep it more general for this study.

The Ram's horn or "Shofar" is symbolic of Jesus. Think about it... In Genesis 22, Abraham was told by God to sacrifice his beloved son Isaac, but at the last second, God miraculously provided a sacrificial lamb to save Isaac. The lamb (ram) was caught by its "horns" in the thicket. Remember also what Abraham told Isaac when he asked, "where is the lamb for the burnt offering?"

Genesis 22:8
And Abraham said, "My son, God will provide for Himself the lamb for a burnt offering."

So, who was ultimately the beloved son who was sacrificed just as the lamb was sacrificed in place of Isaac? Can you see the pattern, and the connection to the Ram's horn, called a Shofar, as a symbol of Jesus and His sacrifice in our place?

Note:
Jesus in Matthew 24, Paul in both 1 Thessalonians 4, and 1 Corinthians 15, as well as John in the book of Revelation associated the blast of a trumpet with the Resurrection, and the Rapture of the Church at the end of our present age.

Yom Teruah

So, as we now know, Yom Teruah, or Feast of Trumpets, is the first day of the Seventh month (Tishrei). In ancient Israel, this feast day began at the official sighting of the new moon by at least 2 witnesses, who then reported back to the Sanhedrin, who then proclaimed the beginning of the holiday, and the new month. Notice that it takes 2 witnesses. That will also be important in the timeline revelation, as we will soon see. Remember that all Jewish months begin on a new moon on the rabbinical calendar. In fact, the Hebrew word for month and new moon are the same word, Chodesh.

Yom Teruah is unique as it is the only feast day appointed to be on the first day of a month. Since Yom Teruah cannot begin until the new moon is spotted and verified, it could fall on the second day of the month if, for some reason, the moon is obstructed by clouds, smoke, etc., on the first day. For this reason, Yom Teruah is also known as the Feast, which means "No one knows the day or the hour" or "The Hidden Day," Yom Hakeseh in Hebrew. Obviously, this particular feast day has a lot of mystery surrounding it, making it highly suspicious with regard to its future fulfillment.

As I have mentioned previously, prior to the Feast of Trumpets, at the beginning of the 7th month, is the 6th month, known as Elul. Elul is also known as the month of Teshuvah, which means "repentance" or "return." In Israel, the Shofar (ram's horn trumpet) is blown every day of the month during Elul, except for Shabbat, to remind the Jews to examine their lives and to repent of their sins prior to the Fall Feast days to come. Teshuvah is actually 40 days long. It includes all of the 30-day month of Elul as well as the 10 days from Yom Teruah to Yom Kippur, or the Day of Atonement as we know it. Remember that the number 40 stands for a time of testing, trial, and probation, which fits perfectly into this time of Teshuvah.

Other Hebrew Names

The Feast of Trumpets is also known by many other names in Hebrew. I think you will see that all of the names have prophetic significance. Of course, we already know that it is called by the name **Yom Teruah**, which is known as the Day of Shouting and the awakening blast to awaken those sleeping in the dust to come to life (resurrection). We see the fulfillment of this pattern in 1 Thessalonians 4:16-17 when the dead in Christ rise first, and then we who are still alive and remain will be caught up (Harpazo, Rapturo) together with them to meet the Lord in the clouds. And from that time, we will forever be with the Lord.

The next name for the 5th feast is **Yom HaDin**, which is a Day of Judgment. This will be the day when believers are given crowns according to Romans 14:10-12, 1 Corinthians 3:13-15, and 2 Corinthians 5:10. Remember that there are two types of final judgments, one for the believer, and one for the non-believer. Our Judgment is for reward, not destruction. It will happen at, or after the rapture. We will stand before the Bema Seat of Christ on that day, and receive our reward for what we did for His Kingdom in this life. Remember, we are supposed to lay up treasures in Heaven, and not here on earth.

The Feast of Trumpets is also known by the name **Yom HaMelech**, which traditionally is known as the day that the Lord will be crowned as the King of the Universe. Because of this, earthly kings were traditionally coroneted on this day as well. The Jews have a hard time understanding this concept since they say that God has always been the King of the Universe, so why does He need a day to be crowned as King? The answer as always, is found in Jesus. When you study the Book of Revelation, you will find many wonderful physical descriptions of the resurrected Jesus. Revelation 1 describes Him as follows.

Revelation 1:13-16
...and among the lampstands was someone like a son of man, dressed in a robe reaching down to his feet and with a golden sash around his chest. The hair on his head was white like wool, as white as snow, and his eyes were like blazing fire. His feet were like bronze glowing in a furnace, and his voice was like the sound of rushing waters. In his right hand he held seven stars, and coming out of his mouth was a sharp, double-edged sword. His face was like the sun shining in all its brilliance.

Notice that John mentions how Jesus' hair was like white wool, but doesn't mention any crowns. That's because the Rapture of Revelation chapter 4 hasn't happened yet, and we, the Bride of Christ, haven't Crowned Him our King yet. Notice that by Chapter 19, there is a different description of Jesus:

Revelation 19:12-16

*His eyes are like blazing fire, and on his head are **many** **crowns**. He has a name written on him that no one knows but he himself. He is dressed in a robe dipped in blood, and his name is the Word of God. The armies of heaven were following him, riding on white horses and dressed in fine linen, white and clean. Coming out of his mouth is a sharp sword with which to strike down the nations. "He will rule them with an iron scepter." He treads the winepress of the fury of the wrath of God Almighty. On his robe and on his thigh he has this name written: KING OF KINGS AND LORD OF LORDS*

Believe it or not, but Yom Teruah is also associated with what the Jews call the birth pangs of the Messiah, also known as the time of Jacobs Trouble, also known as Daniel's 70th week, or as we typically call it, the 7-year tribulation period. In Hebrew, this time of birth pangs leading up to the revealing of the messiah is known as **Chevlai Shel Mashiach**.

Not only is the Feast of Trumpets associated with birth pangs, but oddly enough, it's also known in Hebrew as **Kiddushin/Nesu'in**, which is the wedding ceremony of the Messiah. The Jewish, specifically the Galilean wedding rituals, foretell and pattern the rapture and the subsequent wedding of the Messiah. We see this in part when Jesus was comforting His Disciples prior to His crucifixion in John 14.

John 14:1-4

"Let not your heart be troubled; you believe in God, believe also in Me. In My Father's house are many mansions; if it were not so, I would have told you. I go to prepare a place for you. And if I go and prepare a place for you, I will come again and receive you to Myself; that where I am, there you may be also. And where I go you know, and the way you know."

As if that wasn't enough symbolism of the rapture, the feast day of Yom Teruah is also known in the Jewish custom as The Day of **Natzal**, which means deliverance, to deliver, snatch away, and take away, to rescue. In Greek, this snatching away is called Harpazo, which translates to Natzal in Hebrew. It's the same as the English version of the Latin word Rapture!

On the Feast of Trumpets, there is a special trumpet blast called the **Shofar HaGadol**. It's the "Last Trumpet." This Long blast is the last of the series of 100 trumpet blasts blown on Yom Teruah. Does that sound familiar?

> **1 Corinthians 15: 52**
> *52In a moment, in the twinkling of an eye, **at the last trumpet**. For the trumpet will sound, and the dead will be raised incorruptible, and we shall be changed.*

Many people who believe in a mid or post-tribulation rapture believe that way mainly because of this verse. They think that Paul was alluding to the last of 7 trumpet judgments found in Revelation 11. The reality is that Paul wrote 1 Corinthians prior to John's writing of the book of Revelation, so he could not be alluding to a book that hadn't been written yet. Also, I would say that it would be easy to get confused about the "last trumpet" when studying the end times if you don't also study all of the Jewish connections, idioms, and Hebrew meanings. It seems only natural to associate an end-time "trumpet" in one book to another end-time "trumpet" in another book, but once you dig a little deeper, you will be able to uncover the pattern and the deeper Jewish meaning.

Call the Laborers in from the Fields

In the ancient agrarian Jewish customs, the Shofar was also used to call the workers or laborers in from the fields. It signifies that the harvest is over. Does that sound familiar? We are the laborers in the harvest season right now. Remember what Jesus said in Matthew 9:

Matthew 9:37-38

Then He said to His disciples, "The harvest truly is plentiful, but the laborers are few. Therefore pray the Lord of the harvest to send out laborers into His harvest."

There's a day coming when the harvest season that we are working in now, will come to a close, and we, the laborers will be called in. This day has a certain finality to it. At that time, and on that day, the harvest will be over. However much, or however little fruit our labor brought in is what we will have to show for our time working in God's field. Let's make sure that our baskets are all full!

Finally, Yom Teruah is also known as the **Day of Opening of the Gates**, which refers to both the gates of repentance, and of Heaven. Of course, we already know that the 10 days between Yom Teruah and Yom Kippur are known as the "10 Days of Awe." Those 10 days are the conclusion of the 40 days of Teshuvah**.** The final 10 days of Teshuvah between Yom Teruah and Yom Kippur is when, during Temple times, the High Priest would hide himself in the Temple so that he could be assured of not being tempted to sin, and therefore help guarantee that he wouldn't be defiled. Remember that he had to go into the Holy of Holies on Yom Kippur, and if God found him to be unclean, he wouldn't make it out alive.

So, to break it down, there are a total of 10 days from Yom Teruah until the end of Yom Kippur, including the High Days themselves. There are 7-days in between without the High Days counted. It makes me wonder if that 7-day week in between is figurative of the 7-year tribulation. Does the High Priest who would go into hiding represent the Church, who will be hidden away from the world for at least 7 years? After the High Priest was hidden away for 7 days, he would come out and once again be seen on Yom Kippur, which is symbolic of the future judgment day. To add to the mystery a little, the High Priest, who would normally wear Gold, Blue, Purple, and Scarlet, would only wear white linen on Yom Kippur. After he would enter into the presence of the Lord inside the Holy of Holies he would return from the Tabernacle wearing white linen to be once again seen by all of the people gathered in Jerusalem. Doesn't that sound like us when we will return from heaven to earth, as described in Revelation 19 wearing white linen? And remember that we are Priests according to Peter:

1 Peter 2:4-5
*Coming to Him as to a living stone, rejected indeed by men, but chosen by God and precious, you also, as living stones, are being built up a spiritual house, a **holy priesthood**, to offer up spiritual sacrifices acceptable to God through Jesus Christ.*

You may have noticed that I have been asking a lot of questions over the last few pages related to the Feast of Trumpets. It's because, unlike the spring feasts, the fall feasts have not been fulfilled yet, so there is still plenty of room for speculation. However, I think you will have to admit that there are a lot of very specific prophetic patterns related to this mysterious 5th feast day.

So, there are 10 days from the start of Yom Teruah until the end of Yom Kippur. Within that 10-day period, there is a distinct 7-day period as well. Is there another time when there was a 10-day period between rapture, and another Feast Day? Yes, Jesus was raptured 10 days prior to Pentecost. He ascended into heaven on the 40th day, and the Holy Spirit descended on the 50th day. Is that perhaps a type and shadow of the future rapture and then the establishment of the Millennial Kingdom? We'll have to wait and see.

Now, back to Psalm 121...

Verse 1
¹I will lift up my eyes to the hills- from whence comes my help?

I believe that the writer wants us to understand that our help doesn't come from the hills, from some other place, from Jerusalem, or even from the temple. It only comes from the Lord. That will be especially true in the tribulation period and even during this time leading up to the tribulation and the rapture. At the rapture, in the twinkling of an eye, we will lift up our eyes to see where our help comes from, who rescues us from the trap that has been set for the unbelieving world. As a prophetic pattern, we will lift up our eyes just as John did in Revelation 4, and just as the bride, Rebekah, did to see her groom, Isaac, as told in Genesis 24.

A Bride for Isaac

Do you remember the story of Abraham sending his chief servant to find a bride for his 40-year old son Isaac, detailed in Genesis 24? Abraham was old and wanted Isaac to have a bride, but didn't want him to take a bride from the local Canaanites, who were quite possibly impure in their genes and were Nephilim. We find out later in the book of Numbers that the Canaanites were the sons of Anak, who was a Nephilim.

> ### Numbers 13:31–33
> *But the men who had gone up with him said, "We can't attack those people; they are stronger than we are."[32] And they spread among the Israelites a bad report about the land they had explored. They said, "The land we explored devours those living in it. All the people we saw there are of great size.[33]* **We saw the Nephilim there (the descendants of Anak come from the Nephilim).** *We seemed like grasshoppers in our own eyes, and we looked the same to them."*

The "mingling" of seeds between fallen angels and mankind is one of the main story-lines of the Bible. However, many Christians do not even know about it because it isn't spoken of in a direct sense, but is interwoven, dare I say "encrypted" into the fabric of the Bible in both the Old and the New Testaments.

From the very beginning, Satan was on a quest to taint the pure bloodline or "seed" of the Messiah, which had to run from Adam through Noah, Shem, Abraham, Isaac, Jacob, Judah, and David. If Satan had been successful in tainting the pure Adamic seed, then the prophecy in Genesis 3:15 could never have come true, and there would have been no redeemer, and, therefore, no redemption for mankind.

Genesis 3:15
I will put enmity between you and the woman, and between your "seed" and her "seed." He shall crush your head, and you shall strike his heel.

Jesus is obviously the seed of the woman based on the virgin birth. Keep in mind that women do not have seed, so this prophecy could only be referring to the virgin birth of Jesus some 4000 years after this prophecy was given. We can deduce from this scripture that Satan does have seed, so other fallen angels also have seed, which we also know from other ancient Hebrew texts found in the Dead Sea Scrolls, such as the Book of Enoch. Satan had already struck the heel of Christ at Calvary when the nails were driven into His heels. The snake is also continuously striking at our heels as Christians, but there's a "Head Crushing" coming by the King in Revelation 20!

1 John 3:8
[8] He who sins is of the devil, for the devil has sinned from the beginning. For this purpose the Son of God was manifested, that He might destroy the works of the devil.

So what was the reason that Abraham was adamant about Isaac needing a bride that wasn't from the local Canaanites? He knew that their bloodline was tainted. That's why Abraham sent his servant back to Mesopotamia, where Abraham was originally from, to find a suitable bride for Isaac among his own people.

Who was chosen to be Isaac's bride? Rebekah.

There is another story here hidden in numbers and symbolism just beneath the surface, and as types and shadows in this Old Testament story that patterns the rapture of the Church, believe it or not.

I believe that Rebekah in the story represents the Church, comprised of both Jews and Gentiles. She is delineated and surrounded by the number 10 in the story, and remember that 10, which represents a complete congregation, is often divided as 5 and 5. Isaac represents "the Son of God," and he is associated with the number 40 since his age was stated as being 40 years old. Abraham represents "God the Father." The "Chief Servant" represents the Holy Spirit that was sent out to the bride. In Genesis 24, the Chief Servant does not have a name, just as the Holy Spirit does not have a name, just a title. Let's connect some dots...

We are told earlier in Genesis Chapter 15:24 that the Chief Servant's name was Eleazar of Damascus. Eleazar in Hebrew means God's help, or simply "helper." Jesus said in John 15:26, "But when the "Helper" the "Eleazar" comes, whom I shall send to you from the Father, the Spirit of truth who proceeds from the Father, He will testify of Me. Is this just a coincidence? I don't think so! Can you see how God connects all of these dots when we really search His word?

As I already pointed out, Rebekah (10) was a beautiful and pure virgin bride who represents the Church.

Genesis 24:16
Now the young woman was very beautiful to behold, a virgin; no man had known her.

She was also humble and generous as also described in Genesis 24.

Genesis 24:18-21
[18] So she said, "Drink, my lord." Then she quickly let her pitcher down to her hand, and gave him a drink. [19] And when she had finished giving him a drink, she said, "I will draw water for your camels also, until they have finished drinking." [20] Then she quickly emptied her pitcher into the trough, ran back to the well to draw water, and drew for all his camels. [21] And the man, wondering at her, remained silent so as to know whether the LORD had made his journey prosperous or not.

*²² So it was, when the **(10)** camels had finished drinking, that the man took a golden nose ring weighing half a shekel, and two bracelets for her wrists weighing **ten** shekels of gold, ²³ and said, "Whose daughter are you? Tell me, please, is there room in your father's house for us to lodge?" So she said to him, "I am the daughter of Bethuel, Milcah's son, whom she bore to Nahor." ²⁵ Moreover she said to him, "We have both straw and feed enough, and room to lodge."*

Isn't it interesting that Genesis 24 gives us these seemingly unimportant numbers, such as "10" camels, and 2 bracelets weighing a total of 10 shekels, or 5 shekels each? I believe that these specific numbers interconnect with Jesus' parable of the 5 wise and 5 foolish virgins of Matthew 25, who were also waiting to go to a wedding. The number 10, as it relates to the bride, Rebekah, appears a few more times in the story so that we can be assured that God has connected her to the number 10, the representation of the whole of the Church comprised of both Jews and Gentiles.

Just as the Church should have, Rebekah had initiative and courage, as detailed in Gen 24:54-58. She willingly submitted to the marriage, even though she had never seen or met her groom, just as we, the Church have never actually seen, or met our Bride Groom, Jesus.

> **Note:** This ties in with the story of Thomas meeting Jesus for the first time after His resurrection, as detailed in John 20.

> **John 20:29**
> *Then Jesus told him (Thomas), "Because you have seen me, you have believed; blessed are those who have not seen and yet have believed."*

So, all of us who have never seen Jesus, but still believe in Him, and long to see him have a special blessing. Let's continue the story...

Genesis 24:54-58

*[54] But her brother and her mother said, "Let the young woman stay with us a few days, at least **ten**; after that she may go." [56] And he said to them, "Do not hinder me, since the Lord has prospered my way; send me away so that I may go to my master." [57] So they said, "We will call the young woman and ask her personally." [58] Then they called Rebekah and said to her, "will you go with this man?" And she said, "I will go."*

Skipping over some of the stories at Rebekah's home, Abraham's (the Father) Chief Servant (Holy Spirit) brought Rebekah (the Church) to Abraham and Isaac (Father and Son) to be married by Isaac (the Son).

This part is very important in the imagery and establishes an important pattern. Where was Isaac? Was he with his Father "in the tent" or "tabernacle" waiting for his bride? No, in verse 62, Isaac had left his father, and was **"in the field."**

Genesis 24:62-65

*[62] Now Isaac came from the way of Beer Lahai Roi, for he dwelt in the South. [3] And Isaac went out to meditate **"in the field"** in the evening; and he lifted his eyes and looked, and there, the camels were coming. [64] Then Rebekah **lifted her eyes**, and when she saw Isaac she dismounted from her camel; [65] for she had said to the servant, "Who is this man walking **"in the field"** to **meet** us?"*

So, Rebekah was metaphorically carried (by the camel) to meet her groom Isaac, in the field. Let's expand on "in the field," which is stated twice, so God wanted us to pick up on that.

Remember that the month of Elul is the Hebrew Month known as the time when the King is **"in the field."** I have previously mentioned the month of Elul, but I would like to expand on it as it relates to this story, and to include a few more important details. Elul is the **6th** month on the Jewish ecclesiastical calendar. The following **7th** month is called

Tishri, which is the month of the High Holy Days. These are the Jewish fall feasts.

As we know, in the Jewish custom, the month of Elul is a time of prayer, repentance, and preparation. In ancient times, the king just might make a surprise visit to the fields at harvest time during Elul. Knowing that the King might make an unannounced visit caused the workers to always be ready, working hard, and on their best behavior. What future prophetic event does that sound like?

If the first 7 months, of the God-given unmolested Jewish calendar represent the 7 thousand years of human history just as the creation week does, and Jesus came at the conclusion of the 4th month/day, and it's been 2 months/days since then, what symbolic month or day of the week are we in now? We are in the 6th month, aka the 6th day. In fact, we're at the end of the 6th Day, so one could say that we are at the tail end of the month of Elul, and we're ready to begin the 7th month of Tishri. The 7th month begins with the Feast of Trumpets, which happens to be the next Feast Day that the Lord will fulfill, and as I have already pointed out, it happens to be completely symbolic of the rapture. After that, the seventh day represents the Millennial Kingdom, when Christ will reign for 1000 years. Can you see how God has interconnected everything, the past, the present, and the future through prophecy, and through patterns that He certainly wants us to figure out?

As we have seen in the Genesis 24 prophetic pattern, Rebekah is the bride, who is the symbol of the Church. She lifted her eyes to see her groom in the field. Jesus said in Luke 21 that when we see these certain signs begin, that we should look up and lift up our heads. Can you see how all of these patterns are interconnected? Nothing is coincidental.

Luke 21:28
*28 Now when these things begin to happen, **look up** and **lift up your heads**, because your redemption draws near."*

According to 1 Thessalonians 4 we will be caught up to meet Jesus in the air between earth and heaven. Similarly, as a pattern, Rebekah met Isaac "in the field" between her land and his land. Obviously, they couldn't meet in the air, so I believe that the field, just like the air, represents the space in between. Let's continue...

Genesis 24:67
Then Isaac brought her into his mother Sarah's "tent"; and he took Rebekah and she became his wife, and he loved her.

By the way, Sarah wasn't in the tent with them. That would have been a little weird. She had already passed away by this time. So, the 40-year old Isaac (possibly symbolic of the 40 Jubilees between Jesus' first and second advents) took Rebekah, who is represented by the number 10, "into the tent" and married her and loved her. In addition to all of that imagery, this particular tent is also very special. It wasn't only that it was Isaac's mother's tent, but it was also specifically called ha'ohelah in Hebrew. Ha'ohelah is only written 8 times in the Hebrew Bible, and it always represents the place of the divine presence of God, and His holy dwelling place. Every one of the 8 times Ha'oheloh appears in the Bible, it is always speaking of the sanctuary or tabernacle, including the first and second Temples in Jerusalem. So, why would this tent be associated with the Ha'oheloh, the holy dwelling place of God?

We can see that God is giving us some clues here and telling us that this story is about more than what we see on the surface. We have to ask, why this particular tent is given such an honored position, and why is it spoken of in the same way, and with the same Hebrew word as the Holy Temple? The Temple was God's dwelling place on earth, but as we know from Revelation 11:19 and Hebrews 8:1-5, the earthly temple was symbolic of the real Heavenly Temple.

Revelation 11:19
Then the temple of God was opened in heaven, and the ark of His covenant was seen in His temple. And there were lightnings, noises, thunderings, an earthquake, and great hail.

So there is a temple in heaven, and also an ark of His covenant as well. The book of Hebrews expands on this.

Hebrews 8:1-5

¹ Now this is the main point of the things we are saying: We have such a High Priest, who is seated at the right hand of the throne of the Majesty in the heavens, ² a Minister of the sanctuary and of the true tabernacle which the Lord erected, and not man. ³ For every high priest is appointed to offer both gifts and sacrifices. Therefore it is necessary that this One also have something to offer. ⁴ For if He were on earth, He would not be a priest, since there are priests who offer the gifts according to the law; ⁵ who serve the copy and shadow of the heavenly things, as Moses was divinely instructed when he was about to make the tabernacle. For He said, "See that you make all things according to the pattern shown you on the mountain."

Remember that the special name given to Isaac's mother's tent was Ha'ohelah. This is where Isaac took Rebekah to marry her after he met her in the field. The word Ha'ohelah is only found in the Bible 8 times in the Hebrew Bible, and it always refers to the place of the divine presence of God and His dwelling place. Remember that numbers are important and have special meaning in the Bible. The number 8 in Hebrew is Shemonah, and represents a new beginning, an overflowing abundance, and the **"departure or transcendence from the natural world to the supernatural world."** I do not believe that it is a coincidence that this special word (Ha'ohelah) is only found 8 times in the original Hebrew Bible, no more and no less. God is definitely giving us clues to a deeper meaning if we are willing to dig a little below the surface.

So how does the number 8 or any of this relate to the rapture?

Let's look at one of the main New Testament rapture scriptures in 1 Corinthians.

1 Corinthians 15:50-54

⁵⁰ Now this I say, brethren, that flesh and blood cannot inherit the kingdom of God; nor does corruption inherit incorruption. ⁵¹ Behold, I tell you a mystery: We shall not all sleep, **but we shall all be changed (8)** *— ⁵² in a moment, in the twinkling of an eye, at the* **last trumpet**. *For the trumpet will sound, and the dead will be raised incorruptible, and we shall be changed. ⁵³ For this corruptible must put on incorruption,* **and this mortal must put on immortality (8)**. *⁵⁴ So when this* **corruptible has put on incorruption, and this mortal has put on immortality (8)**, *then shall be brought to pass the saying that is written: "Death is swallowed up in victory."*

You can see how fitting the number 8 is as it relates to our "being changed from the mortal to the immortal, and the fact that Ha'ohelah, represented by the number 8, is God's Holy Temple, which we will be entering into when the Holy Spirit takes us to meet our Bridegroom in the air. We cannot do this in our mortal bodies because flesh and blood cannot inherit the kingdom of God.

So, let's sum up the deeper meaning of the Isaac and Rebekah story. The "helper," "Eleazar," who represents the Holy Spirit, found and chose each of us, and we accepted the marriage proposal to be married to the Son, represented by Isaac. He, the Holy Spirit, is going to return to the "Father," who is represented by Abraham, with us the "Church," represented by the bride, Rebekah. Rebekah is transported to the Father, but before reaching the Father, Rebekah lifts up her eyes and sees the "Son," represented by Isaac. After seeing Isaac, she dismounts, and stands when she meets her groom. Didn't Jesus say that we would "stand" before Him when we meet Him at our escape (Luke 21:36)? Afterward, the Son took the bride "into the tent," the Ha'ohelah, symbolizing heaven. Doesn't that sound like the rapture of the Church?

Let's connect one more dot. How long was the ancient Jewish wedding celebration? Many ancient Jewish texts tell us that their wedding feasts (Seudah) lasted for 7-days, but the Bible is more important than any historical account. So, researching the Bible, I found that both Genesis 29:26-27 and Judges 14:17 tell us that the wedding feasts and celebrations did indeed last for one week, or 7-days. This, of course, matches the 7-year wedding celebration of the Church in heaven during the 7-year tribulation period on earth. Given the choice between tribulation and celebration, I'm going to the celebration!

So, the deeper meaning of the story of Isaac and Rebekah's meeting, and their wedding gives us another symbolic pattern of the rapture followed by a 7-year wedding celebration. The sad reality is that during our celebration, the unbelieving world will be trapped here on earth to endure the worst time that ever was, and ever will be.

As a result of the Rabbinical prophesies that I have mentioned showing the Messiah "standing at the door" in 2021, the symbolism of John seeing an "open door" after the Church Age in Revelation 4, the revelation of John 10 that Jesus is the "Door," and the many prophetic scriptures related to "looking up," and "lifting up our heads and our eyes" to see our rescue, let's look at Luke 21 again in the context of our timeline. Luke 21 is Luke's account of the last day's prophetic teaching by Jesus after His triumphal entry into Jerusalem. After Jesus describes the "birth pains" of the end times, He also uses the idiom of looking up to describe our redemption, as I have previously discussed.

Luke 21:28
When these things begin to take place, stand up and lift up your heads, because your redemption is drawing near."

Besides the pattern and connection to Rebekah in Genesis, and John in Revelation, what else stands out to me in this passage is that Jesus points out that we should be looking for Him, who is our redemption, specifically when these things "begin" to take place. He doesn't say to look for Him in the middle of, or after, but when they "begin." This is just one of the many clues that Jesus gave us to the timing of the rapture.

You may be wondering why I'm talking about the rapture in the chapter devoted to the year 2021 since it didn't happen. No, it didn't happen, but I believe that as of 2021, the Messiah is standing at the "Door" awaiting His Father to tell Him, "Go get your Bride." I believe that 2021 was the opening of the door, and that the rapture can happen at anytime from now until the start of the tribulation, which according to the timeline revelation, starts sometime between 2024 and 2025, with 2025 being the most probable. Hang on, we're getting there...

The Keeper of Israel

God has made promises throughout His word, from Genesis to Revelation, to preserve Israel. At no time was this promise more important than in our present age. What is coming will test the children of Israel to their limit, and separate out a true remnant that will be protected and preserved by God for His glory.

> **Verses 3-8**
> *³He will not allow your foot to be moved; He who keeps you will not slumber. ⁴Behold, He who keeps Israel shall neither slumber nor sleep. ⁵The LORD is your keeper; The LORD is your shade at your right hand. ⁶The sun shall not strike you by day, nor the moon by night. ⁷The LORD shall preserve you from all evil; He shall preserve your soul. ⁸The LORD shall preserve your going out and your coming in from this time forth, and even forevermore.*

Even though there are very troubling years ahead for Israel, God promises to watch over and preserve Israel from this time forward. We see this same end-time promise from God in Ezekiel 38, Joel 3, Isaiah 41 and 43, Zechariah 12, Romans 11, and many more. Based on all of these promises, Israel can rest assured that God will protect His remnant.

CHAPTER 7

Psalm 122 A Song of Ascents of David

The Year 2022 - The Rapture Season Continues, Pray for the Peace of Jerusalem

Of the three "birth pain" patterns of the 15 Songs of Ascent, Psalm 122 is the third type in the theme of God's peace and blessing, primarily for Zion.

Verses 1-2

¹I was glad when they said to me, "Let us go into the house of the LORD." ² Our feet have been standing within your gates, O Jerusalem!

The "Rapture Season" continues in verse 1. Remember that these are the Songs of Ascent which were sung by pilgrims and priests alike as they ascended to the Temple on the High Holy Days. However, prophetically, we can see that they also pertain to the ascension of the Saints into the real Holy Temple in the Heavenly Jerusalem. Remember also that the earthly Temple is only a copy of the Heavenly Temple.

Hebrews 8:5

⁵ who serve the copy and shadow of the heavenly things, as Moses was divinely instructed when he was about to make

the tabernacle. For He said, "See that you make all things
according to the pattern shown you on the mountain."

Verse two, which states that "Our feet have been standing within
your gates, O Jerusalem!" is also twofold prophetically. It refers to both
the physical gates and entryways into Jerusalem and the Heavenly Gates
leading into the Holy City. In Jerusalem the 12 gates were the portals
or entry ways into the city, and each gate had a door or a set of doors
for security against invaders. Remember who the "door" is. Jesus is the
only door, and no one comes to the Father except through Jesus!

Gates in the Bible, as well as in the Jewish tradition, are not just
for access into the city. They are also the place where judgment and
justice were given, civic announcements were declared, and business was
conducted in the open in view of witnesses. Verse 2 says, "our feet have
been standing within your gates," which may indicate that we have been
waiting to gain access into the Holy City since there is no evidence of
any other business being conducted other than "to give thanks to the
name of the Lord" in verse 4 and "judgment" verse 5.

Verses 3-5
³ Jerusalem is built as a city that is compact together, ⁴ where
the tribes go up, the tribes of the LORD, to the Testimony
of Israel, to give thanks to the name of the LORD. ⁵ For
thrones are set there for judgment, the thrones of the house
of David.

Could this be New Jerusalem, as in Heavenly Jerusalem, that we
are going up to and waiting to enter? After all, what is going to happen
as soon as we ascend with Jesus? We will be at the Bema Seat of Christ
to be judged, not for punishment since there is no condemnation for
those who are in Christ (Romans 8:1), but for reward based on our
good works in Christ. No, works do not save us by themselves, but if we
have faith without the fruit of our faith, which is works, we won't have
anything to show for our lives other than ourselves (James 2:14-26).

Pray for the Peace of Jerusalem

Verses 6-9

⁶ Pray for the peace of Jerusalem: "May they prosper who love you.⁷ Peace be within your walls, prosperity within your palaces." ⁸ For the sake of my brethren and companions, I will now say, "Peace be within you." ⁹ Because of the house of the LORD our God I will seek your good.

During the year 2022, God asked that we pray for the peace of Jerusalem. How fitting this was as we draw near to the time of Jacob's trouble, which God designed to ultimately save the Children of Israel. Afterward, in the Millennial Kingdom is when Jerusalem will finally know this peace. For now, the world has a choice to stand with and bless Israel, or stand against them. So far, too many countries have joined with the ones who want to stand against Israel and want to divide the land of Israel, which God gave to His chosen nation. Genesis 12 and Joel 3 are very explicit that nations who bless Israel will be blessed and nations who curse, or try to divide their land will be cursed. The so-called "two-state solution" will never work, and God will not allow it.

Not only should we be praying for the peace of Jerusalem, but we should especially be praying for the salvation of Israel and Jerusalem. There simply is no peace or rest without Jesus. After all, Jesus is the Prince of Peace (Isaiah 9:6)! Time is short, and they are running out of time to accept the real Messiah before it's too late. There is a day coming when this prayer will be fully answered. Peace will finally exist fully in Jerusalem when the Son of God sits on His throne. Until then, let's keep praying for that day and the salvation of God's chosen people.

The Temple isn't specifically mentioned in Psalm 122 because this Psalm was written by King David. During David's reign, there was no temple, but only a tent set up on Mt. Zion where the Ark of the Covenant was kept. Of course, David wanted to build the temple, but God told him that his son would be the one to build the Temple instead.

We know that David's son Solomon built the first temple, which was destroyed by the Babylonians in 586 BC. Then, a new temple was completed in 515 BC, only to be torn down again in 70 AD. After that, the Jews were in exile and without a homeland for almost 2000 years, which, of course, we know ended in 1948. However, they are still waiting and praying for their 3rd temple to be built. They believe by their oral tradition that the new temple will be built by the messiah himself. But of course, we know that their messiah is the Antichrist since the real Messiah came almost 2000 years ago, but they rejected Him.

Obviously, the religious Jews in Israel want desperately to build their 3rd temple in Jerusalem, or more specifically, they want their messiah to build the 3rd temple and usher in what they believe will be their Messianic Age. In anticipation, they have already made all of the provisions, have all of the instruments and priestly garments, and as of 2022, they have held their first Water Libation Ceremony during the Feast of Tabernacles (Sukkot) in expectation of a new temple. This ceremony is revealed in the Jewish Mishnah, and seeks God's blessing for rain in their land.

Also, as I have previously mentioned, in 2022, 5 spotless red heifers were delivered to Israel from Texas, of which one will be slaughtered before a new temple can be built and consecrated. Once slaughtered, the spotless red heifer will be burned together with cedar wood, hyssop, and crimson red wool. Then the ashes will be mixed together with spring water, which will then be used to purify anyone, or any object that has been defiled by contact with, or came into close proximity to a corps. This is necessary since any defiled person would then defile the temple during its construction. Pretty much everybody has been to a cemetery, which means that they are all defiled, so the red heifer is absolutely necessary, according to Numbers 19. Now that at least one red heifer is available for sacrifice, Israel is one step closer to building their temple.

According to Jewish oral tradition, and substantiated by Genesis 15:9, the spotless red heifer must be at least 3 years old before it can be slaughtered and burned for its ashes. It has been revealed in reports that the 5 red heifers from Texas will be 3 years old in the fall of 2024. That means that one of the heifers can be used for the ritual purification requirement prior to the building of the third temple anytime after the fall of 2024. Considering the timing of all of this, can you see how close we are to the building of the third temple and the revealing of the Antichrist?

The signs of the times have been all around us, and the "Rapture Season" continued in 2022. Once the Lord takes His bride out of this world, the trap will be sprung, and the world, including Israel, will be ensnared in a trap with no way out. During these last days, we should make it our mission to pray for and share with our neighbors, including Israel, to bring them all to the saving knowledge of the real Messiah, Jesus, before it's too late.

CHAPTER 8

Psalm 123 A Song of Ascents

The Year 2023 - The Rapture Season Continues and the Spirit of Antichrist Rises

Of the three "birth pain" patterns found in the 15 Songs of Ascent, Psalm 123 brings us back to a time of prayer due to distress, and the realization that the Lord is our only source of help. But first, we find the continuation of the "Rapture Season," and more rapture symbolism in the first verse of this Psalm, just as we saw in the previous 2 Psalms. Of course, those 2 Psalms matched the years 2021, and 2022, and now we've moved into 2023.

Verses 1-2
*¹ Unto You **I lift up my eyes**, O You who dwell in the heavens. ² Behold, as the eyes of servants look to the hand of their masters, as the eyes of a maid to the hand of her mistress, so our eyes look to the LORD our God, until He has mercy on us.*

As I pointed out previously, Jesus is standing at the door and waiting to come for His bride. In the first verse, we once again "lift up our eyes" to see our Lord who dwells in Heaven, similar to the "Rapture Season" language of Psalm 121, where we also "lifted up our eyes." In Psalm 122, the rapture language was "let us go into the house of the Lord."

Also, please notice that the rapture symbolism is specifically found in the first verse of Psalm 123, just as it has been in the previous 2 Psalms. Spoiler alert, this may be important in 2024.

In the second verse of Psalm 123, we look to the Lord's hand until He has mercy on us. My personal interpretation is that 2023 will be a difficult year considering the plea for mercy in the 2nd, and in the 3rd verses for a total of 3 pleas for mercy. Keep in mind that biblically, when God wants to emphasize something, He repeats it 3 times. I am writing this chapter in November of 2022 and not really looking forward to 2023. However, I trust in the Lord and know that He will have mercy on His own!

Verses 3-4
^{3} Have mercy on us, O LORD, have mercy on us! For we are exceedingly filled with contempt.^{4} Our soul is exceedingly filled with the scorn of those who are at ease, with the contempt of the proud.

It is not stated who these persecutors are who are "at ease," and are "proud." For that reason, I believe that the 3rd and 4th verses are prophetic as well as probably historic. I have this hunch that, simply put, God allowed certain prophetic events to happen, then had them written about in a Psalm. At some time later, He inspired those who were constructing the sequence in which the Psalms appear in the Bible so that they would be in an exact order to reveal a prophetic timing pattern. So, even if this Psalm, for instance, wasn't written by a Psalmist who understood that he was writing prophecy, it was certainly inspired to be a pattern of future prophecy, and then placed within the 150 Psalms in a specific position for God's prophetic purpose.

So, who are they who are proud, and have scorn and contempt for God's people as mentioned in verses 3 - 4? Of course, we know that the word "pride" has a whole new meaning in our time. Could verse 4 be prophetic of the "pride" agenda that is being pushed on every citizen through government, media, and even corporations? This agenda is on the rise, and has already been used to try to take down Christians and

Christian-owned businesses. I can see that this is clearly part of the beast system rising, and may have, in fact, been devised by the enemy as the "kill shot" for the true Church, which is certainly in the cross-hairs of our adversary. The acceptance of this perversion of God's design has done more to divide the Church, and even nations than any other matter I can remember in my lifetime.

Also, notice that this Psalm, uncharacteristically, does not mention Israel or Jerusalem. That makes me think that the "scorned" are possibly both Jews and Gentiles. The Prophet Isaiah speaks of the "Day of the Lord," also known as the tribulation period, when the "proud" will be humbled, and the Lord will be exalted.

Isaiah 2:11

[11] The proud looks of man shall be humbled, the haughtiness of men shall be bowed down, and the Lord alone shall be exalted in that day.

As I look at the whole of the timeline revelation encoded in the Psalms, I do not believe that 2023 is in the tribulation period, but the spirit of Antichrist is certainly alive and well and increasing in 2023. I believe that in 2023, we will witness more globalism taking control in the name of climate change, pandemics, failing economies, increased food shortages, supply chain problems, and persecution of anyone who doesn't go along with the globalist agenda, which includes the submission of the masses to the "pride" agenda.

According to the prophesies of Jesus, I expect 2023 to be a year of continued wars and rumors of wars, and it seems that we were hearing rumors of a potential nuclear war almost daily from the news media now even in 2022. I would also expect the world's attention to become increasingly focused on the struggle between Israel, the Palestinians, and their Muslim neighbors. We know from prophecy that Israel, and specifically Jerusalem, will be the focal point of worldwide tension in the last days. It will be like a "heavy stone" for the world according to Zechariah 12. If the encrypted timeline revelation in the Psalms is on target, I would expect to see an increase in global tensions building in 2023 around Israel and Jerusalem, just as we saw in the Israeli-Palestinian Conflict of 2021, which lasted 11 days. Remember that the number 11 symbolizes judgment, rebellion, disorder, and chaos.

Zechariah 12:2-3
2 "Behold, I will make Jerusalem a cup of drunkenness to all the surrounding peoples, when they lay siege against Judah and Jerusalem. 3 And it shall happen in that day that I will make Jerusalem a very heavy stone for all peoples; all who would heave it away will surely be cut in pieces, though all nations of the earth are gathered against it.

Keep in mind that war, famine, and pestilence always go together, just as outlined in the Book of Revelation referring to the 4 Horsemen of the Apocalypse. Even the news headlines of secular, and even socialist news agencies, as well as the World Health Organization in 2022, are warning of coming war, famine, pestilence, and death.

Anyone who is awake can see that everything that is happening is all part of the setup process of the coming "beast" system being established by the global elites who are calling it the "Great Reset," "Build Back Better," "Agenda 21," "Agenda 2030," and the list goes on. Just as new military recruits go to boot camp and are deconstructed by their drill instructors so that they can be rebuilt into what the government wants them to be, so the globalist governments and un-elected elites are trying to tear down the current world systems to rebuild them into their idea of a global utopia where they are at the top, and those who are the "common man" who survive will in their words "own nothing, but be happy." That is not a world that I want to be a part of. Thankfully, we who are in Christ have a "blessed hope" who will soon appear!

While we are still here, according to Psalm 123, we as believers, both Jews and Gentiles should be asking for the Lord to have mercy on us during this time as we are increasingly being scorned and condemned for our beliefs. Just as verse 2 says, we should be looking to our Lord to have mercy on us, help us and provide for us in the same way that a servant looks to his Master for mercy, help, and provision.

Anti-Semitism, as well as the persecution of Christians, is on the rise around the world as our beliefs, and world-view do not align with that of the secular world around us. Persecution certainly has a "weeding out" effect, separating the true believers who have a personal relationship with the Lord and are willing to stand for their faith from those who say they are Christians, but aren't willing to suffer anything unpleasant for the Lord.

If we are in the last few years before the tribulation, which I believe we are, then we should also examine a few of the prophetic New Testament scriptures that speak to our time. Through these scriptures, we will be able to understand what is coming and what to pray for so that we can be better prepared as persecution and difficult times increase.

2 Timothy 3

¹ But know this, that in the last days perilous times will come: ² For men will be lovers of themselves, lovers of money, boasters, proud, blasphemers, disobedient to parents, unthankful, unholy, ³ unloving, unforgiving, slanderers, without self-control, brutal, despisers of good, ⁴ traitors, headstrong, haughty, lovers of pleasure rather than lovers of God, ⁵ having a form of godliness but denying its power. And from such people turn away!

2 Peter 3:3-4

³knowing this first: that scoffers will come in the last days, walking according to their own lusts, ⁴ and saying, "Where is the promise of His coming? For since the fathers fell asleep, all things continue as they were from the beginning of creation."

Apostasy

Apostasy is a falling away from the faith. However, it doesn't have to necessarily be a falling away from attending a church. Entire churches can be in apostasy. Today, there are many churches in the US and around the world that no longer preach the true gospel or repentance. I would say that those two biblical principles should be the basics of any Christian church. We were warned by Paul in his second letter to Timothy that this day would come, and now it is here:

> **2 Timothy 4:3-4**
> *For the time will come when they will not endure sound doctrine, but according to their own desires, because they have itching ears, they will heap up for themselves teachers; and they will turn their ears away from the truth, and be turned aside to fables.*

Today, many churches are preaching a "social gospel" instead of the real gospel truth. This social gospel which actually started in the late 1800s, is based on humanism, social justice, tolerance, inclusivity, and now even environmentalism. Saying that Jesus is the only way to the Father (John 14:6: *Jesus said to him, "I am the way, the truth, and the life. No one comes to the Father except through Me*) and that you must turn from your sinful ways (Matthew 4:17: *From that time Jesus began to preach and to say, "Repent, for the kingdom of heaven is at hand"*) is considered intolerant and is no longer acceptable in modern society. Unfortunately, I don't see this getting any better in these last days.

Social pressure and persecution will certainly increase against Christians during 2023, just as it has been steadily growing over the last decade. At the same time, church attendance has been steadily declining according to a Gallup poll conducted, which shows that as of 2020, only 47% of American adults are part of a Church, Synagogue, or Mosque. That's down from 70% only 20 years earlier in the year 2000. This trend was prophesied by both Jesus and Paul in the New Testament.

Matthew 24:10
¹⁰ At that time many will turn away from the faith and will betray and hate each other.

1 Timothy 4
¹Now the Spirit expressly says that in latter times some will depart from the faith, giving heed to deceiving spirits and doctrines of demons, ² speaking lies in hypocrisy, having their own conscience seared with a hot iron, ³ forbidding to marry, and commanding to abstain from foods which God created to be received with thanksgiving by those who believe and know the truth. ⁴ For every creature of God is good, and nothing is to be refused if it is received with thanksgiving; ⁵ for it is sanctified by the word of God and prayer.

2 Thessalonians 2:3
³Let no one deceive you by any means; for that Day will not come unless the "falling away" (apostasia in Greek) comes first, and the man of sin is revealed, the son of perdition,

It is clear that we are watching the antichrist beast system being birthed and fed all around us today. Satan is birthing one thing, but Jesus is birthing another. What Satan meant for evil, Jesus will set it right and make it good for those who trust in Him. Satan thinks he can be victorious, but Jesus has already won the victory. Satan obviously still has a type of kingdom here on earth, but Jesus already has the keys to a new kingdom, the Kingdom of God, and He will be coming soon to expel the squatters. While we're waiting, our mission is to storm Satan's defenses and pull down his strongholds (2 Corinthians 10), and to win as many souls into God's kingdom as we can while we can. We know what is coming, so let's suit up with the whole armor of God while we're still here and get busy!

CHAPTER 9

Psalm 124 A Song of Ascents of David

The Year 2024 - The Dead Sea Scrolls Shmita Year, Gog Magog War, and the Rapture Season Closes

So far, we have seen that the year 2020 was the year of deception, according to Psalm 120. The years 2021 - 2023 were years of the "Rapture Season" as well as the "birth pains" and continued setup of what is still to come. Of the three "birth pain" patterns found in the 15 Songs of Ascent, Psalm 124 is a song of deliverance. This fits perfectly in place since, according to the timeline revelation, 2024 will be the year that Israel will be delivered by Almighty God from their enemies as prophesied in Ezekiel 38, and the end of the "Rapture Season" when the Church will be delivered from the wrath that will soon be poured out on all the earth.

Verses 1-5
¹"If it had not been the LORD who was on our side," let Israel now say—² "If it had not been the LORD who was on our side, when men rose up against us, ³ Then they would have swallowed us alive, when their wrath was kindled against us; ⁴ then the waters would have overwhelmed us, the stream would have gone over our soul; ⁵ then the swollen waters would have gone over our soul."

Psalm 124 is the second Psalm of the 15 Songs of Ascent that was written by King David himself. This Psalm rejoices over the certainty that the Lord defended Israel from an invading army. It speaks of this miraculous salvation as if it were in the past; however, historically, there is no evidence that this invasion ever happened in the past, especially in David's time. That means that it is either just a metaphor for some unknown spiritual battle, or it has to be prophetic of a future time. I believe that the evidence, as well as Psalm 124s perfect placement within the timeline revelation, indicates that specifically the first 5 of the 8 verses of this Psalm represent the future Gog Magog war as detailed in Ezekiel 38 and 39; then verses 6 through 8 represent the closing of the "Rapture Season." In the previous 3 Psalms, the symbolic "Rapture Season" declaration was in the first verse, but now it starts in the 6th verse after God delivers Israel from the flood of an invading army. I believe that its placement might be very significant.

I cannot find a historical battle, war, or invasion of Israel during David's reign that matches the description of Psalm 124. This Psalm depicts an army that was large enough to "swallow" Israel alive and then uses the imagery of flood waters that would have overwhelmed them if God hadn't been on Israel's side. In the 40 years that David was King of Israel, he fought many battles and conquered many foes such as the Philistines, Edomites, Moabites, Ammonites, and the Amalekites, but none of those enemies ever flooded into Israel as stated in this Psalm. In fact, David typically went out from Israel to conquer his enemies as opposed to having to defend Israel against them. So, I have to conclude that this invasion by an overwhelming force is prophetic, and not historic. I do not believe that it is a coincidence that God prompted King Hezekiah to place this Psalm of David exactly where it is, prophesying of God's future, and miraculous deliverance of Israel.

Beside the fact that this has to be prophetic of a future invasion, how do we know that it's the Ezekiel 38 invasion known as the Gog Magog War? First, both Psalm 124 and Ezekiel 38 are prophesying of an invasion into Israel by a massive army or armies. Remember that King

David wrote Psalm 124, and there was never any such invasion into Israel during his reign. As for Ezekiel 38 and 39, at this time in world history (2022), like no other time, we can see the setup of this coming invasion. Russia, Iran, and Turkey, among others, are all at the doorstep of Israel's northern border in Syria, and as of recently, it appears that we can see a good possibility of what the "hook in the jaw" might be - Natural Gas. Due to Russia's invasion into Ukraine, Europe is no longer trading with Russia, and now it looks probable that Israel will be a major supplier of gas to Europe, thereby becoming a competitor to Russia, but that's not in Psalm 124, so it's just speculation. Another possibility for the "hook in the jaw" could be an escalation to the ongoing Israel-Palestinian conflict. Israel is seen by many who do not have a biblical worldview as an occupier of Palestinian land and an oppressor of the Palestinian people. It wouldn't take much to ignite the region, which has been a powder keg since 1948, giving Russia and a coalition of allied Muslim nations the justification to invade and plunder Israel. After all, remember Psalm 120 forewarned: *⁶ My soul has dwelt too long with one who hates peace. ⁷ I am for peace; but when I speak, they are for war.* That is not an idle warning. God placed it there for a reason, and it will be part of the future regional or global narrative.

Secondly, and most importantly, we see in both accounts that the victory was won because God was on Israel's side. That has not always been the case, which is why Israel has been both in captivity, and exile in their past. Currently, Israel is a very secular society, with around 40% of the population claiming to be non-religious. Christians only make up around 2% of Israel's population. That means that 98% of current-day Jews, both religious and non-religious, reject Jesus as their Messiah. The difference between the victory of the Gog Magog war and past defeats that Israel has suffered due to Israel's unbelief and transgressions is that this time, the Lord says that He's protecting them regardless so that Israel and "the Nations" will know that He is Lord!

Ezekiel 38:18-23

¹⁸ "And it will come to pass at the same time, when Gog comes against the land of Israel," says the Lord GOD, "that My fury will show in My face. [19] For in My jealousy and in the fire of My wrath I have spoken: 'Surely in that day there shall be a great earthquake in the land of Israel, [20] so that the fish of the sea, the birds of the heavens, the beasts of the field, all creeping things that creep on the earth, and all men who are on the face of the earth shall shake at My presence. The mountains shall be thrown down, the steep places shall fall, and every wall shall fall to the ground.' [21] I will call for a sword against Gog throughout all My mountains," says the Lord GOD. *"Every man's sword will be against his brother. [22] And I will bring him to judgment with pestilence and bloodshed; I will rain down on him, on his troops, and on the many peoples who are with him, flooding rain, great hailstones, fire, and brimstone. [23] Thus I will magnify Myself and sanctify Myself, and **I will be known in the eyes of many nations. Then they shall know that I am the LORD."***

Thirdly, David uses the imagery of a flood that could have covered Israel to describe the invading army. Ezekiel uses similar imagery, but he uses a storm covering the land of Israel like a cloud instead of water.

Ezekiel 38:9
*[9] You will ascend, **coming like a storm, covering the land like a cloud**, you and all your troops and many peoples with you."*

Perhaps David and Ezekiel are describing two components of the same invasion, both an air and ground attack. The Old Testament couldn't have stated that men would be flying over to attack Israel since that would have altered God's timing, and, therefore, history, as well as the future. So, it makes sense that God wouldn't reveal too much detail, and the prophets would use similes to poetically describe such a prophetic event. Remember, it's encrypted.

The prophet Isaiah, who was alive during King Hezekiah's reign prior to the Babylonian captivity, also speaks of an invasion into the Land of Israel/Judah that has no historic precedent before or after. It too, uses the imagery of "rushing mighty waters" to symbolize the invading nations. Sure, there have been invasions into the land, but none so large that it could be called "rushing mighty waters," and where God intervened on Israel's behalf and fought back the invaders. Historically, God used the invaders as judgment on the rebellious nations of Israel and Judah, so He specifically did not come to Israel's rescue. Here's what Isaiah has to say about the Gog Magog invasion. Notice that just like the description by Ezekiel, verse 14 mentions that these nations came to plunder and rob God's nation. Notice also that there is a mysterious "he" mentioned in verse 14. Could this be Gog himself?

Isaiah 17:12-14

*12 Woe to the multitude of many people who make a noise like the roar of the seas, and to the **rushing of nations** that make a rushing like the **rushing of mighty waters!** 13 The nations will rush like the **rushing of many waters**; but God will rebuke them and they will flee far away, and be chased like the chaff of the mountains before the wind, like a rolling thing before the whirlwind.*

*14 Then behold, at eventide, trouble! And before the morning, **he** is no more. This is the portion of those who **plunder** us, and the lot of those who **rob** us.*

The Prophet Daniel also has something to say about this war, and similar to David's Psalm and Isaiah's prophecy, Daniel also uses the imagery of a flood. The best thing about Daniel's account is that it is part of a short timeline that helps to put this "flood" invasion into its proper place so that we can be more confident that it happened before the start of the tribulation period. All of these prophecies are connected through similar keywords and imagery.

Daniel's Timeline

Daniel 9:26-27

*²⁶After the sixty-two sevens, the Anointed One will be put to death and will have nothing. The people of the ruler who will come will destroy the city and the sanctuary. The end will come **like a flood**: War will continue until the end, and desolations have been decreed. ²⁷He will confirm a covenant with many for one seven. In the middle of the seven he will put an end to sacrifice and offering. And at the temple he will set up an abomination that causes desolation, until the end that is decreed is poured out on him.*

Here is the timeline from Daniel 9:26-27. Daniel covers 2000 years between verse 26 and the end of verse 27. As we know, Jesus the Messiah was crucified around 2032 at the end of the prophesied 69 weeks (62 weeks plus 7 weeks previously prophesied in verse 25). We know that the Romans destroyed the sanctuary (Temple) in 70 AD and then the city of Jerusalem in 135 AD. So those prophecies in verse 26 have been fulfilled and are now history. The following sentence in verse 26 is still yet prophetic of the future, and connects Psalm 124 (correlating to 2024) with the second sentence of Daniel 9:26, and with the war described in Ezekiel 38 and 39.

Daniel uses the imagery of a "flood" connected to war, just as Psalm 124 does. In Daniel's timeline, this war happens prior to the "confirming of a covenant with many for one seven" by the Antichrist (who is the "He" in the verse). Of course, "one seven" is the 7-year tribulation period. So, based on Daniel's timeline, we can see that the end "comes in like a flood." That means it begins with a flood, but not an actual flood, because there is no prophecy of a last-day flood, but of an invasion that is "like" a flood. We also know that "the end" in verse 26 has to begin with this symbolic flood because it also can't be referring to Armageddon at the end of the tribulation, because there are at least 7 years left after the covenant is confirmed according to the rest of Daniel's timeline. So, I believe it is safe to assume that the meaning of "the end will come like a flood" in verse 26 is that the final 7 years cannot begin until this "flood" war has occurred.

After the 7-year covenant is confirmed, Daniel's timeline indicates that in the middle of the 7 years, the Antichrist will put an end to the sacrifices and offerings at the rebuilt Temple, and then set up the "abomination that causes desolation" just as Jesus also warned about in Matthew 24:15 and Mark 13:14. This is the time that aligns with Revelation 12, but I'm getting ahead of myself.

So, Psalm 124 doesn't reveal any more detail about the Ezekiel 38 war, but together with Daniel 9 it helps to confirm when it occurs in the timeline revelation. Many have wondered if the war happens prior to the tribulation, or if it is the same as what many call the final battle of Armageddon. Not only can we now see where it fits on the timeline, but it also makes more sense now, at least to me.

In Ezekiel 38 verse 23, God exclaims: *"Thus I will magnify Myself and sanctify Myself, and I will be known in the eyes of many nations. Then they shall know that I am the LORD."* It makes sense that God would want the world to know that He is Lord prior to the rapture and the tribulation period. God is good, and He is just, and I believe He will give the world one last chance to repent and believe in His only Son before the trap, that is, the tribulation, is sprung.

More Proof

It is commonly taught by Jewish Rabbis that the beginning of redemption, or the "Messianic Age" as it is known, will be with a war, and with chaos. How much more war and chaos could there be in the wake of God destroying the invading armies as they ascend on Israel, and then a large part of the world's population simply disappears in the rapture? Of course, Rabbis don't teach the rapture, but I believe it's encoded in Psalm 124, but we're not quite there yet.

The Rabbis also teach that historically war and other profound events happen globally, but with a focus on Israel, in the 7th year of the Shmita cycles, which is also known as the Shmita year. As I have previously mentioned, according to the Essene calendar information found in the Dead Sea Scrolls, and my understanding of it, of course, the next 50-year Jubilee will be in 2025, and the end of the age will be in 2075. That makes 2024 a Shmita year. I realize that many Bible scholars and Rabbis have proposed many different years for Shmita years and Jubilee years, but given all of the evidence from the Dead Sea Scrolls, the Daniel timeline of the crucifixion of Jesus, and now the timeline revelation in the Psalms, I believe this is finally correct. Also, keep in mind that the corruption of the Hebrew calendar was prophesied in the Book of Jubilees found among the Dead Sea Scrolls, so we know that we cannot trust the current Jewish Rabbinical calendar.

So, what does this new Shmita and Jubilee calendar do to the many events in Israel over the past 100+ years that many have used to prove that their cycle is correct? Well, if the Essenes were correct, then the Jubilees fall on the 25s and 75s of our Gregorian calendar. Remember that there are 7 Shmitas in each Jubilee, so 7 years x 7 years brings us to the 49th year in the cycle, followed by the 50th year, which is the Year of Jubilee.

Amazingly, this means that the Battle of Jerusalem as well as the writing of the Balfour Declaration of 1917, was on a Shmita year; World War II started on a Shmita year in 1939, which led to the creation of the reborn Jewish State. The Six Day War in June of 1967 was on a Shmita year, the US invaded Iraq in the Shmita year of 2003, the Revelation 12 Sign of September 23rd, and the declaration by President Trump that Jerusalem is the capital of Israel, both occurred in 2017 on a Shmita year. That makes 2024 the final Shmita in the current Jubilee cycle. That means that God gave us a 7-year warning starting in 2017 with the Revelation 12 Sign. Doesn't that sound familiar, as he also gave Joseph and the Egyptians a 7-year warning before the 7-year drought and famine struck? That's a prophetic pattern!

The next Shmita year after 2024, which will be the first Shmita in the new cycle, will be in 2032! That's the 2000-year anniversary of Jesus' crucifixion, which was due to the Jewish rejection of Jesus as their Messiah.

There will be a total of 40 Jubilees between the Jubilee years of 25 AD and 2025. As we know, the time frame of 40 in years, or days, or any time sequence of 40 relates to a time of testing and probation. That means that we have been given 40 Jubilees as a set time of testing and probation during what we call the "Age of Grace." That time is about to come to a close. On the anniversary of the Shmita year on God's calendar that overlaps into our Gregorian calendar year of sometime in late 2031 and into 2032, the armies of the world will gather at a place called Armageddon, and then Jesus will return as King of Kings, and Lord of Lords, and every knee will bow, and every tongue will confess that He is Lord! Guess who is coming back with Jesus on that Shmita anniversary year? We, the Church, the raptured and risen Saints! Can you see how all of this is adding up and how it fits into the timeline revelation encoded in the Psalms?

The Escape!

There are 2 stanzas in Psalm 124. The first stanza depicts the Lord rescuing Israel from the Gog Magog invasion for His glory. The second stanza depicts the Lord rescuing the Church from the coming wrath of the tribulation. For anyone who still wants to believe that there is no rapture, or for anyone who still wants to believe that it doesn't happen before the tribulation begins, you might want to skip this section.

Verses 6-8
6 Blessed be the LORD, who has not given us as prey to their teeth. 7 Our soul has escaped as a bird from the snare of the fowlers; the snare is broken, and we have escaped. 8 Our help is in the name of the LORD, Who made heaven and earth.

Notice that a transition has occurred from the first stanza to the second. The imagery in the first stanza was that of a "flood." The beginning of the second stanza starts with "prey" and "teeth," and then transitions to the "snare of the fowler." I believe that this transition is important. If the flood is the image of the invading army into Israel, then what are the teeth that the Lord saved "us" from? Does He save us or Israel from the teeth? End-time Bible prophecy clearly teaches that there are "teeth" involved in the tribulation period.

Consider the 4th Beast of Daniel's vision written about in Daniel chapter 7, which, as we know, is the kingdom from which the Antichrist rises. Daniel illustrates that this beast had huge iron teeth in Daniel 7:7, and then in Daniel 7:23, it is explained that with these teeth, the beast will devour the whole earth.

Daniel 7:7-8
*7 "After this I saw in the night visions, and behold, a fourth beast, dreadful and terrible, exceedingly strong. **It had huge iron teeth; it was devouring, breaking in pieces**, and trampling the residue with its feet. It was different from all the beasts that were before it, and it had ten horns. 8 I was considering the horns, and there was another horn, a little one, coming up among them, before whom three of the first horns were plucked out by the roots. And there, in this horn, were eyes like the eyes of a man, and a mouth speaking pompous words.*

Daniel 7:23
*23 "Thus he said: 'The fourth beast shall be a fourth kingdom on earth, which shall be different from all other kingdoms, **and shall devour the whole earth, trample it and break it in pieces**.*

I believe that since this 4th beast is the beast from which the Antichrist will rise and devour and break in pieces "the whole earth," the ones who will escape the "teeth" of Psalm 124:6 consist of both the Jewish and Gentile saints who are in Christ. Consider that there will be great persecution of the tribulation saints, made up of both Jews and Gentiles, during the final 7 years. God will not only spare us from His wrath by rapturing us prior to the tribulation, but also from the wrath of the beast.

1 Thessalonians 5:9
⁹For God did not appoint us to wrath, but to obtain salvation through our Lord Jesus Christ,

After verse 6, the imagery transitions once again, now to a very important depiction which aligns perfectly with the words of Jesus, as you will see. According to Psalm 124:7, our souls will escape the trap that has been set. It's important to note that just as God is 3 in 1, which we call the Trinity, we are also 3 in 1. We are body, soul, and spirit. Just as the Father and the Holy Spirit are unseen, our souls and spirits are also unseen. Each soul is personal, and I believe the word "soul" in verse 7 implies the whole person who will escape the trap. We don't have a soul, we are a soul.

How do we know this is the rapture? Well, just as I have pointed out previously, by this year, we will have been in the "Rapture Season" for 4 years. We know this because it has been encoded in the symbolic words used in 4 consecutive Psalms (Psalm 121 - 124). Remember that the number 4 is a dalet in Hebrew, which is the "door." Jesus, the Messiah, and the only "door," has been "at the door" waiting to go get His bride during this season. We have been "looking up" anxiously waiting, and our "feet have been standing in the gate," figuratively, ready to go in.

My hunch is that the rapture will be at the last moment to allow as many to be rescued as possible, but that's just a hunch. During this time between 2021 and 2025, God could at any moment say to His Son, "Go get your bride!" That's why we believers have to be diligent in our efforts to spread the gospel in these last days, and bring in as many as possible for an abundant harvest. That's the Great Commission for the Church Age!

We can compare Psalm 124 verse 7 with Luke 21:34-36 for more scriptural evidence. Of course, we know that Luke 21 is the chapter devoted to Jesus' teaching about what to expect in the end times. These are the last

3 verses of His teaching. They are a warning of what will happen if we are weighed down with the things of the world, and we aren't watching and praying for our escape. Based on many other scriptures in the New Testament, I would also add that we should be conducting the Lord's business until He returns for us. That again is the Great Commission!

Luke 21:34-36
*34 "But take heed to yourselves, lest your hearts be weighed down with carousing, drunkenness, and cares of this life, and that Day come on you unexpectedly.35 For it will come as a **snare** on all those who dwell on the face of the whole earth.36 Watch therefore, and pray always that you may be counted worthy to **escape** all these things that will come to pass, and to stand before the Son of Man."*

I believe that the rapture of the Church is clearly prophesied in Psalm 124 as a foreshadowing of Jesus' prophetic rapture warning in Luke 21. They are both amazingly tied together through the use of a common theme and illustration. Both use the imagery of a snare, or trap for a bird that is set. In Psalm 124:7, the picture is of our souls flying away to escape the snare. The word "flying" doesn't appear in the verse, but based on it being an image of a bird, that would certainly be the context.

Psalm 124:7
*7Our soul has escaped as a bird from the snare of the fowlers; the **snare** is broken, and we have **escaped**.*

Luke 21:35
*35 For it will come as a **snare** on all those who dwell on the face of the whole earth.*

Amazingly, the word used as "snare" in our English translation is the Greek word "pagis." The definition of the Greek word pagis is a snare or trap, **especially for catching birds.**

Can you see how God has interconnected His word from the Old Testament to the New Testament? Jesus wasn't just speaking random thoughts that came to His mind. He was consciously and prophetically connecting the Old Testament to the New Testament to be more fully revealed in our days. It's amazing how many clues He has given us, sort of like bread-crumbs leading us to these important final revelations before He comes like a thief in the night.

Remember that I pointed out earlier that, unlike the previous 3 Psalms where the rapture reference was in the first verse of those Psalms, it is now in verses 6 - 8. As discussed, verses 1 - 5 represent the Ezekiel 38 War in Israel, verse 6 is the escape for both Jews and Gentiles from the coming beast. Verses 7 and 8, at the end of the Psalm, are where the rapture references appear. This is very curious, and I don't think it's by coincidence, so it causes me to believe that this Psalm has a chronological sequence, meaning that the Rapture could possibly take place after the Gog Magog War. That will bring the "Rapture Season" to an end, at which time the "door," by which to escape the wrath, will be closed, and the trap will then be set for those left behind.

Is the Rapture the Setting of a Trap?

I have alluded to this previously, but I think it's important enough to investigate it a little further. In a sense, I believe that the rapture will be like setting a trap. Some will escape from the trap as described in Luke 21 and in Psalm 124, but those who do not escape from the trap will be caught in it. According to the Bible, the only way out will be by death unless you are one of the very few who persevere, believe in Jesus, keep His commandments, survive the tribulation, and do not take the "Mark of the Beast." None of that will be easy, and very few will be able to endure and survive the tribulation to the end.

Of course, there are many scriptures which also depict the rapture as a day when Jesus comes as a "thief" (Matthew 24:43, Mark 13:33, Luke 12:39-40, 1 Thessalonians 5:2, 2 Peter 3:10, Revelation 3:3, Revelation 16:15). This means that He will come unexpectedly when those who are not watching will be caught off guard. The thief analogy is interesting because, on the surface, it's hard to understand why Jesus would relate himself to a thief whom we think of as sinful. However, it does make sense because He is coming like a thief, without warning, at an hour that nobody knows, and He will take the very thing that is the most valuable and precious from the earth. He will remove His children, who are made in His image, along with the Holy Spirit living inside of us. At that time, the Church Age will come to an end, and the whole world will be thrust into chaos. It is out of this chaos that I believe the Antichrist will quickly rise.

The "Spin" of the Rapture

How will the Rapture be explained, or "spun" in the news media to all of those who are unaware that they have been caught in the trap? How will they control the chaos that it will certainly cause in many countries around the world when millions of people vanish from the face of the earth? Perhaps the explanation of the Rapture will be part of the global deception that takes place and helps the Antichrist to rise to power. After all, many Jewish Rabbis expect the world to be at war and in chaos when their messiah arrives. Of course, we know that their messiah is the false messiah, the Antichrist.

Remember that Amos 3:7 tells us that God will do nothing unless He first tells his servants, the prophets. I believe that Satan does the exact same thing but through movies, music, television, books, and through his disciples in the occult and new age movement. Maybe Satan reveals things before they happen because he is a counterfeit to God and imitates what God does. Or, maybe he is also bound by the same rule in Amos 3:7. Remember that no matter what, God is in control of all things.

Don't you know that Satan knows that the Rapture is coming? Just as Satan has deceived many with the global warming narrative, instead of believing that God is shaking the earth to wake us up, Satan has already paved the way for those left behind to believe a lie. So what do you think CNN and other news agencies will report when millions of people suddenly vanish from the face of the earth? Satan has had plenty of time to come up with an answer that suits his plan. He's had a lot of time to try to figure out God's prophetic timing, in the same way that an army general tries to figure out the battle plan of their enemy. Satan is already prepared with a media campaign of lies and deception, and I believe that it relates to the increase in news coverage of aliens, UFOs, and UAPs from all over the world.

New Age Rapture Beliefs (Satanic, Babylonian Gnosticism)

Here are just a few of the many writings from New Age authors describing a time when many will disappear from our planet. You may notice a common "environmental" theme running through all of them. Is this at least part of the "strong delusion" spoken of in 2 Thessalonians 2:9-12?

"Project World Evacuation" published in 1993 by New Age Channeler Thelma Terrell:

"Our rescue ships will be able to come in close enough in the twinkling of an eye to set the lifting beams in operation in a moment. And all over the globe where events warrant it, this will be the method of evacuation; Mankind will be lifted, levitated shall we say, by the beams from our smaller ships. These smaller craft will in turn taxi the persons to the larger ships overhead, higher in the atmosphere, where there is ample space and quarts and supplies for millions of people."

"...We watch diligently, the threat of a polar shift for the planet in your generation. Such a development would create a planetary situation through which none could survive. This would necessitate an evacuation such as I have referred to."

"...Earth changes will be the primary factor in mass evacuation of this planet."

"The Great Evacuation will come upon the world very suddenly. The flash of emergency events will be as lightning that flashes in the sky. So suddenly and so quick in its happening that it is over almost before you are aware of its presence..."

New Age author Kay Wheeler wrote an article in 1994 titled *"The Time is Now"* in the New Age journal *Connecting Link Magazine.* Her information she said came from ETs from the Seventh Celestial Plane of Life who are concerned with helping Earth evolve to full consciousness.

She wrote:

"The Mother is desperately fighting for her life. Many of her vortexes have been drained. She is in critical condition at this time and must turn her thoughts to herself if she is to survive. That is why you see the many crises in the world. Many of these you don't hear about on your "screen of lies.""

"Much of this is necessary. Many of these beings have appointments to leave at this time. Earth's population needs to be decreased to bring forth the necessary changes upon this planet to move into the fourth dimension."

"Many of these beings who are leaving this planet at this time have completed that which they came to do. It is a time of great rejoicing for them. Do not feel sad about their leaving. They are going home. Many are waiting to be with them again... Many beings must move on, for their thought patterns are of the past. They hold on to these thoughts that keep Earth held back."

Here's another book:

"Bringers of the Dawn" by Barbara Marciniak

Written after channeling over 400 hours she wrote:

"The people who leave the planet during the time of Earth changes do not fit in here any longer, and they are stopping the harmony of Earth. When the time comes that perhaps 20 million people leave the planet at one time there will be a tremendous shift in consciousness for those who are remaining."

"If human beings do not change - if they do not make the shift in values and realize that without Earth they could not be here - then Earth, in its love for its own initiation, is reaching for a higher frequency, will bring about a cleansing that will balance it once again. There is the potential for many people to leave the planet in an afternoon."

Can you see how Satan is tying so-called "climate change," saving Mother Earth, and the future rapture together to deceive the nations? It is, and will be a huge deception! Unfortunately, the globalists really believe this stuff and are pushing to "cleanse" the earth on their own by depopulating our planet. That is ultimately what Eugenics and abortion are all about. The actions and agendas of the globalists start to make more sense when you understand their religion and when you can see past their noble-sounding arguments. There are many more articles, book, and websites devoted to this same New Age demonic narrative that you can research for yourself.

Rapture Chronology

If the timeline that J. R. Church discovered in the Psalms is chronologically correct, I think it's safe to say that both the Ezekiel 38 war, which we call Gog Magog, will happen in 2024. Additionally, and if Psalm 124 is chronological within the year itself, the rapture of the Church might happen soon after the Gog Magog invasion in the same year, as I already mentioned.

As a pattern, historically, Israel has been attacked by their enemies, and most recently, by their Arab neighbors in the spring and summer months. In 1948, they were attacked in May by Muslim nations. In 1967, they were attacked in June by Muslim nations. The 1982 Lebanon War was in June. The 2006 Lebanon War was in the summer months. The 2014 Gaza War was in July and August. The 2021 Israeli-Palestinian Crisis was in May. There are a few exceptions, but this pattern is hard to overlook.

The 9th of Av, known in Hebrew as Tisha B'Av, which typically falls in our month of July, is also a date that Israelis know very well. Both Solomon's Temple and the second temple, known as Herod's Temple, were destroyed on the 9th of Av. As if that wasn't "coincidental" enough, let's consider a few more detrimental events that have happened throughout Israel's history on that very same date.

The 9th of Av was the day when the Children of Israel cried out in unbelief and wanted to return to Egypt after hearing a bad report from "10" of the 12 spies who were sent into the promised land for "40" days on a reconnaissance mission. They reported that they saw Nephilim in the land and that they wouldn't be able to take the land. Because of their unbelief, they had to wander in the wilderness for 38 more years until that generation passed away. The history of this event is in Numbers 14.

The Bar Kochba Revolt in 135 AD was crushed by the Romans on the 9th of Av. Subsequently, the Jews were expelled from their homeland. Many Jews migrated to Russia and parts of Europe after their expulsion from Israel. Later, in 1290, the Jews were banished from England on the 9th of Av, and in 1492, from Spain on the 9th of Av. The 9th of Av also marks the beginning of World War I, in which many Jews lost their land and lives. World War I also saw a rise in anti-Semitism, which led to the Holocaust in World War II and the murder of millions of Jews. Based on so much tragic history surrounding this day for the Jews, I believe that the 9th of Av will also play a role in the coming tribulation period since the pattern is well established, and since we have established that there is no such thing as coincidence. Just as Psalm 122:6-9 instructs, we should be praying for the peace of Jerusalem as well as the safety and salvation of God's Children.

As a pattern, it is evident that wars and other terrible events typically occur for the Jews in the spring and summer months. If the Ezekiel 38 invasion occurs based on this pattern, and the rapture occurs afterward, that would potentially place the rapture in the fall, which is, of course, the time of the fall feast days in Israel, which, as I have mentioned before are symbolic of the rapture, 2nd coming, judgment, and the Millennial Kingdom. Of course, I am just speculating, but these pieces do all fit within the prophetic and historical patterns.

Regardless of what month, week, or day the rapture falls on, the year 2024 corresponds to the 10th step down from the Temple court of the 15 steps, matching the 15 Songs of Ascent. Recall that this is the step when the priests would stop and blow their trumpets, which is, of course, highly symbolic of the rapture.

Suppose this timeline revelation and the chronological order of the events in 2024 are correct. In that case, we have but a little time left to prepare ourselves and others before the "blessed hope" and appearing of our Savior. It's really time to get busy!

Titus 2:13-14

[13] looking for the blessed hope and glorious appearing of our great God and Savior Jesus Christ, [14] who gave Himself for us, that He might redeem us from every lawless deed and purify for Himself His own special people, zealous for good works.

Final thoughts about the Shmita and the Rapture

I recently saw a YouTube video of an encounter between a street preacher and an atheist who asked some very intelligent questions in protest of God and Christianity. One of the questions really caught my attention as I had never heard of this specific anti-Christian argument before. The atheist challenged the preacher specifically on the rapture by asking how God could take His own out of the world when that would be sinful because most, if not all, of the Christian escapees would leave behind debt. The atheist was speaking of car loans, mortgages, taxes, and other indebtedness that we might have and would, therefore, leave behind. Wouldn't that make God complicit in theft, the atheist asked? If God cannot sin, then how could this be?

First of all, God is sovereign, and His Law trumps man's law. However, the atheist actually brought up a great point that I had never considered before, and one that ironically might help us to further narrow down the timing of the rapture itself. Secondly, God in His infinite wisdom, has already accounted for this in His word. Remember that according to Deuteronomy 15, the Shmita year is a year for cancelling all debts. God has already proclaimed that the 7th year is the year of release, and according to the Dead Sea Scrolls, 2024 is a Shmita year! So, in 2024, according to God's economy, all of our debts will be erased - glory to God!

Deuteronomy 15:1

[15] At the end of every seven years you must cancel debts.

CHAPTER 10

Psalm 125 A Song of Ascents

Jubilee Year 2025 - Start of the 7-year Tribulation

Of the three "birth pain" patterns of the 15 Songs of Ascent, Psalm 125 is the third type in the theme of God's peace and blessing, primarily for Zion. In the encrypted timeline revelation, Psalm 125 corresponds to the year 2025, and is the year that the tribulation period begins. On the surface, it doesn't really make any sense that 2025 corresponds to God's peace and blessing, but it is also the start of the tribulation period. However, when you look closely at the Psalm, you can see that the promise of peace and blessing is not for the world, but only for those who have put their trust in the Lord. Additionally, 2025 is also the final Jubilee year prior to the Lord's second coming, according to the Essene calendar. However, the Jews are on their own calendar, and do not realize the importance of 2025.

Verses 1-2
¹ Those who trust in the LORD are like Mount Zion, which cannot be moved, but abides forever. ² As the mountains surround Jerusalem, so the LORD surrounds His people from this time forth and forever.

I believe these two verses have a 2 fold prophetic fulfillment. First, they relate to those who have already been resurrected and raptured.

They abide (live) forever, and the Lord surrounds them from that time into eternity. This matches closely to the description that Jesus gave in John 14, where He tells us that when He comes for us, we will live with Him in the place that He prepared for us. It is also very similar to Paul's account of the resurrection and the rapture in 1 Thessalonians chapter 4, where he describes our meeting the Lord in the air, and then always being, or living, with the Lord.

John 14:3

³ And if I go and prepare a place for you, I will come again and receive you to Myself; that where I am, there you may be also.

1 Thessalonians 4:16-17

¹⁶ For the Lord Himself will descend from heaven with a shout, with the voice of an archangel, and with the trumpet of God. And the dead in Christ will rise first. ¹⁷ Then we who are alive and remain shall be caught up together with them in the clouds to meet the Lord in the air. And thus we shall always be with the Lord.

Secondly, Psalm 125:1-2 can certainly also refer to God's "elect," who are those Jewish and Christian Tribulation Saints that weren't ready, but realized after the rapture that all of what the Lord has promised in His word is coming true. They will need to be unmovable to persevere under extreme pressure and hardship to make it through the next 7 years and not give in to the beast system that will certainly be rising to destroy them. I'm already praying for all of the Tribulation Saints for courage, faith, perseverance, and for God's mercy and providence to see them through.

Unfortunately, I'm convinced that during the tribulation period, the truth of God's word will be replaced with deception and lies. God's word may not be found any longer at some point during the 7 years. Thinking about this desolation of God's word reminds me of John

16, where Jesus says that in "a little while, and you will not see Me." Remember that Jesus is the Word of God who became flesh (John 1:14). He went to the Father and will return at the end of the tribulation when, once again, the Word of God will dwell among us.

John 16:16
[16] *"A little while, and you will not see Me; and again a little while, and you will see Me, because I go to the Father."*

Just as books were burned in Nazi Germany, the Bible, along with many other books, like this one perhaps, will be banned. We can already see this coming on the near horizon today as I write in 2022 with the "cancel culture" and the era of so-called "fact checkers" that have already arrived. Any "fact" that doesn't align with their agenda is already being marked or cancelled on the online platforms that "they" control. Consider that so many books are digital nowadays, and then think how easy it will be for those in control, whether global government, 10 regional governments, or corporations, to simply delete them from existence with one keystroke.

I am certain that the Tribulation Saints will have to go "underground" and that the written Word of God will be almost non-existent during that time. That is why God will send the two witnesses, the 144,000 sealed servants of God, and then the 3 Angels to declare the Word of the Lord during the tribulation!

Verse 3
[3] *For the **scepter of wickedness shall not rest on the land allotted to the righteous**, lest the righteous reach out their hands to iniquity.*

Verse 3 is very interesting and revealing. The "scepter" is a ruler's symbol of authority. God is promising that this ruler of wickedness, which I believe is the false messiah, Antichrist, or "beast," will not remain in power for long over "the land allotted to the righteous," meaning Israel. God says that the "scepter of wickedness shall not rest," which means that it does exist; however, it is only temporary. Of course, we know what the fate will be of the one who holds the "scepter of wickedness," as it is described in Revelation 19.

Revelation 19:20

²⁰ And the beast was taken, and with him the false prophet that wrought miracles before him, with which he deceived them that had received the mark of the beast, and them that worshipped his image. These both were cast alive into a lake of fire burning with brimstone.

The latter part of verse 3 states, *"lest the righteous reach out their hands to iniquity."* I believe that this connects with Matthew 24:24, where Jesus said, *"For false christs and false prophets will rise and show great signs and wonders **to deceive, if possible, even the elect**."* Both verses point to the same possibility that deception and the world of iniquity will be so powerful during the tribulation period that it can only be for a set period of time. Satan will do everything in his power to deceive and destroy the Tribulation Saints and the Jews during that time since that is his only possible winning strategy. My educated guess is that much of this deception will be through some means of altering human DNA, rendering those who will accept this alteration (mark of the beast) irredeemable since they will no longer be fully human. Remember, Jesus did not die for transhumans.

Revelation 19:20

²⁰ But the beast was captured, and with it the false prophet who had performed the signs on its behalf. With these signs he had deluded those who had received the mark of the beast and worshiped its image. The two of them were thrown alive into the fiery lake of burning sulfur.

Verses 4-5

⁴ Do good, O LORD, to those who are good, and to those who are upright in their hearts. ⁵ As for such as turn aside

to their crooked ways, the LORD shall lead them away with
the workers of iniquity. Peace be upon Israel!

Similar to verses 1 and 2, in verse 4 we see a plea for the Lord to be good to those who are righteous, those who are His. However, in verse 5 we see the coming fate of those who are unrighteous. Those unrighteous ones who have strayed from the narrow path and turned to "their crooked ways" will find the same fate as the "workers of iniquity." It's not going to be easy during the tribulation period to stay on the narrow path and remain faithful to the Lord. The whole world will be pulling against you, and you may have to literally lose your life to inherit eternal life with the One who died for you. Be courageous, and do not give in! Revelation 7 describes a future scene of an innumerable multitude of Tribulation Saints who will be killed for their faith standing before the Lord in His throne room. Their tears will be wiped away, and the Lord will dwell among them forevermore.

Revelation 7:9-17
A Multitude from the Great Tribulation

⁹ After these things I looked, and behold, a great multitude
which no one could number, of all nations, tribes, peoples,
and tongues, standing before the throne and before the
Lamb, clothed with white robes, with palm branches in
their hands, ¹⁰ and crying out with a loud voice, saying,
"Salvation belongs to our God who sits on the throne, and
to the Lamb!" ¹¹ All the angels stood around the throne
and the elders and the four living creatures, and fell on
their faces before the throne and worshiped God, ¹² saying:
"Amen! Blessing and glory and wisdom, Thanksgiving and
honor and power and might, Be to our God forever and
ever. Amen."
   ¹³ Then one of the elders answered, saying to me, "Who
are these arrayed in white robes, and where did they come
from?" ¹⁴ And I said to him, "Sir, you know." So he said

to me, "These are the ones who come out of the great tribulation, and washed their robes and made them white in the blood of the Lamb. [15] Therefore they are before the throne of God, and serve Him day and night in His temple. And He who sits on the throne will dwell among them. [16] They shall neither hunger anymore nor thirst anymore; the sun shall not strike them, nor any heat; [17] for the Lamb who is in the midst of the throne will shepherd them and lead them to living fountains of waters. And God will wipe away every tear from their eyes."

To connect the prophecy of the fate of those who *"turn aside"* found in verse 5 of Psalm 125 with the words of Jesus during His first visitation, let's focus on the phrase *"workers of iniquity."* Jesus used this same phrase in Luke 13 as He described the fate of those who do not strive to enter through the narrow gate, and then the Master shuts the "door." Remember that Jesus is the only "door!"

Luke 13:24-30

*[24] "Strive to enter through the narrow gate, for many, I say to you, will seek to enter and will not be able. [25] When once the Master of the house has risen up and shut the door, and you begin to stand outside and knock at the door, saying, 'Lord, Lord, open for us,' and He will answer and say to you, 'I do not know you, where you are from,' [26] then you will begin to say, 'We ate and drank in Your presence, and You taught in our streets.' [27] But He will say, 'I tell you I do not know you, where you are from. Depart from Me, all you **workers of iniquity**. [28] There will be weeping and gnashing of teeth, when you see Abraham and Isaac and Jacob and all the prophets in the kingdom of God, and yourselves thrust out. [29] They will come from the east and the west, from the north and the south, and sit down in the kingdom of God. [30] And indeed there are last who will be first, and there are first who will be last."*

According to Jesus and His teaching in Luke 13, the "workers of iniquity" of Psalm 125 are all of those who do not enter through the narrow gate, which is, of course, Jesus. Many in the apostate church today have made up their own version of Jesus. Their Jesus isn't the Jesus of the Bible who has been given all authority and has promised judgment on all of those who try to enter by any other door. If Jesus was only "a" way and not "the" only way to the Father (John 14:6), then why did He have to die for our salvation? The obvious answer is that Jesus is the only way, just as He said He was. No one comes to the Father by their good works or by their religion, but only through a relationship with Jesus coupled with the repentance of their sins. Otherwise, you will hear those fateful words, "I do not know you, depart from me."

In these last days, do not turn aside from the only way to be saved. Nothing is more important! Do not follow the *"workers of iniquity,"* or your fate will be no different than theirs in the end. Do not follow the lies and deception that the world is offering. Your standing for your faith in Jesus will bring suffering and persecution, but stand strong anyway. Remember, they hate you because they hate Him. Also, remember that you should not be afraid of people who can only kill the body, but you should fear the one who can cast your soul into hell (Matthew 10:28, Luke 12:4-5)! That is Jesus, the one who gave us so many warnings, but most people only want to believe what their itching ears want to hear.

CHAPTER 11

Psalm 126 A Song of Ascents

The Year 2026- The Jews Return to Israel

Of the three "birth pain" patterns of the 15 Songs of Ascent, Psalm 126 is again the first type, which is a prayer of distress, or in this Psalm, I would say that it is more of an appeal to God for a merciful response to a dilemma confronting Israel. In Psalm 126, the request is being made for the Lord to bring the Jews back into their Promised Land, specifically after the Lord has "done great things for them."

> **Verses 1-4**
> *¹ When the LORD brought back the captivity of Zion, we were like those who dream.*
> *² Then our mouth was filled with laughter, and our tongue with singing. Then they said among the nations, "The LORD has done great things for them." ³ The LORD has done great things for us, and we are glad. ⁴ Bring back our captivity, O LORD, as the streams in the South.*

Here, we see the Psalmist, possibly King Hezekiah himself, look back on Judea's recent history when thousands from Judea were taken captive during his father's reign. His father, King Ahaz, ruled over Judea for 16 years and was wicked in the eyes of the Lord. Because of his wickedness and Baal worship, the Lord gave him and a multitude from Judea into the hands of Syria, Israel, Edom, and the Philistines. Many were taken captive from Judea during Ahaz's reign; however, Israel returned the ones they had taken captive back to Judea so that the Lord's anger would not increase against them. So, a vast multitude of captives returned from captivity in Israel back to Judea around the time when King Hezekiah took the throne over Judea. There were still many Judeans living in captivity in other lands that had invaded and taken spoils during the time prior to King Hezekiah.

In more detail, this specific return from captivity might also be referring to the Passover celebration at the Temple in Jerusalem when King Hezekiah sent out messengers all over the land of Israel to invite the remnants of all the tribes to the celebration. The interesting history of this event is found in 2 Chronicles 30.

2 Chronicles 30:5
⁵ They decided to send a proclamation throughout Israel, from Beersheba to Dan, calling the people to come to Jerusalem and celebrate the Passover to the LORD, the God of Israel. It had not been celebrated in large numbers according to what was written.

The King's messengers were not always met with kindness from the remnant tribe's people living in Israel. According to 2 Chronicles, many did not want to turn from their wicked ways and their worship of false gods. They mocked and scoffed at the King's messengers. Doesn't that sound like the days that we are living in now? During the tribulation, there will be 2 Prophets in Jerusalem proclaiming salvation along with 144,000 Jews, and many tribulation saints who will have turned to Jesus after the rapture, but they will be hated by those who refuse to humble themselves and turn from their wicked ways.

2 Chronicles 30:10-14
¹⁰ The couriers went from town to town in Ephraim and Manasseh, as far as Zebulun, but people scorned and ridiculed them.¹¹ Nevertheless, some from Asher, Manasseh

and Zebulun humbled themselves and went to Jerusalem.[12] Also in Judah the hand of God was on the people to give them unity of mind to carry out what the king and his officials had ordered, following the word of the LORD.[13] A very large crowd of people assembled in Jerusalem to celebrate the Festival of Unleavened Bread in the second month.[14] They removed the altars in Jerusalem and cleared away the incense altars and threw them into the Kidron Valley.

2 Chronicles 30:26-27

[26] There was great joy in Jerusalem, for since the days of Solomon son of David king of Israel there had been nothing like this in Jerusalem.[27] The priests and the Levites stood to bless the people, and God heard them, for their prayer reached heaven, his holy dwelling place.

Just like the grand Passover celebration in King Hezekiah's time, which brought Israelites flooding back to Jerusalem from all over, it seems certain that the defeat of Israel's enemies in 2024 will have the same effect. National pride will be at an all-time high. The immigration of the Jews back to Israel, known as Aliyah, has been going on for over a hundred years already. Jews from all over the world have returned to their God-given land due to anti-Semitism and persecution, among other reasons. I believe Aliyah will kick into high gear starting in 2025 and 2026 in the aftermath of the miraculous victory over all of the invading nations of the Gog Magog War. It also seems certain that the success of Israel over their enemies will result in the rise of the Antichrist and the signing of a 7-year covenant as well as the rebuilding of the Jewish Temple. It's hard to imagine that these three events are not connected to each other. Somehow, the coming false messiah will step in and possibly take credit for the victory, but that remains to be seen.

The Book of Deuteronomy lays out Israel's future of "life or death," "blessings or curses," depending on their standing in their covenant relationship with God. God entered into a covenant relationship, like a marriage, with Israel at Mt. Sinai. If Israel listened and obeyed God's word, God would be faithful and pour out blessings on His children and on their land. But if they forget God, turn from Him, and pursue other gods, the blessings will be lifted, and they will be left only with death and curses.

> **Deuteronomy 11:26-28**
> [26] *"Behold, I set before you today a blessing and a curse:* [27] *the blessing, if you obey the commandments of the LORD your God which I command you today;* [28] *and the curse, if you do not obey the commandments of the LORD your God, but turn aside from the way which I command you today, to go after other gods which you have not known.*

In addition to the blessings and curses promised in Deuteronomy, God also promised that He would send a future prophet like Moses, a fellow Israelite, who would come in God's name and speak the words that God placed in His mouth. That prophesied representative of God was none other than Jesus, who was the Word of God made flesh. Of course, we know that Israel, in their rebellious state, outright rejected Him. However, just as Jesus prophesied in John 5, they will receive the one who will come in his own name, the Antichrist.

> **John 5:43**
> *I have come in My Father's name, and you do not receive Me; if another comes in his own name, him you will receive.*

In the resulting fervor of the Gog Magog war, where God showed up on behalf of Israel and miraculously destroyed the invading armies, Israel will believe that they are indeed righteous in the eyes of the Lord and that the Lord has blessed them with victory and prosperity. The world will even say: "The Lord has done great things for them," as prophesied in verse 2. This matches Ezekiel 38 perfectly when the Lord spoke, *"I will be known in the eyes of many nations. Then they shall know that I am the Lord."*

Ezekiel 38:22-23

*²² And I will bring him to judgment with pestilence and bloodshed; I will rain down on him, on his troops, and on the many peoples who are with him, flooding rain, great hailstones, fire, and brimstone. ²³ Thus I will magnify Myself and sanctify Myself, and **I will be known in the eyes of many nations. Then they shall know that I am the LORD.**"*

After this great victory, the Children of Israel, who are still scattered all over the world, will be regathered back to their land just as they were before, after their captivity in Babylon and Assyria. This re-gathering is, of course, prophesied many times in the Old and New Testaments, including in Ezekiel 37, Isaiah 11, Jeremiah 31, Zechariah 10, and by Jesus in Luke 21.

I realize that this sounds terrible, but I believe the Antichrist will deceive many after God's victory, and he will encourage, and possibly even eventually demand in some way, that all Jews return to their land. After God's great victory over Gog, and the false messiah's confirmation of the covenant with many, there will be a short time in Israel when everything that the Rabbis have taught about their messiah will seemingly be coming true. The Rabbis will then declare that the Messianic Kingdom has finally come, and that Jews should return to their promised land to be part of a time of blessing like no other. It also makes sense, based on Revelation 6 and the opening of the Seal Judgments by Jesus, that the rest of the world will still be experiencing war, economic collapse, famine, and plagues at that same time, while Israel is prospering. Returning to Israel from all of the struggling nations of the world may seem like the easiest choice for Jews at that time. Simply put, Israel, with the false messiah in control, may seem like a beacon of stability in a tumultuous world in 2026.

The reality is that Satan needs to destroy the Jews, or else he has no possibility of success. This has been one of the central themes of the Bible from Genesis to Revelation, but many have missed it. Satan knows that this will be his final opportunity to corral the Jews and destroy them once and for all. Of course, we know that this will not happen since God has an eternal covenant with them, and He will protect those among them who are His own, just as He promised in the previous Psalm. Jesus warns of this time in Luke 21, Matthew 24, and Revelation 12, but we're not quite there yet...

Verses 5-6
5 Those who sow in tears shall reap in joy. 6 He who continually goes forth weeping, bearing seed for sowing, shall doubtless come again with rejoicing, bringing his sheaves with him.

Verses 5 and 6 have a proverbial ring to them. These two verses may have at least three meanings. As a general rule, work is hard, but the fruit of one's labor brings joy. Let's examine if these verses have any other context to them. In Ezra chapter 3, we read about the restoration of the Temple after the exile, and the weeping over it, as well as the shouts for joy. Psalm 126 is subtly connected with Ezra 3 and the rebuilding of the Temple through the same theme of weeping and rejoicing.

Ezra 3:11-13 - *Restoration of the Temple Begins*
*11 And they sang responsively, praising and giving thanks to the LORD: "For He is good, For His mercy endures forever toward Israel." Then all the people shouted with a great shout, when they praised the LORD, because the foundation of the house of the LORD was laid.12 But many of the priests and Levites and heads of the fathers' houses, old men who had seen the first temple, **wept with a loud voice when the foundation of this temple was laid before their eyes. Yet many shouted aloud for joy**, 13 so that the people could not discern the noise of the shout of joy from the noise of the weeping of the people, for the people shouted with a loud shout, and the sound was heard afar off.*

In the encrypted timeline revelation in the Psalms, I believe that the Temple construction will begin in 2026. The first verses of Psalm 126 were devoted to the return of the exiles. What better way to bring the Jews back to their homeland than the promise of rebuilding the Temple? After all, Jews from all over the world pray regularly for the restoration of their Temple in Jerusalem, the restoration of the temple services, and the restoration of their sacrificial form of worship. Additionally, after the Passover Seder, every year, Jews worldwide say or sing the phrase "next year in Jerusalem" as the very last words of the Seder. It seems that the dream of returning to Jerusalem for the Jews will soon come true, but unfortunately, we know from God's word that the dream will turn into a nightmare for the second half of the tribulation period.

Another meaning of verses 5 and 6 is the future fulfillment of the prophecy of Jesus' return with His saints who, during their time, sowed seeds for the bountiful harvest of our Lord. Jesus used the metaphor of sowing, reaping, and harvesting numerous times to illustrate the multiplication effect of the salvation message to reach all nations. This message culminated with Jesus' last words in Matthew 28, which we call the Great Commission.

Matthew 28:18-20

[18] *Then Jesus came to them and said, "All authority in heaven and on earth has been given to me.*[19] *Therefore go and make disciples of all nations, baptizing them in the name of the Father and of the Son and of the Holy Spirit,*[20] *and teaching them to obey everything I have commanded you. And surely I am with you always, to the very end of the age."*

Ecclesiastes 3 tells us that there is a time for sowing and a time for reaping. Jesus said that He would be with us in our efforts of sowing and reaping as we make disciples of all nations, even until the very end of the age. The age known as the Church Age will end with the rapture of the Church, and all of those who have been, and all of those who will be part of the great harvest will be the sheaves signified in verse 6.

This verse perfectly illustrates the future second coming of our Lord with His Saints.

Verse 6
⁶ He who continually goes forth weeping, bearing seed for sowing, shall doubtless **come again** *with rejoicing,* **bringing his sheaves with him**.

I can't help but wonder if this verse wasn't the inspiration for the old hymn that we used to sing at church when I was a boy called "Bringing in the Sheaves." I believe that this verse has two connotations based on interlinking scriptures. The first is that we believers, who are the hands and feet of the gospel, should be busy growing the Kingdom of God during this final season and "bringing in the sheaves." Keep in mind that Jesus uses several different metaphors for new believers, such as "sheaves" as well as "fruit." The general idea is that fruit is any agricultural produce that can reproduce more of itself such as wheat, barley, corn, or what we consider traditional fruit. They all have seeds and reproduce, thereby multiplying for an abundant harvest. In the Gospel of John chapter 15, Jesus declares that if we abide in Him and He in us, we will bear much fruit and be His disciples. However, it also contains a warning for those who do not abide in Jesus; they will be cast out and thrown into the fire.

John 15:5-8
⁵ "I am the vine, you are the branches. He who abides in Me, and I in him, **bears much fruit**; *for without Me you can do nothing.* ⁶ **If anyone does not abide in Me, he is cast out as a branch and is withered; and they gather them and throw them into the fire, and they are burned.** *⁷ If you abide in Me, and My words abide in you, you will ask what you desire, and it shall be done for you. ⁸ By this My Father is glorified, that you* **bear much fruit**; *so you will be My disciples.*

One day, we will stand before our Lord and receive rewards for all of the hard work that we did while we were "in the field," which is where He placed us along with the gifts that He gave us to sow the seed and reap an abundant harvest. I know I've said this before, but it cannot be overstated, that is the Great Commission, and we are running out of time.

The next aspect of verse 6 is that it is Jesus who is the "First Fruits" of the resurrection, and who will appear at His second coming "bringing His sheaves with Him."

1 Corinthians 15:20
20But now Christ is risen from the dead, and has become the firstfruits of those who have fallen asleep.

Revelation 19:11-14
*11 Now I saw heaven opened, and behold, a white horse. And He who sat on him was called Faithful and True, and in righteousness He judges and makes war. 12 His eyes were like a flame of fire, and on His head were many crowns. He had a name written that no one knew except Himself. 13 He was clothed with a robe dipped in blood, and His name is called The Word of God. 14 And the armies in heaven, clothed in fine linen, white and clean, **followed Him** on white horses.*

The Feast of First Fruits

Remember that Jesus has fulfilled the first 4 of the 7 Feast Days, or Moedim in Hebrew, meaning "appointed times." Three of those four Moedim occurred during Passover week. Passover, when the sacrificial lambs were slain, was fulfilled in Jesus' death, and the Feast of Unleavened bread was fulfilled in Jesus' burial. Guess what important event our Messiah fulfilled at the Feast of First Fruits? *For us believers in Jesus the Messiah, the Feast of First Fruits* honors and commemorates the day when the Messiah rose from the grave. Most call this day Easter, but don't get me started on the pagan origins of that name. I simply call it "Resurrection Day." So, how did Jesus fulfill the Feast of First Fruits? First, let's look at what the Feast of First Fruits was during Temple times and how God instructed Israel to keep it.

Leviticus 23:9-11

*And the Lord spoke to Moses, saying, "Speak to the children of Israel, and say to them: 'When you come into the land which I give to you, and reap its harvest, then you shall bring a **sheaf** of the firstfruits of your harvest to the priest. He shall wave the **sheaf** before the Lord, to be accepted on your behalf; on the day after the Sabbath the priest shall wave it.*

The Feast of First Fruits during Temple times was a wave offering of thanksgiving to the Lord for what God had provided that came up from out of the earth. The priests would literally wave a portion of the first fruits of the harvest, which was barley since it was the first crop of the year to mature. Simply stated, Jesus fulfilled the Feast of First Fruits by being the first fruits of the resurrection. All of us who are in Christ and have died in Christ are also part of the "First Fruits." We will be gathered together to meet our Lord in the air at the rapture and resurrection.

1 Thessalonians 4:16-18

[16]For the Lord Himself will descend from heaven with a shout, with the voice of an archangel, and with the trumpet of God. And the dead in Christ will rise first. [17]Then we who are alive and remain shall be caught up together with them in the clouds to meet the Lord in the air. And thus we shall always be with the Lord. [18]Therefore comfort one another with these words.

What if you were not saved and you missed the rapture? Jesus tells us that many will think they were saved, but were not.

Matthew 7:21-23

21 "Not everyone who says to Me, 'Lord, Lord,' shall enter the kingdom of heaven, but he who does the will of My Father in heaven. 22 Many will say to Me in that day, 'Lord, Lord, have we not prophesied in Your name, cast out demons in Your name, and done many wonders in Your name?' 23 And then I will declare to them, 'I never knew you; depart from Me, you who practice lawlessness!'

If you believed that you were a Christian, but you had no interest in doing "the will of My Father in heaven," and you missed the rapture, I'm sorry to say that the future is set, and the darkest time in the world's history is upon you. However, all is not lost. The Age of Grace, known as the Church Age has ended, but you can still be saved. Here are a few key verses that you should know and understand if you were not ready when Jesus came for His harvest:

Matthew 10:28

28 And do not fear those who kill the body but cannot kill the soul. But rather fear Him who is able to destroy both soul and body in hell.

Matthew 24:9-25

9 "Then they will deliver you up to tribulation and kill you, and you will be hated by all nations for My name's sake.10 And then many will be offended, will betray one another, and will hate one another.11 Then many false prophets will rise up and deceive many.12 And because lawlessness will abound, the love of many will growcold.13 But he who endures to the end shall be saved.14 And this gospel of the kingdom will be preached in all the world as a witness to all the nations, and then the end will come.

The Great Tribulation

[15] "Therefore when you see the 'abomination of desolation,' spoken of by Daniel the prophet, standing in the holy place" (whoever reads, let him understand), [16] "then let those who are in Judea flee to the mountains. [17] Let him who is on the housetop not go down to take anything out of his house. [18] And let him who is in the field not go back to get his clothes. [19] But woe to those who are pregnant and to those who are nursing babies in those days! [20] And pray that your flight may not be in winter or on the Sabbath. [21] For then there will be great tribulation, such as has not been since the beginning of the world until this time, no, nor ever shall be. [22] And unless those days were shortened, no flesh would be saved; but for the elect's sake those days will be shortened. [23] "Then if anyone says to you, 'Look, here is the Christ!' or 'There!' do not believe it. [24] For false christs and false prophets will rise and show great signs and wonders to deceive, if possible, even the elect. [25] See, I have told you beforehand.

Revelation 3:5
[5] He who overcomes shall be clothed in white garments, and I will not blot out his name from the Book of Life; but I will confess his name before My Father and before His angels.

Revelation 14:6-13
[6] Then I saw another angel flying in the midst of heaven, having the everlasting gospel to preach to those who dwell on the earth—to every nation, tribe, tongue, and people— [7] saying with a loud voice, "Fear God and give glory to Him, for the hour of His judgment has come; and worship Him who made heaven and earth, the sea and springs of water." [8] And another angel followed, saying,

"Babylon is fallen, is fallen, that great city, because she has made all nations drink of the wine of the wrath of her fornication."⁹ Then a third angel followed them, saying with a loud voice, "If anyone worships the beast and his image, and receives his mark on his forehead or on his hand, ¹⁰ he himself shall also drink of the wine of the wrath of God, which is poured out full strength into the cup of His indignation. He shall be tormented with fire and brimstone in the presence of the holy angels and in the presence of the Lamb. ¹¹ And the smoke of their torment ascends forever and ever; and they have no rest day or night, who worship the beast and his image, and whoever receives the mark of his name."¹² Here is the patience of the saints; here are those who keep the commandments of God and the faith of Jesus.¹³ Then I heard a voice from heaven saying to me, "Write: 'Blessed are the dead who die in the Lord from now on.'" "Yes," says the Spirit, "that they may rest from their labors, and their works follow them."

Revelation 20:4

⁴ And I saw thrones, and they sat on them, and judgment was committed to them. Then I saw the souls of those who had been beheaded for their witness to Jesus and for the word of God, who had not worshiped the beast or his image, and had not received his mark on their foreheads or on their hands. And they lived and reigned with Christ for a thousand years.

If you missed the rapture, don't lose hope. The "birth pains" will continue until and through the Great Tribulation, when things will increasingly become more and more difficult. But don't give in; Jesus is on your side, and He will come back very soon!

CHAPTER 12

Psalm 127 A Song of Ascents of King Solomon

Year 2027 - The Third Temple Is Complete, but the Lord Isn't in the Temple

Of the three "birth pain" patterns found in the 15 Songs of Ascent, Psalm 127 is once again a song of trust and deliverance, just as Psalm 124 was. The year 2024 was a pivotal year of trust and deliverance for Israel from the Ezekiel 38 invaders, and for all of those who were found in Christ and were raptured to meet the Lord in the air. Psalm 127 is the only Psalm of the 15 Psalms of Ascent that was written by King Solomon, and it is the center point of the 15 Psalms. There are 7 Psalms of Ascent before Psalm 127 and 7 Psalms after Psalm 127. Besides being well known for his wisdom, King Solomon was, and is, still known by the Israelites as the builder of the first temple in Jerusalem.

Verses 1-2
¹Unless the LORD builds the house, they labor in vain who build it; unless the LORD guards the city, the watchman stays awake in vain. ² It is vain for you to rise up early, to sit up late, to eat the bread of sorrows; for so He gives His beloved sleep.

The opening of Psalm 127 speaks a great general truth of God, and has certainly been used in many great sermons over the centuries. In general, all works of man separate from God are ultimately in vain. That doesn't mean that the unrighteous are not profitable, powerful, and prosperous for a time. However, they and their temporary accomplishments will ultimately be burned in the coming fire.

Considering that this Psalm was written by King Solomon, it isn't any wonder that Psalm 127 contains timeless wisdom, but is there more to it? When I first started researching the Psalms for future prophetic patterns for myself, based on the fulfillment of past prophecies in the Psalms from 1901 - 1990 found in the work of J. R. Church and his book *Hidden Prophecies in the Psalms*, I knew that if the encrypted pattern was correct, there would have to be a Psalm before Psalm 128 with a strong linkage to the building of a new Jewish temple. I was hopeful when I found the subtle hint at the rebuilding of the temple in Psalm 126, but overwhelmed when I read Psalm 127, especially with the understanding that it is the only Psalm of Ascent written by King Solomon, the original builder of the temple. That is simply too much of a coincidence to be a coincidence!

For a little more clarity, I knew, based on the long established pattern, that Israel has never made it past 80 years as a sovereign, undivided nation, which means that based on this pattern, they will not survive past 2028. Also, we know from Jesus and Daniel (Matthew 24:15 and Daniel 9:27) that there will be a rebuilt temple prior to that time, and the sacrificial system will be re-established. Remember, it's at the Temple where the Antichrist will declare that he is god and will end the sacrificial system in the middle of the tribulation period. Logically, the temple and the sacrificial system have to exist before the Antichrist can take them over. I have previously established that this should take place in, or around 2028. Therefore, there has to be a rebuilt temple standing before, and during 2028. And if the timeline revelation is correct, then it should be foretold in the 15 Psalms of Ascent for this pattern to hold up. God did not disappoint with Psalm 127!

The opening of this important Psalm says, *"Unless the Lord builds the house, they labor in vain who build it."* What house is the Psalm referring to? Generally, it could be any house. However, based on its perfect placement in the Psalms, as well as the fact that this is the builder of the first Temple, King Solomon speaking, my educated guess is that this "house" is the House of God! The Hebrew word here is "bayith," which can mean house or temple. I read over some statistics that stated that bayith, as "House of God" or "House of the Lord," is used in the Old Testament 80 times. Is it just me, or is the number 80 even further confirmation?

During the time of the building of the first Temple by King Solomon, the Temple was routinely referred to as "house," as we see in 1 Kings 5 and 6, as well as many other scriptures.

1 Kings 5

*¹Now Hiram king of Tyre sent his servants to Solomon, because he heard that they had anointed him king in place of his father, for Hiram had always loved David. ² Then Solomon sent to Hiram, saying: ³ You know how my father David could not build a **house** for the name of the LORD his God because of the wars which were fought against him on every side, until the LORD put his foes under the soles of his feet.⁴ But now the LORD my God has given me rest on every side; there is neither adversary nor evil occurrence.*

*⁵ And behold, I propose to build a **house** for the name of the LORD my God, as the LORD spoke to my father David, saying, "Your son, whom I will set on your throne in your place, he shall build the **house** for My name."*

1 Kings 6:1

And it came to pass in the four hundred and eightieth year after the children of Israel had come out of the land of Egypt, in the fourth year of Solomon's reign over Israel,

> *in the month of Ziv, which is the second month, that he*
> *began to build the **house** of the LORD.*

I believe that the numbers listed in 1 Kings 6:1 are important. I don't think that our God wasted any words or numbers in His word, and I believe that they all have an encoded meaning beyond what's on the surface. It's our job to figure out what that encoded meaning is to gain a better understanding of the text. The number 480 is certainly interesting to me in verse 1 of 1 Kings 6. Think about it, according to Daniel chapter 9, Israel owed God 490 years for not honoring God's Law or the land that God gave them. We know that Jesus rode into Jerusalem as the Messiah at the 483rd year after a 3-year ministry, which leaves the 7-year tribulation period yet to be fulfilled. So, if you take the 3 years of Jesus' ministry off of the 483 years, you also arrive at a 480! Jesus' ministry started 480 years after the command was given to rebuild the temple as prophesied in Daniel 9:25. Is it any wonder that Jesus likened Himself to the temple when He said, *"destroy this temple, and in three days I will raise it up"* in John 2:19? Can you see the encoded pattern based on the number 480?

There is also a prophetic pattern about the "2nd month" encoded throughout the Bible. The 2nd month on God's calendar was called Ziv, which in Hebrew relates to brightness, radiance, brilliance, and prominence, all of which I would ascribe to the countenance of Jesus. The 2nd month also relates to a new beginning and a second chance, which is also certainly part of the narrative in the building of Solomon's temple. The 2nd month is also mentioned in Genesis 7 and 8 in relationship to the beginning and the ending of Noah's flood. I realize on the surface, Noah's flood doesn't sound much like a new beginning, but that's exactly what it was. According to Genesis 6 mankind had become so sinful and genetically corrupted by the fallen "sons of God," and the earth and mankind needed a new start through the seed of someone whose genes weren't corrupted. That was Noah, according to Genesis 6, which says that Noah was perfect in his "generations," meaning that he wasn't genetically corrupted. So, it was through Noah that mankind received a second chance.

Genesis 6:9

⁹ This is the genealogy of Noah. Noah was a just man, perfect in his generations. Noah walked with God. ¹⁰ And Noah begot three sons: Shem, Ham, and Japheth.

The second month also relates to having a "second chance" because it is in the second month that any Israelite could have a second chance at celebrating the Passover if they were ritually unclean in the first month or if they were on a journey and couldn't keep the festival at its appointed time according to Numbers chapter 9. So, you can see that the number 480, as well as the 2ⁿᵈ month both relate to the temple, the Messiah, new beginnings, and second chances. At the building of the 3ʳᵈ temple, which may also begin on the 2ⁿᵈ month, the Jews will believe that they have been given yet another new beginning. According to both the Old and the New Testaments, that will be true; however, it will only be through the fire of the 7-year tribulation that they be given a second chance to accept Jesus, Yeshua HaMashiach, as their true Redeemer.

Jesus was the awaited Messiah 2000 years ago, but the Jews rejected Him. Based on the prophecies of Daniel, they should have known exactly when the Messiah would come. If they had been watching, they could have literally known what day He would ride into Jerusalem, but they weren't. Even Jesus pointed out while He wept over the city of Jerusalem prior to His crucifixion that they should have known the time of His visitation. Let's not make that same mistake!

Luke 19:41-44

*⁴¹ Now as He drew near, He saw the city and wept over it, ⁴² saying, "**If you had known, even you, especially in this your day**, the things that make for your peace! But now they are hidden from your eyes.⁴³ For days will come upon you when your enemies will build an embankment around you, surround you and close you in on every side, ⁴⁴ and level you, and your children within you, to the ground; and they will not leave in you one stone upon another, **because you did not know the time of your visitation**."*

Because the Jews were not watching, and because they rejected Jesus as the Messiah, He prophesied that the city and the Temple would be destroyed, and that not one stone would be left upon another. Of course, we know that the temple was destroyed in 70 AD, then the city was destroyed in 135 AD, and the Israelites were exiled from their land. Since God allowed that temple to be destroyed because of their unbelief, it's obvious that God's glory no longer dwelt in that temple. Nothing has changed; the Jews still reject Jesus as their Messiah, so why would God's glory be found in a new temple in Jerusalem?

God will not be in the new temple. God does not want the temple services and sacrifices because His one and only son was already sacrificed once and for all to atone for all of our sins if we only accept Him. Prophetically, we know that the Jews will eventually accept Jesus as their Messiah, but not until after the 7 years of sorrows. That is what the 7 years are primarily all about:, salvation for the Jews.

First, however, the Jews will invite the devil into the city and into the temple thinking that he is their long-awaited messiah. In fact, because of the writings of their sages, they believe that he will be responsible for the rebuilding of the new temple. Again, why would God be in this new temple built by the Antichrist? He won't!

Bread of Sorrows

I think it's wonderful how God has encoded and connected prophetic times and events together in His word with the use of keywords, phrases, numbers, patterns, and interconnected imagery for us to uncover. In verse 2 of Psalm 127, there is one such key. God tells us that *"It shall be like the bread of mourners."* There is one other scripture in the Bible that corresponds to this "bread of mourners," where it is stated as "bread of mourners" in some translations, and "bread of sorrows" in others. This key is located in the book of Hosea and is directly related to the temple and the temple sacrifices not being accepted or desired by God. There are also many other scriptures related more generally to God's displeasure with the temple sacrifices and offerings of unrighteous Israel from times past in Isaiah 1:11-15, Amos 5:21, Jeremiah 6:20, Proverbs 21:3, Matthew 9:13, Mark 12:33, and many more.

Hosea 9:4
*They shall not offer wine offerings to the L*ORD*, **nor shall their sacrifices be pleasing to Him**. It shall be like **bread of mourners (sorrows)** to them; all who eat it shall be defiled...*

Why will the sacrifices offered at the new temple not be pleasing or accepted by God? Why will God not dwell in this new tribulation temple? Why will their sacrifices be like the "bread of sorrows?"

Jesus is the temple who sacrificed His life to save our lives once and for all (John 2:13-21)! Jesus, with His own blood, and not the blood of goats and calves, has already entered the Most Holy Place once and for all (Hebrews 9:12)! Jesus is the bread of life broken for us once and for all (Luke 22:19)! Simply put, if you are worshiping at any other temple, or eating any other bread, it will be in vain.

144,000 "Sons?"

Verses 3-5
*³ Behold, sons (Hebrew - banim, sons, noun masculine) are a heritage from the L*ORD*, the fruit of the womb is a reward. ⁴ Like arrows in the hand of a warrior, so are the sons of one's youth. ⁵ Happy is the man who has his quiver full of them; they shall not be ashamed, But shall speak with their enemies in the gate.*

Many of our English translations say "children" in verse 3, however, in the original Hebrew it was specifically "sons." In the context of the timeline revelation I think it's safe to say that I believe verses 3 thru 5 are speaking of the 144,000 sons from the 12 Tribes of Israel foretold in

Revelation 7 and 14. The tribe of Dan has been replaced by Manasseh, who was one of the sons of Joseph, but that's another story.

Psalm 127:5 has long been a mystery, and many have asked the question, "how many is a quiver full?" There's no biblical consensus on how many arrows equates to a "quiver full." A full quiver of a warrior in the time of Solomon could have been perhaps 30 to 50, but we don't know for sure. If I were a warrior and an archer of that time, I would have wanted as many arrows as I could stuff into my oversized quiver so that I didn't run out during battle. After all, a bow without an arrow is pretty useless! So, there is no exact number to tie this verse to anything prophetic. If this Psalm said, it's 12 or 144, then this mystery wouldn't be a mystery. Every prophecy scholar and student since the writing of the Book of Revelation would have surmised that this verse is speaking of the 12,000 from each of the 12 Tribes, which equals 144,000.

There are no direct numerical links between the "sons" of Psalm 127 and the 144,000 sons of Israel of Revelation 7 and 14 that I can find. Regardless of the fact that there are no exact prophetic numbers to connect these "sons" of Psalm 127 to the 144,000 "sons" of Israel from Revelation, there are still several interesting and important word connections contained in the texts that allow us to decode it.

Behold

Psalm 127:3 begins with the word *"**Behold**."* Revelation 14 begins with *"Then I looked, and **behold**, a Lamb standing on Mount Zion, and with Him one hundred and forty-four thousand, having His Father's name written on their foreheads..."* I realize that the word behold is used a lot in the Bible, and is typically used to point out something very important. Behold is the Bible telling you not only to look at something, but more importantly, to "pay attention to it." So, on its own, the fact that "behold" is used in both Psalm 127 and in Revelation 14 isn't much of a connection, but there's more...

Fruit

Psalm 127:3 also makes reference to these "sons" as being "**fruit**." Revelation 14:4 explains that *"these are the ones who were not defiled with women, for they are virgins. These are the ones who follow the Lamb wherever He goes. These were redeemed from among men, being first **fruits** to God and to the Lamb."*

Reward

Revelation 14 reads as though these sons are a reward to God since they were redeemed from the earth from among men because they had not been defiled and were found to be without fault before the Lord. Psalm 127 proclaims that they are a heritage and a reward. Also, the use of the word "fruit" to describe these "sons" in both Psalm 127 and in Revelation 4 suggests that they are a reward. After all, the reward of a season of planting, growing, and harvesting is the fruit.

Arrows in the Hand of a Warrior

"Like arrows in the hand of a warrior," these "sons" have a target and a mission. They are evangelists sent out from the Lord. Jesus is the "Warrior," as we see in Revelation 19 at the end of the tribulation period. However, in 2027, there is still a multitude to be evangelized and saved. In the absence of the Church, they will proclaim the testimony of the Lord, which will save a vast multitude, which we see in Revelation 7.

Revelation 7:9-10
[9] After these things I looked, and behold, a great multitude which no one could number, of all nations, tribes, peoples, and tongues, standing before the throne and before the Lamb, clothed with white robes, with palm branches in their hands, [10] and crying out with a loud voice, saying, "Salvation belongs to our God who sits on the throne, and to the Lamb!"

They shall not be Ashamed

Psalm 127 verse 5 tells us that these "sons" *"shall not be ashamed."* This reminds me of Paul's comment in Romans 1:16, where he said *"For I am **not ashamed** of the gospel of Christ, for it is the power of God to salvation for everyone who believes, for the Jew first and also for the Greek.* Can you imagine 144,000 evangelists like Paul boldly proclaiming the gospel to both Jews and Gentiles, even in the face of severe persecution during the tribulation period?

Revelation 14:5 tells us that *"they are without fault."* Not only are the 144,000 sons righteous in God's eyes, but they do not fail at their mission of evangelism. Psalm 127 indicates that these sons shall not be ashamed, and in context, I believe that they are not ashamed of God, or the word of God, which is, of course, ultimately the gospel message. Combined, they are not ashamed of the gospel, and they carry out their mission without fail until its conclusion, at which time they are seen standing with "The Lamb" on Mount Zion, and before the throne singing a new song, which no one else can learn, because they are unique and have fulfilled their unique mission.

Revelation 14:1-5
[1] Then I looked, and behold, a Lamb standing on Mount Zion, and with Him one hundred and forty-four thousand, having His Father's name written on their foreheads. [2] And I heard a voice from heaven, like the voice of many waters, and like the voice of loud thunder. And I heard the sound of harpists playing their harps. [3] They sang as it were a new song before the throne, before the four living creatures, and the elders; and no one could learn that song except the hundred and forty-four thousand who were redeemed from the earth. [4] These are the ones who were not defiled with women, for they are virgins. These are the ones who follow the Lamb wherever He goes. These were redeemed from among men, being firstfruits to God and to the Lamb. [5] And in their mouth was found no deceit, for they are without fault before the throne of God.

They Shall Speak with Their Enemies at the Gate

I believe that this last comparison goes hand in hand with the previous comparison or complementary descriptions between not being ashamed and being without fault. Psalm 127:5 says, *"Happy is the man who has his quiver full of them; they shall not be ashamed, but shall speak with their enemies in the gate."* According to the Psalm, these sons are not ashamed to speak with their enemies in the gate. In analyzing this passage I think it is important to first consider who their "enemies" are, and what is the significance of the "gate?"

Let's start with the "gate." Historically, a gate was an entryway into a fortified city such as Jerusalem. In those days, civic messages were proclaimed at city gates, prophets spoke at the city gates, and elders gathered and settled matters at the city gates according to scripture (Genesis 19, Deuteronomy 21, Ruth 4, 1 Samuel 4).

Notice that the "sons," who are "like arrows in the hand of a warrior," are not fighting with their enemies; there is no violence implied, they are speaking with their enemies in the gate.

Let's now consider who their "enemies" are. Judging from the fact that these sons are righteous, a logical conclusion would be that their enemies would be the same as God's enemies, which would certainly include the coming Antichrist and the false prophet, but that's just speculation. James 4 indicates that anyone who is a friend of the world is an enemy of God. This once again reinforces my belief that these sons are evangelists on a mission to proclaim the gospel to the lost of the world during the tribulation.

James 4:4
*Adulterers and adulteresses! Do you not know that friendship with the world is enmity with God? Whoever therefore wants to be a friend of the world makes himself an **enemy of God**.*

As I have already pointed out, traditionally, "the gate" would refer to one of the city gates of Jerusalem or another fortified city. However, if Psalm 127 is connected with the 144,000, which I believe it is, and is prophetic of the future, then the "speaking with their enemies at the gate" could reasonably even pertain to an event that we can't even imagine. As a stretch, what if "the gate" is referring to the CERN Large Hadron Collider? Conspiracy theories abound around CERN, and over the last few years, it seems that what was once a conspiracy "theory" has been proven to be a conspiracy "fact." All of this is simply conjecture. If the "sons" of Psalm 127 verses 3 - 5 are referring to the 144,000, then only time will tell what the rest of this prophetic Psalm relates to.

Neither Revelation chapter 7, nor chapter 14, gives us much detail about exactly what the mission of the 144,000 is and how they will carry out that mission. We only surmise that they are responsible for the salvation of a multitude of tribulation saints. This is primarily because also in chapter 7, directly after the announcement of the 144,000 Sons, we read about the saved multitude from every tribe and tongue in heaven. That leaves a lot to the imagination, and to the final revelation of the "who, what, when, and where" as this prophecy unfolds. Will the 144,000 Sons be a part of the prophetic narrative in 2027? Only time will tell. Are the 144,000 the final fulfillment of Matthew 24:14?

Matthew 24:14
And this gospel of the kingdom will be preached in all the world as a witness to all the nations, and then the end will come.

CHAPTER 13

Psalm 128 A Song of Ascents

Year 2028 - The Middle of Tribulation, Israel Turns 80, and the Remnant Escapes!

Of the three "birth pain" patterns found in the 15 Songs of Ascent, Psalm 128 is once again the third type in the theme of God's peace and blessing. Psalm 128 actually contains three categories of blessings. There are individual blessings, family blessings, and national blessings. At first thought, it doesn't make sense that the middle of the tribulation, which starts the "Great Tribulation," would be even remotely associated with a Psalm of peace and blessing. However, if you look closely at the blessing, you will understand that it is specifically for those who fear and walk with the Lord, and peace is expressed at the end of the Psalm exclusively upon Israel. We will be able to decipher from scripture exactly who this pertains to at that time in the timeline.

Verse 1
[1]*Blessed is every one who fears the* LORD, *Who walks in His ways.*

Escape of the Remnant

I don't believe that it's a coincidence that the blessing in verse 1 is specifically for everyone who not only fears the Lord, but who also specifically "walks" in His ways. I recognize that "walking in His ways" symbolizes our relationship with the Lord in a spiritual sense. However, in the context of the middle of the tribulation period, there might be more to it. Jesus said in Matthew 24 that when they see the "abomination of desolation" in the temple, then they should flee from Judea to the mountains. In a spiritual sense, the Jews in Judea will not know to flee if they are not "walking" with the Lord, or if they haven't read Matthew 24 from the New Testament. In fact, Matthew 24:15 literally says, "*let the reader understand.*" They will need to flee immediately without looking back, and even more literally "walk" in the Lord's ways as He guides them so that they know the way to go. How else will they know the way to the refuge that He has set up for them?

Based on the timeline revelation, I believe that this specific blessing in verse 1 is expressly for the remnant of Israel who will flee to the wilderness according to Matthew 24, Revelation 12, and even Daniel 12. As I have already alluded to, it is precisely those Jews, the Messianic Jews, who will know and understand what they are witnessing in Jerusalem during Israel's 80th year and heed the words of Jesus who said, "*Therefore when you see the 'abomination of desolation,' spoken of by Daniel the prophet, standing in the holy place" (whoever reads, let him understand), then let those who are in Judea flee to the mountains.*"

If the timeline revelation in the Psalms is correct, then sometime between 2028 and 2029 will mark the middle point of the tribulation period. That means that according to Revelation 12, Daniel 7, 9, and Daniel 12, at some point during the year, the first 1260 days will be history, and all of the prophesied midpoint events will come to pass. The mask of deception that the Antichrist has been wearing will be removed during that year, and he will break the Daniel 9:27 covenant, set up the "abomination of desolation" in the newly rebuilt temple according also to Matthew 24:15, institute the worship of himself, the beast, and the mark of the beast monetary and surveillance system of Revelation 13 will become a reality. As I previously mentioned, this is also the year that the believing Jewish remnant will flee for their lives to the Judean wilderness, as described in Daniel 12, Zechariah 13, Matthew 24, Mark 13, Romans 11, and Revelation 12.

In Matthew 24 and Revelation 12, you can clearly see that the believing Jewish remnant, which will be 1/3 of Israel according to Zechariah 13, will flee to the mountains to escape being put to death. They will be protected and provided for by God for 3.5 years until the Lord's return at the end of the tribulation.

Matthew 24:15-22

15 "Therefore when you see the 'abomination of desolation,' spoken of by Daniel the prophet, standing in the holy place" (whoever reads, let him understand), 16 "then let those who are in Judea flee to the mountains.17 Let him who is on the housetop not go down to take anything out of his house.18 And let him who is in the field not go back to get his clothes.19 But woe to those who are pregnant and to those who are nursing babies in those days!20 And pray that your flight may not be in winter or on the Sabbath.21 For then there will be great tribulation, such as has not been since the beginning of the world until this time, no, nor ever shall be.22 And unless those days were shortened, no flesh would be saved; but for the elect's sake those days will be shortened.

Revelation 12:13-17

13Now when the dragon saw that he had been cast to the earth, he persecuted the woman who gave birth to the male Child.14But the woman was given two wings of a great eagle, that she might fly into the wilderness to her place, where she is nourished for a time and times and half a time, from the presence of the serpent. 15So the serpent spewed water out of his mouth like a flood after the woman, that he might cause her to be carried away by the flood. ¹⁶But the earth helped the woman, and the earth opened its mouth and swallowed up the flood which the dragon had spewed out of his mouth. ¹⁷And the dragon was enraged with the woman, and he went to make war with the rest of her offspring, who keep the commandments of God and have the testimony of Jesus Christ.

Fly Away

My father-in-law, Johnny, passed away on Friday, January 13, 2023, as I was writing this chapter. He was a humble and godly man, and I have no doubt that he is now with the Lord. In trying to console my wife, Tammy, I couldn't help but read her Psalm 90:10, which explains that a man's life is 70 or perhaps 80 years if by reason of strength. You may recall that I have previously discussed Psalm 90:10 regarding the "Fig Tree Generation" and I explained that Israel has never survived as a sovereign, independent, and unified nation for more than 80 consecutive years. There is definitely a pattern at work here.

Psalm 90:10
The days of our lives are seventy years; and if by reason of strength they are eighty years, yet their boast is only labor and sorrow; for it is soon cut off, and we fly away.

My wife's father lived to be 83 years old so I tried to comfort her with this verse by explaining that anything past 80 is gravy! I realize that I am tragically horrible as a comforter, but at least I tried! However, the events of this past week caused me to really study and once again meditate on this verse, especially the last portion of it, which says, *"and we fly away."* Obviously, Psalm 90:10 is a commentary on the normal life expectancy of mankind. It also reveals that we are not simply asleep, as some believe, but our spirits, those of us who are born again, "fly away" to be with the Lord as Paul described in Philippians 1 and 2 Corinthians 5.

Philippians 1:21-23

²¹For me, to live is Christ, and to die is gain. ²²But if I live on in the flesh, this will mean fruit from my labor; yet what I shall choose I cannot tell. ²³For I am hard-pressed between the two, having a desire to **depart and be with Christ***, which is far better.*

2 Corinthians 5:1-8

¹ For we know that if our earthly house, this tent, is destroyed, we have a building from God, a house not made with hands, eternal in the heavens. ² For in this we groan, earnestly desiring to be clothed with our habitation which is from heaven, ³ if indeed, having been clothed, we shall not be found naked. ⁴ For we who are in this tent groan, being burdened, not because we want to be unclothed, but further clothed, that mortality may be swallowed up by life. ⁵ Now He who has prepared us for this very thing is God, who also has given us the Spirit as a guarantee.

⁶ So we are always confident, knowing that while we are at home in the body we are absent from the Lord. ⁷ For we walk by faith, not by sight. ⁸ We are confident, yes, well pleased rather **to be absent from the body and to be present with the Lord.***

How can we be present with the Lord after death if we do not depart our bodies and "fly away" to be with the Lord? There are many more scriptures that further reveal this mystery, such as Genesis 35:18, Matthew 22:32, Mark 12:27, Luke 16:19-31, 2 Timothy 4:6, and 2 Peter 1:13, to name a few. Additionally, though, is there more to Psalm 90:10 than meets the eye? Is there perhaps also a prophetic aspect to this "flying away" that happens at 80 years? I firmly believe, based on encoded biblical patterns within scripture, the fig tree generation prophecy, as well as the encrypted timeline revelation in the Psalms, that it will be at Israel's 80ᵗʰ year in 2028 that Israel will cease to exist as a sovereign, independent, and unified nation, and will have to flee from Judea to escape certain annihilation by the Antichrist.

Is Psalm 90:10 another confirmation that this will happen in Israel's 80th year? Psalm 90 connects "flying away" to 80 years. Revelation 12:14 says that Israel, who is symbolized by a woman, was given two wings of a great eagle so that she could "fly" into the wilderness to escape. In Matthew 24:20, Jesus says to pray that your "flight" may not be in the winter or on the Sabbath. Daniel 9:27 states that in the middle of the 7-year tribulation period, the Antichrist will end the sacrificial system at the Temple and then says on the "wing" of abomination shall be one who makes desolate. This is certainly a bit cryptic, but in all of these verses related to the middle of the tribulation, we can see a recurring theme and symbolism of "flight," just as in Psalm 90:10. So, the question remains, will this flight happen in Israel's 80th year in 2028? I believe that as we have put all of these puzzle pieces together, the picture has become pretty clear, and the answer is yes!

Answered Prayer

The Lord woke me again this morning at 5 AM and had me tune my ear to the Bible as it was read on the tablet I keep by my bedside. As I have previously mentioned, I keep the Bible playing all night long, and He has routinely awakened me and tuned my ear just before something very important is said, which answers specific questions that I was praying about before going to bed. I believe that it is important to reemphasize that He always wakes me up seconds **before** the scripture that answers the question is spoken! Furthermore, when He wakes me up and tunes my ear to His word, I am completely awake in a split second. Normally, when I wake up in the middle of the night, I'm super groggy, and it takes a few minutes before I have my first lucid thought and figure out where I am. It is clear to me that it hasn't simply been my subconscious hearing the answer and waking me up. First of all, because He wakes me up before the answer is spoken, and secondly, because I'm fully awake in an instant and tuned-in to what's being said as if my life depends on it. I have chuckled many times during the night as I have whispered, "You did it again Lord!"

This morning, He answered three questions, but I'm only going to cover one of them here that pertains to this chapter. Actually, I thought I was finished with this section regarding the importance of 80 years as it pertains to Israel's rebirth and the escape of the remnant of Israel. However, last night, the audio Bible that I have set to play at random was in the Book of Acts, speaking Stephen's Sermon to the Council and High Priest. Stephen explained that Moses was 40 years old when he visited the Israelites in Egypt and struck down the Egyptian. Stephen pointed out that it was 40 years later when the Lord spoke to Moses through the burning bush and instructed him to go back to Egypt and bring the Children of Israel out. This is New Testament confirmation of what we know from Exodus 7. Moses was 80 years old when he spoke to Pharaoh and led the Israelites on their flight from Egypt. Can you see the pattern here? Moses led the Children of Israel out when he was 80 years old. Israel will be 80 years old in 2028. Psalm 90:10 says that at 80 years, we "fly away!" Guess who wrote Psalm 90? Moses!

Verses 2 - 4
*2 When you eat the labor of your hands, You shall be happy, and it shall be well with you. 3 Your wife shall be like a fruitful vine In the very heart of your house, Your sons (Hebrew - banim, sons, noun masculine) like **olive plants** all around your table. 4 Behold, thus shall the man be blessed who fears the LORD.*

I have struggled for days studying and trying to decode verses 2 - 4 of Psalm 128 in light of the timeline revelation. I have been in prayer asking for the Lord to grant me wisdom and understanding of these three verses, but unlike the many times past when He revealed specific answers to me in different inexplicable ways, this time, I believe that He wants some of it to remain sealed to be revealed at its time of fulfillment. However, I do believe that verses 2 - 4 are not only true in a general sense for any generation, but they are indeed also prophetic for Israel in 2028.

There are certainly several keywords and phrases throughout these 3 verses that I would expect to see in a prophecy pertaining to the midpoint of the tribulation period. The problem is that they are used in a very cryptic way, and therefore, the full meaning has been concealed for now. Even though I believe that a full understanding of the meaning of these verses is sealed until their fulfillment, other prophetic scriptures with the same, or similar keywords, phrases, and imagery, in both the Old and the New testaments, give us plenty of connections to gain at least a basic understanding of their place in 2028, at the commencement of the "Great Tribulation."

Starting with verse 2, let's see if we can decode some of what God has encrypted.

Verse 2
² When you eat the labor of your hands, You shall be happy, and it shall be well with you.

Besides the fact that verse 2 offers great wisdom to any generation, I have a sense that there is more to it than that, prophetically speaking. Hard work and providing for one's family are essential and create a sense of happiness, well-being, and accomplishment. However, what stands out to me in this verse is that it is specifically speaking of agricultural labor. In the context of this verse fitting into the middle of the tribulation period, it makes me wonder if it isn't in preparation for hardship and famine. In 2028, according to the timeline revelation in the Psalms, the Great Tribulation will begin, and only those in Israel who are obedient to the Lord will be provided for. Those who do not walk with the Lord will be destroyed.

Isaiah 1:19-20
¹⁹ If you are willing and obedient, you shall eat the good of the land; ²⁰ But if you refuse and rebel, you shall be devoured by the sword"; for the mouth of the LORD has spoken.

Verse 3

*³ Your wife shall be like a fruitful vine In the very heart
of your house, your sons (Hebrew - banim, sons, noun
masculine) like olive plants all around your table.*

From an understanding of Revelation 12 and other prophetic
scriptures, I am not surprised to read about a wife in verse 3, who
typically symbolizes Israel. This wife is compared to a vine and is
specifically a "fruitful vine." It is not a stretch to equate this fruitful vine
to the remnant of Israel who will be saved, as we know from Zechariah
13, Matthew 24, Romans 11, and Revelation 12. Remember that Israel
is the vine that was removed from Egypt and planted in their own land
according to Psalm 80, which amazingly and divinely also corresponds,
and is a second witness to the timeframe of 2028, as we will see in the
coming chapters. I believe that the vine symbolism in the middle of
Psalm 128, and throughout Psalm 80 is a prophetic connection point,
sort of like a mile marker in the timeline revelation, and the "fruitful
vine" represents the 1/3 of Israel who will be saved and sheltered by God
as they flee from certain destruction when they see the abomination of
desolation at the temple spoken of by Jesus and Daniel.

It gets even better. Our English translations render verse 3 to say
that this wife, who is a fruitful vine, is *"in the very heart of your house,"* or
"within your house," or even *"by the sides of your house."* This placement
of the fruitful wife in the heart or middle of the house, makes sense
in a general way; however, it doesn't make sense in a prophetic way at
the midpoint of the tribulation unless you really stretch it to mean in
the middle of the tribulation, but then what does the physical "house"
represent? So, as usual, I decided to study the original Hebrew word that
our translators mostly translated to signify the "middle." It turns out
that the original Hebrew word is "yerekah," which more often has the
meaning of "remote or remotest parts or locations" as well as "extreme
rear" and "recesses." How perfect is that!

Remember that Jesus gave specific instructions in Matthew 24
for the believing Jews to flee to the mountains when they saw the
abomination of desolation standing in the holy place. It will only be the

Messianic Jews, the ones who believe in Jesus, who flee because they will know and understand Jesus' words in Matthew 24.

Matthew 24:16
Then let those who are in Judea flee to the mountains.

It only makes sense that the mountains that they would escape to would certainly have to be remote. They will have to hide in the recesses, or clefts, of the mountains as they are being pursued. However, we know from Revelation 12 that they will be protected.

I cannot help but wonder if Song of Solomon chapter 2 is prophetic of this same event. It is full of some of the same keywords and phrases that we have been discussing, and rich with similar imagery such as the fig tree putting forth her figs, vines fruitful with tender grapes, coming away, cliffs, clefts, and it's spoken from the perspective of an adored Shulamite lover, which is non-coincidentally Hebrew for a "woman from Jerusalem!" It is important to point out that most everything at this point in the tribulation will center around Jerusalem, and Jesus specifically said in Matthew 24, as He was sitting on the Mt. of Olives overlooking Jerusalem, that those in Judea, which is where Jerusalem is located, should flee when they see the abomination of desolation standing in the holy place. The holy place is the newly rebuilt temple, which will be in... you guessed it, Jerusalem!

Song of Solomon 2:10-14
¹⁰My beloved spoke, and said to me: "rise up, my love, my fair one, and come away. ¹¹For lo, the winter is past, the rain is over and gone. ¹²The flowers appear on the earth; the time of singing has come, and the voice of the turtledove is heard in our land. ¹³The fig tree puts forth her green figs, and the vines with the tender grapes give a good smell. Rise up, my love, my fair one, and come away!
¹⁴"O my dove, in the clefts of the rock, in the secret places of the cliff, let me see your face, let me hear your voice; for your voice is sweet, and your face is lovely."

There are so many relevant and prophetic images that I would like to discuss in these passages, but time is short, so I'm only going to touch on a few of them and allow you to do a little digging on your own. In the context of the middle of the tribulation period, when the remnant of Israel will have to flee to the mountains, I can see how Song of Solomon 2 is not only prophetic, but also instructional. The remnant of Israel, who is portrayed as the Shulamite woman, is being called by her Beloved to rise up and come away where she longs to see her Beloved's face and hear His voice in the clefts of the rock, and in the secret places of the cliff.

This imagery reminds me of Moses being placed in the cleft of the rock by the Lord in Exodus 33:12-23 when the Lord promises that His presence will go with Israel and that He will give them rest. In the same way, I believe that the Lord's presence will be with the remnant, and only He will give them rest as He provides for, and protects them. Notice also that in verse 14, the lover of the Shulamite woman is called "my dove" as she calls out to see His face, just as Moses wanted to see His glory, but was specifically told by the Lord that he couldn't see His face. Of course, we know that the dove represents the Holy Spirit, which descended upon Jesus as witnessed by all 4 of the Gospels, and that the Holy Spirit is the "helper," a "teacher," and a "guide" as Jesus described Him in John's Gospel chapters 14 and 16.

There are many similarities between Israel's Exodus flight from Egypt being pursued by Pharaoh and his army, and the remnant of Israel's future flight from Jerusalem, and the surrounding areas while being pursued by Satan, possibly in the embodiment of the Antichrist and his armies. Revelation 12 tells us that *the serpent spewed water out of his mouth like a flood after the woman.* We have already established that typically a flood symbolizes a huge, overwhelming army; however, in a time when the world is able to witness a multitude of supernatural events, it might just be that this is telling of an actual flood of water. Only time will tell. What we do know is that the woman will escape due to the earth's opening, possibly from an earthquake, which will consume the literal flood or army. From that time, the remnant will be protected and cared for over a period of 3.5 years until the Lord's return, which will be sometime between 2031 and 2032, according to the encrypted timeline revelation in the Psalms.

Revelation 12:13-16

[13] Now when the dragon saw that he had been cast to the earth, he persecuted the woman who gave birth to the male Child.[14] But the woman was given two wings of a great eagle, that she might fly into the wilderness to her place, where she is nourished for a time and times and half a time, from the presence of the serpent. [15] So the serpent spewed water out of his mouth like a flood after the woman, that he might cause her to be carried away by the flood. [16] But the earth helped the woman, and the earth opened its mouth and swallowed up the flood which the dragon had spewed out of his mouth.

In addition to all of the interconnected imagery and prophetic patterns between Psalm 128:2-4 and Song of Solomon 2:8-14, the Exodus Story, Revelation 12, and Matthew 24, I believe that the timeline revelation finally shines a light and gives context to many of the debated old testament prophesies found in Isaiah, as well as several other books of the Old and New Testaments. Unfortunately, time is short, and I am not able to research, interconnect, and write about all of them in detail at this time. However, I would like to list several historically misunderstood and debated prophetic scriptures that may now finally be understood relative to the escape of the remnant. A prophetic understanding of these scriptures may become very helpful to those in Judea at the time of the escape.

Here are some of the interconnected scriptures to research and study: Psalm 55, Isaiah 1, Isaiah 3, Isaiah 5:1-7, Isaiah 7:18-25, Isaiah 28, Isaiah 35, Isaiah 61 - 66, Jeremiah 49, Romans 9:27-28, and Romans 11

Escape of the Remnant Summarized

I would like to offer my understanding through a relatively brief summary of the combination of these prophetic scriptures. Hopefully, this will shine some light on this epic mid-tribulation event, and offer some guidance for the remnant in the future. Hopefully, this summary can help to uncover the "who, what, when, and where" of the escape of the remnant.

Who will be part of the Escape of the Remnant?

This is both an easy question and a difficult question. According to Paul's teaching in Romans 11 "all" of Israel will be saved/delivered. That sounds simple enough!

Romans 11:26-27
26 And so all Israel will be saved (delivered), as it is written: "The Deliverer will come out of Zion, and He will turn away ungodliness from Jacob; 27 For this is My covenant with them, when I take away their sins."

Unfortunately, it is more complicated than that. The question is, who "all" will be left of the Israelites after the great tribulation? Remember that they have been regathered back to Israel, under the leadership and deception of the false messiah, like lambs to the slaughter. At least 2/3rds of Israel will be deceived into believing that they have entered into the Messianic Age, which they have been awaiting for thousands of years. The re-gathering of Israel by the false messiah has been completed for the sole purpose of finally destroying all of Israel so that Jesus, the true Messiah, cannot return. Prophetically, a remnant must remain at the end of the Great Tribulation so that they can fulfill prophecy by calling out, "Blessed is He who comes in the name of the Lord!"

The physical destruction of God's chosen people coupled with genetically altering their DNA by "mingling" their genes with that of Nephilim (Daniel 2), probably through the "mark of the beast," which may be some sort of vaccine or biometrics, thereby making them irredeemable, is the serpent's only winning strategy. That also explains why once a person takes the "mark of the beast," they are no longer able to be saved. The warning is to not, under any circumstances, take the mark, no matter what the consequences are.

The 1/3 of Israel that will escape and be saved will at least eventually believe in, and call on the one true Messiah, Jesus. They will not be tainted by the "mark of the beast," and they will be guided by the Holy Spirit. All of those who have heeded the warning of Matthew 24, and fled to the mountains will be saved when Jesus, the Deliverer, comes out of Zion.

> **Isaiah 4:2**
> *² In that day the Branch of the LORD shall be beautiful and glorious; and the fruit of the earth shall be excellent and appealing for those of Israel who have **escaped**.*

> **Joel 2:32**
> *And it shall come to pass that whoever calls on the name of the LORD shall be saved. For in Mount Zion and in Jerusalem there shall be **deliverance**, as the LORD has said, among the **remnant** whom the LORD calls.*

What is the Escape of the Remnant?

The escape of the remnant is the flight of 1/3 of Israel out of Jerusalem and Judea into a place in the wilderness mountains that has been prepared for her. It is necessary for God to preserve a portion of His chosen people (Israel) in order to complete the prophecies, and bring them into the Millennial Kingdom.

Romans 11:4-5

⁴ But what does the divine response say to him? "I have reserved for Myself seven thousand men who have not bowed the knee to Baal." ⁵ Even so then, at this present time there is a remnant according to the election of grace.

Where is the Escape of the Remnant?

The escape of the remnant happens in Israel. Many Christians who at least lean toward replacement theology, where the Church has replaced Israel, look at the scriptures pertaining to this escape as if it pertains solely to the Church. Yes, I would say that the tribulation saints should be aware of this event and realize that extreme persecution is also coming after them. There will certainly be a time to flee for the Tribulation Saints from wherever they are. In fact, Revelation 18 proclaims that God's people should "come out of her," meaning Babylon, but that is not what is prophesied in Matthew 24 or in Revelation 12 until verse 17. So, primarily, these scriptures specifically speak of Jews living in Israel, specifically the area known as Judea, and not the Gentile world.

All we know for sure from scripture is that the remnant will flee from Judea and the Jerusalem area, and into the wilderness mountains. Some say they will go to Petra, Jordan, and that is certainly a possibility. However, we know that Israel will never leave their land again, according to Amos 9.

Amos 9:15

¹⁵I will plant them in their land, and no longer shall they be pulled up From the land I have given them," Says the Lord your God.

One could argue that parts of what we today call Jordan were part of the land that God originally gave to Israel, but Petra is located in an area of Jordan that was once Edom. Edom was one of Israel's enemies, and the Edomites were descendants of Esau. Their land was never part of the land that was given by God to any of the tribes of Israel. Judah was to the west and partially to the southwest of the Dead Sea, whereas Edom was to the south and southeast of the Dead Sea. The area south of the Dead Sea is the dividing line between Judah and Edom, and is called the Arabah, which is part of what is called the wilderness and the Negev.

I believe that Isaiah 35 is like a road map for the escape of the remnant in 2028. It not only describes where they will go, but it also illustrates how God will take care of them while they are there. For this reason, I have provided Isaiah 35 in its entirety. Couple this chapter with Isaiah 7:21-22, and the question of how the Lord will provide for and protect the Remnant during their flight and relocation, becomes much clearer.

Isaiah 7:21-22

[21] It shall be in that day that a man will keep alive a young cow and two sheep; [22] so it shall be, from the abundance of milk they give, that he will eat curds; for curds and honey everyone will eat who is left in the land.

I believe from Isaiah 7 and other chapters that the escaped remnant will live in commune, similar to what we read about in the Book of Acts. No one will lack anything, and God will multiply what they have. There will also be an outpouring of the Holy Spirit and healing for the weak and sick.

Isaiah 35:1-10

[1] The wilderness and the wasteland (desert) shall be glad for them, and the desert (Arabah) shall rejoice and blossom as the rose; [2] It shall blossom abundantly and rejoice, Even with joy and singing. The glory of Lebanon shall be given to it, The excellence of Carmel and Sharon. They shall see the glory of the LORD, The excellency of our God.

[3] Strengthen the weak hands, And make firm the feeble knees. [4] Say to those who are fearful-hearted, "Be strong,

do not fear! Behold, your God will come with vengeance, With the recompense of God; He will come and save you."

⁵ Then the eyes of the blind shall be opened, And the ears of the deaf shall be unstopped. ⁶ Then the lame shall leap like a deer, And the tongue of the dumb sing. For waters shall burst forth in the wilderness, And streams in the desert. ⁷ The parched ground shall become a pool, And the thirsty land springs of water; In the habitation of jackals, where each lay, There shall be grass with reeds and rushes.

⁸ A highway shall be there, and a road, And it shall be called the Highway of Holiness. The unclean shall not pass over it, But it shall be for others. Whoever walks the road, although a fool, shall not go astray. ⁹ No lion shall be there, Nor shall any ravenous beast go up on it; It shall not be found there. But the redeemed shall walk there, ¹⁰ and the ransomed of the LORD shall return, and come to Zion with singing, with everlasting joy on their heads. They shall obtain joy and gladness, and sorrow and sighing shall flee away.

What Happens to Gentile Christians

Unfortunately, the Gentile Christians, whom we call the "Tribulation Saints," are not spared in Revelation 12. After the serpent realizes that he cannot wage war against the protected remnant of Israel, he will then turn his attention to destroy her offspring, which according to verse 17, are the Christian Tribulation Saints who are keeping the commandments of God and the testimony of Jesus. So, both Jews and Gentiles should be awake and watching in 2028 because great persecution is coming.

Revelation 12:17
¹⁷ And the dragon was enraged with the woman, and he went to make war with the rest of her offspring, who keep

the commandments of God and have the testimony of Jesus Christ.

When is the Escape of the Remnant?

According to the encrypted timeline revelation in the Psalms, the Escape will happen sometime in 2028. According to Daniel 7:25, Daniel 9:27, and Revelation 12, coupled with Matthew 24:15-16, this event happens at the midway point of the tribulation since the remnant will be protected for 3 and a half years. I believe that the Word of God also gave us some very important clues to the time of year that this event will take place. First, according to Song of Solomon 2:10-14, it is indicated that the Shulamite lover is called to rise up and come away specifically in the Spring time. It is made quite clear in verse 11 that the "winter has passed" and then again in verse 12, we are told that it is in the time when "flowers appear on earth" and when "the voice of the turtledove is heard in our land." It just so happens that turtledoves are migratory and return to Israel, which is part of their breeding grounds, in the springtime. The imagery of the turtledove is also interesting since they are monogamous and mate for life. Consider how many times in scripture that sinful Israel is compared to a harlot, and how God has called them to be faithfully married to Him only. I believe that this symbolism once again helps to identify the believing remnant of Israel, separate from those who have rejected Jesus the Messiah.

Jesus also said in Matthew 24:20, *"20 And pray that your flight may not be in winter or on the Sabbath."* I believe that this prayer will be answered by our merciful Lord, and it will occur after the winter. That would place the escape, which we know will happen in the middle of the tribulation near Passover, which is a time that prophetically has its merits, as well as precedent, as I will discuss further shortly.

Psalm 55:4-8
4 My heart is severely pained within me, and the terrors of death have fallen upon me. 5 Fearfulness and trembling

*have come upon me, and horror has overwhelmed me. ⁶
So I said, "Oh, that I had **wings like a dove**! I would
fly away and be at rest. ⁷ Indeed, I would wander far off,
and remain in the wilderness. Selah ⁸ I would hasten
my **escape** from the windy storm and tempest."*

Understanding that a better translation from Hebrew to English
of Psalm 128 verse 3 should say, *"Your wife shall be like a fruitful
vine in the [remotest parts or locations] of your house [house of Israel],"*
finally gives context to Isaiah 5:1-7 and 7:18-25 and possibly many other
prophetic scriptures that haven't had a complete fulfillment yet. These
prophetic scriptures describe a time when Israel will be made desolate of
most human inhabitants, agriculture, and economy. However, a small,
pleasant remnant to the Lord will have an abundance to sustain them,
unlike the rest of the land of Israel.

Isaiah 5:1-7

*¹ Now let me sing to my Well-beloved a song of my Beloved
regarding His vineyard: My Well-beloved has a vineyard
On a very fruitful hill. ² He dug it up and cleared out its
stones, and planted it with the choicest vine. He built a
tower in its midst, and also made a winepress in it; So He
expected it to bring forth good grapes, but it brought forth
wild grapes.*

*³ "And now, O inhabitants of Jerusalem and men of
Judah, judge, please, between Me and My vineyard. ⁴
What more could have been done to My vineyard that I
have not done in it? Why then, when I expected it to bring
forth good grapes, did it bring forth wild grapes? ⁵ And
now, please let Me tell you what I will do to My vineyard: I
will take away its hedge, and it shall be burned; and break
down its wall, and it shall be trampled down. ⁶ I will lay
it waste; it shall not be pruned or dug, but there shall come
up briers and thorns. I will also command the clouds
    That they rain no rain on it."*

⁷ For the vineyard of the LORD of hosts is the house of Israel, and the men of Judah are His pleasant plant. He looked for justice, but behold, oppression; For righteousness, but behold, a cry for help.

Isaiah 7:18-25

¹⁸And it shall come to pass in that day that the LORD will whistle for the fly that is in the farthest part of the rivers of Egypt, and for the bee that is in the land of Assyria. ¹⁹ They will come, and all of them will rest in the desolate valleys and in the clefts of the rocks, and on all thorns and in all pastures.

²⁰ In the same day the Lord will shave with a hired razor, with those from beyond the River, with the king of Assyria, the head and the hair of the legs, and will also remove the beard.

²¹ It shall be in that day that a man will keep alive a young cow and two sheep; ²² So it shall be, from the abundance of milk they give, that he will eat curds; for curds and honey everyone will eat who is left in the land.

²³ It shall happen in that day, that wherever there could be a thousand vines worth a thousand shekels of silver, it will be for briers and thorns. ²⁴ With arrows and bows men will come there, because all the land will become briers and thorns.

²⁵ And to any hill which could be dug with the hoe, you will not go there for fear of briers and thorns; but it will become a range for oxen and a place for sheep to roam.

Verse 3 (continued)

...Your sons (Hebrew - banim, sons, noun masculine) like olive plants all around your table.

The second part of verse 3 is still somewhat of a mystery to me since I cannot be certain who these specific "sons" are, who are like olive plants all around the table. The reference to olive plants naturally makes me think of the two olive trees of Zechariah 4, and the two olive trees of Revelation 11. However, the mystery is that it doesn't make sense that these are olive plants, not trees, and that if it is referring to the 2 olive trees, why would they be described as being "all around" the table. I believe these are young men of Israel being described as olive plants, which certainly matches the context of the Psalm.

The table in verse 3 can symbolize several things in the Jewish tradition. It represents family, community, fellowship, provision, abundance, and more. However, in the Messianic Jewish/Christian tradition, a table more often represents the Passover meal that Jesus celebrated with His 12 disciples around the table, known as the Last Supper. That not only brings us back to Passover in the springtime, but could also represent the 12,000 young men from each of 12 tribes of Israel mentioned in Revelation 7 and 14.

Every year at Passover Jewish families around the world set the table to celebrate the Passover Seder with one extra cup of wine. This cup of wine is known as Elijah's Cup, and it remains untouched in the hopes that one day Elijah will come and drink from the cup to usher in the Messianic Age. I believe that the false prophet of Revelation 13 will come and deceive the Jews, posing as their long-awaited "Elijah," and usher in the reign of the Antichrist over Israel and the world for 42 months.

In context, at the heart of the 7-year tribulation period, we Christians expect that the two witnesses spoken of in Revelation 11 (possibly Moses and Elijah or Enoch and Elijah), who have by this time been prophesying for 3 and a half years, will be killed by the beast who ascends out of the bottomless pit. Their bodies will be resurrected after 3 and a half days, and they will then be raptured to heaven.

I realize that none of this is very clear from my viewpoint in January of 2023. However, from the keywords and phrases in Psalm 128:3 and other scriptures, which in the timeline revelation correspond to sometime during 2028, I do fully expect that the escape of the remnant, and the rapture of the 2 witnesses will occur during 2028. I also believe that the 144,000 have a larger role to play in that year as well. However, the details of their witness have not been revealed, and will have to remain a mystery until their appointed time.

I have one more possible explanation to add as a "maybe" to the question of the "table" mentioned in verse 3. In the Negev desert, there are a few mountains that have "table top" features. Could it be that these "sons," "olive plants," will gather around a physical "table" mountain, and that is one more piece of the puzzle that will be completed during 2028/2029?

Verses 5 - 6
*⁵ **The LORD bless you out of Zion**, And may you see the good of Jerusalem All the days of your life. ⁶ Yes, may you see your children's children. Peace be upon Israel!*

Just as I have previously discussed, I believe that this is the year when the believing remnant of Israel will have to flee from Judea and will be supernaturally protected and provided for by God. I also believe that Psalm 128 verse 5, although certainly cryptic, is prophetic of this flight and the promise of blessing, protection, and provision. In general, verses 5 and 6 are a blessing of peace, long life, and the goodness of Jerusalem, which I believe all point to the Millennial Kingdom that is to come. However, what must come first before the Millennial Kingdom is the tribulation period with Israel as the focus, which is why it begins with "The Lord bless you out of Zion."

I believe that the phrase "out of Zion" in this passage means that this is the time when the Jews will have to flee to the hills, possibly to Petra, but as I have already hinted at, possibly to the Negev Desert. As I point out a lot in my prophecy teachings, "prophecy is a pattern." For instance, David fled to the Negev desert when he was being pursued by King Saul, who wanted to kill him as we know from 1 Samuel 27. Jerusalem is certainly part of what was Judea and David was from the line of Judah. As a pattern, it is likely that Jerusalem, just like David, will flee south to the Negev away from the ruler who is seeking to destroy them.

The prophet Obadiah wrote, *"...the exiles from Jerusalem who are in Sepharad will possess the towns of the Negev"* -Obadiah 1:20. No one can say for sure where Sepharad was, or is. Many think that it's Spain; some think it's in Turkey, some Greece, but most agree that the European Sephardic Jews are the ones from Jerusalem being discussed. I think it's interesting that Obadiah points out that specifically, exiles from Jerusalem will possess the towns in the Negev. I realize that Obadiah was probably referring to the return of the exiles, and the demise of Edom, but this could certainly be a prophetic pattern as well. In fact, it could be argued that Obadiah, Isaiah 63, and Jeremiah 49 all speak of the final destruction of Edom, which is still yet to come.

In addition to other biblical evidence and patterns pointing to the Negev as the place of refuge, the religious Zealots also fled to the Negev to escape the Romans after the destruction of the Temple in 70 AD. The Zealots specifically fled to the tabletop-like mountain fortress known as Masada in the Negev desert. This mountain fortress was built by King Herod the Great not only as a fortress, but also as a palace for his own personal retreat. Masada made for a perfect and almost impenetrable fortification for the Zealots, but the Romans eventually breached the outer wall and entered into the fortress to find all of the Zealots dead by their own hands. That leaves the question of what would have happened to them if they had fully trusted God for their protection, and didn't take their lives into their own hands.

Back to verse 5 which says, "*The Lord bless you out of Zion.*" "Out of Zion" in this case can mean both from Zion, but can also literally mean "out of Zion" as in "to come out of Zion." Consider that the Lord isn't in Zion at this time because the third temple is the Antichrist temple, so He's not there... For several reasons, I take Psalm 128:5 to mean that the Lord will bless you (Israel) as you come out of Zion, or in other words, flee from Zion or Jerusalem, which we know will happen from several scriptures, including Revelation 12, as previously discussed.

Revelation 12:13-17
¹³ Now when the dragon saw that he had been cast to the earth, he persecuted the woman who gave birth to the male Child.¹⁴ But the woman was given two wings of a great eagle, **that she might fly into the wilderness to her**

place, where she is nourished for a time and times
and half a time, from the presence of the serpent. ^{15} *So*
the serpent spewed water out of his mouth like a flood after
the woman, that he might cause her to be carried away by
the flood. ^{16} *But the earth helped the woman, and the earth*
opened its mouth and swallowed up the flood which the
dragon had spewed out of his mouth. ^{17} *And the dragon was*
enraged with the woman, and he went to make war with
the rest of her offspring, who keep the commandments of
God and have the testimony of Jesus Christ.

From Matthew 24, in connection with Revelation 12, we know that the children of Israel will flee from Judea, and specifically Jerusalem, since that's where the temple will be located, and the abomination of desolation will be witnessed firsthand. Once you understand God's appointed feast days, or Moedim, and also understand that in temple times, all of the Israeli males were required to make a pilgrimage to Jerusalem 3 times per year at Pesach (Passover), Shavuot (Pentecost), and at Sukkot (Tabernacles), you can start to see a clearer picture of the Antichrist's plan of destruction for Israel. Since there will be a rebuilt temple in 2028, the pilgrimage requirement will once again be in effect, and at least most of the Jews will journey to Jerusalem on those three feasts. If the Antichrist plans to destroy God's chosen people, which as I have already pointed out, is the only way that Satan can be victorious in the end, then it would make sense to corral them into one place like lambs led to the slaughter. After all, this has already happened before, and prophecy is a pattern.

It was at the time of the Passover festival in 70 AD when the Romans besieged Jerusalem, which led to the destruction of the Temple and the death of over one million Jews. Most of those Jews did not live in Jerusalem, but had made their pilgrimage there only to be trapped and eventually killed at the hands of the Roman soldiers. Following this pattern, will it be at Passover in 2028 when the Antichrist will declare that he is God in the newly rebuilt temple and seek to destroy the Jewish pilgrims? Passover 2028 will be on April 10th, and Israel's

80th birthday will be less than a month later on May 1st, according to our Gregorian calendar, or 5 Iyar on the Jewish calendar. This makes sense to me since there are 3 Moedim yet to be fulfilled, and all of them are in the timeframe of 6 months after Passover. That means that if the Great Tribulation starts at Passover, and you add the remaining 3.5 prophesied years to the end of the tribulation, you land at the time of the final unfulfilled feast days.

From the timeline, we can see that the Jews will be re-gathering back to Israel during the first 3.5 years of the 7-year tribulation period. We know that Satan's plan is to gather them in order to destroy them, and that he will succeed in destroying 2/3rds of them, according to Zechariah 13. The remaining 1/3rd will be the remnant which God foreknew and reserved for Himself. He will protect them as they come out of Jerusalem and surrounding areas in Israel during their flight, and will bless them with sanctuary and nourishment during the following three and a half years. God will also test and refine them, according to Zechariah 13 during this time, and all of them will be saved, according to Romans 11.

For further clarification of "out of Zion," let's also look at the wording and meaning in Micah 4, which is also a description of the Millennial Kingdom.

Micah 4:2
*For **out of Zion** the law shall go forth, and the word of the LORD from Jerusalem.*

In Micah the phrase "out of Zion" obviously doesn't mean that it stayed in Zion, but that it came forth from Zion in the same way that the Jews will have to come "out of Zion" when they see the False Messiah standing in the temple.

We've already established that this is the middle point of the tribulation, and the beginning of the "Great Tribulation" as Jesus pointed out. This time also connects with the Fig Tree Generation in that the flight of the Children of Israel and the takeover of the country by the fully revealed Antichrist will coincide with Israel not making it to 81 years old. As I have previously pointed out, that prophetic pattern has been well established throughout history. Essentially, when the Antichrist takes over the country and declares that he is god, and, therefore, is also fully in control as a dictator, Israel will cease to exist as a unified, free, and self-governing state. This has to happen before Israel's 81st birthday, which will come in the spring of 2029, for the biblical prophetic pattern to be fulfilled.

CHAPTER 14

Psalm 129 A Song of Ascents

Year 2029- The Refuge

Of the three "birth pain" patterns found in the 15 Songs of Ascent, Psalm 129 once again corresponds to a year of distress. It establishes that God always protects and preserves a remnant of Israel when they are afflicted by their enemies. It is also a prayer and a petition for God's help to destroy, turn back, and put to shame the attacking forces. How could the first year in refuge for Israel in the Great Tribulation be described any better in just a few verses? Furthermore, historians, nor scholars know if this Psalm necessarily corresponds to any known time period in Israel's history, nor are they certain who penned it, when it was written, or why it's part of the 15 Psalms of Ascent. But God does...

Verses 1-4
¹"Many a time they have afflicted me from my youth," let Israel now say—

² "Many a time they have afflicted me from my youth; yet they have not prevailed against me. ³ The plowers plowed on my back; they made their furrows long."

⁴ The LORD is righteous; He has cut in pieces the cords of the wicked.

I believe that Psalm 129 (year 2029), as well as the next few Psalms, correspond to the 3.5 years of the "Great Tribulation," which will end with the return of our Lord. You will notice that there is a consistent theme of affliction, grief, waiting, and longing until Psalm 132, corresponding to 2032 (spoiler alert), when Jesus establishes His eternal dwelling place in Zion.

According to verses 1 and 2, during 2029, the remnant of Israel will be in a sort of protective custody, or "refuge," shielded and nurtured by God. They will say, "many a time, they have afflicted me from my youth." After witnessing God's supernatural protection and guidance, they will realize that the many enemies of Israel have never prevailed against them, and never will! Even though in 2028 and 2029, it will seem that Israel will be annihilated, God will once and for all time protect and shelter a remnant for Himself (Romans 11). No matter what the scheme of the Devil is in his effort to destroy the remnant of God's people, they can rest assured that it will not succeed.

Proverbs 19:21
21 Many are the plans in a person's heart, but it is the LORD's purpose (plan) that prevails.

As described in verse 2 of Psalm 129, we know that at this time, prophetically, Israel will still be in their youth. Keep in mind that Israel only became a nation-state again in 1948, so as nations go, they are still a very young nation. The Jewish people have been the target of evil, working toward their destruction for thousands of years. The Pogroms in Russia in the late 19th and early 20th century, and then the Holocaust at the hands of the Nazi regime, were only the latest of many large-scale efforts throughout history to exterminate the Jewish people. Those efforts by the serpent and his tools have only served to reduce their numbers, but God's children still live!

Israel has also been threatened and attacked by its many Muslim neighbors since their rebirth in 1948. Since then, Israel has been called a "cancerous tumor" that should be removed from the region, a "parasite," an "illegal state," an "occupier," and has been threatened to be wiped off the map by Iran and other Muslim nations. Additionally, the U.N. has routinely voted against tiny Israel in favor of their much larger neighbors for decades, and many nations, including the US, have consistently tried to push Israel to divide their land in the hopes of peace. Israel has truly become a stumbling block to the nations even though they are the smallest country in the Middle East with a land mass of about the same size as New Jersey. No matter what nation comes against Israel and tries to remove them, God prophesied that their enemies will not prevail, and Israel will never again be removed from their land.

Amos 9:15
¹⁵I will plant them in their land, and no longer shall they be pulled up from the land I have given them," says the LORD your God.

Satan's final knockout blow will start in 2028 to totally annihilate God's chosen people after deceptively returning them back to their land. As previously stated, it's his only winning strategy. However, we see Israel proclaiming in verse 2 of Psalm 129 that *"They have not prevailed against me."* Just as prophesied, God will step in and save the remnant from certain destruction, and He will continue to supernaturally shelter them in 2029. Just as so many of the Psalms declare, God is truly their refuge!

Verses 3-4
³ The plowers plowed on my back; They made their furrows long."⁴ The LORD is righteous; He has cut in pieces the cords of the wicked.

The imagery of plowers plowing on Israel's back, and making their furrows long is reminiscent of the prophecy of Micah 3, which was fulfilled by the Roman Empire between 70 AD and 135 AD when they plowed under not only the Temple, but also the city itself. In the Jewish oral tradition, it is believed that the Romans literally took a plow to the city and the ruins of the temple after their destruction.

Micah 3:12

*¹²Therefore because of you Zion shall be plowed like a field,
Jerusalem shall become heaps of ruins, and the mountain
of the temple like the bare hills of the forest.*

Verse 3 can also be seen as symbolic of how Jesus was scourged
for our transgressions before being nailed to the cross. He has already
suffered this disgrace and mistreatment in place of His remnant people.

In the context of verse 3, plowing expresses thorough and deep
destruction in an effort to plant or start something new. Satan certainly
has a plan to destroy Israel, cancel the prophecies of the Messiah, and
establish his wicked kingdom over the world. However, his plan cannot,
and will not prevail. Jesus has already won this victory, and the remnant
of Israel will be sheltered and preserved to enter into the Millennial
Kingdom.

Verses 3 and 4 depict two very distinct but different scenes. Verse
3 describes the awfully real decimation of the land of Israel. The
"plowing" probably indicates a military conquest and the destruction
of the land of Israel, similar to the destruction of Israel and Jerusalem
by the Romans in the First and Second Centuries. As previously stated,
the temple was literally plowed under by Rome when it was destroyed.
This total destruction of the temple in 70 AD was also prophesied by
Jesus, who said, *"not one stone shall be left here upon another, that shall
not be thrown down."* In opposition to Verse 3, verse 4 purports that the
enemy's efforts have failed, and that the righteous Lord has cut "the
cords of the wicked." Notice that He not only cut the cords, but He cut
them in pieces. This represents the slave-like control that the "wicked"
had over God's people, which has now been completely cast off of the
remnant. This means that the "beast system" has no control over them
and cannot touch them. God is their rock, fortress, deliverer, refuge,
shield, salvation, and stronghold. You can't get better than that!

Psalm 18:1-2

*I love you, Lord, my strength. The Lord is my rock, my
fortress and my deliverer; my God is my rock, in whom I*

take refuge, my shield and the horn of my salvation, my stronghold.

Verses 5-8
⁵ Let all those who hate Zion be put to shame and turned back. ⁶ Let them be as the grass on the housetops, which withers before it grows up, ⁷ With which the reaper does not fill his hand, nor he who binds sheaves, his arms. ⁸ Neither let those who pass by them say, "The blessing of the LORD be upon you; we bless you in the name of the LORD!"

Verse 5 is a petition to the Lord to put all of those who are coming against Israel and Jerusalem into a shameful retreat. This verse interplays with Isaiah 28, Isaiah 63, Jeremiah 49, and Obadiah 1, which are all rich in descriptions of this very time in future history, and opens the door to a greater understanding, as well as a lot more questions.

Isaiah 28:5-6
⁵In that day the LORD of hosts will be for a crown of glory and a diadem of beauty to the remnant of His people, ⁶ For a spirit of justice to him who sits in judgment, and for strength to those who turn back the battle at the gate.

In Isaiah 28 we see how beautiful the Lord will be to the remnant of His people. We also see His strength being given to those who turn back the forces coming against Zion. What is confusing is that it mentions "those" who turn back the battle at the gate. Is the Lord of Hosts giving His strength to the "hosts," meaning angelic powers, who will turn back the battle at the gate, or is His power given to the remnant for this purpose? The gate typically indicates a city gate, but it could be a metaphorical gateway into a valley as well. It could also possibly be a dimensional gate. Keep in mind that the Bible is a book of the supernatural. Just because we haven't seen a lot of what we would today call supernatural events during the Church Age doesn't mean that they aren't going to be prevalent during the tribulation. In fact, if you read the prophesies of the book of Revelation, and take what John saw at face value, you have to conclude that many miraculous and supernatural events are on the near horizon. Add to that what Paul wrote in 2 Thessalonians 2, and you should have a pretty clear understanding that the supernatural will not be as unusual during the tribulation as it is during these last days of the Church Age.

2 Thessalonians 2:9-11
[9]The coming of the lawless one is according to the working of Satan, with all power, signs, and lying wonders, [10]and with all unrighteous deception among those who perish, because they did not receive the love of the truth, that they might be saved. [11]And for this reason God will send them strong delusion, that they should believe the lie,"

So, those who are alive during the tribulation can expect plenty of deception along with visible, seemingly miraculous signs and wonders from the "lawless one" (note: the Book of Enoch calls Nephilim the "Lawless Ones"). Having said that, what exactly those signs and lying wonders are, we do not know. They will be understood by those who have the love of the truth and are being saved. Who is the Truth? Jesus is the truth (John 14:6). As a reminder, it will only be those Jews who know and take heed of Matthew 24:15-16 who will understand when they see the "abomination of desolation" that they must flee to the mountains. It will only be those Christian, Messianic Jews who would even know of these verses in the New Testament. Jews who have rejected Jesus as their Messiah and who only study the Torah will have no knowledge of the events that they are witnessing and will be deceived into following the guidance of their false Messiah until it's too late.

In speaking of supernatural signs and wonders, remember that according to Paul in Ephesians 6:12, *"we do not wrestle against flesh and blood, but against principalities, against powers, against the rulers of the darkness of this age, against spiritual hosts of wickedness in the heavenly places."* We have been at war with these powers and rulers of darkness "of this age." This age is the Church Age. During this age, these "hosts of wickedness" have been defined as being "spiritual" and in "heavenly places." During the tribulation, however, these rulers of darkness may not always be hidden from view any longer. They may inhabit our dimension according to Revelation chapter 9 as well as other prophesies. The point is that God has a battle plan, and He will not reveal so much of His plan that the enemy can fully understand it, and then defend against it.

So, in the battle plan relevant to the refuge of the remnant of Israel, what we know from Revelation 12, together with the timeline revelation in the Psalms, is that in 2028, the serpent will try to destroy Israel with something "like" a flood, which probably represents an invading army based on known prophetic symbolism. We see in the 16th verse that the remnant will be protected by the earth, which will open and swallow the oncoming flood or army.

Revelation 12:15-16

15 So the serpent spewed water out of his mouth like a flood after the woman, that he might cause her to be carried away by the flood. 16 But the earth helped the woman, and the earth opened its mouth and swallowed up the flood which the dragon had spewed out of his mouth.

Verses 5-8

5 Let all those who hate Zion be put to shame and turned back. 6 Let them be as the grass on the housetops, which withers before it grows up, 7 With which the reaper does not fill his hand, nor he who binds sheaves, his arms. 8 Neither let those who pass by them say, "The blessing of the LORD be upon you; we bless you in the name of the LORD!"

We have covered verse 5 as a petition to the Lord to turn back those coming against Israel. Verses 6 - 7 go on to call for their total destruction. According to the typology, there will be virtually nothing left of them.

I have the inclination to point out a few interconnecting words, phrases, and agricultural references in these passages because I believe there is a lot more revealed here than what I can decipher at this time.

Verse 6 mentions "housetops," as did Jesus in Matthew 24:17 in speaking of the escape of the remnant. Verse 6 also mentions grass that has withered before it has grown up. Call me crazy, but I believe that this typology is tied to several other prophesies related to this same time period specifically the destruction of Esau and his land of Edom. I don't want to get too far off into the weeds on this possibility, but I have to point out that in Obadiah 1, we see Esau as the stubble that will be burned up in judgment for their mistreatment of Israel. In Isaiah 34, we also see Edom burned up in retribution of Zion, In Isaiah 63, we see Jesus having trampled Edom as in the winepress of God's wrath out of vengeance for His redeemed.

Obadiah 1:17-18
¹⁷ "But on Mount Zion there shall be deliverance, and there shall be holiness; the house of Jacob shall possess their possessions. ¹⁸ The house of Jacob shall be a fire, and the house of Joseph a flame; but the house of Esau shall be stubble; they shall kindle them and devour them, and no survivor shall remain of the house of Esau," for the LORD has spoken.

All of this can be a bit confusing since there isn't a land called Edom any longer, and there isn't a people group who are called Edomites. Most Jews associate Edom with Christianity since there was an intermarrying between descendants of King Herod, who was an Edomite, and the Roman Emperors. For the most part they do not understand that Bible-believing Christianity and Romans are not the same. So, the question is, who is God referring to as Edom, or the house of Esau in many of the last days prophesies who will be destroyed? Will it be an enemy of the remnant of Israel to the southeast in physical Edom, but is today part of Jordan? Or does it refer to a revised Roman Empire, which would match Daniel 9:26? Or is Esau/Edom symbolic of all of Israel's enemies? This mystery has not yet been revealed.

The binding of sheaves also stands out to me in verse 7. There are two harvest seasons in Israel when sheaves are bound. The first is for the barley harvest, which starts around the Feast of First Fruits, usually in March or April, and ends in April or May. The second harvest season when sheaves are bound is the wheat harvest, which usually begins in May or June and ends in June or July. That coincides with Shavuot or Pentecost, as we call it. Backing up for a moment, verse 3 of Psalm 129 mentioned "plowing." Plowing occurs in Israel around September to October, which happens to coincide with the Feast of Trumpets. In like manner, Isaiah 28 also makes reference to plowing, planting wheat in rows, and barley in the appointed place. What does all of that mean? Well, I don't know, but I know that God doesn't waste any words. My hope is that by pointing these possible clues out, someone will be blessed and will have a greater understanding at the right time.

Just as it seems that there are several seasons represented in Psalm 129, Isaiah 28 also has a reference to time during the escape and refuge of the remnant, as well as some very troubling revelations.

Isaiah 28:17-19
¹⁷ Also I will make justice the measuring line, and righteousness the plummet; the hail will sweep away the refuge of lies, and the waters will overflow the hiding place. ¹⁸ Your covenant with death will be annulled, and your agreement with Sheol will not stand; when the overflowing scourge passes through, then you will be trampled down by it. ¹⁹ As often as it goes out it will take you; for morning by morning it will pass over, and by day and by night; it will be a terror just to understand the report."

We know from Isaiah 28:14-15 who will be swept away, who made a covenant with death, and who will be trampled down by the overflowing scourge when it passes through. As disturbing as it sounds, these are the rulers of the people of Israel and Jerusalem. Have the Jewish people been sold out by "elite" ruling Jews who have made this covenant with death to allow the Jewish citizens to be destroyed? If this is true, then it seems that according to Isaiah 28, it is ultimately these same wicked rulers who are destroyed by this "flood." As mentioned before, it could also be referring to the Edomites mentioned in Obadiah, Isaiah, and Jeremiah.

Isaiah 28 calls it an "overflowing scourge" that passes through daily and then continues to use language that is symbolic of a flood, waves, and tides that will trample them down. "Overflowing scourge" is an interesting phrase. It connects the flood element of Revelation 12 with a type of brutal punishment. A scourge is a type of whip used to inflict torment and suffering, just like the one that was used on Jesus prior to the cross. It seems that all of those "rulers" who sold out their own brothers, as well as the unbelievers, will be scourged and destroyed, leaving the land "desolate" except for the protected remnant. That is why the trigger for this time is called the "abomination that causes desolation." After the abomination at the holy place is witnessed, the land will become desolate through this overflowing scourge.

The last verse of Psalm 129 is verse 8. It puts the proverbial icing on the cake for those who have come against the remnant of Israel, and who have been destroyed. No one will ever say that those who were put to shame, turned back, and destroyed, have the blessing of the Lord. I believe that this connects with Jeremiah 49:17, which details the prophetic destruction of Edom and says, *"Edom also shall be an astonishment; everyone who goes by it will be astonished and will hiss at all its plagues."*

God has put it on my heart to insert Isaiah 65 at the closing of this chapter. May it be a blessing to you in this time.

Isaiah 65
[1]"I was sought by those who did not ask for Me; I was found by those who did not seek Me. I said, 'Here I am, here I am,' to a nation that was not called by My name. [2] I have stretched out My hands all day long to a rebellious people, who walk in a way that is not good, according to their own thoughts; [3] A people who provoke Me to anger continually to My face; who sacrifice in gardens, and burn incense on altars of brick; [4] who sit among the graves, and spend the night in the tombs; who eat swine's flesh, and

*the broth of abominable things is in their vessels; ⁵ who say,
'Keep to yourself, do not come near me, for I am holier than
you!' These are smoke in My nostrils, a fire that burns all
the day.*

*⁶ "Behold, it is written before Me: I will not keep silence,
but will repay—Even repay into their bosom— ⁷ Your
iniquities and the iniquities of your fathers together," Says
the Lord, "Who have burned incense on the mountains
and blasphemed Me on the hills; therefore I will measure
their former work into their bosom." ⁸ Thus says the Lord:
"As the new wine is found in the cluster, and one says, 'Do
not destroy it, for a blessing is in it,' so will I do for My
servants' sake, that I may not destroy them all. ⁹ I will bring
forth descendants from Jacob, and from Judah an heir of
My mountains; My elect shall inherit it, and My servants
shall dwell there.¹⁰ Sharon shall be a fold of flocks, and the
Valley of Achor a place for herds to lie down, for My people
who have sought Me.*

*¹¹ "But you are those who forsake the Lord, who forget
My holy mountain, who prepare a table for Gad, and
who furnish a drink offering for Meni. ¹² Therefore I will
number you for the sword, and you shall all bow down to
the slaughter; because, when I called, you did not answer;
when I spoke, you did not hear, but did evil before My eyes,
and chose that in which I do not delight."*

*¹³ Therefore thus says the Lord God: "Behold, My
servants shall eat, but you shall be hungry; Behold, My
servants shall drink, but you shall be thirsty; behold, My
servants shall rejoice, but you shall be ashamed; ¹⁴ behold,
My servants shall sing for joy of heart, but you shall cry for
sorrow of heart, and wail for grief of spirit. ¹⁵ You shall
leave your name as a curse to My chosen; For the Lord God
will slay you, and call His servants by another name; ¹⁶ So
that he who blesses himself in the earth shall bless himself
in the God of truth; and he who swears in the earth shall*

swear by the God of truth; because the former troubles are forgotten, and because they are hidden from My eyes.

[17] "For behold, I create new heavens and a new earth; and the former shall not be remembered or come to mind. [18] But be glad and rejoice forever in what I create; for behold, I create Jerusalem as a rejoicing, and her people a joy. [19] I will rejoice in Jerusalem, and joy in My people; the voice of weeping shall no longer be heard in her, nor the voice of crying.

[20] "No more shall an infant from there live but a few days, nor an old man who has not fulfilled his days; for the child shall die one hundred years old, but the sinner being one hundred years old shall be accursed. [21] They shall build houses and inhabit them; they shall plant vineyards and eat their fruit. [22] They shall not build and another inhabit; they shall not plant and another eat; for as the days of a tree, so shall be the days of My people, and My elect shall long enjoy the work of their hands. [23] They shall not labor in vain, nor bring forth children for trouble; for they shall be the descendants of the blessed of the Lord, and their offspring with them.

[24] "It shall come to pass that before they call, I will answer; and while they are still speaking, I will hear. [25] The wolf and the lamb shall feed together, the lion shall eat straw like the ox, and dust shall be the serpent's food. They shall not hurt nor destroy in all My holy mountain," says the Lord.

CHAPTER 15

Psalm 130 A Song of Ascents

Year 2030 - Waiting on the Lord's Return

Of the three "birth pain" patterns found in the 15 Songs of Ascent, Psalm 130 is once again a song of hope, trust, and deliverance similar to Psalm 121, 124, and 127. The remnant of Israel has been in a place prepared for them now since 2028 and is waiting on the Lord's return. It seems to me that we need a name that embodies where the remnant is currently, as well as what the place is, but most importantly, Who it is! The best term that I can come up with for this refuge is, well, "refuge." This seems fitting since Psalm 46 might just sum up many of the troubles being experienced by the remnant during their time as they wait upon the Lord.

> **Psalm 46:1-3**
> *God is our refuge and strength, a very present help in trouble. ² Therefore we will not fear, even though the earth be removed, and though the mountains be carried into the midst of the sea; ³ Though its waters roar and be troubled, though the mountains shake with its swelling. Selah*

Obviously, their world has turned upside down since their escape in 2028 to the refuge. Now in 2030 they cry out to the Lord for forgiveness of personal sins as well as the national sins of Israel as they hope in, and wait on, the Lord.

Verses 1-2

¹Out of the depths I have cried to You, O LORD; ² Lord, hear my voice! Let Your ears be attentive to the voice of my supplications.

Even though the remnant of Israel is in a place of refuge, and their protection during their escape to the mountains was by the hand of God, and their survival as well has been filled with many miracles, they are still in despair during the Great Tribulation, so they call out to the Lord from the depths.

The Lord did it again! He woke me up this morning from a deep sleep and tuned my ear at around 5 AM, hearing Paul's words of comfort for those who are in tribulation. I pray that this brings hope and comfort to those in distress during this time of trial.

2 Corinthians 1:3-11

³ Blessed be the God and Father of our Lord Jesus Christ, the Father of mercies and God of all comfort, ⁴ who comforts us in all our tribulation, that we may be able to comfort those who are in any trouble (Greek - thlipsis: tribulation, persecution, affliction, distress), with the comfort with which we ourselves are comforted by God. ⁵ For as the sufferings of Christ abound in us, so our consolation also abounds through Christ. ⁶ Now if we are afflicted, it is for your consolation and salvation, which is effective for enduring the same sufferings which we also suffer. Or if we are comforted, it is for your consolation and salvation. ⁷ And our hope for you is steadfast, because we know that as you are partakers of the sufferings, so also you will partake of the consolation.

⁸ For we do not want you to be ignorant, brethren, of our trouble (tribulation) which came to us in Asia: that we were burdened beyond measure, above strength, so that we despaired even of life. ⁹ Yes, we had the sentence of death in ourselves, that we should not trust in ourselves but in God who raises the dead, ¹⁰ who delivered us from so great a death, and does deliver us; in whom we trust that He will still deliver us, ¹¹ you also helping together in prayer for us, that thanks may be given by many persons on our behalf for the gift granted to us through many.

Out of the Depths

I cannot help but be clued in to the word "depths" in the opening sentence of Psalm 130. As you have probably recognized by now, I focus on the keywords, phrases, numbers, and imagery that I believe God has placed throughout His word to make prophetic connections. The word "depths" really jumps off of the page to me.

Over the years that I have been studying God's end-time prophetic word, I have always had this simplistic image in my mind that the remnant of Israel would be carried off to a place of refuge that had been prepared for them, and they would then live in peace and tranquility while the world was literally burning down around them. I didn't think about the fact that going into the "wilderness" biblically signifies a distinct pattern of testing. I suppose that I didn't pay close attention to the words of the prophet Zechariah, which certainly paints a very different picture.

Zechariah 13:8-9
*⁸ And it shall come to pass in all the land," says the L*ORD*, "that two-thirds in it shall be cut off and die, but one-third shall be left in it: ⁹ **I will bring the one-third through the fire, will refine them as silver is refined, and test them as gold is tested.** They will call on My name, and I will answer them. I will say, 'This is My people'; and each one will say, 'The L*ORD *is my God.'"*

I no longer have that naive view. After all, this is the tribulation, and the time of Jacob's trouble! The Children of Israel in God's refuge are the one-third who are left of Jacob, and this is a time of testing like no other. Perhaps it will be a lot like Israel's 40-year journey through the wilderness in the exodus, only a condensed version? The children of Israel could not enter into the promised land until they were tested for 40 years, which as we know, is the time of biblical probation, trial, and testing. Just as it was during the time of the exodus, according to the prophets Zechariah and Ezekiel, who says that God *"will purge the rebels from among you, and those who transgress against Me,"* the remnant of Israel will be tested in a trial by fire, and only those who are refined will remain. During this time, Israel must have faith and trust in God's protection and provision no matter what, or who comes against them.

The word "depths" in Hebrew in verse 1 of this Psalm is "maamaqqim." According to Strong's concordance, there are 5 instances where this word is used throughout the Bible. In every case, it is specifically in reference to deep water and not deep in the earth. It is used both literally and figuratively, but always in the context of water. Deep water is also very symbolic of God's judgment, just think of the great flood in Noah's time. Obviously, in Psalm 130, the word depth is referring figuratively to a time of trouble or affliction, but could it also be referring to something in the literal sense in 2030?

Are there any water-related judgments coming on the earth during the tribulation? Yes, of course there are!

The Second Trumpet Judgment:

Revelation 8:8-9
[8] Then the second angel sounded: And something like a great mountain burning with fire was thrown into the sea, and a third of the sea became blood. [9] And a third of the living creatures in the sea died, and a third of the ships were destroyed.

The Third Trumpet Judgment

Revelation 8:10-11

[10] Then the third angel sounded: And a great star fell from heaven, burning like a torch, and it fell on a third of the rivers and on the springs of water. [11] The name of the star is Wormwood. A third of the waters became wormwood, and many men died from the water, because it was made bitter.

The Second Bowl Judgment

Revelation 16:3

[3] Then the second angel poured out his bowl on the sea, and it became blood as of a dead man; and every living creature in the sea died.

The Third Bowl Judgment

Revelation 16:4-7

[4] Then the third angel poured out his bowl on the rivers and springs of water, and they became blood. [5] And I heard the angel of the waters saying:

"You are righteous, O Lord, the One who is and who was and who is to be, Because You have judged these things. [6] For they have shed the blood of saints and prophets, and You have given them blood to drink. For it is their just due."

[7] And I heard another from the altar saying, "Even so, Lord God Almighty, true and righteous are Your judgments."

The Sixth Bowl Judgment

Revelation 16:12-16

[12] Then the sixth angel poured out his bowl on the great river Euphrates, and its water was dried up, so that the

way of the kings from the east might be prepared. [13] And I saw three unclean spirits like frogs coming out of the mouth of the dragon, out of the mouth of the beast, and out of the mouth of the false prophet. [14] For they are spirits of demons, performing signs, which go out to the kings of the earth and of the whole world, to gather them to the battle of that great day of God Almighty.

[15] "Behold, I am coming as a thief. Blessed is he who watches, and keeps his garments, lest he walk naked and they see his shame."

[16] And they gathered them together to the place called in Hebrew, Armageddon.

Here's another possibility for this place of refuge. Keep in mind that I am reading the Psalms in the context of time, understanding that they fit as years on God's calendar. However, God has certainly reserved many aspects of the tribulation period for future understanding. All I can do is to study the scriptures using the new revelation of the timeline in years, and connect some of the dots. On some things I am still applying a large dose of speculation, and this is one of them.

As I have previously pointed out, many believe that Israel will flee to Petra, but Petra is not in Israel and has never been part of Israel. They cannot leave Israel according to prophecy. Where did they flee to in the past, which, as we know, could be a prophetic pattern? They fled to the Negev. What body of water is in the Negev? The Dead Sea! Isn't there a prophecy about the Dead Sea coming to life when Israel is restored?

Ezekiel 47:8-12

[8] He said to me, "This water flows toward the eastern region and goes down into the Arabah, where it enters the Dead Sea. When it empties into the sea, the salty water there becomes fresh. [9] Swarms of living creatures will live wherever the river flows. There will be large numbers of fish, because this water flows there and makes the salt water fresh; so where the river flows everything will live.

¹⁰ Fishermen will stand along the shore; from En Gedi to En Eglaim there will be places for spreading nets. The fish will be of many kinds—like the fish of the Mediterranean Sea. ¹¹ But the swamps and marshes will not become fresh; they will be left for salt. ¹² Fruit trees of all kinds will grow on both banks of the river. Their leaves will not wither, nor will their fruit fail. Every month they will bear fruit, because the water from the sanctuary flows to them. Their fruit will serve for food and their leaves for healing."

Notice that the Ezekiel prophecy points out En Gedi and En Eglaim. What place of refuge is located between these two ancient cities? Masada. I cannot ignore the many verses that proclaim in similar fashion *"The name of the LORD is a strong tower; The righteous run to it and are safe"* - Proverbs 18:10, and *"The God of my strength, in whom I will trust; my shield and the horn of my salvation, my stronghold and my refuge; my Savior, You save me from violence"*(2 Samuel 22:3). There are many more verses that carry this same theme of the Lord being a strong tower, a stronghold, and a refuge where the righteous can run to for safety. Yes, this is figurative, but perhaps it's also prophetic of a place of refuge for the righteous remnant of Israel in the tribulation. Also, keep in mind that according to Genesis 24, Isaac, for some unknown reason, was in the Negev when he saw his bride for the first time, which is also cryptically associated with the rapture of the Church. It seems to me that there is a definite prophetic pattern at work here.

Again, I'm only following the patterns in God's word and speculating since there is no way to know exactly where this place of refuge is located that has "been prepared" for the remnant of Israel. I just know that there is no pattern revolving around Petra, but there are many that point to the Negev as a place of safety for God's children. One last note: not only is Petra in what was Edom, and not Israel, but it is also much farther away than the Negev area around the Dead Sea, which would make for a longer and more perilous journey for the fleeing remnant.

Verses 3-4

3 If You, LORD, should mark iniquities, O Lord, who could stand? 4 But there is forgiveness with You, That You may be feared.

After praying and asking the Lord for help with this section, He woke me up in the night again as this scripture began to be read on my nightstand tablet:

1 Kings 8:37-40

37 "When there is famine in the land, pestilence or blight or mildew, locusts or grasshoppers; when their enemy besieges them in the land of their cities; whatever plague or whatever sickness there is; 38 whatever prayer, whatever supplication is made by anyone, or by all Your people Israel, when each one knows the plague of his own heart, and spreads out his hands toward this temple: 39 then hear in heaven Your dwelling place, and forgive, and act, and give to everyone according to all his ways, whose heart You know (for You alone know the hearts of all the sons of men), 40 that they may fear You all the days that they live in the land which You gave to our fathers.

As you can see, there are some keywords and prophetic events foreshadowed in these verses, which were written at the original dedication of King Solomon's temple in Jerusalem. Not only do they match many of the judgments expected during the tribulation period, but other keywords also match our Psalm for the year 2030. Specifically, Psalm 130 and 1 Kings 8 reinforce that the Lord is willing to forgive anyone, and even all of Israel, if they will only confess their sins and spread out their hands toward the temple. It's not the Antichrist temple that they should spread out their hands toward, but the one who declared Himself to be the temple, Jesus. Then, the Lord will then forgive all of their iniquities so that they will fear Him, who already knows their hearts. I pray that these verses are a blessing to you at this time.

Verses 5-6
*⁵ I **wait** for the Lord, my soul **waits**, and in His word I do hope. ⁶My soul **waits** for the Lord More than those who **watch** for the morning— Yes, more than those who **watch** for the morning.*

Could there be a more perfect couple of verses to sum up what the remnant of Israel must be feeling while they are in the refuge, waiting and watching for the Lord's return to rescue them from the horrors of the Great Tribulation period? At the start of the tribulation period in 2025, in the wake of the Gog Magog war and the rapture in 2024, we saw in Psalm 125 that the "scepter of wickedness would not rest on the land allotted to the righteous" for long. In Psalm 126, matching 2026, we saw the re-gathering of the Israelites back into their land from all over the world as they said, "the Lord has done great things for us." In Psalm 127, matching 2027, we saw the temple rebuilt, but God wasn't in this temple. In Psalm 128, matching 2028, we saw the remnant of Israel fleeing "out of Zion." In Psalm 129, matching 2029, we saw the remnant of Israel "afflicted," and their land "plowed," but they were protected as their enemies were turned back in shame. Now, in Psalm 130, matching 2030, we see the remnant of Israel still in a time of darkness, eagerly waiting and watching for the "Light of the world" to appear on the horizon. The darkness of the night will be broken soon by the "Bright Morning Star" - Revelation 22:16, and the "Sun of Righteousness" - Malachi 4:2, who is unmistakably Jesus the Messiah!

Hold on a little longer, remnant of Israel. Keep watching; your salvation is coming...

Revelation 16:15
¹⁵ "Behold, I am coming as a thief. Blessed is he who watches, and keeps his garments, lest he walk naked and they see his shame."

Isaiah 62

[1] For Zion's sake I will not hold My peace, and for Jerusalem's sake I will not rest, until her righteousness goes forth as brightness, and her salvation as a lamp that burns. [2] The Gentiles shall see your righteousness, and all kings your glory. You shall be called by a new name, which the mouth of the LORD will name. [3] You shall also be a crown of glory in the hand of the LORD, and a royal diadem in the hand of your God. [4] You shall no longer be termed Forsaken, nor shall your land any more be termed Desolate; but you shall be called Hephzibah, and your land Beulah; for the LORD delights in you, and your land shall be married. [5] For as a young man marries a virgin, so shall your sons marry you; and as the bridegroom rejoices over the bride, so shall your God rejoice over you. [6] I have set watchmen on your walls, O Jerusalem; they shall never hold their peace day or night. You who make mention of the LORD, do not keep silent, [7] and give Him no rest till He establishes and till He makes Jerusalem a praise in the earth.

[8] The LORD has sworn by His right hand and by the arm of His strength: "Surely I will no longer give your grain as food for your enemies; and the sons of the foreigner shall not drink your new wine, for which you have labored. [9] But those who have gathered it shall eat it, and praise the LORD; those who have brought it together shall drink it in My holy courts."

[10] Go through, go through the gates! Prepare the way for the people; build up, build up the highway! Take out the stones, lift up a banner for the peoples!

[11] Indeed the LORD has proclaimed to the end of the world: "Say to the daughter of Zion, 'Surely your salvation is coming; behold, His reward is with Him, and His work before Him.'" [12] And they shall call them The Holy People, the Redeemed of the LORD; and you shall be called Sought Out, a City Not Forsaken.

Verses 7-8

*⁷ O Israel, **hope in the Lord**; for with the Lord there is mercy, and with Him is abundant redemption. ⁸ **And He shall redeem Israel From all his iniquities**.*

Keep your hope in the Lord! Israel's redemption is at hand, and a new era will soon dawn when Israel will be free from their iniquities and sinful ways, and will finally *"be a crown of glory in the hand of the Lord."*

CHAPTER 16

Psalm 131 A Song of Ascents of David

Year 2031 - Israel is Humbled and Hopeful

Of the three "birth pain" patterns found in the 15 Songs of Ascent, Psalm 131 is once again the third type in the theme of God's peace and blessing. At only 3 verses long Psalm 131 doesn't give us much detail into what life is like in the refuge, but it does give us a sense that the remnant of Israel is, by this time, humble and at peace in God's care.

Verse 1

¹*LORD, my heart is not haughty, Nor my eyes lofty. Neither do concern myself with great matters, Nor with things too profound for me.*

By this time, the remnant of Israel is truly approaching the last minutes of the last days. If the encrypted timeline revelation in the Psalms continues to be as accurate as it has already proven itself to be, then Psalm 131 will coincide with the year 2031. It will be the last full year that the remaining children of Israel will be in the refuge. By this time, they that remain will have no more pride or rebellion in their hearts. Just as Zechariah prophesied in chapter 13, they have been refined through the fire and tested as gold. They are ready to call on Jesus' name since they have accepted Him as their true Messiah. Jesus, "Yeshua," will soon declare, "This is My people."

Zechariah 13:8-9

⁸And it shall come to pass in all the land," says the LORD, "That two-thirds in it shall be cut off and die, but one-third shall be left in it:⁹I will bring the one-third through the fire, will refine them as silver is refined, and test them as gold is tested. They will call on My name, and I will answer them. I will say, 'This is My people'; and each one will say, 'The LORD is my God.'"

It is important to understand the key role of humility for God's people. Notice that in verse 1, Israel is described as not being haughty. Of course, we know from many scriptures that Israel has notoriously been haughty and proud. Isaiah 3 likens Israel to daughters of Zion who walk about with outstretched necks, thinking they're all that. God is not looking for a prideful people. He's looking for a humble people. Again, according to verse 1, the Remnant of Israel is finally no longer haughty or proud. That means that they will soon be victorious and lifted up! Here are a few examples from scripture that promise that it is only after His people humble themselves before Him that He will give them victory, and grace, lift them up, forgive their sins, and heal their land.

Psalm 149:4

⁴For the LORD takes delight in his people; He crowns the humble with victory.

Proverbs 3:34

³⁴ Surely He scorns the scornful, but gives grace to the humble.

1 Peter 5:6

⁶ Humble yourselves, therefore, under God's mighty hand, that he may lift you up in due time.

James 4:10

¹⁰ Humble yourselves before the Lord, and he will lift you up.

2 Chronicles 7:13-14

¹³ When I shut up heaven and there is no rain, or command the locusts to devour the land, or send pestilence among My people, ¹⁴ if My people who are called by My name will humble themselves, and pray and seek My face, and turn from their wicked ways, then I will hear from heaven, and will forgive their sin and heal their land.

And most importantly...

Malachi 4:1-3

¹ "For behold, the day is coming, burning like an oven, and all the proud, yes, all who do wickedly will be stubble. And the day which is coming shall burn them up," Says the LORD of hosts, "That will leave them neither root nor branch. ²But to you who fear My name the Sun of Righteousness shall arise with healing in His wings; and you shall go out and grow fat like stall-fed calves. ³You shall trample the wicked, for they shall be ashes under the soles of your feet on the day that I do this," says the LORD of hosts.

Malachi 4 is the final chapter of the Old Testament. It prophesies of a day that is coming when all of the proud and wicked will be completely consumed. According to Psalm 131, the Remnant of Israel will no longer be among the proud. They are now humble and trust in the Lord Jesus, and on "that day," they shall trample the wicked under their feet. That day is the day that we call Armageddon!

Armageddon

According to the timeline and Revelation 16 the nations will soon gather in the valley of Armageddon to make their futile last stand against the Lord. Armageddon is not specifically encrypted in this Psalm, but it is encrypted in the second witness that matches this time period, which we will discuss in detail in a later chapter. Additionally, there is a third witness as well all the way back in Psalm 2.

Psalm 2, as you will see, is so very important prophetically. It is not only a Psalm that contains key Messianic prophecy that points to Jesus, but it also contains prophecies regarding the nations, and their thoughts that came against the reborn Israel in 1948-1949. Even further, it contains prophecy about the second coming of our Lord and Savior. Similar to Matthew 24, in Psalm 2, we find a prophetic pattern of multiple, similar, related, but separate events interwoven into one discourse or Psalm. Without having the timeline revelation for context, the rebirth of Israel would not be understood in Psalm 2, but we will get to that soon in another chapter.

Psalm 2
¹ Why do the nations rage, and the people plot a vain thing? ² The kings of the earth set themselves, and the rulers take counsel together, against the LORD and against His Anointed, saying, ³ "Let us break Their bonds in pieces and cast away Their cords from us."

⁴ He who sits in the heavens shall laugh; the Lord shall hold them in derision. ⁵ Then He shall speak to them in His wrath, and distress them in His deep displeasure: ⁶ "Yet I have set My King on My holy hill of Zion."

⁷ "I will declare the decree: the LORD has said to Me, 'You are My Son, Today I have begotten You. ⁸ Ask of Me, and I will give You The nations for Your inheritance, and the ends of the earth for Your possession. ⁹ You shall break them with a rod of iron; you shall dash them to pieces like a potter's vessel.'"

¹⁰ Now therefore, be wise, O kings; be instructed, you judges of the earth. ¹¹ Serve the LORD with fear, and rejoice with trembling. ¹² Kiss the Son, lest be angry, and you perish in the way, when His wrath is kindled but a little. Blessed are all those who put their trust in Him.

For now, let's focus on the Messianic elements of Psalm 2, and then we'll look at it in the context of the timeline. To all of the Jews who still say that God has no Son, Psalm 2 has presented a theological problem for thousands of years now. Many prominent Rabbis throughout the past 2000 years have claimed that the "Son," who is described in verse 7, is symbolic of the children of Israel. Against Christian popular belief, they are at least partially correct! However, it is first and foremost a Messianic prophecy declaring that God's only begotten Son is the true Messiah. His name is Yeshua!

John 3:16-17
¹⁶ For God so loved the world that He gave His only begotten Son, that whoever believes in Him should not perish but have everlasting life. ¹⁷ For God did not send His Son into the world to condemn the world, but that the world through Him might be saved.

At the beginning of the tribulation period, which according to the encrypted timeline revelation will start in 2025, many of the Jews will be misled by the false messiah and believe that they are finally entering into the prophesied Messianic Age. He will seem to match all that had been written about him by the Jewish sages such as Maimonides over the centuries, but they were not written by the inspiration of the Holy Spirit. That brings up the question, under whose inspiration were they writing?

By 2031, most of what I can only see dimly lit through the timeline revelation from my place in time in 2023, will be fully revealed to the remnant, and will be past history. Today, I can only interpret and imagine from the scriptures how things will happen, and what they will actually look like in real time. However, by 2031, the remnant will have a full understanding of these events and their consequences for the world. In the wake of the Gog Magog War in 2024, at a time of chaos, catastrophe, corruption, and economic woes, the false messiah stepped into the spotlight and seemingly redeemed Israel. Over a few years time, he brought back the exiles of Israel from around the world, ruled over Israel and beyond, and brought prosperity to an increasingly chaotic world. Then, to complete his deception against God's children, he rebuilt the temple, restored the Priesthood, and the sacrificial system. It seemed that the promised Messianic Age had finally arrived!

After completing his mission of returning the Jews back to Israel and consolidating his power over them and the world, he turned on Israel to destroy her once and for all. Two-thirds of the children of Israel have now been destroyed, and the remnant is still being preserved by the Lord in the refuge in 2031. At this time, as we can see by Psalm 131, they are fully trusting in the Lord. They know that He has brought them through the darkest days imaginable and that they don't even have to know what's happening outside of the refuge because they are now fully reliant on the Lord.

Verse 2
2 Surely I have calmed and quieted my soul, Like a weaned child with his mother; Like a weaned child is my soul within me.

It is evident from verse 2 that the remnant of Israel is fully trusting in the Lord at this time and is at peace regardless of what is happening around them. Furthermore, the imagery of their soul likened to a "weaned child" is significant in several ways. Firstly, it represents peace. Secondly, it represents spiritual growth. Thirdly, it represents a continued dependence. Fourthly, it represents an aspect of time.

Traditionally, a child is fully weaned between the ages of 2 to 4 years of age. I say "traditionally" because things are done differently now in our modern age from what was normal historically speaking. In any event, at this time in 2031, according to the timeline revelation in the Psalms, the remnant has been in the refuge for around 3 years, which matches the historic weaning of a child. We can also deduce that this is the age of full weaning from scripture. In 2 Chronicles 31, it is specifically stated that provision isn't given to the children of the Levites until the age of 3. It is reasonable to assume that the unwritten explanation for this specific age is that children younger than 3 were still being nourished through their mothers, and were not in need of meat and produce. Can it be mere coincidence that Psalm 131, which represents the 3rd year in the refuge, is the Psalm that uses the imagery of a weaned child, which also matches a 3-year period of time as well as their spiritual state in the same period?

Verse 3
3 O Israel, hope in the LORD From this time forth and forever.

The use of the word forever is perfectly placed in Psalm 131 at the tail end of the tribulation period, as eternity is literally within view in 2031. The remnant of Israel has been provided for and protected by our Lord. They have been humbled and have finally given their cares and their future over to the Lord. They know that their only hope is in the Lord at this time and forever more.

CHAPTER 17

Psalm 132 A Song of Ascents

Shmita Year 2032 - The Year of the Lord's Return!

Of the three "birth pain" patterns found in the 15 Songs of Ascent, Psalm 132 is the final year of distress. Interestingly, as you read Psalm 132, you will not get an overwhelming sense of distress. That's because the child has now been born!

> ### John 16:21
> *²¹ A woman, when she is in labor, has sorrow because her hour has come; but as soon as she has given birth to the child, she no longer remembers the anguish, for joy that a human being has been born into the world.*

You will notice that Psalm 132 is not only longer than the previous Psalms of Ascent, but it is also distinctly different in character from them as well. That's because the tribulation period is now over, and the fulfillment of the Feast of Tabernacles has begun. For anyone who still wants to believe that there is no Kingdom, or that we're already living in it, or that it will be in heaven and not on earth, you might want to skip the next few chapters because they will shatter your beliefs.

We have transitioned through the Psalms of Ascent from deception in 2020, to the opening of the rapture door in 2021, to praying for the peace of Jerusalem in 2022, to the spirit of the Antichrist rising in 2023, to the Gog Magog war and the closing of the rapture door in 2024, to the start of the tribulation in 2025, to the Jews returning to Israel in 2026, to the completion of the Temple in 2027, to the remnant of Israel escaping "out of Zion" in 2028, to the remnant being protected in 2029, to the remnant waiting on the Lord's return in 2030, to the remnant humbled and hopeful in 2031. Now, in 2032, we will see the Kingdom being born and the Messiah, the seed of David, seated on His throne in Zion forevermore!

It is noteworthy to point out that if these prophetic Psalms were organized in any other order, they wouldn't make sense or match the overarching biblical end-time narrative. The fact that they do fit perfectly into place, like pieces of a jigsaw puzzle, once again gives me overwhelming confidence in the accuracy of the encrypted timeline revelation. After all, can all of this simply be a coincidence?

The year 2032 is also a Shmita year, and according to the Dead Sea Scrolls and the Essenes, this is the 2000-year anniversary of the first coming of the Messiah. Remember that according to Jewish Rabbinical tradition, it is understood that war happens on the seventh year of a Shmita cycle, which is the year 2032. Remember also that it was in the last Shmita year that the Gog Magog War occurred in 2024. It has now been 7 years since the start of the 7-year tribulation period. We know, according to the Book of Revelation, and the prophecies of Daniel, that this is the time of the final conflict of this age.

With all of the prophetic timeline indicators taken into consideration, and considering God is most likely on the calendar that He instructed Moses to keep, it is my conclusion that the nations will gather at Armageddon to make war against the Lord sometime from the fall season of 2031 through the year 2032. There is no way to know the day or the hour, but just as the Israelites should have known the year of our Lord's first advent, according to Jesus Himself, so should we at least know the reasonable timeline of His second advent. As we know from Revelation, His second advent begins with the defeat of the nations who have gathered together to make war against Him.

Revelation 16:16

16 And they gathered them together to the place called in Hebrew, Armageddon.

Revelation 19:19-20

19 And I saw the beast, the kings of the earth, and their armies, gathered together to make war against Him who sat on the horse and against His army. 20 Then the beast was captured, and with him the false prophet who worked signs in his presence, by which he deceived those who received the mark of the beast and those who worshiped his image. These two were cast alive into the lake of fire burning with brimstone. 21 And the rest were killed with the sword which proceeded from the mouth of Him who sat on the horse. And all the birds were filled with their flesh.

Psalm 132 doesn't directly mention war since the fulfillment of this Psalm is after the war that we call Armageddon. As I have previously mentioned, that final conflict is detailed in the second witness in the timeline revelation, which will be covered in a subsequent chapter.

Psalm 132 is both a historical account of a specific time and event in King David's life (verses 1-10) as well as a prophetic revelation of the second coming of our Messiah, King Jesus (verses 11-18). However, as a pattern, both are specifically about the Lord's establishment of an eternal dwelling place in Jerusalem.

Verses 1-5

*1 LORD, remember David And all his afflictions; 2 How he swore to the LORD, And vowed to the Mighty One of Jacob: 3 "Surely I will not go into the chamber of my house, or go up to the comfort of my bed; 4 I will not give sleep to my eyes or slumber to my eyelids, 5 **Until I find a place for the LORD, A dwelling place for the Mighty One of Jacob**."*

Again, there is no war or the aftermath of war mentioned in Psalm 132, so how do we know that Psalm 132 represents a period of time after the war has ended? Verses 1-5 of Psalm 132 specifically connect with 2 Samuel 7, which affirms that this event in King David's life was after his military conquests at a time when the Lord gave him peace from his enemies. There is a pattern at work here...

> **2 Samuel 7:1-2**
> *¹King David was living in his palace, **and the LORD had given him peace from all his enemies around him.**² Then David said to Nathan the prophet, "Look, I am living in a palace made of cedar wood, but the Ark of God is in a tent!"*

Clearly, at a time of rest, King David wanted to build a temple for the Lord, but it wasn't time yet, and David wasn't the right man for the Job. That job was to fall to a future successor in the bloodline of David. Of course, we know that it was David's son Solomon who was chosen to build the first temple for the Lord. However, in verses 12-14 of 2 Samuel 7, as Nathan is prophesying and speaking to David the words of the Lord, clearly, the Lord wasn't only speaking of David's future son Solomon.

> **2 Samuel 7:12-14**
> *¹² When your days are over and you rest with your ancestors, I will raise up your offspring to succeed you, your own flesh and blood, and I will establish his kingdom.¹³ He is the one who will build a house for my Name, and I will establish the throne of his kingdom forever. ¹⁴ **I will be his father, and he will be my son**.*

The words "I will be his father, and he will be my son" did not find completion in Solomon, but were thoroughly and perfectly fulfilled in the "only begotten Son" of God, Jesus the Savior of the world! From these verses in Psalm 132 as well as 2 Samuel, you can see how God seamlessly interwoven the prophecy of Solomon and the first Temple with the coming of His one and only Son, and the establishment of His eternal resting place in Zion. Of course, we know from many scriptures that this eternity will begin on the "3rd day." Don't be confused. The 3rd day is also the 7th day Sabbath rest, the 1000 years known as the Millennial Kingdom.

Hosea 6:1-3

1 Come, let us return to the LORD. For He has torn us to pieces, but He will heal us; He has wounded us, but He will bind up our wounds. 2After two days He will revive us; on the third day He will raise us up, that we may live in His presence. 3So let us know—let us press on to know the LORD. As surely as the sun rises, He will appear; He will come to us like the rain, like the spring showers that water the earth.

In the 7-day/7000 year "week" of man's time on earth since Adam, the Millennial Kingdom represents the 7th day Sabbath rest (remember also that Jesus is our rest). However, Hosea's prophecy is Messianic, and relates to the "2 days" or 2000 years from Jesus' first advent, which ties directly into Daniel's 70 weeks prophecy, and Zechariah 9:9 at Jesus' triumphal entry into Jerusalem in 32 AD (32 AD according to Essene prophecy).

I believe that Hosea is speaking directly to the remnant of Israel in his prophecy. He's calling the remnant to return to the Lord. Israel was torn to pieces, but now, in this time, at the end, the Lord will revive them and heal them.

Our Lord is so good! As I was writing this section and meditating on God's word for guidance to piece all of this together with the 3rd day understanding, He gave me an unexpected miracle! Just yesterday, I found an amazing family group of singers and musicians called the Petersen's on YouTube. Don't judge me because I love Bluegrass music, and I grew up in Alabama! I had them playing in the background, and they sang a song called "Sweet Beulah Land." I had forgotten what

"Beulah" meant in Hebrew, so I looked it up. It's Hebrew for "married!" and in Isaiah 62, Beulah is the new name that God gives to the land of Israel around Jerusalem after the remnant returns to her. Verse 4 says, "*the LORD will take delight in you, and your land will be married.*" How amazing is that? Beulah ties it all together! Without the Lord's help, I would not have been able to make these connections. Let me try to briefly explain and recap how the "3rd day" relates to marriage a little better.

God married Israel on the "3rd day." Exodus 19 specifically declares that it was on the 3rd day when the Lord came down for their wedding.

Exodus 19:10-11
*^{10} Then the LORD said to Moses, "Go to the people and consecrate them today and tomorrow, and let them wash their clothes. ^{11} And let them be ready for the **third day**. For on the **third day** the LORD will come down upon Mount Sinai in the sight of all the people.*

Even though it didn't sound or look like a traditional wedding scene on this "3rd day" with God's thundering and lightning, dark cloud, loud trumpet blasts, and a trembling bride, we can be certain that it was. How? Simply put the Old Covenant was a marriage contract, and Israel said "I do" in Exodus 24:3. Also, because we are specifically told so by the prophets Isaiah and Jeremiah.

Isaiah 54:5
*^{5}For your Maker is your **husband**— the LORD Almighty is his name— the Holy One of Israel is your Redeemer; he is called the God of all the earth.*

Jeremiah 31:31-32
^{31} "The days are coming," declares the LORD, "when I will make a new covenant with the people of Israel and with the people of Judah. ^{32} It will not be like the covenant I made with their ancestors when I took them by the hand to lead

them out of Egypt, because they broke my covenant, though **I was a husband to them,"** *declares the* LORD.

Jeremiah 3:20
[20] But like a woman unfaithful to her **husband**, *so you, Israel, have been unfaithful to me," declares the* LORD.

Unfortunately, Israel was hardly ever faithful to her Husband. Jeremiah 3 ties all of this together along with Hosea 3. Remember that God told the prophet Hosea to marry a harlot, who symbolized Israel. She left him to shack up with another man, and Hosea had to buy her back for **15** shekels of silver (15 shekels of silver represents redemption, while the 15 Psalms of Ascent represent the 15 years after which Israel will be redeemed).

Hosea 3
[1] Then the LORD *said to me, "Go again, love a woman who is loved by a lover and is committing adultery, just like the love of the* LORD *for the children of Israel, who look to other gods and love the raisin cakes of the pagans." [2] So I bought her for myself for* **fifteen shekels of silver**, *and one and one-half homers of barley. [3] And I said to her, "You shall stay with me many days; you shall not play the harlot, nor shall you have a man—so, too, will I be toward you." [4] For the children of Israel shall abide many days without king or prince, without sacrifice or sacred pillar, without ephod or teraphim. [5] Afterward the children of Israel shall return and seek the* LORD *their God and David their king. They shall fear the* LORD *and His goodness in the latter days.*

In Hosea 3 verse 4 we see the past 2000 years spoken of as a time when the Children of Israel had no king or prince, temple to make their sacrifices, ephod, which is part of the priestly garments, or teraphim, which were small pagan idols. All of that is true of the past 2000 years, including the teraphim. Israel always went after foreign gods in times past, but now the majority of Israel is secular and claims no god other than perhaps materialism.

Hosea 3 verse 5 says that after the 2000 years spoken of in verse 4 (2 days in Hosea 6), the children of Israel will once again return to her Husband and "David," which is a code name for the seed of David, which is Jesus. Remember that David had long been dead by the time Hosea wrote this, so he couldn't be referring to the literal David.

Hosea 3 verse 6 says that the children of Israel will once again fear the lord in the "latter days," which I believe refers to the remnant that will be saved and redeemed through the tribulation period.

OK, we know that the "3rd day" represents a wedding in the Old Testament, but how about the New Testament? Did you ever wonder why John, under the inspiration of the Holy Spirit, specifically pointed out in John chapter 2 that Jesus attended a wedding specifically on the "3rd day?"

John 2:1-3
*[1] **On the third day there was a wedding** in Cana of Galilee, and the mother of Jesus was there. [2] Now both Jesus and His disciples were invited to the wedding. [3] And when they ran out of wine, the mother of Jesus said to Him, "They have no wine."*

Can you see how God encodes prophetic times and events by the use of keywords, phrases, numbers, patterns, and interconnected imagery so that we can figure it out? I have heard many good theories about what the water, water pots, and wine symbolize in John's account of the wedding that happened on the 3rd day. But I haven't heard the one I'm about to offer, which is based on the connection with the timeline revelation that I have just illustrated.

Could it be that the 6 stone water pots, which were traditionally used for ritual purification, but Jesus used to miraculously transform water into wine, represented the 6 days or 6000 years of man? After which, on the 3rd day, which is the same as the 7th day, we will "Tabernacle," or literally dwell with Jesus. This is the time when He comes back and finally drinks the last of 4 cups of wine with us. Remember that Jesus said in Matthew 26:29, *"but I say to you, I will not drink of this fruit of the vine from now on until that day when I drink it new with you in My Father's kingdom."* During the Passover Seder, Jesus would have already drank the first 3 cups. The first cup is known as the Cup of Sanctification, meaning "set apart." The second cup is the Cup of Wrath, Plagues or Deliverance. The third cup of wine is poured after the meal is eaten and is known as the Cup of Redemption. This is the cup that Jesus used for the first communion. We know this because Luke 22 specifically says that Jesus "took the cup **after** supper."

Luke 22:20
*Likewise He also took the cup **after** supper, saying, "This cup is the new covenant in My blood, which is shed for you."*

There is so much that I want to connect here, but for time sake, I will shorten it. Jesus established the 3rd cup of wine, known as the "Cup of Redemption," as His blood of the New Covenant, but also said that He would not drink from it again until that day when we share in Communion in His Father's Kingdom. That means that Jesus never drank the 4th cup. The 4th cup is called the Cup of Hallel, which means "praise." When the 4th cup, the Cup of Hallel, is drunk at the Passover Seder, Exodus 6:7 is read aloud.

Exodus 6:7
"I will take you as My people, and I will be your God..."

As you can see, this is wedding language again, but without the imagery! I would like to point out also that Jesus is returning, and by this time in 2032, according to the timeline revelation, He has returned. After His return, He will drink the 4th cup with us. Remember who is associated with the Hebrew number 4? Jesus is! He is the number 4, the dalet, the door, the only way to the Father, the Lion of the tribe of Judah, who was the 4th son born to Jacob, and He is our Sabbath rest, the 4th Commandment, He was the 4th man in the fiery furnace with Daniel's 3 friends, who Nebuchadnezzar exclaimed looked like a "Son of God!" I'll stop there, but understand that Jesus is our Savior who has been ever-present throughout the Bible, and as our Sabbath rest, Jesus is coming back to Tabernacle, or dwell, with us. That is the Kingdom! From this, you can see how the 4th cup of the Passover Seder is connected to the Millennial Kingdom reign of Jesus the Messiah when He dwells with us.

According to John's Gospel, it was at the end of the Passover Seder, that Jesus comforted His disciples after describing that He would be betrayed by one of them, that Peter would deny Him 3 times, and that Jesus was going away to a place where they could not follow at that time.

The disciples must have been very confused. This was supposed to be a time of singing, praise, and rejoicing in celebration and memory of the Exodus as well as the coming Kingdom of God. I'm sure the disciples thought they were about to witness the beginning of the Kingdom Age with Jesus, their Messiah on the throne. However, Jesus changed the tone of the Seder, and prophesied bad news instead, without ever drinking from the 4th Cup of Hallel.

After all of the bad news that He gave them at the conclusion of the Seder, here's how Jesus comforted them:

> **John 14:1-4**
> *"Let not your heart be troubled; you believe in God, believe also in Me. In My Father's house are many mansions (another translation from the Greek is dwellings); if it were not so, I would have told you. I go to prepare a place for you. And if I go and prepare a place for you, I will come again and receive you to Myself; that where I am, there you may be also. And where I go you know, and the way you know."*

Jesus tied the 4th cup of wine, the "Cup of Hallel," to His future return when He will dwell with us in His Kingdom. The disciples and all of the saints who have passed away are already dwelling with the Lord. At the rapture, we will be there as well. Then, at His second coming, we will dwell with Jesus for 1000 years in His Kingdom, where He will reign from Jerusalem, or "Beulah" (married to God - Isaiah 62), which is still just a shadow of what is to come afterward, when all sin and death is eliminated from existence, and God himself will dwell with us in His New Jerusalem. The New Jerusalem will come down out of heaven, as we read about in Revelation 21. This will be the start of the 8th day. The letter "Chet" is also the number 8 in Hebrew and represents transcendence beyond the physical or natural. It also represents fatness, as in an overabundance, and mostly, it represents marriage with God as the head of the marriage. That brings us back to "Beulah." After the 1000 year Millennial Kingdom reign, the entire world will be renewed and will finally be in an unconstrained marriage relationship with God.

Revelation 21:1-7

1 Then I saw "a new heaven and a new earth,:" for the first heaven and the first earth had passed away, and there was no longer any sea. 2 I saw the Holy City, the new Jerusalem, coming down out of heaven from God, prepared as a bride beautifully dressed for her husband. 3 And I heard a loud voice from the throne saying, "Look! God's dwelling place is now among the people, and he will dwell with them. They will be his people, and God himself will be with them and be their God. 4 'He will wipe every tear from their eyes. There will be no more death' or mourning or crying or pain, for the old order of things has passed away."

5 He who was seated on the throne said, "I am making everything new!" Then he said, "Write this down, for these words are trustworthy and true."

6 He said to me: "It is done. I am the Alpha and the Omega, the Beginning and the End. To the thirsty I will give water without cost from the spring of the water of life. 7 Those who are victorious will inherit all this, and I will be their God and they will be my children

In 2032, Jesus will dwell, or "tabernacle" with us! Do you remember the temple that the false messiah built back in Psalm 127 (2027); the one where he did something that was an abomination to God, at which time the land became desolate? That false temple where God never dwelt has been destroyed by this time in 2032, the city of Jerusalem will now be lifted up high above the other cities (Zechariah 14:10-11), and a new Millennial Temple for the Lord will be built in accordance with Ezekiel 40 - 48.

Verses 6-10
⁶ *Behold, we heard of it in Ephrathah; We found it in the fields of the woods.*

⁷ *Let us go into His tabernacle; Let us worship at His footstool.* ⁸ *Arise, O* LORD, *to Your resting place, You and the ark of Your strength.* ⁹ **Let Your priests be clothed with righteousness, and let Your saints shout for joy.**
¹⁰ *For Your servant David's sake, do not turn away the face of Your Anointed.*

I'm starting to really feel the pressure of time while I'm writing this book. It's now February 2023, and at the rate I'm going, this will end up being a history book instead of a prophecy book! For that reason, I'm going to skip over some sections and try to shorten others because I believe that time is really short. I have a tendency to want to explain every detail as clearly as possible, which ends up being sort of like a "spoon-feeding." I'm going to try to let you, the reader, dig into God's word a little deeper to discover some of the additional details for yourself. That sounds good in theory, anyway. Hopefully, I can actually do that! OK, back to Psalm 132...

Verses 6-10 hearken back to when King David brought the Ark of the Covenant back to Jerusalem and thereby united the Nation of Israel once again under God. It was brought back with great fanfare, singing, and dancing as we read in 1 Chronicles and 2 Samuel. There are some keywords in these verses that I won't be able to cover, such as "Ephrathah, footstool, and Anointed," which is, of course, the Messiah.

I would like to start by focusing on some of the interconnecting details that relate Psalm 132 to 1 Chronicles 15. In 1 Chronicles, we see that David and the Levites wore robes of fine linen, and the Israelites shouted and played instruments.

> **1 Chronicles 15:25-28**
> *25 So David, the elders of Israel, and the captains over thousands went to bring up the ark of the covenant of the LORD from the house of Obed-Edom with joy. 26 And so it was, when God helped the Levites who bore the ark of the covenant of the LORD, that they offered seven bulls and seven rams. 27* ***David was clothed with a robe of fine linen, as were all the Levites who bore the ark, the singers, and Chenaniah the music master with the singers.*** *David also wore a linen ephod. 28 Thus* ***all Israel*** *brought up the ark of the covenant of the LORD* ***with shouting and with the sound of the horn, with trumpets and with cymbals, making music with stringed instruments and harps.***

In Psalm 132, we see the "priests" clothed with "righteousness" and the "saints" shouting for joy. Both 1 Chronicles 15 and Psalm 132 are very similar, but I would say that Psalm 132 better matches the day of our Lord's triumphal return as described in Revelation 19 than it does the historical account of David returning to Jerusalem with the Ark.

> **Revelation 19:6-8**
> *6 Then I heard what sounded like a great multitude, like the roar of rushing waters and like loud peals of thunder,* ***shouting: "Hallelujah!*** *For our Lord God Almighty reigns. 7 Let us rejoice and be glad and give him glory! For the wedding of the Lamb has come, and his bride has made herself ready. 8* ***Fine linen, bright and clean, was given her to wear." (Fine linen stands for the righteous acts of God's holy people.)***

In Revelation 19, the saints are seen shouting "Hallelujah!" Remember the 4th Cup of Hallel? Hallelujah in Hebrew means "praise Yah." Yah is, of course, the short form for YHWH or Yahweh, or "LORD" in our English translations. As previously mentioned, the short form of the Name Yah is the number 15 numerically in Hebrew, and we're reading the 15 Psalms of Ascent. Did you know that the word "Hallelujah" only appears in the Bible in one place? You guessed it! It only appears in Revelation 19, and in that chapter, it appears exactly 4 times. When will the 4th Cup of Hallel be drunk, and who is associated with the Hebrew number 4, the dalet? The 4th Cup of Hallel will be drunk in the Kingdom of God according to Mark 14:25. These interconnected details are not by coincidence. This is one of the ways that our Lord shows Himself to be simply amazing and in control of every last detail in scripture. Nothing, not one word or detail, is wasted or excessive, but we won't see it unless we dig deeper into His word and start connecting all of these details together.

Maybe I'm splitting hairs here, but speaking of details, I can't help but continue to notice some of the detailed differences between the Old Testament accounts of the Ark returning to Jerusalem as compared to Psalm 132:9, versus the future fulfillment of Jesus returning to Jerusalem in Revelation 19.

Psalm 132:9 says, *"Let Your priests be clothed with righteousness, and let Your saints shout for joy."* So, in verse 9, we have the word "righteousness," which connects with Revelation 19:8, which specifically tells us that fine linen stands for the "righteous" acts of God's holy people. In addition, verse 9 indicates that it's the saints who are "shouting" for joy. God's holy people are the saints, those of us who have a relationship with Him. In the account of David returning the Ark, it's only the Israelites who were shouting. Also, notice that there are no instruments depicted in the Psalm, just as there are no instruments mentioned in Revelation 19, but on the contrary, there are many instruments detailed in 1 Chronicles and 2 Samuel, which may indicate that it's two separate, but similar events.

Can you see how 2 Samuel, 1 Chronicles, and Revelation 19 are interconnected? But it takes Psalm 132 in context with the timeline revelation to connect all of the pieces together. My point is this, I believe that even though Psalm 132 has historical significance as a poetic retelling of David's desire to build a temple, and his return of the Ark of the Covenant to Jerusalem, it has more significance than we have recognized as a prophetic account of a soon but still future event.

Verses 11-18

*[11] The LORD has sworn in truth to David; He will not turn from it: **"I will set upon your throne the fruit of your body.** [12] If your sons will keep My covenant and My testimony which I shall teach them, Their sons also shall sit upon your throne **forevermore."** [13] For the LORD has chosen Zion; He has desired it for His dwelling place: [14] "This is My resting place forever; here I will dwell, for I have desired it.*

[15] I will abundantly bless her provision; I will satisfy her poor with bread. [16] I will also clothe her priests with salvation, and her saints shall shout aloud for joy.

[17] There I will make the horn of David grow; I will prepare a lamp for My Anointed. [18] His enemies I will clothe with shame, but upon Himself His crown shall flourish."

Verses 11-18 are so clearly prophetic of the coming Messiah that I hesitate to add much in the way of comment. As prophesied, Jesus is unmistakably the fruit of David's body, who will sit upon David's throne forevermore in Jerusalem. Psalm 132 in the timeline revelation not only gives us these details of what is to come, but also prophesies of the time in which it will happen. According to the encrypted timeline revelation, all of the events and blessings pictured in Psalm 132 will happen soon after the second coming of our Lord in 2032 at the establishment of His Millennial Kingdom.

There is one last, but very important element of Psalm 132 that I would like to point out. It's a theme that runs throughout this Psalm, and silently through the next one, when seen in the context of the timeline revelation. It's the fact that there is still no temple! One could argue that Jesus is the Temple, but we know that according to Ezekiel 40-48 there will be a literal new temple built in Jerusalem during the Millennial Kingdom reign of the true Messiah.

CHAPTER 18

Psalm 133 A Song of Ascents of David

Year 2033 - Unified Under the King of Kings

Of the three "birth pain" patterns found in the 15 Songs of Ascent, Psalm 133 is once again a song of hope, trust, and deliverance similar to Psalm 121, 124, 127, and 130. By 2033, the desolation of the land of Israel is over, and the Messiah, Jesus is on the throne of David. And the world has been delivered from the evil that had taken over the globe just a few short years ago. This is the year when the world becomes unified under the only One who has the power and authority to rule, and bring peace and prosperity to all.

Verse 1
¹Behold, how good and how pleasant it is for brethren to
dwell together in unity!

I know I say this a lot, but I get excited about the revelation of encoded biblical mysteries. How perfect is this verse, considering how perfectly Psalm 133 fits into the timeline revelation? First of all, this Psalm was written in the present tense. I believe it will be in the present tense in 2033. I point this out because the previous Psalm 132 was written in the past, present, and future tenses. Some of the prophetic aspects of Psalm 132 were written in the future tense. I take that to mean that even in 2032, some of what was written is yet future. Since there are two more Psalms of Ascent after it, it makes sense that at least some of what was prophesied in Psalm 132 will actually occur over the next few years.

Secondly, The time of division is over! The time of many different religions and even Christian denominations is over. At this time and forevermore, we will live together, and worship together in unity. Remember that in Luke 12, Jesus pointed out that He hadn't come to bring peace to the earth.

> **Luke 12:51-53**
> *Do you suppose that I came to give peace on earth? I tell you, not at all, but rather division. ⁵²For from now on five in one house will be divided: three against two, and two against three. ⁵³Father will be divided against son and son against father, mother against daughter and daughter against mother, mother-in-law against her daughter-in-law and daughter-in-law against her mother-in-law."*

In 2033, those days will finally be behind us! We will be unified under our Savior and King. All of the "decoy" religions that the enemy had set up to take us off of the one path to the Father will all be cast away, and only the worship of the Father and Son, our Savior, will remain.

I can't help but notice some of the allusions in Psalm 133 to something "descending," or coming down. It's a short Psalm with only 3 verses, but 2 of those verses both describe this "descending" with different metaphors. My first thought was of the New Jerusalem coming down, but that's not for another 1000 years. I'm not sure what will be coming down in 2033, but this Psalm certainly illustrates it, as well as the "anointing." Is this the year that Jesus will be anointed? Remember that Jesus is not only anointed by God as the Messiah, and the High Priest, but He will also need to be anointed by the free choice of the nations just as David was chosen and anointed by the people to be King for all of Israel in 2 Samuel chapter 5.

Verse 2

*² It is like the **precious oil upon the head, Running down on the beard, The beard of Aaron**, running down on the edge of his garments.*

Aaron was the first High Priest of the nation of Israel. Jesus is our greater High Priest who offered Himself as the sacrifice for our eternal salvation.

Hebrews 5:8-10

⁸ though He was a Son, yet He learned obedience by the things which He suffered. ⁹ And having been perfected, He became the author of eternal salvation to all who obey Him, ¹⁰ called by God as High Priest "according to the order of Melchizedek,"

Verse 3

*³ It is like the **dew of Hermon**, descending upon the mountains of Zion; for there the LORD commanded the blessing— **Life forevermore**.*

In verse 3, we have another reference to something "descending." This time, it is the "dew of Hermon." Hermon is the tallest mountain in Israel, and at its base was a city known to us through the New Testament named Caesarea Philippi, which featured a large cave that was literally known as the "Gates of Hell!" This was the location, oddly enough, where Jesus proclaimed that He would build His Church in Matthew 16.

This location was a hub of Pagan practices, cult rituals and demon worship during the time of Jesus and all the way back to the time of Enoch and Noah. In fact, it is believed that Mt. Hermon is the location where the fallen angels agreed together, and intermingled with the daughters of men, producing the Nephilim of Genesis 6. This was also the site where the apostate tribe of Dan relocated and worshiped the false god Baal, and later, the Greeks and Romans worshiped the half-human, half-goat fertility god Pan, who is also known today as Baphomet, and is symbolic of Satin himself. No religious Jew would have been caught dead at this defiled place in Jesus' time. However,

Jesus didn't ever concern Himself with such trivial things. He was, and is, after all, the Son of God!

In 2033, it will be clear that the gates of hell did not prevail, Satan and his evil deceptions will be locked away for 1000 years, and the Kingdom of God is finally underway.

Revelation 20:1-3

[1] And I saw an angel coming down out of heaven, having the key to the Abyss and holding in his hand a great chain.[2] He seized the dragon, that ancient serpent, who is the devil, or Satan, and bound him for a thousand years.[3] He threw him into the Abyss, and locked and sealed it over him, to keep him from deceiving the nations anymore until the thousand years were ended. After that, he must be set free for a short time.

Verse 3 uses "dew" as an illustration. Dew is symbolic of God's blessing in the Bible and healing for the land. In the context of Psalm 133, after the brutal tribulation period, the word "dew" connects perfectly with Hosea 14. Not only will God forgive Israel from all of their past transgressions against Him, He will also cause their land to blossom like never before to heal the scars of their turbulent past.

Hosea 14:4-7

*[4]I will heal their apostasy; I will freely love them, for My anger has turned away from them. [5]**I will be like the dew to Israel**; he will blossom like the lily and take root like the cedars of Lebanon. [6]His shoots will sprout, and his splendor will be like the olive tree, his fragrance like the cedars of Lebanon. [7]They will return and dwell in his shade; they will grow grain and blossom like the vine. His renown will be like the wine of Lebanon.*

Take note that in the context of the encrypted timeline revelation, we are now in the second year since the return of the King, and there is still no mention of a temple.

CHAPTER 19

Psalm 134 A Song of Ascents

Year 2034 - Fulfillment of Tabernacles

Of the three "birth pain" patterns found in the 15 Songs of Ascent, Psalm 134 is the final type and the final year of the 15 years. The third and final type in the "birth pain" pattern is in the theme of God's peace and blessing. This Psalm also represents the 15th and final step for the pilgrims and priests ascending up to the temple of God to worship at the final feast of the year, the Feast of Sukkot, or Tabernacles as we know it in English.

Psalm 134 is once again a very short Psalm at only 3 verses. However, the 3 verses simply couldn't possibly be more perfect for the final year in the 15 years of Ascent up to worship and bless the Lord in His Holy Sanctuary. Yes, finally, there is a Holy Temple! We have ascended up through the 15 steps to reach the temple, and it's finally a reality! The 15 steps have been 15 years to finally reach the year of the completion of the Millennial Temple.

Is it any wonder that just as Jesus said in John 2, "destroy this temple, and in 3 days I will raise it up," referring to His resurrection, that He would follow the same pattern, and raise up the new Millennial Temple in 3 days/years since His return, and even on the 3rd day as prophesied in Hosea 6?

Hosea 6:2

² After two days He will revive us; on the third day He will ***raise us up****, that we may live in His sight.*

I realize that Hosea 6:2 is talking about raising up the remnant of Israel, but that would also certainly include the temple, and there is once again a prophetic pattern at work here.

Ezekiel 40-48 gives a detailed description of the new temple, sort of like a written blueprint, but I cannot cover all of that here. However, I would suggest studying those chapters to gain a more comprehensive understanding of the Millennial Temple that is coming. In addition, if you want to know what has been happening in the land since Jesus' return, Isaiah 60-66 gives some descriptions of the rebuilding of the land.

Isaiah 61 is one of the keys that Jesus used for our understanding of His first advent as well as His second advent. Remember that in Luke 4 Jesus went into the Synagogue and read from Isaiah 61, but He didn't read from the entire scripture. He stopped at a certain point, at a comma, in verse 2 after reading *"to proclaim the acceptable year of the Lord."* We now understand that there would be 2000 years between that comma and the next part of the sentence, which reads *"and the day of vengeance of our God."* That day of vengeance was the tribulation period that Jesus spoke about in Luke 21:22 saying, *"For these are the days of vengeance, that all things which are written may be fulfilled."*

After the vengeance, according to Isaiah 61, comes comfort and consolation for those who mourn in Zion. That's the start of the Millennial Kingdom, which, as we know according to the timeline revelation in the Psalms, started at Jesus' return in 2032, or possibly the late part of 2031. Isaiah 61 then continues to say that He will give them *"beauty for ashes, the oil of joy for mourning, the garment of praise for the spirit of heaviness; that they may be called trees of righteousness, the planting of the Lord, that He may be glorified."*

According to Isaiah 61, the years following the tribulation will be a time of healing for Israel, as well as for all of the nations. Isaiah then gives us a further description of what will be happening at this same time of healing:

Isaiah 61:4

⁴And they shall rebuild the old ruins, they shall raise up the former desolations, and they shall repair the ruined cities, the desolations of many generations.

All that was desolate will be rebuilt. That certainly includes the Holy Temple, which I believe will be completed between 2034 and 2035. How do I know that? Because Psalm 134 finally speaks of the Temple! As we know from a previous chapter, the "house of the Lord" is the Temple, and not a tent. In fact, 2 Samuel 7 clears this matter up for us:

2 Samuel 7:4-7

*⁴ But it happened that night that the word of the L*ORD *came to Nathan, saying, ⁵ "Go and tell My servant David, 'Thus says the L*ORD*: "Would you build a **house** for Me to dwell in? ⁶ **For I have not dwelt in a house** since the time that I brought the children of Israel up from Egypt, even to this day, **but have moved about in a tent and in a tabernacle.**⁷ Wherever I have moved about with all the children of Israel, have I ever spoken a word to anyone from the tribes of Israel, whom I commanded to shepherd My people Israel, saying, 'Why have you not built Me a house of cedar?'"*

As you will see, verse 1 of Psalm 134 speaks of "the house of the Lord" and not a tent or tabernacle.

Verse 1-2

*¹Behold, bless the L*ORD*, all you servants of the L*ORD*, **who by night stand in the house of the L*ORD*!** ² Lift up your hands in the sanctuary, and bless the L*ORD*.*

Another very interesting word that is used in verse 1 is "Behold." I realize that I have pointed out once before that the word behold is used a lot in the Bible, and for good reason. Behold is typically used to point out something very important that God really wants you to notice. Behold is the Bible telling you not only to look at something with your eyes, but more importantly, to actually pay attention to it as well. This Psalm could have simply started off with "Bless the Lord, All you... However, God intentionally started it off with "Behold" for a reason.

So, in 2034, it seems that God wants us to focus on these servants, and on the house of the Lord, where they are literally standing and blessing the Lord. He also wants us to see and understand that they are specifically worshiping at night. I cannot find any Old Testament biblical or Jewish historical reference to night worship at the Temple. There were evening services, but Psalm 134 appears to convey that they are truly worshiping around the clock and through the night. There is, however, one very similar verse in the New Testament. It's found in Revelation 7 and speaks of the martyred tribulation saints.

Revelation 7:15
*15 Therefore they are before the throne of God, and serve Him day and **night in His temple**. And He who sits on the throne will dwell among them.*

I find it very interesting that Psalm 134 and Revelation 7:15 share so many similarities, including the "servants" serving the Lord during the night as well as during the day. I realize that the scene of Revelation 7 takes place during the tribulation period, as John sees it. By the way, this scene also begins with "behold." There is no mention that these same martyred saints will stop serving the Lord day and night at some later time, so our glimpse into the future through John's writing, as well as that of the Psalmist, may in fact, be of the same "servants."

Verse 3
3 The LORD who made heaven and earth Bless you from Zion!

I can't help but think that verse 3 almost sounds like a post card that you receive after a family member has arrived at a great holiday destination. In fact, those Gentiles who are alive in the Millennial Kingdom will have an opportunity to visit our Lord in Zion at least once a year at the feast of Tabernacles, according to Zechariah 14. Don't forget to send a post card!

Zechariah 14:16
16 And it shall come to pass that everyone who is left of all the nations which came against Jerusalem shall go up from year to year to worship the King, the LORD of hosts, and to keep the Feast of Tabernacles.

We also know that at least Passover will also be celebrated in the Millennial Kingdom from Ezekiel 45, but it isn't clear if all the nations will go to the temple in Jerusalem to celebrate or just the Jews. Keep in mind that the Millennial Kingdom is a type of Sabbath rest, and a type of Tabernacle as well since our Lord will be physically dwelling, or put another way to Tabernacle with us.

If the last verse of the 15 Psalms of Ascent doesn't make you realize that Jesus is now physically in Jerusalem, then nothing will! But here's one more attempt to wake up those who still can't see it... As a prophetic pattern, it was around the middle of the 7-day Feast of Tabernacles when Jesus "went up into the temple," where He taught and marveled at the Jews according to John 7.

John 7:14
14 About the middle of the feast Jesus went up into the temple and began teaching.

Around the middle of the 7-day feast would be sometime during the 3rd day. Why did the Holy Spirit have the need to point this out? I believe that it's one more hidden prophetic treasure encoded in God's word that He wanted us to find that helps us to connect all of these puzzle pieces together. The middle of the new 7-year Shmita cycle, which started sometime in 2031/2032, depending on which calendar God is operating by, would be in the 2034 timeframe. That matches Psalm 134. So, according to the pattern from John 7, and the timeline revelation in Psalm 134, Jesus will go up into the new temple during or around 2034 and begin to teach. I want to be there for that!

OK, here's one more... In His infinite wisdom, God has also connected this last verse of the 15 Psalms of Ascent, which represents a new beginning at the start of the Millennial Kingdom, to the first verse of the entire Bible! Psalm 134 Verse 3 says, *The LORD who made heaven and earth...*" Of course, Genesis 1:1 also tells us who made "heaven and earth." Isaiah 46:9-10 tells us that God declares the end from the beginning. He's the only one who can do that. Isn't it fitting that God has connected Genesis 1:1, when He (Elohim) created all things perfectly, with this final verse showing that all things will once again be perfect under the rule of His Son, Jesus? For the next 1000 years, the world will be better than we could ever imagine. I don't know about you, but I can imagine a lot! Remember what Paul wrote in 1 Corinthians chapter 2:

1 Corinthians 2:9
⁹ But as it is written: "Eye has not seen, nor ear heard, nor have entered into the heart of man the things which God has prepared for those who love Him."

This prophetic time when our eyes will finally see and our ears will finally hear is the time that we are quickly moving toward. Just a few more years, according to the encrypted timeline revelation in the Psalms, and then all of these prophecies will be sealed up and completed.

As you have seen, there is a lot of evidence that suggests that the 15 Psalms of Ascent relate year by year to the 15 years leading up to, and then into, the Kingdom of our Lord. Just as the 15 Psalms were sung by priests and pilgrims alike on their way up to the temple at the Feast of Tabernacles, these 15 years have led the way to the ultimate fulfillment of the Messianic Temple, and the Feast of Tabernacles, when mankind will finally, and physically dwell with our Redeemer, our Lord and Savior, the King of Kings and Lord of Lords, Jesus Christ, Yeshua HaMashiach!

CHAPTER 20

Psalm 135 (Not a Song of Ascents)

Year 2035 - Recap of the History of Israel and Praise and Worship for the House of the Lord From Where He Now Dwells!

Psalm 135 isn't a Psalm of Ascent. The Millennial Kingdom is here in 2035, and this Psalm is perfectly, but not coincidentally, placed at the glorious start of the new Millennial Kingdom. It has historical references and forward-looking references, even future judgment references, which we know will be at the Great White Throne Judgment after the Millennial Kingdom. Most of all, it ends with the confirmation that Jesus now "dwells in Jerusalem." Enjoy!

> *¹Praise the LORD!*
>
> *Praise the name of the LORD; praise Him, O you servants of the LORD! ² You who stand in the house of the LORD, in the courts of the house of our God, ³ Praise the LORD, for the LORD is good; sing praises to His name, for it is pleasant. ⁴ For the LORD has chosen Jacob for Himself, Israel for His special treasure. ⁵ For I know that the LORD is great, and our Lord is above all gods. ⁶ Whatever the LORD pleases He does, in heaven and in earth, in the seas and in all deep places. ⁷ He causes the vapors to ascend from*

the ends of the earth; He makes lightning for the rain; He brings the wind out of His treasuries.

⁸ He destroyed the firstborn of Egypt, both of man and beast. ⁹ He sent signs and wonders into the midst of you, O Egypt, upon Pharaoh and all his servants. ¹⁰ He defeated many nations and slew mighty kings— ¹¹ Sihon king of the Amorites, Og king of Bashan, and all the kingdoms of Canaan— ¹² and gave their land as a heritage, a heritage to Israel His people.

¹³ Your name, O Lord, endures forever, Your fame, O Lord, throughout all generations. ¹⁴ For the Lord will judge His people, and He will have compassion on His servants.

¹⁵ The idols of the nations are silver and gold, the work of men's hands. ¹⁶ They have mouths, but they do not speak; eyes they have, but they do not see;

¹⁷ They have ears, but they do not hear; nor is there any breath in their mouths.

¹⁸ Those who make them are like them; so is everyone who trusts in them.

¹⁹ Bless the Lord, O house of Israel! Bless the Lord, O house of Aaron! ²⁰ Bless the Lord, O house of Levi! You, who fear the Lord, bless the Lord! ²¹ Blessed be the Lord out of Zion, **Who dwells in Jerusalem!**

Praise the Lord!

CHAPTER 21

It Takes Two Witnesses

As previously stated, according to God's word you need at least two or three witnesses for a matter to be established as trustworthy and true. One witness simply will not do. I am only covering two witnesses encoded in the Psalms in this book. However, I believe that there are at least three. If time permits I will work on the third, but that will have to wait for now since I believe that time is very short.

There are many verses in the Old and New Testaments of the Bible which reveal that it takes two or three witnesses to settle a matter. Having at least two witnesses is God's designed method of confirmation. Ironically, or should I say perfectly by design, the fact that there are two "testaments," the old and the new, both of which point to Jesus as the Messiah, prove the point precisely.

Don't forget that there are also two witnesses spoken of in Revelation 11, and Jesus always sent out His disciples two by two (Mark 6:7).

Revelation 11:3
And I will give power to my two witnesses, and they will prophesy one thousand two hundred and sixty days, clothed in sackcloth."

Here are a few more verses from the Old and the New Testaments regarding God's requirement for no fewer than 2 or 3 witnesses to establish the trustworthiness of any matter:

Deuteronomy 19:15

...by the mouth of two or three witnesses the matter shall be established.

Matthew 18:15-16

...'by the mouth of two or three witnesses every word may be established.'

John 18:17

It is also written in your law that the testimony of two men is true.

2 Corinthians 13:1

...By the mouth of two or three witnesses every word shall be established."

Both Jesus and the Apostle Paul repeat the established old covenant law regarding the need for two or three witnesses, thereby making it apply equally under the new covenant or "Church Age" in which we are living. Oh, and one more thing, there will certainly be both Jews and Gentiles involved in the final days...

So, how can we know if the 15 Psalms of Ascent are truly a type of calendar for the end times, including the 7-year tribulation period? The Biblical answer is, we need another witness! If the 15 Psalms of Ascent line up with the Gregorian Calendar as a witness for the Gentiles, shouldn't there be a set of Psalms that are also chronological witnesses for the Jews? The answer is yes. How do I know that this set of Psalms is connected directly with the Jews and Israel?

It's all about Israel!

As I have mentioned before regarding the "Fig Tree Generation," Israel became a nation again on May 14, 1948. They were attacked by the surrounding Arab nations of Jordan (Transjordan), Egypt, Lebanon, Syria, Iraq, Saudi Arabia, and Yemen only one day after their rebirth. On

May 15th, 1948, they were attacked with firepower and manpower far greater than what the newly founded nation of Israel could muster. Israel miraculously fought off all of their attackers and managed to hold their fledgling nation together. The Arab-Israeli War, as it is known, lasted from May 15, 1948 until March 10, 1949. So their young life hung in the balance for almost one year until they prevailed over their enemy attackers. Just before the official end of the war, on February 14th, 1949, Israel seated their first Knesset, which is their constituent assembly, sort of like our Congress in the US, or Parliament in Great Britain.

Suppose the fig tree generation started in 1948/1949, and is truly as important of an event as many of us believe. The Psalms do contain a prophetic pattern or sequence, as many Bible scholars have believed throughout the ages. Wouldn't it be reasonable to expect to find a Psalm that announces this, the most important generation, and then also foretells annual prophetic events in a chronological sequence? Let's look at Psalm 1 and see if it matches with the rebirth of Israel in 1948/1949.

You could argue that no one, or no nation, is 1 year old until their first birthday, and you would be correct. The prophetic dating encoded in the Psalms gets complicated because we are dealing with no less than 4 different calendars to figure this out. I made many charts in my study time, and tried to simplify it for the book. However, it's just really complicated! So, instead of making charts, I'm going to focus more on the sequence of the Psalms, point out how they align in order, and give a span of time instead of a single Gregorian year. There's really no other way to approach this, mainly because the calendar that God gave to Moses doesn't align perfectly with the Gregorian calendar.

Here's another example to show you how confusing this can get:

The Israeli 6-Day War was in June of 1967. If you look up the 6-Day War historically on the Israeli calendar, you will find that it was in the month of Iyar of the year 5727. However, that's on the secular calendar, which starts the year on what God called the 7th month. So, if you follow the Jewish religious calendar, you will see that the war took place in the month of Iyar in the year 5728. Then, if you go by God's calendar, the one He gave to Moses and Aaron, it will be different again, but most similar to the Jewish religious calendar. The best that I can figure is that there can be up to a 19 month difference when trying to nail down a specific year for this prophetic timeline, so there just isn't any way of being totally accurate unless you are God. Again, I am reminded of what Jesus said: "No man knows the day or the hour." How true that is. How could anyone know with so many different calendars? But I do expect that He wants us to know the year and maybe even the Moedim. We just can't be certain what day that falls on, or whether it's on His calendar, or on one of ours.

I've given you two examples. So, I will stick with those two to make the case that this decoded prophetic sequence can be trusted. The first example was the rebirth of the Nation of Israel. Based on Jesus' teaching in Matthew 24, we call the Jews who would be alive to see the rebirth of Israel, the "Fig Tree Generation." The second example was the 6-Day War of 1967. As I mentioned previously, for this sequence to be accurate, I would expect to find some prophetic truth about both events in sequence in the Psalms. And guess what, there is!

Let's go back to Israel's rebirth in 1947/1948 and compare it to Psalm 1. I include the year 1947 because it was very significant in the rebirth of the nation, and it appears from the timeline revelation that God also includes it in His timeline. In 1947, the United Nations agreed to the establishment of a Jewish State, but it wasn't until May 14, 1948 when it became a reality. If the final generation spoken of in the Gospels is symbolized by a fig tree, or for that matter any tree as it is in Luke 21:29, then I would expect to see a reference to a tree in Psalm 1 to anchor it in the timeline revelation. And guess what, there it is! In Psalm 1, a man, or symbolically Israel in this case, is described as being like a tree, but it gets even better.

Psalm 1:3
*³ He shall be like a **tree** planted by the rivers of water, that brings forth its fruit in its season, whose leaf also shall not wither; and whatever he does shall prosper.*

Did you pick up on some of the encoded hidden prophetic treasures that God left sprinkled throughout Psalm 1? The "tree" is the first one, "rivers of water" is the next, then "fruit in its season," then "leaf shall not wither," and finally "whatever he does shall prosper."

I don't have time to unpack all of them, and I need to stay focused on the "tree" for this chapter, so I would like to invite you to also review John 7:37-39 along with Ezekiel 47 to have a better understanding of the coming "rivers of water." And by the way, John 7 is also a historical account of Jesus attending and teaching at a certain Moedim, you guessed it, Tabernacles!

I believe, and I think it's self-evident, that Israel is the "tree planted by the rivers of water" in Psalm 1. God uses "He" instead of "They" or the "Nation" because it's encrypted. If He said, "Israel shall be like a tree..." then it wouldn't be encrypted, and this timeline would have been discovered and understood at least decades ago. That clearly wasn't God's plan.

Israel has blossomed and "prospered" during this generation, just as many prophecies foretold. Psalm 1 uses all of the necessary keywords, phrases, and imagery to connect it with Jesus' cursing of the fig tree, and the fig tree prophecy, such as "withered" and "brings forth fruit in its season." In Psalm 1, we see that this tree isn't "withered," and it does "bring forth its fruit in its season." It's literally the opposite of the cursed fig tree described in the Gospels.

The problem with the fig tree that Jesus encountered on His way into Jerusalem was that Jesus wanted to find fruit on it, but it wasn't in its fruit-bearing season yet; it had beautiful leaves and looked good on the outside, but just like Israel at the time, it bore no fruit. So, Jesus cursed it, and caused it to wither.

Mark 11:12-14, 20-24

[12] Now the next day, when they had come out from Bethany, He was hungry. [3] And seeing from afar a fig tree having leaves, He went to see if perhaps He would find something on it. When He came to it, He found nothing but leaves, for it was not the season for figs. [14] In response Jesus said to it, "Let no one eat fruit from you ever again." And His disciples heard it.

20 Now in the morning, as they passed by, they saw the fig tree dried up from the roots. 21 And Peter, remembering, said to Him, "Rabbi, look! The fig tree which You cursed has withered away."

That season is now over! Well, almost... The fig tree was withered and dead for almost 2000 years, but as of the rebirth of Israel, the fig tree is now alive! It's not alive in and of itself, but because it was planted by God by the "rivers of water." It is no longer withered, but it also isn't bearing any fruit because it isn't in season yet, but remember that Jesus connected that as well to the time in which we are now living.

Matthew 24:32
*32 "Now learn this parable from the fig tree: **when its branch has already become tender and puts forth leaves, you know that summer is near.** 33 So you also, when you see all these things, know that it (He) is near—at the doors!*

Summer is the time in Israel when figs are ripe and good to eat. Summer is symbolically the time when Israel will finally bear fruit. There is a lot more that I could say about Psalm 1, but I have to move on. The important point is that in the timeline revelation in the Psalms, Psalm 1 is God's announcement that the curse of the fig tree is over, and summer is on its way!

So, we can see some evidence that Psalm 1 matches the timeline of the rebirth of Israel around 1948. You may be wondering if there is any further evidence of the accuracy of this new second witness to the timeline revelation.

Let's look at a few more Psalms in the sequence and see if they fit into the timeline where they should. I'll try to keep this brief. Please understand that these are encoded patterns. Many of these Psalms have multiple prophetic fulfillments, and do not always speak of a singular time or event.

Psalm 1 matches Israel's rebirth between the Gregorian Calendar years 1947/1948, as already discussed. I would like to point out that in

Luke's Gospel, which is primarily for the Gentiles, in Luke 21:29-30 he adds to the fig tree symbol of Israel and also states, *"look at the fig tree, **and all the trees**.*[30] *When they are already budding, you see and know for yourselves that summer is now near."*

God often symbolizes nations as trees. Israel was reborn out of the Holocaust of World War II. In 1947, the world was still in ruins in the wake of the war, and there were only 99 recognized nations at that time. Since then, all of the nations have been budding in a sense, and today, there are 193 recognized nations in the world. It would be hard to make a case that this prophesy in Luke has not come true over the past 7 decades.

The nations around Israel were specifically known symbolically by their native trees. For instance, you will find that Lebanon was always biblically associated with the cedar tree and is still so even today, as you can see by their flag. The nation of Israel is, as we know, the prophetic and symbolic fig tree. The fig tree has been "putting forth leaves" or blossoming and re-gathering against all odds since its re-birth in 1948. Even though they are surrounded by enemy Arab nations that all want their destruction, they have thrived and continue to thrive just as prophesied in Psalm 1, which says, "whatever he does shall prosper." As I have mentioned before, since 1948 Israel has been in 8 recognized wars and countless armed conflicts with their Arab neighbors. Miraculously, no nation, regardless of how big or powerful, has ever prevailed against them.

Psalm 2 matches Israel's Arab-Israeli War from May 15, 1948 to March 10, 1949, when all of the nations around Israel plotted and conspired against them to destroy them before they could become a nation again.

> **Verses 1-3, 7**
> [1] *Why do the nations rage, and the people plot a vain thing?* [2] *The kings of the earth set themselves, and the rulers take counsel together, against the LORD and against His Anointed, saying,* [3] *"Let us break Their bonds in pieces and cast away Their cords from us."*

*⁷ "I will declare the decree: The LORD has said to Me,
'You are My Son, Today I have begotten You.*

In verses 1-3 you can see the nations around Israel conspiring to destroy God's anointed people, which is exactly what they did in 1948 -1949.

Christians recognize Psalm 2, as either prophetic of the Gog Magog invasion, or even of Armageddon. We also recognize it as a Messianic Psalm, especially verse 7. Rabbis recognize Psalm 2 as it relates to the birth of Israel. I'm saying that based on how God encoded prophecy in the Psalms, and based on the timeline revelation, all of the above are correct. These are repeating prophetic patterns. I'm starting to see that so many of the things that we believers, both Jews and Gentiles, argue about the meaning of do not necessarily have only one meaning, but they establish a pattern. God is so much higher and amazing than we have ever given Him credit for. We think in a small singular sense as if we're in a box when it comes to prophecy, but God doesn't. He established repeating patterns so that we can see the bigger picture, and have a greater understanding if we would only get out of the box we've placed ourselves in.

Psalm 3 perfectly matches the years 1949 to 1950. In the wake of the Arab-Israeli War, Israel finally had some peace and could rest even though they were still surrounded by enemies. That scenario was clearly foretold in Psalm 3 when David was able to rest even though he was still surrounded by enemies at the time when Absalom was attempting to take over the kingdom, and trying to kill him.

Verses 5-8
⁵ I lay down and slept; I awoke, for the LORD sustained me. ⁶ I will not be afraid of ten thousands of people Who have set themselves against me all around. ⁷ Arise, O LORD; Save me, O my God! For You have struck all my enemies on the cheekbone; You have broken the teeth of the ungodly. ⁸ Salvation belongs to the LORD. Your blessing is upon Your people. Selah

Notice also that in Psalm 3, God "struck" David's enemies on the "cheekbone" and "broke" their "teeth." God did not destroy the enemies, but wounded them and turned them back, just as He did in the Arab-Israeli War.

Psalm 4 verse 8 continues the same theme of peace and rest into the years 1950 - 1951.

Verse 8
I will both lie down in peace, and sleep; for You alone, O LORD, make me dwell in safety.

For time sake I cannot cover all of the Psalms in this sequence, so I'm going to jump ahead to the most important ones, historically speaking. The next big event after their rebirth would be the Six-Day War in 1967, when Israel was once again attacked by their Muslim neighbors. In the timeline revelation, I would expect to find a Psalm that matches this conflict around Psalm 20 since Psalm 1 matched the years 1947/1948. Basically, 1947 + 20 = 1967.

As expected, Psalm 20 matches the timeline revelation for 1967 and the Six-Day War in many ways. It literally starts out with the theme of "the day of trouble."

Psalm 20
[1]May the LORD answer you in the day of trouble; may the name of the God of Jacob defend you; [2] may He send you help from the sanctuary, and strengthen you out of Zion; [3] may He remember all your offerings, and accept your burnt sacrifice. Selah

[4] May He grant you according to your heart's desire, and fulfill all your purpose. [5] We will rejoice in your salvation, and in the name of our God we will set up our banners! May the LORD fulfill all your petitions.

[6] Now I know that the LORD saves His anointed; He will answer him from His holy heaven with the saving strength of His right hand.

⁷ Some trust in chariots, and some in horses; but we will
remember the name of the LORD our God. ⁸ They have bowed
down and fallen; but we have risen and stand upright.
⁹ Save, LORD! May the King answer us when we call.

I'm going to try to keep this brief. God defended Israel in the 6 day war in 1967, just as stated in Psalm 20 verse 1. They rejoiced at the victory and set up their banners over new territory, including Jerusalem as stated in verse 5. At least the religious Jews recognized that the Lord saved His anointed (Israel) with the strength of His right hand. God's right hand is always associated with His power and victory over His enemies. Verses 7 -8 related specifically to a military victory over their enemies with the concept of their enemies trusting in "chariots," and in "horses." Clearly, in verse 8, Israel has risen, while their enemies have fallen. You may think that military victory is a common theme in the Psalms, but it isn't. However, I believe that this Psalm was perfectly placed by the hand of God to represent the 6-Day War of 1967 and to help prove the validity of the timeline revelation encoded in the Psalms.

So, today, at the start of 2023, Israel is 74 years old, and they will turn 75 in the spring of this year. I would expect from the timeline revelation that has already been established with the Psalms of Ascent, Psalm 120 - 134 matching years 2020 - 2034, that I will find Psalms in this new sequence starting from the rebirth of Israel in 1947/1948 + 74 years that also match, or complement the time in which we are now living. That was a mouthful, but basically, if you add 74 Psalms/years to Psalm 1, which represents the rebirth of Israel, you should end up at a Psalm matching 2023. Then the question is, do both sets match, or work together in a prophetic way that we can discern now in these last days? The answer is absolutely!

Just as we have a certain set of Psalms that match the Gregorian calendar years, God has also provided us with another set of Psalms, as a second witness, that matches the Jewish "fig tree generation" timeline. They are called the Psalms of Asaph, and they have been miraculously encoded to match our time perfectly, as you will see.

CHAPTER 22

Decoding the Psalms of Asaph

Now that I have established that there is another "witness" in the timeline revelation, let's move forward in time away from the 1940s, '50s, and '60s to the present time to see what God wants us to understand about the years we are now living in.

As I mentioned in the last chapter, at the time of writing this book in 2022 through the early months of 2023, we are in the 74th year of the reborn Israel. In May of 2023, Israel will turn 75. That means according to the timeline revelation, that the "second witness" Psalms that fit our present year would be Psalm 74 to Psalm 75. Before we look at any of these Psalms, I would like to point out that coincidentally, wink-wink, once again, we find that God gave us a special "set" of sequential Psalms for these special years that we are living in. They are called the Psalms of Asaph. Asaph in Hebrew means: "ingathering" and "harvest." I'm sure that is also just a coincidence, right?

There are a total of 12 Psalms of Asaph, but oddly, they are not all located together. Psalm 50 is the first Psalm of Asaph, with the remaining 11 numbered 73-83. As you may recall, the number 11 represents Judgment!

Hebrew Gematria

As we have already discovered, numbers are very important to God. He uses numbers to interconnect scripture and to tell a broader story hidden below the surface. Basically, numbers help us to connect the dots. Gematria is the name of the study of the numerical values of letters, names, words, and phrases in the Bible. The understanding of numbers in the Bible can help us to find the deeper meanings of Biblical texts and how they are interconnected with other texts.

So, as we have already learned, there are 15 special, sequential, and prophetic Psalms of Ascent that match the Gregorian calendar years from 2020 through 2034. In summary, they symbolize our ascent up to the Holy Temple. As you may recall, the number 15, which is made up of 5 and 10, is significant because it is the sum of the short form of God's name. Remember that every Hebrew letter has a number associated with it. So, the two letters that make up the short form of Yahweh (YHWH) are Yod and Hey, which have the numerical values of 10 and 5, respectively. Of course, 10 and 5 equals 15. Isn't it interesting that there are 15 Psalms of Ascent, and the sum of the short form of God's name is also 15? The full Hebrew name for God, however, comprises 4 letters. They are YHWH, which is written almost 7000 times in the Tanakh. The remaining two letters that we have not yet covered are Vav and a second Hey. Vav has a numerical value of 6, and as we already know, Hey has the numerical value of 5 for a sum of 11. The total sum of God's Hebrew name, YHWH, is 26.

It's hard enough to believe that there are two sets of Psalms that interconnect to give us a sequential last-day timeline, but there are. Imagine if it were discovered that those two sets of Psalms were also stamped with God's numerical signature of 26. They are! As unbelievable as it sounds, God validated and signed these two sets of Psalms with his numerical name of 15+11, or 26. How could that be a coincidence?

You may say "Aren't there 12 Psalms of Asaph?" Yes, there are, but as you will soon see, there are only 11 of those in the sequential timeline. As you will also soon see, the 12th is set apart for an important historical and prophetic reason. Regardless, the encrypted, overlapping, and sequential timeline revelation is made up specifically of 26 Psalms matching the signature of God!

Asaph?

Who, or what, is Asaph? Asaph was a Levitical music leader, singer, song writer, and prophet in the time of King David and his son King Solomon (1 Chronicles 15:17, 19; 16:4-7, 25:2; 2 Chronicles 29:30). Asaph's descendants were also music leaders and singers later in the Second Temple time. So, Asaph and his descendants were musicians and singers in both the first and the second Temple periods in Israel. Psalms 50 and then Psalms 73-83 are all in this special category, and are all attributed to Asaph.

The Psalms of Asaph all seem to have different meanings and are distinct from one another. For this reason, it has been difficult for scholars to ascribe a central theme to them, or to summarize them as a set. Why are they even a set? Why is one located separately from the rest?

Within the Psalms of Asaph, there are Psalms with historical significance and some with obvious prophetic significance. There are Psalms within the set that range from destruction and distress to testing and judgment to mercy and salvation. Some appear to be of past events, and some still of future events. Regardless of whether some of them appear to be historic in nature, I believe that all of these special Psalms are none the less prophetic, and that the historical accounts contained within them are also encoded patterns of events yet to come.

Different scholars have categorized this special set of Psalms in different ways as they have tried to focus on a central theme or themes. However, it seems clear to me now, looking through the lens of the timeline revelation, that each one of these Psalms is so distinct from one another because they are, at least in part, like individual, self-contained freight train cars, each carrying unique cargo related to certain prophetic events in time, but all being pulled along headed for the same destination.

It's only within the encrypted timeline revelation, that all of these Psalms start to make sense as a set. So, I would say that the only way to summarize them is in the context of the last days, and as individual years. The reason why I said earlier, "at least in part," is because not every verse within these Psalms pertains specifically to the end times. They also represent different historical timelines and events from Israel's past that spoke to different generations. They also fit into the timeline that J. R. Church discovered in his book, so needless to say, they are all very multifaceted. God is simply amazing with a capital "A!" He isn't one-dimensional the way we tend to think of Him. His thoughts and ways are truly so far above our own that it's unimaginable for us. Only He could encode so much into these Psalms to be revealed in these last days through keywords, phrases, numbers, and imagery, which all connect back to other prophetic verses and chapters in a circular dynamic.

Psalm 50

Even though I would love to jump right into the Psalms of Asaph that correlate to our current time, obviously, I should start at the beginning and take a close look at Psalm 50 first. There is so much to dig out of Psalm 50 that it's hard to know where to begin. First of all, I don't think that it is a coincidence that this Psalm is Psalm "50" in the Masoretic text. Remember that numbers have special meaning in God's prophetic patterns. The number 50 represents a Jubilee, and it's also symbolic of first fruits, freedom, release, and fullness. There are 50 days between the Feast of First Fruits and Pentecost. It was at Pentecost in the Old Testament when the Mosaic Covenant was given at Mt. Sinai. Moses was on Mt. Sinai 3 times at 40 days each time, which equals 120. It was at Pentecost in the New Testament when the Holy Spirit was poured out on 120 followers of Jesus. Can you see how God encoded a pattern of hidden prophetic treasures and tied them all together? God wanted us to see and figure out the connection between 50 and 120 as they relate to the end of the age. There are many more occasions when 120 and 50 appear in the Bible, but that's a study for another day. However, here's one more just for us at the end of our current age. When you multiply 120 by 50, you get 6000. That brings us to the completion of the 6th day. The 7th day is the Millennial Kingdom. The Church Age must conclude at the end of the 6th day. The Church Age is about to end, and it is being foretold through two sets of Psalms, starting with Psalm 50 and Psalm 120.

I hope that you can see how, on the very day when the Old Covenant came to a final close, and the New Covenant had fully come at Pentecost in Acts chapter 2, God connected the two covenants with the number 50 which interconnects with 120. Do you think God wants us to notice the number 50 and the number 120? Is it just a coincidence that these two special sets of Psalms just happen to begin with Psalm 50 and Psalm 120?

As I have mentioned before, but I think it's worth repeating, after studying God's prophetic word for many years, I have concluded that everything down to the smallest detail is deliberate, and there are no coincidences. Many will say that there are different versions of the Old Testament based on the Masoretic texts verses the Greek Septuagint, but I believe that God has a reason for that as well.

It is true that there are different versions of God's word that have different orders. For instance, the Jewish Masoretic text is different from the Greek Septuagint in many ways. One example is that in the Masoretic text, the Psalms of Asaph are numbered 50 & 73-83, and in the Septuagint, they are numbered 49, 72-82. So, if we are to align certain Psalms with certain years, which one is it? I cannot tell you for sure why that is, and why God wanted it that way, but if we are to believe that God is in control of all things, and He has established every little detail, and Him alone, there are no mistakes or coincidences. He planned it that way! Perhaps it is to cause us to dig deeper into his word as an archeologist would after finding a small artifact that tells of a greater hidden treasure buried deeper below the surface. Maybe it's to let us know that the prophecies within these Psalms do not align strictly within a year, but may bleed over into the next year. I don't think that anyone knows the answer for sure, but God does.

The details that we cannot figure out are called "Chukim" by the Jewish Rabbis. That simply means that God is so much greater than we are, and that there are many things that our minds simply cannot comprehend. It reminds me of Isaiah 55, where God declares:

Isaiah 55:8-9

⁸"For My thoughts are not your thoughts, Nor are your ways My ways," says the LORD. ⁹ "For as the heavens are higher than the earth, so are My ways higher than your ways, and My thoughts than your thoughts.

So, there are just some things that we may not figure out until they come to pass. But that doesn't mean that we should quit digging for the truth in God's prophetic word. So, let's keep digging...

The Separation

Earlier, I pointed out that the twelve Psalms of Asaph are in two sections, with Psalm 50 being separated from the remaining eleven. The eleven other Psalms of Asaph start at Psalm 73 and continue to Psalm 83. Isn't that odd? First of all, notice that there are a total of twelve Songs of Asaph, but one is missing from the group. Doesn't that remind you of Revelation 7, where the tribe of Dan is missing from the list of 12 tribes of Israel times 12,000, which equals 144,000 evangelizing and sealed Jews in the Tribulation Period? Also, doesn't it remind you of Jesus' twelve disciples, where there was one who was also thought to be from the tribe of Dan, who was no longer among the other eleven? That was, of course, Judas Iscariot, who betrayed Jesus for 30 pieces of silver he had received from the chief priests (Matthew 26:14-16).

Thirty pieces of silver were ten more than what Joseph's brothers received for him when he was sold into slavery to the Ishmaelite traders. Of course, Joseph was a "pattern" in many ways of the true Messiah Jesus. It always puzzled me that there were 10 pieces of silver difference between how much Joseph was sold for, and how much Jesus was sold for. I pondered if this could have been a mistake in translation, or some other oversight. If Joseph was a type of pattern for the true Messiah, wouldn't God make the amounts the same to tie them together in a definite way? Some scholars have theorized that the difference may have been due to inflation. Personally, I think that's funny, and I don't see biblical evidence that God ever tells his story in that way. I believe that there are two answers to this conundrum... The first is that God wants us to notice the difference between the two, which is "10"! Secondly, what is the sum of 20 pieces of silver plus 30 pieces of silver? It's 50! And if that wasn't enough, 20 times 30 equal 6000! So, the Old Testament Messianic figure, times the New Testament true Messiah, equals 6000, which brings us to the close of the age just as I described previously. You just can't make this stuff up!

Can you see how God has orchestrated all of this so that one points to the other in a circular manner? Obviously, God wants us to look at the Psalms of Ascent starting with Psalm 120, but now we can also see that He wants us to look at both Psalm 10 and 50 as well in relation to the end times. It just so happens that Psalm 10 is an extensive description of the Antichrist, and Psalm 50 is a picture of the tribulation period, but instead of reading from beginning to end, it's structured from end to beginning. That ties directly to Isaiah 46, where God announces that He declares the "end from the beginning!"

Isaiah 46:9-10

9Remember the former things of old, for I am God, and there is no other; I am God, and there is none like Me,10 declaring the end from the beginning, and from ancient times things that are not yet done, saying, 'My counsel shall stand, and I will do all My pleasure,'

The Number 11

As I have mentioned, the Psalms of Asaph are comprised of a total of 12 Psalms. However, there is 1 of the Psalms that is separated from the rest. Psalm 50 is the "1" that is separated from the rest, similar to Judas, who was one of the prototypes of the Antichrist. That leaves 11 Psalms in one group and then 1 separated from the group.

The number 11 in the Bible is associated with the Antichrist, rebellion, chaos, disorder, judgment, betrayal, idolatry, bribery, lack of trust in YHWH, incomplete and false government, imperfection, and counterfeit. The lunar calendar, which the Jews currently and falsely follow, is 11 days shorter than the solar calendar per year. God gave Moses a solar calendar, and not a lunar calendar. The Jews adopted the lunar calendar when they were in Babylonian captivity. The Antichrist is the 11th horn of Daniel 7; Moses' 11 day journey lasted 40 years due to rebellion by the Children of Israel. Genesis 11 is the chapter that gives the account of the Tower of Babel, and the list goes on and on.

The 11th Hebrew letter is Khaf, which has a meaning of "similar." The number 11 in Hebrew can be made up of a 10 + 1. The number 10 is the letter Yod in Hebrew, which has the meaning of work and deeds, among others. Yod can be both good and bad since there were 10 Commandments given to Israel, but only after 10 Plagues were sent upon Egypt. The number 1 is the letter Aleph in Hebrew, which has the meaning of strength, prince, and leader. It can be said that it will take discernment through the Holy Spirit to judge who is good, and who is bad. Is the "prince" of Daniel 9:26 the real prince, or is he the false prince?

The number 11 can also be made up of 5 + 6. The number 5 is the letter Hey in Hebrew, which has the meaning of power and strength, among other things. The number 6 is the letter Vav in Hebrew, which has the meaning of man and beast, among other things. Together, they are once again equal to the Antichrist, a powerful man or beast, who is rebellious against God and a counterfeit.

Commentary on Psalm 50

Within Psalm 50 there are 23 verses broken down into 6 stanzas that make up 3 distinct scenes of the 7-year tribulation period. However, they are inverted, so the stanzas can be read from bottom to top in chronological order. There are also 23 Psalms in between Psalm 50 and the remaining 11 Psalms, which, of course, starts with Psalm 73. Can that just be a coincidence, or does God want us to also notice the number 23?

I find it very interesting that there are specifically 23 verses in Psalm 50, and 23 Psalms, which are also 23 years, between Psalm 50 and the remaining Psalms of Asaph. As if that weren't enough, the number 23 in the Bible, and in the Hebrew tradition relates to wickedness, lust, idolatry, immorality, stubbornness, grumbling, and complaining.

According to Jeremiah 25, the people of Judah were about to go into captivity for 70 years, but they would not listen to the prophets who tried to warn them, and they would not turn from their wicked ways. Jeremiah warned them every day for 23 years, as did other prophets, but the people still would not listen. I believe that Psalm 50 has been a warning to Israel in our time to turn from their unrighteousness, and to accept the true Messiah, Jesus. However, they are anxiously awaiting a man who they will accept as their messiah, but he will ultimately deceive them, turn on them, and try to destroy them.

Jeremiah 25:3
³*"From the thirteenth year of Josiah the son of Amon, king of Judah, even to this day, this is the **twenty-third** year in which the word of the LORD has come to me; and I have spoken to you, rising early and speaking, but you have not listened.*

I believe that the 50th year after the rebirth of Israel, which landed around 1998/1999, and the 23-year warning since then, has more Antichrist connections than I can expose here now. That will have to be a study for a later chapter. For now, it is important to understand that Israel did not recognize their true Messiah, who was sacrificed for their sins, once and for all, 2000 years ago. So, by not believing in and worshipping Jesus, any form of worship is rebellion and idolatry against God, since our Heavenly Father put all things under His only Son's feet (1 Corinthians 15:27, Ephesians 1:22).

Within Psalm 50, there is one verse that I'll call the "beginning verse," not because it is numerically at the beginning, but because it describes the beginning of the tribulation period as "the day of trouble" when Israel is to call upon the Lord for deliverance and glorify God.

This verse happens to be verse 15! The number 15 brings us back to the 5, the 10, and the 50, and, of course, the 15 Songs of Ascent! Can you see how God has connected all of these dots for us? If God had not revealed the 5 and 10 to me that night in answer to my prayer, none of this would have been decoded, but He did!

I believe that verse 15 is the key to the tribulation period for the Jews. The purpose for the entire 7- year tribulation is summed up in one sentence. Verse 15 says, *"call upon Me in **the day of trouble**; I will deliver you, and you shall glorify Me."* The "day of trouble is the start of the 7-year tribulation period, although most Jews will not realize it at that time. At the middle point of the tribulation, which is the three-and-a-half-year mark from the confirming of the covenant by the Antichrist, the Antichrist will stand in, or on, the Temple and declare that He is god. He will then end the sacrifices and make the land desolate according to Daniel 9:27, Matthew 24:15, and Mark 13:14. At that time, the Jews will have to flee to a place that God has prepared for them according to Revelation 12:14. If you have read the previous chapters regarding the 15 Psalms of Ascent, you will know that I'm calling the place that God has prepared for them, the "refuge." At the time when they will have to flee to the refuge, they will finally realize that they were deceived into thinking that this "man of sin" was their messiah. The fleeing remnant will finally know beyond any doubt that Jesus was, and is, the true Messiah. They will "call upon" Him, He will "deliver" them, and they will "glorify" Him. My daily prayer is that many of them will realize this prior to the rapture and the tribulation so that they do not have to go through this horrible time that is literally just around the corner.

CHAPTER 23

Psalm 50 A Psalm of Asaph.

Years 1998/1999 - A Prophetic Last Day's Warning to Israel

Remember I stated in the previous chapter that it appears to me that Psalm 50 is chronologically inverted? It makes sense to me that a Psalm, which speaks to the last days and the satanically inspired false messiah, would be inverted. After all, Satanism is the inversion of Christianity. That should get our attention!

> **Verse 1**
> *¹The Mighty One, God the LORD, has spoken and called the earth from the rising of the sun to its going down.*

I believe that this first verse represents the Millennial Kingdom after the tribulation period when the Lord will rule over all of the nations of the earth and all of the heavens which is represented by the phrase *"from the rising of the sun to its going down."* This phrase connects with Psalm 113, which expands on this same concept.

> **Psalm 113:2-4**
> *²Blessed be the name of the LORD from this time forth and forevermore! ³From the rising of the sun to its going down the LORD's name is to be praised. ⁴The LORD is high above all nations, His glory above the heavens.*

Verse 2
²Out of Zion, the perfection of beauty, God will shine forth.

Before Jesus can rule from Zion, which we know will happen from many prophetic scriptures, Jesus has to actually be in Zion. Verse 2 tells us that He is shining forth from a literal Zion. Remember, just as Isaiah 46 tells us, God tells the end from the beginning. Psalm 50 is also telling the end from the beginning.

So, before Jesus can shine forth from Zion, He first has to destroy the armies who have amassed against Him. Verse 3 tells of Jesus' return and victory at Armageddon.

Verse 3
³Our God shall come, and shall not keep silent; a fire shall devour before Him, And it shall be very tempestuous all around Him.

This is a view of the second coming of our Lord. It carries some of the same symbolism of many of the Old Testament scriptures, which are also prophetic of that coming day, such as Zechariah 9. Notice the use of the word "tempestuous" in verse 3, and the word "whirlwinds" in Zechariah 9. These verses are not overlapping, but are complementary and paint a broader view of the same event.

Zechariah 9:14-15
¹⁴ Then the LORD will be seen over them, and His arrow will go forth like lightning. The Lord GOD will blow the trumpet, and go with whirlwinds from the south.¹⁵ The LORD of hosts will defend them; they shall devour and subdue with slingstones. They shall drink and roar as if with wine; they shall be filled with blood like basins, like the corners of the altar.

On that same day, Zechariah also writes in Zechariah 12 that the remnant of Israel will finally see Jesus, *"the one whom they pierced,"* and

mourn for Him for what their forefathers did to Him. Then Zechariah
ties that day together with Megiddo, which is Armageddon.

Zechariah 12:10-11

*¹⁰ "And I will pour on the house of David and on the
inhabitants of Jerusalem the Spirit of grace and supplication;
then they will look on Me whom they pierced. Yes, they
will mourn for Him as one mourns for his only son, and
grieve for Him as one grieves for a firstborn. ¹¹ In that
day there shall be a great mourning in Jerusalem, like the
mourning at Hadad Rimmon **in the plain of Megiddo**.*

Verses 4-6

*⁴He shall call to the heavens from above, and to the earth,
that He may judge His people: ⁵ "Gather My saints together
to Me, those who have made a covenant with Me by
sacrifice." ⁶Let the heavens declare His righteousness, for
God Himself is Judge. Selah*

Verses 4 - 6 also correlate with many prophetic second-coming
verses in Matthew, Mark, and the Book of Revelation.

Revelation 19:11

*¹¹ Now I saw heaven opened, and behold, a white horse.
And He who sat on him was called Faithful and True, and
in righteousness He judges and makes war.*

Matthew 24:29-31

*²⁹ "Immediately after the tribulation of those days the sun
will be darkened, and the moon will not give its light; the
stars will fall from heaven, and the powers of the heavens
will be shaken.³⁰ Then the sign of the Son of Man will
appear in heaven, and then all the tribes of the earth will
mourn, and they will see the Son of Man coming on the
clouds of heaven with power and great glory.³¹ And He will*

send His angels with a great sound of a trumpet, and they will gather together His elect from the four winds, from one end of heaven to the other.

Mark 13:27

²⁷ And then He will send His angels, and gather together His elect from the four winds, from the farthest part of earth to the farthest part of heaven.

Verses 7-11

⁷ "Hear, O My people, and I will speak, O Israel, and I will testify against you; I am God, your God! ⁸ I will not rebuke you for your sacrifices or your burnt offerings, Which are continually before Me. ⁹ I will not take a bull from your house, Nor goats out of your folds. ¹⁰ For every beast of the forest is Mine, and the cattle on a thousand hills. ¹¹ I know all the birds of the mountains, and the wild beasts of the field are Mine.

Israel is once again making sacrifices during the tribulation period, but God rebukes them just as He does in Isaiah chapter 1.

Isaiah 1:11-17

¹¹ "To what purpose is the multitude of your sacrifices to Me?" Says the LORD. "I have had enough of burnt offerings of rams and the fat of fed cattle. I do not delight in the blood of bulls, or of lambs or goats.

¹² "When you come to appear before Me, who has required this from your hand, to trample My courts? ¹³ bring no more futile sacrifices; incense is an abomination to Me. The New Moons, the Sabbaths, and the calling of assemblies—I cannot endure iniquity and the sacred meeting.

¹⁴ Your New Moons and your appointed feasts My soul hates; they are a trouble to Me, I am weary of bearing them. [15] When you spread out your hands, I will hide My eyes from you; even though you make many prayers, I will not hear. Your hands are full of blood.

[16] "Wash yourselves, make yourselves clean; put away the evil of your doings from before My eyes. Cease to do evil, [17] learn to do good; seek justice, rebuke the oppressor; defend the fatherless, plead for the widow.

Verses 12-14

[12] "If I were hungry, I would not tell you; For the world is Mine, and all its fullness.

[13] Will I eat the flesh of bulls, or drink the blood of goats? [14] Offer to God thanksgiving, and pay your vows to the Most High.

Verses 12-14 are further proof that Israel is once again conducting the sacrificial system of atonement at either a temporary tabernacle structure or at the temple at this time in our upside-down tribulation sequence. However, Jesus was the fulfillment of the sacrificial system, and no longer requires empty sacrifices to atone for Israel's transgressions. Israel's offerings and sacrifices are clearly not what the Lord wants. He wants true worship and thankfulness from His chosen people, and not empty religion.

Just as it was 2000 years ago, it seems that the religious leaders of Israel once again will appear to be righteous by their outward show, garments, sacrifices, and symbols, but inside, they will be spiritually dead. Jesus pointed this out many times in His confrontations with the Pharisees, just as in Matthew 23.

Matthew 23:27-28

[27] "Woe to you, scribes and Pharisees, hypocrites! For you are like whitewashed tombs which indeed appear beautiful outwardly, but inside are full of dead men's bones and all uncleanness. [28] Even so you also outwardly appear righteous to men, but inside you are full of hypocrisy and lawlessness.

Verse 14 makes a special point to say that If someone makes a vow to make a special offering they need to keep it. Maybe that relates to a specific person in the future and will be important during that specific time. In general, Ecclesiastes tells us that if we do make a vow, we need to fulfill it promptly and completely.

Ecclesiastes 5:4-7

[4] When you make a vow to God, do not delay to fulfill it. He has no pleasure in fools; fulfill your vow.[5] It is better not to make a vow than to make one and not fulfill it.[6] Do not let your mouth lead you into sin. And do not protest to the temple messenger, "My vow was a mistake." Why should God be angry at what you say and destroy the work of your hands?[7] Much dreaming and many words are meaningless. Therefore fear God.

Verse 15

*[15]Call upon Me in **the day of trouble; I will deliver you, and you shall glorify Me**."*

I believe that verse 15 signifies the start of the tribulation period. The "day of trouble" is synonymous with the "day of the Lord," "day of wrath," "days of affliction," and all of the other synonymous phrases used in the Bible for the time of God's judgment on the earth. In addition, it ties directly to another Psalm of Asaph, Psalm 77, which we will see matches the years 2025/2026 in the timeline revelation. Remember that Psalm 50 appears to be sort of a mini version of the tribulation period condensed inside of just one Psalm, and then inverted.

Psalm 77:2-3

*In the **day of my trouble** I sought the Lord; my hand was stretched out in the night without ceasing; my soul refused to be comforted. [3] I remembered God, and was troubled; I complained, and my spirit was overwhelmed. Selah*

Verses 16-21

[16]But to the wicked God says: "What right have you to declare My statutes, or take My covenant in your mouth, [17] Seeing you hate instruction and cast My words behind you? [18] When you saw a thief, you consented with him, and have been a partaker with adulterers. [19]You give your mouth to evil, and your tongue frames deceit. [20]You sit and speak against your brother; you slander your own mother's son. [21]These things you have done, and I kept silent; you thought that I was altogether like you; But I will rebuke you, and set them in order before your eyes.

Verses 16 through 21 are the "6" verses of the Antichrist. How fitting for there to be "6" dedicated verses within this condensed tribulation account to give us a little more detail about the "man of sin" who is coming. If Psalm 50 is as chronological as I believe it to be, the fact that these 6 Antichrist verses come after the start of the tribulation actually means that he will start to rise prior to it, since this is in reverse chronological order. Of course, we know that he cannot fully come to power until after the rapture, and the removal of the restrainer, according to 2 Thessalonians 2. When taking all of the corresponding prophetic scriptures together with the encrypted timeline revelation, it appears that the Antichrist rises prior to the start of the tribulation, but around the time of the Gog Magog invasion of Israel. I cannot fully declare when the rapture takes place within the timeline revelation, because, as you may recall, it gives us an "open door" timeframe from 2021 until the end of 2024. It may actually be after the Gog Magog invasion, but God didn't intend for it to be known. So, as I'm writing this, I'm also praying that the Lord will allow me to finish this work, and that it will be received by those who the Lord intends for it to be received by. Every day, and with everything happening in the world today pushing us toward the end, I have an overwhelming sense that I'm running out of time.

There is so much to unpack in these 6 verses that I'm not quite sure where to start, so I'll just start with verses 16 and 17 and take the verses two at a time.

Verses 16-17

[16] But to the wicked God says: "What right have you to declare My statutes, or take My covenant in your mouth, [17] seeing you hate instruction and cast My words behind you?

There are so many Western prophecy teachers who say that the Antichrist will be European based on what Daniel 9:26 says.

Daniel 9:26

*[26] "And after the sixty-two weeks Messiah shall be cut off, but not for Himself; and the **people of the prince** who is to come shall destroy the city and the sanctuary. The end of it shall be with a flood, and till the end of the war desolations are determined.*

At first glance it appears that the Antichrist will be European/Roman since "the people" who destroyed the temple and Jerusalem back in 70 AD and 135 AD were Romans. Logically, then, if "the people" of "the prince" are Roman, then "the prince" is also Roman. I'm not going to go into the argument of whether the actual soldiers who destroyed Jerusalem were European Romans, or perhaps Syrian Romans, because I don't think it really matters too much. The reality is that the tribulation period, Daniel's 70th week, is all about Israel (Daniel 9:24). Yes, it's a time of wrath and judgment for the world, but the central focus is Israel. Israel, or at least the religious Jews, are awaiting the person who they believe will be their messiah. Their oral and written tradition is concrete, and there's simply no way that Israel will accept a "Gentile" messiah. The Bible teaches this, and the Jewish rabbis have historically all taught that the messiah must be from the blood-line of David. The Rabbinical leaders have already stated that they will test his blood to ensure that he is from the Davidic bloodline, but that doesn't mean he must be born in Israel. He could certainly come from one of the European nations, and thereby meet all of the qualifications.

There is so much that I want to write about this, but it may end up being a separate chapter or maybe even a separate book. For now, let me just say that the coming Antichrist will have to have Davidic blood, he will come out of one of the countries that we know were part of the Roman empire, which I believe still exists today in the shadows, and he will also be a hybrid. So, in a sense, everyone is correct. I liken it to how the religious leaders before Jesus' time couldn't quite figure out the origin of the Messiah. Obviously, He had to be a descendant of David. Further, one messianic prophecy showed Him being born in Bethlehem, yet another said He would come out of Egypt, and yet another indicated that He would be called a Nazarene according to Matthew 2:23. So which one was correct? All of them! He was born in Bethlehem, escaped to Egypt, and then moved to Nazareth. It's that simple, but only in hindsight.

Ok, back to verse 16 now that I have established that the Antichrist must be at least in part from the bloodline of David and that everyone is at least partially correct about his origin. Just as with Jesus, his origin won't be crystal clear until after he has arrived. We know from scripture that the Antichrist will be a wicked deceiver (Daniel 8:25, 2 Thessalonians 2:10). We also know that he will not have any regard for the God of his fathers from Daniel 11:37. That means that he will not believe in the teachings of the Hebrew Bible, the Tanakh. However, that doesn't mean that he will not know the scriptures, or pretend to follow them in order to deceive and control the religious leaders in Israel who are currently restlessly waiting for their messiah to appear. That is what I believe is being described in Verses 16 and 17. The "wicked" is the Antichrist who will use the Torah to deceive the religious leaders as well as the masses, and once he becomes firmly in control, he will remove the veil of deceit as well as any pretense that he was one of them, and a follower of the Torah.

If all of that wasn't enough confusion about the coming Antichrist, I have to add one more significant possibility to his bloodline. That would be through Ishmael and Esau. Remember that there has been a family feud going on for thousands of years between Jacob and Esau. Esau married into the family of Ishmael (Genesis 28), who was the first-born of Abraham, not through Sarah, but through Hagar, her handmaid. They are part of the "many nations" that would come out of Abraham (Genesis 17). It is understood that the Muslim nations surrounding Israel are made up of, at least in part, the descendants of these two patriarchs. That brings us to Islam and its Eschatology, which shares some similarities with that of Rabbinical Judaism and Christianity. Once again, that would be an entire book on its own, so I will try to narrow it down in a few sentences. Islam, as well as Judaism, claims that God has no son. In 1 John 4:3, we read, *"and every spirit that does not confess that Jesus Christ has come in the flesh is not of God. And this is the spirit of the Antichrist, which you have heard was coming, and is now already in the world."* So, is Jesus Christ the Son of God? A few verses later, John continues and clarifies by saying, *"In this the love of God was manifested toward us, that God has sent His only begotten Son into the world, that we might live through Him."*

By their "anti" Son of God beliefs, Islam is at least a part of the coming Antichrist. It seems likely that the Antichrist and his sidekick, the false prophet, will deceive many, both Jews and Gentiles, by using their prophets and oral traditions against them. Coming on the scene and mesmerizing them with his knowledge of their written scriptures, the Antichrist could easily fool them into following him in unity to their own demise. In fact, it seems self-evident that Satan established false religions for this very purpose. It isn't clear today how Islam's eschatology fits in with the tribulation period, but I'm certain that the Antichrist will deceive many through both Judaism and Islam in the last days. Basically, at some point, he will convince the world that he is the fulfillment of the world's religions. Only those "elect" who hold tight to the teachings of the real Messiah, Jesus, will be able to see through his deception.

Verses 18-19
When you saw a thief, you consented with him, and have been a partaker with adulterers. [19] You give your mouth to evil, and your tongue frames deceit.

The first part of verse 18 matches Isaiah 62, which is part of Isaiah's 7 chapters in a row from chapters 60 - 66 devoted to the last days, and the coming Millennial Kingdom. In those 7 chapters God gives us many specifics, but it's hard to find any chronological order to them. In many cases, they certainly retell the same time periods, but with emphasis on different events. In speaking of the Antichrist, Psalm 50 verse 18 refers to his consenting with a thief and partaking with adulterers. I have to say that I wrestled with the "thief" part of verse 18 all day. In my mind, I kept thinking of the thief as an individual. I just couldn't figure out, or find the answer to who this is referring to in God's word on my own. So, I prayed about it last night and asked the Lord to once again give me a wake-up call in the night when the answer to the question was about to be revealed on my nightstand tablet, which I have set to play random books of the Bible all night long. And once again, God woke me up just in time to hear Isaiah 62:8-9 at around 1:30 in the morning! Here's what God has to say through the prophet Isaiah about these "thieves" that the Antichrist has consented with:

Isaiah 62:8-9
⁸The Lᴏʀᴅ has sworn by His right hand and by the arm of His strength: "surely I will no longer give your grain as food for your enemies; and the sons of the foreigner shall not drink your new wine, for which you have labored. ⁹But those who have gathered it shall eat it, and praise the Lᴏʀᴅ; those who have brought it together shall drink it in My holy courts."

It appears to me that the Antichrist will allow Israel to be plundered by their enemies, which would fit into the timeline revelation between 2028 and 2031. That's the time when the remnant of Israel will go to the "refuge," and the land will be "plowed" by their foreign enemies (Psalm 129). And, as we know, according to Zechariah 13, two-thirds of Israel will be killed during that time. The good news is, according to Isaiah 62, this will be the last time that such a terrible thing will ever happen to His children, Israel.

The second part of verse 18 says that you, in the context of the Antichrist, "*have been a partaker with adulterers.*" This makes perfect sense when you read Revelation 17 and see that the kings of the earth and the inhabitants of the earth committed fornication with the great harlot who rides the beast.

Revelation 17:1-2
¹ Then one of the seven angels who had the seven bowls came and talked with me, saying to me, "Come, I will show you the judgment of the great harlot who sits on many waters, ² with whom the kings of the earth committed fornication, and the inhabitants of the earth were made drunk with the wine of her fornication."

The Antichrist will be a "partaker" in this adultery, but only for a time until the kings, who hate the harlot, destroy her and give their kingdom over to the beast, as described in Revelation 17:16-17.

Now let's consider verse 19, which says, *"You give your mouth to evil, and your tongue frames deceit."* This verse wasn't too hard to figure out since it is an easily discerned and accurate description of the Antichrist. We know from many different prophetic scriptures that he, the Antichrist, will have a mouth full of lies, deceit, and blasphemy. According to Revelation 13, he will be allowed to continue his lies and blasphemies through the first three and a half years, then for another three and a half years until his end.

Revelation 13:5-6
⁵ And he was given a mouth speaking great things and blasphemies, and he was given authority to continue for forty-two months. ⁶ Then he opened his mouth in blasphemy against God, to blaspheme His name, His tabernacle, and those who dwell in heaven.

Verses 20-21
²⁰ You sit and speak against your brother; you slander your own mother's son. ²¹ These things you have done, and I kept silent; you thought that I was altogether like you; but I will rebuke you, and set them in order before your eyes.

I think verse 20 is really interesting from a literary and historical viewpoint. God really has a way with words! Without the context of the timeline revelation, this verse really doesn't make any sense. However, when you view it through the end-time lens, and realize that this Psalm is not just general truth, but also specific truth for a specific time period, it all starts to come into focus.

In verse 20 we see the subject "you," who I believe is the Antichrist, speaking against his brother. That brings up the question of, "who is his brother?" And, if this were just a general reference to anyone's brother, it would seem out of context within this Psalm, which is ultimately about the intervention of Christ in the world at His second coming, and about His judgment. Certainly, James 4:11 tells us not to speak against, or slander a brother, but in context, I believe that there is a whole lot more going on here in verse 20. Notice that our subject is both sitting, and speaking against his brother. To "sit" many times in the Bible represents a position of power, authority, and judgment. If we use the word "sit" as a key word to connect it to other prophetic scriptures, we find 2 Thessalonians 2 which is directly speaking of the Antichrist.

2 Thessalonians 2:4
*⁴ who opposes and exalts himself above all that is called God or that is worshiped, so that he **sits** as God in the temple of God, showing himself that he is God.*

Not only do we see the Antichrist sitting in the Temple in 2 Thessalonians 2, but he's also slandering God and exalting himself above God, which further correlates with the previous verse, verse 19.

There are two possibilities as to the identity of who the "brother" is in the first part of verse 20. The first is Jesus, since He would be considered a brother in the Hebrew custom through the patriarch Judah. Remember that the Antichrist has to be from the line of Judah through David, or he will not be accepted by the Jews. The second possibility is that the "brother" is referring to Israel, all of Israel, since he will also be kin to them. There's no way to be certain at this point, but my hunch is that the first part of verse 20 is referring to Jesus, because the second part of the verse strengthens, and focuses in a little narrower on the "brother's" identity.

In the second part of verse 20, the brother is called "your own mother's son." We know from Revelation 12, Isaiah 54, Isaiah 66, and Micah 4:10 that the mother is Israel. Again, from Revelation 12 we know that "your own mother's son" has to be Jesus. It's a really interesting way of connecting both of them together through a common bloodline, which aligns with prophetic scripture.

Verse 21 is the final of the six verses of the Antichrist in Psalm 50. This verse continues the connections between these verses and many other prophetic "Antichrist" verses. It states, "*these things you have done, and I kept silent; you thought that I was altogether like you; but I will rebuke you, and set them in order before your eyes.*" Remember that in Revelation 13, God allows the Antichrist, also known as the "beast," to continue for another 42 months unopposed. He thinks, therefore, that he is like God, and is a god, but his days are literally numbered. That number is 42 more months, and then he will find out who God really is.

Revelation 19:19-20

[19] And I saw the beast, the kings of the earth, and their armies, gathered together to make war against Him who sat on the horse and against His army. [20] Then the beast was captured, and with him the false prophet who worked signs in his presence, by which he deceived those who received the mark of the beast and those who worshiped his image. These two were cast alive into the lake of fire burning with brimstone.

Verse 22

[22] "Now consider this, you who forget God, lest I tear you in pieces, and there be none to deliver:

In context, verse 22 is a stern warning before the tribulation begins. Remember that this Psalm is inverted, so the end is the beginning. Remember also that Jesus is returning, not as the suffering servant, but as the conquering King. There are many scriptures that I could use to illustrate how powerful and frightening His return will be for those who do not know Him, and are not called by His name. I decided to use Nahum chapter 1, which sums it up pretty well and uses much of the same imagery as found in verse 3 of Psalm 50.

Nahum 1:2-6

[2] God is jealous, and the LORD avenges; the LORD avenges and is furious. The LORD will take vengeance on His adversaries, and He reserves wrath for His enemies; [3] The LORD is slow to anger and great in power, and will not at all acquit the wicked. The LORD has His way in the whirlwind and in the storm, and the clouds are the dust of His feet. [4] He rebukes the sea and makes it dry, and dries up all the rivers. Bashan and Carmel wither, and the flower of Lebanon wilts. [5] The mountains quake before Him, the hills melt, and the earth heaves at His presence, yes, the world and all who dwell in it. [6] Who can stand before His indignation? And who can endure the fierceness of His anger? His fury is poured out like fire, and the rocks are thrown down by Him.

Think of all of the horrible things that mankind has done throughout history. Think of all of the martyrs who have given their lives, and who will give their lives in the coming tribulation period at the hands of wicked men, all to honor God. Now, think about how patient God has been all this time. His patience will finally run out, and those who are not sealed will suffer His overwhelming wrath. Trust me, you do not want to be in His crosshairs when His anger crushes the wicked who have taken the mark of the beast and dare to stand against Him.

Verse 23

[23] Whoever offers praise glorifies Me; and to him who orders his conduct aright I will show the salvation of God."

After the strong warning of verse 22, the ever-merciful God gives hope and instruction to those living today as well as throughout the tribulation period, just as He also did in Nahum 1. In Nahum 1, after 6 verses of horror and devastation at the hand of the most powerful being in existence, God then simply says in the following verse, "*7The LORD is good, a stronghold in the day of trouble; and He knows those who trust in Him.*"

So, offer Him praise and glorify His name, keep your path straight, and do not turn from it no matter what comes against you. If you are reading this prior to the start of the tribulation period, please put your trust in Jesus before it's too late. Call out to Him and make Him the Lord of your life. Remember that God the Father put all things, including judgment, under His Son's feet. If you are reading this during the tribulation, He knows who you are, and whether you have placed your trust in Him or not. If you have, you are sealed, and on the day of His wrath at His return, you will be spared, according to scripture. Please, at any cost do not accept the mark of the beast! Do not worship the beast! Do not allow them to put anything inside of you that can alter your DNA! Stay away from anything "Bio!" Once you accept anything that alters your genetics, you will not be redeemable. Remember, Jesus came as a man to die for mankind, not for transhumans. And above all, don't forget to pray, pray, pray!

CHAPTER 24

Psalms of Asaph 73 - 83

Now that we have studied the Psalms of Ascent, and the all-important and purposefully displaced Psalm 50, let's dig into the remaining Psalms of Asaph and discover what else God has encoded, and what else He wants to reveal to us. Keep in mind that these 11 Psalms of Asaph do not mimic, or necessarily parallel the Psalms of Ascent, but they complement them and give them more context. They do follow a sequential year-to-year pattern, just like the Psalms of Ascent, but I would say that they almost seem to fit in between the years represented by the Psalms of Ascent instead of overlapping them.

What I have found in the Psalms of Asaph is that God uses keywords, phrases, and imagery to make connections in certain verses rather than the entire verse being the connection. I think you will see what I am talking about in Psalm 73. Some of the keywords and phrases you will notice in Psalm 73 that match perfectly with the years 2021 and 2022 are: "pangs," "plagued," and "wash my hands." You might think that those words are mere coincidences in long streams of words and sentences that I have probably taken out of context. You could be right, but when you consider that those keywords and phrases only show up in certain Psalms, which perfectly match the timeline revelation, as well as connect with other prophetic scriptures that further fill-in the prophetic events in the timeline, it's a little hard to believe that they are there simply by coincidence. What I'm trying to say is, "you just can't make this stuff up!" It's part of God's revelation of the times that we are in, but it wasn't intended to be easily decoded or understood. Remember, God's word for this time is as much a battle plan as it is nourishment for our souls. Our military doesn't reveal their battle plans to their enemy, and neither does God!

Even though I believe that God has allowed me, and aided me in decoding the timeline revelation, there are still so many aspects of the last days that remain hidden. For example, I cannot tell you for sure from the timeline revelation in the Psalms what year Damascus will be destroyed as prophesied in Isaiah 17 and Jeremiah 49. However, when I apply the interconnecting keywords and phrases, my best guess would be in the year of distress of 2029, which covered in the Psalms of Ascent. I could do an entire teaching on that, and connect many scriptures to the timeline revelation to show that 2029 is the most obvious year, but for what purpose? It simply isn't clear enough to state conclusively. However, after saying that, I have to also say that if I currently lived in Damascus, I would be making plans to move as soon as possible. Regardless of what year, your time is very short!

As we navigate through the remaining 11 Psalms of Asaph, and put them into the context of the timeline revelation, it's good to realize that the entire Psalm isn't going to be prophetic of their associated years the way that most of the Psalms of Ascent were. I cannot stress this enough. The Psalms of Ascent are primarily prophetic relative to the final 15 years as they progress up the steps to the ultimate Temple in Zion, and our Lord Jesus Christ. The Psalms of Asaph only offer, more or less, prophetic glimpses hidden inside of each of them. In order to bring those glimpses into greater focus, to see them more clearly, it takes biblical prophetic literacy, but most of all, the Holy Spirit.

Dating the Psalms of Asaph

There are major differences between the Gregorian Calendar, which most of the world uses, and the Jewish Calendar. Even the Jewish Calendar has two start dates, one at the 1st month according to God, and one at the 7th month according to Rabbis. I tried to create tables and lists to correlate the different calendars until my head just about exploded, and I decided that it just wasn't feasible. So, what I have done instead with the Psalms of Asaph was to give more of a range between two years. They are still sequential, but based on my calculations, there could be a shift of around 19 months to accommodate the calendar differences.

As a reminder of an example that I have previously given, I would like to use the Six-Day War, which was in June of 1967. That was Iyar 26, 5727, on the Jewish secular calendar that starts on the 1st of the 7th month. However, that war took place on Iyar 26, 5728, on their religious calendar since the year had already changed on that calendar. So, which calendar do you go by? Personally, I think this is one reason why Jesus said that "no man knows the day or the hour." How could you since there are so many calendars?

Another option is to simply take the date when Israel became a nation again, which is, of course, May 14, 1948, and then add the Psalm number to it. So, Psalm 73 is 1948 + 73 = 2021. That gets us close anyway. Where I ran into trouble with this simple way of calculating the year was for the Six-Day War that I mentioned before. It is clearly prophesied in Psalm 20, but if you add 20 to 1948, you get 1968. That gets into the semantics of when Israel was really born. Some say it was in 1947 with the UN Resolution 181. Others say it wasn't until the end of the Palestine War in 1949, and others say that it wasn't until the first Knesset (government assembly) met, which was also in 1949. So, as you can see, it gets a little confusing, but we'll try to get as close as we can anyway.

CHAPTER 25

Psalm 73 A Psalm of Asaph

Years 2021/2022 - Plague and Israel's Harlotry

In General, Psalm 73 teaches us to not be envious of the prosperity of the world, or worldly people. However, when you view this Psalm in its place within the timeline revelation, many keywords, phrases, and word pictures jump off of the page that overtly relates to the time in which we are now living. For the sake of time, I'm not going to go through each verse in detail as I did in the Psalms of Ascent, but I'm going to try my best to hit the highlights, the prophetic words and verses, that pertain directly to this time. I'm sure that I will miss some things, but I hope you, the reader, will also do some digging into these Psalms to uncover more of the prophetic treasures that God has encoded within them. Because of the fact that what I am currently writing may be a helpful tool during the tribulation period, I'm going to include each Psalm in its entirety; however, I won't necessarily have comments on every verse. From my vantage point in 2023, I realize that I simply cannot see, or understand every verse that may have future relevance in the timeline revelation.

Verses 1-3

*¹Truly God is good to Israel, to such as are pure in heart. ²
But as for me, my feet had almost stumbled; My steps had*

nearly slipped. ³ For I was envious of the boastful, when I saw the prosperity of the wicked.

Right after stating that I'm not going to review each Psalm verse-by-verse, I start by going verse-by-verse! However, I need to fully review these first three verses because they represent, and summarize this Psalm as a whole.

God has certainly been good to Israel since their rebirth in 1948. It seems that everything that they put their hand to has been blessed. Despite many obstacles and hindrances, their land has blossomed, their cities have grown, and their people have prospered. This has happened all during a time when Israel is primarily a secular society and has largely forgotten the God who chose them to be His people. Much like most nations today, Israel is in a backslidden state of apostasy. God intended for Israel to be set apart from the gentile nations around them, but time and time again throughout history, they have chased after the gentile ways and gentile gods. Today is no different, although instead of chasing after gods made of wood and metal, in this generation they are in pursuit of worldly goods, entertainment, and all forms of immorality. Not much different from America, or any other nation of the world today.

Verses 4-9

*⁴ For there are **no pangs** in their death, but their strength is firm.⁵ They are not in trouble as other men, nor are they **plagued** like other men.⁶ Therefore **pride** serves as their necklace; **violence** covers them like a garment.⁷ Their eyes bulge with **abundance**; they have more than heart could wish.⁸ They **scoff** and speak wickedly concerning **oppression**; they speak **loftily**.⁹ They set their **mouth against the heavens**, and their tongue walks through the earth.*

Before I go any further, first things first, I have to point out all of the keywords and phrases within the verses of Psalm 73 that relate specifically to the years between 2020 and 2022. You'll notice words and phrases like pangs, plagued, washed my hands, violence, scoff, and oppression. All of those perfectly fit and define the first few years of the 2020s. The only terms that seem to be missing are "toilet paper," "masks," and "vaccines!"

Pangs: As previously discussed in the Psalms of Ascent, Jesus likened the end times to birth pangs (pains). It seems fitting to me that the first word that really struck me when studying Psalm 73 in light of the timeline revelation was the word "pangs." It also seems fitting that it's in the context of how the pains that the world is feeling aren't bothering the elites of the world. Let me just go ahead and say it, Psalm 73 is a behind-the-scenes look at the global elites who are conspiring to "build back better" the world into the utopia that they want for themselves, which is not at all what the people want. They use "climate change" and "social justice" as their tools to deceive, and thus build this ungodly utopia. And it seems that most people are asleep. They have no idea what is being conspired against them because they are too busy trying to just make a living and too busy being distracted with entertainment and social media. What a perfect plan by the enemy, or is it? These pangs will result in a birth alright, but it won't be the birth that they are working towards, the birth of their demonic kingdom. Yes, they will have their day, or so it will seem. But there is a day reserved for judgment, where their end is confirmed and their short-lived kingdom will be crushed as Paul describes in Acts 17:31 *"Because He has appointed a day on which He will judge the world in righteousness by the Man whom He has ordained. He has given assurance of this to all by raising Him from the dead."* What will then follow is the birth of God's glorious Kingdom with the King of Kings and Lord of Lords on the throne forevermore!

Plagued: Well, if you were alive and not in a coma during the first part of the 2020s, you would recognize that the whole world was at the mercy of a plague. Obviously, the world was being deceived as to the lethality of the plague that turned into a pandemic unlike anything the world has ever witnessed. But its grip over the world wasn't because of its lethality, -it was because of the deceptive fear that was perpetuated by governments and the media, which was used to shut down and control the world. Fear is a very useful tool in Satan's tool box. Perhaps the most useful tool he has against mankind. How many times did Jesus say, "fear not?" I wonder why He said that so much? There's a lesson in there somewhere...

While the world was giving up their livelihoods and freedoms to enable the building of the beast system, the globalists, who never miss an opportunity, were rejoicing. They were writing books and giving speeches about "resetting" the world and even using terms like "new world order," but most of the world was still asleep and unaware of what all of this meant because they hadn't considered that the God of all things took the time to reveal these mysteries to them in His word.

Washed my hands: Obviously, this was a central theme during the pandemic, which makes it another connection point to the timeline revelation. This phrase is found in verse 13, which I will expand on in the next section. It has a different meaning in the Jewish ritual context, but you can see how it interconnects with the timeline nevertheless.

Pride: Verse 6 says, "therefore pride serves as their necklace." First of all, let me say that God hates man's pride. These elites who have joined together in many different, but interlinked global institutions, who are being spoken of in verses 4-9, wear pride around their necks as if it's an award. However, God's word tells us many times that pride is evil. Proverbs 16 is the perfect verse befitting these global elites conspiring together. In one brilliant sentence, it gives their description and points out their sin, union, God's view, and His future judgment on them.

Proverbs 16:5
5Everyone proud in heart is an abomination to the LORD;
though they join forces, none will go unpunished.

I would be remiss if I didn't point out the obvious, which is that once upon a time, the word "pride" had a certain meaning, which was not necessarily good. It meant arrogant and conceited, which are terms that most of us do not wish to be associated with. However, in this upside-down Isaiah 5:20 world that we now live in, pride, over time, became a term that reflects a positive characteristic. Then, if that weren't enough, the word pride was hijacked along with God's covenant sign to all mankind, the rainbow, to denote something completely different, wicked, and perverted.

How does this type of "pride" fit in with the globalist agenda? It's another tool, or should I say weapon, that is being used to try to silence God-fearing people, and, therefore, the gospel. The global elites at the World Economic Forum as well as many other globalist organizations, are a large part of the push toward normalizing sinful lifestyles in the culture, and punishing anyone who dares to object. All of this is being done in the name of equality and inclusion. If you follow this to its obvious conclusion, you will be able to see that it is only a matter of time before the Bible is branded as "hate speech," and anyone caught sharing God's word will be punished - even in America!

Violence: Let's face it, the world is a violent place, and it's not getting any better as time marches on. The pandemic and subsequent lockdowns and vaccine mandates sparked more violence and clashes between governments and their citizens all around the world during 2021 and into 2022 than I had ever seen before. Protests flooded the streets from wealthy nations like Australia and France to poorer nations like Mexico and Nigeria, and don't forget China's "Zero Covid" policy that even Chinese citizens eventually revolted against. Increasingly, governments resorted to the use of violence against their own people to maintain control and power in the face of public unrest and dissent. Unfortunately, as the birth pangs of the last days continue to rise and fall and ever increase, I believe that the violence that we've seen has only been a foretaste of what is yet to come.

Scoff: The prideful elites scoff at the world's populace and God. I cannot help but remember some of the outrageous and blasphemous things that have been said at the World Economic Forum, as well as at other likeminded globalist gatherings over the last few years by Yuval Noah Harari, an Israeli Historian, who some are claiming to be a prophet. Here are just a few of his many quotes that I have taken from his speeches:

"Fake news has been with us for thousands of years, just think of the Bible."

"The only thing the God of the Bible managed to create is organic beings. Now we try to go beyond the God of the Bible and create inorganic life, something He never managed to do."

"Now humans are developing even bigger powers than ever before. We are really acquiring divine powers of creation and destruction. We are really upgrading humans into gods. We are acquiring the ability to reengineer life."

"We don't have to wait until Christ's second coming in order to overcome death, a couple of geeks in a laboratory can do it, if you give them enough time and money."

"God is dead, it just takes a while to get rid of the body."

All I can say is that mocking God in these last days isn't a good life plan, and certainly isn't good for your long-term health. This type of prideful and blasphemous global elite is exactly what Psalm 73 is referring to. Paul sums up this type of arrogant, godless person in Galatians 6:

Galatians 6:7
7 Do not be deceived, God is not mocked; for whatever a man sows, that he will also reap.

The other types of mockers that are prevalent in our day hide behind their smart phones and laptops and mock God and scoff at His Son's second coming over the internet. Unfortunately for them, God knows who they are. I pray that they find the truth before it's too late. These mockers and scoffers unwittingly fulfill Bible prophecy every day as they fill the internet with their ridicule of the one true God who only wants to save them and give them eternal life.

2 Peter 3:3-7
3 knowing this first: that scoffers will come in the last days, walking according to their own lusts, 4 and saying, "Where is the promise of His coming? For since the fathers fell asleep, all things continue as they were from the beginning of creation." 5 For this they willfully forget: that by the word

of God the heavens were of old, and the earth standing out of water and in the water, ⁶ by which the world that then existed perished, being flooded with water. ⁷ But the heavens and the earth which are now preserved by the same word, are reserved for fire until the day of judgment and destruction of ungodly men.

If you ever want to see this last day's prophecy in action, just make a post on any social media platform that says that the rapture is imminent, or that Jesus is returning soon, and watch it be fulfilled in front of your very eyes.

Oppression: The global elites, from both government and industry, spoken of in Revelation 18, have a goal to oppress the world, tear it down, and then rebuild it in their image, with them as the masters, and those who are left alive as their servants. They used terms like "Great Reset" and "Build Back Better" to sum up their agenda. These elites go by many monikers, such as Globalists, Humanists, Transhumanists, Environmentalists, Socialists, Communists, Eugenicists, and Luciferians to name a few. Their vision for the world, which looks very humanitarian at first glance, can only result in the oppression of the masses, with them as the supposed benevolent masters ruling over those whom they refer to as the "useless eaters" of the world.

> **Verses 4-9 (continued)**
> ⁴ *For there are* **no pangs** *in their death, but their strength is firm.* ⁵ *They are not in trouble as other men, nor are they* **plagued** *like other men.* ⁶ *Therefore* **pride** *serves as their necklace;* **violence** *covers them like a garment.* ⁷ *Their eyes bulge with* **abundance***; they have more than heart could wish.* ⁸ *They* **scoff** *and speak wickedly concerning* **oppression***; they speak* **loftily.** ⁹ *They set their* **mouth against the heavens***, and their tongue walks through the earth.*

During the Covid crisis, the elites shut down the world, but certainly not their own world, only the world of the regular people.

While small merchant businesses were forced into seemingly endless lock downs, ultimately ending in their demise, the merchant giants of the world never had to abide by these same mandates, allowing them to grow and become even more wealthy and empowered. Of course, they are all on the same team and are interconnected through the World Economic Forum, the United Nations, and countless other globalist elite networks. Just as verses 4-9 prophetically indicate, while the world suffered, they flourished.

Revelation 18 speaks of the fall and destruction of Mystery Babylon and makes some very interesting and misunderstood connections.

Revelation 18:23
23 The light of a lamp shall not shine in you anymore, and the voice of bridegroom and bride shall not be heard in you anymore. For your merchants were the great men of the earth, for by your sorcery all the nations were deceived.

God placed this very important prophetic sentence in verse 23, which has been difficult to understand, especially for us English speakers. God tells us that in these days, the "merchants" will be the "great men of the earth." He then reveals that it will be by their "sorcery" that they will deceive the nations. When our English Bible was translated, sorcery was probably the obvious choice for the original Greek word. However, in light of the COVID-19 pandemic and the enormous power of the Pharmaceutical industry over our world today, I believe that we now should have a better understanding of this "sorcery." The Greek word that was translated to "sorcery" was originally "pharmakeia." Even up until the last decade, many Bible prophecy teachers would say that this is probably related to the prevalent use and abuse of mind-altering drugs.

I'm not saying that was necessarily wrong, but in light of current world events and the dominant control that Big Pharma now has over the world, I think it's safe to say that the real last days "sorcery" is the mandating of mRNA/DNA vaccines and endless boosters, which further enriches the pharmaceutical industry, and gives them and governments more totalitarian control over their subjects. Now that this system of control over the population is in place and has been proven to work on the majority of the world's population, it will be easier in the future to declare pandemics, roll out more vaccines, and take more power and wealth from the world. Couple that with what the globalists are calling the Fourth Industrial Revolution when man and machine will merge and technology will be embedded into the human body. This will link everything together to include artificial intelligence, cloud computing, bid data, biometrics, banking, and more, all in the name of safety, security and convenience, but at the expense of personal privacy, human rights, and autonomy. If that doesn't sound like the "mark of the beast" system, then I don't know what does. This Fourth Industrial Revolution isn't a possibility, it's a fact, and it's growing closer and closer with every day that passes.

In recent days, there has been an outcry against the continuation and implementation of more artificial intelligence systems. Some have called for a halt and an evaluation period before proceeding further with the development of "AI," as many are fearful that AI systems will eventually become sentient and work against humanity. Just a thought: could it be that AI becomes a problem over the next few years, adding to the chaos of the opening scenes of the tribulation period? Could it then be that the coming Antichrist will cancel AI development only to secretly harness AI for his own use, making him seem superhuman? My thought process on this is simple. If AI makes him better than others, why would he want to share it with the world? Once he has control over the world, he could declare AI to be a threat to global peace and then implement it for his own deceptive and nefarious initiatives.

I believe the globalists, both in government and industry, who are behind all of this, are the ones signified by the verse in Revelation 6, that says, "and do not harm the oil and the wine." The third seal that Jesus opens releases the Black Horse, which represents scarcity, extreme inflation, poverty, and famine. The elites, represented by the "oil and the wine," will not be harmed in this coming economic disaster, and more than likely use the crisis to consolidate more power, wealth, and control over the world.

The good news is that according to the timeline revelation, those who are in Christ will not be here to be oppressed by this total control system, and it will be the shortest-lived "revolution" in history thanks to the return of our King! However, we should be praying now for our brothers and sisters around the world who will fall victim to this evil technological tyranny. Pray that they are given strength, power, and endurance to survive, and keep the faith until the Lord's certain return.

Verses 10-14

¹⁰ Therefore his people return here, and waters of a full cup are drained by them.

¹¹ And they say, "how does God know? and is there knowledge in the Most High?"

¹² Behold, these are the ungodly, who are always at ease; they increase in riches.

*¹³ Surely I have cleansed my heart in vain, and **washed my hands** in innocence. ⁴ For all day long I have been **plagued**, and chastened every morning.*

Who is "his" referring to in "his people return here" and where is "here?" Since I cannot find any biblical historical reference, I can only speculate that it is prophetic, and has to do with the last days in which we are living. Could it be that this unknown "his" is referring to the false messiah? Could it be that the place that they "return" to is Davos, Switzerland, where the world's elites meet at the World Economic Forum every year to discuss how to rule over, and deceive the masses in order to bring about a one world government and a global economy while promoting the "alphabet" agenda, social justice, transhumanism, and all manner of ungodly agendas designed by Satan, himself to divide and conquer the world?

Verse 10 describes these elites draining the waters of a full cup. That is certainly an interesting and confusing passage, but it does interlink with another scripture to give it some clarity. In 2 Samuel 14, we are shown that water is a symbol of life. No one can live without water.

Water poured out is a symbol of death, just as Jesus' life was poured out for us on the cross, and then both water and blood flowed from His side.

2 Samuel 14:14

14 Like water spilled on the ground, which cannot be recovered, so we must die.

In verses 13 and 14, we see imagery of "hand washing" as well as "plagued" again. Of course, we can see how those images apply to the last few years in the timeline revelation, but I wanted to point out a few more underlying details in the context of the way they were written. The phrase "washed my hands in innocence" brings to mind Pontius Pilot, who washed his hands of the deed of ordering Jesus to be nailed to the cross. It was the religious Jews, the ones who Jesus spoke to saying, "you are of your father the devil," who arrested Jesus and then accused Him to the Roman Governor. They used Rome as a tool to destroy the true Messiah because they couldn't do it themselves. That, of course, brings to mind the prophetic verse in Zechariah, which reads:

Zechariah 12:10

10 "And I will pour on the house of David and on the inhabitants of Jerusalem the Spirit of grace and supplication; then they will look on Me whom they pierced. Yes, they will mourn for Him as one mourns for his only son, and grieve for Him as one grieves for a firstborn.

It is interesting to me how the Lord ties Zechariah 12:10 to the plagues that were poured out on Egypt by saying, *"they will mourn for Him as one mourns for his only son, and grieve for Him as one grieves for a firstborn."* It's the reference to the "first-born" that brings us back to the 10 plagues that crippled Egypt and ultimately led to the release of captive Israel. I believe that Psalm 73, written thousands of years ago, is not only prophetic of 2021, 2022, and the Covid plague, but it is also prophetic of things still to come within the next handful of years leading up to the day when Israel sees their true messiah, and will mourn over him, who, as a nation, they have rejected for 2 millennia.

Verses 15-19

15 If I had said, "I will speak thus," Behold, I would have been untrue to the generation of Your children. 16 When I thought how to understand this, It was too painful for me— 17 Until I went into the sanctuary of God; then I understood their end.

18 Surely You set them in slippery places; You cast them down to destruction.

*19 Oh, how they are brought to desolation, as in a moment! They are utterly consumed with terrors. 20 As a dream when one awakes, so, Lord, **when You awake, You shall despise their image.***

As you can see once again, there are still future prophesies built into many of the Psalms that relate to certain years in the timeline revelation. The author is certain that God will not let the wealthy and powerful global elites, who are driving the world toward subjugation, go unpunished. But that punishment is still in the future.

Two phrases really stand out to me in these verses. The first is *"when you awake,"* and the second is directly after it, stating, *"You shall despise their image."*

There are many prophetic scriptures, especially in the Psalms, that use the word "awake" or "arise" to paint a mental picture of the Lord rising up to finally put an end to wickedness. These terms signify the day of the Lord's return and vengeance (Isaiah 61:2) on the ungodly.

Psalm 7:6

Arise, O LORD, in Your anger; lift Yourself up because of the rage of my enemies; Rise up for me to the judgment You have commanded!

Psalm 35:23

Stir up Yourself, and awake to my vindication, to my cause, my God and my Lord.

Isaiah 33:10-11

[10] *"Now I will rise," says the LORD; "now I will be exalted, now I will lift Myself up.* [11] *You shall conceive chaff, you shall bring forth stubble; your breath, as fire, shall devour you.*

If I were reading Psalm 73 without having any end-time Bible prophecy context in mind, I'm sure I would read right past the verse that says, *"You shall despise their image"* and maybe only stop and ponder for a moment, who they are, and why does it say "image?" Why not just say, "you will despise them?" Those would be good questions, but I'm sure I would just move on from there and not think too much about it. However, in the context of the last days, this has a lot more meaning. Is God using keywords sprinkled throughout these Psalms to connect them to other passages and prophecies? What would be the chance that you would find the term "image" in a Psalm, which seems so out of place, and then 2 verses later find the term "beast," which also seems out of place?

Verses 21-28

[21] *Thus my heart was grieved, and I was vexed in my mind.* [22] *I was so foolish and ignorant; I was like a **beast** before You.* [23] *Nevertheless I am continually with You; You hold me by my right hand.* [24] *You will guide me with Your counsel, and afterward receive me to glory.* [25] *Whom have I in heaven but You? and there is none upon earth that I desire besides You.* [26] *My flesh and my heart fail; but God is the strength of my heart and my portion forever.* [27] *For indeed, those who are far from You shall perish; You have destroyed all those who **desert You for harlotry**.* [28] *But it*

is good for me to draw near to God; I have put my trust in the Lord GOD, that I may declare all Your works.

Finally, I would like to point out that Israel has deserted God for harlotry repeatedly since their Exodus from Egypt thousands of years ago. The marriage of the prophet Hosea to his harlot wife in the book of Hosea is ultimately a metaphor for the relationship that God, as the husband, has with his adulterous wife, Israel. As we know, God instructed Hosea not only to buy back his adulterous wife from her lover for **15** shekels of silver, but also to love her. In kind, even after Israel's continuous unfaithfulness, God still loves her, and wants her to be His.

As a secular nation, they are currently going after the things of the world, and not the things of God, just as they have in centuries past. This will certainly continue into the tribulation period, where the majority will fall for the seduction of the false messiah since they rejected the true Messiah, Yeshua HaMashiach, two thousand years ago, and continue to do so even today. However, we know from scripture that God has reserved for Himself a remnant that will remain true to Him.

CHAPTER 26

Psalm 74 A Psalm of Asaph

Year 2022/2023 - Enemies Rising

Psalm 74 continues the narrative of how Israel got to where they are today at the precipice of the "time of Jacob's trouble." In Psalm 73, we read how Israel has been envious of, and has been seduced by, the wealth of the world. Now, in Psalm 74, I believe that we find primarily a prophetic depiction of the past 2000 years after the Romans destroyed the Temple, and then destroyed Jerusalem, which was followed by the exile of the children of Israel from their land. It is a further illustration of the "many days" that Hosea describes that Israel will live without the legal and traditional accoutrements that set them apart from the other nations. As you will see, there is a strong central theme present throughout Psalm 74 relating to Israel's enemies who have risen against God's children in the past, as well as those who are rising today.

> **Hosea 3:4-5**
> *⁴For the Israelites must live many days without king or prince, without sacrifice or sacred pillar, and without ephod or idol. ⁵Afterward, the people of Israel will return and seek the LORD their God and David their king. They will come trembling to the LORD and to His goodness in the last days.*

Verses 1-8

[1]O God, why have You cast us off forever? Why does Your anger smoke against the sheep of Your pasture? [2] Remember Your congregation, which You have purchased of old, The tribe of Your inheritance, which You have redeemed— This Mount Zion where You have dwelt. [3] Lift up Your feet to the perpetual desolations. The enemy has damaged everything in the sanctuary. [4] Your enemies roar in the midst of Your meeting place; They set up their banners for signs. [5] They seem like men who lift up Axes among the thick trees. [6] And now they break down its carved work, all at once, with axes and hammers. [7] They have set fire to Your sanctuary; they have defiled the dwelling place of Your name to the ground.[8] They said in their hearts, "Let us destroy them altogether." They have burned up all the meeting places of God in the land.

Verses 1 - 8 are a remembrance of the destruction of Jerusalem at the hands of the Babylonians as well as prophetic of the Roman Empire. However, if this Psalm was written by the person named "Asaph," who was a musician and a prophet during the time of King David and his son King Solomon, then it was purely prophetic since none of the destruction that this Psalm reveals had happened before or during his lifetime. It could have also been written by one of his descendants or "sons of Asaph." That would mean that it would have probably been from the perspective of looking back at the Babylonian destruction of the first temple and Jerusalem. However, it would still be considered a prophetic account and a pattern looking forward to the Roman Empire, and the destruction of the second temple as well, especially because no name is given to the enemy who caused all of the destruction and ruin described in this Psalm.

I believe that it is a prophetic pattern, and, therefore, is equally prophetic of the exile caused by the Roman Empire. That exile is also the most relevant to the timeline revelation, and to the current Jews of this age. As I have previously mentioned, Israel was exiled from the land around 135 AD, and the land became desolate until the end of the 1800s. In the late 1800s, Jews began returning to their homeland in what was called the "first Aliyah." Then, finally, Israel became a nation again officially after World War II, which, of course, miraculously fulfilled many prophecies, including Ezekiel 36.

Ezekiel 36:24

24 For I will take you from among the nations, gather you out of all countries, and bring you into your own land.

The Ezekiel 36 prophecy had to be talking about the exile after the Roman Empire expelled them from the land of Israel because it was the only time when the Jews were scattered among "all of the countries."

Verses 9-17

9 We do not see our signs; there is no longer any prophet; nor is there any among us who knows how long. 10 O God, how long will the adversary reproach? Will the enemy blaspheme Your name forever? 11 Why do You withdraw Your hand, even Your right hand? Take it out of Your bosom and destroy them. 12 For God is my King from of old, working salvation in the midst of the earth. 13 You divided the sea by Your strength; You broke the heads of the sea serpents in the waters.

*14 You broke the heads of Leviathan in pieces, and gave him as food to the people inhabiting the wilderness. 15 You broke open the fountain and the flood; **You dried up mighty rivers**. 16 The day is Yours, the night also is Yours; You have prepared the light and the sun. 17 You have set all the borders of the earth; You have made summer and winter.*

Verses 9 - 17 continue the lament over the destruction and exile of Israel. However, now it gets personal. The author asks God if He will allow the enemy to blaspheme His name forever, and why God hasn't destroyed this adversary. As we know from the timeline revelation, that day is coming very soon.

Within these verses, one verse in particular really jumps out at me. It's verse 15, which says, "You dried up mighty rivers." Historically, this could be referring to when Joshua led the Israelites across the Jordan River and into the "promised land." However, that is just one river and not plural. It could also be referring to the crossing of the Red Sea, but that's first of all, not a river, and secondly, that account was already covered in verse 13. Personally, I think it's very revealing in the timeline revelation that the Tigris and Euphrates Rivers have both dried up in 2022 due to drought and other factors, and they are continuing to dry up even in 2023. This was big news in 2022, not necessarily on American news networks, but global news, and certainly all over social media. Of course, we know that this is in preparation for the "kings of the east," as spoken of in Revelation 16.

Verses 18-21

¹⁸ *Remember this, that the enemy has reproached, O L<small>ORD</small>, and that a foolish people has blasphemed Your name.* ¹⁹ ***Oh, do not deliver the life of Your turtledove to the wild beast****! Do not forget the life of Your poor forever.* ²⁰ *Have respect to the covenant; for the dark places of the earth are full of the haunts of cruelty.* ²¹ *Oh, do not let the oppressed return ashamed! Let the poor and needy praise Your name.*

The verse that really stands out to me here is verse 19, which says, *"oh, do not deliver the life of Your turtledove to the wild beast!"* If you recall from a previous chapter on Psalm 128, we saw similar imagery with regard to the escape of the remnant of Israel to the refuge. It sounds like the author is appealing to our Lord to spare Israel from being delivered into the hands of the "beast," whom we know as the Antichrist. We also know that this event will happen at the midpoint of the tribulation, so this could certainly be a preemptive petition to the Lord to spare them from this future disaster. It's also prudent to point out that the term "beast is used again in this Psalm, similar to the previous Psalm. Has the Lord placed this key-word in these two Psalms to awaken us to an understanding that the Antichrist "beast" is rising?

Could verse 19 be a possible prophetic rapture verse wrapped in a poetic metaphor? Remember that Jesus used the symbolism of a bird escaping a snare in Luke 21 to depict the rapture, which we also found in Psalm 124. There is a possibility then that verse 19 is referring to the future escape of the Church, therefore not falling into the hands of the "beast." Of course, we know from the Psalms of Ascent that we are already in the "Rapture Season" as of 2021, so we'll have to wait and see...

Verses 22-23
*22-**Arise**, O God, plead Your own cause; remember how the foolish man reproaches You daily. 23 **Do not forget the voice of Your enemies; the tumult of those who rise up against You increases continually**.*

In verse 22, we have another appeal to the Lord to "arise" and take action against His enemies, just as in the previous Psalm. Of course, we know that the time when the Lord does "arise" and take action will be at His second coming. Then, in verse 23, we see that the enemy is rising once again. Is this speaking of the "beast" and his followers rising and readying themselves for their last stand against the King?

CHAPTER 27

Psalm 75 A Psalm of Asaph

Year 2023/2024 - The Horns Rising and Judgment Coming

Psalm 75 in the timeline revelation marks the year sometime between the Gregorian calendar years of 2023 and 2024. The world has changed so rapidly in the last few years, and it seems that its rate of change is increasing exponentially. I wish I could say that this change has been for the good of the world, but it's clear from anyone with a biblical worldview that the world's trajectory is distinctly in the direction of final tribulation and judgment. According to this Psalm, God will choose His appointed time to judge this earth, and from my view, as I write this in 2023, I cannot imagine that day can be too far away. So many things are taking place right now, things that I never thought I would be here to witness, such as the development and implementation of national digital currencies as well as a global digital currency to usher in a cashless surveillance system of all buying and selling worldwide, social credit scores, rapid transhuman and AI developments, the steady roll out of UFO/UAP information by the government and the media, wars and more wars on the horizon, the glorification and normalization of sin coupled with the exponential rise of the "alphabet" agenda, which seems to trump all other belief systems, religions, and even common sense. How much longer can the Lord wait to judge this world? If He doesn't come soon, I'm afraid that there won't be any world left to return to, or actual humans left to abide with! I know He has all of this under

His control, but it does seem that He's waiting until the last minute. Honestly, I should have expected that since He is merciful, and does not want anyone to perish. So, until He comes for us, we'll have to be patient and keep busy going about the Father's business adding to the coming harvest.

Verses 1-2
¹ We give thanks to You, O God, we give thanks! For Your wondrous works declare that Your name is near. ² "When I choose the proper time, I will judge uprightly.

The beginning of the tribulation period has to be close at hand. God's name is near, and so is His time to judge the inhabitants of the earth. I believe that it's important at this time, so I would like to reiterate something that I have pointed out before. When you see the title of "God" in the Bible, it was translated from the word Elohim, which is a plural form of the singular word for God. In short, it represents the Trinity. So anytime you see "God," Jesus is implied as one of the Trinity.

In verse 2, the author prophesies and declares for Elohim, *"when I choose the proper time, I will judge uprightly."* The phrase "proper time" in Hebrew was originally "Moed," which, of course, we know means "appointed time" and relates directly to God's appointed feast days. I believe that Jesus is returning on one of the 7 Moedim to judge the world, which I believe will be on Yom Kippur, known as the Day of Atonement in English. Remember that Jesus has fulfilled the first 4 Moedim at His first coming. The final 3 will certainly be fulfilled soon upon His return.

In Judaism, metaphorically, the door or gate is opened on Yom Teruah (Feast of Trumpets) but then closed on Yom Kippur (Day of Atonement), at which time they believe that your fate is sealed. So, once the door is opened on the Feast of Trumpets, you have 7 final days, not including the feast days themselves, to get right with the Lord until your time runs out, the door is closed on you, and your name is not written in the Book of Life. Of course, you had all year, so the 7-days in between is truly your final opportunity. Doesn't that sound like a yearly pattern of the 7-year tribulation?

After studying this verse in the Orthodox Jewish Bible, I found a link to the "Moed" or "Appointed Time" in English that connects this verse back to Habakkuk chapter 2, which was prophetic in Habakkuk's time as Judea was in captivity by the Babylonians, but is also as a pattern, prophetic for the end times as well.

Habakkuk 2:2-3
² Then the LORD answered me and said: "Write the vision and make it plain on tablets, that he may run who reads it. ³ For the vision is yet for an appointed time (Moed); but at the end it will speak, and it will not lie. Though it tarries, wait for it; because it will surely come, it will not tarry.

God has an appointed time for everything and the annual Feast Days of Israel are dress rehearsals for what is to come. God clearly says that these prophecies will speak and be understood, and the end will seem to tarry, but it will not, it will come to pass exactly at God's appointed time. I would suggest studying Habakkuk chapter 2 more in-depth as I believe it has tremendous prophetic significance of the last days and the Antichrist, who will soon be revealed to the world.

Verse 3
³ The earth and all its inhabitants are dissolved; I set up its pillars firmly. Selah

As I pray, study, and write this chapter now in February 2023, and knowing that the verses that I'm now reviewing are literally related to the time that we are living in right now in 2023, I'm finding myself acutely aware of the possibilities of coming catastrophic events possibly encoded within these verses. Up until now, Psalms 73 and 74 have been fairly benign, and primarily gave a historical review as well as the promise of coming tribulation and judgment, especially on the wicked wealthy elites of the world. However, now, in Psalm 75, I'm starting to see glimpses of possible apocalyptic events starting with verse 3.

Verse 3 says, *"the earth and all its inhabitants are dissolved."* I have stated before that the Bible has proven itself to be perfectly reliable, and that it's best to take prophecy as literally as possible, along with the understanding that it is mostly encrypted. To get a better understanding, you need to find and study all of the other connected and matching scriptures. That takes a lot of study, wisdom, and spiritual discernment. However, when I read that the *"earth and all of its inhabitants will be dissolved,"* I have to lean toward an understanding that this is related to a real event, but described, or "encrypted" in a figurative way. I was studying this verse in the New King James as well as in the Hebrew Interlinear Bible. When I looked at the same verse in the English Standard Version, it really gave me chills. It says, *"when the earth totters, and all its inhabitants, it is I who keep steady its pillars."* I'll be honest with you, I don't know how they came up with that translation when I compare it to Hebrew, but I'm not a Hebrew scholar. It certainly makes me wonder about the year 2023 that we've just entered, especially since there was a series of large earthquakes that recently rocked both Syria and Turkey, killing thousands and leaving only ruins where cities once stood.

The root of the original Hebrew word that we have translated into "dissolved" in the New King James Version is "mug," which means "to melt." However, it is also used figuratively in many other verses to mean helpless, fainthearted, and terrified. My hope is that it is being used figuratively in verse 3 to express an upcoming event when everyone is helpless, fainthearted, and terrified, but not actually melted or dissolved. Then, the second part of the same verse says, *"I set up its pillars firmly."* It's still speaking of the earth, and then God gives us a very interesting key word, which is "pillars."

Using "pillars" as a key word to find interconnecting scriptures that may give us more context to this verse has proven to be very fruitful. Job makes a statement in Job chapter 9 that may give us an indication of something soon to come.

Job 9:5-6

*⁵ He removes the mountains, and they do not know when
He overturns them in His anger; ⁶ He shakes the earth out
of its place, and its **pillars** tremble;*

According to Job, it seems that when you see pillars and earth
together, the context is that of an earthquake. However, we need at
least two witnesses to settle this matter, which brings me to 1 Samuel
chapter 2 and Hannah's prayer.

Hannah was barren and could not conceive a child. In sorrow, she
appealed to the Lord that if she could have a son, she would give him
to the Lord all the days of his life. God granted her petition, and that
son was Samuel. When Samuel was weaned, she brought him to the
Tabernacle in Shiloh, to Eli the priest, and dedicated him to God and to
stay with Eli to serve in the Tabernacle. On the day when she brought
Samuel to the tabernacle, she prayed:

1 Samuel 2

*¹ And Hannah prayed and said: "My heart rejoices in
the LORD; my horn is exalted in the LORD. I smile at my
enemies, because I rejoice in Your salvation.*

*² "No one is holy like the LORD, for there is none besides
You, nor is there any rock like our God.*

*³ "Talk no more so very proudly; let no arrogance come
from your mouth, for the LORD is the God of knowledge;
and by Him actions are weighed.*

*⁴ "The bows of the mighty men are broken, and those
who stumbled are girded with strength. ⁵ Those who were
full have hired themselves out for bread, and the hungry
have ceased to hunger. Even the barren has borne seven,
and she who has many children has become feeble.*

*⁶ "The LORD kills and makes alive; he brings down to
the grave and brings up. ⁷ The LORD makes poor and makes
rich; He brings low and lifts up. ⁸ He raises the poor from*

the dust and lifts the beggar from the ash heap, to set them among princes and make them inherit the throne of glory.

*"For the **pillars** of the earth are the LORD's, and He has set the world upon them. [9] He will guard the feet of His saints, but the wicked shall be silent in darkness.*

"For by strength no man shall prevail. [10] The adversaries of the LORD shall be broken in pieces; from heaven He will thunder against them. The LORD will judge the ends of the earth.

"He will give strength to His king, and exalt the horn of His anointed."

Wow, it never struck me before just how amazing, and yet out of place, Hannah's prophetic prayer was and is! After giving her son to the Lord, from a human point of view, her prayer should have been all about the inner struggle that she was going through after raising and loving her first-born son, only to turn him over to a stranger and walk away. Unlike pretty much everyone else on the planet, Hannah kept her word to the Lord. Instead of praying, "I know what I said three years ago Lord, but can I just keep my son anyway," she prayed the most amazing yet seemingly unrelated prayer without any regard for herself. And I'm glad she did because it gives us so much context for Psalm 75 that we wouldn't have otherwise. There are so many interconnecting keywords between the two. There are also so many interrelated prophetic points and themes connecting them that prove they must be divinely inspired and linked. It's now obvious to me that the Lord intended for her 3,000-year-old prophetic prayer to be studied in connection with Psalm 75 in relation to our current day.

Her prophecy seems to indicate that God is going to turn everything over at some point in time. Is that time in 2023/2024, as these connections seem to indicate? In the beginning of 2023, we already see a world heading for turmoil. There is daily talk of hyper inflation, economic collapse, possible nuclear war, spy balloons, UFOs, food shortages, the eradication of free speech, and the list goes on and on. It is clear that the world that we knew only a few years ago is over, dead, and buried. We have moved into a very different time, a time when it feels like we are on a run-a-way train, and there simply is no stopping it. Prophetically, I know that is the case, but I have the comfort of knowing from God's word that we aren't going to be here much longer, or will have to go through the worst of what is coming. This means that now is the time, like no other, to spread the Gospel and bring as many with us as possible!

Here is a list of some of the keywords that Hannah's prayer has in common with Psalm 75: Horn, exalted, pillars, earth, wicked, and judge. In addition, there is also a key concept present in both. That is the concept of God bringing one down and lifting another up, which we will see in verse 7 of Psalm 75. All of that cannot be a coincidence.

Verses 4-5
4 "I said to the boastful, 'Do not deal boastfully,' and to the wicked, 'do not lift up the horn. 5 Do not lift up your horn on high; do not speak with a stiff neck.'"

There are several different types of "horns" mentioned in the Bible. There are literal animal horns, there are horns on the altar in the temple, and there are horns that are symbolic of power and of kings. Think of the horns on a powerful and noble horned animal with its head held high for the entire world to see. The horns or "keren" in Hebrew that are lifted up in verses 4 and 5 are symbolic of an increase in power, strength, honor, and authority. "Lifted up" has the same meaning as exaltation. Of course, we also know that the Antichrist is associated with a "little horn" in Daniel chapter 7, and then in chapter 8, we see a broken horn followed by 4 more horns rising, but without the power of the first. Then the Antichrist follows as prophesied in the following verses from Daniel 8:

Daniel 8:23-25
23 "And in the latter time of their kingdom, when the transgressors have reached their fullness, a king shall arise,

having fierce features, who understands sinister schemes. [24] His power shall be mighty, but not by his own power; he shall destroy fearfully, and shall prosper and thrive; he shall destroy the mighty, and also the holy people.

[25] "Through his cunning he shall cause deceit to prosper under his rule; and he shall exalt himself in his heart. He shall destroy many in their prosperity. He shall even rise against the Prince of princes; but he shall be broken without human means.

The Antichrist is the wicked ruler who is rising to power in the shadows even today. We know, according to Paul (2 Thessalonians 2), that he will not be revealed until after the "Restrainer" is removed, which I believe happens at the rapture. It's also important to point out that the encrypted timeline revelation in the Psalms of Ascent also indicates that the rapture will happen by the end of 2024, and then by the end of 2025, the tribulation will begin, and the Antichrist will come to power. Remember that in Psalm 125, corresponding to 2025, we were told that *"the scepter of wickedness shall not rest on the land allotted to the righteous,"* which indicates that the Antichrist will have power over Israel in 2025, but it will be short-lived (7 years). So, in 2023, we can only speculate as to the identity of the future false messiah. Personally, I believe that we have all been wrong over the decades as to his identity. I have heard everything from King Charles to Barack Obama, but according to prophetic patterns, he will not be an elderly statesman. He will be young, and he'll be "King David-like" at first; then, after consummating his power, he will be revealed as the "seed of the serpent."

Verses 6-8

[6] For exaltation comes neither from the east nor from the west nor from the south. [7] But God is the Judge: He puts down one, and exalts another. [8] For in the hand of the LORD there is a cup, and the wine is red; It is fully mixed,

and He pours it out; surely its dregs shall all the wicked of
the earth drain and drink down.

Verses 6 - 8 are very interesting and may reveal the subject matter for future news reports all over the globe in 2023/2024. After reading these three verses, I think you will agree that they are very cryptic, and it's pretty obvious that they are hints at prophetic events. I find it fascinating that in verse 6, "north" is specifically omitted. So, does this "exaltation," which doesn't come from the east, west, or south, come from the north? In addition, the word translated as "exaltation" is the original Hebrew word "harim," which means promotion, lift, or rise. Could verse 6 be referring to the rise of the Antichrist? After all, it appears that the previous two verses were related to the Antichrist. So, that could certainly still be the context. If it's not about the Antichrist, it could also be about an invasion from the north before the Gog of Magog invasion. I can't help but wonder if this "exaltation," which means "rise," isn't alluding to an "escalation," which is also associated with a "rise." After all, there have been ongoing tensions and skirmishes between Israel and its northern neighbors for decades. It could also be a forewarning of the soon-to-come Ezekiel 38 invasion, which I will expand on shortly.

Verse 7 is perhaps even more intriguing than verse 6! So, to examine this a little closer, it could be prophetically revealing that God is the Judge of someone or some group who rises from the north, and it is God who takes one down and lifts up another. I think we will have to wait and see what this really means, but I do find it very interesting that 2023 has already been a year of powerful people being replaced and others voluntarily stepping down from their positions of power.

On December 29th, just a few days before 2023, on our Western Gregorian calendar, Benjamin Netanyahu was sworn in as Israel's new prime minister. I say new, but he has served as Israel's prime minister longer than any other person in the modern era, just not consecutively. He served as prime minister from 1996 to 1999 and then again from 2006 until 2021, at which time both Naftali Bennett and Yair Lapid had short runs at being prime minister. However, as of the start of 2023, Benjamin Netanyahu is once again the leader of Israel.

In my list of those who have been replaced or stepped down already this year, I, of course, started with Israel since Israel is the focus of end-time prophecy. Nevertheless, they aren't the only country or powerful organization to see such a change so far this year. At the beginning of the year, New Zealand's prime minister Jacinda Arden, a known globalist and part of the World Economic Forum's Young Global Leaders, stepped down citing personal reasons. Then, in February of 2023, Nicola Sturgeon, Scotland's first minister and member of the World Economic Forum, also stepped down, citing that the job was taking its toll on her and that some of her globalist policies had caused her to become polarizing. She didn't say "globalist policies," I did, but that's what they are.

Also in February, YouTube's CEO Susan Wojcicki also announced that she was stepping down from her position to focus on other things. Of course, it is well known that YouTube has played the role of another globalist puppet and silencer of free speech over the past few years. Susan is also a member, speaker, and contributor to the World Economic Forum.

You might think that I'm ganging up on the World Economic Forum, and you would be correct, because they are in this present time, the very epitome of the spirit of the Antichrist. Between them and the United Nations, of which they are very intertwined, I would say that they are the center hub of the rising beast system.

With all of the globalist leaders stepping down this year so far, I'm left with a couple of questions: who's next, and will 2023 be the year that we see huge shifts in power around the world as God puts His chess pieces in place? It seems that big changes are encoded in Psalm 75, and if the timeline revelation is correct, then I believe that we will certainly see more changes to global power during 2023.

It may be, however, that this big change in global power isn't just about global leaders. It could be that a powerful nation is brought down, and another is lifted up on the world stage. It could be a monetary system that is replaced as the dominant world currency. It could be that it is time for nations to start accepting digital currency over cash, or this verse could even be referring to a religious system or systems being replaced by a one-world religion. The point is that God didn't tell us for certain who, or what it would be, He only said, *"He puts down one, and exalts another,"* so we'll have to be patient and wait and see unless, of course, He was only talking about Benjamin Netanyahu, then we've already witnessed at least a partial fulfillment of this prophecy. However, I believe that more is yet to come this year as the global stage is being set for the final act that is about to play out on the world stage.

Ok, as if that wasn't enough prophetic mystery built into one Psalm, let's take a closer look at verse 8, which says, *"For in the hand of the LORD there is a cup, and the wine is red; it is fully mixed, and He pours it out; surely its dregs shall all the wicked of the earth drain and drink down."*

Biblically, a cup of wine can represent life and the fullness of life, a covenant, salvation, and other positive and spiritually powerful certainties. However, when the cup of wine is red, fully mixed, and poured out, it no longer has a positive meaning. Then, if you add to the metaphor the description of drinking the dregs, you know that it means trouble! It's pretty obvious through all of the keywords and symbols that verse 8 means business, and is an ominous prophecy of coming wrath and judgment.

Taken as a whole, I believe that verses 6 - 8 prophesy the coming Ezekiel 38 invasion of Israel and the wrath of God that will be poured out very soon on the earth. Remember that verse 6 cryptically alludes to a "rise" coming out of the "north." Let's consider what Ezekiel prophesied in Ezekiel 38:

> **Ezekiel 38:14-18**
> *[14] "Therefore, son of man, prophesy and say to Gog, 'Thus says the Lord GOD: "On that day when My people Israel dwell safely, will you not know it? [15] Then you will come from your place out of the far **north**, you and many peoples with you, all of them riding on horses, a great company and a mighty army. [16] You will come up against My people Israel like a cloud, to cover the land. It will be in the latter days that I will bring you against My land, so that the nations may know Me, when I am hallowed in you, O*

Gog, before their eyes." [17] Thus says the Lord GOD: "Are you he of whom I have spoken in former days by My servants the prophets of Israel, who prophesied for years in those days that I would bring you against them?

Where does Ezekiel say that the mysterious Gog comes from? He comes from the far north! Let me stop here and point out something very important, I am not a prophet. I have simply been allowed by my Lord to stand on the shoulders of His servant, J. R. Church, whom I've never met, and at least partially decode the timeline revelation that God placed within the Psalms. God obviously wanted us to find this pattern at this time, or He wouldn't have so carefully placed it, hidden in plain sight for millennia, right in front of us. All I'm doing is prayerfully trying to interpret what I'm reading in these perfectly placed Psalms, and compare them to what I'm seeing in the world today. Furthermore, I'm trying to follow the patterns that I'm finding in the timeline, compare them with present world events, and follow them to their logical conclusions based on scripture.

Now that I have that off my chest, I'm going to prognosticate, but not prophesy, a possible outcome based on these few verses, along with other prophetic scriptures throughout the word of God. If I'm wrong, I'm wrong. I'm just looking at the timeline and thinking through several possible scenarios to figure out what seems to be the most likely outcome based on the world's current trajectory. I, however, firmly believe that the person of the Antichrist is rising right now, hidden from the world, but known by a select few.

The proof is all around us. I believe that he will quite possibly have something to do with the prophecy of Ezekiel 38. Perhaps, much like David became a hero when he slew Goliath in Israel's war against the Philistines, the "little horn" will be seen as a national hero in the wake of the Ezekiel 38 invasion of Israel. Based on the timeline revelation, I believe that the Gog Magog attack doesn't happen until at least the end of 2023, but most likely sometime later in 2024. Considering the placement of verse 7, which says, *"but God is the Judge: He puts down one, and exalts another,"* coupled with the global trend this year in 2023 of world leaders being replaced, I can't help but wonder if "Gog" isn't hiding in the shadows as well, waiting to replace the current leader in the land of the "far north?"

Most prophecy teachers think that Magog is Russia, which seems very likely, but it isn't 100% crystal clear as of today. Currently, Russia is at war with Ukraine, and they are staged in Syria along with Iran and Turkey just north of Israel's border. It appears that the US destroyed Russia's natural gas pipeline into Europe in 2022. At the same time, Israel is working on a natural gas pipeline, along with European nations, to connect Israel's Leviathan gas field, which is located off of Israel's shore in the Mediterranean Sea, to supply European nations with Israel's abundant natural gas resources. So Russia, which was the major supplier of natural gas into Europe, has been cut off, and Israel's gas will possibly soon replace it. Could this be a "hook in the jaw" (Ezekiel 38:4) that leads Gog of Magog to attack Israel? According to the timeline revelation, I don't think we will have to wait very long to find out.

Verse 9-10
⁹ But I will declare forever, I will sing praises to the God of Jacob. ¹⁰ "All the horns of the wicked I will also cut off, but the horns of the righteous shall be exalted."

The God of Jacob will have the last word in all of the plans of the wicked. They exalt their horns against God's chosen people, and against God Himself, but He has promised that He will bring them down and cut them off. As for Gog, I believe that his end is described in Joel 2:20, but we're not quite there yet in the timeline.

Joel 2:20
"But I will remove far from you the northern army, and will drive him away into a barren and desolate land, with his face toward the eastern sea and his back toward the western sea; his stench will come up, and his foul odor will rise, because he has done monstrous things."

I cannot help but take special notice of the fact that the "10th" and final verse of Psalm 75 refers again to the *"horns of the wicked"* and also refers to the *"horns of the righteous."* Of course, we know what the ultimate demise will be of the wicked who are rising up during 2023 and 2024. Their fate is sealed, and they will be *"cut off"* (destroyed) during, and at the conclusion of the upcoming 7-year tribulation. But what about the righteous? Notice that verse 10 also says, *"the horns of the righteous shall be exalted."* The original Hebrew word translated into English as *"exalted"* also means to "lift up," similar to how the ark was "lifted up" above the earth as described in Genesis 7:17. Could this be a prophetic hint at the rapture? Of course, we know from the Psalms of Ascent that we're already in the "Rapture Season" during 2023 and 2024, and that Jesus is already standing at the "door."

CHAPTER 28

Psalm 76 A Psalm of Asaph

Year 2024/2025 - Gog Magog and the Rapture of the Church

By September of 2024, 7 years will have passed since the Revelation 12 Sign was seen in 2017. If the Essenes were correct, and historically, they were known to be 100% accurate, then 2024 will once again be a Shmita year. The Shmita year is a Sabbatical year, and a year of release, but historically, according to the Rabbis, the Shmita year is also a year of war. Many have postulated that Psalm 76 was written after a great victory in Israel over one of their many enemies. Even though we do not have any historical certainty as to which conflict this Psalm specifically pertains to, I'm certain that it was written in celebration, and in honor of God, who gave them the victory. I'm also certain that God took this Psalm and perfectly placed it in the timeline revelation in the Psalms, because it was written not only to tell of a past great victory, but also as a prophetic pattern of a great victory yet to come. It is only through the lens of the timeline revelation that Psalm 76 comes to life, and, in fact, takes its place on the prophetic calendar.

Warning! Just as I said for Psalm 124, I'll say it again for its second witness, Psalm 76. For anyone who still wants to believe that there is no rapture, or that it doesn't happen before the tribulation begins, you might want to skip this chapter.

Verses 1-3
¹In Judah God is known; His name is great in Israel. ² In Salem also is His tabernacle, and His dwelling place in Zion. ³ There He broke the arrows of the bow, the shield and sword of battle. Selah

If someone asked me, "What was God's number one intended outcome of the Ezekiel 38-39 invasion of Israel?" I would say that God Himself answered that question in the last verse of chapter 38, and then again in chapter 39.

Ezekiel 38:23
²³ Thus I will magnify Myself and sanctify Myself, and I will be known in the eyes of many nations. Then they shall know that I am the LORD."

Ezekiel 39:7
⁷ So I will make My holy name known in the midst of My people Israel, and I will not let them profane My holy name anymore. Then the nations shall know that I am the LORD, the Holy One in Israel.

According to the wording of verses 1 - 3 of Psalm 76, God was known in Judah, Israel, and Jerusalem after "He broke the arrows of the bow, the shield and sword of battle." This matches what Ezekiel 39 tells us; that God will make His holy name known in the midst of His people through the victory that He will win for them. God wants to be known by Israel, but as we can clearly see in Ezekiel, He also wants to be known by all of the nations in the last days. I believe that the Lord wants to make sure that no one has any excuse when He comes back. Those who want to know Him will receive Him, and those who have hardened their hearts against Him will reject Him.

I wouldn't say that Psalm 76 could replace Ezekiel 38 - 39, but I would say that it is supplemental. In addition to fitting this coming invasion into the timeline, it gives us a little more clarity as it adds a few more pieces to an incomplete puzzle. After studying the words of Psalm 76 in Hebrew, I noticed a few translation oddities, which I will go over. There are actually two in the first three verses of the Psalm. The first one is the word *"tabernacle"* in verse 2. Verse 2 says; *"In Salem also is His tabernacle, and His dwelling place in Zion."* The first problem that I had with the word tabernacle was that I can't see there being a tabernacle in Jerusalem by 2024 if the timeline revelation is correct. This word could have been a potential deal breaker in the timeline if it were to be speaking of the literal temple, because that wouldn't be plausible by 2024, and I can't find any other "witness" to there being a temple built in Jerusalem by 2024. What I found is that typically, the Hebrew word that is translated into English as tabernacle is the word Mishkan. Mishkan means "dwelling" and is known as the dwelling place of God on earth. However, the Hebrew word in verse 2 of Psalm 76 is Sukkow and not Mishkan. Sukkow is only translated once in the entire Bible as tabernacle, which is what we see in Psalm 76. I have to assume that it's the only thing that made sense to the translators since they didn't have any other context. However, in the other verse where "sukkow" appears, which is Jeremiah 25:38, it is translated as a lion's covert hiding place. So, according to Jeremiah, what "sukkow" actually means is more akin to a "covert lion's lair." That changes everything!

Not only does it now make sense in the timeline revelation, but it also makes much more sense in the overall context. When the invading armies come against Israel, they won't be thinking that the creator God, the most powerful being ever to exist, is going to be fighting Israel's battle. The "Lion of the tribe of Judah" is literally going to be crouched and ready as the unsuspecting armies invade the promised land (see also Genesis 49:8-12). Once again, through the power of God Almighty, tiny Israel will defeat the Goliath that comes against them.

The next word that I had trouble with was the word "arrows" in verse 3. Verse 3 says, *"There He broke the arrows of the bow, the shield and sword of battle."* After researching all of these words in Hebrew, I found that the original Hebrew word for arrows is "resheph," which actually means "sharp flames" or even "fire-bolt." Again, the translators did the best that they could within their understanding of the text as it related to a bow, but they missed the important details of flame and fire. Figuratively, it's an arrow as it relates to a bow, but literally, it's not a wooden arrow at all; it's what the author described as a sharp flame or fire-bolt. That doesn't sound like a battle fought over Jerusalem thousands of years ago to me, but a battle that is coming in our modern age of high-tech missiles and military technology. Regardless of the semantics, I believe the point of these verses is that God will defeat the coming enemy completely. He will thoroughly break their offensive weapons, as well as their defenses, to His glory!

Verses 4-6
⁴ You are more glorious and excellent than the mountains of prey. ⁵ The stouthearted were plundered; they have sunk into their sleep; and none of the mighty men have found the use of their hands. ⁶ At Your rebuke, O God of Jacob, both the chariot and horse were cast into a dead sleep.

Knowing the prophecy of Ezekiel 38 and 39, the words "mountains" and "prey" of verse 4 made my little antennas go up. Both of these words are also used in Ezekiel 39 in connection with the demise of the armies of Gog. Ezekiel paints a picture of Gog coming into the land of Israel from the north, and then being soundly defeated, in fact "slain" in the mountains of Israel. There they will be as pray to the birds and beasts that dwell there. Obviously, they will also be "prey" to the Lion of the tribe of Judah, who defeats them. Verse 4 also declares that the Lord is, of course, far superior to those who will come against Israel by stating that He is "more glorious and excellent than the mountains of prey." He is, after all, above all!

Ezekiel 39:1-4
¹ "And you, son of man, prophesy against Gog, and say, 'Thus says the Lord GOD: "Behold, I am against you, O Gog, the prince of Rosh, Meshech, and Tubal; ² and I will turn you around and lead you on, bringing you up from the far north, and bring you against the mountains of

*Israel. ³ Then I will knock the bow out of your left hand,
and cause the arrows to fall out of your right hand. ⁴ You
shall fall (be slain) upon the mountains of Israel, you and
all your troops and the peoples who are with you; I will
give you to birds of prey of every sort and to the beasts of
the field to be devoured.*

Psalm 76, verse 5, is really interesting as it describes how the warriors
of Gog will themselves be plundered. Recall that the reason that Gog
will invade Israel is to take plunder and booty, as it is described in
Ezekiel 38:12. There's a lesson in there somewhere! Then, in Ezekiel
39:10, we also see that *"they (Israel) will plunder those who plundered
them, and pillage those who pillaged them."*

After the destruction of the "mighty army" there will be a cleanup
mission to cleans the land that will last for 7 months, and they will use
the weapons of the enemy that remain for fuel for 7 years afterward. I
believe that the "7-year" period is an undeniable clue that God gave us,
signifying that this invasion will happen prior to the 7-year tribulation.
That, of course, also fits perfectly into the encrypted timeline revelation
in the Psalms.

Psalm 76, as well as Ezekiel 39, uses the term "mighty men" to
describe the warriors of the invading army, which tells us that this
army is well-trained, brave, and more than likely they are seasoned
warriors. They're no pushovers! Obviously, they will think that they
can dominate a small country like Israel, but they won't understand
that Israel has a secret weapon. These "mighty men" will be no match
when the Lord strikes.

From Ezekiel 38:18 - 23 we understand that the Lord will cause a
great earthquake in the land that will consume the invading army as
well as "flooding rain." Again, I can't help but see parallels between
Psalm 76 and Ezekiel 38, not necessarily with the exact words used, but
with a corresponding result. As mentioned, Ezekiel 38 reveals that there
will be an earthquake, flood, and other deadly forces that will come
against the invaders. Psalm 76 uses phrases like "sunk into their sleep"
and "cast into a deep sleep" to illustrate the type of death that awaits

the intruders in the land of Israel. What I'm trying to point out is that Ezekiel 38 describes the deadly force that the Lord will use, and Psalm 76 describes the deadly outcome.

One last curious description of the demise of the coalition army led by Gog of Magog in Psalm 76:5 is that it is stated they will not be able to "find the use of their hands." This seems to indicate that they cannot use the weapons they brought to bear against Israel. Then, in Ezekiel 39, God says, "Then I will knock the bow out of your left hand, and cause the arrows to fall out of your right hand," which seems to indicate the exact same thing, just expressed in a different way.

> **Verses 7-9**
> *7 You, Yourself, are to be feared; and who may **stand in Your presence** when once You are angry? 8 You caused judgment to be heard from heaven; The earth feared and was still, 9 when God arose to judgment, to deliver all the oppressed of the earth. Selah*

Call me crazy, but I believe that verses 7 - 9 indicate the rapture of the Church! I have to admit that without finding the chronological rapture pattern in the 15 Psalms of Ascent that started in Psalm 121 and ended in Psalm 124 after the Gog Magog War, I probably wouldn't have noticed it here in Psalm 76. I would have assumed that verses 7 - 9 were simply follow-up verses to the military victory that was previously described. But God is very clever. I can't help but notice that He loves to encode these little prophetic treasures and interconnect them with keywords, phrases, and imagery, sort of like a breadcrumb trail leading to a greater understanding. I am 100% confident that none of this is by coincidence, but by divine design.

So, let's dissect these verses and pull out the keywords and phrases. Verse 7 uses the phrase "stand in Your presence." Doesn't that sound familiar? Didn't Jesus use similar language in one of our most key rapture verses in Luke 21?

Luke 21:36
*36 Watch therefore, and pray always that you may be counted worthy to escape all these things that will come to pass, and to **stand before the Son of Man.***"

Verse 8 clues us in that prophetically, something will be "heard from heaven." This means that it will be heard here on earth, and it will be understood that it came from heaven. Of course, we know from many rapture verses that there will be a loud sound heard from heaven at the rapture/resurrection. Here are just a few:

1 Thessalonians 4:16-18
*16 For the Lord Himself will descend **from heaven with a shout, with the voice of an archangel, and with the trumpet of God**. And the dead in Christ will rise first. 17 Then we who are alive and remain shall be caught up together with them in the clouds to meet the Lord in the air. And thus we shall always be with the Lord. 18 Therefore comfort one another with these words.*

1 Corinthians 15:52
*52 In a moment, in the twinkling of an eye, at the last trumpet. For **the trumpet will sound**, and the dead will be raised incorruptible, and we shall be changed.*

Revelation 4:1
*1After these things I looked, and behold, a door standing open in heaven. And the first voice which I heard was **like a trumpet** speaking with me, saying, "Come up here, and I will show you things which must take place after this."*

Continuing the rapture language in verse 8, and into verse 9, we are told that after the sound is heard from heaven that, *"The earth feared and was still, when God arose to judgment to deliver all the oppressed of the earth."* I can only imagine that once the rapture/resurrection happens the earth will tremble in fear and collectively gasp in disbelief that it actually happened, and millions of people from around the world have vanished. This "silence" indicates that the "day of the Lord" is at hand, according to the prophet Zephaniah. Of course, we know that the "day of the Lord" is synonymous with the tribulation period, and as we know, it is not a literal day, but a 7-year period of God's judgment on the earth.

Zephaniah 1:7

7Be silent in the presence of the Lord GOD; for the day of the LORD is at hand, for the LORD has prepared a sacrifice; He has invited His guests.

I couldn't help but notice the part in Zephaniah 1:7 that says, "He has invited His guests." Interestingly, the Hebrew word for "invited" is "qadash," which means set apart, consecrated, and sanctified. The root word in Hebrew for "guests" is "qara," which means "called." That paints a very wonderful, but also a very fearful picture depending on your salvation status. On one hand, if you are not saved, you are part of the sacrifice that has been prepared. It isn't a pretty sight if you've ever seen an animal sacrificed. Please trust me; you don't want to be part of the 7-year continual sacrifice that has been prepared. However, you do want to be part of the called, consecrated, and sanctified quests on God's guest list who have been invited to the wedding supper of the lamb.

The word "judgment" in verse 8 in Hebrew is actually different than the word translated to "judgment" in verse 9. The difference is worth pointing out. In verse 8, the Hebrew word is "din," which means something more akin to a sentence at a trial. Then, in verse 9, the original word that is rendered as judgment in our English Bible is the Hebrew word "mishpat," which is a word that has a meaning of justice, or giving people what is due them, both good and bad. So both bases are covered by these two verses, both judgment on the earth, which is what the tribulation period is all about, and justice for the believer who will stand before the Lord on the day of the rapture. Both are also covered in Luke 21:35-36. The snare in Luke 21:35 is the beginning of judgment or "din," and being judged to be worthy to escape and stand before the Son of Man is covered by the word "mishpat."

Luke 21:35-36

35 For it will come as a snare on all those who dwell on the face of the whole earth.36 Watch therefore, and pray always that you may be counted worthy to escape all these things that will come to pass, and to stand before the Son of Man."

We also know from God's word that those who are escaping will receive rewards at the glorious coming of our Lord, as Jesus described in Matthew 16.

Matthew 16:27

27 For the Son of Man will come in the glory of His Father with His angels, and then He will reward each according to his works.

Paul, at the end of his life, also described this event in 2 Timothy 4. Notice the word "appearing." That is the rapture!

2 Timothy 4:7-8

*7 I have fought the good fight, I have finished the race, I have kept the faith. 8 Finally, there is laid up for me the crown of righteousness, which the Lord, the righteous Judge, will give to me on that Day, and not to me only but also to all who have loved His **appearing**.*

Finally, I would like to look at verse 9 as a whole, which says, *"when God arose to judgment, to deliver all the oppressed of the earth."* That begs the question, who are the oppressed of the earth who are being delivered? First of all, notice that we aren't talking about the land of Israel, so this once again isn't discussing the victory in Israel when God rose up and defeated the invading army that we saw in the previous verses, as well as in Ezekiel 38 and 39. This is specifically describing the oppressed of the "earth," not just Israel. OK, we know that the context is the entire earth and not just Israel. Next, verse 9 tells us that God arose to "deliver" a group of people known as the "oppressed." The word in Hebrew that we see translated to "deliver" is from the root word "yasha," which has the meaning of deliver, but also "save" and "rescue." I would certainly say that the general purpose of the rapture of the Church is that it is a rescue mission to pull the Church out of this world before the trap is sprung and God's wrath is poured out for 7 years on the earth. The tribulation is a trap that the world will not escape after the trap is sprung. The evidence of this is in 1 Thessalonians 5, among other scriptures:

> **1 Thessalonians 5:3**
> *³ For when they say, "Peace and safety!" then sudden destruction comes upon them, as labor pains upon a pregnant woman. **And they shall not escape**.*

> **1 Thessalonians 5:9-10**
> *⁹ For God did not appoint us to **wrath**, but to obtain salvation through our Lord Jesus Christ, ¹⁰ who died for us, that whether we wake or sleep, we should live together with Him.*

Now we know that we who are on the "guest list" will be saved out of the world prior to the tribulation period, and according to verse 9, we are called the "oppressed of the earth," but why? According to a combination of definitions from several different dictionaries, "oppressed" means those who are subject to unjust, harsh, and authoritarian treatment, are in a state of bondage and burden, and have a loss of freedom.

From an American perspective, that description doesn't seem to fit. However, that is changing rapidly even in our country. Around the world, Christian believers have been subjected to harsher treatment, persecution, and even martyrdom over the last few years. I'm not going to go into the rising statistics, but you can look those up for yourself.

The main point is that persecution is increasing around the world, even in first-world countries.

In Hebrew, the root word that our English Bibles translated into "oppressed" is "anav," which means poor, afflicted, humble, and meek. As Christians, all of those descriptors should apply to us, and are basically a summation of the "Beatitudes" that Jesus gave to describe His followers in the Sermon on the Mount in Matthew 5.

Matthew 5:1-12

[1] And seeing the multitudes, He went up on a mountain, and when He was seated His disciples came to Him. [2] Then He opened His mouth and taught them, saying:

[3] "Blessed are the poor in spirit, for theirs is the kingdom of heaven.[4] Blessed are those who mourn, for they shall be comforted.[5] Blessed are the meek, for they shall inherit the earth.[6] Blessed are those who hunger and thirst for righteousness,

For they shall be filled.[7] Blessed are the merciful, for they shall obtain mercy.

[8] Blessed are the pure in heart, for they shall see God.[9] Blessed are the peacemakers, for they shall be called sons of God.[10] Blessed are those who are persecuted for righteousness' sake, for theirs is the kingdom of heaven.

[11] Blessed are you when they revile and persecute you, and say all kinds of evil against you falsely for My sake.[12] Rejoice and be exceedingly glad, for great is your reward in heaven, for so they persecuted the prophets who were before you.

Verses 10-12

[10] Surely the wrath of man shall praise You; with the remainder of wrath You shall gird Yourself.[11] Make vows to the LORD your God, and pay them; Let all who are around Him bring presents to Him who ought to be feared. [12] He shall cut off the spirit of princes; He is awesome to the kings of the earth.

The wrath of man against God and against His Children is essential. I realize that that sounds a bit ridiculous, but think about it in the sense of the aftermath of the Gog Magog invasion of Israel, especially in the timeline. If "man" doesn't come against the nation of Israel, which God has declared protection over during this time, God would not be able to show His glory and be known by all nations these days.

Ezekiel 39:7-8

7 So I will make My holy name known in the midst of My people Israel, and I will not let them profane My holy name anymore. Then the nations shall know that I am the LORD, the Holy One in Israel. 8 Surely it is coming, and it shall be done," says the Lord GOD. "This is the day of which I have spoken.

In this day of broadcast media and social media in the palms of everyone's hands, this event will be seen in real-time all over the world. I think it's safe to say that this will be the most amazing and miraculous footage ever recorded in our modern age, and in one day, the entire world will witness God's awesome power as He defends His children and annihilates their attackers. After witnessing this spectacle, there can only be two types of people on this planet. Those who believe in the one true God of Heaven, and those who still reject Him even in the face of all that their eyes have seen. I believe, according to the timeline revelation, and Ezekiel 39:7, that this event will spark a last-minute planetary revival just in time for the rapture of the Church.

2 Peter 3:9

9 The Lord is not slack concerning His promise, as some count slackness, but is longsuffering toward us, not willing that any should perish but that all should come to repentance.

Verse 11 tells us to *"make vows to the LORD your God, and pay them; let all who are around Him bring presents to Him who ought to be feared."*

God has shown Himself to the world. The world's response should be to worship Him. But He demands to be worshipped with a pure heart and not through a religious act.

Isaiah 1:12-17

12 "When you come to appear before Me, who has required this from your hand, to trample My courts? 13 Bring no more futile sacrifices; incense is an abomination to Me. The New Moons, the Sabbaths, and the calling of assemblies— I cannot endure iniquity and the sacred meeting. 14 Your New Moons and your appointed feasts My soul hates; they are a trouble to Me, I am weary of bearing them.5 When you spread out your hands, I will hide My eyes from you; Even though you make many prayers, I will not hear. Your hands are full of blood.

16 "Wash yourselves, make yourselves clean; Put away the evil of your doings from before My eyes. Cease to do evil, 17 learn to do good; seek justice, rebuke the oppressor; defend the fatherless, plead for the widow.

I do not believe that verse 12 of Psalm 76, which says, *"He shall cut off the spirit of princes; He is awesome to the kings of the earth,"* is only referring to earthly princes. I believe that the "spirit of princes" also relates to Ephesians 6:12, where Paul tells us that *"we do not wrestle against flesh and blood, but against principalities, against powers, against the rulers of the darkness of this age, against spiritual hosts of wickedness in the heavenly places."*

In the wake of the sound defeat of Gog and his armies, as well as the astonishing rapture of the Church, the kings, and princes of this world, including those of the unseen spiritual realm, have been put on notice that their days are numbered and that there is only One to be feared, and it isn't them!

Following this teaching on the defeat of Gog, and the armies that he gathered together to come against Israel, and then the disappearance of millions of people from the earth; to bring this teaching to a close, I would like to point out a few things that I have not previously mentioned. I realize that as I'm writing this now, in the beginning of 2023, the world is fearful of what is coming, even if they don't have the Word of God in their lives to really understand what future events are waiting for them just over the horizon. The world has a sense that perilous times are coming, and for good reason. There doesn't seem to be any good news from day to day, and the future for the common people of the world seems to be beyond hope. However, there is hope, and His name is Jesus!

In Luke 17, Jesus described that the world in which we are now living would be like the days of Noah and the days of Lot, meaning very corrupt and sinful. Within His description, it is understood that the world will be moving along, and for most, it will be daily life, sort of business as usual. Then, suddenly, they will be trapped, and a period of destruction will come upon them, but not for everyone.

Luke 17:26-30

26 And as it was in the days of Noah, so it will be also in the days of the Son of Man: 27 they ate, they drank, they married wives, they were given in marriage, until the day that Noah entered the ark, and the flood came and destroyed them all. 28 Likewise as it was also in the days of Lot: they ate, they drank, they bought, they sold, they planted, they built; 29 but on the day that Lot went out of Sodom it rained fire and brimstone from heaven and destroyed them all. 30 Even so will it be in the day when the Son of Man is revealed.

Luke 17:34-36

34 I tell you, in that night there will be two men in one bed: the one will be taken and the other will be left. 35 Two women will be grinding together: the one will be taken and the other left. 36 Two men will be in the field: the one will be taken and the other left."

So even after seeing God arise and supernaturally protect Israel, most of the world will still be carrying on their usual course, not watching or waiting on the Lord. Then suddenly, with a shout and a trumpet call from heaven, the dead in Christ will rise, and then those of us who are "In Christ" will be "taken" (Greek - paralambano: to take to one's side as a companion), and will be "caught up" (Greek - harpazo, Latin - rapturo) in the air to finally meet our lord and savior.

I sense that in my day right now, in 2023, the world is standing at the edge of a cliff. Sometime in 2024/2025, which corresponds to Psalm 76, we'll go over that cliff. The fall will take 7 years, and the world will hit a lot of jagged rocks on the way down to the bottom. For now, even though things aren't looking great prior to the rapture of the Church, there is still a restraining force, as we know from 2 Thessalonians 2, that is holding back the worst of what is to come. Things may seem bad in these birth pains that we are in today, but we haven't gone over the cliff yet, and the Lord is using all of these troubled times to wake people up, and raise people up to fulfill their calling. So, while people are waking up and asking "what is going on," it's a great opportunity for us to share the gospel and explain that God has proven himself by telling us the "end from the beginning." You don't have to go over that cliff with the rest of the world, and in fact, the best is yet to come for those who are in Christ!

CHAPTER 29

Psalm 77 A Psalm of Asaph

Jubilee Year 2025/2026 - The Day of Trouble - Start of the 7-year Tribulation

I have been seeking and praying for wisdom and discernment from God. I have also been praying that the Lord would open these last days' prophetic mysteries to me so I can complete the work that the Lord has entrusted to me. As I have mentioned before, I have found that He gives me insight into His own time. That time often happens in the middle of the night, which is why I now keep a notebook and a pen by my bed. Early one morning, while writing this book, God woke me up and tuned my ear instantly to what was about to be said on the tablet that I had left playing all night with spoken Bible verses. He gave me 3 revelations that morning. One of them pertained to this chapter, and was from Matthew 18 when Peter asked Jesus "how many times he should forgive his brother for sinning against him."

> **Matthew 18:21-22**
> *²¹ Then Peter came to Him and said, "Lord, how often shall my brother sin against me, and I forgive him? Up to seven times?" ²² Jesus said to him, "I do not say to you, up to seven times, but up to **seventy times seven**."*

There has been a long-standing debate on whether the number at the end of verse 22 should be 70 X 7, which is of course, 490, or if it should be 77. Some translations render it one way, and others the other way. Both are prophetic, and I believe that God is in control and intended it to be rendered in both ways. However, on the morning when I awoke with my ear tuned to the tablet, I specifically heard "77." In my spirit, I instantly understood that this was a clue regarding Psalm 77. Psalm 77 represents the 77th year since the re-birth of Israel and the start of the 7-year tribulation period according to the timeline revelation. By 2025, God will have been forgiving, protecting, and even prospering Israel for the past 77 years, all while they were living in unbelief and transgression against Him. As of the year 2025, judgment will begin to fall upon Israel, but they may not see it right away.

At the end of the 490 years, which is the end of Daniel's 70 weeks, God will forgive and save Israel. Remember that 483 years were completed at the crucifixion of Jesus; from that time forward there has been a 2-day/2000-year "Church Age" gap, and then there will be a final 7-year tribulation period to bring Israel back to the Lord, and to accept the one true Messiah, Jesus. That 7-year period starts this year, the 77th year, 2025.

Verses 1-3
¹I cried out to God with my voice— To God with my voice; And He gave ear to me.
  *² In **the day of my trouble** I sought the Lord; My hand was stretched out in the night without ceasing; My soul refused to be comforted. ³ I remembered God, and was troubled; I complained, and my spirit was overwhelmed. Selah*

There isn't much that I can add to the first three verses to better express that the day of trouble has arrived. I believe that God, in His sovereignty and wisdom has placed this Psalm in this exact position within the Psalms to mark the beginning of the final tribulation. Even though the author might have been penned it under other historical circumstances, it fits perfectly as a marker for this exact time.

Asaph calls this time of turmoil the "day of trouble," which we know is synonymous with the tribulation period and many other titles in the Old and New Testaments. For instance, Jeremiah calls it the "time of Jacob's trouble" in Jeremiah 30, Daniel calls it "the time of trouble such as never was" in Daniel 12, and Isaiah calls it "the day of the Lord" in Isaiah 2. Jesus referred to it as "tribulation" in Matthew 24, and "the great day of His wrath" in Revelation 6. Regardless of the terminology used, they all mean the same thing, the 7 years of tribulation that will be poured out on this world in judgment of the wicked, and to bring Israel back to God. As of 2025, that fearful time has come.

Verses 4-6
[4] *You hold my eyelids open; I am so troubled that I cannot speak.* [5] *I have considered the days of old, the years of ancient times.* [6] *I call to remembrance my song in the night; I meditate within my heart, and my spirit makes diligent search.*

It strikes me that many in Israel will not even know that this time of trouble has begun. Many will be celebrating their newfound, seemingly glorious, but false messiah. They will believe that they have entered into what they call the Messianic Age, only to soon find out that they have jumped into bed with the Devil himself. However, just as Asaph recognized his day of trouble, there will be those who know what time it is, and what is ahead. They may understand the calamity of the coming wrath of God through their own studies in God's word, which may no longer be easy to obtain, or they may already hear the 2 Witnesses preaching in Jerusalem and have opened their hearts to receive the truth. Either way, it is with this spirit of understanding that I believe this Psalm was written and chosen for that time to come. The beauty of it is that God is still good! The author searches his memory of the scriptures that tells of God's goodness even through tragic times, and he meditates on those to find comfort and strength. The days ahead will be perilous, no doubt. Study the Word if possible, listen to the 2 Witnesses, follow the teachings of the 144,000 as well, and most of all, listen to the Holy Spirit inside of you.

Verses 7-9

⁷ Will the Lord cast off forever? And will He be favorable no more? ⁸ Has His mercy ceased forever? Has His promise failed forevermore? ⁹ Has God forgotten to be gracious? Has He in anger shut up His tender mercies? Selah

As you read and really meditate on this Psalm, it becomes clear that it was written from a very personal and deeply despairing perspective in view of an overwhelming calamity that was coming against not just the author, but also against the people. The author, who is either Asaph or perhaps a son of Asaph, asks 6 questions in verses 7-9. I believe that all of them are out of a sense of hopeless abandonment, similar to the cries of an orphaned child.

Verse 9 clarifies whether this is a time of man's wrath or a time of God's wrath. Verse 9 clearly says, *"has He in anger shut up His tender mercies?"* It is due to God's anger that He is allowing the coming turmoil to befall Israel. Similar to times of old, God will use those who are even more wicked to steer Israel back to Himself, but only for a time. It must be confusing after such a great victory that God won for Israel at the Gog invasion, to now feel hopeless and abandoned to the point of despair, but remember that God will always save His remnant.

Verses 10-15

¹⁰ And I said, "This is my anguish; but I will remember the years of the right hand of the Most High." ¹¹ I will remember the works of the LORD; surely I will remember Your wonders of old. ¹² I will also meditate on all Your work, and talk of Your deeds. ¹³ Your way, O God, is in the sanctuary; who is so great a God as our God? ¹⁴ You are the God who does wonders; You have declared Your strength among the peoples. ¹⁵ *You have with Your arm redeemed Your people, the sons of Jacob and Joseph. Selah*

The Psalmist answers the 6 questions that he ponders. Looking back, God has always protected Israel and kept a remnant of His people for Himself, just as Paul writes about in Romans 11.

Romans 11:5
⁵ *Even so then, at this present time there is a remnant according to the election of grace.*

Remember that the Psalmist previously asked 6 questions in despair over what was coming over him and over God's people? In verse 1, he asks a final, a 7th question, but this time it's not out of despair, but in victory! He asks rhetorically, *"who is so great a God as our God?"* He knows who this God is, and the entire world will know who this God is in the 7th Day Millennial Kingdom. All of human history is laid out in this same manner as 6 days of trouble and strife, but on the 7th day, we will definitely find rest!

In this time of trouble, lean on Jesus, Yeshua HaMashiach. He is the one who has done great wonders, and gave you the victory over your enemies. It was with His outstretched arm that He led His people out of Egypt after the first Passover, and it was with His outstretched arms on the cross that He redeemed you, and all of His people, as the final Passover Lamb of God. It has been Jesus all along.

It was Jesus, the Son of God, who was written about in Proverbs 30.

Proverbs 30:4
⁴ *Who has ascended into heaven, or descended? Who has gathered the wind in His fists? Who has bound the waters in a garment? Who has established all the ends of the earth? What is His name, and **what is His Son's name**, If you know?*

His Son's name is Jesus, Yeshua!

It was through Jesus whom all things were made (Genesis 1, John 1). It was Jesus who walked in the garden in the cool of the day (Genesis 3). It was Jesus who walked with Enoch and took him (Genesis 5). It was Jesus who closed the door of the ark (Genesis 7). It was Jesus who ate at Abraham's tent (Genesis 18). It was Jesus who wrestled with Jacob (Genesis 32). It was Jesus who appeared to Moses in a burning bush (Exodus 3). It was Jesus who wrote the 10 commandments with His finger (Exodus 31). It was Jesus who was the 4th man in the fiery furnace (Daniel 3), and it was Jesus who said, *"I am the way, the truth, and the life. No one comes to the Father except through Me"*(John 14).

Verses 16-19

[16] *The waters saw You, O God; the waters saw You, they were afraid; the depths also trembled.* [17] *The clouds poured out water; the skies sent out a sound; Your arrows also flashed about.* [18] *The voice of Your thunder was in the whirlwind; the lightnings lit up the world; the earth trembled and shook.*[19] *Your way was in the sea, Your path in the great waters, and Your footsteps were not known.* [20] *You led Your people like a flock by the hand of Moses and Aaron.*

At first glance as you read through verses 16-19 you will automatically assume that the author is giving a poetic account of the crossing of the Red Sea found in Exodus 14. However, on closer inspection, there are many details that do not match those found in Exodus 14. Many of these details are also not found in recounting the Red Sea crossing events, which were incorporate into a song Moses and Miriam sang in Exodus 15.

It appears that the first verse of this stanza in Psalm 77 represents the Red Sea crossing, as do the last two verses, but the middle verses tell of another event, possibly a prophetic event, or events that haven't yet occurred as of the writing of the Psalm. Verses 17 and 18 are foreign to the Exodus story, but are not foreign to the prophetic happenings of the year prior to this one in the timeline revelation. I believe that they are speaking of the victory that God won over Gog and his armies in the previous year as well as the rapture of the Church all wrapped up together! Notice that these verses continue to speak in the past tense of events that have not yet come in the Psalmist's day, or even in our day in 2023, but will be in the past in 2025.

In verse 17, we read, *"the clouds poured out water; the skies sent out a sound; Your arrows also flashed about."* This description does not fit the Exodus of the Children of Israel from Egypt, but it does fit the previous year's victory and also New Testament descriptions of the rapture of the Church. These three phrases in verse 17 represent visual themes that are present in the Gog invasion detailed in Ezekiel 38 as well as other associated verses relevant to the invasion and then also to our being "caught up" together with Jesus in the clouds. Let's start with the written descriptions of the Ezekiel 38 attack on Israel and compare them to Psalm 77, verses 17 and 18.

Ezekiel 38:22

²² And I will bring him to judgment with pestilence and bloodshed; **I will rain down** *on him, on his troops, and on the many peoples who are with him,* **flooding rain, great hailstones, fire, and brimstone***.*

The Psalm reads, *"the clouds poured out water"* and Ezekiel reads *"I will rain down,"* and *"flooding rain."* You can certainly see the similarities. Then the Psalm reads, *"Your arrows also flashed about,"* which could certainly be another way of describing *"great hailstones, fire, and brimstone,"* found in Ezekiel 38. Again, the similarities are absolutely uncanny.

In Ezekiel 38:17 we are told that God has spoken of Gog and the events surrounding his invasion of Israel to other prophets of the past. He says, *"thus says the Lord GOD: "Are you he of whom I have spoken in former days by My servants the prophets of Israel, who prophesied for years in those days that I would bring you against them?"* I've searched the scriptures high and low and found some hints here and there, but there is one that I am certain pertains to the Ezekiel 38 invasion of 2024. That is found in Jeremiah chapter 30.

After a lengthy description of the return of the Israelites and the restoration of Israel and Judah in Jeremiah 30, God ends His discussion of the end times with the following two verses, which I believe also relate to the Gog Magog invasion that sets up the final events of the final 7 years.

Jeremiah 30:23-24
²³Behold, the whirlwind of the LORD goes forth with fury, a continuing whirlwind; it will fall violently on the head of the wicked. ²⁴The fierce anger of the LORD will not return until He has done it, and until He has performed the intents of His heart. In the latter days you will consider it.

Notice how Jeremiah described the Lord's fury as a "whirlwind" in verse 23. Psalm 77 also uses the same description stating, *"the voice of Your thunder was in the whirlwind."* Then the Psalm continues and states, *"the lightnings lit up the world; The earth trembled and shook."* We know from Ezekiel 38:19 that there will be a great earthquake in the land of Israel associated with the destruction of the Gog army. So, once again our Lord has connected all of these scriptures together for us to find and understand. He is so amazing!

Ezekiel 38:19-20
*¹⁹ For in My jealousy and in the fire of My wrath I have spoken: 'Surely in that day there shall be a **great earthquake in the land of Israel**, ²⁰ so that the fish of the sea, the birds of the heavens, the beasts of the field, all creeping things that creep on the earth, and all men who are on the face of the earth shall shake at My presence. The mountains shall be thrown down, the steep places shall fall, and every wall shall fall to the ground.'*

Here's where I believe it gets really interesting. Notice how there is a shift. In Ezekiel 38, the prophecy is specifically about Israel; however, unlike Ezekiel 38 or Exodus 14, Psalm 77 indicates that at least part of what is being prophesied is global and not just a local event. The Psalmist says, *"the lightnings lit up the **world**"* and *"the **earth** trembled and shook."* In the Hebrew Bible, Psalm 77 uses the term "eretz," which usually means "world" or "earth," as in *"in the beginning, Elohim created the heavens and the earth,"* so it seems that the prophecy might possibly pertain to two separate events in the same year. I cannot prove this, but it is interesting, and I do not believe that this difference is there by mistake.

So, what other event is associated with a "voice of thunder," "lightning that lights up the world," and that will cause the "world to tremble and shake?" Of course, in Ezekiel 38, the land of Israel will literally tremble and shake, but in Psalm 77, this phrase could have an encrypted twofold fulfillment, literal and metaphoric. In Psalm 77, the rapture event would cause the world to tremble and shake out of fear of what happened.

Luke 21:26
26 *People will faint from terror, apprehensive of what is coming on the world, for the heavenly bodies will be shaken.*

We know that the rapture is associated with a loud call like thunder and a trumpet from 1 Corinthians 15:52, Revelation 4:1, 1 Thessalonians 4:16, etc... This also matches Psalm 77:18 as well as the description of lightning lighting up the world, which matches Matthew 24:27 where Jesus prophesied of His coming and described it as lightning coming from the east and flashing to the west. I have always associated verse 27 of Matthew 24 with the second coming of our Lord, but it could pertain to both His glorious appearance to us at the rapture as well as to the world at the second coming. We'll have to wait and see. I simply find all of the interconnections amazing and well worth mentioning.

Matthew 24:27
27 *For as the lightning comes from the east and flashes to the west, so also will the coming of the Son of Man be.*

We started the final stanza of Psalm 77 with a clear reference to the Exodus of the Children of Israel from Egypt. Then we took a prophetic detour with the Psalmist away from the Exodus and to the Gog Magog invasion of Israel, and possibly the rapture of the Church encoded in there as well, as the Psalm looked back on the previous year. Verses 19 and 20 bring us back to the Exodus and the supernatural parting of the Red Sea.

Verses 19-20

19 Your way was in the sea, Your path in the great waters, and Your footsteps were not known. 20 You led Your people like a flock by the hand of Moses and Aaron.

Here's what I can't help but notice about the final verse in Psalm 77. In the first year of the tribulation period, when we should expect to see the appearance of the 2 witnesses, according to Revelation 11, to lead Israel into truth, even in the face of the rising Antichrist, we have verse 20 indicating exactly that! However, most scholars have always assumed that the 2 witnesses will be either Moses and Elijah or Moses and Enoch, perhaps, but I don't believe I have ever heard of anyone suggesting that it could be Moses and Aaron, just like in the days of the Exodus. Is verse 20 of Psalm 77 telling us that it will be Moses and Aaron as of old? If the timeline revelation in the Psalms is correct, the world will find out soon enough.

CHAPTER 30

Psalm 78 A Psalm of Asaph

Year 2026/2027 - The Lord Has Done Great
Things for a Rebellious Nation

Psalm 78 consists of 72 verses and is the longest Psalm of Asaph. Even though it is the longest, I would say that on the surface, it has the least amount of detail and interconnection with the timeline revelation. It has definite connections; however, the overall connection is more general from a surface view than the other Psalms of Asaph, and those of the Psalms of Ascent. However, there might be plenty of encrypted hidden details below the surface that will become more evident as the year approaches. For time sake, I cannot cover all of the verses of this Psalm, but I will hit the highlights in view of the timeline revelation, and point out the most significant connecting details as well as the overall theme.

Let's start with the overall theme of this Psalm, which I would say is God's mercy, guidance, and protection for His rebellious Children, Israel, as well as a warning to them. Let's consider how that applies to the end times, specifically the year that God connected this Psalm to in the timeline revelation.

To arrive at a conclusion for our question, we have to go back in history and evaluate how Israel got to where they are today, which is, at least in part, what this specific Psalm also accomplishes. Once again, for time sake, I'm going to try to shorten Israel's history down to just a few sentences. As we review Israel's history through the Bible in the overall sense, we see a stubborn, "stiff-necked" people who have God's favor, but repeatedly reject Him and His laws. As a simplified pattern, they receive Him, then they reject Him, God uses other nations to come against them so that they will return to Him, then God steps in and restores them, they receive Him again, and the pattern repeats. So, is it any wonder that the pattern continued 2000 years ago, and that they rejected their Messiah when He was sent to them, then another nation came against them (Rome), then God restored them in 1948, and here we are today. This time, however, God restored them without them receiving Him, which was prophesied in Ezekiel's dry bones prophecy in Ezekiel 37, where we see Israel reborn, but without God's spirit in them at first. The day when the Spirit of God is breathed into them is still yet future when Jesus returns and they cry out, *"Blessed is He who comes in the name of the Lord!"*

Matthew 23:38
[38] See! Your house is left to you desolate; [39] for I say to you, you shall see Me no more till you say, 'Blessed is He who comes in the name of the LORD!'"

At this time in the timeline revelation, which is the second year of the tribulation period, the Jews in Israel will be evaluating whether or not the one who "confirmed" the covenant with many is their Messiah or not (Daniel 9:27). Ultimately, they will receive him just as Jesus prophesied in John 5:

John 5:43
[43] I have come in My Father's name, and you do not receive Me; if another comes in his own name, him you will receive.

However, they will not be able to receive him fully just yet because he has not yet satisfied all of the needed signs to be exalted as Messiah in the eyes of the Sanhedrin. According to the Mishneh Torah by Rabbi Moshe ben Maimon, "Maimonides," aka Rambam, which Rabbis quote from regularly today, the messiah must accomplish 5 primary missions before being anointed king. He must restore the Davidic dynasty to its former sovereignty and glory. Of course, that means that he himself must be from the line of David. He must rebuild the temple and restore the sacrificial system and observance of the Torah. He must bring the remaining exiles back to Israel, which I believe will be ongoing this year. He must improve the entire world, motivating all the nations to serve God together. He must also "fight the wars of God" and be victorious. If he is killed, or isn't successful at accomplishing these requirements, then according to the Mishneh Torah, he cannot be the messiah. This brings me to Jesus...

Rabbi Maimonides, whose writings today are considered to be almost equal to scripture itself, specifically wrote about "Jesus of Nazareth" as a hopeful, but failed Messiah, and about Christianity as a "stumbling block" for Jews.

Here is a section of the Mishneh Torah, Sefer Shoftim, Melachim Milchamot, translated by Elihahu Touger:

> *"Jesus of Nazareth who aspired to be the Mashiach and was executed by the court was also alluded to in Daniel's prophecies, as ibid. 11:14 states: 'The vulgar among your people shall exalt themselves in an attempt to fulfill the vision, but they shall stumble.'*
>
> *Can there be a greater stumbling block than Christianity? All the prophets spoke of Mashiach as the redeemer of Israel and their savior who would gather their dispersed and strengthen their observance of the mitzvot (commandments). In contrast, Christianity caused the Jews to be slain by the sword, their remnants to be scattered and humbled, the Torah to be altered, and the majority of the world to err and serve a god other than the Lord."*

So, according to Rabbi Maimonides, Jesus could not have been the Messiah because He was killed, He did not redeem Israel from their enemies (Rome), He did not gather the exiles back to the land, and He did not strengthen the observance of the Torah commandments. In the same way that the Pharisees rejected Jesus 2000 years ago, through the writings of Maimonides, the Rabbis of today continue to reject Jesus as the true Messiah. Because of Maimonides' writings, they need not investigate the scriptures for themselves to discover the hundreds of messianic prophesies that Jesus fulfilled at His first coming, and how He will fulfill those that remain at His second coming.

This is going to sound a little harsh, but the fact that Maimonides rejected Jesus as the Messiah, and spoke of a future Messiah yet to come, means that his writings are not inspired by God, but are inspired by the Devil himself. Through this highly esteemed Jewish sage, Satan has already set the stage for his coming Antichrist in the hearts and minds of the children of Israel.

1 John 2:22-23
22 Who is a liar but he who denies that Jesus is the Christ? He is antichrist who denies the Father and the Son. 23 Whoever denies the Son does not have the Father either; he who acknowledges the Son has the Father also.

After stating something so harsh against God's chosen people, I have to soften the blow by turning the mirror on ourselves as Christians. Our collective history as "Christians" hasn't exactly been kind to the Jewish people. So, is it any wonder that they reject what they perceive as "Christianity?"

Unfortunately, I can partly understand how many of them have rejected the one whom they perceive to be Jesus. First of all, without any investigation, they reject the name Jesus because it isn't a Jewish name. How could the Jewish Messiah not have a Jewish name? Considering that not every Jew is a religious scholar, I understand that most Jews do not know that the name "Jesus" is a transliteration of the Hebrew name Yeshua or Yashua, which means "God's Salvation." So, right off the bat, to the average Jew, the Christian religion appears to be worshiping a false god. Why would they investigate such a religion any further, just as most Christians haven't taken the time to investigate other religions, such as Buddhism, for instance? Then, if you add to that the fact that they believe God doesn't have a Son, you can see how easy it is for them to simply dismiss Christianity as a false religion.

It gets worse... Considering the centuries of anti-Semitic history between so-called

> "Christians" and Jews, and the still fresh memories of the crusades, pogroms, as well as the holocaust carried out by supposed "Christian" nations against the Jewish people, is it any wonder that they reject Jesus and Christianity?

Now, when you look at the churches that exist in and around Jerusalem today through the lens of what I just described - a perceived false messiah, false religion, and brutal killers of Jews, the "Church" doesn't look that inviting. Add to that the "holy" facade and perceived forbidden idol worship of many of the historic churches in the area, with their leaders dressed in priestly robes, gaudy necklaces, big hats, staffs adorned with serpents, golden crucifixes, pagan symbols, and graven images, and you have a recipe for a total rejection made to order. All I can say is that Satan has been very clever to use these churches to hide true Christianity from the eyes of Israel.

As we know from the New Testament, most of the religious leaders of Israel rejected Jesus 2000 years ago, and they continue to reject Him to this day, at least in part, based on the evidence that I just laid out. However, Jesus wants to be known by Israel. He wants them to understand that He is the Word of God made flesh, and He is the fulfillment of the Law as well as the Law Giver Himself. After living a sinless life represented by the spotless Passover lamb, He became the final Passover Lamb and sacrificed Himself to atone for sins once and for all for all those who believe in Him. After fulfilling the Old Covenant, which was based on works, He offered us a New Covenant of grace through faith.

Ephesians 2:8-9

[8] For by grace you have been saved through faith, and that not of yourselves; it is the gift of God, [9] not of works, lest anyone should boast.

It was prophesied in Jeremiah 31 that He would make a new covenant with His people. Only it hasn't been fully implemented yet, because, similar to a marriage covenant, it takes both parties to agree before it is binding. Israel hasn't yet agreed to the proposal, but the day when they will finally agree is fast approaching.

Jeremiah 31:31-34

[31] "The days are coming," declares the LORD, "when I will make a new covenant with the people of Israel and with the people of Judah. [32] It will not be like the covenant I made with their ancestors when I took them by the hand to lead them out of Egypt, because they broke my covenant, though I was a husband to them," declares the LORD. [33] "This is the covenant I will make with the people of Israel after that time," declares the LORD. "I will put my law in their minds and write it on their hearts. I will be their God, and they will be my people. [34] No longer will they teach their neighbor, or say to one another, 'Know the LORD,' because they will all know me, from the least of them to the greatest," declares the LORD. "For I will forgive their wickedness and will remember their sins no more."

Verses 1-4

[1] Give ear, O my people, to my law; incline your ears to the words of my mouth. [2] I will open my mouth in a parable; I will utter dark sayings of old, [3] Which we have heard and known, and our fathers have told us. [4] We will not hide them from their children, telling to the generation to come the praises of the LORD, and His strength and His wonderful works that He has done.

It was and is imperative that each generation teach their children about the Lord and the great things He has done. Otherwise, a nation quickly descends into sin and corruption, as Israel has repeatedly done throughout their history and as we are witnessing in America in this generation. Ultimately, self-destruction is inevitable. God gave us boundaries for a reason, just as good parents set boundaries for their children. Those rules were never intended to rob the joy from us, but to protect us from harming ourselves.

I want to point something out in the first 2 verses of this Psalm. The Psalmist says in verse 1, *"Give ear, O my people, to my law; incline your ears to the words of my mouth."* Did you notice that the word "my" appeared 3 times in this first verse, yet it isn't ever capitalized? If this were the Lord speaking, the first letter would be capitalized. I find that odd right from the start. So, who is speaking and proclaiming "my law?" Later, in verse 4, it speaks of the Lord and the words "His" and "He" are then capitalized. In verse 2 it says "I will open my mouth in a parable; I will utter dark sayings of old." Doesn't that sound familiar? Who is it who understands "dark sayings" according to Daniel 8:23?" It's none other than the Antichrist!

Daniel 8:23
[23]And in the latter time of their kingdom, when the transgressors are come to the full, a king of fierce countenance, and understanding dark sentences, shall stand up.

In Hebrew the root word used in both Daniel 8:23 and in Psalm 78:2 for "dark sentences" or "dark sayings," respectively is the same. It is "chidah," which also means perplexing riddles or even intrigue. The point is that Daniel 8:23 is clearly speaking of the Antichrist, and I believe that Psalm 78 verses 1 and 2 are also speaking of the Antichrist, and how he will come to power by deceiving the Rabbis in Jerusalem who are eagerly awaiting the one who can bring clarity to the scriptures apart from Jesus. The false messiah will certainly use their Torah and the "Babylonian" Talmud, coupled with the writings of their sages, such as Maimonides, against them to convince them in an underhanded way that he is their messiah, all while claiming that he isn't. Remember, he's a deceiver.

Verses 5-8

5 For He established a testimony in Jacob, and appointed a law in Israel, which He commanded our fathers, that they should make them known to their children; 6 that the generation to come might know them, the children who would be born, that they may arise and declare them to their children, 7 that they may set their hope in God, and not forget the works of God, but keep His commandments; 8 And may not be like their fathers, a stubborn and rebellious generation, a generation that did not set its heart aright, and whose spirit was not faithful to God.

When I was a much younger lad, I worked for an electronics engineering firm with offices in California as well as in Ottawa, Canada; however, they were owned by a company from Tel Aviv, Israel. On one occasion, I was attending a trade show, and several of the managers from the corporate headquarters in Israel came as well. As I mentioned, I was young and, of course, very naive. I thought, "wow, these are God's chosen people!" I assumed they were all very devout because, why wouldn't they be? I found out, however, much to my dismay, that I was wrong. They were all very nice, and we got along great, but they explained to me that most Jews in Israel are secular, and no longer hold to any of the teachings of the Bible. I was simply in shock! I would have never guessed such a thing... I thought it was such an honor to be one of God's chosen people that they would never turn away from Him. Obviously, at the time, I didn't really understand the scriptures or Israel's history of turning from the One who called them His own.

Unfortunately, we Christians have done the same thing. It seems that most of the nations around the world that were considered to be predominantly Christian are now in full-blown apostasy just as prophesied. We failed to teach our children about the goodness and the glory of God. We allowed our children to be taught the ways of the world through the education systems, television, and the endless stream of worldly garbage flowing through their hand held devices. Lord, forgive us and help us to win back this generation before it's too late!

Verses 9-11

⁹ The children of Ephraim, being armed and carrying bows, turned back in the day of battle. ¹⁰ They did not keep the covenant of God; they refused to walk in His law, ¹¹ and forgot His works and His wonders that He had shown them.

I find it interesting that Ephraim is specifically mentioned in this Psalm. Remember that Ephraim was the younger brother of Manasseh, but Jacob gave him the greater blessing as if he were the first-born (Genesis 48). Later, it was the young warriors of the Tribe of Ephraim, who according to ancient Hebrew texts, left Egypt on their own with disastrous results before God's planned exodus for Israel (Book of Jasher 75). After that, the Tribe of Ephraim disobeyed God and failed to drive out all of the Canaanites from the Land that God gave to them (Judges 1). They weren't the only tribe to fail the Lord at this task, however. The tribes of Manasseh, Zebulon, Asher, Naphtali, and Dan also failed to completely drive out the inhabitants of the promised land, according to Judges 1.

According to Hosea 7, Ephraim is a symbol of Israel's disobedience to God, and the reason why God didn't heal Israel. Remember, it only takes a little leaven to leaven the whole lump of dough (Galatians 5:9).

Hosea 7:1

"When I would have healed Israel, then the iniquity of Ephraim was uncovered, and the wickedness of Samaria.

The Prophet Hosea goes on to describe Ephraim as being mixed and half-baked with "aliens," taking his strength away from him without him even realizing that it happened.

Hosea 7:8-9

[8] "Ephraim has mixed himself among the peoples; Ephraim is a cake unturned. [9] Aliens have devoured his strength, but he does not know it;

I can't help but wonder if there is a connection between Ephraim and the end-time prophecy of Daniel 2:43.

Daniel 2:43

[43] As you saw iron mixed with ceramic clay, they will mingle with the seed of men; but they will not adhere to one another, just as iron does not mix with clay.

I also find it interesting that in addition to the Tribe of Dan, the Tribe of Ephraim is missing from the 12 tribes listed in Revelation 7. I've heard it said that the two tribes through Joseph's sons are covered by Joseph, but that doesn't really make any sense, considering that Manasseh is on the list. So, it's not just the tribe of Dan that is missing from the 12 Tribes list, but Ephraim as well. What is the significance of these revelations about the Tribe of Ephraim? Nothing is by mistake or oversight in God's word, so I know that it's important, and perhaps it will become apparent this year in the timeline revelation, but that mystery hasn't been revealed to me in 2023.

Verses 12-16

[12] Marvelous things He did in the sight of their fathers, in the land of Egypt, in the field of Zoan. [13] He divided the sea and caused them to pass through; and He made the waters stand up like a heap. [14] In the daytime also He led them with the cloud, and all the night with a light of fire. [15] He split the rocks in the wilderness, and gave them drink in abundance like the depths. [16] He also brought streams out of the rock, and caused waters to run down like rivers.

Verses 12-16 are a reminder to the Children of Israel that God has done great things for them, pointing out specific events from their exodus from captivity in the land of Egypt. Of course, we saw this same theme in the other witness to this year, which was Psalm 126. Accordingly, Israel's national identity will be at an all-time high in the wake of Gog Magog and their excitement over their possible messiah and their perception that the long-awaited Messianic Age is about to begin.

Verses 17-20

17 But they sinned even more against Him by rebelling against the Most High in the wilderness. 18 And they tested God in their heart by asking for the food of their fancy. 19 Yes, they spoke against God: they said, "Can God prepare a table in the wilderness? 20 Behold, He struck the rock, so that the waters gushed out, and the streams overflowed. Can He give bread also? Can He provide meat for His people?"

No matter how much God gave Israel, how much He did for them, or how many miracles He performed for them, they always wanted more. It seems that it's just our human nature to always want more than what we have. It's pretty obvious from scripture that God wants to give His children good gifts, but there's a test involved to find out if we trust Him, and His timing completely or not. I have certainly been guilty of this same character flaw throughout my life. I have to say, though, that once I realized how short time is, none of what I thought I wanted out of this life seemed to matter any longer. I suppose that knowing the timeline could make you turn one of two ways. You can let go of the things of the world that seemed important to you before, and focus on fulfilling the mission that God called you to in the life that He gave you. Or, you can ignore it, hold on tighter to the world, and hope that it's all a huge coincidence. Unfortunately, this world is headed downward in a death spiral anyway, so what is there to even hold on to?

Verses 21-31

*²¹ Therefore the L*ORD *heard this and was furious; so a fire was kindled against Jacob, and anger also came up against Israel, ²² Because they did not believe in God, and did not trust in His salvation. ²³ Yet He had commanded the clouds above, and opened the doors of heaven, ²⁴ had rained down manna on them to eat, and given them of the bread of heaven. ²⁵ Men ate angels' food; he sent them food to the full. ²⁶ He caused an east wind to blow in the heavens; and by His power He brought in the south wind. ²⁷ He also rained meat on them like the dust, fathered fowl like the sand of the seas; ²⁸ And He let them fall in the midst of their camp, all around their dwellings. ²⁹ So they ate and were well filled, for He gave them their own desire. ³⁰ They were not deprived of their craving; but while their food was still in their mouths, ³¹ The wrath of God came against them, and slew the stoutest of them, and struck down the choice men of Israel.*

I think the brief lesson here is that God will allow us to have the lusts of our flesh for a time, but all the while, we are digging our own graves. This is very similar to what Paul wrote in Romans 1, which is very appropriate to this day in 2023, and I'm sure it will even be more appropriate in 2026/2027.

Romans 1:18-32

¹⁸ For the wrath of God is revealed from heaven against all ungodliness and unrighteousness of men, who suppress the truth in unrighteousness, ¹⁹ because what may be known of God is manifest in them, for God has shown it to them. ²⁰ For since the creation of the world His invisible attributes are clearly seen, being understood by the things that are made, even His eternal power and Godhead, so that they are without excuse, ²¹ because, although they knew God, they did not glorify Him as God, nor were thankful, but became futile in their thoughts, and their foolish hearts were darkened. ²² Professing to be wise, they became fools, ²³ and changed the glory of the incorruptible God into an image made like corruptible man—and birds and four-footed animals and creeping things.

²⁴ Therefore God also gave them up to uncleanness, in the lusts of their hearts, to dishonor their bodies among themselves, ²⁵ who exchanged the truth of God for the lie, and worshiped and served the creature rather than the Creator, who is blessed forever. Amen.

²⁶ For this reason God gave them up to vile passions. For even their women exchanged the natural use for what is against nature. ²⁷ Likewise also the men, leaving the natural use of the woman, burned in their lust for one another, men with men committing what is shameful, and receiving in themselves the penalty of their error which was due.

²⁸ And even as they did not like to retain God in their knowledge, God gave them over to a debased mind, to do those things which are not fitting; ²⁹ being filled with all unrighteousness sexual immorality, wickedness, covetousness, maliciousness; full of envy, murder, strife, deceit, evil-mindedness; they are whisperers, ³⁰ backbiters, haters of God, violent, proud, boasters, inventors of evil things, disobedient to parents, ³¹undiscerning, untrustworthy, unloving, unforgiving, unmerciful; ³² who, knowing the righteous judgment of God, that those who practice such things are deserving of death, not only do the same but also approve of those who practice them.

Verses 32-39

³² In spite of this they still sinned, and did not believe in His wondrous works.

³³ Therefore their days He consumed in futility, and their years in fear. ³⁴ When He slew them, then they sought

Him; and they returned and sought earnestly for God.
[35] Then they remembered that God was their rock, and
the Most High God their Redeemer. [36] Nevertheless they
flattered Him with their mouth, and they lied to Him with
their tongue; [37] for their heart was not steadfast with Him,
Nor were they faithful in His covenant. [38] But He, being
full of compassion, forgave their iniquity, and did not
destroy them. Yes, many a time He turned His anger away,
and did not stir up all His wrath; [39] For He remembered
that they were but flesh, a breath that passes away and does
not come again.

Thank you, Lord, for not giving us what we all deserve. We've all sinned against God and fallen short. We all deserve death, but through His Son Yeshua's sacrifice, we are not condemned.

Romans 8:1-8

There is therefore now no condemnation to those
who are in Christ Jesus, who do not walk according to
the flesh, but according to the Spirit. [2] For the law of
the Spirit of life in Christ Jesus has made me free from
the law of sin and death. [3] For what the law could not
do in that it was weak through the flesh, God did by
sending His own Son in the likeness of sinful flesh, on
account of sin: He condemned sin in the flesh, [4] that the
righteous requirement of the law might be fulfilled in
us who do not walk according to the flesh but according
to the Spirit. [5] For those who live according to the flesh
set their minds on the things of the flesh, but those who
live according to the Spirit, the things of the Spirit. [6]
For to be carnally minded is death, but to be spiritually
minded is life and peace. [7] Because the carnal mind is
enmity against God; for it is not subject to the law of
God, nor indeed can be. [8] So then, those who are in the
flesh cannot please God.

Not only are we not condemned, but through Yeshua HaMashiach, we are made coheirs of the Kingdom that is soon coming.

Colossians 3:24

24 knowing that from the Lord you will receive the reward of the inheritance; for you serve the Lord Christ.

Verses 40-55

40 How often they provoked Him in the wilderness, and grieved Him in the desert!

41 Yes, again and again they tempted God, and limited the Holy One of Israel.

42 They did not remember His power: the day when He redeemed them from the enemy, 43 When He worked His signs in Egypt, and His wonders in the field of Zoan;

44 Turned their rivers into blood, and their streams, that they could not drink. 45 He sent swarms of flies among them, which devoured them, and frogs, which destroyed them. 46 He also gave their crops to the caterpillar, and their labor to the locust. 47 He destroyed their vines with hail, and their sycamore trees with frost.

48 He also gave up their cattle to the hail, and their flocks to fiery lightning. 49 He cast on them the fierceness of His anger, wrath, indignation, and trouble, by sending angels of destruction among them. 50 He made a path for His anger;

He did not spare their soul from death, but gave their life over to the plague, 51 and destroyed all the firstborn in Egypt, the first of their strength in the tents of Ham. 52 But He made His own people go forth like sheep, and guided them in the wilderness like a flock; 53 And He led them on safely, so that they did not fear; but the sea overwhelmed their enemies. 54 And He brought them to His holy border, this mountain which His right hand had acquired. 55 He also drove out the nations before them, allotted them an

inheritance by survey, and made the tribes of Israel dwell
in their tents.

The narrative of verses 40 - 55 is that even though Israel provokes God to anger time and time again, God will defend His children. Of course, we know that during the tribulation period, many plagues will be cast upon the earth, but God will always save a remnant of His people. And, as we see in verses 52 - 55, God led them like sheep to safety and destroyed their enemies behind them. I believe that this is a foreshadowing of Revelation 12 and Matthew 24, when the remnant will flee to a place prepared for them to escape the wrath of the Antichrist who wants to destroy them.

Verses 56-64

*56 Yet they tested and provoked the Most High God, and did not keep His testimonies, 57 But turned back and acted unfaithfully like their fathers; they were turned aside like a **deceitful bow**. 58 For they provoked Him to anger with their high places, and moved Him to jealousy with their carved images. 59 When God heard this, He was furious, and greatly abhorred Israel, 60 So that He forsook the tabernacle of Shiloh, the tent He had placed among men, 61 and delivered His strength into captivity, and His glory into the enemy's hand. 62 He also gave His people over to the sword, and was furious with His inheritance.63 The fire consumed their young men, and their maidens were not given in marriage.64 Their priests fell by the sword, and their widows made no lamentation.*

Verses 56-64 are clearly a warning to Israel, and they continue to allude to Ephraim through the use of the term "deceitful bow" and the location of Shiloh, although I'm not able to understand the connection with Ephraim in the context of the timeline revelation. My thought is that at the appropriate appointed time, it will be understood, but as of today, it remains a mystery.

Shiloh was the original location of the Ark of the Covenant and the Tabernacle of God after the Israelites had come into their land, and it was located in the land that was given specifically to the Tribe of Ephraim. During that time, Israel was not following God, which is pretty obvious in verses 58 -64. Israel and the Philistines were at war with each other, and the Philistines were prevailing against them. According to 1 Samuel 4, after returning to camp, *"the elders of Israel asked, "Why did the* LORD *bring defeat on us today before the Philistines? Let us bring the ark of the* LORD's *covenant from Shiloh, so that he may go with us and save us from the hand of our enemies."* It seems that they considered the Ark to be like a magic box that would bring them victory regardless of their wickedness or lack of relationship with the Lord. Needless to say, they were soundly defeated, and the Ark was captured by the Philistines. However, the Philistines lived to regret it.

The Psalmist uses the term "deceitful bow," which brings us back to Ephraim once again through the prophet Hosea, who also used this term in describing how the Tribe of Ephraim continued to turn away from God.

Hosea 7:16
[16] They return, but not to the Most High; they are like a **deceitful bow**. *Their princes shall fall by the sword for the rage of their tongue; this shall be their derision in the land of Egypt.*

I can't help but wonder if this connection with a "deceitful bow" in this Psalm and in Hosea has something to do with the bow in the hands of the rider on the White Horse of Revelation 6, whom we associate with the Antichrist himself.

Revelation 6:1-2
[1] I watched as the Lamb opened the first of the seven seals. Then I heard one of the four living creatures say in a voice like thunder, "Come!" [2] I looked, and there before me was

*a white horse! Its rider held a **bow**, and he was given a crown, and he rode out as a conqueror bent on conquest.*

Verses 65-72

[65] Then the Lord awoke as from sleep, like a mighty man who shouts because of wine. [66] And He beat back His enemies; He put them to a perpetual reproach.

[67] Moreover He rejected the tent of Joseph, and did not choose the tribe of Ephraim, [68] But chose the tribe of Judah, Mount Zion which He loved. [69] And He built His sanctuary like the heights, like the earth which He has established forever. [70] He also chose David His servant, and took him from the sheepfolds;

[71] from following the ewes that had young He brought him, to shepherd Jacob His people, and Israel His inheritance. [72] So he shepherded them according to the integrity of his heart, and guided them by the skillfulness of his hands.

In verses 65 and 66 we once again see that the Lord continues to fight Israel's enemies, who are also His enemies. God has allowed enemies to come against and prevail against Israel time and time again to bring Israel back to Himself. This is part of the pattern that I discussed earlier. As Israel pushes God away and seeks after the world, and the gods of the world, it seems as if God is asleep to them, but all the while He's giving them more and more rope to hang themselves with, which they inevitably do. Then they cry out, and God rescues them. That same pattern is repeating itself once again, and for the final time, even in our day.

The Ark never returned to Shiloh after being given back by the Philistines. Eventually, David was made king over Judea, and then over all of Israel. He had the Ark brought to Jerusalem in preparation for the eventual building of a temple for the Lord. So, through a series of events, God removed the Ark from Ephraim, the son of Joseph, and gave it to Judah, just as the Psalm describes.

There are many interesting contextual possibilities cryptically hidden just beneath the surface of Psalm 78 that may be further revealed, and better understood at their appointed times within the timeline revelation. Ephraim seems to play a prominent role as a "deceitful bow" who turns back and loses his position. Although not specifically mentioned, the Ark of the Covenant is certainly a hidden theme within this Psalm. And then there is the demotion of Joseph and Ephraim, and the promotion of Judah through David. Furthermore, I find it very fascinating that there are specifically 72 verses in this Psalm. Maybe I'm way out in the weeds, but it stands out to me that it has 72 verses.

Does the number 72 have any prophetic meaning for this year in the timeline revelation? Let's consider the number 72 in Bible history. Moses and Aaron were told to select 70 elders to help lead Israel. If you add Moses and Aaron to the 70 elders, you get 72. Depending on the translation of Luke 10, Jesus sent out 72 disciples, 2 by 2, into the towns and villages to preach and prepare the way for Him. In Judaic Kabbalah, there are 72 names for God. The Sanhedrin is made up of 70 members plus 2 scribes, which totals 72. And there were 70 nations born from Noah plus God's kingdom Israel, and Edom, making 72 according to some ancient Jewish interpretations of Genesis 10.

Here's where it gets a little crazy... According to *The Lesser Key of Solomon*, which is an ancient textbook on demonology of sorts, there are 72 demons in leadership positions over hundreds of legions of other demons. Interestingly, Muslim martyrs are specifically promised 72 beautiful virgins when they get to heaven. Surprise!

Baal is known as the prince, or king of the 72 demons in leadership positions, and he also controls 66 legions of demons directly under his command. Baal is associated with water, rain, the sea (chaos), seasons, war, teaching of science, and is often represented by a bull.

Last summer, the Commonwealth Games were held in Birmingham, England. These games are similar to, but a smaller version, of the Olympic games. It was attended by then Prince, now King Charles, as well as "72" nations. During the extravagant opening ceremony, which was complete with a mock tower of Babel, music, dancing, and an elaborate video of stars falling from heaven, a gigantic beast in the form of a mechanical bull was rolled out and was promptly worshiped by performers holding crystals, and then tamed and ridden by the main heroin in the show. You just can't make this stuff up!

I'm mentioning the demonic side of the number 72, because, according to Ephesians 6:12, *"we do not wrestle against flesh and blood, but against principalities, against powers, against the rulers of the darkness of this age, against spiritual hosts of wickedness in the heavenly places.* Ironically, 6 X 12 is 72! Obviously, it pays to know your enemy, and we just might be able to piece some things together as well, things that have been mysteries for a long time. The more puzzle pieces you have, the clearer the final image becomes.

The number 72 is also a very important number in Freemasonry symbolism. The Great Pyramid of Giza, which is depicted on the back of our US 1 dollar bill, is made up of 72 stones with a flat top and a floating "all-seeing eye" of the Egyptian god Horus above it. The exoteric reason for the specific 72 stones is that they represent the Hebrew names of God. The esoteric reason is a little harder to come by. Let's just say that their "Great Architect of the Universe" isn't the God that I serve.

Furthermore, the Freemasons have a prominent symbol of a coffin with a pentagram on its cover against an Acacia Tree. If you ever study the Osiris mythology, you'll find that the god Osiris was tricked by his brother Set into placing himself into a specially made coffin, which was then shut on him and nailed shut by 72 accomplices. He was then sent down the river, where he ran aground by hitting an Acacia tree. This also ties to the Egyptian god Horus, but that's another study for another day.

CHAPTER 31

Psalm 79 A Psalm of Asaph

Year 2027/2028 - The Temple Defiled

This is probably a good time to recap the 7 Psalms of Asaph that we have already covered. The dislocated Psalm 50 was an inverted view of the tribulation period with 6 verses specifically devoted to the Antichrist. I do not believe that it was by accident that Psalm 50 was placed in its particular location within the timeline revelation as it relates to the Antichrist. The timeline period between 2027 and 2028 represents the 80th year of the reborn nation of Israel. That means as of 2028, it will have been 30 years ago when Israel celebrated their 50th anniversary. So, the number 50 relates to the number 30 in the timeline of Israel's 80 years. Remember that Israel has never made it past 80 years, and I do not expect this pattern to be broken. So, what is significant about 30 years? It is connected with all types of "messiah" figures in the Bible as well as from other ancient Jewish texts.

The first Psalm of Asaph, in the main group of 11, Psalm 73 (2021/2022), revealed Israel as once again envious of the world, and following after it, as well as many perfectly located keywords, phrases, and imagery matching our recent past, such as "pangs," "plagued," "washed my hands," and "beast" to name a few. Psalm 74 (2022/2023) highlighted the rising of the enemy against God and His Children, as well as the drying up of mighty rivers, which we witnessed in 2022 all over the world from the Mississippi River to the prophetic Euphrates

River. Psalm 75 (2023/2024) prophesied the continued rise of the "horn" that God will "cut off," the bringing down of one, setting up of another, and possible earth-shaking natural events. God also promises that He will judge "uprightly" at the "appointed time." I also believe that it prophesies the coming invasion of Israel from the north. Psalm 76 (2024/2025) indicates God's victory over the Gog Magog invasion of Israel as well as the rapture of the "oppressed of the earth." Psalm 77 (2025/2026) represents the beginning of the "day of trouble," also known as the tribulation period. Psalm 78 (2026/2027), as placed within the tribulation period on the timeline, is a recap of Israel's history of rebellion against God, and of His anger against them, followed by His repeated mercy, guidance, and protection for them. It is also a prophetic tribulation warning for Israel to repent, follow God, and not be as stubborn as their fathers were. Psalm 78 also highlights Ephraim's fall and the selection of Judah, which I'm certain, will play out in some prophetic way in the 2026/2027 time period. It makes me wonder what tribe Benjamin Netanyahu is from.

That brings us to Psalm 79 (2027/2028), which represents the middle of the tribulation period. Clearly, I do not know exactly the "day or the hour" when the rapture will take place, nor do I know the date of the start of the tribulation period. The timeline revelation in the Psalms indicates a general time frame as time progresses through the tribulation. The fact that God gave us 2 witnesses in the Psalms is very helpful; however, since they are on two separate calendars, it can get very confusing as well. Of course, I'm speaking of the Psalms of Ascent, and the Psalms of Asaph, which follow the same pattern of progress through the tribulation, but in many instances, highlight different aspects of the associated years, almost as if a Psalm of Ascent fits in between two Psalms of Asaph instead of directly overlapping one. More confusion comes from the overlap of the calendars, and the fact that a year isn't a single point in time, but is in fact, 12 months long. If the start of the tribulation occurs sometime in 2025, as indicated by the encrypted timeline revelation in the Psalms, then I would expect the middle of the tribulation to fall sometime between 2027 and 2028 if you count the entire year of 2025 in the calculation as I believe we should. According to the prophetic language of the Psalms of Asaph, it appears as well that sometime between Psalm 79 and Psalm 80 will be the three-and-a-half-year mark, or in other words, the middle of the tribulation, which aligns with Psalm 128 as well. Psalm 80 represents the 80th year of the reborn Israel, and according to the prophetic pattern, I do not expect Israel to reach their 81st birthday, so that fits on the timeline perfectly as well.

Now, I'm going to give some of my "hunches" about God's "appointed times" to try to make some better sense of the timeline at this middle point. Jesus fulfilled Passover, which is in the first month of God's calendar. He has yet to fulfill the Feast of Trumpets, Day of Atonement, and Tabernacles. If the Feast of Trumpets is fulfilled in 2023 or 2024 with the rapture, then the next "appointed time" on God's prophetic calendar will be the Day of Atonement, which is always roughly 6 months, or a half year after Passover. What that means is that I would anticipate that Jesus will return on the Day of Atonement in the fall to fulfill that "appointed time," which also means that the half-way point within the tribulation would then be at the time of Passover in the spring. Let's say hypothetically that the Antichrist sets himself in the temple at the end of God's calendar year, which is in the spring. As an illustration, let's say that that day will be on March 31, the last day of that calendar year, and the Antichrist announces that He is god at the end of that day. Remember that in Israel, a day ends at sundown, and a new day begins once it's dark. Then, only minutes later, which will be considered the following day, April 1, the first day of the new calendar year, the remnant of Israel flees to the wilderness according to Matthew 24 and Revelation 12. With this illustration, I hope that you can see how it would appear, on a timeline of years, as if there could be an entire year between these events, but in reality, they are only minutes apart.

Now that we've cleared that up, and it's probably as clear as mud, let's see what our Lord wants to reveal to us about the middle of the tribulation period, as seen through Psalm 79. According to other prophesies within God's word, we know, and have already covered the reality that the middle of the tribulation will be the time when the Antichrist declares that he is god, defiles the temple, and tries to destroy the Jews in Judea. Based on this understanding, and if the timeline revelation is correct, at the middle of the tribulation period, I wouldn't expect to read about daisies and butterflies, but instead, I would expect to read about death, destruction, and the defilement of the temple. Don't say that I didn't warn you...

Verses 1-4
¹O God, the nations have come into Your inheritance; your holy temple they have defiled; they have laid Jerusalem in heaps. ² The dead bodies of Your servants they have given as food for the birds of the heavens, the flesh of Your saints to the beasts of the earth. ³ Their blood they have shed like water all around Jerusalem, and there was no one to bury them. ⁴ We have become a reproach to our neighbors, a scorn and derision to those who are around us.

It seems that we're off to a rough start in 2027/2028! Just as expected, Psalm 79 depicts a devastating scene of death and destruction and the defilement of the temple. This also means that the temple has been built by this time in the timeline. After all, you can't defile a temple that hasn't been built!

Placing this particular Psalm historically is a bit difficult. The original Asaph served during the reign of King David and into the reign of David's son, King Solomon. During that time, there were no wars matching the description of Psalm 79. Asaph had sons, and it is certainly possible that one of his sons wrote this Psalm under the name Asaph after witnessing the Babylonian conquest of Judea and the destruction of Jerusalem and the temple. However, there is no mention of the temple being destroyed in Psalm 79, but only defiled, which we know will happen at the midpoint of the tribulation from Daniel 9:27 in conjunction with Matthew 24:15. Psalm 79 also mentions "armies" plural and not Babylon. I realize that in those times, an army could have been made up of many different conquered nations, but it still seems a little out of place to me. I'm not suggesting that this Psalm isn't regarding the siege of Jerusalem by the Babylonians. Still, I believe that, as with all of these Psalms, the Holy Spirit guided the Psalmists to write in a way that established a pattern of events instead of specific details regarding a singular event. Then, God made sure that they were placed exactly where He wanted them for His prophetic purposes.

The Two Witnesses

Verses 2 and 3 paint a dreadful picture of God's servants and saints who have been killed at the same time that the temple was defiled, and who lie in the streets of Jerusalem with no one to bury them. Their bodies suffer the ultimate disgrace and humiliation by becoming food for the birds and for the animals. Verse 3 seems to indicate that a multitude of God's saints will be killed at this time, but could 2 of those servants and saints actually be the 2 witnesses described in Revelation 11 who are killed by the beast in the middle of the tribulation, and who are also specifically not allowed to be buried? According to Revelation 11, their bodies are seen by the world, which certainly implies today's interconnected technology, and people from all over the world will celebrate their deaths by sending gifts to one another as if it were Christmas. Sending gifts as described also implies today's shipping and transportation abilities.

Revelation 11:7-10
⁷ Now when they have finished their testimony, the beast that comes up from the Abyss will attack them, and overpower and kill them. ⁸ Their bodies will lie in the public square of the great city—which is figuratively called Sodom and Egypt—where also their Lord was crucified. ⁹ For three and a half days some from every people, tribe, language and nation will gaze on their bodies and refuse them burial. ¹⁰ The inhabitants of the earth will gloat over them and will celebrate by sending each other gifts, because these two prophets had tormented those who live on the earth.

Verse 4 says, *"We have become a reproach to our neighbors, a scorn and derision to those who are around us."* That verse brings us to a similar verse, also prophetic of not only the Babylonian exile of the Jews, but quite possibly of a yet future event as well.

Ezekiel 5:14

¹⁴ Moreover I will make you a waste and a reproach among the nations that are all around you, in the sight of all who pass by.

Many say that Ezekiel 5 was written to warn the Jews of the coming destruction of Jerusalem by the Babylonians. I'm not a historian, but it seems to me that Ezekiel was already in captivity in Babylon after that destruction when he wrote his prophesies. I'm basing that on what Ezekiel himself declared about his being called to prophesy in Ezekiel chapter 1.

Ezekiel 1:1-2

*Now it came to pass in the thirtieth year, in the fourth month, on the fifth day of the month, **as I was among the captives** by the River Chebar, that the heavens were opened and I saw visions of God. ² On the fifth day of the month, which was in the fifth year of King Jehoiachin's captivity, ³ the word of the LORD came expressly to Ezekiel the priest, the son of Buzi, in the land of the Chaldeans by the River Chebar; and the hand of the LORD was upon him there.*

Clearly, Ezekiel was already in captivity. If Ezekiel wasn't prophesying of the future Babylonian destruction of Jerusalem because it had already taken place, then what was he prophesying about? It stands to reason that he was prophesying about the Roman destruction, and I would contend that he was, by pattern, also describing the future calamity that would soon come upon Jerusalem. In fact, it seems that Ezekiel 5 matches Zechariah 13:8-9 in many ways, which most believe, myself included, is yet future prophecy.

Zechariah 13:8-9

[8] And it shall come to pass in all the land," says the LORD, "that two-thirds in it shall be cut off and die, but one-third shall be left in it:[9] I will bring the one-third through the fire, will refine them as silver is refined, and test them as gold is tested. They will call on My name, and I will answer them. I will say, 'this is My people'; and each one will say, 'The LORD is my God.'"

Let's compare Zechariah's prophecy to Ezekiel's prophecy.

Ezekiel 5:12

[12] One-third of you shall die of the pestilence, and be consumed with famine in your midst; and one-third shall fall by the sword all around you; and I will scatter another third to all the winds, and I will draw out a sword after them.

You can see the same math in both prophecies, only described a little differently. The sum total is that 2/3rds will perish, and 1/3 will be saved. Notice also that in Zechariah's prophecy, the 1/3 is tested through the fire, and in Ezekiel's prophecy, the 1/3rd is scattered to the winds, and a sword is sent after them. Can both prophesies describe the same event, and the same people group, and be so different? By pattern, they are the same, but one could have more of an emphasis on the events of the first century AD, and the other could have more of an emphasis on the future mid-tribulation episode. The 1/3rd remnant will be "tested"(Zechariah 13:9) during their escape to the refuge (Matthew 24:15-22, Revelation 12:6, 13-17), but we're not told specifically how they are tested. In Ezekiel's account, a "sword" is sent after the 1/3, but it never says that they are slain by that sword. In fact, it is pretty obvious that they are not. Is that "sword" the same as the "like a flood" that spews out of the serpent's mouth to carry away the remnant as prophesied in Revelation 12:15? Remember that a "flood" is sometimes used in prophecy as a metaphor for an army in the same way that a "sword" is also used in scripture to represent an army.

Also, you may say that Zechariah's prophecy is for "all the land" of Israel, and Ezekiel's prophecy is only for Jerusalem and Judea, so how do they match? That's a good question with a good historical answer. The answer has to do with God's Moedim, or "appointed times." We know historically that it was at Passover, when millions of Jews from all over Israel had made their pilgrimage, and were in and around Jerusalem, when the Romans besieged the city and killed over a million Jews who had come to participate in the festival. So, God used the festival to gather the Jews from around Israel, and then used Rome to punish Israel for rejecting the Messiah, and for their numerous sins and bloodshed (Ezekiel 22). So, the prophecies are both at least partially fulfilled since Israelis from all over Israel were in Jerusalem at the time of the siege. Will those prophecies have a future fulfillment in the same way at Passover, or one of the other "appointed times?" My hunch is "yes." Was this gathering of Israel into Jerusalem to be punished for their sins prophesied in scripture, and may it once again come to pass as a prophetic pattern? According to Ezekiel 22, I believe that the answer is Yes.

Ezekiel 22:19-20

*19 Therefore thus says the Lord GOD: 'Because you have all become dross, therefore behold, **I will gather you into the midst of Jerusalem**. 20 As men gather silver, bronze, iron, lead, and tin into the midst of a furnace, to blow fire on it, to melt it; so I will gather you in My anger and in My fury, and I will leave you there and melt you.*

Verses 5-7

5 How long, LORD? Will You be angry forever? Will Your jealousy burn like fire? 6 Pour out Your wrath on the nations that do not know You, and on the kingdoms that do not call on Your name. 7 For they have devoured Jacob, and laid waste his dwelling place.

Once again it seems that the Psalmist is referring to many different nations who have attacked Israel rather than just a single nation or empire. In addition, in many ways, this Psalm could refer to the siege of Jerusalem by the Babylonians around 597 BC, the siege by the Romans in 70 AD, and the future coming "desolation." In addition, the Psalmist is petitioning God to "pour out His wrath" on those nations who have "devoured Jacob," but that never happened; God hasn't "poured out His wrath" on those nations, so it would have to be considered an unanswered prayer concerning ancient Babylon, as well as the Roman Empire. Both empires ended. Well, Rome is still alive in a sense, but either way, I wouldn't say that they ever experienced an outpouring of God's wrath, at least not yet!

I would like to point out how similar Jeremiah 10 is to our Psalm, and how many keywords, phrases, and word pictures they share, so that we can possibly glean some extra understanding and context.

Jeremiah 10:25

25 Pour out Your fury on the Gentiles, who do not know You, and on the families who do not call on Your name; for they have eaten up Jacob, devoured him and consumed him, and made his dwelling place desolate.

Now let's compare Jeremiah 10:25 with Psalm 79:6-7:

Verses 6-7

6 Pour out Your wrath on the nations that do not know You, and on the kingdoms that do not call on Your name.
7 For they have devoured Jacob, and laid waste his dwelling place.

I'm not a world-renowned Bible scholar, nor do I play one on TV, but I think these verses match each other almost perfectly. That makes me want to investigate Jeremiah 10 a little more to see if there are any prophetic patterns that can shed more light on this year in the timeline revelation.

Jeremiah 10 is instructional to Israel, warning them not to follow after other nation's false gods. Of course, we know that Israel has always had this problem, and has done so as a pattern throughout their history. Will Israel worship a false god or gods in the future? Yes, in fact, they are doing it even today. Unfortunately, so is the United States as well as every other nation, just not in the same form as the ancients did. In ancient times, they even sacrificed their children to the idols of false gods such as Baal. Behind every idol that was worshipped and given sacrifices to throughout history, there was actually a demon in disguise.

Psalm 106:35-39
35 But they mingled with the Gentiles and learned their works; 36 they served their idols, which became a snare to them. 37 They even sacrificed their sons and their daughters to demons, 38 and shed innocent blood, the blood of their sons and daughters, whom they sacrificed to the idols of Canaan; and the land was polluted with blood. 39 Thus they were defiled by their own works, and played the harlot by their own deeds.

1 Corinthians 10:20-21
20 Rather, that the things which the Gentiles sacrifice they sacrifice to demons and not to God, and I do not want you to have fellowship with demons. 21 You cannot drink the cup of the Lord and the cup of demons; you cannot partake of the Lord's table and of the table of demons.

Does Israel sacrifice their children to demons today? Yes, you may find this hard to believe about the Holy Land, but abortion, which is a child sacrifice to demons, whether people know it or not, is legal in Israel today, and has been since 1977. It has to be approved by a pregnancy termination board, so it's not as easy to obtain as it is in other countries, but it is legal, and from my research, it appears that hardly anyone has ever been denied. Of the approximately 20,000 abortions requested per year in Israel, only around 1% is denied. And, of course, there are other avenues to receive an abortion without government authorization, so we really don't know the true number of abortions performed in Israel annually.

Is God happy about this? No, of course not. In fact, these practices will ultimately lead to their downfall as well as ours. From God's word, we know that He will not put up with this detestable practice much longer. We also know from Revelation 13 that there will be idol worship of the beast and his image during the tribulation period.

Revelation 13:11-15

[11] Then I saw another beast coming up out of the earth, and he had two horns like a lamb and spoke like a dragon. [12] And he exercises all the authority of the first beast in his presence, and causes the earth and those who dwell in it to worship the first beast, whose deadly wound was healed. [13] He performs great signs, so that he even makes fire come down from heaven on the earth in the sight of men. [14] And he deceives those who dwell on the earth by those signs which he was granted to do in the sight of the beast, telling those who dwell on the earth to make an image to the beast who was wounded by the sword and lived. [15] He was granted power to give breath to the image of the beast, that the image of the beast should both speak and cause as many as would not worship the image of the beast to be killed.

According to many other scriptures, we know that there will be a lot of demonic activity around the world during the tribulation. They will be unleashed to cause destruction, and to torment the inhabitants of the earth for a period of time. So, what does God want us to understand from Jeremiah 10 concerning these false idols, which are actually demonic false gods? No matter how they are portrayed, or how much power they are said to have, there is only one God who created the heavens and the earth, and He will be victorious, and they will perish. Choose who you will serve very carefully.

Jeremiah 10:11

[11] Thus you shall say to them: "The gods that have not made the heavens and the earth shall perish from the earth and from under these heavens."

Verses 8-10

[8] Oh, do not remember former iniquities against us! Let Your tender mercies come speedily to meet us, for we have been brought very low. [9] Help us, O God of our salvation, for the glory of Your name; and deliver us, and provide atonement for our sins, for Your name's sake! [10] Why should the nations say, "Where is their God?" Let there be known among the nations in our sight the avenging of the blood of Your servants which has been shed.

The Psalmist cries out for God to "come speedily" and then to "deliver us," but that also never happened during the ancient Babylonian exile, which lasted 70 years, nor did it happen after Israel was expelled from their land by the Roman Empire, which has lasted almost 2000 years. So, there is still an expectation that God will "come speedily" at some time in the future and "deliver" Israel. I find verse 9 very interesting as the Psalmist calls for "deliverance" and "atonement" for Israel's sins for the glory of His name. That actually did happen 2,000 years ago, but just not in the way that they expected.

Verses 11-13

[11] Let the groaning of the prisoner come before You; according to the greatness of Your power preserve those who are appointed to die; [12] and return to our neighbors sevenfold into their bosom their reproach with which they have reproached You, O Lord. [13] So we, Your people and sheep of Your pasture, will give You thanks forever; we will show forth Your praise to all generations.

As we progress through the sequence of events in the last days in these Psalms, we know from many prophetic verses that the Lord will return, and will avenge the remnant of Israel. In verses 11-13, the Psalmist is calling out for that day, the day when the Lord pours out His wrath on those who are left and still unrepentant including all of Israel's neighbors who have turned on them. However, according to the timeline, we still have at least three and a half years of tribulation left.

At the beginning of this Psalm, we read about the defilement of the temple. That means that the temple once again stands in Jerusalem by this time in the timeline. We know from Daniel 9 and Matthew 24 that when the temple is defiled, the believing remnant must flee from Jerusalem and Judea. We also know from Revelation 12 that they will flee to a place that has been prepared for them, and that they will be kept and nourished for three and a half years. How do you think that the remnant will know the way to the "refuge" if they are not led there like sheep by a Good Shepherd?

CHAPTER 32

Psalm 80 A Psalm of Asaph

Year 2028/2029 - Israel is 80! - God Leads the Remnant Like a Shepherd - Plea for Salvation

Psalm 80 picks up right where Psalm 79 left off. At the end of Psalm 79, we saw Israel described as "the sheep of Your pasture." The remnant of Israel, aka the "sheep," after witnessing the abomination of desolation in the temple, must flee from Judea and the Antichrist, who pursued them just as Pharaoh pursued the Israelites as they fled Egypt. But how will they know the way? Fortunately for them, there is only One who is "The Way," and He is also the Good Shepherd who will, according to the first 2 verses of Psalm 80, lead the remnant of Israel to safety. What exactly that will look like at that time, I don't know. Will He guide them similar to how He guided Israel during their exodus, with a pillar of cloud by day, and a pillar of fire by night? I don't know, but I'm positive that He will reveal the way in the most perfect way, and none of His people will miss it.

Verses 1-2
¹Give ear, O Shepherd of Israel, you who lead Joseph like a flock; you who dwell between the cherubim, shine forth!
² Before Ephraim, Benjamin, and Manasseh, stir up Your strength, and come and save us!

During the reign of King Hezekiah, from whom we have the other timeline witness through the 15 Psalms of Ascent, the Assyrian king came into the land to make war against Judea. The Assyrian king sent a message to king Hezekiah telling him basically that the God of Israel would not save them, and that Assyria would take Jerusalem. King Hezekiah cried out to God, as we see in Isaiah 37:

Isaiah 37:14-17

14 And Hezekiah received the letter from the hand of the messengers, and read it; and Hezekiah went up to the house of the LORD, and spread it before the LORD. 15 Then Hezekiah prayed to the LORD, saying: 16 "O LORD of hosts, God of Israel, the One who dwells between the cherubim, You are God, You alone, of all the kingdoms of the earth. You have made heaven and earth. 17 Incline Your ear, O LORD, and hear; open Your eyes, O LORD, and see; and hear all the words of Sennacherib, which he has sent to reproach the living God.

You may be wondering why I'm bringing up Isaiah 37, and what it has to do with the remnant of Israel fleeing from the Antichrist. The main reason why I was prompted to refer back to Isaiah 37 was because of a key interconnecting description of God found in both Psalm 80, and Isaiah 37. That description is *"You who dwell between the cherubim,"* which is also describing the Ark of the Covenant. There are other chapters in the Bible that also use this description, but Isaiah 37 stands out to me because it has this odd little section that doesn't seem to fit within the history of the events being described.

Suppose your understand the history of the events of Isaiah 37. In that case, you will know that the Assyrian king did not overtake Jerusalem, and in fact, he didn't even shoot a single arrow at Jerusalem. The Angel of the Lord went into the Assyrian military camp and slew 185,000 Assyrians, causing the king to return to Nineveh. That means that the inhabitants of Jerusalem were saved by the hand of the Lord, and none of them had to flee the city and live in the wilderness for 3 years. I realize that is a very specific and odd thing to say, and it is! Like

I said, it's this little odd section that stands out to me after finding the interconnection between these two texts. Here's what Isaiah says:

Isaiah 37:30-32
[30] "This shall be a sign to you: you shall eat this year such as grows of itself, and the second year what springs from the same; also in the third year sow and reap, plant vineyards and eat the fruit of them. [31] And the remnant who have escaped of the house of Judah shall again take root downward, and bear fruit upward. [32] For out of Jerusalem shall go a remnant, and those who escape from Mount Zion. The zeal of the LORD of hosts will do this.

In reviewing verse 30 of Isaiah 37, I understand that the field workers in Judea at that time probably weren't able to plant while the king of Assyria and his troops were camped around Jerusalem, and therefore, they would have had a year with a bad harvest unless God supernaturally stepped in and provided for them. That doesn't mean that they couldn't plant the next year unless maybe it was a sabbatical, "Shmita" year, for the land, but we're not told. Regardless, it seems a little odd on its own, but then, when you keep reading in verses 31 and 32, it becomes even more of a head-scratcher. If the city was never assaulted, why is there a remnant who has escaped from Jerusalem for at least 3 years? Maybe that is answered in another book, but I haven't found it. This, to me, seems like a prophecy, or at least a pattern pertaining to another time, the end-time, which matches this year in the timeline revelation perfectly. Regardless, God is going to watch over His remnant and provide for them during their time in the refuge, as well as protect them from the threats that will surely come against them during the next 1260 days, as stated in Revelation 12.

Revelation 12:6
[6] Then the woman fled into the wilderness, where she has a place prepared by God, that they should feed her there one thousand two hundred and sixty days.

Verse 3
³ Restore us, O God; cause Your face to shine, and we shall be saved!

I find verse 3 extremely interesting because the Lord has gone out of His way to highlight this verse so that we'll notice it. Not only this verse, but there are 2 others in this Psalm just like it, also set apart in the format. Each of these 3 verses, or "refrains," call for God to "restore" Israel and to "save" Israel. Could it be that those 3 repeating verses interconnect with the 3 years in Isaiah 37? I think you know by now that God is very clever at these things. If we're just reading through the Bible, it's easy to miss these details, but when you start scratching just below the surface, a whole new world of understanding is opened up. You may say, but wait; shouldn't it be 3.5 years, aka 1260 days? Yes, that is correct. Notice that in verse 2 of Psalm 80, the Psalmist says, *"stir up Your strength, and come and save us!"* It's half of the call to "restore" and "save." I know that sounds crazy, but I keep finding that God loves to encrypt these prophetic treasures in His word so that we can seek and find them (Proverbs 25:2).

The other interesting aspect about this is the thought that He has possibly encoded this in Psalm 80 in chronological order. The half-year is encoded first, then the other three. For the sake of argument, let's just say that the prophetic pattern continues, and that the Antichrist will try to destroy the Jews around the time of the spring feasts as his predecessors did. It will then be another half year until the fall feasts, and then exactly 3 years after that will be when the Lord will return and set up His Kingdom. Either way, if you put the half year at the beginning or the end, the 6 months represent the time between the spring and the fall feasts or "Moedim," but I have a hunch that there is a reason why God assembled this Psalm the way He did.

Verses 4-6
⁴ O LORD God of hosts, how long will You be angry against the prayer of Your people? ⁵ You have fed them with the bread of tears, and given them tears to drink in great

measure. ⁶ You have made us a strife to our neighbors, and
our enemies laugh among themselves.

Verse 4 asks the Lord, "how long will You be angry against the prayer of Your people? Well, I can answer that question - it's 3.5 years! In verses 5 and 6, there is a "them" versus "us" dynamic going on that most miss. I certainly did until I really started digging into this Psalm. We read these two verses and assume that the Psalmist is talking about the same group of people, which in this case would be the escaping Israelites. However, the Israelites would be an "us" from the perspective of the writer and not a "them," as we see in verse 5. So, who is the "them?" In the context of the escape of the remnant, I can only suggest that "them" is the army that was sent out to destroy the fleeing Israelites, as described in Revelation 12, who will be defeated. I have stated before that a "flood" can be a metaphor for an army.

Revelation 12:16
¹⁶ But the earth helped the woman, and the earth opened
its mouth and swallowed up the flood which the dragon
had spewed out of his mouth.

Just in case this was a translation error, I looked these two verses up in the Orthodox Jewish Bible, and it also renders the words as "them" and "us," so I do believe that the Psalmist is talking about two different people groups.

Verse 7
⁷ Restore us, O God of hosts; cause Your face to shine, and
we shall be saved!

This is the second refrain calling out for God's restoration and salvation, which I believe is representative of the second full year of the Israelites in the refuge.

Verses 8-11

⁸ You have brought a vine out of Egypt; you have cast out the nations, and planted it. ⁹ You prepared room for it, and caused it to take deep root, and it filled the land. ¹⁰ The hills were covered with its shadow, and the mighty cedars with its boughs. ¹¹ She sent out her boughs to the Sea, and her branches to the River.

Israel, depicted as a "vine" removed from Egypt and planted, is a familiar theme in many Old Testament books of the Bible, which was discussed in the chapter related to Psalm 128. Psalm 128 in the timeline revelation is related to the same timeframe as Psalm 80 at the midpoint of the tribulation, so I would have expected to see some interconnecting symbolism.

Verses 8 - 11 portray God's chosen people as the "vine" historically moving into the land of Israel and prospering by the Lord's hand. However, all good things must end, especially when you reject your Creator, and chase after false gods, which is, of course, exactly what the Israelites did.

Verses 12-13

¹² Why have You broken down her hedges, so that all who pass by the way pluck her fruit? ¹³ The boar out of the woods uproots it, and the wild beast of the field devours it.

Whether this Psalm was written by the Asaph of David's time, or one of his sons of a later generation is unknown. Personally, I believe that all of the Psalms of Asaph were written by the original Asaph, just as their names suggest, "A Song of Asaph." The only reason why scholars believe that many of these 12 Psalms must have been written later after the Babylonian conquest of Judea is that it's easier to believe that the original Asaph could not have known the future in such detail, but his distant relatives known as the "sons of Asaph" would have, because they lived it. But knowing the future is what prophecy is! I would even go a step further and proclaim that although many of the verses of Asaph's

Psalms relate to now historical events, they speak even clearer of still future events.

In commenting about Psalm 80, Charles Spurgeon wrote, *"A later Asaph we should suppose, who had the unhappiness to live, like the 'last minstrel,' in evil times. If by the Asaph of David's day, this Psalm was written in the spirit of prophecy, for it sings of times unknown to David."*

I agree that they were written in the spirit of prophecy; furthermore, I believe that they were placed by the hand of God exactly where He wanted them to create a prophetic timeline for the last days. Now that I've cleared that up, let's look at verses 12 and 13 through a future lens. Disclaimer - This next section is my own conjecture based on scripture and the timeline revelation.

It appears that God will allow the hedges of protection that He had around His vineyard, Israel, to be broken down, thus allowing the enemy inside of His vineyard. In today's terms, I would suggest that what that means is that Israel's defenses will be taken down and that the land will be overrun by the enemy. It stands to reason also from several different prophetic scriptures that this enemy will be allowed inside at the command of the Antichrist so that they can destroy God's vine.

Remember that this year is the year of the "abomination of desolation." Verse 12 says, *"all who pass by the way pluck her fruit."* That seems to describe desolation since there is no one there to protect the fruit. Where is the farmer? Where are his hired helpers? Then in verse 13 we see that *"the boar out of the woods uproots it"* (the vine). I've said before that I do not believe that any words are wasted in God's perfect word. Notice that this ultra-destructive force is represented by a "boar," which comes from "the woods." Remember that trees represent nations. Could the "boar" represent a global coalition force under the control of the Antichrist? Or worse, could the "boar" represent a demonic force in some way that comes out of the nations to uproot Israel? Remember that Jesus cast the legion of demons into pigs in Matthew 8. Is that a prophetic connection?

In the very same sentence where we see the boar uprooting the vine, we also see "the beast." Have you ever asked yourself when reading this verse, "self, why would a wild and hungry "boar" uproot a vine only to allow another "beast" to eat it?" I have to reason that this dynamic implies some dominance and control. So, who is this "beast" who takes the vine uprooted by the "boar" and then devours it?

Hang on, because here's where it gets crazy! All of these questions and interconnecting words bring me to Joel chapter 2. I've long tried to figure out where Joel 2 fits in with end-time events. Is it describing Gog Magog? Is it describing Armageddon? Or is it describing another destructive event still to come at sometime in between those two events? It does have some similarities to both, but I would have to say that the invasion that Joel describes cannot be either because there are too many conflicting elements. Joel 2 can also not be a description of the demon locust army of Revelation 9 for the same reason, even though it shares a few similarities with it as well.

Considering that in this year in the timeline revelation, we are in the middle of the tribulation, which starts what is known as the "Great Tribulation," I would expect to find certain interconnecting words and phrases encrypted in Joel 2 if it does relate to the middle of the tribulation as described in Psalm 80, and other prophetic passages related to this time. I would expect to find words and phrases like beast, beast of the field, remnant, vine, devours, day of the Lord, earthquake, Jerusalem, Zion, reproach among the nations, and deliverance, among others. All of those are found in Joel 2 and more!

We know that Joel 2 is describing the last day for many reasons, but most of all because, it concludes with a picture of the Millennial Kingdom. In the aftermath of all that has happened during the tribulation, the Lord God declares that He will restore His land and His people, and that they shall never be put to shame again. That can only be a description of the Millennial Kingdom.

Joel 2:25-27

25 "So I will restore to you the years that the swarming locust has eaten, the crawling locust, the consuming locust, and the chewing locust, My great army which I sent among you.
26 You shall eat in plenty and be satisfied, and praise the name of the Lord your God, Who has dealt wondrously

with you; and My people shall never be put to shame. [27]
Then you shall know that I am in the midst of Israel: I am
the LORD your God and there is no other. My people shall
never be put to shame.

There is so much more that I want to discuss in Joel 2, but this is supposed to be about the encrypted timeline revelation in the Psalms, so I must move on. Perhaps in light of the timeline revelation, you can study Joel 2 for yourself.

I'm not totally sure why, but I must add this section here. Daniel 2 indicates that the final empire will be partly iron and partly clay. Then Daniel describes the following:

Daniel 2:43

[43] *As you saw iron mixed with ceramic clay, they will*
mingle with the seed of men; but they will not adhere to
one another, just as iron does not mix with clay.

Have you ever wondered why, in Leviticus, God was so adamant about not mixing the seed of livestock, mixing seed in the field, or even wearing a garment mixed with two types of material? I have my hunches, but I can only imagine that these are related, and that this will be completely understood at this time in the timeline of the tribulation.

Leviticus 19:19

[19] *'You shall keep My statutes. You shall not let your livestock*
breed with another kind (mixed seed). You shall not sow
your field with mixed seed. Nor shall a garment of mixed
linen and wool come upon you.

Verses 14-16

[14] *Return, we beseech You, O God of hosts; look down*
from heaven and see, and visit this vine [15] *and the vineyard*
which Your right hand has planted, and the branch that

You made strong for Yourself. ¹⁶ *It is burned with fire, it is*
cut down; they perish at the rebuke of Your countenance.

"Return!" What an interesting thing to say. How can He return if
He hasn't already come at least once before? These five verses are all
about the true Messiah, the Son of God, who sits at the right hand of
the Father. The Psalmist, Asaph, pleads with God to return and visit
the vineyard "which His right hand has planted." Who is it who sits at
Yahweh's right hand? There are many verses that I could cite that show
that the Son sits at the right hand of the Father, but perhaps none sums
it up better than Hebrews chapter 1.

Hebrews 1:1-4
¹ God, who at various times and in various ways spoke in
time past to the fathers by the prophets, ² has in these last
days spoken to us by His Son, whom He has appointed heir
of all things, through whom also He made the worlds; ³ who
being the brightness of His glory and the express image of
His person, and upholding all things by the word of His
power, when He had by Himself purged our sins, sat down
at the right hand of the Majesty on high, ⁴ having become
so much better than the angels, as He has by inheritance
obtained a more excellent name than they.

Verse 15 concludes with the statement, *"and the branch that You*
made strong for Yourself." Of course, we know that Jesus is the "branch"
from the root of Jesse from Isaiah 11:

Isaiah 11:1-2
There shall come forth a Rod from the stem of Jesse, and
a Branch shall grow out of his roots. ² The Spirit of the
LORD shall rest upon Him, the Spirit of wisdom and
understanding, the Spirit of counsel and might, the Spirit
of knowledge and of the fear of the LORD.

N. KARL LAWLEY

Similar to the vine, the people of God planted in Israel, specifically in the Millennial Kingdom, are also known as a "branch" in Isaiah 60. Christ's return and the establishment of the Millennial Kingdom are what these verses in Psalm 80 are crying out for. I think you will see how similar Psalm 80 verse 15 is to Isaiah 60 verse 21, which brings me to the conclusion that they are interrelated and interconnected.

Isaiah 60:21

²¹ Also your people shall all be righteous; they shall inherit the land forever, the branch of My planting, the work of My hands, that I may be glorified.

Verse 16, which says, *"It is burned with fire, it is cut down; they perish at the rebuke of Your countenance,"* once again matches the description in Joel chapter 2. Joel describes Israel before the invasion and the land in the aftermath of the invasion. The invaders come into a land that is "like the Garden of Eden," but they leave behind a burning desolate wasteland. There's that word "desolate" again. We know directly from Matthew 24 and Daniel 9 that the middle of the tribulation will leave Israel "desolate." This is another connection leading me to believe that Joel 2 is partly about the invasion in the middle of the tribulation.

Joel 2:3

³ A fire devours before them, and behind them a flame burns; the land is like the Garden of Eden before them, and behind them a desolate wilderness; surely nothing shall escape them.

I want to point out one more interesting detail in verse 16. Notice that the Psalmist shifts from "it" to "they." He says, "it is burned," "it is cut down," then switches to "they perish..." As you read through this Psalm casually, you will probably assume that we're still talking about the "vine," the "vineyard," and/or "the branch," but the Psalmist might be shifting his focus to the invading army instead. Wouldn't it make more sense for symmetry's sake to say, "it perishes at the rebuke of Your countenance?" So, why the shift? Remember that according to Revelation 12, *"the earth opened its mouth and swallowed up the flood which the dragon had spewed out of his mouth."* Who do you think controls the earth and all things? That would be the Lord! Also, in Joel 2, there is an odd shift between verses 9 and 10. Verse 9 is a continuation of the description of the army that appears like horses that have invaded the land. Then, in Joel 2 verse 10, we're told that "the earth quakes before them," and that's the last time we hear about these invaders. That suggests to me that it's at least possible that an earthquake is their final end, just as it is described in Revelation 12.

Joel 2:9-11

⁹ They run to and fro in the city, they run on the wall; they climb into the houses, they enter at the windows like a thief.

¹⁰ The earth quakes before them, the heavens tremble; the sun and moon grow dark, and the stars diminish their brightness. ¹¹ The LORD gives voice before His army, for His camp is very great; for strong is the One who executes His word. For the day of the LORD is great and very terrible; who can endure it?

I believe that Joel 2 verse 10 reflects the demise of this army with an earthquake, which is confirmed to me in the following verse, which speaks about the Lord's army and His command, which would certainly be the end of the invaders. We see Jesus once again as the "One" who executes His word. Not even this great and powerful army, which is described as something that no one has ever seen before, can stand before our Lord.

Many will say that we do see these invaders again in Joel 2 verse 20, which says:

Joel 2:20

²⁰ "But I will remove far from you the northern army, and will drive him away into a barren and desolate land, with his face toward the eastern sea and his back toward the western sea; his stench will come up, and his foul odor will rise, because he has done monstrous things."

I do not believe that this is the same army for many reasons. First of all, the army of Joel 2:2-9 has already been defeated by the Lord in verse 10 if the Psalm is in chronological order. The tense shifts from the present tense to the future tense. Notice that the first 17 verses are written consistently in the present tense, then in verse 18, there is a shift into the future tense, which suggests to me that these events, although perhaps similar, are, in fact, separate. The soldiers are also described differently as well. The first army is likened to horses, and the other is likened to locusts. I realize that in Revelation chapter 9, we're told that the "locusts" from the bottomless pit were shaped like horses, but in Revelation 9, they are not allowed to harm anything green on the earth. However, in Joel 2, it is quite the opposite. However, I believe it's entirely possible that we're dealing with the same demonic army, just at different times and events. It is also not stated where the first army comes from, but it is expressly stated that the future tense army comes from the north. In addition, the description of the northern army in verse 20 adds a "him." There was no "him" mentioned in Joel's original army description, which begs the question, who is "him?"

Joel 2:20

*"But I will remove far from you the northern army, and will drive **him** away into a barren and desolate land, with his face toward the eastern sea and his back toward the western sea; his stench will come up, and his foul odor will rise, because he has done monstrous things."*

I believe that the most compelling evidence to suggest that we are reading about two separate armies, and two separate events is that the demise of the northern army, and the "him" is followed up immediately by a description of the restoration of the land, an outpouring of abundance, and a promise that the Lord's people will no longer be put to shame. All of those descriptions suggest that Joel concludes with a description of the Millennial Kingdom directly after the destruction of the northern army and the "him." That would indicate that the "him" is the beast, and the northern army is his army that will be gathered together to make war against the Lord and His army.

Following the destruction of the invading army, verses 17 and 18 are all about Jesus, the one who destroyed the invaders who came into God's vineyard.

Verses 17-18

17 Let Your hand be upon the man of Your right hand, upon the son of man whom You made strong for Yourself. 18 Then we will not turn back from You; revive us, and we will call upon Your name.

Jesus is, as I have pointed out before, the one at the right hand of the Father, and Jesus often referred to himself as the "Son of man" in the gospels. I believe that the term "Son of man," referring to Jesus as the Messiah, links Jesus with Psalm 80 as well as with Daniel 7, which reveals Jesus receiving His kingdom and authority over all things.

Daniel 7:13-14

13 "I was watching in the night visions, and behold, One like the Son of Man, coming with the clouds of heaven! He came to the Ancient of Days, and they brought Him near before Him. 14 Then to Him was given dominion and glory and a kingdom, that all peoples, nations, and languages should serve Him. His dominion is an everlasting dominion, which shall not pass away, and His kingdom the one which shall not be destroyed.

Verse 18, which says, *"then we will not turn back from You; revive us, and we will call upon Your name,"* is foreshadowing of the end of the tribulation when the remnant of Israel will call upon His name just as Jesus and Zechariah prophesied.

Zechariah 13:9

⁹I will bring the one-third through the fire, will refine them as silver is refined, and test them as gold is tested. They will call on My name, and I will answer them. I will say, 'This is My people'; and each one will say, 'The LORD is my God.'"

Matthew 23:39

³⁹ for I say to you, you shall see Me no more till you say, 'Blessed is He who comes in the name of the LORD!'"

Verse 19

¹⁹ Restore us, O LORD God of hosts; cause Your face to shine, and we shall be saved!

This is the third and final refrain calling out for God's restoration and salvation representing the third full year of the Israelites in the refuge. Remember that the first half year has already been accounted for. So, Psalm 80 is perhaps foreshadowing the coming three-and-a-half-year period leading up to the Return of our Lord and Savior.

CHAPTER 33

Psalm 81 A Psalm of Asaph

Year 2029/2030 - Time of Testing for the Remnant

It is noticeable that all of the Psalms that make up the timeline revelation are centered specifically around the land of Israel, as well as the people of Israel. In context, as of 2029/2030, most of the land of Israel is desolate by this time, and the surviving remnant is in the refuge that God prepared for them to keep them safe for the remaining years of the Great Tribulation. Since these Psalms are focused on Israel, what they do not reveal is the worldwide outpouring of the wrath of God against those who are still alive outside of the refuge. So, I haven't found it possible to correlate these Psalms with many global catastrophic events detailed in the Book of Revelation.

I wish that I could say that these Psalms reveal the timing of events, such as when the stellar object known as wormwood strikes the earth found in Revelation 8, or when the demon army from the bottomless pit torments the unsealed masses that we read about in Revelation 9. It is evident to me at this point that revealing such details of future apocalyptic events is clearly not God's purpose in these Psalms within the timeline. I believe that their primary purpose during this time in the Great Tribulation is to guide the remnant, and strengthen their faith as they realize that it is only our God who tells the end from the beginning, and is therefore proven to be totally in control of all things. They are also for the purpose of showing Israel that He will continue to protect and preserve them until His soon return. And most of all, these Psalms along with all of the interconnected scriptures in the Old and New Testament, reveal that Jesus is the Son of God, and is their one true Messiah and Redeemer. It is only through Jesus that all of these interwoven Old and New Testament prophecies can be understood.

Psalm 81 is no different from those Psalms before it in the timeline since it also doesn't reveal what is happening outside the refuge. Instead, it gives the remnant comfort by reflecting back on how God rescued the children of Israel from Egypt during the exodus, but also how He tested them while they were in the wilderness. That is a perfect parallel to this time in the encrypted timeline revelation.

Through Psalm 80, which represented the previous year, we witnessed the remnant being led like a flock by the "Shepherd of Israel" as they fled from Judea at the witnessing of the defilement of the temple spoken of in Psalm 79. This year, the remnant is seen in the congregation singing and rejoicing in praise and worship of the Lord their savior.

Verses 1-5

¹Sing aloud to God our strength; make a joyful shout to the God of Jacob. ² Raise a song and strike the timbrel, the pleasant harp with the lute.

³ Blow the trumpet at the time of the New Moon, at the full moon, on our solemn feast day. ⁴ For this is a statute for Israel, a law of the God of Jacob. ⁵ This He established in Joseph as a testimony, when He went throughout the land of Egypt, where I heard a language I did not understand.

From these verses, we can see a gathered Israel celebrating during the final 3 festivals of the year. The trumpet and the New Moon indicate the Feast of Trumpets at the beginning of the 7th month, according to God's calendar that He gave to Moses and Aaron. The full moon represents the Feast of Tabernacles 15 days later. Between those two celebrations is the Day of Atonement, which falls on the 10th of the 7th month. During normal temple times, this would be a time of pilgrimage up to the Temple, as represented by the 15 Psalms of Ascent. However, in this Psalm, there is oddly no mention of the Temple. Of course, there's no mention of the Temple since the remnant of Israel is no longer in Jerusalem, but in the refuge!

There are 3 specific instruments mentioned together in verse 2, possibly representing that the Lord will return within the next 3 years, or on the "3rd day," according to Hosea 6. Prophetically speaking, we know that a day can represent a day, a year, or even a millennium, according to scripture.

Hosea 6:1-3

¹Come, and let us return to the LORD; for He has torn, but He will heal us; He has stricken, but He will bind us up. ²After two days He will revive us; on the third day He will raise us up, that we may live in His sight. ³Let us know, let us pursue the knowledge of the LORD. His going forth is established as the morning; He will come to us like the rain, like the latter and former rain to the earth.

The 3rd day of Hosea 6 primarily represents the very beginning of the third millennium after Jesus died and rose again to pay our sin debt, and to redeem us from the wages of our sin, which is death according to Romans 6.

Romans 6:23

²³For the wages of sin is death, but the gift of God is eternal life in Christ Jesus our Lord.

Again, it's all about Israel. Notice from Hosea that God is keeping exact time! Hosea is speaking to Israel when he says that, *"after two days He will revive us; on the third day He will raise us up."* Using a day for a thousand years according to Psalm 90 and 2 Peter 3, along with the understanding that according to the Dead Sea Scrolls, it was in 32 AD when Jesus the Messiah was *"cut off, but not for Himself"* (Daniel 9:26), we know that, as of this year in the timeline revelation, which is 2029/2030, it will have been almost a complete 2 days/2 thousand years since Jesus' death, burial, and resurrection. We can also see that the "3rd day" begins in 2032.

Let me just point out how amazing this prophecy is! First of all, it recognizes long before Israel was cast out that there would be 2 days/2 thousand years when Israel would be dead and in need of being "raised up." Israel was dead for almost 2 thousand years, but became a nation again in 1948, as we know. That was a miracle in itself; however, they are not yet fully "revived" yet as they do not have the Spirit of God breathed back into them per Ezekiel 37. We know from Hosea 6 that the Spirit of God will come back into them after the 2 days/2 thousand years, and they will be revived just as it says, *"after two days He will revive us."* It is this remnant that God is watching over that will soon be revived and "raised up" on the 3rd day. Isn't it amazing how all of these prophecies are perfectly interconnected and can finally be understood through God's encrypted timeline revelation in the Psalms?

Verses 6-7
6 "I removed his shoulder from the burden; his hands were freed from the baskets. 7 You called in trouble, and I delivered you; I answered you in the secret place of thunder; I tested you at the waters of Meribah. Selah

The Lord delivered, in fact, "redeemed" Israel from slavery in Egypt. That is such a powerful statement, but I think we miss it sometimes. Isaiah 43 gives us a behind-the-scenes look at the Lord's heart for Israel, and similar to Psalm 81, I believe that Isaiah also speaks about this re-gathered generation of the last days.

Isaiah 43:1-7
But now, thus says the LORD, who created you, O Jacob, and He who formed you, O Israel: "Fear not, for I have redeemed you; I have called you by your name; you are Mine. 2 When you pass through the waters, I will be with you; and through the rivers, they shall not overflow you.

When you walk through the fire, you shall not be burned, nor shall the flame scorch you. ³ For I am the LORD your God, the Holy One of Israel, your Savior; I gave Egypt for your ransom, Ethiopia and Seba in your place. ⁴ Since you were precious in My sight, you have been honored, and I have loved you; therefore I will give men for you, and people for your life. ⁵ Fear not, for I am with you; I will bring your descendants from the east, and gather you from the west; ⁶ I will say to the north, 'Give them up!' And to the south, 'Do not keep them back!' Bring My sons from afar, And My daughters from the ends of the earth— ⁷ Everyone who is called by My name, whom I have created for My glory; I have formed him, yes, I have made him."

Can you see how treasured Israel was, and is in the Lord's sight? He literally gave others in exchange for them and will certainly continue to do so. That's why the final 7 days/years of Daniel's 70ᵗʰ week prophecy is all about Israel, and why these timeline revelation Psalms are also all about Israel. Keep in mind that Israel's exodus from Egypt was about 600 years before Isaiah penned this love letter from our Lord to Israel. That means that when he says that the Lord will be with Israel through the rivers, and through the fires, he is speaking prophetically of future events.

Because of His love for Israel, the Lord has promised to protect them and never leave them; even as they walk through the flames, they will not be burned. I can see that scene vividly in my mind as the world is burning all around them during this time of the Great Tribulation, but they aren't harmed at all because of Jesus' supernatural protection over His chosen people.

Verse 7 says, *"I answered you in the secret place of thunder; I tested you at the waters of Meribah."* The "secret place of thunder" refers to Mt. Sinai, when on the 3ʳᵈ day, God entered into a marriage covenant with Israel. Can you see in this pattern that there is another "3ʳᵈ day" fast approaching for Israel?

The original Hebrew word used for the "secret place" is from the root word "cether," which is also associated with a covert hiding place such as a refuge. Could this be yet another prophetic pattern at work? Verse 7 continues and reminds Israel that they were tested at the "waters of Meribah." If you remember your Sunday or Sabbath school lessons, you'll recall that in Exodus 17, the Israelites contended with Moses, and tempted the Lord because they complained mightily about being thirsty. The Israelites were so enraged that Moses even thought they were going to stone him to death over it. God then instructed Moses to take his rod and strike a rock so water could miraculously flow from it.

Allowing Israel to feel their parched throats for a while was certainly a little test from the Lord. Obviously, He was never going to allow them to die of their thirst, but He had to test them first, shine a light on their lack of faith, and then prove His power and provision to build up their faith in Him. But of course, they were difficult and "stiff-necked" as they continued to repeat the same unfaithfulness over and over. I would love to say "shame on them" for not learning to trust in the Lord, but I've been proven to be just as bad time and time again myself, even through the process of writing this book. I've asked the Lord so many times to prove Himself so that I can know for sure that the encrypted timeline revelation is from Him and not from my own imagination. He proved Himself many times, but as of recently, I think He's finished proving Himself, and is probably tired of me asking. I would be! I've finally backed off and looked back over all of the times that He showed Himself to be faithful and real in this process. Even though I'm just as "stiff-necked" as the Israelites, or maybe more, I've finally moved into a time and place where I fully trust in Him. I've also finally concluded without a doubt that He is in this and wants this encrypted timeline revelation in the Psalms to be revealed. There's a lesson in there somewhere...

Verses 8-10
8 "Hear, O My people, and I will admonish you! O Israel, if you will listen to Me! 9 There shall be no foreign god among you; nor shall you worship any foreign god. 10 I am the LORD your God, who brought you out of the land of Egypt; open your mouth wide, and I will fill it.

The remnant of the Children of Israel is gathered all together in the refuge that the Lord prepared for them. A high holy day festival is in progress, and the praise and worship service, complete with music, singing, and dancing, has ended. The Lord then reminds them of the love and devotion that He has always had for His children. He also reminds them of some of the mighty things He has done for them throughout their entire history, many of which they didn't even realize or understand. He points out how He faithfully provided for them in the desert, miraculously bringing water from stone, even though they were a difficult and grumbling people. Now that He has their attention, the Lord gives them a warning and says, *"Hear, O My people, and I will admonish you! O Israel, if you will listen to Me! There shall be no foreign god among you; nor shall you worship any foreign god."*

The more I think about verse 9, the more I can't help but wonder if there might be some who have received the "mark of the beast," and have slipped into the congregation like wolves in sheep's clothing. If the mark of the beast turns out to be what I think it will be, then it will be part of the "transhumanist" agenda. By taking the mark, a person may possess some "godlike" abilities in the eyes of man, but they will no longer be redeemable, as I have explained before. Even worse, if some were able to infiltrate the remnant, their "seed" could eventually defile the pure bloodlines of those in the refuge. After all, that has been Satan's plan and tactic ever since Genesis 3:15. It makes sense that he will continue to try to alter man's genetics so they are no longer fully made in the image of God. If there are any such transhumans found among the congregation, they must be removed.

It's time to end Israel's long pursuit of foreign gods! Their mission has always been to destroy God's children, even now in the tribulation period. Throughout history, they have been able to seduce Jews and Gentiles alike because they appeal to man's fleshly lusts. However, their promises are ultimately always empty, and only lead to death and destruction. It has always only been the Lord who has cared for His children, and who has fought, and even died for His children. It's time for Israel to see the foolishness of their ways, and turn from these demonic fraudsters once and for all.

This is the time written about by Zechariah in his 13th chapter:

Zechariah 13:1-6
1 "In that day a fountain shall be opened for the house of David and for the inhabitants of Jerusalem, for sin and for uncleanness.

*2 "It shall be in that day," says the L*ORD *of hosts, "that I will cut off the names of the idols from the land, and they shall no longer be remembered. I will also cause the prophets and the unclean spirit to depart from the land.*
*3 It shall come to pass that if anyone still prophesies, then his father and mother who begot him will say to him, 'You shall not live, because you have spoken lies in the name of the L*ORD*.' And his father and mother who begot him shall thrust him through when he prophesies.*

4 "And it shall be in that day that every prophet will be ashamed of his vision when he prophesies; they will not wear a robe of coarse hair to deceive. 5 But he will say, 'I am no prophet, I am a farmer; for a man taught me to keep cattle from my youth.' 6 And one will say to him, 'What are these wounds between your arms?' Then he will answer, 'Those with which I was wounded in the house of my friends.'

I have a hunch that in the tribulation period, these "foreign gods" will no longer be idols made by hand out of wood and metal, or even the worldly things that we tend to idolize currently in our modern age, like money or entertainment, but they will be revealed for the demonic presences that have always been hiding behind them. I believe Ephesians 6:12 will take on a whole different meaning in the years to come.

Ephesians 6:12
12 For we do not wrestle against flesh and blood, but against principalities, against powers, against the rulers of the darkness of this age, against spiritual hosts of wickedness in the heavenly places.

Fortunately their time is almost over, and they will soon be cast into a place reserved for their judgment, proving that they never actually wielded any real power or control, only deception. Can you imagine how much it broke God's heart every time His children walked away from Him, the only one who actually cared for them, and defiled themselves with these false gods? Think about the reality that Jesus gave up His life and died on the cross to save all of mankind, and man rejects Him and His gift every single day. Do not reject His gift. He redeemed you with His own blood. No other supposed "god" has, or will ever do that for you.

Verses 11-12

¹¹ "But My people would not heed My voice, and Israel would have none of Me. ¹² So I gave them over to their own stubborn heart, to walk in their own counsels.

A few New Testament verses come to mind as I read verses 11 and 12. These New Testament verses are from John chapter 1, and Romans chapter 1.

John 1:10-11

¹⁰ He was in the world, and the world was made through Him, and the world did not know Him. ¹¹ He came to His own, and His own did not receive Him.

Romans 1:28-32

²⁸ And even as they did not like to retain God in their knowledge, God gave them over to a debased mind, to do those things which are not fitting; ²⁹ being filled with all unrighteousness, sexual immorality, wickedness, covetousness, maliciousness; full of envy, murder, strife, deceit, evil-mindedness; they are whisperers, ³⁰ backbiters, haters of God, violent, proud, boasters, inventors of evil things, disobedient to parents, ³¹undiscerning, untrustworthy, unloving, unforgiving, unmerciful; ³² who, knowing the righteous judgment of God, that those who practice such things are deserving of death, not only do the same but also approve of those who practice them.

The Lord desires for us to have a real and personal relationship with Him, and that we make Him the Lord of our lives, which is actually for our own benefit, but He never pushes Himself on us. He desires that we recognize His love for us and that we want to be filled with that love. However, because of our own sinful nature, we would rather pursue worldly things, all of which are designed to take us farther and farther away from the one who created us in His image, and who desires to walk with us and guide us throughout all our days. We, by listening to the powerless false gods of this world, become our own worst enemies by granting them power over our lives. There inevitably comes a point in time when the Lord takes a "hands-off" approach, and allows us to walk fully in our sin. Today, in 2023, as I'm writing, this can be seen everywhere. Just take a walk in a public space, and you will see people who are proud of their sins and love to advertise them to the world in as many ways as they can imagine. If that weren't bad enough, even many churches today have fallen into the trap of accepting anyone, and everyone, no matter what sinful lifestyle they are living. Instead of helping them out of the sin that will lead to their destruction, they approve of their lifestyle, and actually "feel" that approving of their sin is the loving thing to do. Approving of a sinful and destructive lifestyle, and not being willing to lead those trapped in that lifestyle to repentance signifies that these enabling churches foolishly discount the very word of God. They refuse to believe that the judgment of God is actually coming, and, in fact, has already begun.

Verses 13-16

[13] *"Oh, that My people would listen to Me, that Israel would walk in My ways!* [14] *I would soon subdue their enemies, and turn My hand against their adversaries.* [15] *The haters of the LORD would pretend submission to Him, but their fate would endure forever.* [16] *He would have fed*

them also with the finest of wheat; and with honey from the rock I would have satisfied you."

At this time in the tribulation, the enemies of the remnant of Israel have not gone away. Remember that Satan has to destroy the children of Israel, or he simply cannot win. During the first few years of what Israel thought was the beginning of the prophesied "Messianic Age," the Antichrist was fulfilling his role as the one who returned the exiles back to Israel. Then, more than likely, on Passover, while the city of Jerusalem was packed with excited pilgrims, he declared that he was god, and defiled the temple, causing those who knew to flee into the refuge. We know from Revelation 12 that even though he wasn't successful in destroying the remnant that fled, his thirst for their destruction didn't diminish, so he temporarily turned his destructive attention to the "offspring."

Revelation 12:17
[17] Then the dragon was enraged at the woman and went off to wage war against the rest of her offspring— those who keep God's commands and hold fast their testimony about Jesus.

One-third of Israel is now walking in submission to the Lord in the refuge. Their enemies outside of the refuge are being subdued by the Hand of God, which is against them, according to verse 14. What an amazing revelation! If the Hand of God is protecting you, no matter what things look like outside, you have absolutely nothing to fear. Nothing from heaven or earth can harm you when the Creator of all things is on your side. Could there ever be a better body-guard than the One protecting the remnant right now in 2029/2030?

Verse 15 is fairly odd, which makes it really stand out to me. It says, *"The haters of the LORD would pretend submission to Him, but their fate would endure forever."* If you apply that verse to the timeline, it definitely sounds like a prophecy of something specific that is still a mystery. The word "haters" is used not only in this Psalm, but also in its corresponding Psalm of Ascent, which is Psalm 129, which also matches the timeline of 2029/2030. How can that be a coincidence?

Psalm 129:5 says, *"may all who hate Zion be turned back in shame."* This verse is speaking of those who are seeking to destroy Zion and the Children of Israel. From these two Psalms, it is clear that there is a very real faction who truly hates the Lord, His earthly abode, and His people. Also, notice in verse 15 of Psalm 81 that these haters "pretend submission" to Him. This indicates deception and intrigue, so if you are reading this during the tribulation, be aware that not everyone who seems to be one of you, or seems to want to ally with you really is on your side.

The final verse of Psalm 81 concludes the warning regarding these "haters." It says, *"He would have fed them also with the finest of wheat; and with honey from the rock I would have satisfied you."* This means that if they would only turn from their wicked ways of hatred against the Most High, the Lord would also invite them in and provide abundantly for them as well. Our Lord is full of mercy and grace, but it appears that these "haters" do not take Him up on His offer, and their fate is sealed.

Notice the phrase *"honey from the rock"* along with some of the previous phrases like *"the secret place of thunder."* These last few verses of Psalm 81 continue to use verbiage from the exodus account to connect God's past provision for the children of Israel to His future provision for the remnant children of Israel. He has not only established a prophetic pattern linking these two ages, but also, throughout their history, He has required Israel to celebrate the past exodus event through the Passover Seder. This is so they would not only remember God's total provision in the past, but also use it as a "dress rehearsal," so they will be ready, and trust in Him in their own last days exodus into the refuge prepared especially for them. Our God is so exceedingly amazing!

CHAPTER 34

Psalm 82 A Psalm of Asaph

Year 2030/2031 - God Judges the "gods"

The importance of a literal translation of Psalm 82 cannot be overstated. By this time in the tribulation, everyone on earth has witnessed many supernatural events, as well as the outpouring of the wrath of God onto a wicked world. The Augustinian view-point that has for centuries sought to spiritualize the events of the Book of Revelation has by now been totally rejected by those who remain and who are in Christ. They have no doubt accepted that God gave His literal prophetic word to warn His own of the things to come so that they can be prepared. In this case, prophecy was encrypted in the timeline, but not in types and shadows, as with many other prophecies. God has proven that these events depicted in His prophetic word are real, and even though they are often encrypted, they should still be interpreted as real events. This understanding also means that they can have faith, and know that He is fully in control. By now, He has proven Himself through many fulfilled prophetic events, which they have personally witnessed with their own eyes. In fact, the remnant of the Children of Israel, who are living in the refuge, are a literal fulfillment of prophecy themselves, and no one can tell them that what they have been through, and the events they have witnessed have all been allegories.

In the last Psalm we saw the remnant of Israel in the refuge during the Fall festivals, worshipping the Lord all together as a community.

The Lord then gave them a warning not to follow foreign gods, which, of course, Israel has struggled with for most of their existence. I believe that it's no coincidence that the Lord warned them about foreign gods at this time in the timeline, which is especially evident when you read the following Psalm for the following year, our current Psalm, Psalm 82. Of course, we understand from scripture that these foreign gods are not just imaginary deities formed into idols by the hands of craftsmen. But that they are, In fact, demonic entities seeking to deceive and destroy both Jew and Gentile believers, all of those of the seed of Abraham who are under a covenant relationship with God, and ultimately all of the image bearers of God who are of pure seed, that's pretty much every human with the exception of those who have by this time taken the mark of the beast and altered their DNA.

In Psalm 82, we turn our attention away from the congregation of the remnant on earth, and to a heavenly congregation of the "gods" presided over by the one true God, the creator of the heavens and the earth.

Verses 1-2
¹God stands in the congregation of the mighty; He judges among thegods.² How long will you judge unjustly, and show partiality to the wicked? Selah

Psalm 82 has been the subject of debate by scholars, both Jewish and Gentile, for many centuries. It is a hard Psalm to digest for those who have been fed a steady diet of strict monotheism. My goal is to simplify these difficult and challenging scriptures without using a lot of words, and without any fancy theological terms. That last part is easy since I don't know any.

I think the easiest way to understand who God is in relation to the little "g" gods is to see who God is through the "Echad" in the Passover Seder. There are three special pieces of Matzo at the Seder. All three are placed in a pouch, which was historically called an Echad, which means "one," in the sense of the unity of oneness between a husband and wife as in Genesis 2:24. The interesting thing is that this pouch, which is called "one" has three chambers inside. So, it's three in one.

At an appointed time in the Seder, the middle piece of unleavened bread, or Matzo, is removed from the middle compartment and broken into 2 pieces by the father, who is the head of the Seder. One half, the larger half of the middle piece of Matzo, is wrapped in a linen cloth and hidden somewhere in the home. The other smaller half is placed back into the middle compartment of the Echad to be eaten later. It is very important that the first piece of matzo remains unseen in the Echad throughout the Seder, and it is never eaten. The third piece of Matzo is eaten with the Seder meal.

As Christians, it seems pretty evident that the unseen, and uneaten Matzo represents "The Father" (Col 1:15). The middle piece of Matzo which is broken, then half hidden and half eaten, represents "The Son" (Isaiah 53:5, Luke 22:19) And the bottom piece of Matzo, which is eaten represents "The Holy Spirit" since we partake of Him, and He dwells inside of us.

After dinner, the half of the middle piece of Matzo, which was wrapped in the linen cloth and hidden away, becomes very important to the children at the Seder. It is called the Afikoman, which means "that which comes after," or "the coming one." Now is the time when the children play a hide-and-seek type game and hunt for the hidden piece of Matzo. Once the Linen-wrapped Afikoman is found, it is brought back to the Father.

The Seder cannot be completed without it because it is the final food eaten after the festive Seder meal. To the Jews, it is very important because it is eaten in remembrance of the sacrificial lamb that was sacrificed and eaten during temple times. Since the temple's destruction in 70 AD, they can no longer sacrifice a lamb, so they have substituted pierced, striped, bruised, and broken unleavened bread as a stand-in. Because of its importance, the child who finds the Afikoman has great power, and can hold it for ransom in exchange for a free gift from the Father.

Just like the Afikoman is broken and eaten by Jewish families in remembrance of their Passover lamb at their Seder, we believers in the Messiah also break and eat bread in remembrance of our Passover Lamb who was broken for us. We call it "communion," but it's easy to see that

Jesus is the true fulfillment of both. Only the Jews still cannot see it (2 Corinthians 3:14), even though the symbolism is overwhelming.

Just like the Jews, I believe that much of the church has been in spiritual blindness as it relates to the "gods" mentioned in the Bible. It all boils down to this; God is symbolized by the Echad of the Passover Seder, which is "three in one." He consists of the Father, Son, and Holy Spirit. Anything, anyone, or any god outside of that Echad was created by the "Three in One" God.

These other little "g" gods show up throughout the Bible, but unfortunately, due to some translational inconsistencies, we've had a hard time connecting the dots and understanding who they are. So, let's try to connect some of the dots and figure out who these little "g" gods really are.

First, let me point out that I think it's more than a coincidence that every ancient civilization has stories of "gods" coming down from heaven; many of them have left behind details of these gods intermingling with humans, which created hybrids. We know these hybrids as Nephilim in the Bible. By 2030/2031, the argument of whether the sons of God who married the daughters of men in Genesis 6, were fallen angels, or simply the descendants of Cain will be over. The "descendants of Cain" argument is so ridiculously weak, and has so many holes in it that I'm not even going to give it any validity through debate. Simply stated, the "sons of God" are the same as the little "g" gods that are presented here in Psalm 82. They are the angelic forces that God created, which are also mentioned in Genesis 3:22, Genesis 6, Deuteronomy 10:17, Deuteronomy 32:8-9 (Dead Sea Scrolls), 1 Kings 22:19-23, Job 1:6, Job 2:1-7, Job 38:7, Isaiah 24:21, Isaiah 34:4, Jeremiah 10:11, Daniel 10:13, 1 Corinthians 15:24, 2 Corinthians 4:4, Ephesians 6:12, Colossians 2:15, 1 Peter 3:22, and Jude 1:8-10, among many others I'm sure.

If you study all of these scriptures, you will begin to understand more fully that God has a hierarchy of rulers under Him, and His Son Jesus. Some have fallen, and some have remained loyal to the Throne. It's the fallen little "g" gods who are being questioned and judged in verses 1 - 2, where the Psalmist says: *"He judges among the gods. ² How long will you judge unjustly, and show partiality to the wicked?"*

At this time in the timeline revelation, the rule of these gods over the nations is finally coming to a close. Just as all of mankind will be judged, these created beings will also be judged for the evil they have perpetrated over the world. Of course, we know who will be their judge. According to 1 Corinthians 15, Jesus will be their judge since all things have been placed under His control.

1 Corinthians 15:27

[27] For "He has put all things under His feet." But when He says "all things are put under Him," it is evident that He who put all things under Him is excepted.

Verses 3-4

[3]Defend the poor and fatherless; do justice to the afflicted and needy. [4] Deliver the poor and needy; free them from the hand of the wicked.

These fallen angelic beings are instructed by the Most High to turn from their wicked ways and to serve and protect mankind, especially the "least of these." However, it seems that they are more apt to serve and promote the "wicked" of the world until their final end.

Verse 5

[5] They do not know, nor do they understand; they walk about in darkness; all the foundations of the earth are unstable.

In context, the beginning of verse 5 seems to be referring to mankind who does not know about, or understand all of the spiritual battles that are being waged around them. Most people do not even know that another dimension exists where the fallen "gods" of this world do battle over the souls of men on a daily basis. Here are a few of the texts that I mentioned earlier to illustrate this point, the first of which is perhaps the most commonly known and referred to by Christians.

Ephesians 6:12

¹²For we do not wrestle against flesh and blood, but against principalities, against powers, against the rulers of the darkness of this age, against spiritual hosts of wickedness in the heavenly places.

Job 1:6-7

⁶ One day the angels (Bnei HaElohim: sons of God) came to present themselves before the LORD, and Satan also came with them.⁷ The LORD said to Satan, "Where have you come from?" Satan answered the LORD, "From roaming throughout the earth, going back and forth on it."

1 Peter 5:8

⁸ Be sober, be vigilant; because your adversary the devil walks about like a roaring lion, seeking whom he may devour.

From Job 1, 1 Peter 5, and might I add Genesis 3, when Satan manifested as a serpent and deceived Adam and Eve, we can clearly see that we have a hidden adversary who has been working for our destruction from the very beginning. The good news is that Jesus has already won the victory over Satan and all of the wicked fallen sons of God at the cross. The world is His, and He's returning soon to claim it! Metaphorically speaking, Jesus holds the title deed to the house, but He hasn't come back to kick the squatters out and move in yet. But He's coming back oh so soon to finally claim what is legally His and to make an end to all of the armies of wickedness who have deceived the nations.

The second part of verse 5 seems to be out of place, which makes me all the more interested in it. Wait, weren't we reading about people who cannot see the spiritual battle around them? Seemingly out of nowhere, God adds, *"all the foundations of the earth are unstable."* We've been looking behind the veil into the spiritual dimension up until now in Psalm 82, and now our attention has shifted back to earth because God wants us to know something important that will happen at this time in the timeline. I believe that something "earth-shaking" is coming in this year. Could this be a foretelling of the 7th and final bowl of wrath poured out by God just before the great battle?

Revelation 16:16-21

*16 And they gathered them together to the place called in Hebrew, **Armageddon**.*

*17 Then the seventh angel poured out his bowl into the air, and a loud voice came out of the temple of heaven, from the throne, saying, "It is done!" 18 And there were noises and thunderings and lightnings; and there was a great **earthquake**, such a mighty and **great earthquake** as had not occurred since men were on the earth. 19 Now the great city was divided into three parts, and the cities of the nations fell. And great Babylon was remembered before God, to give her the cup of the wine of the fierceness of His wrath. 20 Then every island fled away, and the mountains were not found. 21 And great hail from heaven fell upon men, each hailstone about the weight of a talent. Men blasphemed God because of the plague of the hail, since that plague was exceedingly great.*

Verses 6-7

6 I said, "You are gods, and all of you are children of the Most High. 7 But you shall die like men, and fall like one of the princes."

Verses 6 and 7 refocus on the sons of God and on their ultimate judgment and fate. God points out that He still considers them His sons, but because of their transgressions, they will suffer the same fate as those among the wicked and unrepentant of mankind. Of course, we know that it's only through Jesus' sacrifice, and our acceptance, relationship, and repentance that we are separated from those who will perish. Unfortunately, the wicked, unbelieving, and unrepentant of mankind will suffer the same fate as the fallen angels.

Verses 6 - 7 lead me to Jude 1:6-7. Jude, who was obviously familiar with the Book of Enoch, described the fallen angels from the time of Jared. According to the Bible, and the Book of Enoch, Jared was the father of Enoch, and it was during his lifetime when the angelic sons of God, whom Enoch called the "Watchers," left their proper place and came down to Mt. Hermon. This mountain later became part of northern Israel. It was on Mt. Hermon where the fallen angels made an agreement together to do a sinful deed by taking wives from the daughters of men so they could have offspring of their own. Jude 1 and Genesis 6 describe that same event.

Jude 1:6-7

6 And the angels who did not keep their proper domain, but left their own abode, He has reserved in everlasting chains under darkness for the judgment of the great day; 7 as Sodom and Gomorrah, and the cities around them in a similar manner to these, having given themselves over to sexual immorality and gone after strange flesh, are set forth as an example, suffering the vengeance of eternal fire.

Genesis 6:1-4

6 Now it came to pass, when men began to multiply on the face of the earth, and daughters were born to them, 2 that the sons of God saw the daughters of men, that they were beautiful; and they took wives for themselves of all whom they chose.

3 And the LORD said, "My Spirit shall not strive (abide) with man forever, for he is indeed flesh; yet his days shall be one hundred and twenty years." 4 There were giants (Nephilim) on the earth in those days, and also afterward, when the sons of God came in to the daughters of men and they bore children to them. Those were the mighty men (gibborim) who were of old, men of renown.

Genesis 6 is the origin story of many of the fallen sons of God. The children that they bore with the daughters of men were the giant

Nephilim that we read about in much of the Old Testament, as well as through the writings and artifacts of most ancient civilizations. Notice that it says *"on the earth in those days, and also afterward,"* meaning before the flood and after the flood. The adversary's plan has always been to corrupt the seed of mankind ever since he found out that it would be through the "seed of a woman" that his head would be crushed all the way back in Genesis 3. The fallen angels, as well as the disembodied spirits of the Nephilim, are irredeemable and are subject to Satan. The Book of Enoch describes that God would not forgive the angels because they corrupted His prized creation, which is mankind. The fate of their hybrid offspring was to become evil spirits, which we also know as demons. This is described in chapter 5 of 1 Enoch.

1 Enoch 5:28-31

[28] *And now, the giants (Nephilim), who are produced from the spirits and flesh, shall be called evil spirits upon the earth, and on the earth shall be their dwelling.*

[29] *Evil spirits have proceeded from their bodies; because they are born from men and from the Watchers is their beginning and primal origin; they shall be evil spirits on earth, and evil spirits shall they be called.* [30] *And the spirits of the giants afflict, oppress, destroy, attack, do battle, and work destruction on the earth, and cause trouble. They take no food, but nevertheless hunger and thirst, and cause offences.* [31] *And these spirits shall rise up against the children of men and against the women, because they have proceeded from them.*

Now we know who these little "g" gods are, who the demons are, and where they come from. We know that their mission is primarily to destroy man, especially the children of God, by corrupting their genetics. Deception is the primary weapon they have, and will use to achieve that goal. Remember, in verse 5, we learned what we already pretty much knew that man is blind to the things that are happening all around in the spiritual domain. That means we can be easily deceived if we do not know God's word.

During the tribulation, I do not expect God's word to be easily accessible. I'm certain that the Bible, along with books like this one, will be banned, and that the internet will be scrubbed of all Christian literature. The enemy will not allow people to have access to the truth because he knows it will thwart his deceptive plot. We have already seen the tactical push to eliminate our freedom of speech worldwide ever since 2020, and I don't see that trend changing or getting better as the years go by. It's only a matter of time before the Bible is considered "hate speech" and removed from the internet. For this reason, it is imperative that we Christians today purchase, print, copy, or handwrite hardcopies of important Bible verses and literature that can help our "Tribulation Saint" brothers and sisters who will be trapped during that time. We need to leave God's printed word behind for them because they will need it more than we can even imagine right now so that they will not be deceived.

According to Psalm 82 in the timeline, and many other prophetic scriptures, we can see clearly that these fallen angels and demonic spirits will play a large role in the last days of the tribulation period. The apostle Paul gives us a clear-cut warning about this in his first letter to Timothy. Once again, it's a warning to not be deceived by these evil spirits.

1 Timothy 4:1
¹ The Spirit clearly says that in later times some will abandon the faith and follow deceiving spirits and things taught by demons.

Demonic deception will be nearly impossible to discern without God's word in the last days of the tribulation. That's why Jesus said in Matthew 24; *"For false christs and false prophets will rise and show great signs and wonders to deceive, if possible, even the elect."* From where do you think these false christs and false prophets will be getting their powers to deceive?

Sons of God over the Nations

Since I do not fully know what form these entities will take during the time of the tribulation, I believe that it's prudent to add this last part to this short teaching on fallen angels and demons. We know that Jesus connected false messiahs and false prophets with these deceiving evil spirits, as did the Apostle Paul, but will they possess normal men, pose as normal men, pose as gods from the heavens, or pose as aliens from other galaxies? That part remains yet to be seen, but we know from scripture, and from history that these gods are real, and that they have a ranking system. Think about it: the dark principalities, who are over entire nations, are certainly not the same entities that have found a host in the homeless drug addict on the street corner. So, who are these higher-order "princes" who are ruling over the wicked of the earth? We'll have to take a look at the Book of Deuteronomy and Daniel to find out.

Deuteronomy 32:8

[8]*When the Most High divided their inheritance to the nations, when He separated the sons of Adam, He set the boundaries of the peoples according to the number of the* ~~children of Israel~~ *(sons of God).*

The Dead Sea Scrolls, which contains the oldest copy of Deuteronomy 32 in existence, clearly says **"sons of God,"** and not "children of Israel." This correction changes everything! Honestly, it never made any sense as "children of Israel" to me, but I won't go into that. It is, however, essential to know that, in God's view, there are 70 nations in the world according to Genesis 10. Putting Deuteronomy 32 together with Genesis 10 would seem to indicate that there are 70 nations, and therefore 70 prince angels over those nations. We know from Daniel chapter 10 that an angel who was dispatched to help Daniel was hindered for 21 days by the prince of Persia until he was helped by the Archangel Michael, who appeared to be over the nation of Israel. This same angel then spoke of the coming of the prince of

Greece as well. What that indicates to me is that there are also fallen angelic princes over the 70 nations of the world. And quite frankly, of course, there are! Satan mimics and perverts everything that God has established. Daniel gives us a small glimpse into the angelic realm, and the battles that they wage, which we know very little about. Thankfully, through these two books of the Bible, we have a further understanding that there really are certain angelic forces operating in the spiritual dimension over each of the 70 original nations. Some of these are working for our benefit and restoration, and their wicked counterparts are working for our ultimate destruction.

Verse 8
⁸ Arise, O God, judge the earth; for You shall inherit all nations.

The last verse of this very important Psalm calls on the Lord to arise, take action, judge the earth, and then inherit all of the nations of the earth! This will be the ultimate fulfillment of Jesus' words in John 12:31 when He said, just prior to going to the cross, *"Now is the judgment of this world; now the ruler of this world will be cast out."* The adversary's rule over this world will finally come to an end! Jesus took away Satan's power as well as that of all of the fallen gods of this world at the cross, but for His own purposes. He has allowed them to continue for the past 2 thousand years during the Church Age, which is rapidly coming to a close. Part of that purpose has been to bring the gentiles into His family, and to make the Jews jealous by doing so. How do we know this? Let's look at Isaiah 65 and then Romans 11 to answer this question.

Isaiah 65:1
"I was sought by those who did not ask for Me; I was found by those who did not seek Me. I said, 'Here I am, here I am,' to a nation that was not called by My name.

Romans 11:11

[11] I say then, have they stumbled that they should fall? Certainly not! But through their fall, to provoke them to jealousy, salvation has come to the Gentiles.

In Isaiah it is understood that the nation mentioned is the Gentile nation as a whole, which has received salvation in Jesus' name. Remember that the Church was a mystery in the Old Testament, so the believing Gentiles are never referenced in such simple terms in the Old Testament scriptures. In Romans 11, Paul points out that it was because of Israel's failure by constantly chasing after false gods, such as Baal, that allowed the Gentiles to be grafted into the Kingdom of God.

This final verse in Psalm 82, verse 8, is the setup for the next Psalm, which is the final Psalm of Asaph. It represents the end of the tribulation period in the timeline, and the defeat of the wicked of man, demons, and of the fallen sons of God. In several places, the prophet Isaiah speaks of the coming punishment of the fallen angelic armies of darkness and the earthly kings and their armies. Remember that verse 7 of Psalm 82 says that the little "g" gods will die just like men.

Isaiah 24:21-23

[21] It shall come to pass in that day that the LORD will punish on high the host of exalted ones, and on the earth the kings of the earth. [22] They will be gathered together, as prisoners are gathered in the pit, and will be shut up in the prison;

After many days they will be punished. [23] Then the moon will be disgraced and the sun ashamed; for the LORD of hosts will reign on Mount Zion and in Jerusalem and before His elders, gloriously.

Isaiah 34:1-4

[1] Come near, you nations, to hear; and heed, you people! Let the earth hear, and all that is in it, the world and all things that come forth from it. [2] For the indignation of the LORD is against all nations, and His fury against all their

armies; He has utterly destroyed them, He has given them over to the slaughter. [3]Also their slain shall be thrown out; their stench shall rise from their corpses, and the mountains shall be melted with their blood. [4]All the host of heaven (Tz'va HaShomayim: armies of heaven) shall be dissolved, and the heavens shall be rolled up like a scroll; all their host (armies) shall fall down as the leaf falls from the vine, and as fruit falling from a fig tree.

The prophet Jeremiah also wrote about the coming battle, the demise of the wicked nations, and the demise of the fallen "gods."

Jeremiah 10:11

[10]*But the LORD is the true God; He is the living God and the everlasting King. At His wrath the earth will tremble, and the nations will not be able to endure His indignation. [11]Thus you shall say to them: "The gods that have not made the heavens and the earth shall perish from the earth and from under these heavens."*

Two thousand years ago the unseen wicked foes of this world were made aware by the true Messiah that their time was running out. Psalm 82 in the timeline revelation is their final notice.

CHAPTER 35

Psalm 83 A Psalm of Asaph

Year 2031/2032 - All Roads Lead to Armageddon

Psalm 83 is the final Psalm of Asaph. It marks the final year of the tribulation according to the encrypted timeline revelation. The first Psalm of Asaph, Psalm 73, matching 2021/2022, foresaw Israel still in their longstanding condition of being envious of the other nations, wealthy nations, and wanting to be part of them instead of being set apart from them. Unlike other Psalms, Psalm 73 uses phrases like "washed my hands," and "I have been plagued," bringing to mind the Covid crisis that was plaguing the world during that time. It also gives a stern warning of destruction to those who follow after harlotry, which certainly brings to mind the whore of Babylon depicted in Revelation 17. In Psalm 74, matching 2022/2023, we see the enemy of God rising, who is also the enemy of God's people, and mighty rivers being dried up, which has been happening worldwide during this time. In Psalm 75, matching 2023/2024, we see God prepared to judge the earth at His "appointed time," and God declaring that He will cut off the "horns" of the wicked.

During this same year, we see the prophetic possibility that God will remove one from power, or control, and put another in its place, as well as the possibility of something earthshaking on the horizon in this year in which I am writing. There has already been a devastating earthquake in Turkey and Syria this year that has leveled whole cities and killed thousands. In Psalm 76, matching 2024/2025, we see types and shadows of the Gog Magog invasion, as well as the rapture of the Church. In Psalm 77, matching 2025/2026, we see the "Day of Trouble" beginning. In Psalm 78, matching 2026/2027, God reminds Israel of the great things that He has done for them, of the plagues that He sent upon Egypt for their deliverance, how He brought the Children of Israel into their land, and how they even still continued to be unfaithful and provoked the Lord to anger and judgment. He then also proclaims in Psalm 78 that He will wake up and beat back Israel's enemies, and shepherd them by the bloodline of Judah and David, which is the line of Yeshua. In Psalm 79, matching 2027/2028, we see the Temple defiled by the nations, which means that the temple has already been rebuilt by this time at the midpoint of the tribulation. We see Jerusalem left in ruins and countless dead in Israel with no one left to bury them.

In Psalm 80, matching 2028/2029 we see the Lord Shepherding the remnant of Israel and their land ravaged as they cry out for the Lord's return. In Psalm 81, matching 2029/2030, we see the remnant of Israel being tested and God once again declaring that they should not worship any foreign gods. Also, God affirms that if Israel will walk in His ways, He will subdue their enemies "soon." In Psalm 82, matching 2030/2031, God declares that He judges among the fallen angelic "gods" and that they will die like men. We see the "foundations" of the earth being unstable, and the Lord prepared to "arise" and judge the earth! That brings us to the final Psalm of Asaph, Psalm 83, which is also the final Psalm that represents the climax of the final year of the tribulation period in the encrypted timeline revelation.

Scholars have long debated whether Psalm 83 fits into the last day's timeline, or if it has already been fulfilled at some time in the past. Some believe that it was fulfilled in 1948 during the Arab-Israeli War, and others believe that it has to happen just prior to, or even during the tribulation. Others believe that it's the same as the Ezekiel 38, 39 war, also known as Gog Magog. I believe that the timeline revelation encrypted in the Psalms finally answers that hotly contested age-old question... it's absolutely Armageddon!

Verses 1-4

*¹Do not keep silent, O God! Do not hold Your peace, and do not be still, O God!² For behold, Your enemies make a tumult; and those who hate You have lifted up their head. ³ They have taken crafty counsel against Your people, and consulted together against **Your sheltered ones.** ⁴ They have said, "Come, and let us cut them off from being a nation, that the name of Israel may be remembered no more."*

From the view point of the timeline revelation, we can now see how this Psalm makes perfect sense as a prophetic tale of the final battle against God's tribulation remnant of Israel, who has by this time been in the refuge for 3.5 years. Verse 3 literally calls them **"Your sheltered ones!"** The Hebrew root word for "Your sheltered ones" is tsaphan, which means **hidden treasure.**

A while ago, I listened to a teaching by the late great Chuck Missler wherein he gave some ideas about the timing of the war described in Psalm 83. Of course, we know many scholars believe it will occur, or has already occurred, before the rapture of the Church. But he conjectured it might happen after the rapture because the "sheltered ones" could refer to the raptured saints. However, he did realize that all of the various hypotheses had problems and that it was very difficult to say for sure when it would occur. I believe the encrypted timeline confirms its timing and by the end of this chapter, you will know beyond a shadow of a doubt that Psalm 83 describes the future battle of Armageddon.

At the end of the tribulation, after massive waves of death and destruction, the remainder of the nations will blame Israel and their God for the sufferings that they have endured (Revelation 16). They will truly hate the God of Israel, Who has continued to pour out His wrath on their wicked and rebellious lands, and they will conspire together to attack, and finally destroy God's "sheltered ones" in the refuge of God. They will bring all of their technology and manpower, and stage it in the Valley of Megiddo, also known as the Jezreel Valley, and most notoriously as Armageddon!

The Valley of Megiddo is a 150 square mile, flat, fertile plain located in the northern part of Israel to the southwest of the Sea of Galilee. It is 57 miles north of Jerusalem and makes a perfect staging point for a large offensive against an enemy that has no airstrike capabilities. I'm no military strategist, but it seems to me that in this modern era of warfare, it wouldn't make sense for all of the world's armies to gather together at one location unless they knew that their opponent had no means of carrying out an airborne strike against them. Of course, we know that the remnant will have very little, or even no, offensive or defensive military capabilities since they fled into the refuge with only the clothes on their backs, according to Matthew 24:17-18.

In Revelation 16, we see three unclean demonic spirits that go out from the Devil, the Antichrist, and the false prophet to the rulers of the world to deceive them through signs to convince them to gather for battle against the remnant of God's people.

Revelation 16:12-14

[12] The sixth angel poured out his bowl on the great river Euphrates, and its water was dried up to prepare the way for the kings from the East. [13] Then I saw three impure spirits that looked like frogs; they came out of the mouth of the dragon, out of the mouth of the beast and out of the mouth of the false prophet. [14] They are demonic spirits that perform signs, and they go out to the kings of the whole world, to gather them for the battle on the great day of God Almighty.

Remember, if they are successful at destroying the remnant of Israel through genetic hybridization or military annihilation, then the Lord's promises cannot be fulfilled (Zechariah 12:10-14, Matthew 23:37-39), which would give the enemy the victory. That's the enemy's only hope at this point because all of his other plans throughout the ages have failed. Once again, his plan will not succeed against God or against His people because the King of Kings and Lord of Lords is mounting up to do battle, and no one can stand against Him!

Verses 5-8

[5] For they have consulted together with one consent; they form a confederacy against You: [6] The tents of Edom and the Ishmaelites; Moab and the Hagrites; [7] Gebal, Ammon, and Amalek; Philistia with the inhabitants of Tyre; [8] Assyria also has joined with them; they have helped the children of Lot. Selah

The scholarly sort has focused on this list of names, as have I until recently, to decipher what current nations these represent, and to figure out if this list represents a time past, or a time that is still in the future. Now that I'm looking through the lens of the encrypted timeline revelation in the Psalms, I realize that this list isn't necessarily a list of specific past, present, or future enemies that will form a confederacy against Israel. Sure, we can map out where these enemies lived in relationship to Israel. We can make educated guesses about who intermarried with which other tribe or nation to try to decipher who the Amalekites are today as an example. That will take us down a path of utter confusion and guesswork.

For instance, some historians believe that the Amalekites existed even before Abraham, and others believe that Amalek was a descendent of Esau, while others believe that there might have been two tribes named the Amalekites. We know from Exodus 17 that a nation named the Amalekites was the first nation to attack Israel after their exodus from Egypt. Israel defeated them, but did not destroy them completely, and possibly never did throughout history. The Amalekites may, or may not have been hybrid Nephilim. There's evidence in Numbers 13 that suggests that they might have been. They may, or may not, have been shape shifters. The Jewish Midrash explains that they were sorcerers who could shift their appearance into that of animals to evade capture. This is said to be why God instructed Israel to destroy all of the Amalekites, including their animals. Today, we simply do not know if they were ever totally destroyed. The Amalekites appeared as enemies of Israel throughout the Old Testament all the way through the time of King Saul and King David. It is even believed by Jews that the evil

Haman, who tried to destroy the Jews in Queen Esther's time, was an Amalekite.

The point is this, we don't know who the Amalekites are today. However, we do know that they are an archetype of the sworn enemies of Israel. We also know that they are listed as one of "10" sworn enemies that plan to totally destroy Israel, so that the name Israel will no longer be remembered. There's that number 10 again.

I realize that if you add up the names listed in verses 5 - 8 you will arrive at a total of 11. However, the final group of people listed by name, which are the children of Lot, have already been included in the 10 previously listed names. The children of Lot are the Moabites and the Ammonites, so they are already included.

Notice that after verse 8, the word "Selah" appears. The meaning of the word: "Selah" has long been debated among Bible scholars. Some believe that it gives musical direction to either pause or, on the contrary, to lift your voice louder in praise as you sing the Psalm. There are a few other possible meanings, one of which seems to have the most merit, in my opinion, especially since the word "Selah" also appears in the prophetic writing of Habakkuk. It could be interpreted that "Selah" means there is an additional encrypted meaning that takes wisdom to discern, sort of like a riddle. So, if that is the case, what is the hidden meaning of these 10 historical arch-enemies of Israel?

Keep in mind that numbers are important. Just as the golden image of Daniel chapter 3 is linked to the Antichrist through the numbers associated with it, which are 666, so also is this list of 10 nations in verses 6 - 8. Remember that the golden image Nebuchadnezzar had erected was specifically 60 cubits high, 6 cubits wide, and everyone had to bow down to it when they heard 6 instruments play.

Daniel 3:1-6
¹ Nebuchadnezzar the king made an image of gold, whose height was sixty cubits and its width six cubits. He set it up in the plain of Dura, in the province of Babylon. ² And King Nebuchadnezzar sent word to gather together the satraps, the administrators, the governors, the counselors,

the treasurers, the judges, the magistrates, and all the officials of the provinces, to come to the dedication of the image which King Nebuchadnezzar had set up. ³ So the satraps, the administrators, the governors, the counselors, the treasurers, the judges, the magistrates, and all the officials of the provinces gathered together for the dedication of the image that King Nebuchadnezzar had set up; and they stood before the image that Nebuchadnezzar had set up. ⁴ Then a herald cried aloud: "To you it is commanded, O peoples, nations, and languages, ⁵ that at the time you hear the sound of the horn, flute, harp, lyre, and psaltery, in symphony with all kinds of music, you shall fall down and worship the gold image that King Nebuchadnezzar has set up; ⁶ and whoever does not fall down and worship shall be cast immediately into the midst of a burning fiery furnace."

Just as the number 666, which is hidden in plain sight, is important relative to the golden image of Nebuchadnezzar, so also is the number 10 hidden in plain sight in Psalm 83. They are both testifying of something prophetic regarding the last days, and something greater than what is seen on the surface. Through both sets of numbers, God wants us to see the archetype of the Antichrist, who is an enemy of Israel, as well as the archetype of all of the nations of the world who will be the enemies of Israel at the end.

Remember that biblically speaking, 10 represents a complete congregation, or the whole of a larger number. A tithe, for instance, which is a 10th, represents someone's entire flock, crop, property, or income. So too, the 10 arch-enemies of Israel listed in verses 6 - 8 represent the entirety of the enemy nations of the world who have gathered together at a place called Armageddon.

Revelation 16:16
¹⁶ And they gathered them together to the place called in Hebrew, Armageddon.

Revelation 19:19

¹⁹ And I saw the beast, the kings of the earth, and their armies, gathered together to make war against Him who sat on the horse and against His army.

Also, 10 unknown kings, regions, or nations appear in many other last-day prophesies in Daniel and in Revelation. In Daniel, chapter 2, the image that Nebuchadnezzar sees in his dream that Daniel interprets contains 4 empires, with the last empire as the feet made of iron and clay. Of course, feet have 10 toes. The beast that Daniel sees in chapter 7 has 10 horns, and the beast that rises up from the sea that John sees in Revelation 13, and again in Revelation 17, also has 10 horns. An angel explains to John that the 10 horns represent 10 kings who do not yet have kingdoms, and who give their power over to the beast. They also hate the harlot and try to destroy her.

Revelation 17:16-17

¹⁶ And the ten horns which you saw on the beast, these will hate the harlot, make her desolate and naked, eat her flesh and burn her with fire. ¹⁷ For God has put it into their hearts to fulfill His purpose, to be of one mind, and to give their kingdom to the beast, until the words of God are fulfilled.

Regardless of the murky details of exactly who these 10 kings are, one thing is clear; these 10 kings represent 10 regions of total global control in the last days. Be they politicians, bankers, or industrial elites, these globalists control the world for a short time and unwittingly fulfill God's plan by destroying the harlot, and then willingly bow down under the authority of the beast. So, in my humble opinion, the 10 historical enemies of Israel found in Psalm 83, as well as the 10 toes, or 10 horns of Daniel and Revelation, all represent the same thing. They represent the entirety of the nations of the world who hate God and hate His inheritance. I believe that the world will be divided into 10 kingdoms, representing the global power structure for a time, but today, it is impossible to see how they will be delineated in the apocalyptic years to come. The bottom line is this: 10 enemies representing all of Israel's enemies, past, present, and future, will come against Israel to destroy her so that she will be remembered no more.

Verses 9-12
⁹ Deal with them as with Midian, as with Sisera, as with Jabin at the Brook Kishon, ¹⁰ Who perished at En Dor, who became as refuse on the earth.¹¹ Make their nobles like Oreb and like Zeeb, yes, all their princes like Zebah and Zalmunna, ¹² Who said, "Let us take for ourselves the pastures of God for a possession."

In verses 9 - 12, Asaph is petitioning God to deal with this confederation of world powers, who will be the final enemies of Israel, in the same way that He did with Midian, Sisera, and Jabin. How did we not see the clues before now? They all scream that Psalm 83 is all about Armageddon! Hang on, and you'll see why I ask that as we go through the history around these names and events described in verses 9 - 12.

Let's start with Midian and discover how God dealt with them. Midian is notable in the Old Testament for several different reasons, but there are two that are specific to how God dealt with them at two different times related to the Children of Israel. Both accounts are prophetic of the final battle of the tribulation.

In the Book of Numbers, during the Exodus from Egypt, Israel was camped in Moab. Balak, the king of Moab, and the elders of Midian joined together to hire the prophet Balaam to curse Israel (Numbers 22) so that Israel could be driven from their land. Balaam, who was ultimately a wicked man, and a prophet-for-hire, prophesied the words of the Lord 4 times, but could not curse Israel, because the Lord would not curse Israel. Remember that 4 relates to the Messiah. There is so much that I would like to write about Balaam, but that will take us in another direction. Suffice it to say that Balaam tried to outsmart and manipulate God, and gave Israel's enemies knowledge of how to bring about Israel's downfall. He showed them how to use God's wrath against

His children by leading them into the worship of false gods and sexual immorality, which would then cause God to punish Israel for their evil deeds. In the New Testament, Peter makes mention of this in 2 Peter 2:15, as well as Jude in Jude 1:11. Then Jesus Himself in Revelation 2:14. This same spirit of idolatry and perversion certainly exists in our fallen culture today, and it's growing exponentially in these last days. I expect this same spirit to be at a pinnacle in the 7-year tribulation ahead, and the coming false prophet will be of this same spirit against Israel and against all of God's children. Here are Balaam's 3rd and 4th prophesies:

Numbers 24:3-9 - Balaam's Third Prophecy

3 Then he took up his oracle and said: "the utterance of Balaam the son of Beor, the utterance of the man whose eyes are opened, 4 The utterance of him who hears the words of God, who sees the vision of the Almighty, who falls down, with eyes wide open: 5 "how lovely are your tents, O Jacob! Your dwellings, O Israel! 6 Like valleys that stretch out, like gardens by the riverside, like aloes planted by the LORD, like cedars beside the waters. 7 He shall pour water from his buckets, and his seed shall be in many waters.

"His king shall be higher than Agag, and his kingdom shall be exalted.

8 "God brings him out of Egypt; He has strength like a wild ox; He shall consume the nations, His enemies; He shall break their bones and pierce them with his arrows. 9 'He bows down, He lies down as a lion; and as a lion, who shall rouse Him?'

"Blessed is he who blesses you, and cursed is he who curses you."

When reading verses 7 - 9, you have to ask yourself, "who is 'He' referring to?" Are we still talking about Israel, or are we talking about the coming Messiah? The exact same question arises when studying Hosea 11.

Hosea 11:1
*"When Israel was a child, I loved him, and out of Egypt
I called My son.*

We know from the Gospel of Matthew chapter 2 that Hosea 11 relates not only to Israel's exodus from Egypt, but also to the young Messiah's exodus from Egypt after the death of Herod. There is a pattern at work here. Both the Children of Israel, and the Messiah of Israel had to come "out of Egypt."

Matthew 2:14-15
*[14] When he arose, he took the young Child and His mother
by night and departed for Egypt, [15] and was there until the
death of Herod, that it might be fulfilled which was spoken
by the Lord through the prophet, saying, "Out of Egypt I
called My Son."*

Likewise, I believe that Balaam's 3rd prophecy also relates to both Israel and the Messiah. Notice the symmetry between Balaam's 3rd prophecy and other Messianic prophecies, such as suggesting that his "King" is higher than other Kings (verse 7), *"God brings Him out of Egypt"* (verse 8), and *"He has strength like a wild ox"* (verse 8). An ox is associated with the strength of God, and is a symbol of God as the pictogram version of the first letter of the ancient Hebrew alphabet, which is Aleph. He is the Alpha and the Omega in Greek, the Aleph and the Tav in Hebrew, the beginning and the end (Revelation 22:13). By the way, the ancient pictogram symbol of the Tav, which is the last letter of the Hebrew Alphabet, is shaped like the cross that Jesus died on. Coincidence?

Verse 8 continues and says that "He shall consume the nations." The word "consume" stands out to me, and I believe that it is a connection point from this prophecy spoken in the distant past to the near future final battle between the nations and the King of Kings. Notice how it interconnects with several other end-time prophesies that speak of the demise of these nations, and the beginning of the Millennial Kingdom.

Daniel 2:44 says, *"and in the days of these kings the God of heaven will set up a kingdom which shall never be destroyed; and the kingdom shall not be left to other people; it shall break in pieces and* **consume** *all these kingdoms, and it shall stand forever.*

Daniel is talking about the Millennial Kingdom and then into eternity, which is symbolically the 8th day, which has no end. Jesus, the returning Messiah, will establish His kingdom, and it will "consume" all other kingdoms that have ever existed. Not only will they be consumed in the sense of being taken over, but they will also be consumed in the sense of being destroyed. The prophet Zephaniah prophesies about this same time and describes how all the nations will be gathered together and will become prey for the Lord as He pours out His "burning anger" on them to consume them.

Zephaniah 3:8
8 "Therefore wait for me," declares the LORD, "for the day when I rise up to seize the prey. For my decision is to gather nations, to assemble kingdoms, to pour out upon them my indignation, all my burning anger; for in the fire of my jealousy all the earth shall be **consumed***."*

Compare Zephaniah's "Armageddon" account, and how he describes the Lord, who is the Lion of the tribe of Judah (Revelation 5:5), rising up to *"seize the prey,"* to Asaph's description in verse 9, and how he also describes the Messiah as a lion who is being roused to awaken and take action.

Verse 9
9 'He bows down, He lies down as a lion; and as a lion, who shall rouse Him?'

It's not just the nations that will be consumed. Daniel 9:27, which speaks of the Antichrist and his ultimate demise at the end of the tribulation period, also uses the terminology of "consummation" to indicate that his reign over the kingdoms of earth will be "consumed" by the true Messiah, and His Kingdom, at His 2nd coming.

Daniel 9:27

*²⁷Then he shall confirm a covenant with many for one week; but in the middle of the week he shall bring an end to sacrifice and offering. And on the wing of abominations shall be one who makes desolate, even until the **consummation**, which is determined, is poured out on the desolator."*

Likewise, in 2 Thessalonians 2:8, which speaks of the end of the Antichrist and his reign, Paul states, *"and then the lawless one will be revealed, whom the Lord will **consume** with the breath of His mouth and destroy with the brightness of His coming."*

Of course, we know of the Antichrist's end, along with the false prophet, their armies, and all of those who accepted the mark of the beast. Their ultimate destruction is revealed in Revelation 19.

Revelation 19:19-21

¹⁹ And I saw the beast, the kings of the earth, and their armies, gathered together to make war against Him who sat on the horse and against His army. ²⁰ Then the beast was captured, and with him the false prophet who worked signs in his presence, by which he deceived those who received the mark of the beast and those who worshiped his image. These two were cast alive into the lake of fire burning with brimstone. ²¹ And the rest were killed with the sword which proceeded from the mouth of Him who sat on the horse. And all the birds were filled with their flesh.

Even though the word "consume" isn't used in Revelation 19, I think we can all agree that the beast, false prophet, mark of the beast bearers, and worshipers of the beast's image will all be "consumed" by the lake of fire.

Balaam's third prophecy ends with *"Blessed is he who blesses you, and cursed is he who curses you."* Obviously, this final statement in Balaam's third prophecy will find its fulfillment at the 2ⁿᵈ coming of our Messiah.

As we know from Joel 3, at His second coming Jesus will judge the nations for how they treated His children, the children of Israel.

> **Joel 3:1-2**
> *[1] "In those days and at that time, when I restore the fortunes of Judah and Jerusalem, [2] I will gather all nations and bring them down to the Valley of Jehoshaphat. There I will put them on trial for what they did to my inheritance, my people Israel, because they scattered my people among the nations and divided up my land.*

Can you see how God used the name "Midian," in Psalm 83, an end-time prophecy, even though that nation doesn't even exist any longer on any current map or list of nations, to open up so much more than what is on the surface? Can you also see how interconnected the Word of God is, and how He wants us to dig deeper to discover the mysteries that He has encrypted and hidden below the surface?

Now, let's look at Balaam's fourth prophecy and discover some more hidden prophetic treasures and insights into the final year of the tribulation period and beyond. I think it's important to note that prior to Balaam's 3rd and 4th prophesies that, he was on top of Mt. Peor overlooking the camp of Israel as expressly stated in Numbers 24. This is important because the layout of the camp was specifically designed by God to be in the shape of a cross when viewed from above (Numbers 2). This, of course, points to the One who was to come, and who is returning, Jesus.

> **Numbers 24:2-3**
> *[2] When Balaam looked out and saw Israel encamped tribe by tribe, the Spirit of God came on him[3] and he spoke his message:*

While overlooking the camp of Israel, just prior to revealing his final oracle, Balaam made this statement about the timing of his last prophecy regarding his people and God's people:

Numbers 24:14

*14 And now, indeed, I am going to my people. Come, I will advise you what this people will do to your people **in the latter days**."*

By this, we know that this prophecy pertains to the "latter days," regardless of whether Midian, Moab, or any of the other ancient nations still exist on modern-day maps. The God who has each hair on our heads numbered still knows who they are, and where they are, scattered among the nations.

Numbers 24:15-24 - Balaam's Fourth Prophecy

15 So he took up his oracle and said: "the utterance of Balaam the son of Beor, and the utterance of the man whose eyes are opened; 16 The utterance of him who hears the words of God, and has the knowledge of the Most High, who sees the vision of the Almighty, who falls down, with eyes wide open:

17 "I see Him, but not now; I behold Him, but not near; a Star shall come out of Jacob; a Scepter shall rise out of Israel, and batter the brow of Moab, and destroy all the sons of tumult.

18 "And Edom shall be a possession; Seir also, his enemies, shall be a possession, while Israel does valiantly. 19 Out of Jacob One shall have dominion, and destroy the remains of the city."

20 Then he looked on Amalek, and he took up his oracle and said: "Amalek was first among the nations, but shall be last until he perishes."

21 Then he looked on the Kenites, and he took up his oracle and said: "firm is your dwelling place, and your nest is set in the rock; 22 Nevertheless Kain shall be burned. How long until Asshur carries you away captive?"

23 Then he took up his oracle and said: "alas! Who shall live when God does this? 24 But ships shall come from the coasts of Cyprus, and they shall afflict Asshur and afflict Eber, and so shall Amalek, until he perishes."

Balaam's fourth prophecy has a lot to digest, so I will try to keep it brief. Starting with verse 17, it is easy to see that this is a Messianic prophecy as well as a "latter days" prophecy. Balaam says, *"I see Him, but not now; I behold Him, but not near; a Star shall come out of Jacob; a Scepter shall rise out of Israel, and batter the brow of Moab, and destroy all the sons of tumult.* This verse can be speaking of none other than Jesus. From Balaam's time, standing on top of Mt. Peor overlooking the symbol of the cross made up of the camp of Israel, he could see the Star that would come out of Jacob (Israel) who would one-day rule (scepter), and who would, as it says *"batter the brow of Moab, and destroy all the sons of tumult."* That last part brings us to Jeremiah 48, which is a prophecy regarding the destruction of Moab and the inhabitants of Moab (verse 43), which is modern-day Jordan. Jeremiah uses almost the exact same language in verse 45, where he says, *"shall devour the brow of Moab, the crown of the head of the sons of tumult."*

Jeremiah 48:45
45*"Those who fled stood under the shadow of Heshbon because of exhaustion. But a fire shall come out of Heshbon, a flame from the midst of Sihon, and shall devour the brow of Moab, the crown of the head of the sons of tumult.*

At the tail end of Jeremiah 48 God declares that in the latter days, He would bring back the captives of Moab, who, as we know, fled from their land after being conquered by the Babylonians around 580 BC.

Jeremiah 48:47
47 *"Yet I will bring back the captives of Moab in the latter days,"* says the LORD.

Can this be part of Jesus' end-time prophecy in Luke 21:29-31, which talks about the fig tree (Israel) budding, as well as "all" of the trees? All nations around Israel have been budding since the rebirth of the Jewish state in 1948. For example, Moab and Edom were located in what is the nation of Jordan today. Census information confirms that Jordan only had a population of around .5 million people in 1950. Today, they have grown to over 11 million people.

Luke 21:29-31

*"Then He spoke to them a parable: "Look at the fig tree, and **all the trees**.[30] When they are already budding, you see and know for yourselves that summer is now near.[31] So you also, when you see these things happening, know that the kingdom of God is near?"*

If Israel, and all of the surrounding nations are once again budding, then according to Jesus, we know that the kingdom of God is near. Of course, we already recognize this, but it's amazing to see how all of these prophecies are so interconnected between the Old and the New Testaments.

Remember, I said that Midian was notable in the Old Testament for several different reasons. So far, we've only covered one of those that interconnected it with the coming of the Messiah, and with the latter days through the prophecies of Balaam. I'll try to briefly cover one more reason why Midian was notable in the Old Testament that I believe is very significant to end-time prophecy. In the time of the Judges, Midian oppressed Israel for 7 years. God allowed this because His children had once again gone astray and sinned against the Lord by worshiping Baal. There's a lesson in there somewhere...

Judges 6:1-6

[1] Then the children of Israel did evil in the sight of the LORD. So the LORD delivered them into the hand of Midian for seven years, [2] and the hand of Midian prevailed against Israel. Because of the Midianites, the children of Israel made for themselves the dens, the caves, and the strongholds which are in the mountains. [3] So it was, whenever Israel

had sown, Midianites would come up; also Amalekites and the people of the East would come up against them. ⁴ Then they would encamp against them and destroy the produce of the earth as far as Gaza, and leave no sustenance for Israel, neither sheep nor ox nor donkey. ⁵ For they would come up with their livestock and their tents, coming in as numerous as locusts; both they and their camels were without number; and they would enter the land to destroy it. ⁶ So Israel was greatly impoverished because of the Midianites, and the children of Israel cried out to the LORD.

In response to Israel's cry for help, the Lord met with Gideon and commissioned him to save Israel out of the hands of the Midianites. First, let me say that I do not believe that it's a coincidence that the Israelites were delivered into the hands of the Midianites, who oppressed them for specifically "7" years. As we know, they were allowed to be oppressed by the Midianites for these 7 years because of their propensity to once again chase after foreign gods. So, God used the Midianites to oppress Israel for 7 years to wake them up, repent, and bring them back to Him. Doesn't that sound like God's plan for Israel in the tribulation period?

I also find it very interesting that in Judges 6:11, the word of God made sure to mention that the Angel of the Lord, who I'm certain was the pre-incarnate Jesus, sat under a terebinth tree in Ophrah. **It just so happens that Ophrah is in the Jezreel Valley, which is the valley of Megiddo, the same area we call Armageddon.** Coincidence? Also, why would the word of God mention a specific type of tree if it wasn't important? Does the Lord want us to find out what this tree represents based on other times when it shows up in scripture? I had no idea that I would be writing about horticulture when I started writing today, but let's see where this takes us.

The terebinth tree is mentioned specifically in the Bible in Genesis, Judges, Isaiah, 1 Samuel, and Hosea. It is a tree that can reach around 30 feet tall, and up to 20 feet around, is native to the Mediterranean area, and is found in Morocco, Greece, Portugal, Turkey, Syria, Lebanon,

Israel, and others. It provides good shade, is drought resistant, and can thrive in arid areas where other vegetation cannot. It has a very long lifespan and can live to be thousands of years old. There is currently a terebinth tree in Cyprus that is said to be at least 1500 years old. In fact, the first-century Jewish historian, Josephus, even wrote about a specific terebinth tree of his time that was said to have been as old as the world itself.

The terebinth tree's fruit is rich in organic nutrients, giving it medicinal values to reduce pain, chest congestion, and other useful properties. In addition to medicine, the fruit of the terebinth tree has been used for ages to produce the solvent turpentine. It's also used in food as a flavoring, in wine as a sweetener, in cosmetics, and soaps, and it is still used today to make a very popular coffee in Turkey.

When a leaf of a terebinth tree is bitten, or irritated by an insect such as an aphid, the leaf develops abnormal growths called "galls." Many trees and plants produce galls in response to similar stimulation, but what is unique about the galls that are produced on the terebinth tree, unlike other trees, is that they are specifically shaped like a ram's horns. Wasn't there a ram caught by its horns in a thicket when the Lord stopped Abraham from sacrificing his son Isaac in Genesis 22?

The terebinth tree is one of the varieties of trees that will regenerate after being cut down. New branches will begin to grow out of the stump. Doesn't Isaiah 11 mention that *a shoot will come up from the stump of Jesse, and a branch from his roots will bear fruit* in speaking of the future Messiah, who was to be, and is, from the line of David?

One more notable characteristic of the terebinth tree is that it can naturally produce hybrids with another tree called the mastic tree. The terebinth tree and the mastic are closely related, so it is common to find the hybrid offspring of the two trees when they are located close to each other. It can be difficult to distinguish between the real tree and the hybrid descendants unless you know the subtle differences between the two. So, in a spiritual and metaphoric sense, the terebinth and the mastic are two related species that participate in a type of adultery and prostitution, which creates an impure hybrid lookalike replica. The understanding of this characteristic reminds me of several prophetic parallels. The first is Israel's religious prostitution with foreign gods, who are none other than fallen angels and disembodied hybrid Nephilim. The second is the coming antichrist, who will be a false "lookalike" of the true Messiah, probably a hybrid himself similar to Nimrod, but that's another study. For now, I believe that both of these parallels will be interwoven together in the tribulation period based on numerous prophetic scriptures from Genesis 3, Genesis 6, Daniel 2, Revelation 13, Revelation 17, and many more.

Now that we know more than we ever thought we wanted to about the terebinth tree, let's see how else it relates to Bible prophecy. As I have already pointed out, in Judges 6, the terebinth tree that the Lord was sitting under was specifically the area we call **Armageddon**. Genesis 22 it relates to the substitutional sacrifice of the Messiah, and in Isaiah 11 it connects to the then-future Messianic offspring of Jesse and his son David, who is Jesus. That's significant enough, but what else can this tree tell us? In Genesis 12"4-5, just after the Lord spoke to Abram and told him to leave his country, and said, *"I will make you a great nation; I will bless you and make your name great; and you shall be a blessing. I will bless those who bless you, and I will curse him who curses you; and in you all the families of the earth shall be blessed,"* we find Abram, Sarai, Lot, Abram's nephew, and all of their people moving to Shechem as far as the "terebinth tree" of Moreh, which would later become part of Israel. Again, why is a terebinth tree mentioned?

In Genesis 13:18, we find Abram moving to another location in Hebron, once again by terebinth trees. Then, in Genesis 18, we read that the Lord and 2 angels appeared to Abram, now Abraham, by the "terebinth trees," where they rested under them, and then also ate under the terebinth trees. Later in Genesis 35:2-4 we find Jacob proclaiming to his household to put away their foreign gods and purify themselves. Then Jacob hid all of the foreign gods and their earrings specifically under, you guessed it, a terebinth tree.

In 1 Samuel 17:2, we find that king *"Saul and the men of Israel were gathered together, and they encamped in the Valley of Elah, and drew up in battle array against the Philistines."* Elah, in Hebrew, is a terebinth tree. This means that there was an entire valley populated by terebinth trees, only about 24 miles from Jerusalem. It was at this location where David slew the Nephilim giant, Goliath. The name Elah in Hebrew begins with "El," which is the short form of Elohim, and suggests the power and strength of God, which correlates perfectly to the slaying of the Nephilim giant by the supernatural power of the Lord.

Later, in 2 Samuel 18, King David's son, Prince Absalom, who formed a rebellion against his father, was caught in a terebinth tree by his hair as he was fleeing his father's army. Absalom was a wicked son who wanted to overthrow his father through deception, and then become king himself, but that wasn't God's plan. He was killed while he was hanging by his hair in the terebinth tree, suspended between heaven and earth. Many Bible interpretations say it was an "oak" tree, but in the original Hebrew, the word used is clearly "Elah," which is a terebinth tree. So Absalom, the offspring of Jesse and David, died hanging on a tree for his own sin of rebellion against his father David, and against God's plan. Doesn't Deuteronomy 21:23, and Galatians 3:13, say something about *"cursed is everyone who is hanged on a tree."* Wasn't Jesus, the Messiah, also hanged on a tree, not for His own sins, but for our sins?

Isaiah 1:27-31 uses the terebinth tree as a symbol of rebellion and sin that will wither, be consumed, and be destroyed at the time when Jerusalem is finally redeemed. There's that word "consumed" again! We know that Jerusalem will finally be redeemed at the 2nd coming of our Messiah, which is 2031/2032 in the timeline revelation. That's why we pray for the peace of Jerusalem.

Isaiah 6:8-13 also uses the terebinth tree as a symbol of the Lord's return. In addition, Isaiah 6:13 also uses specific connecting words such as "consuming," "stump," and "seed" all in the same verse. The last part of verse 13 says, *"as a terebinth tree or as an oak, whose stump remains when it is cut down. So the holy seed shall be its stump."* I believe that this relates to the small remnant left in the land at the exile. Still, it also certainly has Messianic overtones, as well as the rebirth of Israel in 1948, and again in the Millennial Kingdom as a prophetic pattern.

If you recall, it was under a terebinth tree where Jacob buried the false idols from his people. Of course, God views the worship of foreign false gods as a terrible and destructive sin, so, in a sense, their sins were buried at the foot of the terebinth tree. In Hosea 4, we see Israel returning to their false gods and idol worship, specifically under the terebinth trees, oaks, and poplar trees. Once again, the majestic terebinth tree is associated with the sins of Israel and their history of chasing after false gods, who we know are fallen angels, as well as the spirits of the dead Nephilim. As we saw in Psalm 82, these little "g" gods will die at the end, just like the foolish people who worshiped them and did not repent.

Hosea 4:11-13

11 "Harlotry, wine, and new wine enslave the heart. 12 My people ask counsel from their wooden idols, and their staff informs them. For the spirit of harlotry has caused them to stray, and they have played the harlot against their God.

13 They offer sacrifices on the mountaintops, and burn incense on the hills,

*Under oaks, poplars, and **terebinths**, because their shade is good. Therefore your daughters commit harlotry, and your brides commit adultery.*

It's the idolatry and harlotry of Israel spoken of in Hosea chapter 4 that brings about God's judgment in chapter 5, which then begets the prophetic call to repentance of the remnant of Israel of the last days in Hosea chapter 6.

Hosea 6:1-3

1 Come, and let us return to the LORD; For He has torn, but He will heal us; He has stricken, but He will bind us up. 2 After two days He will revive us; On the third day He will raise us up, That we may live in His sight. 3 Let us know, Let us pursue the knowledge of the LORD. His going forth is established as the morning; He will come to us like the rain, like the latter and former rain to the earth.

It is clear from scripture that the terebinth tree is important, not only as a landmark in fundamental biblical stories, but also as a marker of prophetic patterns. Otherwise, I don't believe that it would have been specifically mentioned so many times by name in association with the pre-incarnate Messiah, Abraham, David, and his offspring. As you have seen, the terebinth tree is also associated with **Armageddon**, Nephilim, false worship, the antichrist, and the redemption of sin. All of those have last day's significance and are part of our continuing prophetic study into the encrypted timeline revelation.

In conclusion of my unexpected dendrology (study of trees) course, and because I can imagine what you might be thinking, I would like to add that there is no Biblical evidence of what type of wood the cross of Calvary was made of. Many types have been suggested throughout the centuries, from pine to palm to olive. However, with all of the prophetic signs pointing to the terebinth tree throughout scripture, it wouldn't surprise me at all to find out that the tree that Jesus rested under when He met with Abraham, the father of many nations, was also the tree that He was hung on when He took away the sins of the world.

That was quite a journey. We started with the mention of Midian in Psalm 83, which took us on a prophetic tour through some of the ancient enemies of Israel, including Balaam, and learned how they are connected with Israel through many last days prophesies that will soon play out in the timeline revelation. As if that weren't enough, we then learned way more about a tree than we wanted to, and how that tree, in particular, points to the Messiah, past, present, and future. We still have a few more people and places to discuss from the list in Psalm 83 to see how they point to the coming of what we call Armageddon. As a reminder, here are verses 9 - 12 of Psalm 83 again:

Verses 9-12

⁹ Deal with them as with Midian, as with Sisera, as with Jabin at the Brook Kishon, ¹⁰ Who perished at En Dor, who became as refuse on the earth. ¹¹ Make their nobles like Oreb and like Zeeb, yes, all their princes like Zebah

and Zalmunna, ¹² Who said, "Let us take for ourselves the
pastures of God for a possession."

After Midian, we see Sisera and Jabin on the list, and the Psalmist, Asaph, asking the Lord to deal with the final "10" enemies of Israel as He did with Sisera and Jabin in the past. Sisera and Jabin, unlike Midian, aren't nations, but men. Let's look at who these two enemies called, Sisera and Jabin were, and how God dealt with them to find out how they relate to the final chapter of this age. Sisera was the commander of the Canaanite army during the time of the Judges in Israel, and specifically during the time of the prophetess and Judge Deborah. Jabin was the king of Canaan who oppressed the children of Israel for 20 years.

Judges 4:1-3
¹ When Ehud was dead, the children of Israel again did evil in the sight of the LORD. ² So the LORD sold them into the hand of Jabin king of Canaan, who reigned in Hazor. The commander of his army was Sisera, who dwelt in Harosheth Hagoyim. ³ And the children of Israel cried out to the LORD; for Jabin had nine hundred chariots of iron, and for twenty years he had harshly oppressed the children of Israel.

Once again, the Israelites turned back to their evil ways, causing the Lord to once more give them over to their depravity. Time and time again, it was only when the Lord allowed Israel to be subjugated by their enemies that they would finally remember their Lord and call out to Him for help. And, as any good Father, He always helps them but teaches them a lesson in the process. There's a lesson in there somewhere for all of us and for all of the nations today.

The first thing I would like to point out is that Commander Sisera specifically lived in Harosheth Hagoyim, north of Megiddo, which is, of course, in the Jezreel Valley, otherwise known as **Armageddon**. The second thing I would like to point out is that verse 9 mentions the Brook

Kishon, and then verse 10 mentions En Dor, both of which are located where? The Jezreel Valley, **Armageddon,** of course!

So, here's what happened. The Israelites went to see the prophetess Deborah for help, and she summoned Barak, the Israeli military commander. She said to him that the Lord commanded him to deploy 10,000 troops at Mt. Tabor, on the border of the Jezreel Valley. Jabin's army, led by Sisera, was deployed at the River Kishon, which runs through the Jezreel Valley. On the day of battle, according to Judges 5, which was written by Deborah after the battle as a blessing to the Lord, there was a spiritual battle raging as well as a physical battle.

> **Judges 5:19-21**
> *19 "The kings came and fought, then the kings of Canaan fought in Taanach, by the waters of Megiddo; they took no spoils of silver. 20 They fought from the heavens; the stars from their courses fought against Sisera. 21 The torrent of Kishon swept them away, that ancient torrent, the torrent of Kishon. O my soul, march on in strength!*

According to Judges 4, the Lord put Sisera and his army to flight. However, Judges 4 doesn't exactly tell us how the Lord did that. In Judges 5:21, listed above, we saw that it was through a torrent that swept them away, but it's hard to know and understand because it isn't clear which verse is speaking of the battle from a physical location, and which is speaking of the battle from the spiritual realm. The main understanding that I take away from this historic, yet also prophetic event, is that all of the armies of the enemy were physically killed by the edge of the sword, down to the very last man (Judges 4:16). Similarly, all of the armies that will come against the Lord at the final battle, which will also be in this historic valley (**Armageddon**), will likewise be killed by the edge of the sword, but this time it's with the sword that comes from the mouth of the Lord (Revelation 19:21).

Judges 4:15-16

15 And the LORD routed Sisera and all his chariots and all his army with the edge of the sword before Barak; and Sisera alighted from his chariot and fled away on foot. 16 But Barak pursued the chariots and the army as far as Harosheth Hagoyim, and all the army of Sisera fell by the edge of the sword; not a man was left.

Revelation 19:21

21 And the rest were killed with the sword which proceeded from the mouth of Him who sat on the horse. And all the birds were filled with their flesh.

Notice that Revelation 19 describes the carcasses of the slain being eaten by birds, which is also revealed in Matthew 24 and Revelation 19. This means that none of them will be buried. They will be left like litter, or refuse, left to rot on the ground. Psalm 83 verse 10, describes this very same scene after the final battle in the Jezreel Valley of **Armageddon**.

Verse 10

10 Who perished at En Dor, who became as refuse on the earth.

In the context of ancient Israel, and the Law of Moses, it is considered a curse for a dead body to be left uncared for lying on the ground. The image of these bodies lying on the ground, becoming like refuse, reveals that they were reviled and dishonored.

Deuteronomy 28:26

26 Your carcasses shall be food for all the birds of the air and the beasts of the earth, and no one shall frighten them away.

Recall that we weren't only dealing with the demise of the Canaanite army, but also with the commander and the king as well. All we know from scripture is that the Canaanite king named Jabin was eventually destroyed by the Israelites. More importantly, perhaps, we know that the Canaanite commander Sisera abandoned his iron chariot, and fled on foot from the Israelites. He found his way north to Kedesh, where he came across the tent of Heber the Kenite, and his wife, Jael. Their tent happened to be located near a certain type of prophetic tree. Can you guess what type of tree it was? Yes, of course, it was once again a terebinth tree!

Judges 4:11
*¹¹ Now Heber the Kenite, of the children of Hobab the father-in-law of Moses, had separated himself from the Kenites and pitched his tent near the **terebinth** tree at Zaanaim, which is beside Kedesh.*

Heber's wife, Jael, invited the Canaanite commander inside the tent and gave him milk to drink. Eventually, when Sisera fell asleep, Jael pounded a tent peg through his temple, killing him. It was not the most hospitable way to treat a guest, but it did fulfill God's purpose of defeating the enemy of God's people. It also fulfilled a prophecy that was given to the prophetess and judge Deborah, who prophesied that Barak, who would not go to battle without Deborah, would not be the hero in his journey. She further prophesied that it would be a woman who would get the glory that would have otherwise been due Barak. The story of Deborah and Jael proves that our Lord is an equal opportunity employer, and since prophecy is pattern, it makes me believe that women are going to once again play a vital role in the last day's battle at Armageddon. Even more importantly, all of this took place in the area of **Armageddon**.

Verses 11-12
¹¹ Make their nobles like Oreb and like Zeeb, yes, all their princes like Zebah and Zalmunna, ¹² Who said, "Let us take for ourselves the pastures of God for a possession."

These next two verses of Psalm 83 do not relate to the battle that took place in the Jezreel Valley (Armageddon) between the army of Barak, the Israelite commander, and the Canaanite army led by Sisera, but once again, they also relate to **Armageddon**. The names Oreb, Zeeb, Zebah, and Zalmunna refer to the Midianite princes and kings who oppressed the Israelites in the days of Gideon, who was a Judge of Israel after Deborah. However, just as I already pointed out, it is true that, once again, this episode also took place at **Armageddon**. Coincidence?

Judges 6:33
*33 Then all the Midianites and Amalekites, the people of the East, gathered together; and they crossed over and encamped in the **Valley of Jezreel**.*

According to the history of Gideon in Judges 6 - 8, with just 300 warriors, Gideon slew 120,000 eastern enemies. That means that each one of Gidion's 300 warriors killed an average of 400 enemy soldiers with apparently no losses on the Israeli side. I think my arm would get tired after the first 100, but I certainly have to believe that there was a supernatural battle taking place as well. The reality is that when God plans a victory for His people, He doesn't do it half-way. He has proven that at Armageddon in the past, and He will prove it again at the final Armageddon battle in the future.

The two princes, Oreb and Zeeb, fled from the battle and were eventually found and killed by the tribe of Ephraim, who then brought their heads to Gideon. According to Judges 8, the two kings, Zebah and Zalmunna, were also found after they fled with 15,000 remaining troops. In Judges 8, we find a lot of prophetic patterns related to the last days, and it may take someone a lot smarter than I am to extract all of them. However, through the timeline revelation, I now have an understanding that these verses are patterns of the future final battle, whereas I never saw that before. I'll try to shorten this and simplify it as much as possible so that we do not get lost in a maze of prophetic parallels.

After the battle at **Armageddon**, in pursuit of the remaining army of the east, an exhausted Gideon and his army came to the town of Succoth, according to Judges 8:4-5. He asked the men, or specifically 77 elders of Succoth, for some bread to feed his hungry warriors. The men of Succoth denied them bread because Gideon's army had not yet captured the two fleeing kings. In response, Gideon told the 77 men that when he returned with the two kings, he would *"tear their flesh with the thorns of the wilderness and with briers!"* Succoth was a city, but coincidentally, the name Succoth, or in Hebrew Sukkot, is also the name of the final Feast Day, or Moedim, to be fulfilled at the Millennial Kingdom after the battle of **Armageddon**. As stated several times previously, we call that day the Feast of Tabernacles. After being rejected at Succoth, Gideon and his army went to the city of Penuel. Once again, Gideon asked for bread for his hungry army, with the same response from the men of Penuel as he received from the men of Succoth. In response, Gideon said, *"When I come back in peace, I will tear down this tower!"* Penuel in Hebrew means the "Face of God." This is the same location where Jacob wrestled face-to-face with the Angel in Genesis 32.

Genesis 32:30
30 So Jacob called the name of the place Peniel (also: Penuel): "For I have seen God face to face, and my life is preserved."

After the battle at **Armageddon**, and after capturing the two kings, Gideon, a messianic type, judge, warrior, and savior of Israel, returned to the city of Succoth (Millennial Kingdom), and to the city of Penuel (Face of God) where Gideon made good on his promises to those two cities who did not offer his men any food, and who in fact mocked and ridiculed them.

Judges 8:13-17
13 Then Gideon the son of Joash returned from battle, from the Ascent of Heres. 14 And he caught a young man of the men of Succoth and interrogated him; and he

wrote down for him the leaders of Succoth and its elders, seventy-seven men. [15] Then he came to the men of Succoth and said, "Here are Zebah and Zalmunna, about whom you ridiculed me, saying, 'Are the hands of Zebah and Zalmunna now in your hand, that we should give bread to your weary men?'" [16] And he took the elders of the city, and thorns of the wilderness and briers, and with them he taught the men of Succoth. [17] Then he tore down the tower of Penuel and killed the men of the city.

Realizing through the timeline revelation, and its connection through Psalm 83, that Gideon is a prefigure of the returning Messiah, and that his story is a foretelling of the final battle at Armageddon, as well as a glimpse into the beginning of the Millennial Kingdom, all of the imagery finally makes more sense. It brings so many of the prophetic scriptures to life, more than what I can cover here and now, but here are just a couple. After the battle of Armageddon, and the capture of the false messiah, and the false prophet (Revelation 19:19-21), the returning Messiah will meet "face to face" and punish those scoffers who did not offer any help to His people (Matthew 25:31-46).

Can you see all of the prophetic parallels to the 7-year tribulation encrypted in this historic account hiding just below the surface? There are many more than what I have covered, and I cannot cover them all here. It could literally be a separate book all on its own. However, I would ask you to take some time and study Judges 6, 7, and 8 on your own, and look for as many prophetic connections and patterns to the tribulation as possible. It's well worth the time and effort, but you will have to meditate on the scriptures to find the prophetic meanings. Then, just for kicks, take a look at Judges 9 and the story of Gideon's wicked son Abimelech for more prophetic last-day's parallels.

When you are studying these chapters, look for key numbers such as 7, 10, 15, 70, 77, 120, etc. Some may have zeros after them, but what they represent is typically the same. Also, look for keywords, phrases, patterns, interconnected imagery, and anything that seems out of place. For instance, Gideon was threshing wheat at a winepress. That's prophetic imagery of the second coming of our Lord. I believe another prophetic treasure that seems out of place is the phrase "Ascent of Heres" in Judges 8:13. Bible translators and scholars have had a difficult time trying to figure out what to do with it. Is it the name of a place? Does it simply mean that Gideon returned before the sun rose in the morning? There has never been a consensus on the meaning of "Ascent of Heres" among the scholars to this day. However, since it is obvious, to me anyway, that the Gideon account is full of parallels to the second coming of our Lord, and the final battle after the 7-year tribulation, the term "Ascent of Heres" seems perfectly placed to get our attention, and to remember what other prophets wrote. We all know what "ascent" means. The Hebrew word used is from the Hebrew root word maaleh, which means "ascent," as in the climbing of a "staircase." That certainly brings to mind the 15 Psalms of Ascent, which lead to the temple and the Millennial Kingdom. The Hebrew word used for "Heres" is "he hares," which means "sun." So, it's the "Ascent of the Sun." That brings us to another prophetic scripture that is also about the second coming of our Lord and the Millennial Kingdom found in Malachi 4.

Malachi 4:2
2But to you who fear My name the Sun of Righteousness shall arise with healing in His wings; and you shall go out and grow fat like stall-fed calves.

In addition to Malachi 4, it also parallels back to Judges 5 and the song that the prophetess Deborah wrote after the Lord's victory over Israel's enemies in her time. Of course, as we know, her story of **Armageddon** also ties in with Psalm 83. She also uses the imagery of the rising sun, but in her ode, she is referring to those who love the Lord coming out like the sun in full strength. I believe that she is prophesying of the remnant coming out of the refuge at the Lord's return when He, the "Sun of Righteousness," arises and returns for them.

Judges 5:31

*³¹ "Thus let all Your enemies perish, O L*ORD*! But let those who love Him be like the sun when it comes out in full strength." So the land had rest for forty years.*

Perfectly Suited to Fulfill God's Purpose

I want to interject something that happened to me last night. I have been struggling with several things lately while writing this book. First, I didn't intend for it to be this long or to take as much time to write as it has. Since I have been researching and writing for many hours most days, I have had to sacrifice work, income, family, and other necessities of life to make the time to complete this work. Lately, as time has been speeding by, and so many prophetic events have been happening, propelling the world at an ever-increasing rate to the final 7 years, I've been wondering if I will finish this work before it's too late. It's now the beginning of April 2023, and elements of prophetic things to come seem to be happening at a lightning-fast pace.

For example, I hear daily now about the coming economic collapse and the coming programmable central bank digital currencies that will soon replace cash. A cashless society will certainly propel the world into a fully controlled totalitarian globalist system. It seems that nothing can stop what's coming, and of course, I know that nothing will stop it because it has all been prophesied in God's word. Naturally, having an understanding of the time that we are living in, knowing the approximate start of the tribulation, and seeing it accelerating ever closer and closer is making me nervous. Not for what's coming, but because I am wondering if I can fulfill my duty as a watchman to sound what will perhaps be the final warning and wake-up call to the world. I also have no idea how God wants me to publish this work, or how He plans to get it into the hands of those whom He has chosen, but I have faith that He has all of that covered. However, as I see the clock ticking by everyday as I'm doing more studying than writing; it is a little worrying that I may fail at this mission because time is clearly running out. I can't help but think that maybe God should have chosen someone a lot smarter than me who doesn't have to read more than write. That way, this work could have already been published, and in the hands of the world. I'm thankful, though, that He placed his trust in such an imperfect person, and I am fully dedicated to seeing this work through to completion.

Last night, while I was sleeping, I was repeatedly awakened enough to hear what I knew to be a Hebrew word. I kept hearing, and then in a half-sleep, repeating in my mind the word "Tov" over and over as if it were the most important word in the world. Of course, I had no idea what Tov meant, so the first thing this morning, as I began my daily studying and writing routine at my shop, I looked it up and did a study on the word to fully understand it. It turns out that Tov is the very word that God used repeatedly during the creation week in Genesis 1 to express that what God, "Elohim," had made "was very good." So, Tov, in its simplest English translation, it means "good." Since I know that I'm not "good," I know that He couldn't have been referring to me as "Tov!" That would have been a joke.

However, in Hebrew, it means so much more than just "good." Our English language doesn't quite do the word justice. In Genesis 1, the Hebrew word "Tov" actually expresses the much fuller meaning that the specific creation was not only good, but that it was perfectly suited for what God had planned for it. Even though I haven't asked for any more signs from God to make sure that He wanted me to write this, or that it would be completed in time. He gave me one Hebrew word in the still of the night to help me to be able to rest assured that He is in this, and that His divine plan will be fulfilled, even through someone as imperfect as me. Through this one little Hebrew word with a big meaning, I now have the peace of mind to carry on and complete this mission that He has given me. I'm going to take a deep breath every morning and remember that He is in control of everything, even the timing of this work. Thank you Lord!

Back to Psalm 83

As we proceed through the details of Psalm 83, I don't want to lose sight of the fact that there are so many interconnecting elements between Psalm 83 and other verses throughout the Bible that link it to the upcoming attempted last stand of the Antichrist and his armies in the Jezreel Valley, known as Armageddon. In actuality, based on all of these connections, it's hard to imagine that most of us didn't figure out sooner that this prophetic Psalm has to be speaking of none other than Armageddon. Seriously, every single nation, person, or location mentioned between verses 9 and 12 has a direct connection to Armageddon! As if that weren't enough, verses 13 through 18 offer us even more prophetic connections to the final conflict of our age at the historic valley known as Armageddon.

Verses 13-18
¹³ O my God, make them like the whirling dust, like the chaff before the wind!¹⁴ As the fire burns the woods, and as the flame sets the mountains on fire,¹⁵ So pursue them with Your tempest, and frighten them with Your storm.¹⁶ Fill their faces with shame, that they may seek Your name, O LORD.¹⁷ Let them be confounded and dismayed forever; yes, let them be put to shame and perish,¹⁸ That they may know that You, whose name alone is the LORD, are the Most High over all the earth.

So far we've seen that all roads have led to Armageddon in Psalm 83. Our Lord has placed many specific historical references to people, places, and things within this Psalm to compare past God-given victories of Israel with the yet future final victory of this age. Through these exact references, all of which pertain to the area of the Jezreel Valley in some way, and then through the fact that this Psalm fits perfectly within the encrypted timeline revelation, I am 100% confident that the Lord has finally revealed that Psalm 83 is unmistakably a placeholder for the final battle that we call Armageddon!

In the conclusion of this Psalm, and continuing in the trend of prophetically pointing to the final conflict of this age, verses 13 - 18 do not disappoint. We'll have to separate the verses to better navigate through their interconnections with other prophetic verses so that we don't get lost. Starting with verses 13 and 14, they jump right out of the gate with more imagery of the final destruction of the wicked used in many other prophetic passages throughout the books of the prophets, which, of course, once again connects this Psalm directly to the final conflict of our age, which will be the ultimate victory of our Messiah over the wicked nations of this world.

Notice in verse 13 that the Psalmist uses "whirling dust" and "chaff" as similes to portray the demise of the defeated foes. This is almost too easy! There are so many prophetic scriptures throughout God's word that use this same visual imagery in relation to the final destruction of the kingdoms of this world that, once again I have to scratch my head and wonder how I didn't recognize this before. It has only been through the decoding of the timeline revelation, which started with two simple numbers, 5 and 10, that God spoke to me one night, which has unlocked an entirely new depth of knowledge. After the discovery of the encrypted timeline revelation hidden in the Psalms, it became evident that every word that God placed in these Psalms matters and interconnects with other counterparts throughout the Old and the New Testaments to unlock more of the hidden mysteries now in the last of the last days. God is so good and faithful! He said that "knowledge shall increase" in the last days (Daniel 12:4), and it certainly has, not just through the timeline revelation, but also through so many good men and women who have been watching and studying, discerning and proclaiming to let the world know that time is short and that the Day of the Lord is at hand. May God bless them all!

Sorry, I get excited sometimes about how good God is, and how He is pouring out His Spirit of wisdom and understanding in this final act of the greatest story ever told. Ok, back to Psalm 83 again...

Whirling Dust

The apocalyptic image of whirling dust or a whirlwind doesn't just show up in Psalm 83, but it is used as an illustration of the annihilation of man in many other parts of the Bible. Dust itself is a metaphor for death since Adam was formed from the dust of the earth (Genesis 2:7), and we all must return to it after death (Genesis 3:19). The image of "whirling dust" brings to my mind a picture of instant annihilation instead of the slow process of post-mortem decomposition. Do you remember the movie "Raiders of the Lost Ark?" There was a scene when the wicked Nazi Gestapo officer looked at the death angel that had come out of the Ark of the Covenant, which caused his face to melt and instantly decompose. Some of the wicked who were around the Ark were killed in a similar fashion, and others were killed with lightning bolts that went through them. Then a mighty swirling whirlwind rose up from the Ark like a pillar of smoke and blew all of them away up into the atmosphere, and they were no more. That's the image that comes to my mind. Is such a dramatic scene even scriptural? It is according to the prophets Zechariah and Isaiah, but not during the pre-World War II era as depicted in the movie, and it is still yet to come.

Zechariah 14:12
12 And this shall be the plague with which the LORD will strike all the people who fought against Jerusalem: their flesh shall dissolve while they stand on their feet, their eyes shall dissolve in their sockets, and their tongues shall dissolve in their mouths.

Isaiah 40:24
24 Scarcely shall they be planted, scarcely shall they be sown, scarcely shall their stock take root in the earth, when He will also blow on them, and they will wither, and the whirlwind will take them away like stubble.

I think you can see how once again, Psalm 83 relates to the end of the tribulation period and the triumphant return of the King of Kings and Lord of Lords, through so many prophetic interconnecting words, phrases, numbers, and imagery. Here are a few more scriptures related to God's wrath being released on His enemies, which is then likened to a whirlwind or blowing dust:

Proverbs 1:23-27

23 Turn at my rebuke; surely I will pour out my spirit on you; I will make my words known to you. 24 Because I have called and you refused, I have stretched out my hand and no one regarded, 25 because you disdained all my counsel, and would have none of my rebuke, 26 I also will laugh at your calamity; I will mock when your terror comes, 27 When your terror comes like a storm, and your destruction comes like a whirlwind, when distress and anguish come upon you.

Proverbs 10-25

25 When the whirlwind passes by, the wicked is no more, but the righteous has an everlasting foundation.

Jeremiah 23:19-20

19 Behold, a whirlwind of the LORD has gone forth in fury— a violent whirlwind! It will fall violently on the head of the wicked. 20 The anger of the LORD will not turn back until He has executed and performed the thoughts of His heart. In the latter days you will understand it perfectly.

Jeremiah 24:32-33

32 Thus says the LORD of hosts: "Behold, disaster shall go forth from nation to nation, and a great whirlwind shall be raised up from the farthest parts of the earth. 33 And at that day the slain of the LORD shall be from one end of the earth even to the other end of the earth. They shall not be

*lamented, or gathered, or buried; they shall become refuse
on the ground.*

Jeremiah 30:23

*23 Behold, the whirlwind of the LORD goes forth with fury,
a continuing whirlwind; it will fall violently on the head of
the wicked. 24 The fierce anger of the LORD will not return
until He has done it, and until He has performed the
intents of His heart. In the latter days you will consider it.*

Nahum 1:2-3

*2 God is jealous, and the LORD avenges; the LORD avenges
and is furious. The LORD will take vengeance on His
adversaries, and He reserves wrath for His enemies; 3 The
LORD is slow to anger and great in power, and will not
at all acquit the wicked. The LORD has His way in the
whirlwind and in the storm, and the clouds are the dust
of His feet.*

Chaff in the Wind

Chaff is one of those common symbols used in the Bible to indicate
the destruction of the wicked. Chaff is the refuse left behind during the
separation of wheat husks from the grain. After the chaff is separated
from the valuable portion of the wheat, the grain is gathered together and
stored, and the chaff is usually eliminated by burning it. According to
Jesus Himself (Matthew 11:11), John the Baptist, the greatest prophet of
all, also prophesied about the coming of the Messiah and His judgment
at the end of our age in Matthew 3. He, too, used the symbol of
separating the wheat from the chaff, and the chaff's destruction by fire.

Matthew 3:12

*12 His winnowing fan is in His hand, and He will
thoroughly clean out His threshing floor, and gather His*

wheat into the barn; but He will burn up the chaff with unquenchable fire."

The Lord reminded me today through a teaching that I was listening to from author Ken Johnson, Th.D. that one of the most important scriptural accounts relating to the destruction of the final world empire also specifically describes the remains of that empire, as well as all other empires that came before it, to chaff. That account is found in Daniel 2, which is the chapter regarding Daniel's interpretation of the dream that God gave the Babylonian king Nebuchadnezzar. As you may recall, Nebuchadnezzar saw in his dream a statue with a head of gold, chest and arms of silver, belly and thighs of bronze or brass, legs of iron, and feet of iron mixed with clay. Daniel explained that the different metals represented world empires from his time and throughout history, ending with the final empire, which we know as the Antichrist empire or kingdom. King Nebuchadnezzar also saw a stone, which was not carved by hands, strike the feet of the statue, resulting in the total destruction of not only the final kingdom, but all of the previous kingdoms as well. Of course, we know that this particular "Stone" is Jesus, the Stone which the builders rejected (Psalm 118:22, Matthew 21:42). The meaning is that when Jesus returns, He will strike the final world kingdom, which we know happens at Armageddon, and destroy that kingdom so completely that what will remain of it is likened to chaff that the breeze can easily blow away. Once again, the word "chaff" is encoded in the Bible and used to connect the prophetic scriptures from the Psalms, as well as from the prophets, to Jesus' final victory at Armageddon.

Daniel 2:32-35

[32] *This image's head was of fine gold, its chest and arms of silver, its belly and thighs of bronze, [33] its legs of iron, its feet partly of iron and partly of clay. [34] You watched while a stone was cut out without hands, which struck the image on its feet of iron and clay, and broke them in pieces. [35] Then the iron, the clay, the bronze, the silver,*

*and the gold were crushed together, and became like chaff
from the summer threshing floors; the wind carried them
away so that no trace of them was found. And the stone
that struck the image became a great mountain and filled
the whole earth.*

Here are a few more prophesies describing the same event foretold
through 3 different Old Testament prophets who all use very similar
imagery to describe the future great victory of Jesus over the nations,
which will be at Armageddon:

Isaiah 66:14-16

*[14] When you see this, your heart shall rejoice, and your
bones shall flourish like grass; the hand of the LORD shall
be known to His servants, and His indignation to His
enemies. [15] For behold, the LORD will come with fire and
with His chariots, like a whirlwind, to render His anger
with fury, and His rebuke with flames of fire. [16] For by fire
and by His sword the LORD will judge all flesh; and the
slain of the LORD shall be many.*

Zephaniah 3:8

*[8] "Therefore wait for me," declares the LORD, "for the day
when I rise up to seize the prey. For my decision is to gather
nations, to assemble kingdoms, to pour out upon them my
indignation, all my burning anger; for in the fire of my
jealousy all the earth shall be consumed.*

Malachi 4:1

*[1] "For behold, the day is coming, burning like an oven,
and all the proud, yes, all who do wickedly will be stubble.
And the day which is coming shall burn them up," Says
the LORD of hosts, "That will leave them neither root nor
branch.*

Now that we understand the imagery and the meaning of the dust and of the chaff, which will be burned up by the wrath of God, let's move on to the next two verses to glean some more understanding of the Lord's victory on the last day.

Verses 15-16

15 So pursue them with Your tempest, and frighten them with Your storm. 16 Fill their faces with shame, that they may seek Your name, O LORD.

We know that there will be survivors of the Gentile nations who will inhabit and populate the Millennial Kingdom. It stands to reason that these Gentiles will only be those who not only persevere, and survive the tribulation, but most importantly, do not take the "mark of the beast." Those who receive the mark of the beast are damned and cannot be redeemed, most likely because they are no longer fully human, as I have discussed in a previous chapter, which is consistent with (Revelation 19:20-21, 20:4-5). Verses 15 and 16 gives me some hope that even in the climactic battle when the Lord's wrath is being finally, and fully, poured out on this world, He is still willing to save those who are genetically still pure, and who call on His name! Judging by these two verses, the sight of the Lord's apocalyptic storm will be so terrible that it will literally scare the hell out of them, and many of them will repent and cry out for the Lord's salvation. Talk about cutting it close! The Lord is so full of mercy and grace that He will even accept those who planned to fight against His remnant, and Himself, even as He is treading them in His winepress of fury. They will be like the thief on the cross, literally spared in the last seconds of their mortal existence.

Verses 17-18

17 Let them be confounded and dismayed forever; yes, let them be put to shame and perish, 18 That they may know that You, whose name alone is the LORD, are the Most High over all the earth.

In verse 17, I believe that our attention has been turned back to those who have not called out to the Lord for salvation at the last second, and to those who have taken the mark of the beast. These are the ones who will perish at the hands of the returning King for all of the wickedness that they have committed against the Lord and His children.

Zephaniah 3:8

8 "Therefore wait for Me," says the Lord, "until the day I rise up for plunder;

My determination is to gather the nations to My assembly of kingdoms, to pour on them My indignation, all My fierce anger; all the earth shall be devoured with the fire of My jealousy.

Keep in mind that this Psalm was written from the perspective of the future remnant of Israel, who has been in the refuge by this time for around three and a half years. We know that because the Psalmist speaks from the view-point of God's "sheltered ones" in verse 3. It's important to understand that context because, based on that context, we can connect other prophetic scriptures that clearly teach about the same moment in time. One such is found in Zechariah 12. I'm going to include it in its entirety.

Zechariah 12:1-11
The Coming Deliverance of Judah

1 The burden of the word of the Lord against Israel. Thus says the Lord, who stretches out the heavens, lays the foundation of the earth, and forms the spirit of man within him: 2 "Behold, I will make Jerusalem a cup of drunkenness to all the surrounding peoples, when they lay siege against Judah and Jerusalem. 3 And it shall happen in that day that I will make Jerusalem a very heavy stone for all peoples; all who would heave it away will surely be cut in pieces, though all nations of the earth are gathered against it. 4

In that day," says the LORD, "I will strike every horse with confusion, and its rider with madness; I will open My eyes on the house of Judah, and will strike every horse of the peoples with blindness. ⁵ And the governors of Judah shall say in their heart, 'The inhabitants of Jerusalem are my strength in the LORD of hosts, their God.' ⁶ In that day I will make the governors of Judah like a firepan in the woodpile, and like a fiery torch in the sheaves; they shall devour all the surrounding peoples on the right hand and on the left, but Jerusalem shall be inhabited again in her own place—Jerusalem.

⁷ "The LORD will save the tents of Judah first, so that the glory of the house of David and the glory of the inhabitants of Jerusalem shall not become greater than that of Judah. ⁸ In that day the LORD will defend the inhabitants of Jerusalem; the one who is feeble among them in that day shall be like David, and the house of David shall be like God, like the Angel of the LORD before them. ⁹ It shall be in that day that I will seek to destroy all the nations that come against Jerusalem.

Mourning for the Pierced One

¹⁰ "And I will pour on the house of David and on the inhabitants of Jerusalem the Spirit of grace and supplication; then they will look on Me whom they pierced. Yes, they will mourn for Him as one mourns for his only son, and grieve for Him as one grieves for a firstborn. ¹¹ In that day there shall be a great mourning in Jerusalem, like the mourning at Hadad Rimmon **in the plain of Megiddo**.¹² And the land shall mourn, every family by itself: the family of the house of David by itself, and their wives by themselves; the family of the house of Nathan by itself, and their wives by themselves; ¹³ the family of the house of Levi by itself, and their wives by themselves; the family of Shimei by itself, and their

wives by themselves; [14] all the families that remain, every
family by itself, and their wives by themselves.

Did you notice that verse 11 brings in another connection to Megiddo,
aka Armageddon? I believe the good Lord placed that in Zechariah's
prophecy just to make sure that we didn't miss the connection. We'll
have to wait and ask the Lord about "Hadad Rimmon," because I have
no idea what that means. I've done some Biblical and historical research,
but have not found a satisfactory answer so far. Some say that there
was public mourning at a place called Hadad Rimmon in the Valley
of Megiddo after the death of King Josiah, but no one is sure where
that exact location is in the valley. Some say that Hadad and Rimmon
were two Syrian gods. Some say that Hadad refers to the Edomites,
and some say that Rimmon is a pomegranate, which represents fertility.
Personally, I don't really care who or what Hadad Rimmon is, or was.
The main point is that the Lord of Heaven and Earth will return to
the Valley of Megiddo for the entire world to see. And at that time, no
matter what side a person is on, according to the final verse of Psalm
83, they will all fully know, and fully understand whose name alone is
the Lord, and who is the Most High over all the earth - Jesus, Yeshua
HaMashiach!

There are many more scriptures that match the timeline of the
battle of Armageddon that I would love to cover. However, I've tried to
keep this study as brief and to the point as possible by staying focused
mainly on the wording and prophetic imagery found in Psalm 83,
and matching that to all of the other similar interconnected passages
throughout the Bible. As you have seen, Psalm 83 is full of connections
to Armageddon through the Biblical characters and nations mentioned
within its verses, as well as the "10" nations listed, which may well
signify and represent all of the "nations" and enemies of Israel and of
our God.

I wanted to end this chapter with a pertinent and prophetic chapter
from the prophet Zephaniah. I don't believe that this chapter, or for
that matter the Prophet Zephaniah himself, receives enough attention

for the wealth of insight that they share. This chapter paints a perfect prophetic written picture of the last days that will soon culminate with the glorious return of our Lord, and the restoration of His faithful remnant. Enjoy!

Zephaniah 3
The Wickedness of Jerusalem

¹ Woe to her who is rebellious and polluted, to the oppressing city!² She has not obeyed His voice, she has not received correction; she has not trusted in the Lord, *She has not drawn near to her God.*

³ Her princes in her midst are roaring lions; her judges are evening wolves that leave not a bone till morning.⁴ Her prophets are insolent, treacherous people; her priests have polluted the sanctuary, they have done violence to the law. ⁵ The Lord *is righteous in her midst, He will do no unrighteousness. Every morning He brings His justice to light; He never fails, but the unjust knows no shame.*

⁶ "I have cut off nations, their fortresses are devastated; I have made their streets desolate, with none passing by. Their cities are destroyed; there is no one, no inhabitant. ⁷ I said, 'Surely you will fear Me, you will receive instruction'— so that her dwelling would not be cut off, despite everything for which I punished her. But they rose early and corrupted all their deeds.

A Faithful Remnant

⁸ "Therefore wait for Me," says the Lord, *"until the day I rise up for plunder; My determination is to gather the nations to My assembly of kingdoms, to pour on them My indignation, all My fierce anger; all the earth shall be devoured with the fire of My jealousy. ⁹ "For then I will restore to the peoples a pure language, that they all may call*

on the name of the LORD, to serve Him with one accord.
[10] From beyond the rivers of Ethiopia My worshipers, the
daughter of My dispersed ones, shall bring My offering. [11]
In that day you shall not be shamed for any of your deeds
in which you transgress against Me; for then I will take
away from your midst those who rejoice in your pride, and
you shall no longer be haughty in My holy mountain. [12] I
will leave in your midst a meek and humble people, and
they shall trust in the name of the LORD. [13] The remnant
of Israel shall do no unrighteousness and speak no lies, nor
shall a deceitful tongue be found in their mouth; for they
shall feed their flocks and lie down, and no one shall make
them afraid.”

Joy in God's Faithfulness

[14] Sing, O daughter of Zion! Shout, O Israel! Be glad and
rejoice with all your heart,

O daughter of Jerusalem! [15] The LORD has taken away
your judgments, He has cast out your enemy. The King of
Israel, the LORD, is in your midst; you shall see disaster no
more.

[16] In that day it shall be said to Jerusalem: “Do not fear;
Zion, let not your hands be weak. [17] The LORD your God
in your midst, the Mighty One, will save; He will rejoice
over you with gladness, He will quiet you with His love,
He will rejoice over you with singing.”

[18] “I will gather those who sorrow over the appointed
assembly, who are among you, to whom its reproach is a
burden. [19] Behold, at that time I will deal with all who
afflict you; I will save the lame, and gather those who were
driven out; I will appoint them for praise and fame in every
land where they were put to shame.

[20] At that time I will bring you back, even at the time
I gather you; for I will give you fame and praise among all

the peoples of the earth, when I return your captives before your eyes," Says the LORD.

OK, I know that I said that I would end this study of Psalm 83 with the prophet Zephaniah, but I've been reminded of how pertinent the first chapter of the Book of Enoch is to the time of the end. So, I have provided the first chapter of Enoch for you below. You will notice that even though Enoch lived prior to the flood of Noah, he starts his book with a prophecy specifically for the end times in which we are now living, calling us, a "Generation," which is a "Remote one which is for to come."

In Enoch's first chapter, you will notice that he sums up and paints a perfect picture of the final battle that we have been discussing. Depicted is Jesus, the "Holy Great One," leaving His heavenly dwelling place with His "holy ones" to physically return to earth to protect the "elect" in the refuge and to bring judgment to all the world. According to Revelation 19, we, the raptured and resurrected saints, will be the "holy ones" that make up the army returning with the Lord. The little "g" gods of Psalm 82 are mentioned as "Watchers" who will tremble in fear at His return. No matter how powerful they appear in the tribulation period, even they will have to bow down to the Almighty and confess that He is the true Lord of all when He returns with us to establish His new Kingdom over all of the earth.

Enoch 1:1-9

¹ The words of the blessing of Enoch, wherewith he blessed the elect and righteous, who will be ² living in the day of tribulation, when all the wicked and godless are to be removed. And he took up his parable and said -Enoch a righteous man, whose eyes were opened by God, saw the vision of the Holy One in the heavens, which the angels showed me, and from them I heard everything, and from them I understood as I saw, but not for this generation, but for a remote one which is for to come. ³ Concerning the elect I said, and took up my parable concerning them:

The Holy Great One will come forth from His dwelling, [4] and the eternal God will tread upon the earth, (even) on Mount Sinai, [And appear from His camp] and appear in the strength of His might from the heaven of heavens. [5] And all shall be smitten with fear and the Watchers shall quake, and great fear and trembling shall seize them unto the ends of the earth. [6] And the high mountains shall be shaken, and the high hills shall be made low, and shall melt like wax before the flame. [7] And the earth shall be wholly rent in sunder, and all that is upon the earth shall perish, and there shall be a judgment upon all (men). [8] But with the righteous He will make peace. And will protect the elect, and mercy shall be upon them. And they shall all belong to God, and they shall be prospered, and they shall all be blessed. And He will help them all, and light shall appear unto them, and He will make peace with them. [9] And behold! He cometh with ten thousands of His holy ones to execute judgment upon all, and to destroy all the ungodly: and to convict all flesh of all the works of their ungodliness which they have ungodly committed, and of all the hard things which ungodly sinners have spoken against Him.

CHAPTER 36

Psalm 84 A Psalm of the Sons of Korah (bonus)

Year 2032/2033 - The Blessedness of Dwelling in the House of God

I couldn't help myself! I know that Psalm 83 was the last of the Psalms of Asaph, but this first Psalm of Korah is just so perfectly placed by the providential hand of God that I had to study it and write about it. I believe that you will also see how after the tribulation period outlined in the previous Psalms of Asaph, along with the vivid depiction of the final battle found in Asaph's last Psalm, Psalm 84 is perfectly placed as a picture of the glorious beginning of the Millennial Kingdom reign of our Lord.

The Psalms of the sons of Korah represent the fulfillment of an amazing redemption story. The account of Korah is found in Numbers 16, during the exodus from Egypt as the Israelites were in the wilderness. Korah and his family, who were of the Levitical priesthood line, rebelled against God by insisting that Moses and Aaron should not have any authority over them. They believed that the whole community was holy, and that Moses and Aaron should not be over any of them. Korah was the leader of this rebellion, but it also included many other Israelites as well.

Even after witnessing all the miracles of protection and provision that the Lord had accomplished through His servants Moses and Aaron, they still demanded to have things their own way, which was not the Lord's way. Ultimately, the Lord destroyed most of them by opening the earth, which swallowed them along with all of their belongings. The remaining 250 men in this rebellion, who were well-respected council members, were consumed by fire in front of the Tabernacle. There's a lesson in there somewhere...

Fast forward about 500 years and we find some "sons of Korah" serving during the 40-year reign of King David along with Asaph as worship leaders in the Tabernacle. Keep in mind that the Temple had not been built yet in David's time, but was built later during the 40-year reign of his son Solomon. Apparently, God was gracious and allowed some of Korah's line to survive His wrath, find redemption in the Lord, and become renowned song-writers and worship leaders in the House of God. The sons of Korah have an amazing character arc, from rebelliousness and destruction to grace and glory. We don't know much about what happened in between, but I believe that we will one day soon.

> Jude 1:11 says, *"woe to them! For they have gone in the way of Cain, have run greedily in the error of Balaam for profit, and perished in the rebellion of Korah."*

Jude was speaking of false teachers who, like Cain, made up their own offering, or way of worship, contrary to the Lord, and even despised his brother, who followed the right path. He was speaking of false teachers who like Balaam sought to profit from his gift, using it also to manipulate the Lord's ways against His own. He was also speaking of false teachers who like Korah rebelled against the Lord and His anointed, not wanting any authority placed over him, other than himself.

As we study Psalm 84 in the context of the timeline revelation, keep the contrast in your mind between Korah, the fallen rebel against the Lord, and the redeemed sons of Korah, who wrote this amazing prophetic Psalm. I think you will see that the redeemed descendants of this notorious rebel truly loved the Lord, His ways, and His Tabernacle on a higher level than we can even imagine. Remember that in Luke 7:47, Jesus explains that those who are forgiven much love much, and those who are forgiven little, or love little. I believe that reality certainly applies to the sons of Korah.

Verses 1-2
¹How lovely is Your tabernacle, O LORD of hosts! ²My soul longs, yes, even faints for the courts of the LORD; my heart and my flesh cry out for the living God.

I cannot think of a better way to start the Millennial Kingdom reign of our Lord, which will be the fulfillment of the 7ᵗʰ annual feast (Leviticus 23), the Feast of Tabernacles, than with a Psalm which is wholly devoted to His dwelling, or tabernacling with us. The Hebrew root word "mishkan," which is a dwelling or tabernacle, is literally in the first verse! It makes me wonder again, how did we not see this before? How did we not realize that these Psalms were placed in a sequence that matches and gives a final certainty to the prophetic last day's timeline?

Looking at it now, it's easy to see that I should have picked up on this sooner. A great battle prophesied in a Psalm, which has "Armageddon" hidden throughout, followed by a Psalm about "tabernacling" with our Lord, should have given me enough evidence to work backwards to see if there was a timeline hidden in the sequence of the previous Psalms. However, I believe that the Lord did not intend for this sequence to be revealed until now. That's really the only explanation that makes any sense, because it's really hard not to see it now that I know it's there.

For almost 2,000 years, Jews and Christians alike have had to allegorize, or spiritualize these verses. We've thought of entering into the courts of our Lord only through prayer, studying His word, through praise, and worship, but not literally and physically. Certainly, we cannot actually see our Savior, right? According to this Psalm, and its placement in the timeline revelation, the Psalmist is not just being poetic or speaking of a longing to see our Lord in His courts in a

496 N. Karl Lawley

spiritual sense, but finally, in a physical sense right here on earth after
His second coming. I believe that in these first two verses of Psalm 84, the Psalmist, a redeemed son of Korah, is crying out prophetically to see the one true Redeemer with his own eyes of flesh, and not just his spiritual eyes. He says in verse 2, *"my heart and my flesh cry out for the living God."* In Hebrew, this verse could also be translated "my inner man as well as my outer man, or my body cries out for the living God." Notice also that he's crying out for the "living God." I realize that there are many verses that speak of our God as the living God, so why do I think this verse might be an encrypted prophecy and should be taken more literally? Let's look at the next two verses.

Verses 3-4
³Even the sparrow has found a home, and the swallow a nest for herself, where she may lay her young— even Your altars, O LORD of hosts, my King and my God.
    ⁴Blessed are those who dwell in Your house; they will still be praising You. Selah

Verse 3 removes any uncertainty for me by including a scene of a physical lowly little sparrow, as well as a swallow, which has found a place to nest at a physical tabernacle so that they can bring new life into this world. I can certainly see the spiritual side of this Psalm, but I have a hunch that there will also literally be little birds nesting in the Tabernacle in the coming Kingdom. I cannot wait to physically see my Savior seated on the throne of David in Zion. And as silly as it sounds, because of this Psalm, and its placement in the timeline revelation, I also can't wait to see these little prophesied birds inhabiting the Tabernacle of our Lord one day soon. I know this for certain, if God said it, it will come to pass!

Verse 4 is a blessing for those who dwell, or live, in God's house. This invites the question, who gets to live in God's house? And also, where is God's house?

First, let me point out that I do not believe that the Antichrist temple built by 2028 will be used any longer in the Kingdom age, and more than likely, it has been destroyed by now in the timeline. We know from Psalm 127 that God does not build that house. Therefore, He will certainly never dwell in it. I also do not believe that Jesus will snap His fingers and instantly build a new Temple. Many of the "post-apocalyptic" prophetic scriptures speak of a rebuilding process by actual people, and that's the way it has always been. In fact, Ezekiel 40 - 48 is a written blue-print of the Millennial Kingdom Temple that will be built, as well as the restored Jerusalem, Israel, Priesthood, and more.

Think about it, the Lord could have sent down a tabernacle for Moses and the Israelites, but He gave gifts of talents to the people so that they could build it. Also, He could have sent down a Temple for Solomon and the Israelites of his day, but He had them build it. Likewise, He could have sent down a new Temple, or supernaturally rebuilt the ruins of Jerusalem and the Temple in Nehemiah's day, but He didn't. He gave the Israelites the honor of rebuilding both the city and the Temple themselves.

For all of these reasons, I do not expect that a new Temple will be completed in 2032/2033. However, we know that Christ will be living with us, ruling and reigning from Jerusalem. So the only thing that makes any sense in the first year of the Millennial Kingdom is that Psalm 84 describes a physical Tabernacle similar to the one built by the Israelites during the exodus, not a completed Temple. I believe that the Temple project of Ezekiel 40 - 48 will take much more time to complete. This seems to correlate to Amos 9:11, which indicates that the Lord will raise up the Tabernacle of David, and we know that during David's time, there was no Temple.

Many take Amos 9 figuratively, and I can certainly understand that based on Acts 15, when Amos is quoted at the Council at Jerusalem to help them understand that God also chose Gentiles as His own. But I now fully believe, based on the timeline revelation, that it is also to be taken literally as well. Yes, Jesus is the Tabernacle (John 1:14), but at His return, I believe that He will raise up David's actual tent as a temporary dwelling until the new Temple of Ezekiel 40 - 48 is completed.

Amos 9:11

[11] "On that day I will raise up the tabernacle (booth, tent) of David, which has fallen down, and repair its damages; I will raise up its ruins, and rebuild it as in the days of old;"

Judging from scripture, it appears that the new Temple, and Jerusalem will once again be built by the hands of people at the beginning of the new Kingdom age. Here are a few of those scriptures taken from the Book of Isaiah:

Isaiah 60:10

[10] "The sons of foreigners shall build up your walls, and their kings shall minister to you; for in My wrath I struck you, but in My favor I have had mercy on you.

Isaiah 61:4

And they shall rebuild the old ruins, they shall raise up the former desolations, and they shall repair the ruined cities, the desolations of many generations.

Isaiah 62:10-12

[10] Go through, go through the gates! Prepare the way for the people; build up, build up the highway! Take out the stones, lift up a banner for the peoples!
[11] Indeed the LORD has proclaimed to the end of the world: "say to the daughter of Zion, 'surely your salvation is coming; behold, His reward is with Him, and His work before Him.'" [12] And they shall call them The Holy People, the Redeemed of the LORD; and you shall be called Sought Out, a City Not Forsaken.

In Isaiah 65:17 - 18, speaking of this same time, it is clear that the Lord will create a new heavens and a new earth where there is no more sorrow and no more tears. In a sense, He will create a new canvas on which we can rebuild at His direction. This plays out in the following verses.

Notice the word "they," meaning His children who are actual people, in verses 21 - 23. So, the Lord creates new heavens and a new earth, but "they" build, plant, eat, work, and have children. God's plan has never been for us to be idle, sitting around on clouds strumming harps, but to build and to be fruitful in all things.

Isaiah 65:17-23

[17] "For behold, I create new heavens and a new earth; and the former shall not be remembered or come to mind.[18] But be glad and rejoice forever in what I create;

For behold, I create Jerusalem as a rejoicing, and her people a joy.[19] I will rejoice in Jerusalem, and joy in My people; the voice of weeping shall no longer be heard in her, nor the voice of crying.

[20] "No more shall an infant from there live but a few days, nor an old man who has not fulfilled his days; for the child shall die one hundred years old, but the sinner being one hundred years old shall be accursed.[21] They shall build houses and inhabit them; they shall plant vineyards and eat their fruit.[22] They shall not build and another inhabit; they shall not plant and another eat; for as the days of a tree, so shall be the days of My people, and My elect shall long enjoy the work of their hands.[23] They shall not labor in vain, nor bring forth children for trouble; for they shall be the descendants of the blessed of the LORD, and their offspring with them.

If those scriptures do not satisfy the question of who will build the House of the Lord, the final chapter of Isaiah certainly answers the question, and it does so within a question? The Lord asks, "where is the house that you will build Me?" Notice, "You will build Me."

Isaiah 66:1

¹ Thus says the LORD: *"Heaven is My throne, and earth is My footstool. Where is the house that you will build Me? And where is the place of My rest?*

I took us on a detour away from the two obvious questions that arise from reading Psalm 84 verse 4, which says *"Blessed are those who dwell in Your house; they will still be praising You."* The two questions were, who gets to live in God's House, and where is God's house? I believe that we have already answered the second question based on the scriptures from Isaiah. God's house will once again be in Jerusalem since all of the scriptures that I pointed out are in reference to Zion. The first question is a bit more problematic. Obviously, Jesus, Yeshua HaMashiach will reside in His house, but verse 4 relates to "those" who dwell in His house, and not to Him, so it's speaking of others. Historically, we know that Eli and Samuel both lived in the Tabernacle at Shiloh because 1 Samuel chapter 3 tells us so.

1 Samuel 3:1-3

¹ The boy Samuel ministered before the LORD *under Eli. In those days the word of the* LORD *was rare; there were not many visions.*

² One night Eli, whose eyes were becoming so weak that he could barely see, was lying down in his usual place. ³ The lamp of God had not yet gone out, and Samuel was lying down in the house of the LORD, *where the ark of God was.*

I'm not saying that because we know that Eli and Samuel lived in the tabernacle, and that there will be people living in the future tabernacle. However, I suspect there will be those worshipping and blessing the Lord both day and night. I don't believe that there will be a time when there are no praises being offered in the tabernacle of the Lord. Similar to Psalm 84, the first witness in the timeline, Psalm 134, which relates to the following year according to the timeline revelation, also speaks of a blessing on those who stand in the house of the lord offering blessings even by night.

Psalm 134:1-2

Behold, bless the LORD, all you servants of the LORD, who by night stand in the house of the LORD! ² Lift up your hands in the sanctuary, and bless the LORD.

Also, in Revelation 7, John observed in the heavenly temple and during the tribulation period on earth that the ones who are martyred for their faith will be before the Lord "day and night." I cannot imagine that this will end once the Lord is dwelling with us in His tabernacle here on earth. So the best answer that I can give to the question pertaining to verse 4, which was, who will be "dwelling" and "praising" in the Lord's house beside the Lord Himself in the Kingdom, is that of Revelation 7, but honestly, I believe that we will all be blessed and have a turn.

Revelation 7:13-15

¹³ Then one of the elders answered, saying to me, "Who are these arrayed in white robes, and where did they come from?" ¹⁴ And I said to him, "Sir, you know." So he said to me, "These are the ones who come out of the great tribulation, and washed their robes and made them white in the blood of the Lamb. ¹⁵ Therefore they are before the throne of God, and serve Him day and night in His temple. And He who sits on the throne will dwell among them.

Verses 5-7

⁵Blessed is the man whose strength is in You, whose heart is set on pilgrimage. ⁶As they pass through the Valley of Baca, they make it a spring; the rain also covers it with pools. ⁷They go from strength to strength; each one appears before God in Zion.

Everyone is blessed who has their strength in the Lord according to many scriptures. But verse 5 goes on to add, *"whose heart is set on pilgrimage."* According to many scriptures from Isaiah, Zechariah, and more, the peoples of the nations will go to the Lord's house for worship, prayer, teaching, judgment, festivals, and sacrifices.

Isaiah 2:2-4

Now it shall come to pass in the latter days that the mountain of the LORD's house

Shall be established on the top of the mountains, and shall be exalted above the hills; and all nations shall flow to it. ³ Many people shall come and say, "Come, and let us go up to the mountain of the LORD, to the house of the God of Jacob; He will teach us His ways, and we shall walk in His paths." For out of Zion shall go forth the law, and the word of the LORD from Jerusalem. ⁴ He shall judge between the nations, and rebuke many people; they shall beat their swords into plowshares, and their spears into pruning hooks; nation shall not lift up sword against nation, neither shall they learn war anymore.

Isaiah 56:7

Even them I will bring to My holy mountain, and make them joyful in My house of prayer. Their burnt offerings and their sacrifices will be accepted on My altar; for My house shall be called a house of prayer for all nations."

Zechariah 14:16

¹⁶ And it shall come to pass that everyone who is left of all the nations which came against Jerusalem shall go up from year to year to worship the King, the LORD of hosts, and to keep the Feast of Tabernacles.

Verse 6 says, *"As they pass through the Valley of Baca, they make it a spring; the rain also covers it with pools."* Baca in Hebrew is Bakah, which means "weeping." It makes me wonder if this verse, and its reference to the "Valley of Bakah," is related to Isaiah 66 verse 24, which indicates that when the people of the nations make pilgrimages to worship the Lord, they will also go and look at the corpses of the deceased unsaved sinners. Is the Valley of Bakah the same place?

Isaiah 66:22-24

*22 "For as the new heavens and the new earth which I will make shall remain before Me," says the L*ORD*, "so shall your descendants and your name remain. 23 And it shall come to pass that from one New Moon to another, and from one Sabbath to another, all flesh shall come to worship before Me," says the L*ORD*.*

24 "And they shall go forth and look upon the corpses of the men who have transgressed against Me. For their worm does not die, and their fire is not quenched. They shall be an abhorrence to all flesh."

Jesus made reference to Isaiah 66:24 in Mark 9:42-48 three times when He also said, "Their worm does not die, and the fire is not quenched." When Jesus says something three times, you had better pay close attention to what He is saying. It's a matter of eternal life or eternal damnation in this case. The context is sin. He said that if our hand, foot, or eye causes us to sin, it would be better to cut them off, or pluck them out respectively, than to be thrown into the eternal fire of hell. Putting all of this together gives me the impression that along our annual journey to, or from, the Tabernacle in Jerusalem to worship the Living God, we will pass through an area where we will be able to see these remains as a reminder of sin.

Connected to the annual pilgrimage at the Feast of Tabernacles is also what seems to be the renewal of the Old Covenant Law according to Isaiah 66:23, which indicates that in the Millennium, the Sabbath and the other feast days, or Moedim, will once again be instituted. This time, it seems that it isn't just for the children of Israel, but for all of the nations. Keep in mind that many of the laws that are part of the Old Covenant require a Tabernacle or Temple to be in Jerusalem. The renewal of the covenant makes sense to me, because as a pattern, Nehemiah also led Israel in a renewal ceremony of the covenant between them and God. This is documented in Nehemiah chapters 7 - 10, which happens to take place in the 7th month at the Feast of Tabernacles. I do not think that is a coincidence.

Verses 8-9

8O Lord God of hosts, hear my prayer; give ear, O God of Jacob! Selah

9O God, behold our shield, and look upon the face of Your anointed.

Who is the "anointed" mentioned in verse 9? Anointed in Hebrew is Mashiach, which is, of course, Messiah. So verse 9 reads, "O God, behold our shield, and look upon the face of Your Messiah." That would be none other than Yeshua HaMashiach, who, in the context of the timeline revelation, is now seated in the Tabernacle located in Zion, from where He will rule and reign over all of the nations.

Verses 10-12

10For a day in Your courts is better than a thousand. I would rather be a doorkeeper in the house of my God than dwell in the tents of wickedness. 11For the Lord God is a sun and shield; the Lord will give grace and glory; no good thing will He withhold from those who walk uprightly.12O Lord of hosts, blessed is the man who trusts in You!

Once again, the imagery of this Psalm is of a physical place of worship here on earth, and not in heaven. Naturally, there cannot be "tents of wickedness" in heaven, so the Psalmist is certainly speaking of an earthly "house of my God" and not one in heaven. That in itself doesn't prove anything, but taken as a whole, and considering God's placement of this Psalm directly after the 7 Psalms that match the 7 years of tribulation, I have to believe that it is far more than coincidental. This Psalm gives so many beautiful images of the Messiah dwelling among us in His physical Tabernacle in Jerusalem. Through several keywords, phrases, and images, it also ties together the prophetic pilgrimage of all of the nations at the annual Feast of Tabernacles mentioned in Zechariah 14 that will happen during the Millennial Kingdom.

Yesterday was my birthday, and as usual, I came in early to my office to write. In my mind, I had finished with Psalm 84 and was ready to move on with the next chapter of the book even though I had omitted the last two verses of this Psalm. To be honest with you, I wasn't ever planning to write about the last two verses because they didn't jump out at me in any prophetic way, so I figured I would skip them. However, yesterday evening, I got together with some family to have dinner in celebration of my birthday when I was handed a birthday card by my mother-in-law. The card had a Bible verse on it. Guess which verse it was? Yes, Psalm 84, verse 11, the first of the exact two verses I hadn't planned to study or write about.

So, here I am writing about them today because there's no way that was a coincidence! Think about the odds. Out of over 30,000 verses in the Bible, on the very day that I decided not to study or write about the last two verses of Psalm 84, I was handed a birthday card containing the first of those exact two verses. God did it again! Here are verses 11 and 12 again:

> *11For the LORD God is a sun and shield; the LORD will give grace and glory; no good thing will He withhold from those who walk uprightly.12O LORD of hosts, blessed is the man who trusts in You!*

It is interesting that the end of Psalm 84, which is connected to the beginning of the Millennial Kingdom reign of Christ, uses the sun as a metaphor, just as the prophet Malachi did in his last chapter related to the final end of the tribulation, and the beginning of the Millennial Kingdom.

Malachi 4:1-2

[1] *"For behold, the day is coming, burning like an oven, and all the proud, yes, all who do wickedly will be stubble. And the day which is coming shall burn them up," says the LORD of hosts, "that will leave them neither root nor branch.* [2] *But to you who fear My name the **Sun** of Righteousness shall arise with healing in His wings; and you shall go out and grow fat like stall-fed calves.*

Just as our sun is good, and gives us light by day, warmth, and is a vital part of the survival of all that lives and grows on our planet through its radiance, so also the "Sun of Righteousness" lights our path, gives us life everlasting, and radiates God's glory into our lives now and forevermore (Revelation 21:23). However, the sun also has a destructive power as noted in Malachi 4. The same sun that gives life, can also take life away. Its radiating heat can burn up all life that isn't nourished with life giving-water. In the same way, at the second coming of the "Sun of Righteousness," all of those who are not nourished with the "living water" that Jesus freely gave (John 4), will be burned up according to Malachi. He also adds that they will be left with neither "root nor branch," meaning that they will have no more second chances at life and no future descendants. At some time in the near future, all sales will be final (to use a retail metaphor), you're either sold out to Jesus and live, or you're sold out to the world, and perish. Remember that to be a friend of the world is enmity with God (James 4:4). This is why it is more important than ever in these last days to be the watchman on the wall and to warn everyone who will listen about what is coming (Ezekiel 3:16-22). Their eternity depends on it.

Verse 11 also describes our Lord as a shield, who gives us grace and glory. This verse speaks a great, timeless, and general biblical truth about our Savior, but in context, I believe that this is also a hopeful promise to the remnant of Israel in the last days prior to the Millennial Kingdom. Our Lord will be a shield of protection to those in the refuge during the final 3.5 years of the tribulation. I believe they will experience the fullness of His grace, and they will see His glory as He provides for them and protects them from everything that the serpent tries to use to destroy them.

Continuing to the last part of verse 11, the Psalmist reassures us that our Lord will not withhold any good thing from those who walk uprightly. This sounds like a great, timeless, and general biblical truth; however, there have been many throughout history who have "walked uprightly" with the Lord, but who also spent their lives in poverty. So, is this promise of not withholding any good thing, a promise referring to today, or to the Kingdom that is coming? My conclusion is that it mostly refers to the Kingdom that is coming soon. Even Malachi uses a visual image of "growing fat like stall-fed calves" related to that coming time in chapter 4 verse 2 for those who fear God's name, which is another way of saying, have a relationship with/walk uprightly with the Lord. I love the symbolism of growing fat. It's quite funny, actually. A stall-fed calf is pretty well taken care of, and really doesn't have a care in the world. That will be a blessing for all of those who put their trust in the Lord (verse 12) during the Millennium. However, there are also several warnings in God's prophetic Word related to those survivors, and I'm sure also for those born into the Kingdom during the 1000 years, who do not obey and trust in our Lord. Isaiah 65 speaks that anyone who dies at 100 years old will be considered to be accursed, which I take to mean that there will still be some rebellious ones against the Lord during that time to come. Just as Korah and his family rebelled in the wilderness against the Lord during the exodus from Egypt, even though they saw many signs and wonders of the Lord's protection and provision, they still rebelled. Likewise, according to prophecy, it sounds like that rebellious spirit will still exist in the future.

Zechariah 14 also reveals another punishment for rebelliousness in the coming age. For those nations who do not come up to Jerusalem to worship at the Feast of Tabernacles, there will be drought. Of course, drought causes crop failure, and then all sorts of hardship and suffering. Unfortunately, it seems that even in the Millennial Kingdom, when the world will be in perfect harmony and rest under the care of the One who loves us so much that He died for us all, people will still be people, and still rebel against Him.

Zechariah 14:16-19

*¹⁶And it shall come to pass that everyone who is left of
all the nations which came against Jerusalem shall go up
from year to year to worship the King, the LORD of hosts,
and to keep the Feast of Tabernacles. ¹⁷And it shall be that
whichever of the families of the earth do not come up to
Jerusalem to worship the King, the LORD of hosts, on them
there will be no rain. ¹⁸If the family of Egypt will not come
up and enter in, they shall have no rain; they shall receive
the plague with which the LORD strikes the nations who
do not come up to keep the Feast of Tabernacles. ¹⁹This
shall be the punishment of Egypt and the punishment of
all the nations that do not come up to keep the Feast of
Tabernacles.*

Even though rebelliousness will still exist in the Millennial Kingdom,
making the Lord's guidance/correction through various forms of
punishment still necessary, there will still be hope for redemption. Just
as the writers of Psalm 84 would attest to, being redeemed sons of the
rebellious Korah themselves, God will still give His grace, and even
glory to those who will once again choose to trust in Him.

In the timeline revelation this Psalm fits sometime between 2032
and 2033. That's only about 10 years away from the time of writing
this book. Suppose the timeline revelation encoded in the Psalms is
correct, and I believe fully that it is. In that case, it's an amazing
thought to imagine that our Lord and Savior will finally be back in
Jerusalem in less than 10 years from now. That makes me really excited!
However, I'm not excited about what is about to come upon this world.
Regardless of the exact timing of any of the prophetic events that we
have covered in this book, we all know that time is short. There are so
many people who are still unaware of what is coming. It's time to take
our responsibilities as watchmen and women seriously, forget about our
fears of rejection, and even persecution, and warn the world that time is
so very short, Jesus is returning soon, and today is the day of salvation!

CHAPTER 37

Decoding Psalms 5, 10, and 15

Remember the unexpected numbers "5 and 10" that the Lord spoke to me, which started me on this journey. We've already covered Psalm 50, the first Psalm of Asaph, which is also the product of multiplying 5 and 10. Prophetically, Psalm 50 gives an account of the tribulation period to come, but from an inverted perspective. We also discovered that Psalm 50 gives us a 6 verse description of the Antichrist. I also have a hunch that the number 50 may have an important meaning in the life of the Antichrist as well, which I will discuss to some extent in this chapter.

I had originally decided to only study Psalm 10, in addition to the 15 Psalms of Ascent and the 12 Psalms of Asaph, which also includes Psalm 50. I have already mentioned the reasons for studying Psalms 10 and 50 in the context of the timeline in a previous chapter. Basically, Psalm 10 as well as Psalm 50 stood out to me because of their prophetic connections with the Antichrist.

For the sake of time, I really didn't want to include Psalm 5 or Psalm 15 in this study. However, after thinking about it some more, I realized that if God gave me "5 and 10," which has a sum of 15, and I'm only looking at the product of 5 multiplied by 10, which is 50, I'm probably only seeing half of the picture. So, to get a more complete view, I eventually conceded that I had to study Psalm 5 and 15, as well as 10 and 50, to see if they contained any further significant prophetic information that could help bring the last days into a little sharper focus.

I must say that I would have been disappointed if these two Psalms were ordinary. But of course, God is good, and He placed certain Psalms in certain orders, and under certain numbers for us to find and understand. They could have easily been just Psalms of worship that had no connection to the last days. However after studying them, I believe that not only are Psalm 10 and 50 prophetic, but also Psalm 5, along with 5 and 10s sum sister, Psalm 15. It seems to me now that all of them are very important as they enable us to more fully visualize the last day's prophecies. They also help to further substantiate the timeline revelation itself, which is a blessing to me because, half the time, I think I might be nuts.

Because time is short, I'm not going to go too in-depth with these 3 Psalms. I'm just going to hit the highlights. However, I believe that as you study these Psalms, and as time progresses, you will see that these Psalms are related, at least in part, to the tribulation period, and that they help to further establish the validity of the encrypted timeline revelation.

Psalm 5 is known as a prayer of David for guidance from the Lord. To me, it also seems like a subtle snapshot of the tribulation period, not of the specific events of the tribulation, but of the emotions, lamentations, transgressions, and even adversaries. Speaking of adversaries, I believe that the Antichrist is depicted in none other than verse 6, of course!

Verses 1-3
¹ Give ear to my words, O LORD, consider my meditation.
² Give heed to the voice of my cry, my King and my God,
for to You I will pray. ³ My voice You shall hear in the
morning, O LORD; in the morning I will direct it to You,
and I will look up.

In verses 1 and 2 David cries out to God to listen to his prayer 3 times by saying "give ear," "consider," and "give heed." As I have mentioned before, anything repeated 3 times in the Bible should get our attention. Of course, we know that the number 3 can represent many things in scripture, such as divine completion, perfection, and even resurrection. But I believe here, the fact that David cries out for God to hear him in 3 different ways means, get ready for a revelation!

There are also 3 types of rapture imagery used in verse 3. This verse uses keywords such as "voice," and "morning," as well as the phrase "I will look up." However, the "voice" that we would expect to hear in the "morning" will be that of God, and not of David. So, the keywords are present, but the symmetry with other scriptures isn't. For this reason, I cannot conclude that verse 3 is definitely a shadow of the rapture, but I find it an interesting possibility.

Verses 4-6
4 For You are not a God who takes pleasure in wickedness, nor shall evil dwell with You. 5 The boastful shall not stand in Your sight; You hate all workers of iniquity.
6 You shall destroy those who speak falsehood; the LORD abhors the bloodthirsty and deceitful man.

Seemingly in opposition to the above verses, Ezekiel 33 tells us that God takes no pleasure in the death of the wicked.

Ezekiel 33:11
11 Say to them: 'As I live,' says the Lord GOD, 'I have no pleasure in the death of the wicked, but that the wicked turn from his way and live. Turn, turn from your evil ways! For why should you die, O house of Israel?'

How are we to understand these two outwardly opposing statements from Psalm 5 and Ezekiel 33? It's simple, God is a God of justice, and wickedness cannot stand in His presence, but He loves all of His image bearers, that's us, and He wants none of us to perish (2 Peter 3:9). How could He invite the wicked and unrepentant to abide with Him when wickedness cannot abide in His presence?

During Temple times, animals were sacrificed to temporarily atone for the sins of the people of Israel. It was a substitutional sacrificial system that required the life of one to stand in for the life of another.

Jesus, God's only Son, who left His heavenly abode to come down and live among us, became the final blood sacrifice, not just for Israel, but for the entire world. Then, He made it so easy for us during this age. All we have to do is believe in, and call on His name to be saved. After that, the Holy Spirit comes to live inside of us, we start to no longer desire the things of the flesh that the world has to offer, and we move closer and closer to God. That's why Jesus is the only way. Why would God send His Son to suffer and die for us, but then say, "oh well, no big deal, let's make lots of ways to get to heaven." He wouldn't, that would make no sense at all!

The tribulation is God's final offer for people to turn from their sins and call on the name of His only Son. It's going to be a terrible time like no other in all of history, and I'm not going to lie to you, following Jesus will come at a very high cost. It will most likely require you to lose your own life to gain eternal life with Him. It is still not a bad trade though...

Mark 8 ties all of this together with the second coming of Jesus after the tribulation period. If you are reading this during the tribulation period, please do not give in to the system that has been designed to trap and destroy you. Sure, you might live a little longer in your mortal body if you give in and take the mark, but you will be exchanging eternal life for a few more days and then eternal death and damnation.

Mark 8:34-38

34 When He had called the people to Himself, with His disciples also, He said to them, "Whoever desires to come after Me, let him deny himself, and take up his cross, and follow Me. 35 For whoever desires to save his life will lose it, but whoever loses his life for My sake and the gospel's will save it. 36 For what will it profit a man if he gains the whole world, and loses his own soul? 37 Or what will a man give in exchange for his soul? 38 For whoever is ashamed of Me and My words in this adulterous and sinful generation, of him the Son of Man also will be ashamed when He comes in the glory of His Father with the holy angels."

Verse 6 says, *"You shall destroy those who speak falsehood; the* LORD *abhors the bloodthirsty and deceitful man.* Based on the timeline revelation, I believe that verse 6 is speaking of none other than the Antichrist himself. Did you notice that the previous verses spoke of "all" and "those," as in many wicked people? Then, in verse 6, we transitioned to a singular "man?" We also know from many scriptures that the Antichrist is bloodthirsty and has plans to destroy all of the Jews as well as anyone else who worships the true and living God. As for a "deceitful man," Jesus, Paul, and John all warned of deception when discussing the last days and the Antichrist. Deception seems to be the Antichrist's calling card, in fact, and I believe that he will be a master at it. He will have most of the world deceived into following him, as well as the nation of Israel. Then, when he takes control, he will devour Israel and her offspring, those who keep the commandments of God and have the testimony of Jesus Christ (Revelation 12). That would be Christians, aka Tribulation Saints, who will realize after the rapture that the Bible wasn't just a bunch of fairy tales, grandma was right, and they will give their lives to Jesus. It also appears that according to Revelation 12, the commandments of God will once again be required even for Gentiles. However, maybe it will be the Noahide Laws/Commandments since the Law of Moses never applied to Gentile nations. I cannot say for sure, but it makes sense as the Church Age/Age of Grace will end at the rapture of the believing Church. If I were in the tribulation, I would make sure that I listened to the 2 witnesses in Jerusalem (Revelation 11), the Sealed 144,000 Children of Israel (Revelation 7 & 14), the 3 angels (Revelation 14), and most of all, the Holy Spirit of God. I'm pretty sure that anything else will be a deception!

The consequences of not listening and obeying God's word at that time will be eternally horrific. You must be courageous. Do not fall for the lies and deception of the beast, or the beast system that will engulf the world. You will be their enemy, but you will also be God's servant even until death.

Revelation 14:9-13

[9] Then a third angel followed them, saying with a loud voice, "If anyone worships the beast and his image, and receives his mark on his forehead or on his hand, [10] he himself shall also drink of the wine of the wrath of God, which is poured out full strength into the cup of His indignation. He shall be tormented with fire and brimstone in the presence of the holy angels and in the presence of the Lamb. [11] And the smoke of their torment ascends forever and ever; and they have no rest day or night, who worship the beast and his image, and whoever receives the mark of his name."[12] Here is the patience of the saints; here are those who keep the commandments of God and the faith of Jesus.[13] Then I heard a voice from heaven saying to me, "Write: 'Blessed are the dead who die in the Lord from now on.'" "Yes," says the Spirit, "that they may rest from their labors, and their works follow them."

Verses 7-8

[7] But as for me, I will come into Your house in the multitude of Your mercy; in fear of You I will worship toward Your holy temple. [8] Lead me, O LORD, in Your righteousness because of my enemies; make Your way straight before my face.

Verse 7 is interesting because David says that he will come into God's House, but then he says that he will worship toward the Holy Temple. So, which is it, is he in or out? It could be that David is expressing that he will come into God's House to worship, and look up toward the Heavenly Holy Temple. However, during David's time, there was no "House" (Hebrew root word bayith), only a tent/tabernacle (Hebrew root word ohel, or mishkan). So, how could David enter God's "House" if there wasn't one? Sure, we can spiritualize all of this, as many do, but I believe that there is more to this. I believe that the timeline revelation gives this verse some much-needed context. It may be that this is a picture of the remnant children of Israel inside of the refuge, worshiping either toward Zion or toward Heaven. Interestingly, the word used for "House" in verse 7 is the same Hebrew word used in Psalm 128, which represents the year that the remnant of Israel will flee into the refuge prepared by God to sustain them for three and a half years until the Great Tribulation is complete.

Verse 8, which can be over-spiritualized as well, lends more credence to my conclusion, which is that David was not just worshiping, but also prophesying when he wrote this Psalm. Speaking of Psalm 128, which goes hand in hand with Psalm 80 as the middle of the tribulation period, and the time when Israel will need to flee into the refuge (Revelation 12), verse 8 matches perfectly. Psalm 128 uses the phrase "out of Zion," and Psalm 80 speaks of the "Shepherd of Israel, who leads Joseph like a flock," and then goes on to say, "come and save us." In the same context, how perfect is it that Psalm 5 says, *"lead me, O Lord, in Your righteousness because of my enemies; make Your way straight before my face."* If you take away the general poetic and spiritual meaning, and envision this verse with your prophetic eyes, I believe that you will be able to picture Jesus leading the remnant out of Jerusalem and Judea to the refuge with their enemies in pursuit, but Jesus protecting them and guiding them (making His way straight and known before them), to His place of refuge for the remnant.

I now have to add this crazy part. I'm sure that many who study and preach eschatology will push back at what I'm about to say, and I was once such a person as well. However, I still have to discuss Zechariah 14 verses 1 - 5 in the context of the timeline revelation. There are certain parts of the beginning of Zechariah 14 that never made any sense to me as a picture of the final conflict at Armageddon. First of all, it's not at Armageddon, but at Jerusalem. I realize that Armageddon might, in fact, be a staging location for the armies of the world to then strike at Jerusalem or those who fled Jerusalem, but if Zechariah is describing the state of Jerusalem in the 7th year of the tribulation after the remnant has fled, and the land became desolate, then who are these people living in Jerusalem? It doesn't sound like it's desolate at all?

Here's Zechariah 14:1-5 so that we can dissect it a little further to see if we can fit it into its proper place within the timeline.

Zechariah 14:1-5

Behold, the day of the LORD *is coming, and your spoil will be divided in your midst.*

² For I will gather all the nations to battle against Jerusalem; the city shall be taken, the houses rifled, and the women ravished. Half of the city shall go into captivity, but the **remnant** *of the people shall not be cut off from the city.*

³ Then the LORD *will go forth and fight against those nations, as He fights in the day of battle. ⁴ And in that day His feet will stand on the Mount of Olives, which faces Jerusalem on the east. And the Mount of Olives shall be split in two, from east to west, making a very large valley; half of the mountain shall move toward the north and half of it toward the south.*

*⁵ **Then you shall flee through My mountain valley**, for the mountain valley shall reach to Azal. Yes, **you shall flee as you fled from the earthquake in the days of Uzziah king of Judah**. Thus the* LORD *my God will come, and all the saints with You.*

Most prophecy teachers teach that verse 4 relates to the second coming when Jesus will actually once again stand on the Mount of Olives. After all, it was at the Mount of Olives where the Lord ascended into Heaven, and the angels said that He would come back in like manner (Acts 1). I have no problem believing that Jesus will come back and stand on the Mount of Olives at His second coming, but could there be more to this prophetic pattern? Could it be that He will be visible to the remnant either in person, or perhaps in a pillar of cloud by day, and a pillar of fire by night, as He leads them to the refuge, similar to the time of the Exodus?

The reason that Zechariah 14:1-5 has been a problem for me for a while now, especially after discovering the timeline revelation, is that it specifically gives us the reason that Jesus stands on the Mount of Olives, and it's not necessarily to enter into Jerusalem and stay. It's to split the Mount of Olives in half so that the remnant can flee through the valley that He creates, just as He used Moses to part the Red Sea so that the Children of Israel could flee through it to escape the army of Pharaoh. So, the question is, if Zechariah 14:1-5 describes the second coming, why would the Israelites have to flee from Jerusalem when Jesus returns?

Remember that Moses was specifically 80 years old when he led the Israelites through the Red Sea according to Exodus 7:7. Also, remember that according to the timeline and Biblical patterns, the re-born Israel will be 80 years old when the remnant will have to flee from Judea as described in Matthew 24 and Revelation 12. It seems to me, based on Zechariah's description of this event, that the Exodus account would have been the most obvious choice for Zechariah to use as a historic and symbolic "fleeing" reference in verse 5. However, he uses a different, more obscure, historic event in Judea's past as a connection point to the future fulfillment of his prophecy. Obviously, that's not a coincidence.

So, is there also an "80" connection within Zechariah's use of the story of the historic earthquake that took place during King Uzziah reign over Judea that God wants us to pick up on to help prove the encrypted timeline revelation in the Psalms? Well, of course there is!

According to 2 Chronicles 26 and other historic accounts, King Uzziah was a righteous king until later in life when he became prideful. One day he decided to burn incense on the Alter of Incense in the Temple, which was a transgression against God because he was only a king and not a priest. Only Jesus, the Messiah would be both King and Priest, so it wasn't right for King Uzziah to do this. He was confronted by Azariah the priest to stop him from entering and burning incense along with "80" other priests.

2 Chronicles 26:17
*17 So Azariah the priest went in after him, and with him were **eighty** priests of the LORD—valiant men.*

Do you believe it is a coincidence that God interconnected these stories with the number "80" and that it will be in Israel's 80th year when they will have to flee from Judea to the mountains according to the timeline revelation in the Psalms? I don't! Further, I believe that the story of King Uzziah gives us a prophetic glimpse into the future of the day when the Antichrist will also defile the coming temple. As a pattern, I believe there will be valiant priests who will try to stop him from entering just as they tried to stop King Uzziah.

The Jewish historian Josephus gives us a little more insight into this Biblical account and connects King Uzziah's transgression with the earthquake mentioned in Zechariah 14. According to Josephus (Antiquities of the Jews 9:10:4), the earthquake happened on the same day, at the same time, when King Uzziah was being confronted by Azariah and the "80" priests. Furthermore, the earthquake caused a crack in the Temple, and the sun's rays shone through onto Uzziah's face. His face was then immediately stricken with leprosy, which caused him to live outside of the city for the rest of his days.

Revelation 12 adds to the scene of Zechariah 14:5 by describing how the earth will help Israel by opening up its mouth and swallowing the pursuing army. The pursuing army is described as a "flood which the dragon spewed out of his mouth." The entire visual image that I get through the complete timeline revelation plays out something like this:

According to the timeline revelation in the Psalms, sometime between 2027 and 2029, when Israel is 80 years old, the false messiah will stand in the newly rebuilt temple, defile the temple, and declare that he is god. This is the day when he pulls his mask of deception off, and Israel will finally see and realize that they have been played by the one they thought was their messiah. He will then try to destroy Israel, which is his ultimate mission, so that they cannot fulfill God's promise of calling on the name of the true Messiah, Yeshua! After all, if they are all dead, they cannot call on His Name. The believing remnant will know that they must flee when they see these things happening because they know the teaching of Jesus in Matthew 24. Just like Pharaoh, the Antichrist will summon his army, either human, demon, or Nephilim, to pursue and destroy the Children of Israel. Jesus will come and part the Mount of Olives so that the remnant can escape from Jerusalem and the clutches of the man of sin and his army. I have a hunch that his army may not be fully human based on Joel 2. Once the remnant is safely through the valley, the invading army will be consumed by the closing of the earth just as Pharaoh's army was consumed by the water of the closing Red Sea. God established a pattern, but it doesn't have to be exact. He's a lot more interesting and exciting than that!

Verses 9-10

⁹ For there is no faithfulness in their mouth; their inward part is destruction; their throat is an open tomb; they flatter with their tongue. ¹⁰ Pronounce them guilty, O God! Let them fall by their own counsels; cast them out in the multitude of their transgressions, for they have rebelled against You.

Keep in mind that all of these Psalms are Israel-centric. As a Westerner, as I read them, I have to put aside my Western mind and realize that the Psalms are not about the US, or Europe, but all about Israel and the children of Israel. So, in context, who are the faithless, destructive flatterers with throats like open tombs? David asks God to pronounce them guilty so that they would fall and be cast out due to their transgressions and rebellion against God. To be cast "out" seems to indicate that they were once "in."

I can't help but be reminded of one of the times when Jesus taught the multitudes and pronounced 7 woes on the Pharisees and scribes, which was recorded in Matthew 23. Trust me, you do not want the Son of God pronouncing a "woe" on you, and definitely not 7! Could the 7 woes be foretelling of the 7 years of tribulation? Could the ones with "throats like open tombs" be the Jewish religious leaders of our day? In the 6th woe, Jesus said that the Pharisees and scribes were like whitewashed tombs, beautiful on the outside, but full of dead men's bones on the inside, which is very similar in character and metaphor to *"their throat is an open tomb."* As you peer down those throats, you will see inside the tombs full of dead men's bones.

Matthew 23:27-28

27 "Woe to you, scribes and Pharisees, hypocrites! For you are like whitewashed tombs which indeed appear beautiful outwardly, but inside are full of dead men's bones and all uncleanness. 28 Even so you also outwardly appear righteous to men, but inside you are full of hypocrisy and lawlessness.

So, they had an outward appearance of righteousness with their robes, tassels, and phylacteries, but they were filled with hypocrisy and wicked religious spirits on the inside. After pronouncing the 7th woe on the Pharisees and scribes, Jesus described them as a *"brood of vipers,"* and then described how, just like their forefathers, they would persecute and kill the prophets and teachers that He would send to them. Because Jesus knew their evil hearts and their rejection of Him and His New Covenant, He declared that they would be held responsible for all of those past, present, and future sins. Who are the Pharisees today? I hate to say it, but they are the Rabbis who teach not only from the Torah, but also from the oral traditions of their Rabbinical forefathers, and who continue to reject Yeshua HaMashiach.

Matthew 23:33-35

33 Serpents, brood of vipers! How can you escape the condemnation of hell? 34 Therefore, indeed, I send you prophets, wise men, and scribes: some of them you will kill and crucify, and some of them you will scourge in your synagogues and persecute from city to city, 35 that on you may come all the righteous blood shed on the earth, from the blood of righteous Abel to the blood of Zechariah, son of Berechiah, whom you murdered between the temple and the altar.

Jesus used the term "brood of vipers" on the Pharisees one other time as well, as we read from Matthew 12:

Matthew 12:34-35

³⁴ Brood of vipers! How can you, being evil, speak good things? For out of the abundance of the heart the mouth speaks.³⁵ A good man out of the good treasure of his heart brings forth good things, and an evil man out of the evil treasure brings forth evil things.

Jesus clearly labeled them evil, and that they will speak evil because that's what's in their hearts. In fact, I cannot remember one time Jesus had anything good to say about the Pharisees, who were the ancestors of today's Rabbinical leaders. Most Christians like to think fondly of the Jewish Rabbis, and I am one of those; however, we have to understand that they are an enemy of the true Messiah, and they have been for 2000 years. Just last month, the religious leadership in the Israeli Knesset tried to outlaw Christian proselytizing in Israel. Thankfully, the Prime Minister was never going to go along with that bill since he is a friend to Christians, but you can see where this is going. Remember that such an attempt against the Great Commission comes directly from the spirit of the Antichrist.

The Harlot

Here's what I believe may be the fulfillment of these, and many other, prophetic verses. Many Christians who are awake and study Bible prophecy believe that the Roman Catholic Church will be the harlot who rides the beast. The current Pope does seem to be preoccupied with globalism, environmentalism, and unifying the world's religions rather than spreading the gospel of Christ. Therefore, I'm absolutely positive that this Pope at the head of the Roman Catholic Church will play a large part in the move toward a one-world religion and government under the Antichrist. But I do not believe that the Pope is the Antichrist, nor do I believe that the Roman Catholic Church is the harlot riding the beast as described in Revelation 17.

Throughout the Bible, it has always been Israel who has played the role of the harlot by following after other gods. Why would God establish such a strong pattern, and then finish with something totally different? That is why I always point out that the end times are centered around Israel, but from a Western view-point, we always seem to make it about the Church, or Western powers.

So, in my opinion, the harlot (Israel) will once again follow a false religion. To clarify, today's religious Jews are also currently following a false religion in Judaism, since they rejected God's Son, Yeshua HaMashiach, 2000 years ago, and continue to do so. Because of their rejection of the true Messiah, any form of worship is inherently false.

In ancient times Israel strayed away from Yahweh and repeatedly followed after the gods of other nations, such as Baal and Asherah. The difference this time may be that they actually believe that they are following Yahweh due to the deceptions of their oral traditions written in their Talmud. Remember that in Judaism, it is believed that the Torah, the 5 Books of Moses, was only part of what God gave to Moses at Mount Sinai. They believe that the remainder was handed down as oral tradition, which wasn't written down at the time.

Over time, sages added their interpretations and commentaries to the oral traditions, and it was finally written down into a complete work between the 3rd and 5th centuries AD. It is considered to be the oral commentary necessary to better understand the meanings behind the written Torah. The Talmud is also considered to be one of the most important texts in modern Judaism, even as important as the Torah itself to many religious Jews. Can you see how the enemy could use the Jewish sages to falsely interpret the Torah, thereby setting the stage for the coming end-time deception of the false messiah? Perhaps the false messiah and the false prophet are the embodiment of Baal and Asherah?

There are actually two versions of the Talmud. One is known as the Jerusalem Talmud, and the other is known as the Babylonian Talmud. The latter is considered to be more comprehensive and authoritative, and is typically referred to as simply the Talmud. Do you think the fact that it stems from Babylon has any prophetic significance?

Here's how I believe this all could play out based on Bible prophecy combined with the teachings of many current Rabbis. As I have stated before, and believe it's worth repeating, modern-day Rabbis have certain expectations of their long-awaited messiah, which are considered to be absolutes. In other words, they will not consider anyone to be their messiah unless he accomplishes certain tasks written about in their Talmud. This gives us a glimpse of what to expect from the coming false messiah, aka Antichrist.

In the eyes of religious Jews, the coming of their messiah will usher in the long-awaited Messianic Age. For that new age to be recognized, they must first have a messiah. By comparing what we know about the coming Antichrist, to the Rabbinical expectations of their messiah, we can get a pretty good picture of what the ultimate "man of sin" will be like, and what some of his accomplishments and deceptions will be. According to Rabbis, the messiah must be from the line of King David. No Gentile will ever be considered because he must restore the Davidic monarchy. How can he do that unless he has Davidic blood? That begs the question, other than the fact that he will be a descendant of King David, how will they recognize the one they will call their messiah? Here is a list of absolutes based on Rabbinical teachings:

1. They absolutely expect their messiah will be responsible for rebuilding the Jewish Temple.
2. They absolutely expect him to restore the Priesthood to the Temple and reinstate the sacrifices.
3. They absolutely expect him to gather the exiles from all nations back to Israel.
4. They absolutely expect him to be a mortal man, but with super human abilities.
5. They absolutely expect him to triumph over all enemies of Israel, leading the world to accept God and live in universal peace.
6. They absolutely expect Israel and Jerusalem to be the center of government and religion worldwide.

There are also many other expectations that Jewish Rabbis have about their coming messiah that aren't as absolute. These points are

debated, and are not necessarily prerequisites to determining who
qualifies as messiah, however, many still anticipate that their messiah
will possess these qualities as well as the absolutes listed above. Many say
that he will be a Torah scholar, and may know the Torah and Talmud
word for word. He will be wise and righteous, and will lead the nation
of Israel to repentance. Here's a big one. Many believe that he will defeat
the enemies of Israel in the Gog Magog war of Ezekiel 38 & 39, which
will then usher in the Messianic Age. So, in the minds of many Rabbis,
they are expecting that the hero of the upcoming Gog Magog conflict
in Israel will be their messiah!

That fits perfectly in the timeline revelation found in the Psalms
since in both witnesses, the Psalms of Asaph and the Psalms of Ascent,
we can see the Gog Magog war occurring in 2024 and then the rise
of the Antichrist in 2025. There are also several other Rabbinical
predictions that they believe will lead to the arrival of their messiah.
Just as stated in the Seal Judgments of the Book of Revelation, many
Rabbis also believe their messiah will arrive during a time of war, chaos,
high inflation, and poverty. Similar to what the Apostle Paul wrote to
Timothy (2 Timothy 3), they also expect that these things will happen
at a time when people will be arrogant and prideful, and when young
people will not have any respect for their elders.

All of those expectations certainly resemble the world around us
today. Then add to that the fact that we are living in a world full of
wars and conflicts, and in a time when we can already see World War
3 looming on the near horizon. We already have high inflation that
doesn't seem to have an end in sight. In fact, most analysts predict a
worsening as Western powers seem to be stumbling over themselves to
make bad decisions for their people, almost as if it were all planned. I
always say, "of course, it's planned; nobody can be that stupid!" And that
seems to be the reality that we are living in today in 2023.

So what does all of this have to do with Psalm 5 verses 9 - 10? I
believe that these verses are describing the "harlot" of Revelation 17,
who are the Jewish religious leaders in these last days who have rejected
God's Messiah, yet are hungry for their own version of messiah. I believe
that the Talmud that they follow, as well as other Jewish interpretations

and commentaries on the Torah and Tanakh, will lead them to accept, and in many cases, even worship the beast, who will check all of the boxes on their messianic wish list. Satan has devised a perfect setup for his man of the hour to step in, deceive many, and then control the Jews with the ultimate goal of their total annihilation.

Verses 11-12

¹¹ But let all those rejoice who put their trust in You; let them ever shout for joy, because You defend them; let those also who love Your name be joyful in You. ¹² For You, O LORD, will bless the righteous; with favor You will surround him as with a shield.

Here is the contrast. In verses 9 - 10, we saw the "harlot" who will get into bed with the Devil himself, believing him to be their Messiah. Now, in verses 11 -12, we see those who rejected the false messiah, and put their trust in the one true Messiah. Remember that these Psalms are typically Israel-centered, so in context, they can only be referring to those who have fled into the refuge prepared by God, where He "defends them" and "surrounds him as with a shield." They are called blessed, joyful, righteous, and they have God's favor. I can't help but also notice a word that really stands out to me in verse 11, which is "ever." I believe the phrase "let them ever shout for joy," in a subtle way connects God's children, who will be protected in the refuge for three and a half years, with the coming Millennial Kingdom when they will be able to come out and finally be God's children for all of eternity.

Psalm 10

In the context of the timeline revelation, I believe that Psalm 10 is primarily a written portrait of the Antichrist, as well as the false prophet, and all of those who follow them. Their followers are the ones who will be responsible for carrying out the orders to persecute, and even martyr the saints of the Lord, both Jews and Gentiles, during the tribulation. Of all of the 150 Psalms, Psalm 10 is perhaps the most descriptive as it relates to the character and the mindset of the coming false messiah. From prophetic scriptures in the Old and the New Testaments, we know that this false messiah will be a man of sin and iniquity, the deceiver, the teacher of unrighteousness, the wicked counselor, the lawless one, the little horn, and the beast among many other titles. In addition to giving more insight into the nature and temperament of the Antichrist, watch as Psalm 10 also adds a few more descriptive titles to him as well.

In addition to the prophetic descriptions of the Antichrist, I believe this Psalm is also a cry for help by the remnant and all who will reject the mark, and refuse to worship the beast during the tribulation. Those who rebel against the beast and his system of control will be persecuted by him and his allies, and will cry out to God for help and for answers. Spoiler alert! It has a happy ending.

Verses 1-2
¹Why do You stand afar off, O Lord? Why do You hide in times of trouble? ² The wicked in his pride persecutes the poor; let them be caught in the plots which they have devised.

Notice the *"times of trouble"* mentioned in verse 1. Obviously, Israel has been through many times of trouble, but there is one coming that will be like no other.

Jeremiah 30:7
⁷Alas! For that day is great, so that none is like it; and it is the time of Jacob's trouble, but he shall be saved out of it.

Verse 2 uses the possessive personal pronoun "his," indicating a singular person rather than a group when it says, *"the wicked in **his** pride persecutes the poor."* It then transitions to "them" when it says, *"let **them** be caught in the plots which they have devised."* I do not believe that any of this is by accident, but by design. It appears that we are dealing with an individual as well as a group following his lead. In fact, notice that the term "wicked" is frequently paired with "his." The Hebrew word used for this "wicked" man is "reshah." Interestingly, it's the same word used in Psalm 125:3, which you may recall signifies the beginning of the 7-year tribulation period by stating, *"for the scepter of **wickedness** (reshah) shall not rest on the land allotted to the righteous, lest the righteous reach out their hands to iniquity."* Of course, according to the timeline revelation, we know that the "scepter of wickedness" is speaking of the authority and rule of the Antichrist over the land of Israel. So, in context, I believe that the "reshah" and the "his" in Psalm 10 refer to none other than the coming man of sin, the Antichrist.

There is another very interesting "Antichrist" related detail that is easy to miss in verse 2. I only picked up on this because I also studied this Psalm using the Orthodox Jewish Bible, which points out that in verse 2, the original Hebrew word used that our English Bibles translate to "poor," is actually "ani." So, in this context, we see the wicked, prideful Antichrist persecuting the poor (ani). Ani happens to be the very same word used in Zechariah 9:9 for "lowly," referring to the Messiah on the day that He rode into Jerusalem on a donkey, hailed as the Messiah, prior to His crucifixion.

Zechariah 9:9
⁹ *Rejoice greatly, Daughter Zion! Shout, Daughter Jerusalem! See, your king comes to you, righteous and victorious, **lowly** and riding on a donkey, on a colt, the foal of a donkey.*

So, Psalm 10 provides for us a connection between the Antichrist and the true Messiah, and indicates that the "reshah" will persecute the "ani." Obviously, the man of sin, the Antichrist, cannot persecute the true Messiah because he has no power over Him, but he can persecute all of those who are redeemed by the blood of the Messiah, and who have been born again in His image, at least for a time according to Revelation 12:17 and Revelation 13:7:

Revelation 12:17

[17] And the dragon was enraged with the woman, and he went to make war with the rest of her offspring, who keep the commandments of God and have the testimony of Jesus Christ.

Revelation 13:7

[7] It was granted to him to make war with the saints and to overcome them. And authority was given him over every tribe, tongue, and nation.

These are the "Tribulation Saints," those who became Christians during the tribulation period, and did not follow, or worship the beast. According to Revelation 12, during the second half of the tribulation period, when the Antichrist realizes that he cannot destroy the protected "woman," who is the remnant of Israel safe inside of the refuge, he will turn his attention and destructive power toward her "offspring," meaning the Tribulation Saints.

Verses 3-4

[3] For the wicked boasts of his heart's desire; he blesses the greedy and renounces the LORD. [4] The wicked in his proud countenance does not seek God; God is in none of his thoughts.

According to verses 3 and 4, the Reshah boasts about his plans, works with the greedy, and speaks out against God. From both verses, we can see that this Reshah is boastful, proud, and arrogant, and that he wants no part of the Living God except to blaspheme and renounce Him. This same prophetic narrative is also seen in Revelation 13 specifically speaking of the Antichrist and his proud words and blasphemies against God.

Revelation 13:5

[5] The beast was given a mouth speaking proud words and blasphemies, and he was permitted to exercise ruling authority for forty-two months.

"He blesses the greedy." Who are the greedy other than those merchants, pharmaceutical companies, bankers, media moguls, etc., who will become even more powerful and wealthy through their cooperation with the Antichrist during the tribulation? We can see this trajectory in our world today as we near the onset of the time of trouble. We catch a glimpse of these greedy and powerful globalists in Revelation 18 as they are mourning the loss of their beloved "Babylon" after its final fall.

Revelation 18:23
23 The light of a lamp shall not shine in you anymore, and the voice of bridegroom and bride shall not be heard in you anymore. For your merchants were the great men of the earth, for by your sorcery all the nations were deceived.

The Greek word translated as "sorcery" in Revelation 18:23 is pharmakeia, which is of course where we get our English word pharmacy from. After the planned and engineered pandemic, that the entire world had to endure only a few years ago, this verse takes on a whole new meaning in my mind. I believe these same globalist pharmaceutical companies, along with their other industrial globalist partners, will be at least in part responsible for the rise of the Antichrist in a mutually beneficial pact, which will certainly serve their interests over the interests of the population. We see this mindset already developing within the United Nations and the World Economic Forum with their "Agenda 2030" and "Great Reset" agenda, respectively, which promise to bring peace, equality, and prosperity to all, but will only enslave the world's population into a system of total control and tyranny. By now it should be obvious to anyone paying attention to the direction that the world is headed that all of what is happening has been well-planned by the global elites, perhaps even for generations. However, I don't believe that the mastermind who is truly behind all of this is human. The humans are the puppets and Satan is the puppet master behind the scenes, pulling the strings. Most of the puppets don't even know they are being controlled, used, and manipulated because their pride and arrogance closes their eyes to the truth.

Speaking of "planned," we Bible prophecy believers have long understood that the Antichrist couldn't actually take global control as described in Revelation 13, unless there was a system already in place for global government, global surveillance, global religion, and a global cashless currency. We see all four moving toward their final destination today, just as the Bible predicted, but I want to focus on the digital currency aspect of the last days since it has literally arrived at our doorstep this year.

As of now, it's called Central Bank Digital Currency, or CBDC, and I believe it's the last big step in global financial control for the coming super surveillance and control "beast system." A digital currency will give governments, and ultimately a 1-world government, total control over your purchases and unprecedented surveillance power over every aspect of your life. Cash will soon be outlawed, which is already being discussed in Europe. Even today, in the US, many retailers will no longer accept cash in payment of goods and services even though it is still legal tender. One of the most important aspects of digital currency to understand is that it is programmable, so once cash is gone, every government will have the ability to control your purchases by programming the currency with limits and restrictions.

Former Secretary of State and rabid globalist, Henry Kissinger was quoted as saying, "who controls the food supply controls the people; who controls the energy can control whole continents; who controls money can control the world."

Can you see that all three are already being controlled by global powers to our detriment even today? First of all, our food supply is full of chemicals and is highly genetically modified. Recently, food production plants have been mysteriously burning down and exploding in record numbers. Millions of chickens have been destroyed due to a supposed bird flu, which also affects the cost and availability of eggs. The globalists want to drastically limit human consumption of beef due to the supposed environmental impacts of methane emissions from cows, and the list goes on and on.

Also due to environmentalism, energy production and costs are being controlled to push the population into relying on inefficient and unreliable "renewable" energy sources such as wind and solar to power electric cars and our homes, businesses, and industries. So, at this time in history, it appears that a relatively small group of elected and unelected, godless, arrogant and murderous globalists are working behind the scenes to control, and "reset" the world to suit their agenda, which is the agenda that is building the global beast system. So, thanks to globalist puppets like Kissinger, they understood that they needed to control the food supply so that they could control the people. They knew that they needed to control energy to control continents, and they knew that they needed to control money to control the world. To add to Kissinger's wish list, now, with digital/programmable money, the globalists can take total control of all aspects of human existence on this planet, including food and energy. It's sort of the knockout punch to human freedom as we once knew it. For example, if they deem that you have reached their programmed limit of beef purchases this month, your digital currency will simply not allow you to purchase any more beef. The same with energy, weapons, ammunition, and countless other goods and services that they do not want you to have or use.

Verses 5-7

5 His ways are always prospering; Your judgments are far above, out of his sight; as for all his enemies, he sneers at them. 6 He has said in his heart, "I shall not be moved; I shall never be in adversity." 7 His mouth is full of cursing and deceit and oppression; under his tongue is trouble and iniquity.

In verses 5 - 7, we get to see the inner workings of the prideful and callous heart of the Antichrist. I think we can get a pretty good idea of who this wicked one is at heart from Psalm 10, along with many other descriptive passages and patterns found in the Old and New Testaments. Daniel 8 also offers a very good description of the Antichrist and some of his wicked ways. You will notice that Psalm 10 and Daniel 8 have quite a few similarities in their descriptions. For example, both speak of his prosperity and his attitude of invincibility.

I also get an understanding from both Psalm 10 and Daniel 8 that this prophesied wicked prince is so extremely confident in himself, and in his calling that he understands that he was born, might I even say "bred" for this role.

Daniel 8:23-25

[23] *"And in the latter time of their kingdom, when the transgressors have reached their fullness, a king shall arise, having fierce features, who understands sinister schemes. [24] His power shall be mighty, but not by his own power; he shall destroy fearfully, and shall prosper and thrive; he shall destroy the mighty, and also the holy people. [25] "Through his cunning he shall cause deceit to prosper under his rule; and he shall exalt himself in his heart. He shall destroy many in their prosperity. He shall even rise against the Prince of princes; but he shall be broken without human means.*

Notice that Daniel 8 verse 24 indicates that it is not his power that makes him mighty, but by another. Of course, we know that this mighty power comes from Satan himself for a time, according to 2 Thessalonians 2:

2 Thessalonians 2:9

[9] *The coming of the lawless one is according to the working of Satan, with all power, signs, and lying wonders,*

Likewise, Psalm 10 verse 6 has a definite satanic overtone, which is seen more clearly when read in the Orthodox Jewish Bible.

Verse 6 (Orthodox Jewish Bible)

[6] *He hath said in his lev (heart), I shall not be shaken; throughout all generations I shall never be in trouble.*

Notice that the "he" who is speaking is insinuating that he has been around, and will be around "throughout all generations?" That cannot be speaking of a mortal man, but Satan himself, who will indwell the "man of sin" just as he did Judas Iscariot as indicated in Luke 22.

Luke 22:3

³ Then Satan entered Judas, surnamed Iscariot, who was numbered among the twelve.

Verses 8-11

⁸ He sits in the lurking places of the villages; in the secret places he murders the innocent; his eyes are secretly fixed on the helpless. ⁹ He lies in wait secretly, as a lion in his den; he lies in wait to catch the poor; he catches the poor when he draws him into his net. ¹⁰ So he crouches, he lies low, that the helpless may fall by his strength. ¹¹ He has said in his heart, "God has forgotten; He hides His face; He will never see."

There are a few common themes that are evident in most of the prophetic passages concerning the Antichrist and his dark exploits. One of those is that he focuses his destructive power on the common man, the innocent, the poor, and the helpless. Most Bible prophecy students have long realized that there would be an end times divide between the "haves," and the "have-nots." This is evident in many passages including Revelation chapter 6 through the rider on the black horse, who depicts a world in famine.

Revelation 6:5-6

⁵ When the Lamb opened the third seal, I heard the third living creature say, "Come!" I looked, and there before me was a black horse! Its rider was holding a pair of scales in his hand.⁶ Then I heard what sounded like a voice among the four living creatures, saying, "Two pounds of wheat for a day's wages, and six pounds of barley for a day's wages, and do not damage the oil and the wine!"

I believe that the common man is the one pictured as the impoverished wage earner who is only able to earn enough after a full day's work to afford a modest amount of basic provisions for his family. In contrast, notice also that in verse 6, it is specifically stated, "do not damage the oil and the wine," which most believe is a reference to the wealthy elites not being harmed through the same time of famine. This also suggests to me that they, the wealthy elites, will be guilty of orchestrating the famine themselves, and more than likely profiting from it and gaining more global control. Later in Revelation 18, we see these same kings and merchants who were able to profit from the ungodly abuses perpetrated by the beast system and its center of power, Babylon.

Revelation 18:3
3 For all the nations have drunk the maddening wine of her adulteries. The kings of the earth committed adultery with her, and the merchants of the earth grew rich from her excessive luxuries."

Verses 9 and 10 depict the Antichrist as a lion stealthfully waiting to catch his prey, which again are not the wealthy, but are the poor and the helpless. Naturally, the man of sin will ultimately do the opposite of what God's word commands. Initially, I expect that he will appear to be merciful and benevolent to the masses. However, once firmly in power, I believe that his true colors will finally be revealed. God's word says to treat your neighbor as yourself, and to help the oppressed, the widow, and the orphan, so I'm confident that ultimately, the wicked one will do the exact opposite.

I find it interesting that both the true Messiah and the false messiah are depicted symbolically as lions in several Psalms, but with very different principles. As you saw in verses 9 and 10, the false messiah stalks and murders the innocent and the helpless. In contrast, as we covered in a previous chapter, Psalm 76 depicts the Messiah, who is the "Lion of the Tribe of Judah" in His "sukkow," or "covert lion's lair," protecting Israel from an invading army. So the counterfeit "lion" is out to steal, kill, and destroy the weakest among the heard, whereas the true "Lion" is a hidden, but all-powerful protector of His Children.

Revelation 13 also connects the Antichrist, in part, to the most dangerous part of a lion, its mouth! Of course, Revelation 13 also connects back to Daniel 7, but that's another study for another day.

Revelation 13:2
² The beast I saw resembled a leopard, but had feet like those of a bear and a mouth like that of a lion.

To add to the growing mountain of evidence that shows Psalm 10 to be a depiction of the Antichrist, there's one more possible connection between a lion and the Antichrist that comes to mind. In Deuteronomy, just before Moses died, he gave blessings over each of the tribes of Israel. Here's what he said about the tribe of Dan:

Deuteronomy 33:22
²² And of Dan he said: "Dan *is* a lion's whelp; he shall leap from Bashan."

This verse could spark an entire book all on its own, so I'll try to summarize my thoughts, regarding the tribe of Dan and the Antichrist. Dan is the tribe that, just like the fallen angels mentioned in Jude 1:6, and the Book of Enoch, did not keep their proper abode. Due to their lack of faith in God, they moved from the land that was allotted to them, since they did not drive out the occupants of the land as commanded by God. They moved northward to the upper-most region of Israel, north of the Sea of Galilee, into the Bashan and Mount Hermon area. Both of those areas were associated with Nephilim and false god worship. In fact, the tribe of Dan took to idol worship pretty much immediately when they moved north, and was the first to apostatize and worship false gods, according to Judges 18.

Deuteronomy associates the tribe of Dan with a lion's whelp, and them leaping from Bashan. Many believe that Dan became a sea-faring tribe and ultimately "leapt" from their location in the area of Bashan, and moved into many other parts of the globe, including Europe. Although their history isn't certain, many believe that they became the Danes, and also the Vikings.

Of course, we know that the tribe of Dan was specifically omitted as one of the 12 tribes of Israel in Revelation 7, along with Ephraim. Because of Dan's history of false worship, disobedience, lack of faith, and possible move into Europe, many believe that the Antichrist, who comes out of Europe according to Daniel 9, will be a descendant of the tribe of Dan. Personally, I believe that to be only partially true.

Not just the Antichrist, but also his master himself, Satan, is also compared to a lion in 1 Peter 5:8, which says, *"Be sober, be vigilant; because your adversary the devil walks about like a roaring lion, seeking whom he may devour."*

I think it is pretty clear that there is a lot of evidence throughout the Bible that connects with Psalm 10, which suggests that we are, in fact, reading a short biography of the Antichrist himself, as we read through this Psalm. What I find even more intriguing is his state of mind mentioned in verse 11, which implies that he is so arrogant that he thinks he will actually get away with his evil agenda, and that God will not remember, or perhaps that He doesn't care.

Verse 11
[11] He has said in his heart, "God has forgotten; He hides His face; He will never see.

After living a life of prosperity (verse 5), where everything he touches seems to turn into gold, the man of sin, in his self-importance and overconfidence, hasn't yet experienced the biblical principal of "reaping what you sow" found in Galatians 6. He will be able to carry out the serpent's plan with the self-confidence that he has garnered through a lifetime of realizing that nothing ever stands in his way. The false messiah will however find out the hard way that biblical principles apply to everyone eventually. At the return of our Lord after the Antichrist's reign of terror, the man of sin will be annihilated with a simple breath from the mouth of the true and almighty Messiah, as if he were nothing.

2 Thessalonians 2:8

⁸ And then the lawless one will be revealed, whom the Lord will consume with the breath of His mouth and destroy with the brightness of His coming.

Verses 12-13

¹² Arise, O LORD! O God, lift up Your hand! Do not forget the humble. ¹³ Why do the wicked renounce God? He has said in his heart, "You will not require an account."

God will not forget the humble. In fact, He will shelter them, protect them, and provide for them during the final 42 months of the tribulation period. Remember that these Psalms are centered on the children of Israel. Obviously, at the midpoint of the tribulation, many who previously believed in Yahweh will renounce Him as God, and will accept the Antichrist as their god in the wake of his deceiving signs and wonders. I believe that he will use the many interpretations in the Talmud against the Jews to convince them that he is divine. And for those Jews and Gentiles who are inconvincible, and who will not bow down and worship the beast, he will make war on them and destroy them.

Revelation 13:4

⁴ So they worshiped the dragon who gave authority to the beast; and they worshiped the beast, saying, "Who is like the beast? Who is able to make war with him?"

Verses 14-15

¹⁴ But You have seen, for You observe trouble and grief, to repay it by Your hand. The helpless commits himself to You; You are the helper of the fatherless. ¹⁵ Break the arm of the wicked and the evil man; Seek out his wickedness until You find none.

Our Father in Heaven has been keeping an account of all things, good and bad, of all people throughout the ages. Likewise, the wickedness of the Antichrist, his false prophet, and all of those who follow them will not go unreported or unpunished. With God, there will be a reckoning for the unrepentant.

Verse 15, which says, *"break the arm of the wicked and evil man,"* to me, is the final piece of the Psalm 10 Antichrist puzzle. As we know from Zechariah 11, where the Antichrist is called the "worthless shepherd," we find some details that tie into Revelation 13:3, which says, *"and I saw one of his heads as if it had been mortally wounded, and his deadly wound was healed. And all the world marveled and followed the beast."* Revelation 13:3 mentions a mortal wound to the head of the beast, and then in reference to the false prophet, Revelation 13:12 continues and says, *"and he (the false prophet) exercises all the authority of the first beast in his presence, and causes the earth and those who dwell in it to worship the first beast, whose deadly wound was healed."* By these verses, we understand that the Antichrist will suffer a fatal head wound by a "sword" or weapon of some sort (Revelation 13:14).

As I mentioned, Zechariah gives us a little more detail that we can now add to Revelation 13 and Psalm 10 to reveal a fuller impression of a climactic scene still to come in the life of the prophesied man of sin.

Zechariah 11:17
[17] *"Woe to the worthless shepherd, who leaves the flock! A sword shall be against his arm and against his right eye; his arm shall completely wither, and his right eye shall be totally blinded."*

Putting all of these descriptions together, it is reasonable to presume that the Antichrist will suffer an assassination attempt on his life sometime at, or around, the midpoint of the tribulation period. It sounds like one of his arms will be seriously injured, perhaps at least partially amputated, and his head wound will be through his right eye, and will be fatal. Many throughout the centuries have pondered the aftermath of this fatal head wound. Revelation 13 tells us that his fatal injury will be healed, and afterward the whole world will follow the beast, marvel after him, and say, "who is able to make war with him."

In other words, he will appear to be indestructible and unconquerable. Of course, the seed of Satan will have to have a resurrection event to mimic the resurrection of the true Messiah. The question is, does Satan have healing and resurrection power? Personally, I don't believe that he does unless God granted that power to him for this one event to fulfill God's purposes. More than likely, however, this is one of those deceptive "lying wonders" that Paul warned us about in 2 Thessalonians 2.

Could it be that the Antichrist will be the first to have his consciousness uploaded to a machine and thereby continue to live and rule, but only as an "image" of his former self, possibly as a hologram? I pose this question based on current scientific trends and research as well as the use of the word "image" in Revelation 13.

Revelation 13:15

¹⁵ He was granted power to give breath to the image of the beast, that the image of the beast should both speak and cause as many as would not worship the image of the beast to be killed.

Scientists have been working on the technology to be able to upload human consciousness to machines for years. In fact, over 10 years ago, some expected to be able to accomplish this goal within 10 years. Although this seems like the stuff of a science fiction movie, it might not be as farfetched as you might think. All of this is simply conjecture on my part as I look at the biblical narrative and compare it to developing technology. His mimicked resurrection could have something to do with AI, robotics, transhumanism, cloning, demonic forces posing as alien life from other galaxies, or he could be simply used as an animated meat puppet by Satan himself. Only time will tell how this will actually play out. Unfortunately, I haven't found any additional details encoded in the Psalms pertaining to the postmortem "image" of the beast, but it is nonetheless interesting to contemplate.

I have had one more thought regarding the "image" that I would like to add based on connecting a few more prophetic "dots" with current events. The continual revealing of the supposed aliens and alien

UAPs by our government and media cannot be a coincidence in our time, especially when you consider that only a few years ago, you would have been called a nut if you believed in such a thing. However, even the US Congress is taking this phenomenon seriously and asking questions.

I mentioned earlier that some of the possible explanations of the "image" could be based on how demonic forces pose as aliens or that the body of the Antichrist could possibly be reanimated by Satan himself. What if the Antichrist is a hybrid Nephilim, as many of us suspect? Remember, according to the Book of Enoch, that a disembodied Nephilim is an evil spirit, also known as a demon. In other words, when the flesh of a Nephilim dies, his spirit becomes a demon. Of course we know that Demons can inhabit the flesh of humans and animals. It has also been suggested that the little grey "aliens" who abduct humans for experimentation related to "seed" are actually demons inhabiting biometric suits, for the lack of a better term. The term "nonhuman biologics" has been used recently by whistle-blowers who have been involved in government research programs related to alien phenomena. What an interesting term! It makes me think they know that these "aliens" are not real and that they are simply biological "suits" worn and animated by demonic forces.

According to many of the fascinating teachings of L.A. Marzulli, who is an author, film-maker, lecturer, and who has been on the trail of the Nephilim for many years, the demons do wear biologic "suits" to pose as aliens from other galaxies. Perhaps the cattle mutilation phenomena also have something to do with all of this, but that's not what this book is about, so I'm not going to go there. My question is, could it be that when the Antichrist suffers his "mortal" wound, his evil spirit inhabits a biological "suit?" Maybe the suit looks like him, or maybe it doesn't. Either way, we know from Revelation 13 that the second beast, aka the false prophet, will require that everyone must worship the "image" of the first beast and take his mark or be killed. It seems to me that through modern-day technologies, coupled with the evil spiritual component of the beast, the world is finally ready for this 2000-year-old mystery to be solved in the very near future.

Verses 16-18

16 The Lord is King forever and ever; the nations have perished out of His land. 17 Lord, You have heard the desire of the humble; You will prepare their heart; You will cause Your ear to hear, 18 to do justice to the fatherless and the oppressed, that the man of the earth may oppress no more.

I promised a happy ending, and here it is. The conclusion of Psalm 10 sees the Lord as King, not only now, not only in the Millennial Kingdom, but forever into eternity! To achieve this happy ending, there must be justice for all of those who were oppressed, and the Antichrist kingdom must be defeated, and that is the conclusion of Psalm 10.

Additionally, we can be assured once again that this Psalm has been about the Antichrist, and his short-lived kingdom, because it also connects with the aftermath of the tribulation by affirming the demise of the nations of the earth who followed him into battle against the King of Kings and Lord of Lords. Many prophets have had something to say about this coming day. Here are two such verses, one verse by Isaiah and then a little more detail from John and the Book of Revelation:

Isaiah 63:6

6 I trampled the nations in my anger; in my wrath I made them drunk and poured their blood on the ground."

Revelation 19:19-21

19 And I saw the beast, the kings of the earth, and their armies, gathered together to make war against Him who sat on the horse and against His army. 20 Then the beast was captured, and with him the false prophet who worked signs in his presence, by which he deceived those who received the mark of the beast and those who worshiped his image. These two were cast alive into the lake of fire burning with brimstone. 21 And the rest were killed with the sword which proceeded from the mouth of Him who sat on the horse. And all the birds were filled with their flesh.

When you read verses 17 and 18 of Psalm 10, you are left with two questions, who is it referring to as the "humble," the "fatherless," and the "oppressed," and who is this "man of the earth?" I think we're pretty clear at this point about who the "man of the earth" might be since it's probably the same person who has been referenced throughout the Psalm, namely the Antichrist. I have heard that there are 33 different titles given for the Antichrist in the Old Testament, but I have been keeping my own list, and now I have a few more to add to it, namely, the "Rashah" or the "wicked man" and the "evil man," and now also more than likely, the "man of the earth." Keep in mind that the term "Antichrist" only appears in 1 John and 2 John in the New Testament, but the essence of this Rashah is understood through many other terms throughout the Bible, from Genesis 3:15 as the seed of the serpent, through Revelation 19:20 as the beast.

Here are a few more thoughts regarding the "man of the earth." Could this verse be referring to the false prophet, and not actually referring to the beast himself? After all, it's the false prophet who is given the power to cause the world to worship the image of the beast after his death and supposed resurrection. Also, we know from Revelation 13 that the second beast, the false prophet rises up specifically from the "earth," so is it a coincidence that verse 18 of Psalm 10 ends with a reference to the "man of the earth?"

The second thought that I have lingering in my mind about the "man of the earth" is in the context of him being possibly compared to fallen angelic beings who are "not of this earth." So, is the term "man of the earth" a comparative term designating him differently from others who may be prevalent at that time? With the trajectory of talking points in our government and news agencies regarding UFOs and UAPs, from absolute denial only a few years ago to public disclosure, and now stating that they constitute a national security threat, it seems obvious that this narrative will play a key role in the chaos still to come.

Back to the original question regarding verses 17 and 18, who are the "humble," the "fatherless," and the "oppressed?" The Hebrew word translated as "humble" in verse 17 is the plural version of "anav," which also means poor, afflicted, and meek. The Hebrew word translated as "fatherless" is "yathom," which also means orphan, and the Hebrew word translated as "oppressed" is from the root word "dak," which also means crushed and afflicted. In Psalm 9:9, we read that Yahweh will be a "refuge" for the oppressed in times of trouble.

Psalm 9:9
⁹The LORD also will be a refuge for the oppressed, a refuge in times of trouble.

I'm pretty sure by now we all understand that this is not only figurative, but will soon become literal when the oppressed remnant of Israel will flee to the refuge prepared for them by Yahweh in their time of trouble, as detailed in Matthew 24 and Revelation 12. However, with the addition of the "humble/meek," and the "fatherless/orphan," I would have to believe that the final two verses of Psalm 10 are not just indicative of the remnant, but also of all who remain have called on the name of Yeshua, and have, against all odds, resisted taking the mark of the beast for their short term survival. Revelation 13 tells us that it will be the false prophet, or second beast, who oppresses the world and forces them to take the mark.

Revelation 13:16-17
¹⁶He causes all, both small and great, rich and poor, free and slave, to receive a mark on their right hand or on their foreheads, ¹⁷and that no one may buy or sell except one who has the mark or the name of the beast, or the number of his name.

The false prophet will be the one responsible for oppressing the world by demanding that everyone must take this mark, which will almost certainly be biometric and probably vaccine-related. Based on current technology and the direction that the globalists have been pushing the world since even before the pandemic of 2020, it seems obvious that their goal is to create a system of total control and global surveillance, which will be no only external, but also internal, under your skin. This will be necessary to give the Antichrist and his puppet master the illusion of omniscience to mimic the power of God.

All of the technology already exists to fulfill these prophetic scriptures, from the internet, digital currencies, real-time biometric data, etc. And, the world has already been conditioned to bring about Revelation 13:16-17, which says that no one may buy or sell unless you have the mark. It wasn't that long ago that we were told that you couldn't buy, or sell, or even leave your home unless you had a digital passport on your phone indicating that you had been vaccinated. Phones can get lost, stolen, or broken. It only makes sense that the coming version of a digital passport will be biometric and implanted within your body. During the pandemic, every individual was oppressed supposedly for the good of the collective, according to government officials, who were all espousing the same narrative worldwide. They were able to use deception and fear to even turn neighbor against neighbor during a perceived time of crisis and chaos. I don't for a second believe that the world is finished with the crisis and chaos that began in 2020.

It may take on a different form, but unfortunately, it's only going to get worse from here, and resisting the system will get harder and harder over time until it will most assuredly cost you your life. That's why today is the day of salvation before the rapture of the Lord's Church. I believe that the rapture will be the ultimate spark that causes the world to be set ablaze with crisis and unimaginable chaos, allowing one man to step forward who can seemingly bring order out of the chaos. Everything that he needs to rule the world has already been developed; he just needs the right crisis to be able to rise to power. That crisis might just be the instantaneous disappearance of millions of people around the world. For those who disappear, it will be an escape from what's to come, according to Luke 21:36, but for those who will be left, it will be a trap that you can't get out of (Luke 21:34-35). Don't get caught in that trap, call out to Jesus today because time is very short!

Psalm 15

Before studying Psalm 15, I knew that if the timeline revelation was correct, I had to expect that Psalm 15 would be a conclusion to Psalm 5, and Psalm 10. Mathematically, Psalm 15 is the sum of the other 2 Psalms, Psalm 5 and Psalm 10. As such, if God was in control of the sequence and numbering of these Psalms, It would make sense for Psalm 15 to carry the symbolism of the final step in the 15 steps of the ascension up to the temple at the Feast of Tabernacles. That final step is the one that brings the sojourner from the outer court into the inner court, and closest to the presence of God. It represents the passing from the material to the spiritual just like the 15 Psalms of Ascent represent the journey through the birth pains and the tribulation, and then into the presence of God. Put another way, if Psalm 5 was about the Lord leading the remnant through the tribulation, and Psalm 10 was about the enemy of the remnant during the tribulation, then Psalm 15 would certainly have to be about what comes next, which would be about those survivors who will live with the Lord into the Millennial Kingdom. Remember that in John 14, Jesus promised us *that where I am, you will be also.* Even though Psalm 15 is a short Psalm, I was not at all disappointed.

Verses 1
¹Lord, who may abide in Your tabernacle? Who may dwell in Your holy hill?

Just like the conclusion of the 15 Psalms of Ascent, as well as the conclusion of the 12 Psalms of Asaph, which ends with Psalm 83, but is then capped by Psalm 84, we once again have a theme that includes people abiding in the Tabernacle. The Hebrew root word that has been translated as tabernacle is "ohel," which is specifically a tent and not a constructed temple. This makes sense considering that this Psalm was written by King David, who had placed the Ark of the Covenant in a tent. As we know, it was his son Solomon whom God allowed to build the first Temple in Jerusalem. It also makes sense that it's a tent in the timeline revelation. Similar to what has been revealed in Psalm 132, there will be no Temple built in Jerusalem at the very beginning of the Millennial Kingdom in 2032. As shocking as it may seem, Jesus is working out a pattern, and yes, He could simply speak a new Temple into existence, but He clearly doesn't work that way. Why would He give us a written blue-print of the Millennial Temple in Ezekiel 40 - 48 if He was going to make a new one appear out of thin air? And, if that were the case, what would man have to do with it? The idea that mankind will be sitting on clouds strumming harps for an eternity simply isn't biblical. There's work to be done!

Verses 2-5
2 He who walks uprightly, and works righteousness, and speaks the truth in his heart; 3 he who does not backbite with his tongue, nor does evil to his neighbor, nor does he take up a reproach against his friend; 4 in whose eyes a vile person is despised, but he honors those who fear the LORD; he who swears to his own hurt and does not change; 5 he who does not put out his money at usury, nor does he take a bribe against the innocent. He who does these things shall never be moved.

In verse 1, David asks the Lord, who may inhabit the Tabernacle and the holy hill of Zion? Verses 2 - 5 constitute the response to his question. Just as Ezekiel chapters 40 - 48 make up a written blue-print of the future Millennial Kingdom Temple, it appears that Psalm 15 verses 2 - 5 gives us a short job description of those future servants who will inhabit the Tabernacle, and then also the Temple on the holy hill with the Lord.

I believe that it goes without saying that those of us who will be raptured, along with those who will be resurrected, will forever be with the Lord based on 1 Thessalonians.

1 Thessalonians 17
17 Then we who are alive and remain shall be caught up together with them in the clouds to meet the Lord in the air. And thus we shall always be with the Lord.

Based on that understanding, verses 2 - 5 cannot describe the state of the "transformed" of which Jesus was the first fruits. We will have already put off our corruptible bodies, and put on our incorruptible bodies according to 1 Corinthians 15, so the job description for those who may abide in the Tabernacle, and dwell on the holy hill that is given in verses 2 - 5 must be for mortal men.

1 Corinthians 15:52-54

[52] in a moment, in the twinkling of an eye, at the last trumpet. For the trumpet will sound, and the dead will be raised incorruptible, and we shall be changed. [53] For this corruptible must put on incorruption, and this mortal must put on immortality. [54] So when this corruptible has put on incorruption, and this mortal has put on immortality, then shall be brought to pass the saying that is written: "Death is swallowed up in victory."

As incorruptible, sin will no longer plague us. Therefore, this job description surely doesn't apply to us who know no sin and are no longer corruptible, but to those who will still be alive in the Kingdom and will still be in the flesh, and can still choose between righteousness and sin.

You will notice from verses 2 - 5 that this job description is all about character, and not about a person's resume of "works." These 4 verses should also be a model for our lives here and now since they sum up the godly attributes of a person's heart, which is exactly what God is looking for in each of us. Such a heart is fertile ground, out of which an abundance of good fruit can grow. As we know, bearing good fruit is what we are called to do while we await the soon coming of our Lord.

If verses 2 - 5 constitute a job description for the future priests at the coming Millennial Tabernacle, followed by the new Temple, then Ezekiel 40 - 48 tells us who will be hired for the job. According to Ezekiel, the candidates will be from the sons of Zadok.

Ezekiel 40:45-46

45 Then he said to me, "This chamber which faces south is for the priests who have charge of the temple. 46 The chamber which faces north is for the priests who have charge of the altar; these are the sons of Zadok, from the sons of Levi, who come near the LORD to minister to Him."

It was the priestly Levitical line of Zadok who did not fall into sin, as did all of the other Levitical lines. Zadok, who was a descendant of Aaron, was the high priest during the reigns of King David, and his son King Solomon. The descendants of Zadok became known as the Zadok priests, who also became the leaders of the Essenes from whom we have the Dead Sea Scrolls. To summarize hundreds of years of history, the remaining priests who weren't from the line of Zadok became the group we know of through the New Testament as the Sadducees. It was the Sadducees, along with the Pharisees, who were constantly at odds with Jesus and his teachings 2000 years ago.

As a reward for their faithfulness to the Lord, the Zadok priests will even be given a special district in which to live in the Millennial Kingdom. Their special land allotment will have the "sanctuary of the Lord" in the center of it. The Zadok priests and their families will literally surround the holy Tabernacle and then the new Temple during the Kingdom, according to Ezekiel 48.

Ezekiel 48:9-12

9 "The district that you shall set apart for the LORD shall be twenty-five thousand cubits in length and ten thousand in width. 10 To these—to the priests—the holy district shall belong: on the north twenty-five thousand cubits in length, on the west ten thousand in width, on the east ten thousand in width, and on the south twenty-five thousand in length. The sanctuary of the LORD shall be in the center. 11 It shall be for the priests of the sons of Zadok, who are sanctified, who have kept My charge, who did not go astray when the children of Israel went astray, as the Levites went astray.

*¹² And this district of land that is set apart shall be to them
a thing most holy by the border of the Levites.*

So, all of the Temple positions for priests will be apparently filled
by the Zadok priesthood, and what lower level positions will be left will
be filled by the remaining Levitical priestly lines, according to Ezekiel.
Those other priestly lines, who had formerly followed the children
of Israel into sin, and into the worship of other gods, will serve only
as gatekeepers, slayers of the sacrifices and ministers to the people,
according to Ezekiel 44. So, what positions will be left open for all of
us regular folks? Worshipers! But don't expect to come into the Lord's
presence to worship if you do not meet the qualifications set forth in
Psalm 15:2-5 or in Ezekiel 44.

Ezekiel 44:6-9

*⁶ "Now say to the rebellious, to the house of Israel, 'Thus
says the Lord GOD: "O house of Israel, let Us have no more
of all your abominations. ⁷ When you brought in foreigners,
uncircumcised in heart and uncircumcised in flesh, to be
in My sanctuary to defile it—My house—and when you
offered My food, the fat and the blood, then they broke
My covenant because of all your abominations. ⁸ And you
have not kept charge of My holy things, but you have set
others to keep charge of My sanctuary for you." ⁹ Thus says
the Lord GOD: "No foreigner, uncircumcised in heart or
uncircumcised in flesh, shall enter My sanctuary, including
any foreigner who is among the children of Israel.*

According to Ezekiel as well as other prophets, the sacrificial system
will be reinstated in the Millennial Kingdom, and circumcision will
continue to be practiced. It is also apparent that there will still be those
who rebel against the Lord's authority during the 1000-year reign of
Christ, which ends with a mass rebellion when Satan is released for a
short time, according to Revelation 20. All of this brings up a question
in my mind. Are the sacrifices reinstated to provide atonement for the

sins of those living in the Millennial Kingdom, or are they a visual reminder of the Lord's ultimate sacrifice at Calvary 2000 years ago? I believe that the sacrifices that will be offered in the Kingdom represent a lesson of the consequence of sin. The wages of sin will still be death. I believe that Jesus' sacrifice, as a man, was the only sacrifice that could fully remove sins once and for all from mankind. The blood of animals simply covered up those sins, and no amount of animals sacrificed could equal a human's worth, especially the worth of the Son of God.

Ok, we know that most of the jobs have already been filled at the tabernacle and later in the newly built temple of the Lord. The Zadok priests will fulfill their occupational calling, the other priestly Levitical lines will have their predetermined jobs, and we even know that there is a sort of job description of righteousness listed in Psalm 15 and Ezekiel 44 for those who come to worship the Lord during the Millennium. However, there is one more position that still needs to be filled - Singers!

Ezekiel 40:44
[44] *Outside the inner gate were the chambers for the singers in the inner court, one facing south at the side of the northern gateway, and the other facing north at the side of the southern gateway.*

If, according to Ezekiel 40, there is a special chamber for singers at the new temple, then there must also be singers! That's good news for my wife Tammy, who was a professional Christian singer for many years. I'm pretty sure that she would be on the shortlist of applicants. However, I'm also pretty sure that I will be passed over for that job since, as they say, I "can't carry a tune in a bucket." I even have to lip-sync at church so that I don't offend anyone nearby during worship. My only hope is that when I receive my "glorified" body at the rapture/resurrection that I will have a new singing voice to go with my new six-pack abs! I guess we'll have to wait and see...

I thought it would be a good idea to end this short prophetic study on Psalm 15 with two fascinating accounts of Jerusalem, the temple, and the drastic changes that will take place in that area during the Kingdom. Both Isaiah and Micah have very similar things to say about this coming age, which gives us an extra prophetic glimpse into that time, which I believe is fast approaching.

Isaiah 2:1-4

¹ The word that Isaiah the son of Amoz saw concerning Judah and Jerusalem. ² Now it shall come to pass in the latter days that the mountain of the LORD's house shall be established on the top of the mountains, and shall be exalted above the hills; and all nations shall flow to it. ³ Many people shall come and say, "Come, and let us go up to the mountain of the LORD, to the house of the God of Jacob; He will teach us His ways, and we shall walk in His paths." For out of Zion shall go forth the law, and the word of the LORD from Jerusalem. ⁴ He shall judge between the nations, and rebuke many people; they shall beat their swords into plowshares, and their spears into pruning hooks; nation shall not lift up sword against nation, neither shall they learn war anymore.

Micah 4:1-5

¹ Now it shall come to pass in the latter days that the mountain of the LORD's house shall be established on the top of the mountains, and shall be exalted above the hills; and peoples shall flow to it. ² Many nations shall come and say,

"Come, and let us go up to the mountain of the LORD, to the house of the God of Jacob; He will teach us His ways, and we shall walk in His paths." For out of Zion the law shall go forth, and the word of the LORD from Jerusalem. ³ He shall judge between many peoples, and rebuke strong nations afar off; they shall beat their swords into plowshares, and their spears into pruning hooks;

nation shall not lift up sword against nation, neither shall they learn war anymore.

[4] But everyone shall sit under his vine and under his fig tree, and no one shall make them afraid; for the mouth of the LORD of hosts has spoken. [5] For all people walk each in the name of his god, but we will walk in the name of the LORD our God forever and ever.

CHAPTER 38

Both "Witnesses" Combined

The full Timeline Revelation can be seen when you compare both sets (witnesses) of Psalms overlapping each other. I use the word "overlapping" loosely because they do not fully overlap each other. If they did, they would just be repeats of each other. How they correlate with each other is actually even better. They fit in between each other, sort of like when you put your hands together and intertwine your fingers. The pattern that I see when I chart this by putting the prophecies from the chapters of the Psalms of Ascent together with the Psalms of Asaph is that since the Psalms of Ascent are based on the Gregorian calendar years, then in between two chapters of the Psalms of Ascents, you can loosely place the corresponding Psalm of Asaph. That's a lot of words, and maybe I made it more confusing than it actually is. For example, it seems that Psalm 77, which is a Psalm of Asaph, fits in between Psalm 125 and 126, both of which are Psalms of Ascent. There is some carryover between them also, which is helpful in proving the validity of the pattern. I believe that the overlap, or "like themes" found within some of the corresponding Psalms, are also there to act sort of as road markers, or landmarks. So when you see the same event encoded within a Psalm of Ascent as well as in a Psalm of Asaph, you know that the years overlap at that point, and that the event may mark the spot of the overlap.

Believe it or not, when I was in high school, I didn't like to read much at all, especially on subjects that I didn't care anything about. As was typical at most high schools in the 80's, I was supposed to read books like *To Kill a Mockingbird* and *The Grapes of Wrath*, but I never even considered actually reading any of those books. I was much too interested in cars, girls, and other things that were actually fun. To me, back then, spending any amount of time reading those old books would have been a complete waste of my precious time. So, my go-to, get out of reading free card, or almost free, was to just read the *Cliffs Notes* a night before the big test. Granted, I understood that choosing that route was never going to earn me an "A" in the class, but I was ok with that. If it meant that I could goof off as much as possible, I was willing to accept any grade above an "F." However, I'm pretty sure my teachers figured this trick out long before I arrived, so they asked very specific questions on their tests that they knew weren't covered in the *Cliffs Notes*. It seemed that they had read them also. Well, at least I passed anyway.

Because of my love for brevity in reading, which may not come across in my writing, this may be my favorite chapter of the book. It's sort of the *Cliff's Notes* version of my own book, inside of my own book. It's actually going to be more than that, and I will add to the evidence already described in the other chapters so that it's not simply redundant. I'm sorry to say that to get the complete picture of each of the prophetic years in the timeline revelation; you'll want to suck it up and read the entire book.

This is also the chapter where I will be adding in more of my own speculation and conjecture about prophetic events yet to come. These speculations may or may not be accurate, but at least I believe that they will help us to open our minds a little, and maybe look at events in the prophetic future in a new way based on current events and the encrypted timeline revelation in the Psalms.

If you recall, I have mentioned several times that the Psalms are timeless, and that the wisdom that God placed within them is also timeless. They are not just a random collection of hymns, but a perfectly placed guide for life, worship, righteousness, faith, prayer, instruction, history, and prophecy. Some of the prophetic treasures hidden in the Psalms were already uncovered for us by Jesus Himself. For example, Jesus said in Luke 24, just before His ascension to the Father, that He came to fulfill all things that were written about Him in the Law, the Prophets, and the **Psalms**.

Luke 24:44

⁴⁴Then He said to them, "These are the words which I spoke to you while I was still with you, that all things must be fulfilled which were written in the Law of Moses and the Prophets and the Psalms concerning Me."

Consider that at Jesus' death on the cross, He fulfilled what was written about Him in Psalm 22, which begins with the question, *"My God, My God, why have You forsaken Me?"* As we know, Jesus fulfilled these words by speaking them on the cross before He died. Consider also that no one could have known that these words were prophetic of the Messiah's death prior to the day when they heard Jesus speak them on the cross. At that time, a light bulb must have illuminated in the disciples' minds since they knew that they had heard those same words before in the Psalms. Matthew writes in Matthew 27:46, *"And about the ninth hour Jesus cried out with a loud voice, saying, Eli, Eli, lama sabachthani? That is, My God, My God, why have You forsaken Me?"* Afterward, Matthew pointed these words out specifically, and even in Hebrew, which is probably how they would have studied the Psalms, because he then understood that it was a prophecy fulfilled.

So, the very words that Jesus would speak at His death were encrypted in the Psalms long before His first coming. That's amazing! That's just one example, and we know that there are many more prophesies in the Bible regarding His second coming than there were about His first. It stands to reason then that there would be many more second-coming prophesies also encoded in the Psalms, we just couldn't see them, just as no one could see that Psalm 22 verse 1 would be the very words spoken by the Messiah at His death prior to that day. However, our benefit today is that Jesus broke the code for us. By revealing Himself in the Psalms at His first coming, and even stating it in Luke 24, He shined a light on the Psalms for us so that we could find many of His encrypted hidden prophetic treasures that He buried within them. All we needed was a little push in the right direction, which is where the "5 and 10" came in, and an understanding of prophetic patterns, and that He used keywords, phrases, numbers, and images within the Psalms to ingeniously connect them to other prophetic scriptures, thereby revealing His timeline. If that is confusing, hang in there! I think it will be more understandable as we progress through the timeline encoded in both sets of Psalms.

Here is what I found when I studied the 15 Songs of Ascent together with the 12 Psalms of Asaph in the context of the encrypted timeline revelation. Again, I'm also adding my own 2 cents worth of speculation based on the current trajectory of the world compared to Bible prophecy. Since these events are close at hand in 2023, they are easier to understand than ever before. Daniel did say that "knowledge would increase" (Daniel 12:4), so we certainly should have understood that as we approach "the day," the things that were but fuzzy images in our minds even a few years ago, would start to become much clearer and sharper as we race toward the end. I will make sure to say "I believe" before any of my opinions so that you will know that what I'm saying isn't necessarily exactly how things will play out, just my educated guess based on prophecy, the current world trajectory, and the timeline revelation.

A few last notes, keep in mind that there are 15 consecutive Psalms of Ascent, but only 11 consecutive Psalms of Asaph, so there isn't a 1 to 1 relationship between them. All of these Psalms are Israel-centric. Also, keep in mind that they seem to correspond to two different calendars, the Psalms of Ascent with the Gregorian calendar, and the Psalms of Asaph with the Jewish Religious calendar. Now, let's get started...

Year: 1998/1999 as Seen Through the Lens of Psalm 50

The Building of the Antichrist

I'm going to be super controversial right from the start on this one! If you add 50 years to Israel's re-birth date, you arrive at sometime around 1998/1999, depending on the calendar that you use. I believe that was the timeframe when the Antichrist was born.

Remember that there are 6 "Antichrist" verses in Psalm 50, and that Psalm 50 is primarily an inverted view of the tribulation period. Doesn't it make sense that God would encode this Psalm in this manner? After all, it is said that Satanism is the inversion of Christian beliefs and values. Even the term "antichrist" means an "inversion," or "opposite to" Christ, as well as "opposed to" Christ. That's why our world seems upside down in these last days; what is good is now bad, and what is right is now wrong. We were forewarned about this thousands of years ago in Isaiah 5:20.

Isaiah 5:20
20 Woe to those who call evil good, and good evil; who put darkness for light, and light for darkness; who put bitter for sweet, and sweet for bitter!

Doesn't it seem that the inverted Satanic agenda of the Antichrist has been alive and well over the last few decades? Since the turn of the century, we've watched our world spiral out of control and into sin, chaos, and calamity. During that same time, we've also witnessed the rise of the technocratic state as an unelected technological overlord, watching every move we make in preparation for the inevitable handover of power and control to the coming Antichrist. But be encouraged; this is why God gave us Bible prophesy, so that we would be warned, and so that we could understand that we need to be watching and waiting, be prepared, and most importantly, prepare others by leading them to Christ.

In the 6 Antichrist verses in Psalm 50, he is called the "Evildoer." We can add that perfect one-word description to our list of Antichrist terms. Doing evil is his ultimate mission in rebellion against God with the intent of pulling the entire world into this same evil along with him. Those who will not go along, who will not reject the true and living God, will have to be destroyed so that there will be none left who will cry out to God for salvation. That's his plan anyway.

So, could it be that the Antichrist was born in 1998/1999? The problem with this theory of mine is that if he was born in, let's say 1999, he would be 1 year old in the year 2000 and would then be 30 years old in 2029. According to the Songs of Ascent, the midpoint of the tribulation would be in 2028/2029 before Israel turns 81 years old, so my theory seems to be about a year off. Here's the simplified math: Israel was re-born in 1948/1949, depending on which Jewish calendar you follow. Add to that 50 years (Psalm 50) and you arrive at 1998/1999. Add to that another 30 years, for a total of 80 years, and you arrive at 2028/2029. We know that Israel has never survived more than 80 years, which also brings us to this same time on the timeline. As of this week in which I am writing, Israel turned 75 years old. That gives me chills!

My expectation is that the false messiah should be 30 years old when he declares that he is god at the midpoint of the tribulation. You may be wondering why he needs to be 30 years old when he declares that he is god. You may also be thinking, "that sounds really young?" I believe that most people have an older, more "statesman" appearing antichrist in mind. However, that doesn't align with the prophetic messianic patters given to us in the Bible or through other historical texts.

There is a clear Biblical pattern of "messianic" type rulers who all came to power at the age of 30. Remember that Jesus, the real Messiah, was 30 years old when He began His ministry. Was that a coincidence? David was 30 years old when he became king over Israel, and Joseph was 30 years old when he became ruler of Egypt under Pharaoh; he was the ruler over all of the known nations at that time since they were all starving, and only through Joseph could they be saved. In addition, the one real "Antichrist" figure from ancient Babylonian history who established a "one world government" similar to the coming world dominated by another Babylon prophesied in Revelation was Nimrod himself. According to ancient (non-Biblical) Jewish writings, he too, became ruler at the age of 30.

The number 30 is also further associated with the Antichrist and Judas Iscariot, whom Satan entered when he betrayed Jesus. Both are seen in Zechariah 11. Remember that it was for 30 pieces of silver that Judas betrayed his Teacher. It was for 20 pieces of silver that the sons of Israel betrayed their brother Joseph (30 + 20 = 50). Coincidence?

Zechariah 11:12

[12] Then I said to them, "If it is agreeable to you, give me my wages; and if not, refrain." So they weighed out for my wages thirty pieces of silver.

Zechariah 11:15-17

[15] And the LORD said to me, "Next, take for yourself the implements of a foolish shepherd. [16] For indeed I will raise up a shepherd in the land who will not care for those who are cut off, nor seek the young, nor heal those that are broken, nor feed those that still stand. But he will eat the flesh of the fat and tear their hooves in pieces.

[17] "Woe to the worthless shepherd, who leaves the flock! A sword shall be against his arm and against his right eye; his arm shall completely wither, and his right eye shall be totally blinded."

In addition to the messianic pattern of being 30 years old, which also fits, at least loosely, within the timeline, I also have a few more messianic mimicking expectations of the coming "Evildoer." Since the coming false messiah will be a complete counterfeit of the real Messiah, Jesus, it would make sense that he was also born under a sign in the heavens similar to Jesus. After all, we know from Genesis 1:14 that God placed the lights in the sky for "signs" and seasons. So, was there a sign in the heavens around the 1998/1999 time frame? Well, of course, there was!

In 1999, there was a full solar eclipse over Europe on August 11th, which happens to be right around the time of Tisha B'Av that year. Tisha B'Av was the notorious day on Israel's calendar when both temples were destroyed, and many other terrible things happened to the children of Israel on that same day throughout history. The solar eclipse of that year passed over parts of England, France, Hungary, Germany, Austria, Romania, and Turkey. The epicenter was in Romania. Of course, we know that the prophet Daniel seems to indicate that the Antichrist will come from what many prophecy teachers call the "revised Roman Empire." Hmm, Romania, named after the Roman Empire (meaning: citizen of the Roman Empire)? What an interesting epicenter! It must be just a coincidence, I'm sure.

Remember that Psalm 50 was the missing "Dan" or "Judas" of the 12 Psalms of Asaph. So, it's the symbol of the Antichrist and a warning to Israel. The remaining 11 Psalms of Asaph start at Psalm 73, which is 23 Psalms later. Coincidentally, according to the timeline revelation, from Israel's 50th birthday, there are 23 years before the season of tribulation begins, which we are already in. Don't take that the wrong way, we're in the season, the birth pangs if you will, but we're not in the 7-year tribulation yet as of 2023. Also, coincidentally, I'm sure; Psalm 50 has 23 verses as well. Actually, I don't think any of this is a coincidence. In fact, I believe that it's really obvious that God wants us to notice the number 23 here for a greater understanding, and to help us to better connect the prophetic puzzle pieces.

As I have previously pointed out, the number 23 in the Bible and in the Hebrew custom stands for immorality, stubbornness, grumbling, complaining, wickedness, and idolatry. This understanding of the number 23 comes from Jeremiah 25:3 and 1 Corinthians 10:6-10, among other scriptures. It can also be said that 23 is the sum of 12 and 11. Of course, we know that 12 represents a perfect and divine government or society (12 tribes, 12 disciples), and God's perfect measurement of time (twelve months, 12 hours of daylight). However, the number 11 represents a false or incomplete government or society, judgment, disorder, betrayal, idolatry, lack of faith, and the spirit of the Antichrist. Remember that the Antichrist is also the 11th horn, according to Daniel 7. So combined, the number 23 represents a choice between the true Messiah and the false messiah, between good and evil, and between heaven and hell. Perhaps it has been a final 23-year wake-up call for Israel and the world to choose wisely.

The Nimrod Connection

I have already mentioned Nimrod earlier in connection with the Antichrist, but is there more to the Nimrod connection?

Here's where I put on my tin foil hat and try to connect some puzzle pieces through historical means as well as the trajectory of the world in which we live. Hang on, because it might get a little crazy! This part is all speculation, but just might possibly prove to be true over time. I have already stated in previous chapters that the modern religious Jewish Rabbis will not even consider accepting a messiah who isn't from the line of David. One of his primary accomplishments will be to re-establish the Davidic Dynasty according to their writings. I have also established that there is a likelihood that he will also be from the seed of Dan based on several prophetic patterns found in the Bible, as well as the fact that the tribe of Dan took up residence in Europe as well as all over the globe. So, if the Antichrist has to be at least, in part, from the seed of David, will more than likely also be from the seed of Dan, where does Nimrod come in?

It is understood, or at least surmised by some historians, that Nimrod is also known as Gilgamesh in other ancient writings and Osiris in others. It is at least probable that the same ancient character is known under different names in different cultures, which makes sense because he was the king of Babylon who oversaw the construction of the Tower of Babel, causing God to divide the people's tongues into 70 different languages. From there, the people were scattered over the earth, and each of the 70 groups would have remembered the king, the builder of Babylon, under a new name in their new language. It's obvious that over time, those different cultures ascribed to him various additional stories, but the essence of the person remains the same. According to the *Epic of Gilgamesh,* which are the written adventures of Gilgamesh inscribed on a set of 12 clay tablets dating to around 2000 years BC, he was two-thirds god, and one-third human. That makes him a hybrid. Based on the Genesis 6 account, the Book of Enoch, as well as other historical texts, we can be certain that the "gods" of the old world were in fact, the fallen angels and their hybrid Nephilim offspring known as giants, mighty men, and men of renown. Doesn't that sound like it connects to Daniel chapter 2 where Daniel speaks of "they" of the final kingdom who will mingle with the seed of man?

Daniel 2:43

[43] As you saw iron mixed with ceramic clay, they will mingle with the seed of men; but they will not adhere to one another, just as iron does not mix with clay.

I believe we have been forewarned that the hybrids are coming back in the last days. I also believe that the Antichrist is a hybrid. In fact, Paul calls the Antichrist the "lawless one" in 2 Thessalonians 2. Thousands of years before Paul wrote to the Thessalonians about the Antichrist, Enoch called the hybrids of his days the "lawless ones" in Enoch chapter 7. Can that be just a coincidence?

Furthermore, every ancient civilization from the Sumerians, Babylonians, Egyptians, Greeks, Romans, and Native Americans, among others, all tell of the same stories of gods coming down from the heavens, mixing with humans, and creating hybrid gods. In addition, they left behind proof of their existence through architecture around the world that even modern man, with all of our technology, simply cannot replicate or explain.

For centuries, Christianity has been very silent about these topics, even though it's only through the Bible that these ancient gods and hybrids can be explained. Modern man calls these tales from ancient civilizations, as well as from the Bible, myths, fables, and fairytales. I might add that Satan has tried, with some degree of success, to hide the truth behind bogus theories and hyper-spiritualization of the biblical text, but it is a central theme interwoven throughout the Bible from Genesis to Revelation. You just have to open your eyes and connect some of the puzzle pieces that God gave us in His word so that you can see it. These hybrid beings mentioned in Genesis 6, and elsewhere in the Bible weren't a metaphor for something else, and they weren't the offspring of Cain intermarrying with the daughters of Seth. They were exactly what the Word of God says they were in Genesis 6. They were giants, who were the hybrid offspring of fallen angels who came down to earth and married women. You may say, "but angles can't have sex because Matthew 22 says they can't."

Matthew 22:30
30 For in the resurrection they neither marry nor are given in marriage, but are like angels of God in heaven.

Actually, Matthew 22 doesn't say that angels can't marry or even have sex on earth. It only says that they don't do that "in heaven." I believe that to correctly divide the word, it is prudent to pay attention to what the text isn't saying, as well as what it is saying, and not read more into it than it actually says unless there is a pattern at work, or interconnecting words, phrases, or imagery that clearly links it with other passages that help to build a better understanding. Think about it, Matthew 22 could have simply stated, "but are like angels of God." Why did Jesus add "in heaven?" I believe every word that Jesus spoke was important, so if He added "in heaven," it was for a reason.

The Book of Enoch gives a more detailed and graphic account of the Genesis 6 narrative on the topic of the fall of some angels who took wives from among humans, and had relations with them, which then produced the hybrids the Bible refers to as Nephilim, Rephaim, Anakim, and so on. I'm not going to go into any of the dirty details from Enoch, but if you think about it, the fact that angels were tempted by the beautiful earth-women that they saw makes sense. We know that at least one-third of the angels fell at some time in the distant past. That means that they aren't perfect beings, and that they too, have choices to make and temptations to overcome. Just like us, it is clear that God also gave them free will to love Him, and obey Him, or to follow their own desires. Otherwise, they would simply be like robots, programmed to love and follow God, and that's not real love or obedience at all. So, to put it in simple terms, perhaps God gave them abilities as a test to separate the good from the bad.

It is important to know and understand that Satan and the other fallen angels have been trying to mix their seed with the seed of mankind for a very long time, and I don't expect that to end until Jesus comes back. Keep in mind that this is a strategy in a war that has been waging for millennia, and prophesied all the way back in Genesis 3:15.

Genesis 3:15
¹⁵ And I will put enmity between you and the woman, and between your seed and her Seed; He shall bruise your head, and you shall bruise His heel."

The "you" that God is speaking of is Satan himself. Apparently, according to Genesis 3:15, Satan has "seed" and can have offspring no different than the other angels who fell and mated with women from earth. I believe that Satan's offspring, literally from his own seed, is none other than the final Antichrist. I do not know how exactly this happens, but by many prophetic indications in the Word, the Antichrist will be more than a normal human and a narcissist who rebels against God. I believe that he will know that he is from the stock of the fallen one, the "god of this world," and that's why he will believe, and declare that he has the right to be called god over all other gods and to be worshiped as God. Paul discusses this "man of sin," "son of perdition," in 2 Thessalonians who exalts himself above God. In his second letter to the Corinthians, he also points out who the "god of this world" is, who blinds the world to the truth of who Jesus is.

2 Thessalonians 2:3-4
³ Let no one deceive you by any means; for that Day will not come unless the falling away comes first, and the man of sin is revealed, the son of perdition, ⁴ who opposes and exalts himself above all that is called God or that is worshiped, so that he sits as God in the temple of God, showing himself that he is God.

2 Corinthians 4:4
*⁴ whose unbelieving minds the **god of this world** hath blinded, lest the light of the glorious Gospel of Christ, who is the image of God, should shine unto them.*

As you can see from 2 Corinthians 4, another part of Satan's war strategy is spiritual blindness and deception. Remember that deception is also the key element in the tribulation, as Jesus Himself revealed in His Olivet Discourse. So, in the time of the tribulation, those who are still here should not believe anything that they see or hear unless it aligns with the word of God.

So, Bible prophecy has established the likelihood that the Antichrist will be a hybrid man, the seed of Satan himself, and Bible history has established a pattern of Nephilim on earth both before and after Noah's flood.

Genesis 6:4
*⁴ There were giants (Nephilim) on the earth **in those days, and also afterward**, when the sons of God came in to the daughters of men and they bore children to them. Those were the mighty men who were of old, men of renown.*

Jesus said that the last days would be like the days of Noah in Matthew 24. Obviously, He was referring to the wickedness that would be upon the earth in the last days, just as it was in the days of Noah. But, was He saying more than that? I believe that He was absolutely saying more with that statement than what is on the surface. His statement connects with the rapture, the fallen angels, and the Nephilim. In my opinion, it also connects the remaining 120 years that God gave them before the flood to the 120th Psalm through a numerical pattern. Of course, Psalm 120 is the first Psalm of Ascent.

Genesis 6:3
*³ And the LORD said, "My Spirit shall not strive with man forever, for he is indeed flesh; yet his days shall be **one hundred and twenty years**."*

Exactly how all of this plays out, I do not know. According to Revelation 12, Satan and his angels will be cast out of the heavenly realm and down to earth.

Revelation 12:7-9

[7] Then war broke out in heaven. Michael and his angels fought against the dragon, and the dragon and his angels fought back. [8] But he was not strong enough, and they lost their place in heaven. [9] The great dragon was hurled down—that ancient serpent called the devil, or Satan, who leads the whole world astray. He was hurled to the earth, and his angels with him.

It appears to me that the tribulation period will be such a time of chaos and upheaval that people aren't going to know what to expect from one day to the next. Between the judgments of God being poured out on the earth, the deception of the Nephilim hybrids, the hybrid Antichrist, and then quite possibly fallen angels appearing from the heavens, I fully believe that men's hearts will fail them because of what is coming on the earth just as Jesus said.

Luke 21:26

[26] men's hearts failing them from fear and the expectation of those things which are coming on the earth, for the powers of the heavens will be shaken.

I believe that the Nephilim hybrids are already among us and are quite possibly in high places. I also believe that when the fallen angels appear, they will deceive most of the world. I'm almost certain they will proclaim that they are gods from another galaxy who seeded us here on earth a long time ago. This coming to earth of the gods matches history and, as a prophetic pattern, matches what is yet to come. It also matches the writings of past New Age channelers as well as the current trajectory of our government's slow release of previously classified UFO documents. They went from saying that there was no such thing for around 70 years to openly stating that they are real, and that they pose a national security threat. As you know, we have been flooded with movies carrying this same theme for decades now. The people of the world have certainly been pre-conditioned for decades to accept what will soon be coming on the earth. But even with all of the conditioning through the various forms of media that we consume, many will still not be prepared for what is coming once they see it. They will be willing to accept any narrative that they are offered to find some peace within themselves. But there won't be any peace.

I would like to turn our attention back to Nimrod (Babylonian), aka Gilgamesh (Sumerian), aka Osiris (Egyptian), who was possibly a hybrid himself. Many times, these hybrids were called "gibborim" in the Hebrew Bible. Gibborim means "mighty men." This term wasn't exclusively applied to the hybrids since other human warriors were also termed as gibborim occasionally in the Bible, but in general, it is associated with the hybrid Nephilim. Remember that Genesis 10 states that Nimrod, whose name is associated with rebellion, became a "mighty one," aka "gibbor," which is the singular version of gibborim. I always thought that God used an interesting choice of words in Genesis 10:8 when He said that Nimrod "became" or "began to be" a gibbor. "Became" could imply a back-story complete with a strict regimen of diet and exercise, along with military and weapons training, but I don't think that's what is being relayed in the text. Considering the genetic tampering, both pre-flood and post-flood, that we know about from Genesis 6, and from the Book of Enoch, it stands to reason that Nimrod somehow "became" a hybrid gibbor through genetic means.

How could that happen you might ask? According to the Bible, as well as other ancient Jewish texts, Nimrod was the first world ruler who united the people in defiance of God. Nimrod was the son of Cush, who was the son of Ham, who was the son of Noah. Interestingly, but not certain, according to ancient tradition, Ham was the first person to summon the help of a demon after the great flood. The Egyptians who enslaved the Hebrews were also descendants of Ham, as well as the Canaanites who possessed the land which God gave to Israel. It just so happens that there were giants, "Nephilim," living in the land of Canaan when the Israelites arrived according to Numbers 13. This is why "10" of the 12 spies that Moses sent into the land gave a bad report after scouting out the land for "40" days. It was only Joshua and Caleb who proclaimed that they could take the land. Wow, 10 faithless

Israelite spies were gone for 40 days and saw hybrid giants in the land (10 + 40 = 50). Remember that God connects prophetic patterns many times through the use of numbers. So, was Nimrod a giant hybrid Nephilim? There's no way to say for sure, but as you can see, there are several connections that can be made that suggest that he was.

You may be wondering, who cares? What does Nimrod, an old dead guy, have to do with anything today, or in the tribulation?" Remember that an angel described the "beast," aka Antichrist, to John in Revelation 17 in a very strange way:

Revelation 17:8
[8] *The beast, which you saw, **once was, now is not, and yet will come up out of the Abyss** and go to its destruction.*

In my humble opinion, he's describing a well-known character from the Bible who once lived, then died, and will come again. This "beast" of Revelation 17 is directly connected with the Babylon of the tribulation period, also spoken of in Revelation 17. The question is then, which historical biblical characters are associated with world rule from Babylon, and who might *"come up out of the Abyss"* and return? We can narrow that down to two individuals, Nimrod and Nebuchadnezzar. Personally, I believe that Nebuchadnezzar's story in Daniel obviously connects with many aspects of the 7-year tribulation period; however, he himself revealed in Daniel 4 that he became a believer and worshiper of the one true God after 7 years of being a "beast."

Daniel 4:37
[37] *Now I, Nebuchadnezzar, praise and exalt and glorify the King of heaven, because everything he does is right and all his ways are just. And those who walk in pride he is able to humble.*

So, Nebuchadnezzar already had his time as the "beast" for 7 years, and at the end, he declared in humility that the God of the Hebrews was, and is, the King of Heaven, and the all-powerful God over heaven and earth, and over all who dwell in them eternally. After Nebuchadnezzar worshiped the Lord, as a sign of God's restoration of His servant, God returned him to his throne, and his kingdom became even greater than it had been in the past. Nebuchadnezzar's proclamation that there is an all-powerful God in heaven, and that he wasn't Him, removes him from the list of the two Babylonian candidates. That only leaves one, Nimrod.

If Nimrod is the same historical character as Gilgamesh and Osiris, which I believe him to be, then how can he be resurrected from the Abyss, as stated in Revelation 17? Doesn't Isaiah 26 tell us that the Rephaim, who are a subset of the Nephilim giants, shall not rise?

Isaiah 26:14 (Orthodox Jewish Bible)

[14] They are mesim (dead ones), they shall not live; they are **refa'im** (dead ones), they shall not rise; therefore Thou hast visited and destroyed them, and made all their zekher (memory) to perish.

This gets a bit confusing since there are so many translations into English. Even the Orthodox Jewish Bible indicates that the Rephaim (refa'im) relates to the "dead ones" and not the giant hybrids. However, there are many verses in the Bible where it is clear that the word Rephaim refers to the hybrid giants. Here are a few: Genesis 14:5, Deuteronomy 2:11, 2:20, 3:13, Joshua 15:8, 18:16

Based on the context, I believe that Isaiah 26 is talking about the giant Rephaim and not simply "dead ones." Also, why would Isaiah say that the "dead ones," meaning dead people, shall not rise when it is clear that all humans will rise, and be resurrected, some to eternal life, and some eternal death, as indicated by Jesus Himself in John 5?

John 5:28-29

[28] *Do not marvel at this; for the hour is coming in which all who are in the graves will hear His voice* [29] *and come forth— those who have done good, to the resurrection of life, and those who have done evil, to the resurrection of condemnation.*

So, I believe that Isaiah is referring to the dead Rephaim giants who shall not rise, and not referring to ordinary dead people. This is unfortunately problematic for my narrative because again, how can a hybrid be resurrected from the Abyss if they do not rise according to Isaiah 26?

First of all, I do not believe that God has granted Satan any resurrection power. That means that he will have to "resurrect" his man of the hour in some other way. That's where modern science comes in. Imagine if you had the DNA from Nimrod, and you knew how to use it to create a life that once was, is not, but will be.

We now live in a time like no other before in history, when man can use genetic engineering to alter the DNA of cells and even produce designer babies, chimeras, clones, and more. I would expect that he, the Antichrist, would have been created as a hybrid through the use of modern technology and not necessarily through breeding. I believe that he was engineered to incorporate all of the necessary genes to create the perfect tyrant king. Haven't we been conditioned to this through films like *Jurassic Park* and others? However, I don't believe that the Antichrist is going to show up and tell everyone that he was genetically engineered in a lab and birthed from a fluid-filled birthing capsule (virgin birth). So then, why is any of this important?

It's important, because God gave us many clues, and He gave us many titles and descriptions of this elusive final false messiah. He must have given us all of that for a reason! He even gave us the number of the man, 666. Did you know that according to the Epic of Gilgamesh, that Gilgamesh was said to be two-thirds god and one-third man? That would make him 66.6% god and 33.3% human. I realize that being three parts doesn't make any sense under natural circumstances, but that's not the point. It's the numbers that make it interesting.

In the Book of Jasher, which is referred to in the Bible in both Joshua and 2 Samuel, there are some very interesting prophetic passages regarding Nimrod in the latter days. In Jasher 11, Abram, when he was specifically "50" years old, was brought before king Nimrod to explain why he destroyed a collection of idols at his father's house. Instead of giving Nimrod excuses, Abram took the opportunity to instruct the king to repent of his sinful ways, and to serve the only true God. The consequence for Nimrod for not following Abram's instructions would be that Nimrod would die in shame, along with everyone who follows him, in the latter days.

Book of Jasher 11:59-60

*59 Now therefore put away this evil deed which thou doest, and serve the God of the universe, as thy soul is in his hands, and then it will be well with thee. 60 And if thy wicked heart will not hearken to my words to cause thee to forsake thy evil ways, and to serve the eternal God, **then wilt thou die in shame in the latter days**, thou, thy people and all who are connected with thee, hearing thy words or walking in thy evil ways.*

Obviously, Nimrod did not heed Abram's warning. So if Abram's prophecy was true, then Nimrod would somehow die in shame in the latter days, along with all of his followers. But how could he die in the latter days when he lived thousands of years ago?

Two years later, Nimrod had a dream similar to the dream that Nebuchadnezzar would have, which Daniel interpreted, and also similar to the one that the Egyptian Pharaoh had, which Joseph interpreted. This time, however, it wasn't a wise and righteous man who interpreted the dream like Daniel or Joseph, but a man who promoted the killing of Abram, which would have destroyed his seed and the future Messiah. Once again, I have to point out that this has been the enemy's game plan ever since Genesis 3:15.

Book of Jasher 12:52-57

*52 And a wise servant of the king, whose name was Anuki, answered the king, saying, This is nothing else but the evil of Abram and his seed which will spring up against my Lord and king **in the latter days**. 53 And behold the day will come when Abram and his seed and the children of his household will war with my king, and they will smite all* *the king's hosts and his troops.* ^{54} *And as to what thou hast said concerning three men which thou didst see like unto thyself, and which did escape, this means that only thou wilt escape with three kings from the kings of the earth who will be with thee in battle.* ^{55} *And that which thou sawest of the river which turned to an egg as at first, and the young bird plucking out thine eye, this means nothing else but* **the seed of Abram which will slay the king in latter days.** ^{56} *This is my king's dream, and this is its interpretation, and the dream is true, and the interpretation which thy servant has given thee is right.* ^{57} *Now therefore my king, surely thou knowest that it is now fifty-two years since thy sages saw this at the birth of Abram, and if my king will suffer Abram to live in the earth it will be to the injury of my lord and king, for all the days that Abram liveth neither thou nor thy kingdom will be established, for this was known formerly at his birth; and why will not my king slay him, that his evil may be kept from thee in* **latter days?**

Both of these prophecies indicate that Nimrod and his cohorts will be killed by the seed of Abram in the last days. Verse 55 even refers to one of his eyes being plucked out, similar to other Antichrist passages such as Zechariah 11:17 and Revelation 13:3

According to the Book of Jasher, Nimrod was indeed killed by the seed of Abram. In fact, according to Jasher 27, it was Abram's grandson Esau who killed him by cutting off his head one day while he was out hunting, which was "coincidentally" the same day that Esau sold his birthright to Jacob. However, Nimrod's death was clearly not a complete fulfillment of these two prophesies. Even though Nimrod was killed by the seed of Abram, there remains major components of both prophesies yet to be fulfilled. All of his followers were not killed, there was no full-scale war between the seed of Abram and Nimrod and his troops, Nimrod was not killed in shame, nothing happened to his eye, and there weren't 3 men with him, but two, both of which died at the hand of Esau. So, is the Book of Jasher correct, and is there a type of future "latter days" fulfillment still to come?

Here's the part where I could talk about the Great Reset of the World Economic Forum, the United Nations and their Agenda 2030, the World Health Organization and their takeover of national sovereignty, central banks, the Freemasons and other secret societies, the role of the US government, the Vatican, Obelisks, the all-seeing eye of Horus, transhumanism, bioengineering, artificial intelligence, and so on. However, that will certainly drive us even farther into the weeds than we already are, so I'll try to be brief and sum it all up without going into too much detail. So, put on your tin foil hat with me and let's try to sum this all up...

I believe that Nimrod, or whatever name you want to ascribe to that biblical character, is coming back. He was the first and will be the last global world leader. Nimrod had children, according to the Book of Jasher. I believe that the DNA of his offspring has been sought out and collected ever since the 1940s when Israel became a nation again, and, coincidentally, when the UFO abduction phenomena began to be reported. "They," be they government operatives, or inter-dimensional "demonic" forces, have used the collected DNA to manufacture, in a sense, the one we know as the Antichrist. The physical signs of the world's desire to "resurrect," or "re-birth" him are all around us. For instance, obelisks, which are Egyptian and Babylonian phallic symbols representing fertility and resurrection, are prominently displayed at the Vatican and in Washington DC, adjacent to domed buildings. Domed buildings are said to be the pregnant bellies, wombs of the female alongside the erect penis of the male, both of which are symbolic of the re-birth of Nimrod/Gilgamesh/Osiris. There is a prominent statue on top of the US Capitol building, which was designed by Freemason Thomas Walter, called the "Statue of Freedom." In case anyone missed the meaning of the dome itself, it is crowned with a stylized 15,000-pound bronze pagan symbol of Libertas, who is none other than the Greek goddess Athena representing the Egyptian goddess Isis. Isis is also known by other pagan cultures and religions mentioned and warned about in the Bible, including Asherah. Asherah (Asherah pole) is always associated with Baal worship, which the Israelites fell into time and time again. And they were punished for it time and time again as well.

Why on earth would such symbols be at our nation's capitol or at the Vatican? The next time you see those images with your family, you'll need to cover your children's eyes! Of course, there are exoteric explanations for such architecture, but the reality is that they are there none the less, and they have nothing to do with Christianity at all. In fact, they are an abomination to God.

It is known that the Washington Monument along with the layout of Washington DC itself, was designed by Freemasons. It has been widely reported that the Washington Monument, an Egyptian obelisk/phallus, stands 555 feet tall. OK, that's not 666 feet tall, you might say. However, according to ancient architecture, a true Egyptian obelisk has to be 10 times as tall as its width. Thus, the height was determined by the width of its base. I haven't personally measured the base, but it is generally reported to be 55.5 feet wide, which makes sense if it has to be 10 times as tall, give or take a little for human error. I would not want to have been the person with the tape measure back in the day! So, if it is 555 feet tall and 55.5 feet wide at its base, that makes it 6660.00 inches tall and 666.00 inches wide. Three sixes in a row in each direction, how coincidental!

According to some of the historic writings that I have been able to read from high-level Freemason writers such as Manly P. Hall, it is evident that they have a thing for Nimrod/Gilgamesh/Osiris. It makes sense because Nimrod is associated with great builders (Masons) since he was the first world ruler to build great cities as well as the tower of Babel.

Without going into too much detail, it is evident to me that enshrouded in their esoteric writings is the secret doctrine of the resurrection of Osiris himself to take back the rulership of the world. They consider themselves to be the avengers of Osiris along with Isis, who was the sister and wife of Osiris, but is now personified by the Mystery School of Freemasonry. It was Osiris' brother Typhon who tricked Osiris and had him killed by "72" conspirators. He later had Osiris' body cut into 14 pieces and scattered over the earth so that he could never be re-born. The incestuous sister/wife, Isis found 13 of the 14 pieces; however, the final piece, which was, as my son used to call it, "his private," was never found because it was eaten by a fish. It is that part of Osiris, which is associated with his "seed," that they consider to be the "Lost Key," according to Manly P. Hall, and if found, would bring him back.

So, have they been looking for this "Lost Key" for centuries in a physical sense, or is this only allegorical of wisdom and spiritual enlightenment? I believe the answer is yes to both counts. They have certainly been seeking wisdom and enlightenment through their ancient mystery schools, but it is obvious through their writings, once you peel back the thin exoteric veneer, that they absolutely wanted to bring the one back to life who personally embodies that wisdom and enlightenment. Not only the Freemasons, but all of the other secret societies are on this same quest, according to Hall. The result of this quest is that most, if not all, of the secret societies are either independently or cooperatively working toward a world, which will be controlled by a ruler who embodies their view of a utopian, and enlightened society. This society is opposed to God and the true Messiah, in favor of Osiris and a pantheon of other deities, and is thereby fully antichrist at its core.

I believe "they" have already found the "Lost Key" and have already been able to accomplish this quest to, in a sense, resurrect their ruler. They know that they are on a timeline and that everything, including technology and society, must be prepared and ready before the year 2030 (UN Agenda 2030, WEF Great Reset) so that he, the Antichrist, can fulfill the messianic pattern of being 30 years old when he declares himself king, which he will do at the Temple in Jerusalem according to Bible prophecy.

If my hunch is correct, and the false messiah was born in 1998/1999, which also aligns with the encrypted timeline revelation in the Psalms, then I would expect to also see other references to this time period as well as it relates to the antichrist.

I hesitate to mention this, but we are at war, and we have an enemy who has knowledge and a battle plan. Doesn't it make sense from a military strategy perspective to intercept and understand the enemy's plans? Now that I've cleared that up, there was a prophetic quatrain penned by Nostradamus that predicted that a "king of terror" would come down in the year 1999. Nostradamus, a French physician and astrologer of Jewish descent, wrote 942 prophetic quatrains which were published in 1555. Not many of them had a reference to an actual date, but quatrain "10:72" did make reference to the year 1999. What a coincidence that it's quatrain 10:72! We've already covered the numbers 10 and 72 previously...

This prophetic quatrain stated:

> "The year one thousand nine ninety-nine seven month
> From the sky shall come a great King of terror,
> [Shall be] revived the great King of Angoulmois.
> Before and after, Mars [shall] reign as chance will have it."

Let me start by pointing out that Mars was the Roman god of war, and closely corresponds to the deified Nimrod of the Babylonians. Based on the timeline revelation, I tend to look at our time now as part of the overall last 120+ years. Just as Noah was told in Genesis 6:3 that man would have 120 years, and there happen to be 120 Psalms corresponding to 1901 - 2020, which started the 15 Psalms of ascent, I believe that this block of time represents the full duration of the "birth pangs" and the "wars and rumors of wars" spoken of by Jesus. During the last 120+ years, we've had two World Wars, we're working on the setup to the Third World War now, and there have been countless other wars, and death and destruction over the same period of time. Blame it on advancements in technology, or man's hearts growing cold, either way, in my estimation, the god of war has truly reigned over the last 120+ years.

The meaning of this quatrain from Nostradamus has been the subject of much debate for hundreds of years, especially as the world moved into the year 1999. However, the basic understanding is that a king of terror was to descend to earth as a revived king in the seventh month of 1999. During the summer of that year, many newspapers around the world presented articles about the quatrain in anticipation of something, or nothing, to happen during the seventh month of that year. Due to the difference between our modern day Gregorian calendar and the Julian calendar of Nostradamus' time, the seventh month could actually mean our 9th month, so for all practical purposes, the entire summer was in the spotlight.

By the end of the summer, several newspaper articles were written, poking a little fun at the supposed prophecy and recognizing that it was good for scaring people and for selling books about the end of the world, but little more. After combing through many articles from that time, I found one that was very interesting, especially in light of modern genetic technology.

In September 1999, Everett F. Bleiler wrote an article for the Washington Post entitled *Nostradamus.* In this article, he mentions an odd interpretation that he found regarding this quatrain, which came through a medium, and was supposedly from the deceased Nostradamus himself. Let me state first of all that as a Christian, I do not normally listen to what demonic forces masquerading as dead people in séances have to say, but we also know from Matthew 8 that the enemy knows something about God's timetable. Not down to the day or hour, just as we don't, but they know more than we do for certain; after all, they've had millennia to study God's word and to try to formulate a strategy against it. So, as I said before, we are at war. We are in God's Army, and I believe we should try to intercept and understand the enemy's plans whenever possible.

Matthew 8:28-29
*28 When He had come to the other side, to the country of the Gergesenes, there met Him two demon-possessed men, coming out of the tombs, exceedingly fierce, so that no one could pass that way. 29 And suddenly they cried out, saying, "What have we to do with You, Jesus, You Son of God? **Have You come here to torment us before the time?"***

Obviously, they were, and are aware of God's timing. They not only knew that Jesus was the Son of God, but they clearly had an understanding of the timeline, and they knew that it wasn't yet time. So, based on Matthew 8 and several other scriptures, it is evident to me that demons know about God's timing. That means it is possible they could have imparted this timing to Nostradamus regarding 1999. That also means that later, they could have added some more clarity to the quatrain. Here's what the author of the article in the Washington Post stated that caught my attention:

"The oddest interpretation that I have run into, however, comes from the spirit of Nostradamus himself, via a medium. He explains the quatrain as describing a **genetic program, perhaps continuing Nazi eugenics programs, for creating super soldiers irresistible in war**. If you cannot see how this reading emerges from the quatrain, do not be discouraged -- neither can I."

In 1999, the author could not understand what the demonic entity was describing about that year. Everyone expected there to be an object, or person/entity descending from the sky that year, but that's not what the esoteric meaning of the quatrain was, according to the demonic interpreter. It described a genetics program beginning to create an army of overwhelming and overpowering super soldiers. Irresistible doesn't just mean wildly appealing, but it also means overwhelming and overpowering, which I believe is the context of the word in this case.

Every army has a leader, and in context, I believe that leader is the individual known as the "king of terror" in the quatrain, and as the "beast" in Revelation. This description of the beast as a genetically created/modified super soldier not only fits my thesis of the re-birthed Nimrod, but it also brings to mind a specific prophecy in Revelation 13:4, which says, "...who *is* like the beast? Who is able to make war with him?" As a genetically modified super-intelligent and super-human god-like character, the beast will be unstoppable to man and nations.

I asked this question before, but it's a good time to restate it. Was there a sign in the heavens around the 1998/1999 timeframe that could have heralded the coming of the beast, the king of terror over what was the Roman Empire? Recall that in 1999, there was a full solar eclipse over Europe on August 11th, which passed over England, France, Hungary, Germany, Austria, Romania, and Turkey, with the epicenter directly over Romania.

So far, I have laid out my case for who I believe the Antichrist to be, and more importantly, when he would come to be. I realize that my views are quite unconventional when compared to most Bible scholars and prophecy teachers. They are different because they come out of the added perspective of the encrypted timeline revelation, which I believe gives a little more clarity to this mysterious figure.

Based on the timeline revelation, I have shown that there is a distinct possibility that his arrival or "re-birth" happened around 1998/1999, which matches Psalm 50, with its 6 Antichrist verses, and the 50th anniversary of the re-birth of Israel. I've also established that I believe the Antichrist will follow the prophetic pattern of other messiah figures of the Bible, which indicates that they were all 30 years old when they began their reign, or in Jesus' case when He began His ministry. Let's just think out loud for a moment, If you think about it from the enemy's perspective, the copycat who was present as the ruler of this world when Jesus the Savior was born, and you at least loosely understand God's timeline, wouldn't you want to try to mimic the timing of the birth of Jesus, but 2,000 years later? After all, you know when He was born, you know when He started His ministry, and you know when He died and rose again. This timing also matches the "fig tree generation" and the fact that Israel has never made it past 80 years, which will bring us to the 2028/2029 timeframe when, coincidentally, the Antichrist will be around 30 years old, and Israel will be in her 80th year. Can you see how all of these timeline events are about to intersect? Then, if you take 3.5 years off of 2028/2029, you arrive at around 2025 for the start of the tribulation period, which also matches the timeline revelation in the Psalms. How can all of this be a coincidence?

Here are a few final thoughts on the "lawless one." Even though he will be partially the genetic repeat of Nimrod, I don't believe that the Antichrist will look like a giant. I believe that would be too obvious, so I'm sure that trait has been genetically removed. He might be tall, but not a giant. It's all about deception! The coming false messiah will probably be a genetic mix from the tribe of Judah through David, the tribe of Dan, and Nimrod/Gilgamesh/Osiris. By virtue of David and Dan's bloodline, he will be a Jew, but will probably not be born in Israel. I believe that he will come out of the revived Roman Empire, just as Daniel 12 indicates. I'm certain that the global elites, secret societies and the infiltrated governments of the world, including the United States, have had all their hands in the creation of this "king of terror." I haven't made much mention of it, but I'm confident that the descendants of Esau will have much to do with the final days and that the eschatology of Islam will be intertwined into the last days to keep them deceived and acting on the enemy's behalf as well. The Antichrist may be the one the Muslims call the Dajjal, or he may be the messianic figure they call the Mahdi; only time will tell.

My vision of the Antichrist is a young leader who is well-spoken, knows the Torah inside and out, and says and does all the right things. One of his missions is to deceive the Jews and bring them back to Israel like lambs to the slaughter. He will sign a covenant for peace, which will allow the temple to be rebuilt in the wake of the Gog Magog war, and he will unite and bring the Jews back to Israel from all over the world to establish his messianic kingdom with Israel as the world power and seat of government. However, it will all be just a deceptive plot to destroy the Jews once and for all. His plan will not fully succeed; however, millions of Jews will lose their lives when he turns on them to crush them in his trap. The remnant will flee to the "refuge" where God will protect them at a place that He has prepared for them (Revelation 12, Ezekiel 39).

In addition to the Torah, I believe he will also know all of the world's other religious books, including the Christian Bible, so that he can deceive "if possible, even the elect" (Matthew 24:24). After all, he has to bring unity to the world's religions so that they can then be consumed by him at the midpoint of the tribulation. Certainly, the false prophet of Revelation 13 will also be highly instrumental in this deceptive work.

I still have my tin foil hat on, so I feel at liberty to say that I believe that UFOs are coming! Although, I'm certain they are demonic inter-dimensional beings, and not from another planet. Every civilization, from the Sumerians to the Native Americans, have similar stories of gods who came down from the heavens and married women to create hybrid gods. The dead disembodied hybrids, or Nephilim, are now demons since they are not redeemable. The mark of the beast will not only control buying or selling, but I believe it will also, in part at least, change one's DNA, making all who take it no longer fully human. This movement has already begun and is being pushed by the World Economic Forum under the name "Fourth Industrial Revolution," which is simply Transhumanism. They envision a world where we are all linked into the system through bioengineering and IA controlled by the world elites. The Bible predicts that this system will be developed and will later be taken over by the Antichrist. This system will give him god-like powers of global control and surveillance, omniscience if you will. Again, a mimic of God.

Gilgamesh Found, Coincidence?

It was reported on April 29, 2003, by the BBC that a German-led archeological team found the tomb of Gilgamesh in Iraq, which is the location of ancient Babylon. Less than three weeks later, the US invaded Iraq and immediately seized them along with thousands of other artifacts from the Iraq Museum in Baghdad. How could that simply be a coincidence?

I believe this ties back to Manly P. Hall and the Freemason's plan to resurrect Nimrod/Gilgamesh/Osiris to be their world ruler. Obviously, 2003 was after 1999, so I'm not sure if they wanted the remains for extra genetic verification, or if they had a way of using the DNA after the birth of the Antichrist. I believe that the Antichrist, just like Jesus, was heralded by a heavenly sign that the Luciferians knew the timing of and were waiting for. This Antichrist is Satan's last hope. He knows he only has a short time left, and that he must destroy the Jews to cancel the covenants that God has with them through Abraham, Isaac, Jacob, and with King David. No matter, he has already lost, but he's certainly not going to go down without a fight.

Only time will tell if any of these Antichrist predictions are correct. They have been pieced together through a lot of study, prayer, and contemplation. Hopefully, this Psalm 50 study on the Antichrist will be helpful to many during the tribulation period as a warning and a guide. Do not be deceived, and do not allow them or put anything in your body that can alter your DNA. No vaccines or therapies! We've been conditioned by Covid, but those who understand that deception will also come in the form of "pharmakeia," know to reject any such thing. Your eternity depends on it!

Year: 2020 as Seen Through the Lens of Psalm 120, a Psalm of Ascent

The Year of Deception

If I had known, prior to the year 2020, that Psalm 120 was a prophetic glimpse into the highlights of that coming year, I believe that I would have been able to glean a lot of insight from its poetic verses. However, I wouldn't have known, or could have even imagined, just how it would all play out, and that a manmade virus would play the leading role in a play set on a global stage that nobody wanted to see. Nobody but the global elites, that is! After all, 2020 was their big opportunity at a self-described "great reset." Although I realize that I wouldn't have been able to foresee exactly what was going to play out over that year, I would have, however, known to anticipate a year full of distress, lies, and deception. And that's from the first verse of the Psalm!

Looking back in the rear view mirror, it is clear to see now that the year 2020 was the beginning of a new dark era on this planet, almost as if it was the first big step in a plan to change the world. It seems that everything changed, almost instantly as the year got underway when the news of a new contagion called COVID-19 spread around the world. Control-hungry politicians, as well as unelected bureaucrats from around the world, wasted no time and seized the opportunity to grant themselves more power at the expense of the rights of the people. Dissenting voices were quickly silenced, and only a controlled narrative was allowed to be heard. Of course, this was all done under the guise of protecting those same people whose rights were being trampled.

Through every imaginable media outlet, the message of fear was disseminated at a record pace and with constant 24-hour nonstop news coverage. Death tolls, which we now know were being greatly exaggerated, were read off by news anchors as if they were sports scores. For the first time in human history, all of the governments and news media organizations from around the world were all speaking with one voice, just as if they were all being handed the same script.

We now know that our rights and even livelihoods were being taken away all for a virus that was little more than a bad flu. That's not to say that it wasn't significant, or that people didn't lose their lives because of it, but there simply was no cause for destroying the lives and futures of so many other people who weren't even sick. It was all part of a planetary "great reset," which could only fully take place after the right puppet was "elected" as the leader of the free world, in the presidency of the world's strongest superpower, the United States of America, which also took place in 2020.

We also know through Psalm 120 that there is a harsh judgment coming for all of the deceivers who have played their part in the global deception of 2020 and beyond. God will not forget them, and their sins will not go unpunished.

Just as foretold by Psalm 120, the year 2020 was indeed a year of unprecedented global distress caused by lies and deception. However, it was just the start of the final prophesied labor pains in the birthing process of the coming Kingdom Age.

In addition to the distress, deception, and lies prophesied in Psalm 120, the year 2020 also marks the near end of the time when Israel must dwell with the "one who hates peace." Israel is surrounded, and infiltrated, by a Muslim religious mindset that is diametrically opposed to the nation of Israel, and that at its core cannot coexist with the Jewish State. Since Israel's rebirth in 1948, they have been living in a time marked by a constant threat of war. However, according to Psalm 120, that time will soon come to an end, and Israel will finally have peace in their God-given land. But first, tribulation must come…

Year: 2021 as Seen Through the Lens of Psalm 121, a Psalm of Ascent

The Rapture Season Begins

As of 2021, I believe that Jesus was standing at the door ready to hear His Father say "Go get your bride!" Jesus, in John 14, likens His return to the traditional Galilean betrothal and wedding rituals, in which, after becoming engaged, the groom goes to his father's house to build a new abode on to it for himself and his new bride. It's only after the father inspects the new addition to the home and approves of it, when at his discretion, he says to his son, "Go get your bride!" It's only then when the groom is allowed to return with his wedding party, usually in the middle of the night, to lift his bride up on a type of royal litter to be carried to the 7-day wedding celebration at the father's house. It's because no one knows the exact "day or the hour" when the father will instruct his son to return for his bride that everyone has to be ready when they see the signs of his soon return. It's signs like the butcher, the vintner, and extra servants who have all been hired and are ready to go that would give them a clue that the groom's return was imminent. Just as they had signs back then to let them know that the groom's return was near, Jesus also gave us many signs to be watching for that tell us that His return is near. All of those signs are looming large all around us today! Regardless of the encrypted timeline revelation in the Psalms, it is safe to say, based on all of the signs around us, His return must truly be imminent.

In the opening verses of Psalm 121, God uses a clever encrypted rapture allegory to usher in the "Rapture Season." Many call this time the "rapture window," which is the time frame when the imminence of the rapture becomes more and more probable based on the "last days" signs detailed in Bible prophecy. I do not call it a "window" because it is never associated with a window in the Bible, but with a "door" instead. That might be splitting hairs, but I don't want to confuse myself with mixed-up metaphors.

Verse 1 says, "I will lift up my eyes to the hills- from whence comes my help?" Watching, and lifting up one's eyes or head, is a common image of the rapture in both the Old and the New Testaments, as I discussed in the Psalm 121 chapter of this book. This could certainly be just a coincidence; however, the subtle rapture symbolism also continues in the first verses of the next 2 Psalms of Ascent as well, then it shifts to the last 3 verses in Psalm 124 and then stops altogether in the following Psalms of Ascent. My theory is that the rapture can happen on any day between now and 2025, but I'm pretty confident that the rapture will also fulfill the next unfulfilled feast day, which is, of course, the Feast of Trumpets. Considering that the 2022 Feast of Trumpets is behind us as of today, as well as Passover, Feast of Unleavened Bread, Feast of First Fruits, and Pentecost, I'll be anxiously watching and hoping as the Feast of Trumpets approaches this fall in 2023, but my hunch is that it will be in 2024 based on the Shmita cycle. Keep in mind that the calendars are all messed up, as I have discussed previously, so it is true that *"no man knows the day or the hour"* of the Feast of Trumpets. That's because it will be based on God's timing, and not on man's corrupted calendars.

Verse 1
¹I will lift up my eyes to the hills— From whence comes my help? My help comes from the LORD, Who made heaven and earth.

I believe that Psalm 121 has a twofold purpose. This Psalm isn't just about the subtle hint to be watching and waiting for His appearing at the rapture, but it's predominantly about God's help for His people. At the rapture, we will be changed in the twinkling of an eye, and then we will lift up our eyes and finally behold our Savior. That's for both believing Jews and Gentiles. From that time forward, He will preserve us from all evil and harm. The rapture will be the ultimate help by allowing all of God's children to escape the terrible events that are about to befall the earth.

Israel will also be helped and preserved. Psalm 121 is largely a promise to help and preserve Israel, and more precisely, the remnant of Israel through the time of Jacobs's trouble.

Year: 2021/2022 as Seen Through the Lens of Psalm 73, a Psalm of Asaph

Plagued and Israel's Harlotry

Psalm 73 subtly uses perfectly placed imagery that relates to some of Israel's religious rituals, such as hand washing, to describe some aspects of life under COVID-19. Verse 13 and 14 say, *"... and washed my hands in innocence. For all day long I have been plagued..."* If that were in any other Psalm, I wouldn't believe that it has a secondary meaning, but in the context of the Covid years of 2021/2022, I am certain of its prophetic connection to the difficult time which we have just survived.

This Psalm was written from an individual's first-person perspective from a time long ago. However, it is also clearly prophetic, and I believe that it also represents the viewpoint of a modern-day Jewish person living in Israel who is being seduced by the world, but who ultimately resists the world's pull, and returns to the Lord. I believe that person represents the 1/3 of the Jews who will be part of the surviving remnant of Israel, who will be protected in the refuge by the hand of the Lord during the second half of the tribulation. It can also pertain to anyone, Jew or Gentile, who resists the new world order developing around us, but it has a definite Israel-centric theme.

The Psalmist likens himself to a "beast" for being envious, and foolishly falling into the deceptions of the world. The world that he describes sounds an awful lot like the coming "beast" kingdom hallmarked by prosperity, abundance, pride, violence, and opposition to God. He also describes those who go along with the world as not being in trouble like other people. According to prophecy, those who go along with the world's beast kingdom will flourish for a time, while those who oppose it will know only trouble. However, just as it is also described in this Psalm, those who follow after wickedness will ultimately be cast down to destruction, while those who resist, and draw near to God will be saved. That salvation spoken of in this Psalm is spiritual, and may or may not mean that he or she will be protected from harm in this world. In fact, there are several verses that lead me to believe that physical protection is not at all guaranteed, but more importantly, eternal salvation is for those who have received the salvation of the Lord. Here are a few of those verses:

Verses 24-26
24 You will guide me with Your counsel, and afterward receive me to glory. 25 Whom have I in heaven but You? And there is none upon earth that I desire besides You. 26 My flesh and my heart fail; but God is the strength of my heart and my portion forever.

In addition to the term "beast" in this Psalm, just for good measure, God employs two more words that are also directly connected with the book of Revelation and the prophetic happenings in the coming beast kingdom. I believe these are warnings of still future events. Both "harlotry" and "image" are used within this Psalm. Verse 20 says that God will *"despise their image,"* and verse 27 says that all of *"those who are far from You shall perish; You have destroyed all those who desert You for harlotry."* As we know from Revelation 13 there will be an "image" that will be worshipped, which is an ultimate form of religious "harlotry" that God will not allow to go unpunished.

Finally, I believe that the majority of Psalm 73 is a warning shot across the bow of humanity just before the beginning of the final 7 years. It's time to realize that there are only two paths in life, one path leads to life, and the other leads to death. It is evident in the prophetic scriptures that at the end of the age, people will be distinctly divided as they travel along one or the other of these two opposing paths. We see this division ever increasing in our current day as we draw closer and closer to the time in which even a "father will be divided against son, mother against daughter," just as Jesus described in Luke 12. It's time to pick the path that you will travel and not depart from it. Perhaps even more importantly, it's time to bring as many as possible onto the right path before it's too late. In the tribulation, it will still be possible to get on the right path that leads to life, but the decision to switch paths will become ever increasingly more difficult as the beast system grows stronger and stronger over time. In fact, switching from the path of ultimate death to the path that leads to everlasting life may result in physical death during the tribulation. As awful as that sounds, death will have no victory over those who are in Christ, and who will gain eternal life with Him in His glory.

Year 2022 as Seen Through the Lens of Psalm 122, a Psalm of Ascent

The Rapture Season Continues, Pray for the Peace of Jerusalem

The "Rapture Season" continues in 2022 through more imagery encoded in the first verse of Psalm 122, and then continuing into verse 2 as well. Verse 1 shows God's people glad to hear that it is time to enter into the *"house of the Lord."* We understand through the Old Testament and the New Testament, especially Hebrews 8, that the house of the Lord on earth was merely a copy and a shadow of the Tabernacle in Heaven. It's that one in heaven that we are most excited to enter into with our Savior, who redeemed us, once and for all, through His blood sacrifice (Hebrews 8-10).

Through the description of verse 2, which says *"our feet have been standing within your gates,"* I can visualize all of us at the end of the

Church Age who are alive and remain, standing within the gate eagerly waiting to enter into His glorious Kingdom. And through whom may we enter? Only through the one and only "Gate" Himself may we enter in (John 10:9).

In verse 6 we are instructed to pray for the peace of Jerusalem. This commandment is perfectly placed right before the beginning of the "time of Jacob's trouble." Jerusalem will finally know "peace," but it will only come after the tribulation period, at the start of the Millennial Kingdom, under the rule of the true Messiah Himself, Yeshua HaMashiach. Until then, many will be fooled as they eagerly await the one they believe to be their messiah. He will tick all of their wish list boxes because he will be made in the image that they wanted for their messiah. Unfortunately for them, the old saying "be careful what you wish for," will seem to come to life through this "man of sin" as he transforms into the Devil himself. By then, it will be too late, and they will be caught in his wicked trap of death and destruction. But God always reserves for Himself a remnant to be saved whom He foreknew (Romans 11). Even when two-thirds of Israel will be *"cut off and perish"* (Zechariah 13), God will spare His remnant of Israel, who will be saved from the wrath of Satan and his false messiah. They will be led under the Lord's protection into the refuge to remain under His care until the time of the Lord's indignation has passed. Then, peace will finally, and fully come to Jerusalem.

Year: 2022/2023 as Seen Through the Lens of Psalm 74, a Psalm of Asaph

Enemies Rising

Psalm 74 is a depiction of Israel's enemies who have risen against her in the past, as well as a call for God to deliver Israel from the enemies who are rising against her today. Those of us who have eyes and ears focused and tuned to God's prophetic word can clearly see and hear the steady rise of the beast system developing all around us today. Even a few years ago, we still had to close our eyes and imagine in our minds who the actors would be, and what they would look like in the final act of the tribulation drama. Today, in 2022/2023, we can simply turn on the television and see them with our own eyes, and hear them with our own ears. We don't have to wonder any longer since the final act has begun to play out all around us in our world today.

The puppets of the UN, WEF, IMF, governments around the world, bankers, and big business "merchants" are all following the script of their wicked master, whether they know it or not. It wouldn't surprise me at all, however, to find out that they are already taking orders from the wicked one, who is still hidden from the world but who has been prophesied to come since the beginning, the seed of the serpent himself, the Antichrist.

Near the end of Psalm 74 the Psalmist Asaph petitions the Lord by saying, *"Arise, O God, plead Your own cause; remember how the foolish man reproaches You daily."* I believe this "foolish man" is none other than the Antichrist, who is already speaking blasphemous things against the Most High (Daniel 7:25); he's doing it from the shadows since it isn't time for him to be revealed yet.

The final verse of this Psalm shows the enemies of God continually increasing and rising up against Him. That means they are also rising up against His children, both Jews and Gentiles, as we are His representatives on earth in this age. As of this year, we have seen unprecedented hostility toward those who still hold true to Godly principles and morals, and reject the "woke" ideology being pushed around the world today. Righteous voices have been cancelled in the name of tolerance and inclusion, which is neither tolerant nor inclusive. It seems that only one side of any debate is acceptable and worthy to be heard in the public marketplace of ideas in these final days. That side is the side who boldly proclaims that evil is good, and good is evil (Isaiah 5:20).

Year: 2023 as Seen Through the Lens of Psalm 123, a Psalm of Ascent

The Rapture Season Continues and the Spirit of Antichrist Rises

The "Rapture Season" continues in 2023, as encoded once again in the first verse of the Psalm. Similar to Psalm 121, we once again find the same imagery of lifting up our eyes to see our Lord and Savior. How exciting to know that the Lord is standing at the door and is ready to come for His bride at any time! Based on prophetic patterns, I believe His appearing will be at one of the "appointed times" detailed in Leviticus 23, but that's far from a certainty from my perspective. All I know for sure is that He is ready to return, and that we should be watching and praying always that we are found worthy to escape what is about to come upon this world (Luke 21:36).

Psalm 123 seems to pick up where Asaph left off in Psalm 74, which makes sense, because, according to the timeline revelation, they are both roughly related to the same year. Specifically, both Psalms describe the same time when the Lord and His children are being reproached and disparaged by the ungodly and proud. The term "pride" has taken on an entirely new meaning in our society today, causing me to wonder if that isn't at least part of the context of those mentioned in this Psalm. It's obvious to me in these last days that the enemy has developed this type of "pride," which is based on being proud of one's own sin, as a weapon against all of those who adhere to biblical morals and authority. And starting in 2022, it became very clear that the loud and proud "alphabet" movement wasn't just a benign faction, but an organized group that wasn't satisfied with having equal rights, but is a highly motivated group bent on shoving their "morals" and their agenda down the throats of every citizen, including children. At this same time the media, as well as large corporations, have proven to be complicit with this weaponized anti-Christian agenda. It's only a matter of time before God's Word is deemed "hate speech" since it offends those who are participating in sin, and those who approve of such sinful behavior.

Weren't we warned about this very time by Jesus Himself as one of the signs of the end times?

Matthew 24:10
*[10] And then many will be **offended**, will betray one another, and will hate one another.*

Year: 2023/2024 as Seen Through the Lens of Psalm 75, a Psalm of Asaph

The Horns Rising and Judgment Coming

I believe that Psalm 75 is a last warning to the world prior to the trap being sprung. That trap is, of course, the rapture. After the rapture, the people of the world that remain will be stuck to endure the worst time in human history, which most will not survive. I know that's really dreary news; however, according to scripture, the tribulation period will spawn the largest revival in history, with a multitude without number coming to the saving knowledge of Jesus (Revelation 7). After the rapture, many people will realize that "grandma" was right all those years when she told of the rapture, and the other events of the end times. They dismissed her, or whoever their "grandma" was in their life, and her crazy-sounding stories as fairytales, but they will finally believe after they witness the rapture for themselves. Unfortunately for them, most of them will be martyred for their faith in Jesus according to Bible prophecy during the 7-year tribulation. This is why I say, "come to Jesus now while salvation is free." In the tribulation, it will probably cost you your life. We still live in the Age of Grace, Jesus paid the penalty for your sin, and all you have to do is repent of your sins, call on Him and accept His free gift of salvation, and simply desire a relationship with the one who knows you, and loves you, better than anyone else.

I am writing these words at the end of May 2023, and Israel has just recently turned 75 years old, which, according to the timeline revelation in the Psalms, matches Psalm 75. In case you haven't read the entire book, and you're only reading the *Cliffs Notes* version like I would here at the end of the book; it is my belief that the numbering of the Psalms of Asaph matches the years of Israel's re-birth. That means Psalm 80, for example, matches Israel's 80th year since they became a nation again in 1948. That means that their 80th year will be in 2028.

According to the encrypted timeline revelation, Psalm 75 corresponds roughly to 2023 and into the beginning of 2024, so it should give us some insight into the year that is still ahead. The problem that I find from a prophetic view-point of Psalm 75 is that it does seem to be, as I indicated earlier, a warning to the world about what is to come after the rapture, and into the tribulation period. As such, I cannot be sure which, if any, of the specifics relate to 2023, or are they all meant as a foreshadowing of the seven final years? However, what I do see from Psalm 75 is that the tribulation is on the near horizon, but so is the return of the King! In fact, verse 1 says, *"Your wondrous works declare that Your name is near."* His return is, in fact, near; He is standing at the door!

Verse 2 indicates that when He chooses the "appointed time," He will judge the world "uprightly." Of course, we know that an appointed time is one of the Moedim, which means that it's one of God's 7 appointed festivals of Leviticus 23. Just as Jesus fulfilled all of the first 4 Moedim exactly at His first coming, I fully expect that He will continue that same pattern, and fulfill the remaining 3 exactly at His "appearing," His "return," and at His "Millennial Reign." Notice also that verse 2 indicates the reason for this "appointed time." That reason is judgment!

Verse 3 gives a strong indication that the world will be shaken. We obviously know that global catastrophes will take place during the tribulation, but is verse 3 a warning that the shaking will begin in 2023? The year already kicked off with a strong earthquake in Turkey and Syria, which killed almost 60,000 people. Are there more to come this year?

I believe that verses 4 - 5 represent the Antichrist's kingdom rising, and a warning to the Antichrist and his followers to "not lift up the horn." We know who the horn is from Daniel chapter 7. A "horn," in this case, also represents a ruler's power and authority. Later in the final verse, which happens to be verse 10, we see God declaring that He will "cut off" all of the "horns of the wicked."

In verses 6 - 7 judgment is coming from the North. Is this prophetic of the coming Ezekiel 38 - 39 war? Also, in verse 7, God *"puts down one, and exalts another."* Here again, I have to ask the question: is that speaking of things still to come later in the Gog Magog war, or maybe in the tribulation, or does this pertain to the year 2023? I also have to wonder if the term "one" refers to an individual, or could it refer to a country, financial system, religion, etc? Several world leaders have already stepped down, or have been replaced earlier this year, which could change the global political landscape moving forward. It also appears that the US dollar is losing its global dominance, which could be replaced by another form of currency to be used in global trade. And at the same time, programmable digital currencies are being developed, and will soon be ushered in by most countries around the world.

Verse 8 is full of tribulation and judgment symbolism. It reads: *"For in the hand of the LORD there is a cup, and the wine is red; it is fully mixed, and He pours it out; surely its dregs shall all the wicked of the earth drain and drink down."* This verse reveals a righteous God ready to pour out His "cup" of wrath on a wicked world, a world that I believe even rivals the depravity of Noah's time before the flood. Imagine the wickedness of the world today, but shifted into high gear after the removal of the "Restrainer" of 2 Thessalonians 2. As of 2023; I have already seen wickedness and depravity that I never thought I would ever see. I can't even imagine what this world will be like when the wicked have their way with no hindrances at all. I'm glad that I won't be here to see it, thank the good Lord! That brings me to the remainder of the final verse which says, *"but the horns of the righteous shall be exalted."* Could this be a reference to the coming rapture? After all, another interpretation of "exalted" is "lifted up." So, is this an indication that the righteous will be lifted up at the end of the tribulation in the Millennial Kingdom, or is this prophetic of the rapture, which has to happen before the wrath of God is poured out on the wicked? I guess we'll have to wait and see.

Year: 2024 as Seen Through the Lens of Psalm 124, a Psalm of Ascent

The Dead Sea Scrolls Shmita Year, Gog Magog War, and the Rapture Season Closes

According to the Essenes and the Dead Sea Scrolls, 2024 will be a Shmita year, which means it's a year for war! According to the timeline revelation and verses 1 - 5 of Psalm 124, this is the year for the Gog Magog invasion into Israel, and God's supernatural victory over Israel's enemies. This invasion is detailed in Ezekiel 38 - 39, Psalm 124, as well as in her sister Psalm of Asaph, which is Psalm 76.

I would like to offer a few observations and speculations: I have some new thoughts after more firmly connecting the notoriously loose-fitting prophetic puzzle pieces using the knowledge gleaned from the timeline revelation in the Psalms. I believe the conflict that has raged for over 70 years between the Palestinians and the Nation of Israel will finally end this year with the defeat of all of the invading armies mentioned in Ezekiel 38 and 39. The militant Palestinians will certainly be involved in this coming conflict. They are not named in Ezekiel 38, probably because they are not a nation, but they may be represented by the statement: "and many peoples with you" found in verse 9. As with the other invading armies, they will also be soundly defeated by God Himself. In the aftermath of their defeat, I can foresee that the land they occupy will return to Israel in preparation for the return of the remaining Jews scattered among the nations.

I also have a hunch that the Palestinians or perhaps another Muslim army may ultimately be responsible for the destruction of their holy sites on the Temple Mount. Think about it - they regularly and indiscriminately launch rudimentary rockets into Israel, not knowing where they will land. It would only take a few of these crude rockets to get through Israel's Iron Dome defense system and strike their own Al Aqsa Mosque and Dome of the Rock shrine to end their hold over the Temple Mount. Problem solved! If that happens, Israel couldn't be blamed by the international community for destroying Islam's holy sites because, in this scenario, they did it to themselves.

After God's victory on behalf of Israel in the Gog Magog War and the possible self-inflicted destruction of the Al Aqsa Mosque compound, the site could finally be cleared in preparation for the building of the third Jewish Temple in Jerusalem. According to the encrypted timeline revelation in the Psalms, the year 2026 will be the height of the re-gathering of the Jewish people back to Israel, and the year 2027 will see the completion of the third Temple. However, God will not be in this Temple.

The year 2024 also sees the close of the "Rapture Season." Personally, I believe that 2024 is the most probable year for the rapture of the Church, but the timeline revelation doesn't define it that way. That's just me hypothesizing. The timeline gives us an understanding of a 4 year "Rapture Season" that ends in 2024. I think this is why so many prophecy teachers have been wondering lately why we are still here. We've definitely been "watching" like no time in history, and the signs are all around us, signifying the end of the age. However, it seems to me that our merciful Father is waiting until the last moment to send His Son to rescue His bride, because that rescue will certainly usher in the "Day of the Lord," also known as the tribulation period. Just as Peter indicated, the Father has been patiently waiting to allow everyone to have an opportunity to come to repentance before it's too late.

2 Peter 3:9
⁹ The Lord is not slow in keeping his promise, as some understand slowness. Instead He is patient with you, not wanting anyone to perish, but everyone to come to repentance.

Psalm 124 contains the strongest rapture imagery yet, as it says in verse 7, *"Our soul has escaped as a bird from the snare of the fowlers; the snare is broken, and we have escaped."* That is remarkably similar to the words of Jesus in Luke 21 verses 34 - 36, which also likens the rapture to the snare of a fowler, which will trap all of those who are fruitless, who are caught up in the things of the world, who are not waiting and watching for the Lord's return, and who are thus not counted worthy to escape.

> **Luke 21:34 - 36**
> *[34] "But take heed to yourselves, lest your hearts be weighed down with carousing, drunkenness, and cares of this life, and that Day come on you unexpectedly. [35] For it will come as a* **snare** *on all those who dwell on the face of the whole earth. [36] Watch therefore, and pray always that you may be* **counted worthy to escape** *all these things that will come to pass, and to stand before the Son of Man."*

There are two distinct prophetic images associated with the Fowler's snare. There are those who are trapped by the snare, and those who escape the snare. In Luke 21, Jesus gives a warning to the world not to be caught off guard by worldly living, and, therefore, become trapped in the snare. Whereas, Psalm 124 chronicles those "souls" who have escaped the Fowler's snare, whose "help was in the name of the Lord." That name is Jesus, Yeshua HaMashiach!

The opening of the "Rapture Season" began in Psalm 121 verse 1, which we've already covered. Verse 1 was followed by *"my help comes from the Lord, Who made heaven and earth"* in verse 2. I believe that statement was metaphorically like a pin stuck in God's calendar, signifying the opening of the "Rapture Season." Here's the amazing thing, it just so happens that there is another pin stuck in God's calendar signifying the end of the "Rapture Season," and it's in Psalm 124. After the rapture imagery in Psalm 124 verses 6 - 7, we find an almost identical passage as the one in Psalm 121. To end the "Rapture Season," Psalm 124 says, "our help is in the name of the Lord, Who made heaven and earth." This time, it's the last verse of the Psalm, possibly signifying that the "Rapture Season" will close near, or at the end of 2024.

What a perfect verse to start and end the "Rapture Season!" I believe that this time is all about God revealing Himself to the nations, and putting His stamp on the supernatural events that the world will witness in 2024. He is the one who will help Israel at the invasion of Gog Magog, and He is the one who will help all of his saved ones at the escape. He is the creator of heaven and earth, and no one else (Isaiah 45 - 46). Certainly not the gods who will also reveal themselves in the tribulation, nor the false messiah, nor the false prophet. They are only cheap imitations of the one true God, who came in the flesh, died, and then rose again so that we can be saved.

Year: 2024/2025 as Seen Through the Lens of Psalm 76, a Psalm of Asaph

Gog Magog and the Rapture of the Church

Just as we saw in Psalm 124, again in Psalm 76, we see the Gog Magog invasion of Ezekiel 38 - 39, as well as the rapture of the bride of Christ. Remember that this is a Shmita year, according to the Essenes and the Dead Sea Scrolls, which means that it's notoriously a year for war. Being a Shmita year also means that it's a year for debts to be forgiven, and an agricultural Sabbath year for the land of Israel. However, Israel has not been observing these Shmita requirements due to their own corruption, but the time of Israel's corruption is quickly coming to a close.

Verses 1 - 6 speaks of the Gog Magog invasion and God's sure victory over the invading forces for His name to be known and feared once again in Israel. It is clear from these verses that it will be God who defeats Israel's enemies, and not Israel through superior military might or technology. Just as indicated in Psalm 76, Ezekiel 38-39 also indicates that God will show his awesome power for His glory, and so that He will be known. The Gog Magog invasion, as well as the rapture of the Church, is a revealing! Both events must take place prior to the tribulation so they can separate the masses that are left. All the world will witness God's glory and will either accept Him, or reject Him; there will no longer be a middle ground. I believe that after God shows the world that He, the God of Abraham, Isaac, and Jacob, is the living and one true God, the world will be without excuses. I also believe that this is the moment when the Antichrist will deceive many, and will try to steal the glory in some way. That glory is due only to the Most High!

Similar to Psalm 124, the rapture is once again encrypted in Psalm 76 after the Gog Magog invasion. Does that mean that it will certainly happen after the Gog Magog invasion? Verses 7 - 9 are the rapture verses in Psalm 76. Verse 7 asks the question, *"and who may stand in Your presence?"* Jesus answered that question in Luke 21. They are the ones who are watching and praying to be counted worthy to escape all of the things that will come upon the earth during the tribulation that Jesus was speaking about in Luke 21.

Luke 21:36
³⁶ Watch therefore, and pray always that you may be counted worthy to escape all these things that will come to pass, and to **stand before the Son of Man.***"*

Year: 2025 as Seen Through the Lens of Psalm 125, a Psalm of Ascent

Start of the 7-Year Tribulation

According to the Essenes and the Dead Sea Scrolls, this will be a Jubilee year. Of course, Israel is still observing a corrupted calendar and doesn't realize that 2025 will be a Jubilee. According to the timeline revelation in the Psalms, this will also be the first year of the tribulation period, which will end 7 years later, which is 2000 years (40 Jubilees) after the crucifixion and resurrection of our Savior.

Since this is the first year of the tribulation, which we know can only start with the confirming of a covenant by the Antichrist for 7 years as spoken of in Daniel 9:27, we should expect to find prophetic "Antichrist" information encoded in Psalm 125 if the timeline revelation is correct. And, of course we do! Verse 3 says, *"for the scepter of wickedness shall not rest on the land allotted to the righteous, lest the righteous reach out their hands to iniquity."*

Thankfully, the power of the Antichrist will not remain long over the land of Israel, or the world. It will be a very short-lived empire for the sake of the elect, just as Jesus foretold in Matthew 24.

Matthew 24:22

²² And unless those days were shortened, no flesh would be saved; but for the elect's sake those days will be shortened.

Psalm 125 is also a promise to all of those who put their trust in the Lord. He will surround them and protect them, and they will stand forever, just as Mount Zion will stand forever. I believe that this applies to everyone who comes to faith in Jesus during the tribulation; whether in life or in death, He will be with them. More specifically however, I believe that this applies to the believing remnant of Israel who will be cared for in the refuge during the last half of the tribulation. The Lord already has His eyes on them, and is ready to surround them, and protect them from the serpent who has devised a wicked plan to destroy them. Those who side with the serpent and his man of the hour, the beast, are dealt with in verse 5, which says, *"As for such as turn aside to their crooked ways, the LORD shall lead them away with the workers of iniquity."*

Finally, Psalm 125 declares, *"Peace be upon Israel!"* That peace, which will only be possible under the reign of Christ, is coming soon.

Year: 2025/2026 as Seen Through the Lens of Psalm 77, a Psalm of Asaph

The Day of Trouble - Start of the 7-Year Tribulation

Just as Psalm 125 indicates the beginning of the tribulation in the timeline revelation, so too does its sister psalm, Psalm 77, which, of course, corresponds to roughly the same time period. Verse 2 says, "in the day of my trouble, I sought the Lord." I believe that this verse is a veiled reference to the time of "Jacob's trouble" spoken of in Jeremiah 30. I also believe that in 2025, the day which has been long feared, the "day of trouble," has fully come.

This Psalm is narrated from the first person perspective, but I believe that "person" is not the author, Asaph, but reflects the combined consciousness of the future righteous remnant of Israel. This is a Psalm of anguish and hopelessness revealed in the first 10 verses, which then becomes a remembrance of God's merciful and redeeming power for Israel in the final 10 verses. In fact, the last 5 verses seemingly reflect on the exodus account when God saved Israel from the Egyptian army by parting the Red Sea, but mixed in with the historical details of the Red Sea crossing are some extra bonus particulars that do not pertain to that event. Could it be that those are in reflection of God's triumph over Gog Magog of the previous year?

Verse 17 makes reference to arrows flashing about, then verse 18 says, *"the voice of Your thunder was in the whirlwind; the lightnings lit up the world; the earth trembled and shook."* I don't recall any of that in the exodus account, so at a minimum, this is referencing another miraculous event when God intervened or will intervene in Israel's history or future. Personally, I believe that this encrypted event is just over the horizon.

Year: 2026 as Seen Through the Lens of Psalm 126, a Psalm of Ascent

The Jews Return to Israel

Psalm 126 brings us to what may be the first full year of the tribulation period, the year 2026. This Psalm is perfectly placed within the timeline revelation in the wake of the Gog Magog victory, and it heralds the prophesied return of the Jews back to their land. Both events are a perfect setup for the plan of the Antichrist. In the aftermath of God's resounding defeat of Israel's enemies, he, the Antichrist, who I believe will position himself to hijack some of God's glory, has confirmed a covenant, which in part promises the rebuilding of the Temple in Jerusalem. That will kick off the final mass exodus of the Jewish people out of all nations, and back to their covenant land.

Verse 4 says, *"Bring back our captivity, O LORD, as the streams in the South."* The Jews, and in fact, the world, will declare that *"the Lord has done great things for them"* (verses 2-3), and there will be a jubilant fervor among the Jews scattered throughout the nations to return to their promised land. Of course, the Antichrist will be the consummate "wolf in sheep's clothing," and will have his own secret agenda and motivation for returning the Jews back to Israel... their destruction!

I also believe Bible prophecy reveals that during the first part of the 7-year tribulation period, Israel will be prosperous under the guidance of the Antichrist while the rest of the world will be suffering. This devised prosperity under the rule of the false messiah will prompt the remaining Jews in foreign lands to return to Israel prior to 2028. It's a perfect setup!

Year: 2026/2027 as Seen Through the Lens of Psalm 78, a Psalm of Asaph

The Lord Has Done Great Things for a Rebellious Nation

Exactly like Psalm 126, Psalm 78 also carries the central theme of remembering the great things that the Lord has done for Israel. After the latest "great thing the Lord has done for Israel," the victory of Gog Magog in 2024, Israel will be on a high, and the dispersed children of Israel will return to their land in record numbers. Israel will prosper while the rest of the world will be in chaos. It will appear that the long-awaited Messianic Age has finally arrived. However, this Psalm also points out in much detail Israel's repeated rebellion against God, and the consequences of their rebellion, which is tribulation and wrath. Isn't that what the time of Jacob's trouble is all about?

Israel's final rebellion started 2000 years ago when they rejected the one and only Son of God, the true Messiah. This has set them up to follow a god of their own making, a god who will ultimately try to annihilate them.

Year: 2027 as seen through the lens of Psalm 127, a Psalm of Ascent

The Temple is Complete but the Lord Isn't in the Temple

Psalm 127 represents the year of the completion of the 3rd temple in Jerusalem, which will be 2027. However, the Lord will not be in this temple; it's the Antichrist temple, the temple of Israel's rebellion and fornication with the beast. Verse 1 says, *"unless the LORD builds the house, they labor in vain who build it..."* Their labor will be in vain, but it will serve the agenda of the Antichrist, who needs the temple to be completed so that he can stand in, or on, the temple and declare himself to be god before Israel turns 81 years old in 2029, which will more than likely also be when the Antichrist is 30 years old according to many prophetic patterns.

Year: 2027/2028 as Seen Through the Lens of Psalm 79, a Psalm of Asaph

The Temple Defiled

Similar to Psalm 127, Psalm 79 pictures a completed temple in Jerusalem; however, it also predicts and envisions the start of the second half of the tribulation period. It prophetically describes the horrors of Revelation 12, and many other apocalyptic prophesies regarding the desolation of Jerusalem, Judea, and Israel after the Antichrist, and his followers defile the temple, end the sacrifices, and set up the "abomination of desolation" in the holy place according to Daniel 9:27 and Matthew 24:15.

The first 4 verses describe the desolation of Jerusalem after the defilement of the temple. Jerusalem will be left in heaps with dead bodies left lying about and no one to bury them. Israel went from the high of believing that their messiah had finally come, and that they were at the beginning of the prophesied Messianic Age to the realization that they were deceived and are now once again a reproach to the nations.

Verse 7 says, *"for they have devoured Jacob, and laid waste his dwelling place.* Jacob is of course, Israel. Zechariah 13 describes this same event and goes on to state that 2/3rds of Israel will be killed. The remaining 1/3rd will be refined through the fire just as silver and gold are refined. This is the same remnant described in Romans 11, who will flee into a place prepared for them according to Matthew 24 and Revelation 12, to be protected by the Lord for the remainder of the tribulation period.

Year: 2028 as Seen Through the Lens of Psalm 128, a Psalm of Ascent

The Middle of the Tribulation, Israel Turns 80, and the Remnant Escapes!

If the 7-year tribulation period begins in 2025, which it does according to the encrypted timeline revelation, that means that sometime in 2028 will be the midpoint of the tribulation. According to Bible prophecy, the midpoint of the tribulation cannot happen unless there is a temple in Jerusalem. It just so happens that the temple will be completed in 2027 according to the timeline encoded in Psalms 79 and Psalm 127.

Just for fun, let's say that the tribulation period begins and ends at the fall festival season in Israel, which makes sense because the fall festivals have yet to be fulfilled by Jesus. That means that the midpoint of the tribulation will be at the spring festival season when most of Israel will be gathered in Jerusalem to worship. It will be an exciting time in Israel because, after almost 2,000 years, there will finally be a new temple standing on the Temple Mount in Jerusalem. Every Jew in the land will want to attend the celebration, and they will flock to the historic first Passover in the new temple era.

As a prophetic pattern, a similar scenario has played out once before. In 70 AD, millions of Jews had journeyed to Jerusalem to celebrate the Passover. Unfortunately for them, that was the year when the Romans besieged the city, destroyed the temple, and killed over 1 million Jews who had come to worship.

Also, as a prophetic pattern, Israel will not survive as a nation beyond 80 years; they never have! On May 14, 2028, the Jews will celebrate the 80th anniversary of their re-born nation of Israel. At the time of that celebration, they will once again have a temple, they will believe that they have finally entered into the Messianic Age according to their sages, and they will believe that they will finally put the 80-year curse behind them. However, it will be at this time, with the entire world watching, that the Antichrist will declare that he is god! Millions of Jews will be killed, and the nation will be ravaged.

Jesus Himself spoke of this day in Matthew 24. This is the day when the remnant of Israel must immediately flee to the mountains to escape certain death.

Matthew 24:15-18
15 "Therefore when you see the 'abomination of desolation,' spoken of by Daniel the prophet, standing in the holy place" (whoever reads, let him understand), 16 "then let those who are in Judea flee to the mountains. 17 Let him who is on the housetop not go down to take anything out of his house. 18 And let him who is in the field not go back to get his clothes.

Psalm 128 is one of the more cryptic Psalms in the timeline revelation, making it more difficult to decipher than most. There are two primary but subtle keys to this Psalm that connect it to the timeline. In verse 1 it says, *"blessed is everyone who fears the LORD, who walks in His ways."* I believe this is the key to being part of the remnant that will escape and survive. I also believe that the line, *"who walks in His ways,"* will prove itself to be literal when Jesus guides the remnant out of danger, and they will literally *"walk in His ways"* as He guides them into the place that He has prepared for them. Remember that Satan must wipe out all of the Jews to have any hope of success, which is why this remnant must survive.

The second subtle key to this Psalm is found in verse 5, which says, *"The LORD bless you out of Zion, and may you see the good of Jerusalem all the days of your life."* When I read this verse in the context of the timeline revelation, the phrase *"out of Zion"* really jumps off the page at me. Is this a blessing from the Lord for the remnant who will *"walk in His ways"* and come *"out of Zion?"* I believe that it is!

Year: 2028/2029 as Seen Through the Lens of Psalm 80, a Psalm of Asaph

The Lord Leads Israel Like a Shepherd - Plea for Salvation

Psalm 80 in the timeline revelation represents Israel's 80th anniversary. As I have mentioned in my previous summary of Psalm 128, Israel has never survived past 80 years as a complete nation, and they won't survive past 80 again this time! The Antichrist will be on a mission to take over and destroy the Israelites starting in 2028. Up until this year, he has convinced them that he is their long-awaited messiah; however, he has been a wolf in sheep's clothing all along, as they will find out.

In 2028, at the midpoint of the tribulation, is when the remnant of Israel must flee for their lives from Judea into the mountains, according to Jesus in Matthew 24. If Psalm 80 represents this period of time, I would expect to find imagery related to such a time of distress, when the remnant will be led out of Judea and into the refuge that has been prepared for them to be able to survive the Great Tribulation. And that's exactly what the first 2 verses of Psalm 80 represent.

Verses 1-2

¹Give ear, O Shepherd of Israel, You who lead Joseph like a flock; You who dwell between the cherubim, shine forth!
² Before Ephraim, Benjamin, and Manasseh,
*   Stir up Your strength, and come and save us!*

These verses are a cry to the Lord as the "Shepherd of Israel" to lead them like a flock to safety. It is interesting to note that this Psalm begins with the "Shepherd and flock" imagery, then shifts to the imagery of the land of Israel, like a vine that has been "burned with fire" and "cut down," which matches the overall biblical narrative of the second half of the tribulation. Also interwoven into the Psalm, after the initial "Shepherd and flock" imagery, is the cry for the Lord to "return" so that Israel can be rescued, revived, and restored. This will be the plea of the remnant of Israel for the next 3.5 years as they are sheltered in the refuge.

Why is all of this happening to Israel? Verse 4 explains that it is because God is angry with them, which also fits the overall biblical narrative perfectly.

Verse 4
⁴ O LORD God of hosts, how long will You be angry against the prayer of Your people?

In the tribulation, God will pour out His wrath on a wicked and unbelieving world, which certainly includes His own, the children of Israel. However, just as Noah and his family were rescued from the wrath of God, Lot and his family were rescued from the wrath of God, and the faithful are to be rescued via rapture from the wrath of God, so also will the faithful remnant of Israel be rescued from the wrath of God at the midpoint of the tribulation. Up until this time, Israel has had it pretty easy over the previous 3.5 years as the rest of the world has suffered. This fits into the narrative that has been portrayed by the ancient Jewish sages, who have written about their messiah, who is the false messiah, which will guide Israel's rabbis to recognize the beginning of their "Messianic Age." Remember that up until this time in the 7-year tribulation, Israel has proclaimed that "God has done great things for them." During that same time before the midpoint, the Jews were focused on building a temple and re-starting the sacrificial system, so logically, things in Israel weren't that bad up until 2028. However, in 2028, when Israel will turn 80 years old, which is also the midpoint of the tribulation according to the timeline revelation, everything is going to change for Israel, and a horrific time like no other will begin. The Antichrist will wage war against the children of Israel to destroy them, and thereby, the covenants that God has with them. After all, if the children of Israel no longer exist, then the covenants can no longer exist.

Just in case we've missed all of the tribulation imagery in Psalm 80, for good measure, verse 13 mentions a "wild beast" devouring the vine, which is symbolically Israel in this Psalm. God is literally spelling it out for us!

Year: 2029 as Seen Through the Lens of Psalm 129, a Psalm of Ascent

The Refuge

As of 2029 the world has moved into the Great Tribulation, and even Israel won't be spared from the wrath that will be poured out on a wicked and unbelieving world. However, the remnant of Israel will be spared. You may notice a consistent theme of affliction, grief, waiting, and longing from this time onward until Psalm 132, which relates to 2032. Spoiler alert, 2032 is when Jesus establishes His eternal dwelling place in Zion.

Psalm 129 is a much-needed reminder to Israel of the many times that God has prevailed against their enemies, and that He will do it again! However, it is clear from the wording of this Psalm that the Psalmist is writing from the view point of a nation that is still waiting and hoping for victory. This perspective falls perfectly within the first full year that the remnant of Israel will be hidden away in the refuge while the rest of Israel, and indeed the whole world, will be suffering the outpouring of the wrath of God.

Keep in mind that all of these Psalms are centered on Israel. From 2029 onward, I believe that they are more specifically centered on the "Romans 11" remnant of Israel who is being cared for in the refuge. The Lord will free them from the control and influence of the outside world during this time. The mark of the beast economic control and monetary system will have no effect on them inside the refuge.

Verse 4
The LORD is righteous; He has cut in pieces the cords of the wicked.

God will *"cut in pieces the cords of the wicked,"* which is symbolically the control that the "wicked" had over them. Picture the cords of control a plowman uses to control an ox pulling a plow. Once those cords are cut, the plowman will no longer have control over the animal.

Since these prophetic Psalms are centered on the remnant of Israel, they do not give much additional information regarding what else is happening in the world around them. However, it does seem clear that in 2029, the enemy of Israel has amassed an army to try to come against the sheltered remnant. My conclusion from verses 5 - 7 is that it won't go well for the attacking army. Word to the wise, God will protect His remnant at all costs, and no weapon formed against them will prosper.

Verses 5-7
[5] Let all those who hate Zion be put to shame and turned back. [6] Let them be as the grass on the housetops, which withers before it grows up, [7] With which the reaper does not fill his hand, nor he who binds sheaves, his arms.

Year: 2029/2030 as Seen Through the Lens of Psalm 81, a Psalm of Asaph

Time of Testing for the Remnant

Just as the Children of Israel were tested during the 40-year exodus from Egypt, so too will they once again be tested in the refuge, however this time for only 42 months. Psalm 81 begins with a Feast of Trumpets celebration and a review of how God rescued the children of Israel from Egypt, which in many ways parallels their upcoming time in the refuge. Remember that the prophet Zechariah specifically points out that during this time, the 1/3ʳᵈ remnant will be refined and tested.

Zechariah 13:9

⁹ I will bring the one-third through the fire, will refine them as silver is refined, and test them as gold is tested. They will call on My name, and I will answer them.

I will say, 'This is My people'; and each one will say, 'The LORD is my God.'

So again, just as they were tested in the wilderness, they will once again be tested and refined while they are in the refuge. And once again, it seems that they will still have an issue with worshiping false gods. It may actually be worse this time since they have more than likely seen these false gods with their own eyes by now. I believe that during the tribulation period, the things that we call "supernatural" today will be far more common, and will be seen by multitudes, and not just a select few. The false gods will seem to be powerful, but not compared to the true God. Just as God does not want "luke-warm" Christians, He also doesn't want His chosen people to have any association with little "g" gods.

Verses 9-12

⁹ There shall be no foreign god among you; nor shall you worship any foreign god.

¹⁰ I am the LORD your God, Who brought you out of the land of Egypt; open your mouth wide, and I will fill it.¹¹ "But My people would not heed My voice, and Israel would have none of Me.¹² So I gave them over to their own stubborn heart, to walk in their own counsels.

You will notice a distinct sense of frustration in Psalm 81. The pattern is that God has repeatedly saved Israel from their enemies by the might of His own hand, and in ways that could only be from Him. Yet, they have repeatedly, and almost instantly, fallen for the perversion of false gods. I have a sense from Psalm 81 that these false gods will continue to be a source of temptation for the remnant, and that God has ordained this as part of their refinement process. Even so, how frustrating and heartbreaking it will be for our Lord who will shepherd His children to safety, cover them with His protection, show them mighty miracles, and provide for them daily, only for them to once again turn their backs on Him, and chase after foreign gods who have nothing but destruction in mind for them.

Year: 2030 as Seen Through the Lens of Psalm 130, a Psalm of Ascent

Waiting on the Lord's Return

The remnant of Israel's time of testing in the refuge continues in 2030. Psalm 130 portrays Israel waiting and hoping for their redemption from the Lord during 2030. At this time, they cry out to the Lord for forgiveness and mercy as they wait and watch for the return of the Lord.

> **Verse 6**
> *My soul waits for the Lord more than those who watch for the morning— yes, more than those who watch for the morning.*

Think about all of the types and themes of the Psalms. This Psalm could have simply been a Psalm of praise, or it could have been a Psalm of thanksgiving. However, it is perfectly placed in the timeline as a Psalm showing a distinct image of Israel watching and waiting for their redeemer, exactly what they will be doing from the refuge in the coming year of 2030.

As they are watching and waiting, God directs them to keep their hope in Him. He is merciful and will redeem them from all of their past sins against Him.

Verses 7-8

⁷ O Israel, hope in the LORD*; for with the* LORD *there is mercy, and with Him is abundant redemption. ⁸ And He shall redeem Israel from all his iniquities.*

Hang on, Israel; redemption is coming!

Year: 2030/2031 as Seen Through the Lens of Psalm 82, a Psalm of Asaph

God Judges the "gods"

Psalm 82 is a very important Psalm that illuminates many other scriptures relating to the hidden principalities and powers that have been at work in this world for thousands of years. It is also a very interestingly placed Psalm in the timeline revelation coming on the heels of Psalm 81 and her sister psalm, Psalm 130. As you may recall, in Psalm 81, the Lord admonished Israel for their continual failure to reject the false gods of other nations, which are the 70 principalities and their subordinates over the other nations according to an accurate reading of Deuteronomy 32:8. Then, in Psalm 130 we found Israel crying out of the "depths" for God to forgive their unspecified iniquities. Of course, we know from the Old Testament that Israel's primary iniquity was always following after and worshipping the false gods. That sin is called "idolatry," and it's the first big sin Israel committed after leaving Egypt in the exodus. There's a pattern at work here. We also know from Zechariah 13 that all of Israel's false god worship will come to a head in the last days, and that God will make a final end of these false gods. I believe that Psalm 82 is in reference to the time of their end.

This Psalm opens with the view of God in a heavenly congregation of the fallen angels who were supposed to help the poor, the needy, the fatherless, and the afflicted of mankind; however, they also have freewill, and ultimately decided to side with the wickedest of mankind instead.

Verses 1-4
¹ God stands in the congregation of the mighty; He judges among the gods.² How long will you judge unjustly, and show partiality to the wicked? Selah

³Defend the poor and fatherless; do justice to the afflicted and needy.⁴ Deliver the poor and needy; free them from the hand of the wicked.

Now is the time for God to judge and drop the hammer on the fallen "mighty ones" who have been active participants in a rebellion against God, and against His creation all along, from Genesis to Revelation.

In verse 5, "they," meaning people, are referenced as the ones who are in darkness and lack understanding of these "powers" and their structured army that is against us.

Verse 5
⁵ They do not know, nor do they understand; they walk about in darkness; all the foundations of the earth are unstable.

I believe this gives a broader meaning to the Apostle Paul's words in 1 Corinthians 13:12 when he said, *"for now we see in a mirror, dimly, but then face to face. Now I know in part, but then I shall know just as I also am known."* Uncharacteristically of the other timeline revelation Psalms, the second part of verse 5 makes a seemingly out-of-place reference to the foundations of the earth being unstable. I say "uncharacteristically" because, as I have mentioned before, these Psalms normally focus on Israel, but in this verse, that pattern is broken, and what appears to be a worldwide event is prophesied for the 2030/2031 time period. There are many terrible and earth-shaking events prophesied in the Book of Revelation, so it's hard to know which event in particular this mention could be in reference to, but my best guess would be that at this time, the "seventh bowl" is ready to be poured out on the earth, which will be the greatest earthquake ever to hit the planet since man has inhabited it according to Revelation 16.

At the conclusion of Psalm 82, it is made clear that the ones who are being judged by God are, in fact, the fallen angels. These are the "gods" who have been worshipped by many nations, and by many different names in various languages throughout the centuries.

Verses 6-8

6 I said, "You are gods, and all of you are children of the Most High.7 But you shall die like men, and fall like one of the princes." 8 Arise, O God, judge the earth; for You shall inherit all nations.

Verse 7 indicates that even though they are angelic "gods," they will "die like men, and fall like one of the princes." I'm not going to discuss in detail the second part of that, even though I have my own thoughts on what is meant, which is that the "princes" spoken of are the offspring of the fallen angels who also died like men. The point is that God is declaring that these immortal fallen angelic "gods" will "die like men," meaning ordinary mortal men. That would seem to indicate that God will alter their state of being from angelic to human. If that sounds crazy to you, then consider that at the rapture of the Church those who are "in Christ" we will be transformed in an instant to be like Jesus, the First Fruits of the resurrection, according to 1 Corinthians 15, as well as the lesser quoted Philippians 3:20-21.

Philippians 3:20-21

20 For our citizenship is in heaven, from which we also eagerly wait for the Savior, the Lord Jesus Christ, 21 who will transform our lowly body that it may be conformed to

*His glorious body, according to the working by which He
is able even to subdue all things to Himself.*

Then, in 1 Corinthians 15:40, it is said *that "There are also celestial
bodies and terrestrial bodies; but the glory of the celestial is one, and the
glory of the terrestrial is another."* So, based on Psalm 82 verse 7, is God
going to transform certain "celestial bodies" into "terrestrial bodies" so
that they can "die like men," possibly just in time for the second half of
the seventh bowl judgment to be poured out on the earth? This second
part of the seventh bowl judgment will be exceptionally horrific and
deadly. It pictures 100+ pound hail stones falling on men, which would
certainly cause men to fall as they are crushed under the weight of the
falling hailstones. What a fitting judgment and degrading end that
would be for the "gods" who, like Satan himself, have been at the root
of everything evil that has plagued the world for countless generations.

Revelation 16:21
*[21] And great hail from heaven fell upon men, each hailstone
about the weight of a talent. Men blasphemed God because
of the plague of the hail, since that plague was exceedingly
great.*

Verse 8, which says *"arise, O God, judge the earth; for You shall
inherit all nations,"* indicates to me that as of the end of this year we are
near the completion of the tribulation period, and that the next event
will be the final judgment of the earth. Remember in Psalm 75 that
God declared that at His "appointed time," He would judge the earth?
Well, it's almost that appointed time! After the judgment, the true
Messiah, Jesus will inherit all nations and rule over them from Zion in
the Millennial Kingdom, which is described in the second part of verse
8. It's so amazing to think that we are really this close to seeing our
Lord and Savior, and the fulfillment of so many prophesies. However,
as exciting as that is, it is heart breaking to think of the millions who
will continue to reject the Son of God and be lost. We only have a short
time left to warn the world!

Year: 2031 as Seen Through the Lens of Psalm 131, a Psalm of Ascent

Israel is Humbled and Hopeful

Psalm 131 is roughly the same time period as the previous Psalm in the timeline revelation, Psalm 82. Whereas Psalm 82 dealt with the hidden fallen angelic "gods" of this world, who may no longer be hidden in 2031, Psalm 131 brings us back to the remnant of Israel still sheltered in the refuge that God has established for their protection.

This is a very short Psalm with only 3 verses. In the context of the remnant of Israel, who has now been in the refuge for 3 years, it is obvious that all who remain have been refined as God promised in Zechariah 13. Verse 1 says, *"Lord, my heart is not haughty, nor my eyes lofty. Neither do I concern myself with great matters, nor with things too profound for me."* During the opening months of the refuge, I can only imagine that the occupants will have great fear and anxiety as they will see the world burning down around them. However, by year 3, they are no longer concerned about those things. They know that God is in control of their protection and their destiny, and not the beast, the serpent, the harlot, Babylon, nor any other evil adversary. Because they will know that it is only through God that they have been protected, they will lose any self-aggrandizing pride that they once had, and place their trust solely in the Lord.

The final verse, I believe really says it all; *"O Israel, hope in the Lord from this time forth and forever."* There is no better One, in heaven or on earth, to rest your hope in than the Lord. And in 2031, the remnant of Israel will be standing at the edge of eternity, the great "forever," and "everlasting" with our Lord and Savior, the One whom we are all hoping and praying for.

Year: 2031/2032 as seen through the lens of Psalm 83, a Psalm of Asaph

All Roads Lead to Armageddon

According to the timeline revelation encrypted in the Psalms, the invasion of Gog Magog happened in the Shmita year of 2024, possibly preceded by, or followed closely by, the rapture of the Church. The Jubilee year of 2025 saw the rise of the false messiah over the land of Israel, and the beginning of the 7-year tribulation period. In 2026, the children of Israel streamed back to their homeland from all corners of the world, believing that their long-awaited Messianic Age had finally begun; not realizing that it was actually the prophesied "time of Jacob's trouble." They completed the new temple in Jerusalem in 2027, just in time for their foreboding 80th birthday in 2028. The middle of the tribulation period also occurred in 2028, or early 2029, along with the Antichrist's proclamation that he was god, and the "abomination of desolation" was set up in the temple, which led to the destruction of two-thirds of the children of Israel and the destruction of their land.

However, as has always been the pattern, God spared a remnant of His people and led them into a refuge where they were protected, cared for, and refined for the remainder of the second half of the tribulation, known as the "Great Tribulation." According to the timeline revelation, the second half of the tribulation, which will last 42 months, will cover the years of 2028/2029 through 2031/2032. That brings us to Psalm 83, which is the final Psalm of Asaph. It matches the time of 2031/2032, which would have been Israel's 83rd anniversary year if they hadn't fallen for the false messiah's deceptions. What it is, instead, is the year of the most infamous prophetic battle ever known to man, the Battle of Armageddon! It's also the first Shmita year in the new Jubilee cycle according to the ancient Essenes and their Dead Sea Scrolls. That also aligns with the common Rabbinical knowledge that war happens on Shmita years. This time, it's the war to end all wars...

According to the prophesies of the Essenes in the Dead Sea Scrolls, as of 2032, it will have been exactly 2000 years since the true Messiah rode into Jerusalem on the back of a lowly donkey fulfilling the prophecy of Zechariah 9:9. He was rejected and crucified, but not for His own sins, but for the sins of the world fulfilling the prophecy of Daniel 9:26. He rose again (Psalm 16) and was seated at the right hand of the Father awaiting His return, which will fulfill many prophesies, including Psalm 110. However, this time, He will not be riding in on a lowly donkey in meekness, but He will return in glory and victory on a white horse, and will be followed by a heavenly army prepared to do battle against the kings of this world and their armies at Armageddon (Revelation 19).

How do we know that Psalm 83 pertains to Armageddon, other than the fact that it fits perfectly in place within the timeline revelation? After all, scholars have speculated many different possible times within the last days for this battle to occur. Some say it's the same as Gog Magog, some say it will be first, some in the middle, some at the end, some say it probably already happened, and I'm sure there are plenty who think it's all a metaphor for something else entirely. Well, it just so happens that Psalm 83 has Armageddon encrypted throughout its verses. It's just that we never noticed it before.

Within Psalm 83, there are many references to historic Israeli military victories, especially from the time of the Judges. All of them mentioned in Psalm 83 are associated with the area that we know as Armageddon. If you would like to read about each one in more detail, please see the chapter on Psalm 83 in this book. However, for now, the important thing is to understand that God did not have the Psalmist simply write about a bunch, or random historic battles and characters that he had heard about; no, they are all very specific, they all relate to Armageddon, and they probably give us even greater prophetic insight than what I have been able to uncover in my studies. I have a feeling that I've only scratched the surface. I'm sure that many of the historic patterns will repeat in the battle still to come, but only time will tell.

Many have been confused about the specific list of 10 notorious enemies of Israel who want to utterly destroy Israel so completely that Israel will no longer even be remembered. It's a very unambiguous list of 10 nations that doesn't seem to fit in with the "whole world coming against Israel" narrative of the great and final battle detailed in the pages of both the Old and the New Testaments. What we have all missed is the fact that it's specifically "10" enemy nations. Just like the number 10 itself, in the Hebrew reckoning, they represent the whole; the same as a tenth (tithe) of your income represents your entire income.

If you're still skeptical, I'll end this quick review of Psalm 83 as it relates to the timeline revelation with this question, who are the "sheltered ones" in verse 3?

Verse 3
*They have taken crafty counsel against Your people, and consulted together against **Your sheltered ones**.*

Remember that one-third of Israel has been "sheltered" in the refuge for the past 3.5 years! The serpent and the beast must destroy them, or all hope is lost for the future of their wicked kingdom. Verses 13 - 18 give us a good idea of what will happen when God and His Army shows up! Understand that according to the timeline revelation, as I'm writing, this is less than 10 years away from now in 2023. Now, go read Psalm 83 again with the timeline knowledge of how soon this might be, and see if it doesn't give you chills to know that we will be there at Armageddon with the Lord, and it's probably not so far away!

Year: 2032 as Seen Through the Lens of Psalm 132, a Psalm of Ascent

The Year of the Lord's Return

As I mentioned in Psalm 83, which corresponds to 2031 and into 2032, this is the first Shmita year in the new Jubilee cycle, and it's a year for war. But according to Psalm 132, it's also the start of something new as well.

As detailed in Revelation 19 and 20, after the defeat of the beast, his kings, and all of the armies who had gathered together to make war against the Lord and His army at Armageddon, the beast, and false prophet will be cast alive, kicking and screaming no doubt, into the lake of fire. Then, Satan will be chained and thrown into a bottomless pit to be imprisoned for the duration of the Millennial Kingdom. According to the timeline revelation, the Millennial Kingdom starts in 2032! That means that if the timeline revelation is correct, then it would make sense for Psalm 132 to be about the Lord finally dwelling/tabernacling, and reigning in person from Zion. And that's exactly what Psalm 132 is about!

The gloomy Psalms of distress, waiting, hoping, and longing related to the remnant of Israel over the last 3+ years are finally over. That means that the Great Tribulation and the time of Jacob's trouble are now in the rear-view, and the prophetic 7th day Sabbath, which is the real Messianic Age, has begun. Verses 13 - 16 sum it up nicely, and undoubtedly position this Psalm as a prophetic Messianic Psalm since it speaks of a time that hasn't come... until now!

Verses 13-16

13 For the LORD has chosen Zion; He has desired it for His dwelling place: 14 "This is My resting place forever; here I will dwell, for I have desired it. 15 I will abundantly bless her provision; I will satisfy her poor with bread. 16 I will also clothe her priests with salvation, and her saints shall shout aloud for joy.

Year: 2033 as Seen Through the Lens of Psalm 133, a Psalm of Ascent

Unified Under the King of Kings

Just as you would imagine, if the timeline revelation is correct, and the Millennial Kingdom has begun by 2033, then Psalm 133 simply cannot be about issues dealt with in previous Psalms, such as war, enemies, hardship, death, judgment, or any other trouble brought about by man's sinful nature. Those sufferings should now all be behind us.

So, instead of those things, this Psalm should be about pleasant things such as peace and unity, and even blessings and life. And once again, just as if God planned it this way, that's exactly what this Psalm is about!

Verse 1
¹Behold, how good and how pleasant it is for brethren to dwell together in unity!

Verse 3
³ It is like the dew of Hermon, descending upon the mountains of Zion; for there the LORD commanded the blessing— Life forevermore.

After all of the previous "tribulation" Psalms, doesn't this one make you want to breathe a big sigh of relief?

Year: 2034 as Seen Through the Lens of Psalm 134, a Psalm of Ascent

Fulfillment of Tabernacles

Psalm 134 is the final Psalm of Ascent. As such, it historically represents the final step for the pilgrims and priests who ascended up the 15 steps to the temple of the Lord for the annual Feast of Tabernacles celebration, which begins on the 15th of the 7th month. Of course, according to the timeline revelation, the 15 Psalms of Ascent also represent the 15 steps of years to reach the Lord, who is now tabernacling with us in Zion after the 7-year tribulation period.

Here's the entire Psalm:

Verses 1-3
Behold, bless the LORD, all you servants of the LORD, who by night stand in the house of the LORD! ² Lift up your hands in the sanctuary, and bless the LORD. ³ The LORD who made heaven and earth bless you from Zion!

You may have noticed verse 3 has a familiarity to it. Remember Psalm 121, which opened the "Rapture Season" with the phrase, *"My help comes from the LORD, **who made heaven and earth**."* And then, in Psalm 124, the "Rapture Season" closed with the phrase, *"Our help is in the name of the LORD, **who made heaven and earth**."* This important phrase relates to who the Creator of heaven and earth is through Genesis 1:1 and John 1:1 - 5, which also connects to the giving and sealing up of prophecy through Isaiah 46:9 - 10 and Daniel 9:24. Additionally, I believe that it connects to man's time of 6,000 years plus a 1,000 year Sabbath, which relates back to Genesis 1 and is also interwoven throughout these, and many more scriptures.

Notice that in the two Psalms, which represented years prior to the tribulation period, and were also related to the rapture, both carried the context of needing help. Now, Psalm 134 also closes with *"**who made heaven and earth**,"* but this time there's no help needed. Why? Because the time of trouble is over, we're in the Millennial Kingdom, and Jesus is on the throne blessing us literally in person *"from Zion!"*

CHAPTER 39

Timeline Mysteries and
Charts Revealed

I am definitely a visual learner. I would much rather see a picture or a chart of something rather than a bunch of words. Here's how the encrypted timeline revelation in the Psalms maps out as a calendar, assuming that God doesn't add a currently unknown amount of time, as He has been known to do.

Realistically, according to the Essenes, the end of the age isn't until 2075, so He could reposition the final years and still be within the numbers. Also, if the Psalms make up a specific timeline, then why are there 150 Psalms and not only 134? Of course, 150 is 10 X 15, or 10 X 5 X 3, which points back to the encrypted timeline as well. The main point I'm trying to make is that God is sovereign, and He can add as much time as He wants regardless of what we believe. However, there is a mountain of evidence that suggests that He has had this planned all along, and that even the timing aspect, and not just the sequence of the encrypted timeline revelation, is important. In my humble opinion, it all fits.

Speaking of "fits," at the end of the Book of Daniel, he writes that there will be 1290 days from the time that the temple sacrifices are taken away, and the abomination is set up until the end.

Daniel 12:11

[11] "And from the time that the daily sacrifice is taken away, and the abomination of desolation is set up, there shall be one thousand two hundred and ninety days.

The 1290 days equates to roughly 3.5 years. This is speaking of the second half of the tribulation period. Then, however, Daniel throws a wrench in the works by stating another number, which has confused Bible students for thousands of years. Here it is:

Daniel 12:12

[12] Blessed is he who waits, and comes to the one thousand three hundred and thirty-five days.

So, Daniel states that the second half of the tribulation will be 1290 days, and then he adds another number of 1335. The difference between them is 45. That's an interesting number. It's not one of the key numbers that we have been dealing with in prophecy, which really makes me wonder about it. So, what happens 45 days after the 1290 days? That's the question that many have been asking, myself included, ever since Daniel wrote this prophecy.

Maybe nothing happens of great prophetic significance 45 days after Jesus returns! That's hard to imagine, but maybe we should be adding the entire 1335 to the 1290 instead of just adding the difference between the two. Maybe they don't overlap as we have suspected? Maybe the new temple, Jerusalem, and the surrounding area will be completed during that time, as I have previously described in the last 3 Psalms of Ascent, and into Psalm 135. After all, Ezekiel 40 - 48 is a written blueprint for the Millennial Temple and the Holy Land. And from other prophetic scriptures, I do not believe that Jesus is going to simply speak it into existence. I believe it will be built over 3 years time, and then possibly completed and consecrated at 1335 days. After all, Jesus did say that he would raise up the temple again in 3 days.

John 2:19

¹⁹Jesus answered and said to them, "Destroy this temple, and in three days I will raise it up."

Obviously, He was talking about His body, but could He have also been giving us clues about a raising up of the Millennial Kingdom Temple? Does this tie into Hosea 6, which says that "on the 3rd day He will raise us up?" The reality is that 3.5 days is still on the 3rd day. There's no way to know for sure where to place the 1335 days, but I believe this, and many other mysteries, will be revealed very soon. For now, I'm going to leave you with my hunch that the 1335 days will fit sometime between 2031/2032 and 2034/2035 after the tribulation period has concluded.

Timeline of the15 Psalms of Ascent

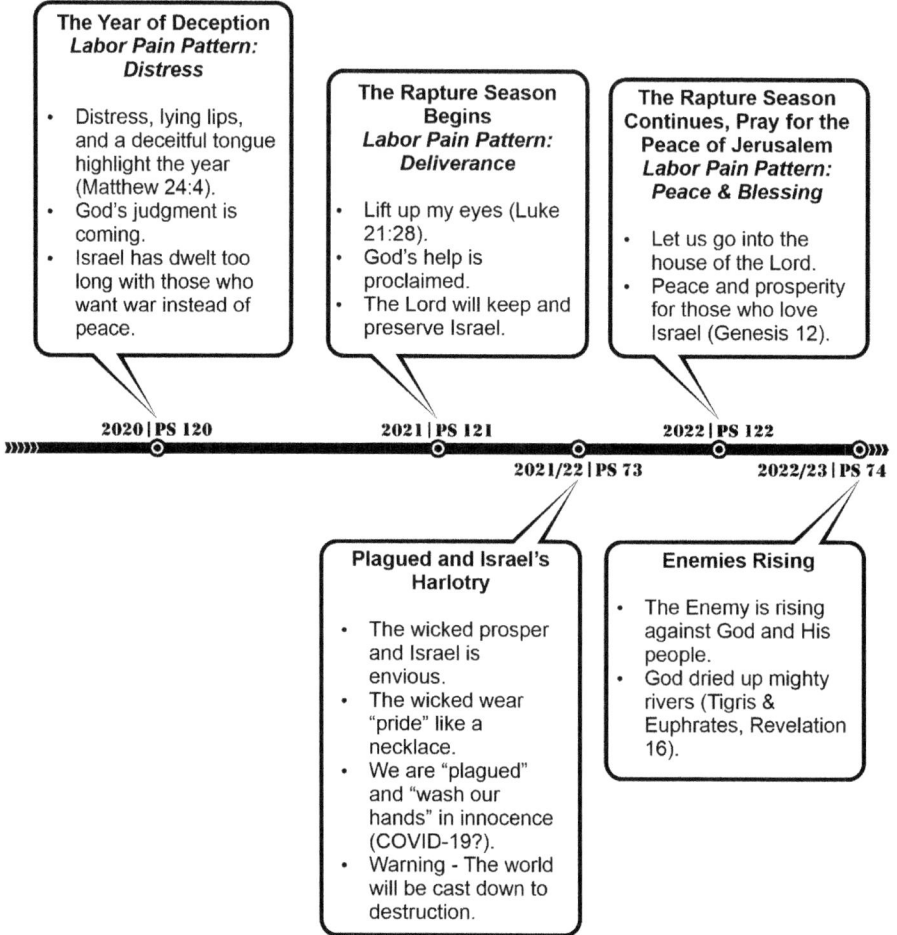

The Year of Deception
Labor Pain Pattern: Distress

- Distress, lying lips, and a deceitful tongue highlight the year (Matthew 24:4).
- God's judgment is coming.
- Israel has dwelt too long with those who want war instead of peace.

The Rapture Season Begins
Labor Pain Pattern: Deliverance

- Lift up my eyes (Luke 21:28).
- God's help is proclaimed.
- The Lord will keep and preserve Israel.

The Rapture Season Continues, Pray for the Peace of Jerusalem
Labor Pain Pattern: Peace & Blessing

- Let us go into the house of the Lord.
- Peace and prosperity for those who love Israel (Genesis 12).

2020 | PS 120 **2021 | PS 121** **2022 | PS 122**

2021/22 | PS 73 **2022/23 | PS 74**

Plagued and Israel's Harlotry

- The wicked prosper and Israel is envious.
- The wicked wear "pride" like a necklace.
- We are "plagued" and "wash our hands" in innocence (COVID-19?).
- Warning - The world will be cast down to destruction.

Enemies Rising

- The Enemy is rising against God and His people.
- God dried up mighty rivers (Tigris & Euphrates, Revelation 16).

Timeline of the 12 Psalms of Asaph (- Psalm 50)

Timeline of the 15 Psalms of Ascent

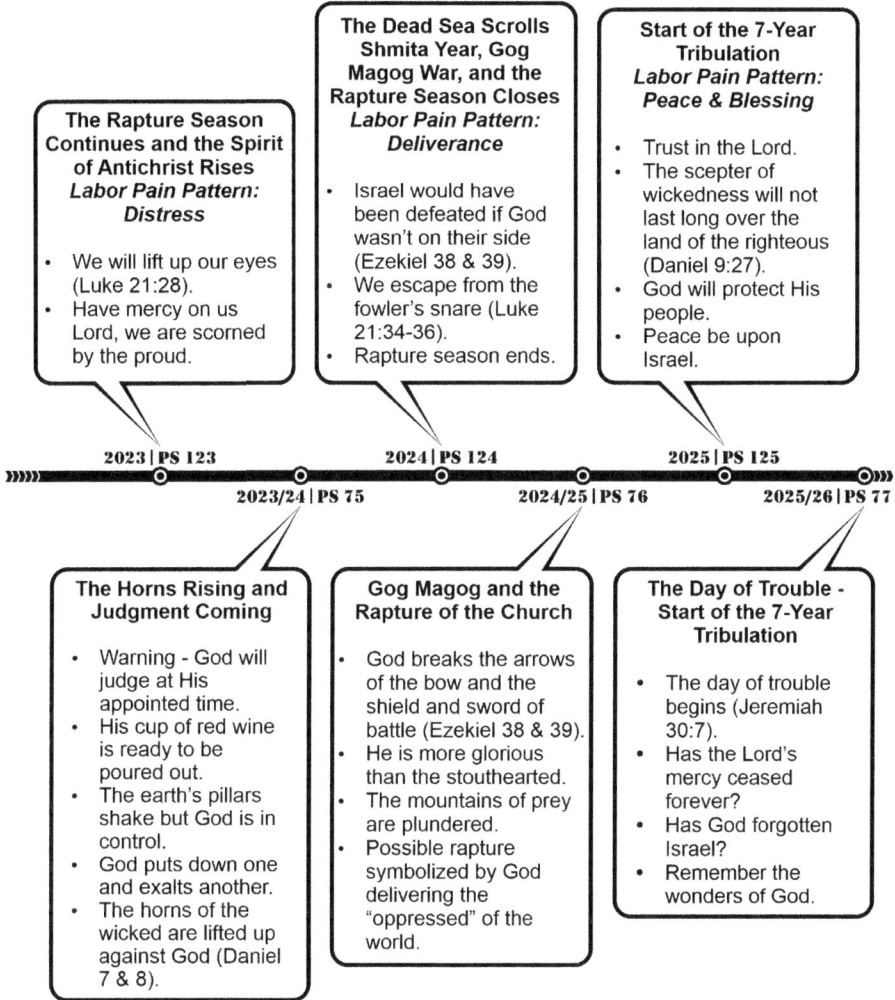

The Dead Sea Scrolls Shmita Year, Gog Magog War, and the Rapture Season Closes
Labor Pain Pattern: Deliverance

- Israel would have been defeated if God wasn't on their side (Ezekiel 38 & 39).
- We escape from the fowler's snare (Luke 21:34-36).
- Rapture season ends.

Start of the 7-Year Tribulation
Labor Pain Pattern: Peace & Blessing

- Trust in the Lord.
- The scepter of wickedness will not last long over the land of the righteous (Daniel 9:27).
- God will protect His people.
- Peace be upon Israel.

The Rapture Season Continues and the Spirit of Antichrist Rises
Labor Pain Pattern: Distress

- We will lift up our eyes (Luke 21:28).
- Have mercy on us Lord, we are scorned by the proud.

2023 | PS 123

2023/24 | PS 75

2024 | PS 124

2024/25 | PS 76

2025 | PS 125

2025/26 | PS 77

The Horns Rising and Judgment Coming

- Warning - God will judge at His appointed time.
- His cup of red wine is ready to be poured out.
- The earth's pillars shake but God is in control.
- God puts down one and exalts another.
- The horns of the wicked are lifted up against God (Daniel 7 & 8).

Gog Magog and the Rapture of the Church

- God breaks the arrows of the bow and the shield and sword of battle (Ezekiel 38 & 39).
- He is more glorious than the stouthearted.
- The mountains of prey are plundered.
- Possible rapture symbolized by God delivering the "oppressed" of the world.

The Day of Trouble - Start of the 7-Year Tribulation

- The day of trouble begins (Jeremiah 30:7).
- Has the Lord's mercy ceased forever?
- Has God forgotten Israel?
- Remember the wonders of God.

Timeline of the 12 Psalms of Asaph (- Psalm 50)

Timeline of the15 Psalms of Ascent

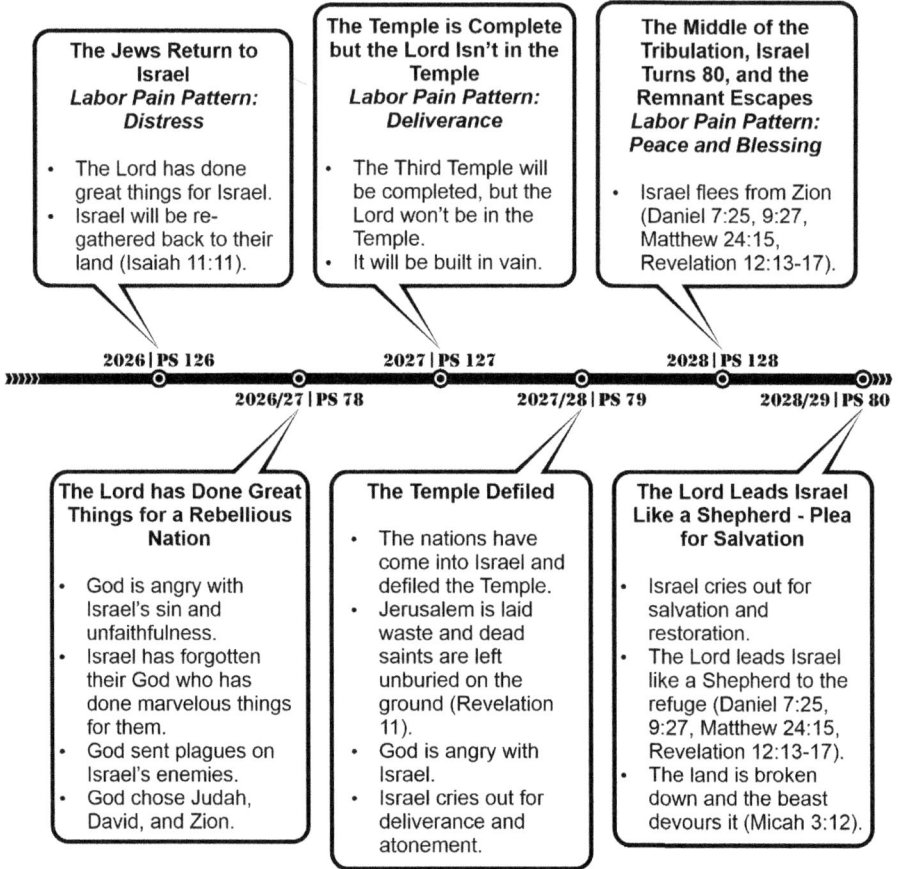

The Jews Return to Israel
Labor Pain Pattern: Distress

- The Lord has done great things for Israel.
- Israel will be re-gathered back to their land (Isaiah 11:11).

The Temple is Complete but the Lord Isn't in the Temple
Labor Pain Pattern: Deliverance

- The Third Temple will be completed, but the Lord won't be in the Temple.
- It will be built in vain.

The Middle of the Tribulation, Israel Turns 80, and the Remnant Escapes
Labor Pain Pattern: Peace and Blessing

- Israel flees from Zion (Daniel 7:25, 9:27, Matthew 24:15, Revelation 12:13-17).

2026 | PS 126   2027 | PS 127   2028 | PS 128

2026/27 | PS 78   2027/28 | PS 79   2028/29 | PS 80

The Lord has Done Great Things for a Rebellious Nation

- God is angry with Israel's sin and unfaithfulness.
- Israel has forgotten their God who has done marvelous things for them.
- God sent plagues on Israel's enemies.
- God chose Judah, David, and Zion.

The Temple Defiled

- The nations have come into Israel and defiled the Temple.
- Jerusalem is laid waste and dead saints are left unburied on the ground (Revelation 11).
- God is angry with Israel.
- Israel cries out for deliverance and atonement.

The Lord Leads Israel Like a Shepherd - Plea for Salvation

- Israel cries out for salvation and restoration.
- The Lord leads Israel like a Shepherd to the refuge (Daniel 7:25, 9:27, Matthew 24:15, Revelation 12:13-17).
- The land is broken down and the beast devours it (Micah 3:12).

Timeline of the 12 Psalms of Asaph (- Psalm 50)

Timeline of the15 Psalms of Ascent

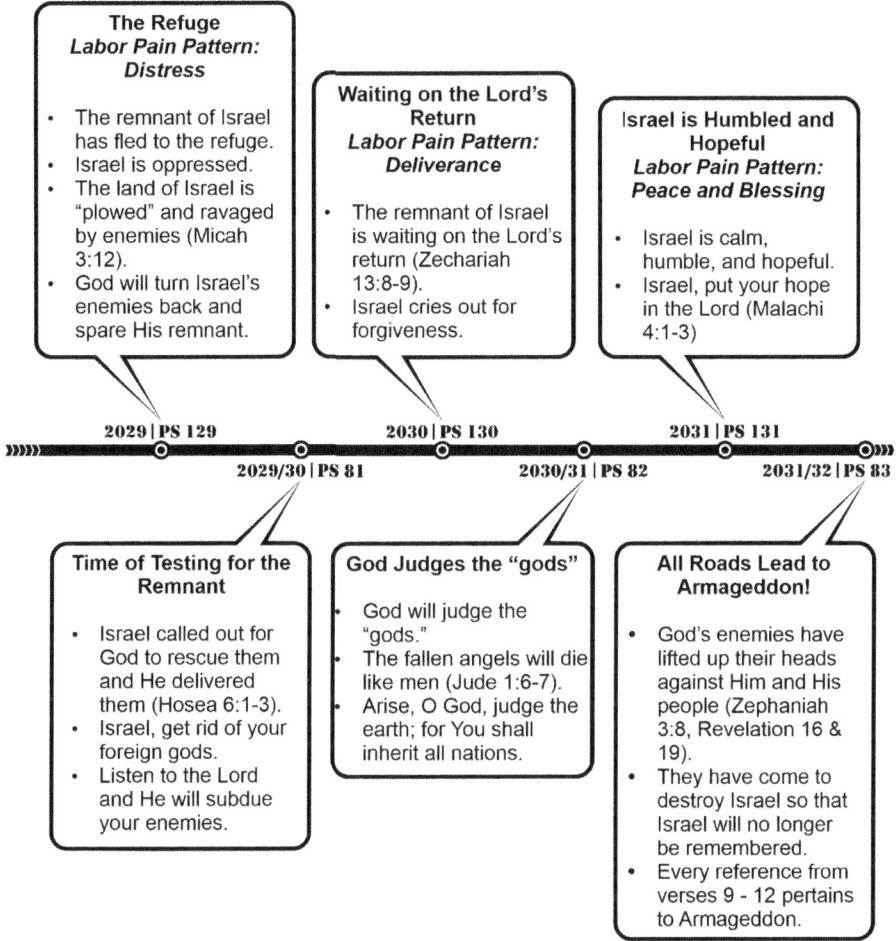

The Refuge
Labor Pain Pattern: Distress

- The remnant of Israel has fled to the refuge.
- Israel is oppressed.
- The land of Israel is "plowed" and ravaged by enemies (Micah 3:12).
- God will turn Israel's enemies back and spare His remnant.

Waiting on the Lord's Return
Labor Pain Pattern: Deliverance

- The remnant of Israel is waiting on the Lord's return (Zechariah 13:8-9).
- Israel cries out for forgiveness.

Israel is Humbled and Hopeful
Labor Pain Pattern: Peace and Blessing

- Israel is calm, humble, and hopeful.
- Israel, put your hope in the Lord (Malachi 4:1-3)

2029 | **PS 129**　　　2030 | **PS 130**　　　2031 | **PS 131**

2029/30 | **PS 81**　　　2030/31 | **PS 82**　　　2031/32 | **PS 83**

Time of Testing for the Remnant

- Israel called out for God to rescue them and He delivered them (Hosea 6:1-3).
- Israel, get rid of your foreign gods.
- Listen to the Lord and He will subdue your enemies.

God Judges the "gods"

- God will judge the "gods."
- The fallen angels will die like men (Jude 1:6-7).
- Arise, O God, judge the earth; for You shall inherit all nations.

All Roads Lead to Armageddon!

- God's enemies have lifted up their heads against Him and His people (Zephaniah 3:8, Revelation 16 & 19).
- They have come to destroy Israel so that Israel will no longer be remembered.
- Every reference from verses 9 - 12 pertains to Armageddon.

Timeline of the 12 Psalms of Asaph (- Psalm 50)

Timeline of the15 Psalms of Ascent

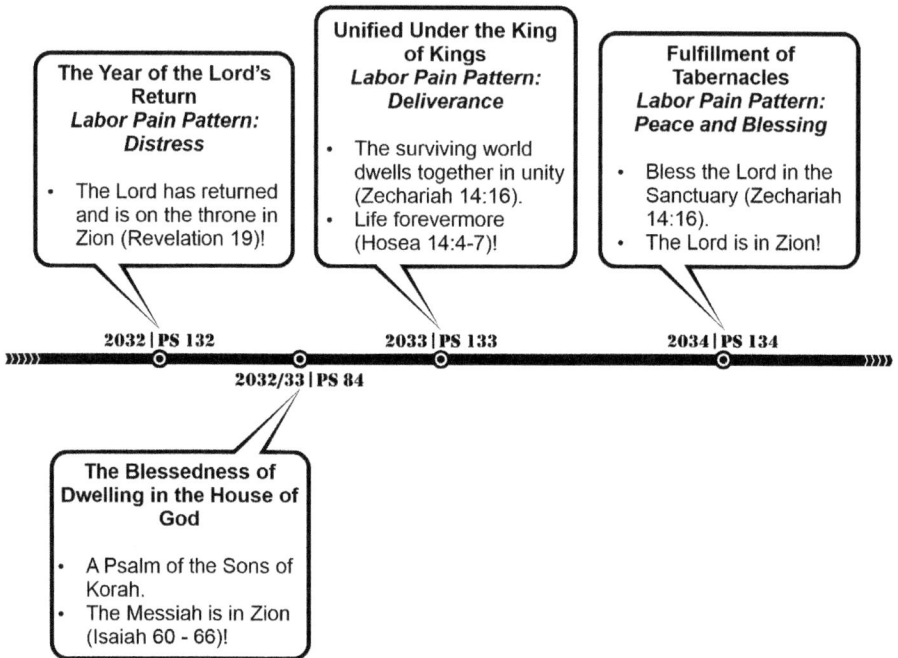

Unified Under the King of Kings
Labor Pain Pattern: Deliverance

- The surviving world dwells together in unity (Zechariah 14:16).
- Life forevermore (Hosea 14:4-7)!

The Year of the Lord's Return
Labor Pain Pattern: Distress

- The Lord has returned and is on the throne in Zion (Revelation 19)!

Fulfillment of Tabernacles
Labor Pain Pattern: Peace and Blessing

- Bless the Lord in the Sanctuary (Zechariah 14:16).
- The Lord is in Zion!

2032 | PS 132   2033 | PS 133   2034 | PS 134

2032/33 | PS 84

The Blessedness of Dwelling in the House of God

- A Psalm of the Sons of Korah.
- The Messiah is in Zion (Isaiah 60 - 66)!

Timeline of the 12 Psalms of Asaph (- Psalm 50)

CHAPTER 40

The Final Jubilee

My journey of researching and writing this book has certainly been a challenging one. I would even say that it has been a time of trial and testing. There have been many hurdles and roadblocks along the way, and my business and my family have both suffered from it. It seems fitting then that the final chapter of this book happens to be chapter "40." The notorious number 40 has always been associated with trial and testing throughout Bible history. The good news is that the number 40 also represents the end of that time of testing. Just as Israel was tested in the wilderness for 40 years, and Jesus was tested in the wilderness for 40 days, the number 40 represented the final completion of that time of testing.

The Church is also at the end of its time of trial and testing. There are 40 Jubilees of 50 years each in a 2000-year period. So, any way you look at it, there have been almost 40 complete Jubilees since Jesus came, died for our sins, was resurrected, and then ascended to the Father "40" days later. Regardless of whether all of that happened in 32 AD as the Essenes prophesied, or even as early as 28 AD as some believe, either way, we're at the very end of the 40th Jubilee cycle since then. That means that we do not have much time left to prepare ourselves and to warn and prepare others of what is coming.

It seems that almost everyone, even in the secular world, at least has a sense that something is coming, something even worse than the 2020 Covid crisis that we have just lived through. Sometimes, I try to listen to non-Christian financial market experts because they seem to have their finger on the pulse of the global banking system, and the direction that it is headed. I think we all tend to live our lives in bubbles of our own making, where we only see, or hear others who are of our own opinion most of the time. Sometimes, I find that it's a good idea to peek outside of my own bubble to see what the rest of the world is up to.

Today, I was listening to a financial investing expert whose company has a YouTube channel dedicated to financial news with an emphasis on gold, silver, and cryptocurrency investing. I was interested in what they had to say because, after all, it's obvious to me that the "mark of the beast," which will control everyone's ability to buy or sell, will certainly be developed, and ready to be implemented, prior to the revealing of the Antichrist. If the encrypted timeline revelation is correct, we should be seeing and hearing about such a system being developed even today as we approach the 40th Jubilee. And that's exactly what is happening!

The host of the show had an interesting fellow on her program who had written a few books about the diabolical origins of what the US government calls the Federal Reserve Bank, which is not actually a federal governmental agency at all, but is part of a private world banking system. However, that's another story. In summary, let's just say that it's all about deception! He was explaining that what is coming is a global financial system collapse, possibly even in 2023, which has been planned for a long time, designed to create the need to usher in central bank digital currencies, or "CBDCs," around the world. The vast majority of nations have been in development of their own CBDCs for several years now, but the end game is to consolidate them all into one global CBDC system where the global banking elites, and their subordinates, control and monitor every transaction through an AI system, effectively eliminating all remnants of personal freedom and privacy. That describes the backbone of what we know as the "mark of the beast" system perfectly!

This system has already been developed. It exists today. The elites need only a global crisis to implement it since they know that there are many of us who will push back against such a system unless they create a situation so desperate that we will beg for it. All that we're really waiting on is the "mark" itself to be implemented, and the "beast" to be in power, demanding to be worshiped through the acceptance of that mark.

As the guest interviewee was talking and describing exactly what we Bible prophecy students have known for ages, I couldn't help but yell at the screen! He was literally quoting from Revelation 13, but didn't even know it! He said that under this coming global digital banking system, cash will be eliminated, and you won't be able to "buy or sell" unless you have sold out to the system, have a good social credit score, and thereby have permission from the "cabal" to use their digital currency. The "cabal," as he put it, is the group of global banking elites who now have the power to regulate entire countries, and even the world because they control all of the money. For decades, he said that their goal has been a cashless society where individuals will no longer have cash money in their pockets because cash can't be monitored, tracked, or traced. People will no longer own money, but will only be allowed to use it if they follow the dictates of the system. Money will be allocated only to those who conform. If not, the money they thought was theirs, even money that they worked for, will simply be turned off. What has been developed is a system of total global surveillance and control over every person on the planet, just as prophesied thousands of years ago.

I already knew about all of what he was describing, so it wasn't shocking to me at all. However, what I found most interesting during this interview was that the host was more interested in asking the guest, and I'm paraphrasing, "what types of investments he is making and recommending to navigate the coming crisis and system collapse to take advantage of the situation, and increase his wealth." She was looking for an angle to be able to beat the system, and profit from what's ahead. She asked if he was buying silver, or gold, or if he was investing heavily in cryptocurrency. His reply was priceless. He said, and I'm paraphrasing again; "you can't eat silver, gold, or crypto, and anyone who has something edible isn't going to want to trade it for something as useless as those."

Isn't that exactly what the prophets Ezekiel and Zephaniah prophesied about the last days?

Ezekiel 7:19

They cast their silver into the streets, and their gold is like an unclean thing. Their silver and gold are not able to deliver them in the day of the wrath of the Lord. They cannot satisfy their hunger or fill their stomachs with it. For it was the stumbling block of their iniquity.

Zephaniah 1:18 ESV

Neither their silver nor their gold shall be able to deliver them on the day of the wrath of the Lord. In the fire of his jealousy, all the earth shall be consumed; for a full and sudden end he will make of all the inhabitants of the earth.

The reality is that you're not going to beat the coming system, and you're not going to profit from it in the long run. It's rigged against you. It's almost here, and time is running out. The only way to profit from what is coming is to realize that there is only one God who warned us of all of this, thereby proving Himself through prophecy to be the only true and living God. It is a fool's errand to put your hope and trust in anything, or anyone, other than Him. He has warned us all about this coming time of trial through His Word, and He wants to set all of us free from the hardship and catastrophe that is coming if we will only wake up and accept His salvation.

Just as He warned Noah and his family, and Lot and his family, this is a warning to you and your family, if you will only listen. There is a price to be paid for sin and wickedness, and our world has accumulated a heavy debt that must be paid. The blood of the righteous cries out from the grave for justice, and the penalty must be paid in full. Thankfully, as a pattern, God's word shows us that He made a way for Noah and Lot to be saved prior to the outpouring of His wrath on the wicked world around them. He has once again promised that He has made a way for us all to be spared and preserved from this dreadful time which is fast approaching. That way is only through the free gift of salvation offered by the One who already invested heavily in you, and paid your price through His own blood. No silver, gold, or cryptocurrency in the world can compare to the price that He already paid to set you free from the trap that is closing in all around us today, and from the eternal trap of separation and damnation.

There is no doubt that this coming system is a trap for humanity. The wicked global elites, who are busy constructing the "beast" system, believe that they will profit from it, and reign supreme over an unsuspecting world. In their pride and arrogance, they don't realize that they too are simply expendable pawns in a game much larger than themselves. God is allowing this evil game to play out, but only for a time. Ultimately, this game will also trap and destroy them as well as everything they have worked for.

Based on the encrypted timeline revelation in the Psalms coupled with countless biblical prophesies, I believe the trap is already set. We were only given a certain amount of time in this final age, and the clock has run out. You don't even have to be a Bible scholar to know that we're quickly approaching the end. Even the group of Atomic Scientists, known as the Science and Security Board, have moved their "Doomsday Clock" forward to 90 seconds to midnight this year in 2023. That's the closest that it has ever been to what they call a "global catastrophe." Even they know that something is coming!

It's time to wake up! The trap that has already been set will be sprung at the instant of the rapture of the Church. After that, the entire world will be caught like an animal in a cage that cannot be escaped. According to the encrypted timeline revelation in the Psalms, the rapture of the Church should happen no later than 2025, and most likely between today and the end of 2024. That means that as of today in June 2023 we only have at most around one and a half years left to complete our mission as believers and as the Church, which is the fulfillment of the Great Commission.

Of course, God is sovereign, and He could grant the world more time just as He did King Hezekiah when He granted him 15 more years of life. However, I believe that the 15 more years started already in 2020, after arguably what has been the 120 bloodiest years in human history. The 15 Psalms of Ascent, which begins with Psalm 120, match those 15 extra years. During those same 120 years, the world has witnessed exponential growth in knowledge and technology (Daniel 12), all leading to this very time, and the final fulfillment of Bible prophecy. In 2 Timothy chapter 3, Paul wrote to his protégé Timothy; *"but know this, that in the last days perilous times will come."* Don't you know that those "perilous times" have already started? They have already begun, there's no way to stop them, and we're at 90 seconds to midnight. Now, what are you going to do with the final seconds that you have left?

I recognize that there is an inherent danger in knowing even roughly when to expect our Lord's appearing at the resurrection/rapture. There is a human tendency to want to just stop what we're doing, put on a white robe, and sit on the rooftop and just wait for the Lord's coming. That actually happened during what is known as the Millerite Movement in the 1800s when a group of believers were told that Jesus was coming for them on October 22, 1844. Their leader, William Miller, with some help, had calculated that Jesus would return for them that year on that certain day. Many of the Millerites sold everything they had and simply waited for the Lord to appear on that day to no avail. What followed was known as the "Great Disappointment." I'll bet it was!

In hindsight, it's pretty easy to see that so many of the necessary "signs" were not visible in their day, but they overlooked those signs in the excitement of going home. The most vivid sign should have been Israel, which didn't even exist yet in the 1800s. Also, how could the Mark of the Beast system have been implemented, monitored, and controlled during a time of coins, horse, and buggy? I have to ask myself, are there signs still missing that I have overlooked, or cannot see from my vantage point? Again, God is sovereign, and He will set the final 7 years in motion at His appointed time no matter what calculations we have made. He will send His Son to come for His bride when He declares it. As I said in the beginning, I am responsible for sharing what has been revealed to me, and I do believe that the timeline revelation does overwhelmingly point to the very time that we are now living in, but that doesn't mean that our sovereign God can't allow the world more time.

So, regardless of the evidence and the timing, the wake-up call remains the same! It's time to wake up and get serious about winning souls for the final harvest, no matter what day that harvest ends. We are the workers in that harvest, but regrettably speaking for myself, I know that I have been lazy for years and haven't been hard at work in my mission field. I was caught up in trying to make a name for myself in my chosen career, live the "American dream," and take care of my family by providing earthly things for them and myself. All of that is fine to a degree, but that can't be our mission. Those are only temporal things that won't last. Aren't we supposed to be storing up our treasures in heaven? For me, the realization through the timeline revelation of how little time may be left to fulfill my true calling has lit a fire under my rear end to finally take my mission seriously and to finish strong.

I have a 16-year-old son at home named Devin, who doesn't necessarily want to hear that his life may be cut short and that he won't be able to do all of the things he has dreamt of doing in his life. I also have a 28-year-old daughter named Joelle, who had her first baby, James, in June of 2022. She's a new mom now, making all sorts of plans for the future for her new family. To a young person, even one who is saved, hearing that we may only have a short time left is very different than to an older person. I'm in my middle 50s, and I think, "Come Lord Jesus, come!" However, they think, "But I have plans, and I still want to do (fill in the blank)!"

The reality is that none of us were promised tomorrow. Just a few weeks back, in a neighboring town, there was a storm, and early in the morning, a tree fell onto the interstate highway and killed a man in a pickup truck as well as another man on a motorcycle. They were both on their way to work, just like every other day, and were more than likely thinking about the things they would do that evening, or on the upcoming weekend, but their lives were over. They didn't wake up that morning thinking that this would be their last day on earth. I pray that they knew the Lord and that they were ready to meet Him. My point is that we should be ready no matter what the encrypted timeline seems to reveal. We should be carrying out the Great Commission wherever God has placed us until the very last second, no matter when we think the Lord is coming for us. In fact, knowing that He is coming soon, should spark a blazing fire in all of us where there was just a small flame before!

Knowing that time is short and that the harvest of souls is almost over, should cause each of us to double and triple our efforts so that no one is lost, and no one is trapped in the terrible time that is ahead.

The reality is also that the world that we knew only a few years ago is now over, and it isn't coming back. The days of making great future plans, fulfilling the "American dream," or even just having some freedom in life are behind us. Technology combined with evil will see to that. What's ahead is already being described by the global elites and world leaders as a time when "you'll own nothing and be happy." How can you be happy without owning anything? If you don't own it, that means that you will owe on it, on everything. You will be beholden to the system. The use of anything will be a service and a privilege as long as you obey the masters, and ultimately the "beast." We have already been conditioned for this by all sorts of apps like Spotify, Netflix, and so many others. We don't purchase the music, or movies any longer, and we just pay a subscription for everything. Think about it, if you don't own it, who does? What they are really saying is that we little people will not own anything, but they will, and we'll have to rent everything or work as a serf for them for our livelihoods in the future. No thanks! Is that a world that you want to live in? On the contrary, the Bible promises a life even beyond our hopes and dreams.

1 Corinthians 2:9
⁹ But as it is written: "Eye has not seen, nor ear heard, nor have entered into the heart of man the things which God has prepared for those who love Him."

So, we all have choices to make. Whether you like it or not, the future looks really horrible on this planet, and you cannot stop what's coming, nor can you profit from it long-term. If it weren't for the "Restrainer" mentioned in 2 Thessalonians 2, I believe that this dystopian future would have already consumed the globe. It's only by the grace of God that this coming, world-consuming, evil has been restrained until now. At the soon rapture of the Church, an evil will be unleashed on earth unlike anything ever witnessed. The trap that is the tribulation period of 7 years will be sprung, and regret will be everyone's unpleasant and terrible bedfellow; everyone who heard this message, but ignored it.

After reviewing all of the evidence laid out in this book; you have had an opportunity to judge for yourself if the encrypted timeline revelation in the Psalms is real or not. I believe that the evidence reveals that God placed interconnecting numbers, words, phrases, and imagery to reveal His prophetic sequence and general timing of the last days. However, all of that is only circumstantial evidence and is open to interpretation, so ultimately, only time will tell. Even if the timing of the encrypted timeline revelation is wrong, I believe that the pattern, or sequence of events is correct, as witnessed by two sets of Psalms that fit together perfectly to match the overall end-time biblical narrative. I also believe strongly in the timing as well, but I believe ultimately far more in the sovereignty of God. He will have the last word, and as the Father, only He will tell His Son that it's time to go and get His bride. Whatever day and hour that is, we need to all be ready, born-again with a strong relationship with the Lord, and we need to have our treasure laid up in heaven, which means that we need to make sure that everyone around us has heard the gospel! During the tribulation, everyone will have a decision to make, a decision that will cost them their lives. Let everyone know now, before it's too late; today, that decision is easy and free, but tomorrow, it might be too late. The price has already been paid by our Redeemer, and there's nothing on this earth worth holding onto.

If you missed the great escape known as the rapture, and you have found this book during the tribulation, whether you are Jew or Gentile, I pray that it will be a comfort and a guide for you as you navigate through such a difficult time. It can't take the place of the complete Word of God, but I did put in as many relevant scriptures in this book as I could. I also pray that you will persevere and share the love of God with as many as possible. Their eternity depends on it. Even amid such a tremendous trial, God has a purpose and a plan for you in His Kingdom. He is with you, and He will guide you through.

Prayer for Salvation

If you believe that it is only through Jesus, the one true Messiah, and that He is the only "Door" to the Father by which you can be saved, and would like to accept Him as your Savior right now, please pray this prayer and allow Him to change your life today and your eternity forevermore.

Heavenly Father, in the name of your Son Jesus, Yeshua HaMashiach, I ask that you come into my heart and my life, fill me with your Holy Spirit, and become the Lord of my life, and my guiding light from this day forward. Forgive me, I am sorry for all the sins I have committed. I repent and turn away from those sins, and today I commit my life to Your service, all for your glory. In faith, I confess that Your Son Jesus shed His blood on the cross and died to atone for my sins, was raised from the dead, and is coming back soon to establish His Kingdom on this earth. I desire to be a part of Your Kingdom, to have a relationship with You, and to never be separated from You again. Please accept me into your eternal Kingdom. I will courageously confess You before others and strive to bear fruit for Your Kingdom. Thank You for your forgiveness, grace, mercy, love, and for never leaving me nor forsaking me. In Jesus' holy name, Amen!

Printed in Great Britain
by Amazon

47371335R00371